SOL JUSTITIAE
LAW
Robert B. L. Murphy

THE CAMBRIDGE HISTORY OF ARABIC LITERATURE

RELIGION, LEARNING AND SCIENCE IN THE ʿABBASID PERIOD

RELIGION, LEARNING AND SCIENCE IN THE ᶜABBASID PERIOD

EDITED BY
M. J. L. YOUNG, J. D. LATHAM AND
R. B. SERJEANT

The right of the University of Cambridge to print and sell all manner of books was granted by Henry VIII in 1534. The University has printed and published continuously since 1584.

CAMBRIDGE UNIVERSITY PRESS
CAMBRIDGE
NEW YORK PORT CHESTER
MELBOURNE SYDNEY

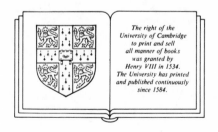

Published by the Press Syndicate of the University of Cambridge
The Pitt Building, Trumpington Street, Cambridge CB2 1RP
40 West 20th Street, New York, NY 10011, USA
10 Stamford Road, Oakleigh, Melbourne 3166, Australia

First published 1990

Printed in Great Britain at the University Press, Cambridge

Religion, learning and science in the ʿAbbasid period. –
(The Cambridge history of Arabic Literature).
1. Arabic literature, 750–1258 – Critical studies)
I. Young, M. J. L.
892.7090034

Library of Congress cataloguing in publication data
Religion, learning, and science in the ʿAbbasid period/edited by
M. J. L. Young . . . [et al.].
p. cm. – (The Cambridge history of Arabic literature)
Includes bibliographical references.
ISBN 0 521 32763 6
1. Islamic Empire – Intellectual life. 2. Civilization, Islamic.
I. Young, M. J. L. II. Series.
DS36.85.R45 1990
909'.097671 – dc 20 90-1549 CIP

ISBN 0 521 32763 6

SE

Minerva mirabilis nationes hominum circuire videtur, et a fine usque ad finem attingit fortiter, ut se ipsam communicet universis. Indos, Babilonios, Aegyptios atque Graecos, Arabes et Latines eam pertransisse iam cernimus.

Richard of Bury, *Philobiblon* (AD 1344)

CONTENTS

		page
List of plates		xiv
Editorial preface		xv
List of abbreviations		xxi
Map Literary, political and religious centres in the ᶜAbbasid period		xxii
1	Sunnī theology *by* SALVADOR GÓMEZ NOGALES†, *Instituto Hispano-Arabe de Cultura, Madrid*	1
	Muslim theology and *fiqh*	2
	Muslim theological schools	3
	Later developments	9
	The pillars of Islam	10
	Wahhabism	12
	Dogma	12
	ᶜAqīdāt	14
2	Shīᶜī theological literature *by* I. K. A. HOWARD, *University of Edinburgh*	16
3	Ibāḍī theological literature *by* J. C. WILKINSON, *University of Oxford*	33
	Ẓuhūr: the expansion of Ibaḍism	33
	Literature of the period	34
	The fourth/tenth to sixth/twelfth centuries	36
4	Quranic exegesis *by* JOHN BURTON, *University of St Andrews*	40
	Traditional exegesis	40
	Written exegesis	43
	Dating (*sabab*) and identification (*taᶜyīn*)	44
	The linguistic approach	45
	The rational approach	49
	The role of intuition	52

5 The prose literature of Ṣufism
by Caesar E. Farah, *University of Minnesota* 56
Moralizing literature 60
Biography 62
Literature of veneration 64
Reference literature 64
Etiquette literature 66
Literature of divine converse 67
The allegorical 68
Literature of the Path (*ṭarīqah*) 68
Apologetic literature 70
The *qaṣaṣ* technique 71
The theme of love 71
The theme of the Logos 72
Other themes 74

6 Philosophical literature
by Muhsin Mahdi, *Harvard University* 76
Al-Fārābī on Plato and Aristotle 78
The philosopher and the city 87
Ibn Ṭufayl on al-Fārābī 98
Ibn Ṭufayl on Ibn Sīnā 100
Ibn Ṭufayl on al-Ghazālī 101
Ibn Ṭufayl's path to truth 103

7 Arabic lexicography
by M. G. Carter, *New York University* 106

8 Arabic grammar
by M.G. Carter 118
The origins of grammar 119
Primitive grammar 120
The creation of grammar 122
The emergence of pedagogical grammar 123
Basrans and Kufans 126
The perfection of method 127
The search for form 132
The great masters 133

9 Islamic legal literature
by P. W. Baker, *University of London*, and I. D. Edge, *University of London* 139

The Qurʾān and books of *tafsīr* 139
The *sunnah* and books of Tradition 140
The early jurists and the development of the schools of law 140
The major legal works of the different schools of law 146
Collections of *fatāwā* 153

10 Administrative literature
by C. E. Bosworth, *University of Manchester* 155
Descriptive, practical manuals on administrative procedure 156
Didactic treatises for the training and guidance of secretaries 161
Biographical material and collections of anecdotes on viziers and secretaries 163
Mirrors for Princes and manuals of statecraft 165

11 Arabic biographical writing
by M. J. L. Young, *University of Leeds* 168
Biographical dictionaries 169
The biographical dictionaries as registers of vital data 176
Individual biographies 177
Characteristics of Arabic biography 178
Medieval Arabic autobiography 183

12 History and historians
by Claude Cahen, *Université de la Sorbonne Nouvelle, Paris III* 188
From the beginnings to the time of al-Ṭabarī 189
The classical period 201
The post-classical period 216
Conclusion 232

13 Faṭimid history and historians
by Abbas Hamdani, *University of Wisconsin, Milwaukee* 234
Faṭimid literature 235
The "Period of Concealment" 236
The North African period of the Faṭimid caliphate 239
Period of al-Ḥākim 240
The reign of al-Mustanṣir 241
The Ṭayyibī *daʿwah* 243
The Nizārī *daʿwah* 244
The last period of the Faṭimid caliphate 245
General histories 246
Later developments 246

14 Mathematics and applied science
by DONALD R. HILL, *University College, London* 248
Mathematics 251
Physics 256
Mechanical technology 260

15 Astronomy
by DAVID A. KING, *Johann Wolfgang Goethe-Universität, Frankfurt am Main* 274
Folk astronomy 275
Religious aspects of astronomy 275
Mathematical astronomy 276
Theoretical astronomy 283
Astronomical timekeeping 284
Astronomical instruments 286
Al-Bīrūnī 288
Conclusion 288

16 Astrology
by DAVID PINGREE, *Brown University, Providence, Rhode Island* 290
The sources of Arabic astrology 290
The earliest astrological works in Arabic 291
The Persian influence 293
Astrology in the third/ninth century 295
Abū Maᶜshar Jaᶜfar al-Balkhī 297
Later Arabic astrology 299

17 Geographical and navigational literature
by J. F. P. HOPKINS, *University of Cambridge* 301
The *Sindhind* 302
Ptolemy 303
Abū Jaᶜfar Muḥammad b. Mūsā al-Khwārazmī 304
Geodesy 306
From geodesy to *adab* 307
Al-Balkhī – al-Iṣṭakhrī – Ibn Ḥawqal – al-Muqaddasī 312
Al-Masᶜūdī 315
Al-Bīrūnī 316
"Post-Classical" geographers: al-Bakrī and al-Idrīsī 317
Dictionaries and encyclopaedias 319
Travellers 322
Navigational literature 324

18 The literature of Arabic alchemy
by DONALD R. HILL 328
The nature and aims of alchemy 328
Alchemical literature 331

19 Arabic medical literature
by HASKELL D. ISAACS, *University of Cambridge* 342
The period of translation and Jundīshāpūr 343
The period of development and original contribution 345
Education, professionalism and specialism 346
Encyclopaedic medical works 354
Synoptic medical literature 358
Ophthalmology 359
Paediatrics and obstetrics 360
Materia medica and materia alimentaria 361
Astrology and medicine 363

20 Al-Kindī
by FRITZ W. ZIMMERMANN, *University of Oxford* 364

21 Al-Rāzī
by ALBERT Z. ISKANDAR, *Wellcome Institute for the History of Medicine* 370
Biography and religious views 370
The philosophy of al-Rāzī 371
The medical writings of al-Rāzī 373

22 Al-Fārābī
by ALFRED L. IVRY, *New York University* 378

23 Ibn Sīnā
by SALVADOR GÓMEZ NOGALES† 389
Biographical sketch 390
Original features of Ibn Sīnā's works 392
Theory of knowledge 395
Emanation or creation? 395

24 Al-Bīrūnī and the sciences of his time
by GEORGE SALIBA, *Columbia University* 405
Biographical background 405
Al-Bīrūnī's works 406
Conclusion 421

25 Al-Ghazālī
by Adīb Nāyif Diyāb, *University of Jordan* 424
Pupil and teacher 424
Spiritual conversion 426
Al-Ghazālī's style 427
The philosophy of al-Ghazālī 429
The Ṣūfī anthropology 437
Morality and education 438
Freedom and politics 441
Divine love and beauty 443

26 Christian Arabic literature in the ʿAbbasid period
by Samir Khalil Samir, SJ, *Pontificio Istituto Orientale, Roma* 446
Biblical exegesis 446
Canon law 449
Christian theology 450
History 455
Religious encyclopaedias 459

27 Judaeo-Arabic literature
by Paul B. Fenton, *Université Jean-Moulin, Lyon III* 461
Origins 463
Scope 465
Theology and philosophy 466
Philology and exegesis 468
Legal literature 470
Belles-lettres 470
Arabic in Hebrew characters 471
The study of Judaeo-Arabic literature 473
Conclusion 475

28 The translation of Greek materials into Arabic
by L. E. Goodman, *University of Hawaii* 477
The beginnings of the translation movement 480
Al-Maʾmūn and the translation of Greek works 484
Thābit b. Qurrah 485
Ḥunayn b. Isḥāq 487
Translation after Ḥunayn 491
The end of the translation movement 494

29 Didactic verse
by ṢAFĀʾ KHULŪṢĪ, *Oxford* 498

Glossary 510
Bibliography 524
Index 549

PLATES

1 Page from a seventh/thirteenth-century manuscript of Ibn Sīnā's *al-Shifā*ʾ. (Cambridge University Library Add. Or. MS 1013, fol. 10b: published by courtesy of the Syndics.) *page* 89

2 Design for a dredging machine. (Staatsbibliothek Preussischer Kulturbesitz, Berlin, Orientabteilung, MS Or. quart. 739, fol. 74a.) 265

3 Design for a pump for raising water driven by a paddle wheel. (Arthur M. Sackler Museum, MS 1965, 476 Mamluk, Harvard University, Cambridge, Mass: bequest of Meta and Paul J. Sachs.) 269

4 A water-raising device. (Topkapi Sarayi Müzesi MS Ahmad III 3472, fol. 161.) 271

5 The constellation Lepus, as illustrated in al-Ṣūfī's *Ṣuwar al-kawākib al-thābitah*. (Bodleian Arabic MS Marsh 144, fol. 342: published by courtesy of the Bodleian Library, Oxford.) 281

6 Map of North Africa and Spain from al-Iṣṭakhrī's *Kitāb al-Masālik wa-ʾl-mamālik*. (Chester Beatty MS 3007, fol. 29v: published by courtesy of the Chester Beatty Library, Dublin.) 313

7 Page from Ibn al-Nafīs' *Sharḥ tashrīḥ al-Qānūn*. (University of California Arabic MS 80: published by courtesy of the History and Special Collections Division, Louise M. Darling Biomedical Library, University of California, Los Angeles.) 349

8 Physicians' dinner party. (Biblioteca Ambrosiana, Milan, Islamic MS LXX, fol. 12b) 352

9 Page from a sixth/twelfth-century manuscript of al-Rāzī's *al-Kitāb al-Manṣūrī*. (Cambridge University Library Add. Or. MS 1512, fol. 128b: published by courtesy of the Syndics.) 355

10 Diagrams from al-Bīrūnī's *al-Tafhīm li-awāʾil ṣināʿat al-tanjīm*. (Chester Beatty MS 3910, fols. 53–4: published by courtesy of the Chester Beatty Library, Dublin.) 414

EDITORIAL PREFACE

The five centuries of the ᶜAbbasid caliphate in Baghdad saw the flowering of Arabic writing over an extraordinary variety of literary fields, from poetry and humane letters to philosophy, law, history and the natural sciences. The second volume of *The Cambridge History of Arabic Literature* is devoted to *belles-lettres* in the ᶜAbbasid period; the present volume takes as its province the literature of the scholarly disciplines broadly delineated by "religion, learning and science".

Arabic scholarship began with the study of the Qurʾān, the *Ḥadīth* and the various fields of learning which were ancillary to these; but the translations from Greek and other languages which began in the second century after the death of Muḥammad and which continued through the third/ninth century greatly extended the horizons of Arabic literature, and the resulting proliferation of learned disciplines led a number of Muslim writers to draw up lists classifying the various "sciences" or fields of learning. These classifications differ in many details, but there was a generally admitted distinction between the "religious sciences" and the "foreign sciences". The former included Quranic exegesis, Tradition, theology, jurisprudence and all those subjects such as philology and historiography which developed from them. The "foreign sciences" included medicine, the natural sciences, mathematics, astronomy, astrology, geography, alchemy and mechanics.

In the present volume the first five chapters deal with the literature of theology and religious experience. *ᶜIlm al-kalām* (theology, or defensive apologia) originated with the dissensions in Islam after the battle of Ṣiffīn, but it needed an external stimulus to develop fully, and this stimulus was provided by the disputations with Christian apologists and the influence of Greek thought. The disagreements among the Muslims resulted in the establishment of the two heterodox sects of the Shīᶜīs (and their later subsects) and the Kharijites (of which the most important surviving body is that of the Ibāḍīs), and this means that the study of Arabic theological literature has to take into account Shīᶜī works (chapter 2) and Ibāḍī works (chapter 3), as well as those of orthodox or Sunnī Islam (chapter 1).

The values of the Islamic religion are enshrined in the Qurʾān, and as with all sacred books, the need was felt at an early stage for guidance in the interpretation of the meaning of the text. The exegetical literature which arose to fulfil this need sought to explain everything down to the smallest detail. It is characteristic of this literature that to a far-reaching extent it has been a vehicle for the expression of differing doctrinal tendencies in Islam, different schools of thought having sought to justify their views through their own particular interpretations of the Quranic text. In the present volume, chapter 4 is devoted to an examination of the main lines of development of this exegetical literature.

Ṣūfī poetry is the subject of a chapter (14) in *CHAL/ABL*, while the prose literature of Ṣufism is examined in chapter 5 of the present volume. Although reckoned among the "religious sciences" by Ibn Khaldūn, Ṣufism or Islamic mysticism had not always been accepted by the orthodox; it was al-Ghazālī who contributed most to breaking down the prejudice of legalistic Islam and to ensuring the full acceptance of mysticism within the mainstream of Islamic thought and practice. Ṣūfī writings came to embody the highest ideals of Islam, and to Arabic literature they contributed flights of brilliant imagination, together with a style of expression free from literary affectation.

Philosophy (chapter 6) occupied a fringe position between the "religious sciences" and the "foreign sciences". Arabic philosophical thought had its beginnings in the third/ninth century as a result of the Muslim encounter with Greek philosophy. This included not only the thought of Plato and Aristotle, but also that of their successors and continuators, above all the neo-Platonism of Plotinus and Proclus. Philosophy (*falsafah*) and theology (*kalam*) were not originally thought of as being opposed to each other, but after the triumph of the teaching of al-Ashʿarī in the fourth/tenth century relations between the two became characterized by a hostility which was epitomized in the celebrated "quarrel of the *Tahāfut*", in which al-Ghazālī's book *Tahāfut al-falāsifah* ("The Incoherence of the Philosophers") was answered by Ibn Rushd's *Tahāfut al-Tahāfut* ("The Incoherence of 'The Incoherence'").

Concern for the correct understanding of the Quranic text was the starting-point of the literature of the Arabic philological sciences, and for more than a millennium Arabic grammar and lexicography have been the objects of constant cultivation. It is this concern for the means of expression provided by the literary *ʿarabiyyah* that has been effective in ensuring the survival and vigorous continuance of a single literary Arabic. With the partial exception of the use of dialects in modern drama, no local Arabic dialect has been able to replace the "eloquent" (*fuṣḥā*) form of the Arabic language as the normal means of literary expression, and no Arabic dialect (with the exception of Maltese) has succeeded in establishing itself as an independent literary and spoken language. Chapters 7 and 8 examine the literary labours which are the basis of this extraordinary achievement.

The sacred law of Islam (*sharīʿah*) is the "epitome of Islamic thought ... the core and kernel of Islam itself".[1] The cultivation of jurisprudence (*fiqh*, lit. "knowledge") gave rise to the extensive body of Arabic legal literature (chapter 9). In its early stages the subject-matter of Islamic law varied from one place to another, and this was responsible for many of the divergences between the later schools of law. Sunnī Islam eventually recognized four schools of law as differing, but equally valid, interpretations of the *sharīʿah*, while the Shīʿīs and the Ibāḍīs developed their own independent interpretations of the law.

Administrative law and constitutional rules in the caliphate and its successor states came to be regarded as matters within the discretionary power of the caliph or sultan. This discretionary power was referred to as *siyāsah* (lit. "policy"), and the *sharīʿah* recognized the right of the sovereign and his agents to exercise this power in matters of public order, taxation and criminal justice. The specialist literature to which this jurisdiction gave rise comprised both works on administrative procedure and treatises on the training of secretaries (*kuttāb*), and a number of other associated genres, which are discussed in chapter 10.

Chapters 11 to 13 are concerned with aspects of Arabic biography and historical writing. Arabic historiography originally grew out of interest in the oral traditions of the Arab tribes in the time before Islam, but the concern of Muslims with the career of the Prophet and the lives of his Companions gave an added impulse to collect and record information about the past. Subsequently historical scholarship expanded to take in the biographies of later Muslims, the events of the Islamic conquests, the annals of dynasties, local history and universal history, and the impressive achievement of the medieval Arab historians is reflected in the great number and variety of their surviving works.

Chapters 14 to 19 are concerned with those areas of natural science which are most prominently represented in medieval Arabic literature. These range from the abstractions of mathematics to the practicalities of medicine. They include the now discarded hypotheses of astrology (which, however, had the merit of provoking astronomical observation), and also those of alchemy (which at least had the merit of involving experimentation). Thanks to the non-confessional nature of such subjects non-Muslims were

[1] Joseph Schacht, *An Introduction to Islamic Law*, Oxford, 1964, 1.

able to participate freely in these areas of Islamic culture, and Christians and Jews made important contributions to Arabic literature in a number of sciences, particularly medical literature.

The extensive scientific literature in medieval Arabic had a strong influence on European thought, a fact illustrated by those terms from the sciences cultivated by the Muslims which have become part of the European vocabulary, such as algebra, algorithm, cipher, alcohol, alembic, alkali, zenith, nadir, azimuth, simoom, monsoon and many others. It was the achievements of Islamic civilization in the natural sciences and medicine that first compelled the interest of Christian Europe in Arabic literature, and led to the movement of translation of Arabic scientific and philosophical works into Latin which began at the end of the fifth/eleventh century and continued until the tenth/sixteenth century.

The admiration which was felt for the Muslim achievement in these fields appears clearly in the widely circulated *Quaestiones naturales* (early sixth/twelfth century) of Adelard of Bath, the first English Arabist. Adelard is at pains at different points in his book to emphasize the contrast between the learning of the Arabs which, he believed, followed the leadership of reason, and the hidebound reliance on established authority among the savants of Christendom in his day.

Chapters 20 to 25 deal with the lives and works of six universal scholars whose careers span 300 years of Islamic history, from the third/ninth to the beginning of the fifth/eleventh century: Yaᶜqūb b. Isḥāq al-Kindī, Abū Bakr Muḥammad al-Rāzī, Abū Naṣr Muḥammad al-Fārābī, Abū ᶜAlī al-Ḥusayn b. Sīnā, Abū ᵓl-Rayḥān Muḥammad al-Bīrūnī and Abū Ḥāmid Muḥammad al-Ghazālī. Of these only al-Kindī was an Arab, while al-Fārābī was a Turk and the remainder Iranians, but the language in which most of their numerous works were written was Arabic. The intellectual range of these polyhistors covered virtually all the knowledge of their time, and their erudition was equalled only by their industry – al-Bīrūnī is credited with 146 scholarly works, al-Kindī with 265, Ibn Sīnā with 276, and so on.

As a result of the Arab conquests Arabic not only became the learned language of non-Arab Muslims, such as the Persians, but also the language of the Christian and Jewish communities of western Asia and north Africa. In this way Arabic literature came to encompass extensive Christian and Jewish writings in theology, philosophy and law, as well as in medicine and the natural sciences, as mentioned above. Moreover the ᶜAbbasid period saw the production of a considerable body of historical works in Arabic composed by Christian authors and these may sometimes record matters unknown to Muslim historians, to whom Greek, Syriac and Coptic sources were usually inaccessible. Chapters 26 and 27 consider Christian Arabic literature and Judaeo-Arabic literature respectively.

The first volume of this *History* (*CHALUP*, chapters 22, 23 and 24) has discussed some of the diverse influences on early Arabic literature; in Chapter 28 of the present volume the processes are examined by which Greek themes and modes of thought were assimilated into Islamic civilization as a result of the widespread translation of Greek materials into Arabic, and the consequent opening of the Hellenic "treasure house of wisdom".

Chapter 29 deals with Arabic didactic verse, that is verse intended to assist the learning process and aid the student's memory. This was not a literary form invented by the Arabs, but it was one which they employed widely; moreover it was but one of various *Hilfsmittel* for the student which Islamic educational methods introduced, other notable ones being the *masāʾil* or catechism (see chapter 19) and the epitome or *mūjiz*.

In how many copies, and how widely, did the literary works discussed in this volume circulate? No precise answer can be given to these questions, although the ʿAbbasid period saw the elaboration of methods of publication, transcription, bookbinding and bookselling to a remarkable degree, and the circulation of books was greatly assisted by the introduction of paper in the second/eighth century. The extensive holdings reported of the great medieval Islamic libraries such as the ʿAbbasid library of Baghdad, the Faṭimid libraries of Cairo, and the library of al-Ḥakam II in Cordova give an indirect indication of the considerable volume of book production before the days of printing. It has recently been estimated that there are some 600,000 surviving Arabic manuscript books, of which half are still uncatalogued;[2] clearly much remains to be learned of Arabic literary history.

Many of the matters discussed in the following pages are relevant to more than one chapter, and the more important instances have been cross-referenced; elsewhere use of the index should help the reader to find further references to topics treated in several places. As in the first volume of this work only abbreviated references to sources are given in the footnotes where the full details are given in the bibliographies.

It has been pointed out in the editorial preface of *CHAL/ABL* that the term "ʿAbbasid" is a cultural rather than a political designation, and in the following chapters literary developments may sometimes be traced well

[2] A. Gacek, "Some remarks on the cataloguing of Arabic manuscripts", *Bulletin of the British Society for Middle Eastern Studies*, x, 1983, 173.

beyond the year 656/1258, the year of the destruction of the ʿAbbasid caliphate in Baghdad. In the cases of the chapters on Judaeo-Arabic literature and didactic poetry, where it is not intended to treat these subjects further in subsequent volumes of this *History*, literary developments have been brought down to the fourteenth/twentieth century.

The plates used to illustrate the present volume are taken from Arabic manuscript books of the ʿAbbasid period or a little later.

The much regretted death of Fr. Salvador Gómez Nogales prevented him from revising his contributions as he would have wished, and it has only been possible to make the most necessary changes in them for the sake of consistency.

Warm thanks are due to Dr Robin Derricourt and Elizabeth Wetton, and latterly to Dr Katharina Brett, of the Cambridge University Press, for their valuable help and advice in the process of preparing this volume. The Executive Editor is also most grateful to Margaret Jean Acland, who has subedited the final typescript and improved its presentation in many ways, and to Barbara Hird, who has compiled the index.

M.J.L.Y.

ABBREVIATIONS

CHALUP	*The Cambridge History of Arabic Literature: Arabic Literature to the End of the Umayyad Period*
CHAL/ABL	*The Cambridge History of Arabic Literature: ʿAbbasid Belles-Lettres*
EI[1]	*The Encyclopaedia of Islam*, 1st edn
EI[2]	*The Encyclopaedia of Islam*, 2nd edn
GAL, *GAL*, S	C. Brockelmann, *Geschichte der arabischen Litteratur*, and Supplements I–III
GAS	F. Sezgin, *Geschichte des arabischen Schrifttums*
IBLA	*Revue de l'Institut des Belles Lettres Arabes*
Shorter EI	*Shorter Encyclopaedia of Islam*

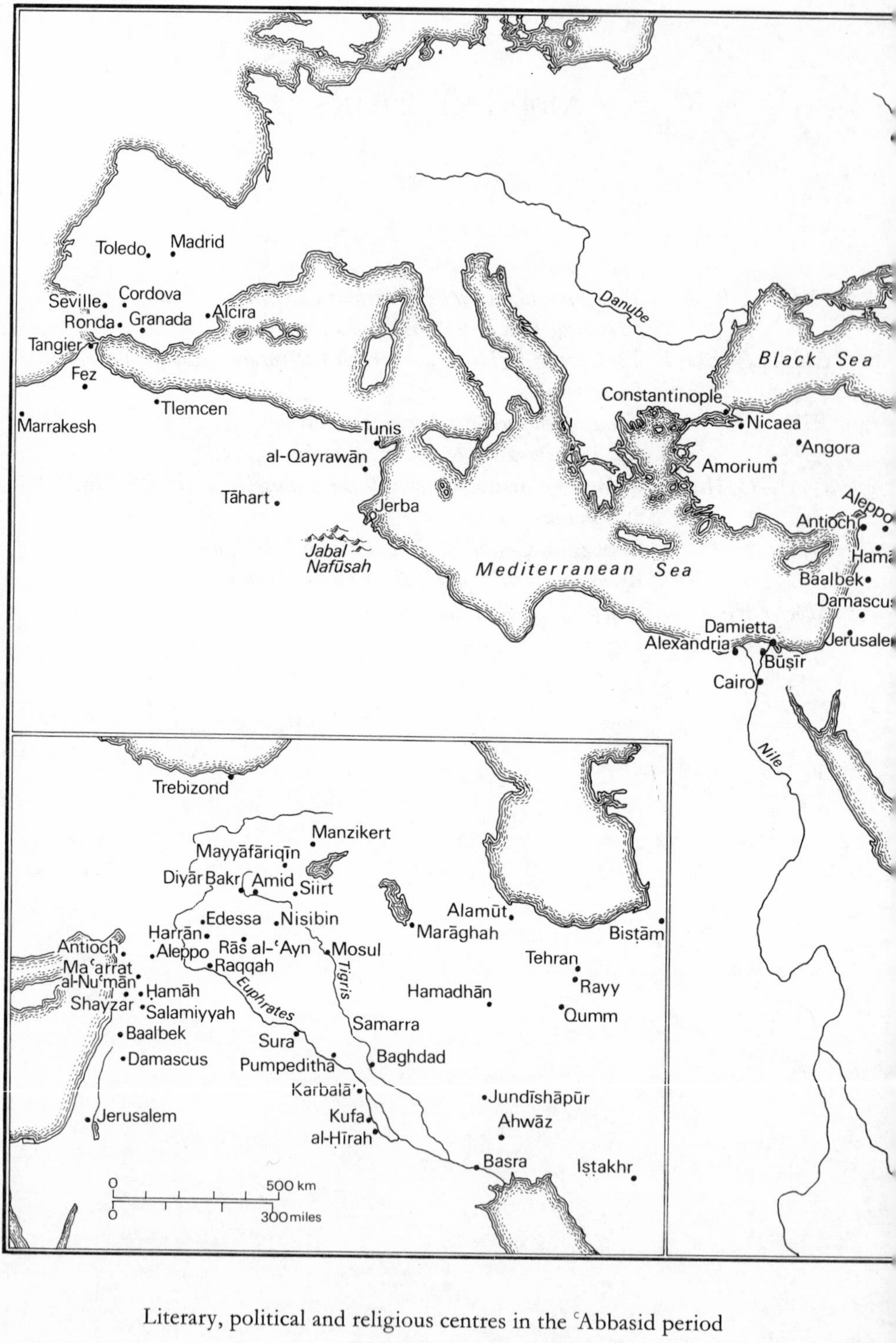

Literary, political and religious centres in the ʿAbbasid period

Kazan
Aral Sea
KHWĀRAZM
Caspian Sea
Samarqand
Afshana
Bukhārā
Fārāb
Nissa
Marw
Balkh
bizond
Manzikert
Ghazālah
Ṭūs
Diyār Bakr
Alamūt
Jurjān
Naysābūr
Marāghah
Tehran
Delhi
Mosul
Hamadhān
Ghaznah
Samarra
Indus
Euphrates
Baghdad
Tigris
Karbalā'
Ahwāz
Ujjain
Iṣtakhr
Shīrāz
Burhānpūr
Basra
Sīrāf
Surat
al-Baḥrayn
Bombay
Nizwā
Medina
OMAN
ḤIJĀZ
Mecca
Red Sea
Arabian Sea
Calicut
YEMEN
Ṣan'ā'
Zabīd
0
1000 km
0
500 miles

CHAPTER 1

SUNNĪ THEOLOGY

The closest equivalent to "theology" in Arabic is *kalām*. It is not an exact translation, however, so we must begin by defining what is meant by "Muslim theology". Provisionally, this can be done negatively by distinguishing it from terms which do not designate Muslim theology and which are the subjects of other chapters of this book.

Theology is not *fiqh*, Muslim jurisprudence; nor, even in its juridical capacity, is it the *sharīʿah*, revealed law. The *sunnah* must be excluded too because, as an oral tradition, it is revealed, like the *sharīʿah*, and constitutes the source of theology, therefore, rather than theology itself. In Christianity, mysticism is a branch of theology, but in Islam not only does it fall outside the domain of theology, in the general sense in which Muslim theology is understood, but is even regarded with some suspicion by the more traditional elements. Besides which, mysticism's unique nature calls for a singularly non-rationalist methodological approach. The term *millah* is synonymous with "religion" as man's expression of divine revelation, or of his relationship with the Deity, and, therefore, comes no closer to conveying the sense of the word "theology". Nor should this be confused with *falsafah*, Muslim philosophy, although arguably their content is the same, for, whereas the starting-point of philosophy in Islam is reason, that of theology is revealed faith. Yet, while Muslim theology cannot be equated with any single one of these subjects, it is rooted more or less directly in all of them.

Abū Zayd ʿAbd al-Raḥmān b. Muḥammad b. Khaldūn (732–808/1332–1406) approaches the understanding of Muslim theology with his definition of *kalām* as the science "that involves arguing with logical proofs in defence of the articles of faith and refuting innovators who deviate in their dogmas from the early Muslims and Muslim orthodoxy".[1] This is to be distinguished from philosophy, which proceeds from the belief "that the essences and conditions of the whole of existence, both the part of it perceivable by the senses and that beyond sensual perception, as well as the

[1] *Muqaddimah*, trans. F. Rosenthal, III, 34.

reasons and causes (of those essences and conditions), can be perceived by mental speculation and intellectual reasoning".[2]

Theology can be said to be a feature of all societies with a cultural expectation of revelation. Having distinguished it from revealed faith, we might describe it, then, as the science which studies the intelligibility of revealed knowledge: the rationalization of revelation in other words. Judaism, Christianity and Islam all became vitally dependent on the development of theology as a science, particularly in the cases of Christianity and Islam, where the appearance of a new religion needed to be explained and justified to the community at large. All three religions subscribe to a monotheistic belief in the oneness of the Deity. Muslims argue, however, that the Hebrew Deity is posited as being the exclusive property of Jews, and that the Christian Trinity violates divine unicity. Only Muslim theology, they contend, preserves the simplicity of the one universal Deity. What is more, Muslims believe that Jewish theology has an exclusively worldly conception of life, while the Christian vision is purely spiritual; only Islam combines both the spiritual and the secular.

We have said already that the appearance of theology in Islam was subsequent to revelation: therein lay the difficulty with which it was faced from the very beginning, namely, the problem of its own possibility. Was it right to allow human reason the privilege of controlling revealed knowledge? One of two positions could be adopted in response to this question. One was the intransigent stance of those whose excessive literalism led them to see in the free exercise of reason the danger of falsifying the data of revelation. At most, allowance could be made for attempts either to render the knowledge intelligible or to make it practically applicable (in the way that the *sharīᶜah* and *fiqh* do). The other position, which later expanded by fragmenting into multiple subdivisions, was to allow the gradual use of reason in pursuance of three objectives: the first of these objectives was the intelligibility which would accrue from a deeper understanding of revelation; the second objective was the elaboration of the knowledge gleaned from revelation (an elaboration which would leave this knowledge essentially unaltered); and the third was the construction of an apologetic in defence of the faith against its opponents and critics.

MUSLIM THEOLOGY AND *FIQH*

The first steps towards rationalizing the faith were taken by *fiqh*, Muslim jurisprudence. Given the impossibility of finding solutions in the Qurʾān to all the problems of life, the Muslim jurists had recourse to various

[2] Ibid., III, 246–7.

procedures employed in the traditional schools of law. These procedures, involving the use of reason and the human faculties, became crystallized in more or less rationalist criteria for interpreting the Qurʾān; such procedures include *raʾy* (individual reasoning), *qiyās* (methodical analogy), *istiḥsān* (discretionary opinion in breach of strict analogy), *istiṣlāḥ* (taking public utility into account) and *istiṣḥāb al-ḥāl* (presumption that an established fact is valid until there is proof to the contrary). Their use of these terms argues further the need felt by these schools to adapt the data of revealed knowledge to the demands of human nature, both at the individual and at the social level. Their procedures, in other words, were the quiet murmurs of an interpretative approach to revelation which was later to develop into an authentic Muslim theology.

MUSLIM THEOLOGICAL SCHOOLS

Despite what has just been said, I would go so far as to say that Muslim theology originated in a series of problems which arose in conditions that were both of religious and of political consequence. Religion and politics are inseparable in Islam; indeed, Islam as a religious movement pervades all quarters of Muslim social life. Not uncommonly, theological controversy begins in response to concrete situations in which prophetic revelation is at issue. It is however the historical question of the Prophet Muḥammad's succession which has provoked not only controversy but also the formation of different theological schools over the ages. Initially, it can be said, the Quranic revelation was a religious experience of relative calm. Only on the Prophet's death did conflict emerge in connection with the problem of his succession, as a consequence of which the different theological conceptions that appeared were crystallized in doctrinal pluralism.

Theological disputation between the parties of Muʿāwiyah, ʿAlī and the Kharijites centred on three basic concepts, namely sin, authority and freedom.[3] The key issue was the concept of sin: the Shīʿīs used it against the Umayyads, arguing that, because of their sin of treachery, the Deity had divested them of authority and had transferred it instead to ʿAlī. The Umayyads themselves suspended judgement on whether or not their leaders had sinned, leaving the decision to the Deity (hence the name Murjiʾites, abstentionists). The Kharijites, lastly, shared the view that the authority of leaders is annulled by sin:[4] since, in this instance, both sides in the dispute were equally culpable, each had been stripped of authority by the Deity. This authority now rested with the community. It was in order to debate the relationship between sin and authority that these first theological

[3] For the political background to this, see *CHALUP*, xii–xiii.

[4] Cf. below ch. 3, 37.

schools in the Islamic community, namely, the Shīʿīs, the Murjiʾites, and the Kharijites, were formed.

One argument which was used to exonerate the leaders centred on the question of freedom: in so far as everything is an act of the Deity, there can be no cause for making men accountable for what they do. Three new groups formed in response to this paradox: the Jabrites, determinists who maintained that all is prefigured by *jabr* (divine destiny), and that man, therefore, has no freedom; the Qadarites, who sought, on the contrary, to reconcile *qadar*, divine decree, with human liberty, by stating that the Deity ordains a course of action only after making prior provision for men to act freely; thirdly, between these two extremes, were placed the middle-ground Ashʿarites, to whom I return below. These, then, were the theological schools which derived from events subsequent to the succession to the Prophet Muḥammad.

The mutakallimūn

There is a further chapter in Islamic history which occasioned the formation of a third set of theological schools, classically known as the *mutakallimūn*, specialists in *kalām* and Muslim theology. The crux of the division between them was the question of the rationality of revealed facts. Similarly structured to the two earlier sets, these schools comprised a pair of opposed groups and a third intermediate one: at one extreme were the rigid traditionalists who acknowledged only Quranic codes of practice and for whom there was nothing created that was not the word of the Deity. Ratiocination is heretical and a real source of danger to faith. Attributes of the Deity which are named in the Qurʾān correspond to real properties, contingent features of divine essence. On the matter of free will, needless to say, they were Jabrites: everything, including human action, is the will of the Deity; men can do nothing that is not predetermined by God.

The Muʿtazilites

At the other extreme, opposite this rigid, anti-rationalist position, stood the Muʿtazilites, defenders of human reason and freedom. Not only were they Islam's earliest intellectuals but in the history of philosophy, also, they have a place of honour. Their name has been interpreted in a number of ways, one of the most usual of which is that it means "the schismatics", or "those who are separate", referring to an occasion on which the school's founder, Wāṣil b. ʿAṭāʾ (d. 131/748), was standing surrounded by a group of followers; it is alleged that when his teacher, al-Ḥasan al-Baṣrī (d. 110/728), saw how this other group had formed at some distance from the column of the mosque where he himself stood, he protested: *iʿtazala ʿannā*, "he has separated himself from us".

Although it is not possible to bracket together under a single head all the Muʿtazilites, since each of the group's members had a distinct and independent system of thought, they did share certain features in common which we shall endeavour to summarize. Despite their importance in the history of philosophy, they were theologians rather than philosophers. Their writings were encylopaedic in scale, ranging in subject from theology and metaphysics to psychology and physics, and even politics and the sciences. Nevertheless, their starting-point was theology, and the perspective from which they reviewed the issues which they wrote about was mainly theological. What distinguishes their doctrine from earlier Muslim theology is the principle of the primacy of reason which they upheld. Reason, prior to and quite independently of revelation, can discover the two fundamental tenets of revealed knowledge. They are the unicity of a perfect, transcendent Deity, which is inferred from the creation of the world, and the freedom of man.

The Muʿtazilite conception of the indivisibility of the Deity was maintained in spite of the pluralist doctrines prevalent both within Islam and outside it. Muʿtazilites were opposed, for example, to the Christian Trinity as well as to the dualism of certain Iranian sects, notably Zoroastrianism. Within Islam, they disagreed with pietistic men of old whose Deity possessed a plurality of attributes, because these were incompatible with the divine essence. Even the terms used in defining this essence could not be granted positive reality, as this would be tantamount to attributing multiplicity to Divinity. One way of understanding the Qurʾān which was propounded by the Muʿtazilites, and later adopted by Muslim philosophers, was the metaphorical interpretation of expressions implying multiplicity, those, that is, which refer to psychic faculties (thinking, wishing, etc.) or to physical properties (touch, hearing, etc.). Muʿtazilites also denied that the Qurʾān is uncreated.

Classically, the Muʿtazilites are known for the five points on which they reached consensus. The common denominator of these points is that they are all demonstrable by recourse to reason, quite independently of revealed knowledge. The first concerned *tawḥīd*, the unity of the Deity; it was a revocation of arguments for (a) the plurality of divine attributes; (b) the uncreated pre-existence of the word of the Qurʾān (Muʿtazilites defended the position that the Qurʾān was created by the Deity); and (c) divine visibility, an aspect of the Deity which was only to be interpreted metaphorically.

The second point concerned ᶜ*adl* (divine justice), the correlate of which is human freedom, curiously, inasmuch as justice, particularly when it is supplemented by the power of sanction, makes demands upon man's sense of responsibility. The Qurᵓān appears to deny human liberty in two ways; by asserting that whatever happens to us is through the divine will, and by affirming the existence of a heavenly register recording past, present and future. In the first case, the Muᶜtazilites interpreted the divine will as being a general divine will whose function is creativity and a concomitant of which is exhaustive knowledge of all that will befall its creations. What is at issue, then, is neither the divine power of mandate (*amr*), nor acts of divine volition (*irādah*), but rather those aspects of Deity which relate to divine knowledge, and which are expressed in the divine capacity for creation and in the Deity's design for eternity. Similarly the metaphysical implications of the existence of the divine register are perfectly compatible with human freedom of action since, although the outcome of a sequence of acts is prefigured in the heavenly record, the acts themselves are presupposed a posteriori, and they are therefore free. It is *qudrah*, the will to act, not *qadar*, the authority with which to decide how to act, that the Deity created in man. The will itself is a divine gift, but not acts of volition or the power of mandate. Furthermore, as a testimony to human freedom, Muᶜtazilite authors cite the Quranic text which reads (*sūrah* iv. 79): "Whatever good comes to thee is from God; whatever evil comes to thee is from thyself." Likewise the cultural, moral and social duties which the Deity imposes in the Qurᵓān imply that man is responsible in a way which would be inconceivable were he not free. The third point which they held in common concerns *waᶜd* (promises) and *waᶜīd* (admonitions), complementing the previous point from an eschatological point of view. The human responsibility implicit in the operation of divine justice entails positive and negative sanctions, in the form of favours for virtue and forfeits for wrong-doing. This was another way of testifying to human freedom, since it would be vain to sanction actions undertaken at the will of someone other than the agent. Their fourth point addressed the issue of an intermediate position (*al-manzilah bayn al-manzilatayn*) between the two classes of sin distinguished by some Muslim theologians, namely *kabāᵓir* and *ṣaghāᵓir*, mortal and venial sins, respectively. According to these theologians, all mortal sins are equally serious and warrant exclusion from the Muslim community; even venial offences, if committed repeatedly, are converted into mortal sins. Muᶜtazilites, in contrast, took human fallibility into account. They distinguished two kinds of serious sin, of which the only kinds that disqualify someone from membership of the Muslim community are sins which implicate a loss of faith: they alone convert a Muslim into a *kāfir*, unworthy of belonging to the community of believers. Grave sins, then, were of two kinds: those involving disbelief (which, additionally, incapacitate a person from governing a Muslim community), and those which incur neither loss of faith nor, therefore, excommunication, but which place a Muslim in an intermediate position. Fifthly, and lastly, there was the point about moral imperative (*al-amr bi-ʾl-maʿrūf*). In the emphasis which they placed on the need for believers to observe the principles of freedom and responsibility in their relations both with the community and with the environment, Muʿtazilites were showing their interest in the social dimension of human behaviour. Ratiocination played a vitally important part in all of this, as the absolute arbiter of truth, including religious truth. This was not to say that revelation is to no avail: on the contrary, it is absolutely indispensable for ordinary people who are unable to think for themselves.

The Ashʿarites

The Ashʿarites stood between these two extremes of either the rejection of reason or its acceptance as the absolute, unique criterion. As exponents of the reasonableness of revealed knowledge, they may be considered as a reaction against the excesses of Muʿtazilite rationalism. In this sense, they represented a return to tradition, though not an unconditional return since the position which they adopted did make allowance for moderate use of theological reasoning.

Ashʿarites derive their name from the *nisbah* of the school's founder, Abūʾl-Ḥasan ʿAlī b. Ismāʿīl al-Ashʿarī (b. Basra, 260/873; d. Baghdad, 324/935). Al-Ashʿarī's life-history is not entirely straightforward. At the close of a fortnight's retreat at the age of forty, having been an active Muʿtazilite all his life, he renounced his former convictions in the great mosque at Basra, entering it like a storm at the hour of prayer. He was frightened by the extreme rationalism of Muʿtazilite beliefs, but found the unmitigated literalism of the rigid traditionalists no less offensive. This change of allegiance complicates the classification of his writings because it is not always clear to which period they belong.

One of his works, entitled *Maqālāt al-Islāmiyyīn* ("Muslim Dogmas"), is worth underlining at this juncture because it is the first known and perhaps, too, the most important history of Islamic dogma. It falls into three parts: in the first, the different Islamic sects and their doctrines are described; the second deals with the literalists (men of *Ḥadīth*); and the various branches of theology, or *kalām*, form the subject of the third section.

Al-Ashʿari was a genuine eclectic whose wish it was to reconcile all the established Sunnī tendencies: at times he would take a Shafiʿite position; at others, he would express himself as a Malikite or even, occasionally, as a Ḥanbalite. All these traditions were agreed on matters of principle but differed in their views on how the principles should be applied. Al-Ashʿarī denied that reason can be the absolute arbiter of the truth in fundamental matters of religious dogma, as this would mean that reason could replace faith. This in itself would not cause any difficulty, were their content the same in both cases. As it is, however, the Qurʾān is committed to *ghayb*, absence, or mystery, that which is invisible and unattainable by processes of reasoning: the mystery, in other words, which it is beyond the powers of human intelligence to decipher, and which must be accepted, therefore, unquestioningly, without having to submit to the arguments and distortions of reason. This eclecticism and, with it, his role of mediator between two extremes, underpins al-Ashʿarī's centuries-old acceptance by all Sunnī parties. A few illustrative cases will exemplify his irenical theology. The position which he held, for instance, in response to one of early Muslim theology's most debated themes, namely, the question of divine attributes, was a middle-ground position which was as much a departure from Muʿtazilite agnosticism as it was from literalist *tashbīh* (anthropomorphism). He used the word *taʿṭīl*, said equally of a garlandless female or of a waterless well, in order to express the view that there can be no Deity without a garland of attributes, for these are the water by means of which the depths of divine essence may be sounded. He thus opposed Muʿtazilites in support of a non-metaphorical interpretation of divine properties: the Deity really does have hands and hearing, as the Qurʾān says. How, though, was this to be made compatible with the unity and simplicity of the Deity? His reply was terse: *bi-lā kayf* (i.e. I know not how. It has no rational explanation. I accept it as an article of faith).

Regarding the origin of the Qurʾān, al-Ashʿarī echoed the Stoic theory which some later Christian theologians were to accept as an explanation of the Logos. There are two aspects to the divine word: it is both *kalām*, language subsisting eternally in Divinity, exempt from articulation and sonority, and it is also the Qurʾān composed of words and phrases addressed to the Prophet. In the first instance, naturally, the word is uncreated; in the second, contrary to the literalist point of view, it is a temporal creation. How was it that these two antithetical aspects could be realized together in the Qurʾān? It must be taken in good faith, without asking how.

On human freedom, finally, after floundering in a sea of perplexity, al-Ashʿarī devised what he saw as a redeeming argument. While wishing to avoid a juxtaposition of human and divine potentiality for action (*qudrah*), he also discounted the *jabr*, or fatalism, of rigid traditionalists. Active potential inheres solely in the Deity, it is not a human attribute; but neither, then, can freedom be, because, if activity is dependent on the will of the Deity, the object of divine creation is deprived of freedom of action. Here, al-Ashʿarī resorted to a new and exclusively human concept, namely *kasb*, or *iktisāb*, the assimilation of the divine will to act. *Qudrah*, action determined by human volition, is superseded by divine mandate, the acceptance of which is free, but passive, like subsequent action taken in response to it. Freedom, therefore, consists in establishing concordance between divine transmission and human reception. Even this liberty, though, he was later to explain as merely nominal since *kasb* is itself a gift to man from the Deity, created by divine decree. How, then, was this apparently absolute occasionalism to be explained? *Bi-lā kayf* (i.e. I know not how; it is what I believe).

LATER DEVELOPMENTS

A long series of works reviewing and systematizing the data of revelation can be assigned to the theological ramifications of intellectuals who were seeking to rationalize revealed knowledge. The interpretative schemes which they employed were traditional in principle, but structured to a degree which made revelation amenable to cultural context. These early reflections on Quranic texts, at once theodicy, anthropology, eschatology and moral law, were later to be crystallized in Sunnī theological treatises. Their systematizations of the interpretation of the Qurʾān gave rise to the traces of what could be called the primitive theology from which derived the various schools at Mecca, Medina, Basra and Kufa. The schools were to be fortified, in turn, by the advent and development of the grammarians, whose aim it was to make a linguistic study of the Qurʾān which, not confined to the merely superficial study of words as such, would penetrate to the deeper level of their ideological content. The title of Arnáldez' book on the Spanish Sunnī author, Ibn Ḥazm (384–456/994–1064), *Grammaire et théologie chez Ibn Ḥazm de Cordoue*, attests the bearing of their interests. Ibn Ḥazm was indeed aware that there was a risk of depriving the revelation of its meaning by interpreting it from the purely humanist perspective of grammatical science. Linguistic analysis aspired to explain Islam's revelation in terms of pre-Islamic poets and Arabic grammar, which was to verge on a dubious naturalism similar to that incurred by Hellenism. This sort of literalist reading of the Qurʾān as a mere work of human grammar did have the advantage of locating it historically against the background of previous civilizations, but was liable to invalidate its absolute, divine origin. As, in fact, Arnáldez makes clear, ʿAlī b. Ḥazm tried to avoid this snag by allowing the Qurʾān to interpret itself; to this end, he drew on its logic and grammar to discover the profound meaning of Islamic theology. Later still, the point was reached at which the systematization of the knowledge revealed in the data presented in the Qurʾān became consolidated in what can be called the official theology of Islam. This, like the earlier systems, covered all areas of Muslim spirituality; here, though, we leave aside its more pragmatic aspects – such as those relating to mystical and ascetic theology, or to liturgical or juridical theology – in order to concentrate solely on dogmatic theology.

THE PILLARS OF ISLAM

The main sources on which Sunnī theology indisputably drew can be limited to four: the Qurʾān, the Sunnah (gradually reduced to permanent form in written *Ḥadīth*), *qiyās* (analogical reasoning) and *ijmāʿ* (the consent of the Muslim community). The frame of the *ummah*, or community, conforms to that of the five "pillars" of Islam, as they have come to be known to Muslims and accepted by them, universally, as constituting what might be defined as the foundation stone of Islam.

The first pillar is the pillar of the *shahādah*, the Muslim creed, which professes that "there is no deity but God; Muḥammad is the Prophet of God". Two fundamental principles are laid down in this declaration of faith: God's *tawḥīd* (uniqueness), and the acknowledgement of Muḥammad as the latest and the most complete divine envoy. This declaration alone is the necessary and sufficient condition of *ummah* membership. The second pillar is *ṣalāh*, prayer. This involves the obligatory performance of five daily prayers. The third pillar is *zakāh*, usually glossed as "alms". The meaning of the word, though, is far broader than this, being more closely equivalent to the tithes and first-fruits of medieval Christian and Hebrew tradition. It signifies the material assistance which it is every Muslim's duty to give to helpless victims of chance, in order to provide for their needs. The fourth pillar is the pillar of *ṣawm*, fasting. This is practised mainly during the month of Ramaḍān. The fifth pillar, the *ḥajj*, is the pilgrimage to Mecca, involving a series of traditional rites, some of which are prior even to Islam.

Al-Ghazālī

There came a time when the two streams of Sunnī theology, based on either rationalist or literal interpretations of the Qurʾān and of the Sunnah (*ahl al-kalām wa-ʾl-ʿaql* and *ahl al-ḥadīth wa-ʾl-naql*, respectively), underwent radical transformation at the instance of one of Islam's most inspired theologians, al-Ghazālī.[5] He threw discredit on reason, on the one hand, by denouncing the fallibility of human faculties: a critique of the revelation in the light of reason, or of a dogmatically rationalist theology, is inherently deficient. Strict adherence to the letter of the text, on the other hand, is conducive to the arid superficiality of sterile formalism. Al-Ghazālī was a bitter opponent of *taqlīd*, acceptance of truth on the authority of a master. Islam needed reviving, and this could be done only if there was a return to the source of revelation, direct contact with the Deity. His systematization of the central truths of the Muslim religion makes al-Ghazālī one of Islam's leading theologians; and yet his system, by restricting doctrinal verification to mystical experience, came closer to Ṣūfī mysticism.

Ibn Tūmart

Gradually, the manifold modes of Islam were transmitted throughout the Muslim west. In the field of jurisprudence, the Malikite school (one of the most conservative, particularly in its Maghribī and Andalusian configurations) consolidated itself at an early stage. Everything understood by the term *kalām*, in the sense of a rational interpretation of the Qurʾān, and Ṣufism likewise, was violently contested by official theologians: in Cordova, al-Ghazālī's works were burned in public by a *qāḍī*. A rigidly anthropomorphic interpretation of Quranic texts was advocated, above all by the Almoravids. It was then that the figure of Ibn Tūmart (d.524/1130) emerged. A Berber of eastern education who had made the pilgrimage to Mecca and who studied in Alexandria, Baghdad and even, possibly, Damascus, Ibn Tūmart felt the need for reform in western Islam very strongly. His reformism was predicated on a synthesis of al-Ghazālī, combined with the ideas of Ibn Ḥazm and even Shīʿī doctrine. In time, his reformist drive developed into an armed movement which, using as its watchword the cause of religious and political unity, overran the whole of the Maghrib and al-Andalus. This was the foundation of the Almohad empire, based on the doctrine of divine unity, which was defended tooth and nail. Ibn Tūmart had the audacity to translate the Qurʾān into Berber, his native language, which he wished to see used also in mosques for prayers and religious preaching.

Ibn Taymiyyah

Another great reformist theologian to emerge in the East was the Syrian Ibn Taymiyyah (d. 728/1328). In adopting the position of a moderate

[5] See below, ch. 25.

anthropomorphist, he expressed an inclination towards Ḥanbalism, an orthodox school committed to a moderate traditionalism which was opposed both to *kalām* and to Ṣufism as much as it was opposed to rigid literalism. The movement which he initiated diverged along two different paths towards Wahhabism, on the one hand, and towards the modernist reformism called the Salafiyyah on the other.

WAHHABISM

Wahhabism takes its name from the founder, Muḥammad b. ʿAbd al-Wahhāb (d. 1206/1791). ʿAbd al-Wahhāb was educated at Mecca, Medina and Basra, before settling in Arabia under the protection of the amir of Dirʿiyyah, Muḥammad b. Saʿūd. After the amir's marriage to one of ʿAbd al-Wahhāb's daughters, the history of this school converges with that of the troubled Saʿūd dynasty. ʿAbd al-Wahhāb's followers, contemptuously referred to by his opponents as Wahhābīs, called themselves *muwaḥḥidūn*, unitarians. The return to primitive Islam which they called for is implied by their name for their teachings, *ṭarīqah Muḥammadiyyah*, the way of Muḥammad. They regarded themselves as Sunnīs and adherents of Ḥanbalism, professing the pure orthodoxy of Ibn Taymiyyah. Doctrinally, their theology can be characterized as follows: religious worship is due solely to the Diety; prayer, therefore, to intercessionary beings of any kind, whether they are angels, prophets or saints, is the expression of *shirk*, polytheism. Someone who denies that human acts are determined by the Deity, or who engages in *taʾwīl*, the allegorical approach to the interpretation of the Qurʾān, is a *kāfir*. The only authority that they accepted was *ijmāʿ*, the consensus of the Muslim community of Muḥammad's Companions; they excluded, therefore, *ijtihād* (reliance on personal judgement as the means of interpreting Islamic sources), which had developed since the fourth/tenth century. The interpretative function was reserved, then, for pre-fourth/tenth century *mujtahid*s, and all subsequent innovation (*bidʿah*) was to be seen as a corruption of orthodox tradition. This restricted understanding of "consensus" was thought to be unduly rigorist in other circles: in some geographical areas, it was observed, innovations which did not impugn the revelation, and which received the consensus of the Muslim community, had always been accepted and acknowledged as the basis of legitimate progress.

DOGMA

It was mentioned above that the presentation of the truths of the Qurʾān is not ordered systematically. Nevertheless theologians demarcate four distinct thematic fields, concerning the faith itself, ritual observances, the moral code and life in society. It is implied that the structure of a believer's life is based on his relationship with the Deity, the Muslim community and the world at large. Another traditional theme of Muslim theology is political philosophy, centred on the caliphate. The doctrinal basis of Islam may be summarized in the following points of dogma:

1 First and foremost, and in sharp contradistinction to the Christian Trinity and the divinity of Jesus, the oneness of a Deity possessing a multiplicity of attributes. The attributes nevertheless do not disrupt the essence.

2 There are subordinate supernatural beings, including angels and *jinn*.

3 The Revelation was transmitted to the prophets by the angel Gabriel. This broaches the issue of prophetology. Islam acknowledges all the prophets of earlier religions: the first was Adam, the father of humanity; then Abraham, father of the faithful, champion of the doctrine of monotheism and accordingly the first Muslim in its etymological sense of one who submits to the Deity. Indeed, Abraham's submission was all the greater for his having gone to the extreme of desiring to sacrifice his own son. His attempt to do so is alluded to not in the Qurʾān but in a relatively recent Tradition, with the difference that the son whom he wishes to sacrifice was not Isaac but Ishmael. The incident occurred in the Kaʿbah at Mecca, the origins of which are not at all certain: some maintain that it was built by Adam; others say that Seth made it. Destroyed in the Flood, it was reconstructed by Abraham and Ishmael before being consecrated by Muḥammad as Islam's holiest shrine. After Abraham came Moses, to whom God gave the Hebrew Torah. David received the book of Psalms, and the Gospel was given to Jesus (who in Islam is simply a prophet, and not the Son of God). According to the Qurʾān Jesus did not die: he ascended to heaven, announced the coming of Muḥammad, and denied that he was God. The last of the prophets, the one to whom God revealed complete knowledge, was Muḥammad.

4 The Revelation is described in full in the sacred texts, that is to say, in the Qurʾān, the Torah and the Gospels. The problem of its relation to the Scriptures is another central theological topic in Islam. For Muslims, the sacred text, by antonomasia, is the Qurʾān, the content of which is wholly revealed. Muḥammad urged that since these revealed works were fully concordant with one another originally, any discrepancies between them must be due to textual falsification by Jews and Christians. The extent to which this is an article of faith for Muslims can be judged from the fact that they believe that theirs is the only authentic holy book.

5 In Islam, it is held that all is of divine origin. The Creation, then, is made a further theme of fundamental bearing since, if Divinity is the source of everything human, this raises the problem of the freedom of mankind. The different schools of Muslim theology have responded in various ways to this problem, each according to its own definition of the relation of divine creativity to human action.

6 Lastly, there is the question of Islamic doctrine on the ultimate end of human life. Implicit is the principle of the resurrection, including the resurrection of the body, Muslim theologians, on the whole, following the Qurʾān in stressing the transcendent role of a day of judgement. This is often referred to antonomastically as "the Day". According to al-Ghazālī's epitome of the course of the afterlife, all men are examined in the grave by the angels Munkar and Nakīr (the punishment of the grave, *ʿadhāb al-qabr*); on the Day of Judgement, the actions of a person's life are weighed in the balance (*al-mīzān*) of divine justice; all will cross the hell-spanning bridge (*al-ṣirāṭ*) from which any who are not chosen will fall. The process begins with the provision of *rizq*, or life-wages, in the form of the aid and means of subsistence which each in his lifetime has received from the Deity. When the wages come to an end, death inexorably ensues. It is a process which conforms to the doctrine of predestination, however variously this has been interpreted by different schools. There is a widespread belief that either Jesus or Muḥammad, or one of Muḥammad's descendants, will appear as a final guide for humanity at the end of time.

ʿAQĪDĀT

Synopses of Islamic theological material are available in the classical *ʿaqīdāt* (compendiums of dogma), which deal with what were considered to be central matters of faith for true Muslims. These works, published by the most illustrious theologians of the times, have no more authority than that which they are granted by the Muslim community. Their value lies in the fact that they are all agreed on basic points of doctrine. The oldest known *ʿaqīdah* is the one which has been attributed to Abū Ḥanīfah (d. 150/767); this is followed by "Abū Ḥanīfah's testament", so-called – although it is unlikely that he was its author – since it is, in part, a reflection of Ḥanbalite tendencies. It is probably an early fourth/tenth-century imitation of early third/ninth-century polemics. The best-known *ʿaqīdāt* are those of Abū Jaʿfar Aḥmad al-Ṭaḥāwī (d. 321/933), two written by al-Ghazālī and incorporated in his *Iḥyāʾ ʿulūm al-dīn*, and those by Abū Ḥafṣ ʿUmar b. Muḥammad al-Nasafī (d. 537/1142), Fakhr al-Dīn abū ʿAbdullāh Muḥammad b. ᶜUmar al-Rāzī (d. 606/1209), Abū ᶜAbdullāh Muḥammad b. Yūsuf al-Sanūsī of Tlemcen (d. 895/1490), and the Egyptian Muḥammad al-Faḍḍālī (d. 1236/1821). It is fair to say that anyone regarding himself as a theologian published his own *ᶜaqīdah*; some came to be used as catechisms in schools.

CHAPTER 2

SHĪᶜĪ THEOLOGICAL LITERATURE

The pioneers of Shīᶜī theology seem to have begun to propagate theological views during the middle of the second/eighth century. By that time, distinct branches of the Shīᶜah had emerged. All of these believed that ᶜAlī b. abī Ṭālib (reigned 35–40/656–61) was the most excellent (*afḍal*) after the Prophet and that he should have been the caliph or imam. The party which supported his claims and the claims of his family (*ahl al-bayt*) for the leadership of the community became known as the Shīᶜah (originally *shīᶜat* ᶜAlī, the party of ᶜAlī). ᶜAlī did eventually attain the caliphate and was succeeded briefly by his elder son al-Ḥasan, whose mother was Fāṭimah, daughter of the Prophet. When al-Ḥasan, who was forced to abdicate by Muᶜāwiyah b. abī Sufyān (reigned 41–60/661–80), died, the Shīᶜah called on his brother al-Ḥusayn to lead them in revolution against Muᶜāwiyah. Al-Ḥusayn did not embark on action until after the death of Muᶜāwiyah, when he answered the call of his supporters in Kufa to lead them in revolution against Muᶜāwiyah's son Yazīd (reigned 60–4/680–3). The revolution proved a catastrophe and al-Ḥusayn and many of his close relatives were tragically killed at Karbalāᵓ by vastly superior forces as they were on their way to Kufa (61/680). Only one son of al-Ḥusayn, ᶜAlī b. al-Ḥusayn (d. 95/713–4), survived this disaster, and for the rest of his life he seems to have followed a quiescent policy towards the Umayyad authorities.

However, the death of al-Ḥusayn did provoke calls for vengeance among the Shīᶜah. In 66/685 al-Mukhtār b. abī ᶜUbayd al-Thaqafī, acting to avenge the blood of al-Ḥusayn, took control of Kufa and claimed to be acting on behalf of Muḥammad b. al-Ḥanafiyyah, a son of ᶜAlī by a wife other than Fāṭimah, whom he declared was the imam and the Mahdī (the rightly guided one) who would remove injustice and bring about an era of justice for the oppressed. The movement, which became known as the Kaysāniyyah, was soon defeated (the support given it by Muḥammad b. al-Ḥanafiyyah was always ambiguous). Yet it does seem to have introduced theological ideas which were to play a significant role in future Shīᶜī thinking. The first of these is a primitive conception of the doctrine of *badāᵓ*. When al-Mukhtār was defeated in a battle after declaring that God would give him victory, he explained this by saying that a different idea had seemed good (*badāʾ*) to God after his initial promise. At this stage *badāʾ* simply means that God could change his mind. After Muḥammad b. al-Ḥanafiyyah's death (81/700), many of the Kaysāniyyah who still believed that he was the imam declared that he was not dead but was in hiding under the protection of God, as he would eventually return as the Mahdī to bring about an end to oppression and an age of justice for the Shīᶜah. These two doctrines, the doctrine of the occultation (*ghaybah*) of the imam and the imam's return (*rajᶜah*) either from death or occultation, were to be constantly recurring ideas among the Shīᶜah.

It was ᶜAlī b. al-Ḥusayn's son Muḥammad al-Bāqir (d. 114/732 or 117/735) who really developed the doctrine of the imamate. He seems to have laid down the principle of designation (*naṣṣ*). The Prophet had designated ᶜAlī, al-Ḥasan and al-Ḥusayn. Al-Ḥusayn had designated his son ᶜAlī b. al-Ḥusayn and the latter had designated Muḥammad al-Bāqir. There was a body of knowledge which was handed down to the imams so that they could safeguard the religion of Islam. Although they should be the political leaders and the Muslims who had rejected ᶜAlī were guilty of unbelief, the imams would not lead their Shīᶜah against the authorities until an appropriate time. For the present all should concentrate on religion and receive their religious instruction from the imams. This doctrine was further elaborated by Muḥammad al-Bāqir's son and successor Jaᶜfar al-Ṣādiq (d. 148/765). In doing this he maintained the doctrine that the imamate could never be held by a brother in succession to a brother after al-Ḥusayn's succession to al-Ḥasan. This doctrine seems to have been in response to the claims of his uncle Zayd b. ᶜAlī. The latter had declared that the imam was a member of the family (*ahl al-bayt*) of al-Ḥusayn who declared his imamate publicly, by force of arms if necessary. The Prophet had not designated ᶜAlī publicly (*naṣṣ jalī*), but privately (*naṣṣ khafī*). Therefore in choosing Abū Bakr, ᶜUmar and ᶜUthmān, the Muslims had not committed unbelief because they had been unaware of the designation. Thus while the imam should be the most excellent (*afḍal*) from the family of ᶜAlī, it was possible to have a less excellent (*mafḍūl*) imam. In this way the rule of Abū Bakr, ᶜUmar and part of ᶜUthmān's rule became legitimate.

Zayd b. ᶜAlī put his doctrine to the test, claimed the imamate and came out in revolution, only to be decisively defeated and killed (122/740)[1] Athough Jaᶜfar al-Ṣādiq lost some of his father's supporters to Zayd and the party that became the Zaydī sect of the Shīᶜah, he did still have a band of devoted followers who were prepared to follow his more quiescent

[1] *CHALUP*, 299.

leadership. During his imamate, the doctrine of *badāʾ* came fully into Shīᶜī theological thinking. It had appeared clear to all the supporters of Jaᶜfar that he had designated his son Ismāᶜīl as his successor. However, Ismāᶜīl died and Jaᶜfar is reported to have explained this premature death by maintaining that after God had ordered the designation of Ismāᶜīl, something different appeared good to him. This doctrine came under severe attack from those opposed to the Shīᶜah, and its defence became an important element in Shīᶜī theology accepted by almost all their theologians, though with differing interpretations. One group accepted the notion of God changing his mind, that new ideas can occur to God, and they compared it to the doctrine of abrogation where one revelation from God can abrogate another. Another group maintained that a change of plan was possible for God in what he knows is going to happen, as long as it has not yet happened.

A group of the Shīᶜah could not accept this and declared that either Ismāᶜīl had not died or that the imamate belonged to his son Muḥammad. This group is known as the Ismāᶜīlīs. Although they emerge in strength later in Faṭimid Egypt, their theological contribution does not belong to mainstream Shīᶜī theology. It is the group who accepted the imamate of Jaᶜfar's son Mūsā al-Kāẓim (d. 183/799) after Jaᶜfar's death in 148/765, who are generally known as the Shīᶜah. However, the succession of Mūsā was not completely smooth, as many of the Shīᶜah thought that Jaᶜfar's successor was his eldest son ᶜAbdullāh, and it was only after Mūsā's claims had been endorsed by leading Shīᶜī scholars that he became generally accepted as imam by the Shīᶜah.

In view of the fact that the Shīᶜah was always an organization which, even at its most quiescent, was in some way at variance with the authorities, it was necessary at times to hide its beliefs from the authorities. This gave rise, from a very early time, to the doctrine of *taqiyyah* (precautionary dissimulation). It was permissible for the Shīᶜah to conceal their true beliefs. This became a distinctive feature of Shīᶜī belief and its use was encouraged more or less as an article of faith.

The early Shīᶜī theologians appear to have been adherents of the sixth imam, Jaᶜfar al-Ṣādiq, and his son Mūsā al-Kāẓim, the seventh imam. The sources which record the views of these early theologians are all hostile to them so that only a very coloured picture of their views emerges. The distinctive doctrine of all these early theologians was, of course, their belief in the imamate. It is this doctrine which, in the main, set them apart from other Islamic thinkers who were seeking to develop a systematic theology for Islam. Otherwise, apart from a few purely Shīᶜī doctrines, these theologians are an integral part of the theological process which was taking place at the time. How the imams reacted to the theological speculation of these followers of theirs is difficult to assess. There are later traditions which put denunciations of many of their views in the mouths of the imams. If these traditions are true, and it is certainly quite possible that they are, it would involve the theologians in a somewhat different theology of the imamate from that which became the standard theology later.

From the account of Shīᶜī beliefs about the imamate given by the heresiographer, ᶜAlī b. Ismāᶜīl al-Ashᶜarī, in his *Kitāb Maqālāt al-Islāmiyyīn*, two distinct trends emerge. On the one hand, there are beliefs which are given prominence by later traditional literature. The imams are not more excellent (*afḍal*) than the prophets but they may be more excellent than the angels. They and the prophets are protected from error because they are proofs (*ḥujaj*) of God to the world. This doctrine is later elaborated to mean that without an imam, the world would cease to exist. Knowledge of the imams is necessary and one who dies without knowing the imam dies a death of those who are ignorant of Islam, because the imams are the ones who preserve the law of Islam (*sharīᶜah*). The imams know everything that was and will be. No knowledge of religion or the world is unknown to them. Thus the imams know all languages and everything else that can be known. The imams and the prophets perform miracles because they are God's proofs, but the imams do not have inspiration.

Clearly anybody who held these views of the imamate and had access to his imam could not indulge in theological speculations. However, the other trend is clearly compatible with theological speculation. The imams know all the matters of legal injunctions and Islamic law, because they are the guardians and preservers of the laws and everything that people need to know. However, the imams do not always know those things which are not necessary for people to practise their religion; the imams' knowledge does not encompass everything. This view is endorsed by al-Faḍl b. Shādhān (d. 260/873–4) who belonged to one of the early schools of theology. He is reported as having maintained that the Prophet brought the complete form of the religion, and he taught the one who was to take his place the knowledge of that religion. This knowledge is concerned with legal matters and understanding the Qurʾān. There must always be someone who knows that and it is passed on as inherited knowledge.[2] The early theologian Hishām b. al-Ḥakam (d. 179/795–6) maintained that the imams were protected from error, whereas the prophets were not, because they could be corrected by revelation. He clearly means this protection from error to involve the imam's preservation of the laws of Islam. Those who would

[2] Kashshī, *Rijāl*, 540–1.

allow theological speculation would also insist on the necessity of recognizing the imam for the proper practice of religion, but they regard it as impossible for the imams to perform miracles.

With this kind of doctrine of the imamate, it was possible for the early Shīᶜī theologians to indulge in theological speculation. One of the earliest of them was Zurārah b. Aᶜyān (d. 150/767). Few of his theological views have survived but it is reported that he wrote books on the ability to act (*istiṭāᶜah*) and determinism (*jabr*). He is said to have maintained that the ability to act must precede the act. This ability to act consisted of physical soundness. From this it would seem that Zurārah was prepared to allow human beings a considerable role in the performance of an act, and that he supported the adherents of free will and opposed determinism. There are a number of traditions in the works of later Shīᶜī Traditionists with the imams denouncing Zurārah's views. Zurārah also seems to have held the view that the attributes of God, like knowing, hearing and seeing, did not exist until God created them for himself.

Two contemporaries of Zurārah, Muḥammad b. Nuᶜmān al-Aḥwal, called Shayṭān al-Ṭāq by opponents and Muʾmin al-Ṭāq by the Shīᶜah, and Hishām b. Sālim al-Jawālīqī, seem to have held similar views. They held an anthropomorphist view of God maintaining that God has the form of a man. Perhaps this view was influenced by a tradition that when Muḥammad was taken into the Divine presence, he saw him in the form of a young man. However, they did not believe that God is a body but regarded him as incorporeal. All other things are bodies, even motions including human acts. They, like Zurārah, believed that ability to act precedes the act, but this doctrine is somewhat modified by al-Aḥwal as he maintains that no act can occur unless God wills it, thus inclining towards determinism. These three theologians together with Hishām b. al-Ḥakam, the most distinguished of all the early theologians, seem to have played an important role in securing the Shīᶜah's acceptance of Mūsā al-Kāẓim after the death of Jaᶜfar al-Ṣādiq.

A somewhat younger theologian, ᶜAlī b. Ismāᶜīl al-Mīthamī, is claimed by Ibn al-Nadīm (fourth/tenth century) in the *Fihrist* to have been the first to elaborate the theology of the Shīᶜah. This claim is clearly false as all the Shīᶜī sources make him a follower of the eighth imam, ᶜAlī al-Riḍā (d. 203/818), and mention his rejection of those who held that Mūsā al-Kāẓim was in occultation and would return. However, he is also claimed to have held views that approximate to those of the Zaydīs, maintaining that, although ᶜAlī was the most excellent and the one entitled to be imam, the Muslims had not erred to the point of sin in appointing Abū Bakr and ʿUmar; however, he renounced ʿUthmān and those who had fought against ᶜAlī as unbelievers. If this Zaydī view is true, perhaps he became a follower of ᶜAlī al-

Riḍā when the latter was made heir apparent by the caliph al-Maʾmūn (reigned 198–218/813–33). Very little is known of his other theological views. He followed al-Aḥwal and Hishām al-Jawālīqī in believing that God is in the form of a man. He is also said to have regarded God's will as motion, which may well accord with the views of the other two theologians.

The most important of these early theologians was Hishām b. al-Ḥakam. He is reported in al-Ashʿarī's *Kitāb Maqālāt al-Islāmiyyīn* to have held that God is a body unlike other bodies but yet with spatial dimensions, a shining light with colour, taste and smell. At first he was not in space; then he created space by his motion. Space is the throne (*ʿarsh*) of God. Hishām maintained that there was a likeness between God and perceptible bodies in one respect, as they gave evidence for him. It seems that Hishām held that anything, including God, must involve some form of substantiality, otherwise it would be nonexistent. Hishām rejected any idea of the attributes of God being eternal. Thus God knows only existing things and therefore could not have known from eternity. God's attributes like knowledge are not God and not eternal, but they are not created. However, such attributes are dependent upon creation. Creation comes about through God's will which is expressed in motion. Acts and motion seem to be understood in the same sense. Thus the concept of motion may involve a temporal connotation.

With regard to the physical universe, Hishām held that different bodies could inhere in one place. Thus heat and colour are bodies which inhere in one place, producing two effects on the senses. God's knowledge of the physical universe is also explained in corporeal terms. God knows what is under the earth by means of rays that come from him. Man consists of body and soul and the soul is light. Human actions are created by God. Human ability to act (*istiṭāʿah*) consists of five things, four of which precede the act: soundness of body, freedom of circumstances (*takhliyat al-shuʾūn*), space in time and the means by which the act can be done; the fifth, which occurs at the moment of the act, is a motivating cause (*sabab*) for doing the act. When God causes all five to occur, the act takes place. It cannot take place without the fifth and it is caused by God. From this understanding of the ability to act, it would seem that Hishām had a rather determinist view.

As far as the conflict concerning the Qurʾān was concerned, Hishām took an intermediate position which was fairly generally adopted by the Shīʿah. He held that the Qurʾān was neither creator nor created.

Hishām's views represent a materialist theology as opposed to the more anthropomorphic views of the other early theologians. This materialism is coupled with a determinist attitude towards human acts.

Shortly after Hishām's death, Mūsā al-Kāẓim died in prison. There had been ideas circulating among Shīʿī groups that the seventh imam would be the Mahdī. Many of the Shīʿah would not accept that Mūsā had died and believed that he was in occultation, and that he would return to bring about a golden age for the Shīʿah. The doctrine of *rajʿah* was also being elaborated along with the return of the imam. It was claimed that the dead would return to the world before the resurrection. The force of this belief was to provide some solace to the Shīʿah since, whether the imam was in occultation or not, they would be present when the Mahdī did bring about the era of justice for the Shīʿah.

There seems to have been a definite Shīʿī school of theology that followed the teachings of Hishām b. al-Ḥakam. The leadership of this was taken up by his student Yūnus b. ʿAbd al-Raḥmān. Yūnus was born at the end of the reign of Hishām b. ʿAbd al-Malik (reigned 105–25/724–43). He was a *mawlā* of the Shīʿī family of Yaqṭīn, and it is alleged that he was a foundling. He seems, after the death of Mūsā al-Kāẓim, to have been influential in advocating the imamate of ʿAlī al-Riḍā. The reports of his theological writings are meagre, though he was a prolific writer on legal matters. It seems clear that he followed the main lines of Hishām's teaching. There is a report that he followed the doctrine that God was a body (*jism*) unlike other bodies, a thing unlike other things, permanent, existing, not nonexistent, beyond the limits of invalidation and anthropomorphism. In this form the doctrine is approved by ʿAlī al-Riḍā, the eighth imam, while he rejects the doctrine of Hishām b. Sālim al-Jawālīqī.[3] Yūnus is also reported as following Hishām b. al-Ḥakam in his view that the Qurʾān was not a creator nor created. This view was also endorsed by ʿAlī al-Riḍā. Although al-Ashʿarī maintains that he followed the views of Zurārah as far as ability to act was concerned, there is a Shīʿī tradition in which he declares himself to uphold the doctrine of determinism.[4] This latter view would fit more appropriately into a school of theology following the teachings of Hishām b. al-Ḥakam. He is also alleged to have held that there were bearers of the throne of God, arguing that this was possible on the basis that the thin legs of a crane are able to bear it. This was probably an attempt to explain Qurʾān, lxix.17, which speaks of eight angels carrying the throne of God. Yūnus is also said to have claimed that heaven and hell had not yet been created. He further seems to have maintained that there was some of the substance of God (*jawhariyyah*) in mankind.[5] Perhaps this is an extension of the materialist views of Hishām b. al-Ḥakam that there was a likeness between God and bodies.

At the death of Yūnus, leadership of the school of Hishām b. al-Ḥakam

[3] Ibid., 284–5. [4] Kulaynī, *al-Uṣūl min al-kāfī*, I, 157–8. [5] Kashshī, *Rijāl*, 495.

was taken over by Muḥammad b. al-Khalīl al-Sakkāk who was also a pupil of Hishām. Although he is said to have opposed Hishām in some things, there is also evidence that in others he followed Hishām fairly closely. He wrote a book on the unity of God (*tawḥīd*) taken from Hishām, which is reported to have erred in the direction of *tashbīh*.

Al-Faḍl b. Shādhān was the next leader of the school. He claimed to be following in the path of the three earlier leaders,[6] and both he and his father were students of Yūnus b. ᶜAbd al-Raḥmān.[7] Al-Faḍl was a prolific writer in both jurisprudence and theology. His extant polemical work, *al-Īḍāḥ* ("The Clarification"), includes a defence of the doctrine of *rajᶜah*. He seems to have carried on the school's definition of God as a body. This doctrine was condemned by the eleventh imam al-Ḥasan al-ᶜAskarī just before he died (260/874).[8]

During the time of the school of Hishām, there had been a further three imams after ᶜAlī al-Riḍā: the ninth imam Muḥammad al-Jawād (d. 220/835), the tenth imam ᶜAlī al-Hādī (d. 254/868) and the eleventh al-Ḥasan al-ᶜAskarī. There were ideas current that the twelfth imam was going to be the Mahdī and al-Ḥasan al-ᶜAskarī was kept under close surveillance. The Shīᶜah claimed that a son was born to him and smuggled out of his house to the Ḥijāz. There that son, Muḥammad, whose name should not be mentioned, remained in hiding, only communicating with the Shīᶜah through a series of four successive leaders who were each called *safīr* (ambassador). This was the "Small Occultation" (*al-ghaybah al-ṣughrā*). The "Great Occultation" (*al-ghaybah al-kubrā*) began in 329/941, when the fourth and last *safīr* announced on his death-bed that the imam would no longer make direct contact with the Shīᶜah.[9] He was in the world but in concealment and he would return as the Mahdī to bring about the golden age.

It was during this time that the Traditionists were able to exert much more authority over the Shīᶜah. As they possessed in their Traditions the various imams' rulings on all aspects of life, they and their Traditions became the source of authority for the lives of the Shīᶜah. They had, too, in the corpus of these Traditions many in which the imams laid down theological doctrines. Thus the Traditionists claimed that their Traditions were the ultimate source of Shīᶜī theology.

In the course of the third/ninth century, Qumm became the principal centre for Shīᶜī Traditions, and it is the Traditionists of Qumm who attempted to lay down the pattern of orthodox Shīᶜī theology. This is most clearly set out in the section on the unity of God in the collection of

6 Ibid., 359. 7 Ṭūsī, *Fihrist*, 254. 8 Kashshī, *Rijāl*, 542. 9 *CHALUP*, 302.

Traditions *al-Uṣūl min al-kāfī* by al-Kulaynī (d. 329/941). The work seems to represent the consensus reached by the Qummī Traditionists, who appear to have been generally extremely hostile to the theological speculations of the early theologians. Although their names are often mentioned with pride for their prowess in theology, their doctrines are frequently rejected. The battle between the theologians and the Traditionists seems to have been fought during the time of al-Faḍl b. Shādhān, and the issue concentrated on Yūnus b. ᶜAbd al-Raḥmān. The Qummī Traditionists showed their hostility to him and declared that his views were at variance with the teachings of the imams. Al-Faḍl b. Shādhān quotes a Qummī Traditionist, ᶜAbd al-ᶜAzīz b. Muhtadā (whom he describes as the best Qummī he has ever seen), as saying that ᶜAlī al-Riḍā had instructed him to take the doctrines of his religion from Yūnus b. ᶜAbd Raḥmān, even though he is opposed by the people of his town. Another pupil of Yūnus, Ibrāhīm b. Hāshim, moved from Kufa to Qumm and established himself there. He is declared to be the first to transmit Kufan Traditions in Qumm.[10] It seems probable that many of these Traditions reflected the philosophical school of Yūnus b. ᶜAbd al-Raḥmān. His son, an important Qummī Traditionist, ᶜAlī b. Ibrāhīm al-Qummī (d. 307/919), wrote a work in defence of Hishām b. al-Ḥakam and Yūnus b. ᶜAbd al-Raḥmān entitled *al-Risālah fī maᶜnā Hishām wa-Yūnus*.[11] In his commentary on the Qurʾān,[12] ᶜAlī b. Ibrāhīm upholds the visibility (*ruʾyah*) of God, suggesting his corporeality.

Although ᶜAlī b. Ibrāhīm al-Qummī is an important authority for al-Kulaynī, it is quite clear from the Traditions the latter has used in his chapter on the unity of God that he has avoided those views which ᶜAlī b. Ibrāhīm held about the doctrines of Hishām b. al-Ḥakam and Yūnus which were in conflict with the Qummī Traditionists' consensus. Where he does use Traditions from ᶜAlī b. Ibrāhīm, they represent those parts of their theology which was in accord with the Qummī view.

The Qummī Traditions in *al-Uṣūl min al-kāfī* maintain that God is a thing, but deny that he is a body or a form. These denials are attributed to Jaᶜfar al-Ṣādiq and Mūsā al-Kāẓim. In repudiating these doctrines, Jaᶜfar and Mūsā specifically mention the names of Shīᶜī theologians contemporary to them who held these doctrines.[13] The Traditions in *al-Uṣūl min al-kāfī* also deny the possibility of being vouchsafed the vision of God.[14] The attributes of God are divided into essential attributes (*ṣifāt al-dhāt*) and attributes of action (*ṣifāt al-fiᶜl*), according to the theological system that had become established. The essential attributes are described by al-Kulaynī, in a personal interpretation of the Traditions, as those attributes of God

[10] Najāshī, *al-Rijāl*, 13. [11] Ibid., 197. [12] See below, ch. 4, 48.
[13] Kulaynī, *al-Uṣūl min al-kāfī*, 1, 82–3. [14] Ibid., 95–100.

whose opposite could never be used of him. They include such attributes as knowledge, hearing, seeing, power, wisdom, might, mastery and eternity.[15] The attribute of will is regarded as an attribute of action; God's will came after such attributes as knowledge, which belong to his divine essence.[16] This gives some scope for the retention of the doctrine of *badāʾ*. In his section on *badāʾ*, the Traditions which al-Kulaynī uses emphasize the importance and wonderful nature of *badāʾ*. However, he does not include the Tradition about Jaʿfar al-Ṣādiq and Ismāʿīl. *Badāʾ* is a kind of knowledge that only God knows which implies a rejection of the Tradition about Ismāʿīl. The knowledge that God gives to angels, prophets and imams will come to be because God does not lie against himself. However, it must be accepted that God will bring forward whatever he wishes and delay whatever he wishes.[17] As far as the created or uncreated Qurʾān is concerned, al-Kulaynī does not present any explicit Traditions on the subject. The report that Jaʿfar al-Ṣādiq maintained, along with Hishām b. al-Ḥakam, that the Qurʾān is neither creator nor created is not included. Al-Kulaynī does, however, include a Tradition in which Jaʿfar states that speech (*kalām*) is an attribute which has been caused to be (*muḥdathah*) and which is not eternal; God was, when he was not speaking.[18] This would seem to imply that the Qurʾān is created even if the term *muḥdath* (caused to be) is used instead of *makhlūq* (created).

The Traditions of *al-Uṣūl min al-kāfī* concerning free will and determinism seem to tend towards a compromise position. A Tradition is attributed to ʿAlī al-Riḍā which gives a very similar account of *istiṭāʿah* to that given by Hishām b. al-Ḥakam, so that the ability to act is only made available to a man at the moment of acting, and he does not have the ability either to act or to refrain from acting until the moment he does or does not do so. The deterministic tendency of this is further emphasized by a Tradition from Jaʿfar al-Ṣādiq, which maintains that God does not lay duties upon men which they do not have the ability to perform, but that they can do anything by virtue of his will.[19] Despite this seeming determinism, there is a degree of consensus in the Traditions that the position is neither one of determinism nor free will. The position is summed up in a Tradition from ʿAlī al-Riḍā in which he maintains that God is too mighty (*aʿazz*) to give his creatures free will and too just to compel them to sin.[20]

The view of faith (*īmān*) presented by the Traditions in *al-Usūl min al-kāfī* is akin to the general Islamic view of the time. The Traditions distinguish between faith and Islam. Islam is prior to faith and achieved by belief in Islam and the recitation of the *shahādah*. On the other hand, faith involves

[15] Ibid., 111–2. [16] Ibid., 109. [17] Ibid., 146–9. [18] Ibid., 107. [19] Ibid., 160–2.
[20] Ibid., 157.

giving full effect to the requirements of religion and may increase or decrease. A sinner may cease to be a believer (*muʾmin*) but will remain a Muslim. Repentance may help to restore his faith.[21]

In al-Kulaynī's treatment of the imams, there is great emphasis on the miraculous nature of the imams. Al-Kulaynī also has to address the problem of the occultation of the twelfth imam. As already mentioned, the idea of the occultation of an imam had been well known among the Shīʿah. In *al-Uṣūl min al-kāfī* al-Kulaynī presents a brief chapter with Traditions on this subject. In a Tradition attributed to Jaʿfar al-Ṣādiq, the latter explains the predicament that the Shīʿah would face after the death of the eleventh imam al-Ḥasan al-ʿAskarī. He explains that the occultation of the imam must occur before he rises up. This occultation is necessary because otherwise the authorities would destroy the imam, something that could not be allowed to happen. The occultation was also designed to test the faith of the Shīʿah, especially against those who denied the imam had ever been born. At the appropriate time when the appropriate signs and circumstances appeared, the imam would appear to bring about the golden age.[22] He does also have a Tradition that there will be two occultations.[23] As one of the reasons for the occultation is that the hidden imam fears for his life, there is an element of *taqiyyah* (precautionary dissimulation) in it in so far as the occultation is taking place as a precaution against the destruction of the imam. Al-Kulaynī also presents Traditions from the imams on *taqiyyah*. Muḥammad al-Bāqir declares in one of them that *taqiyyah* is his and his fathers' religion, and that anyone who does not have *taqiyyah* has no faith.[24] The emphasis given to *taqiyyah* in such Traditions indicates the imams' concern to protect themselves and their followers from persecution by the authorities. There are other Traditions which imply that *taqiyyah* should not be applied in such legal matters as the drinking of *nabīdh* (a kind of date wine) and *masḥ ʿalā ʾl-khuffayn* (rubbing the shoes, instead of taking them off. In ablutions before prayer, the Sunnīs consider the Prophet to have allowed the rubbing of the shoes instead of washing the feet; whereas the Shīʿīs insist that no such concession had been allowed and require that the feet should be rubbed. The difference in interpretation came to be emphasized as a distinction between the two).[25] These Traditions also come from Muḥammad al-Bāqir and may well belong to the time when such subjects, particularly *masḥ ʿalā ʾl-khuffayn*, were still under discussion among the schools of law and were not therefore identifiably Shīʿī. Nowhere does al-Kulaynī deal with the doctrine of *rajʿah* in the sense of the return of the believers before the end of the world. The fact that he ignores this doctrine

[21] Ibid., II, 25–33. [22] Ibid., I, 337. [23] Ibid., 339. [24] Ibid., II, 219. [25] Ibid., 217.

implies that he did not think it particularly significant. Perhaps al-Kulaynī was influenced by the anticipated imminent return of the hidden imam, so that he was not disposed to deal with the more tendentious idea of a more general return of the dead Shīᶜīs.

Apart from the more extreme Traditions on the imamate, the theological Traditions presented by al-Kulaynī in *al-Uṣūl min al-kāfī* could almost be described as belonging to the mainstream discussions of Islamic theology. Many of these doctrines could well belong to the imams to whom they are attributed. One of al-Kulaynī's purposes was to establish the Qummī consensus of the imams' views on theology as the source of Shīᶜī theology. In attempting to clear Shīᶜī theology from accusations of anthropomorphism and materialism, he may have been influenced by a small group of the Muᶜtazilah who had been converted to Shiᶜism in the latter half of the third/ninth century.

This group of theologians, who combined Muᶜtazilah theology[26] with Shiᶜism, broadly accepted the doctrine of the imamate, probably in the version which was put forward by the early theologians and which has already been described. The strictly theological doctrines of the early Shīᶜī theologians had once been in the vanguard, but ideas had moved on and it was now the Muᶜtazilah who had the leadership in Islamic theology. Although they succeeded in ridding Shiᶜism of the early materialistic and anthropomorphical ideas of God, they were still at odds with the Traditionists on several matters, particularly the Traditionists' deterministic tendencies and some of the latter's more extreme views of the imams. They were eager to bring about a synthesis between Shiᶜism and general Muᶜtazilite doctrines.

It was the family of Nawbakht, in the persons of Abū Sahl Ismāᶜīl (d. 311/923) and his nephew Abū Muḥammad al-Ḥasan b. Mūsā (d. between 300–10/912–22), which took up the task. Although their theological writings have not survived, we have reports that they adopted the Muᶜtazilite doctrine concerning the attributes of God and human free-will. They also naturally rejected the materialism and anthropomorphism of the early theologians and rejected the idea of the vision of God.

Shortly after the death of al-Kulaynī, the Buwayhids (or Buyids) took control at the centre of the ᶜAbbasid empire. During the period of the Buwayhids, from 334/945 to 447/1055, the Shīᶜīs enjoyed considerable freedom as the Buwayhids were sympathetic to their views. As a result the centre of Shīᶜī learning shifted from Qumm to Rayy and then eventually to Baghdad. Without the restraint of persecution, there was a flowering of

26 See above, ch. 1, 4–7.

Shīʿī scholarship. For a period, the Traditionists who claimed to preserve the teachings of the imam were in the ascendancy in Shīʿī theology. A leading proponent of this Traditionist theology which opposed Muʿtazilite influences on Shīʿī theology was Abū Jaʿfar Muḥammad b. ʿAlī b. Bābawayhi (or Bābūya) al-Ṣadūq (d. 381/991).[27]

In his works on theology, notably *Risālat al-Iʿtiqādāt* and *Kitāb al-Tawḥīd*, he presents Shīʿī traditions from the imams which he comments on and explains. He shows himself to be hostile to theology using Traditions from the imams denouncing theology, but yet is at pains to try to reconcile the Traditions as far as possible with the Muʿtazilite theology whose influence was growing among the Shīʿah. However, without the constraint of the consensus of Qummī Traditionists, or at least that group of it that al-Kulaynī represented, Ibn Bābawayhi's task was much more difficult.

Ibn Bābawayhi has used much the same Traditions as al-Kulaynī to deny the possibility of the vision of God, thus following on this subject the Qummī consensus as interpreted by al-Kulaynī. He gives some space to his own rejection of any idea of the vision of God, clearly rejecting those Traditions which had supported the idea.

As far as the doctrine of attributes is concerned, he follows al-Kulaynī, even interpreting the distinction between essential attributes and attributes of action in the same way as al-Kulaynī. However, he finds that the Tradition about *badāʾ*, concerning Jaʿfar al-Ṣādiq and his son Ismāʿīl, has re-established itself in the accepted corpus of Tradition. In both books, he gives the Tradition and attempts to explain it away. In his later work he has found another Tradition which refers not to Jaʿfar's son Ismāʿīl but to Abraham's son Ismāʿīl, and therefore the different idea occurring to God is the abrogation of the command to Abraham to sacrifice Ismāʿīl. (In Islamic Tradition, this command to Abraham to sacrifice his son is usually interpreted as referring to Ishmael, Ar. Ismāʿīl, not Isaac.) This allows him to interpret *badāʾ* as the equivalent of abrogation. However, his explanation is unsatisfactory, as the Arabic is *badā li-ʾllāh* (something different appeared to God) not *badā min Allāh* (something different appeared from God). On the question of the Qurʾān he reintroduces the Traditions that al-Kulaynī had ignored in favour of the statement that the speech of God was caused (*muḥdath*). He reports a statement from Mūsā al-Kāẓim that the Qurʾān is neither a creator nor created, but the word of God. Another Tradition from ʿAlī al-Riḍā states that only God is the creator and everything else is created, but the Qurʾān is the word of God and one should not apply a term to it.

[27] *CHALUP*, 304.

This idea of not entering into the controversy is also endorsed by another Tradition from Mūsā al-Kāẓim. Ibn Bābawayhi, under Muᶜtazilite pressure, feels obliged to enter the controversy. He explains that the meaning of *ghayr makhlūq* (normally understood as "not created") is ambiguous, and could be understood in the sense *ikhtalaqa* which means "fabricated" or "forged". Thus what Jaᶜfar al-Ṣādiq was saying was the Qurʾān is not something forged. Ibn Bābawayhi goes on to assert that the Qurʾān is caused (*muḥdath*). Thus his position is the same as al-Kulaynī's, but he had to involve himself in a rather artificial interpretation of the Tradition in order to conform to the Muᶜtazilite position, whereas al-Kulaynī had merely ignored the Tradition.

With regard to free-will and determinism, Ibn Bābawayhi's position is very similar to al-Kulaynī. He uses the same Tradition as al-Kulaynī to explain the ability to act but attributes it to Mūsā al-Kāẓim. He also adopts the intermediate position between determinism and free-will. His position with regard to faith and Islam is also similar to al-Kulaynī.

Ibn Bābawayhi has the same position with regard to the imams as al-Kulaynī. For him, the hidden imam had now been absent for over 100 years. Therefore he is concerned to explain the background and reasons for this, particularly as opponents of the Shīᶜah were holding them up to ridicule. He wrote a book on the occultation of the hidden imam entitled *Kamāl al-dīn wa-tamām al-niᶜmah* ("Perfection of Religion and Completeness of Benefaction") in which he sought to justify the occultation by presenting Traditions from the imams on the subject. He also reintroduces the doctrine of *rajᶜah* into theology on the basis of Traditions which al-Kulaynī had not used, arguing in its favour on the basis of the interpretation of Quranic verses, on the claim that it was a Jewish belief and on Traditions from the Prophet. Ibn Bābawayhi preserves the Traditionists' attitude to *taqiyyah*, maintaining that it is an obligation on the Shīᶜah until the time of the return of the hidden imam.

Ibn Bābawayhi is very much a Traditionist. His contribution to the development of Shīᶜī theology is a greater retreat to the Traditionists' position. However, many of the advances of al-Kulaynī have been preserved. It was a pupil of Ibn Bābawayhi's who was to develop Shīᶜī theology in a much more Muᶜtazilite direction: Shaykh al-Mufīd Muḥammad b. Muḥammad b. al-Nuᶜmān (d. 413/1022). Although educated as a Traditionist, he came very much under the influence of the Muᶜtazilites in Baghdad where he lived. His early works show a bias towards Tradition, notably his work on the lives of the imams, *Kitāb al-Irshād fī maᶜrifat ḥujaj Allāh ᶜalā ʾl-ᶜibād*. However, he later develops a much more rationalistic approach to theology. He wrote a correction to Ibn Bābawayhi's *Risālat al-Iᶜtiqādāt* entitled *Kitāb Sharḥ ᶜaqāʾid al-Ṣadūq* or *Taṣḥīḥ al-iᶜtiqād*, and he also elaborated on his own theology in a work entitled *Awāʾil al-maqālāt fīʾl-madhāhib al-mukhtārāt*.

Al-Mufīd does not accept Ibn Bābawayhi's strictures against theology, saying that the use of reason is absolutely necessary in religion, as otherwise there would simply be blind imitation (*taqlīd*). On the other hand, public disputes might need to be avoided at certain times. This brings him directly into conflict with Ibn Bābawayhi's interpretation of *taqiyyah*. Al-Mufīd does not regard *taqiyyah* as an obligation at all times, but only as being appropriate in situations where there is danger. He further considers that *taqiyyah* is more applicable to ordinary Shīᶜīs rather than experts. However, al-Mufīd, for all his espousal of reason, regards it very much as secondary to revelation. He does not believe that one can arrive at knowledge of God or moral behaviour without the aid of revelation. Al-Mufīd reduces the number of essential attributes of God mentioned by the Traditionists to three, in line with the Muᶜtazilite attempts to reduce their number. They are knowledge, power and life. He subsumes hearing and seeing under knowledge. God's will is not an essential attribute but an attribute of action. He only accepts the doctrine of *badāʾ* because of Traditions which he regards as ones which have to be accepted. He then sets about trying to reconcile *badāʾ* with reason and makes it accord with abrogation. By emphasizing its use with *min* (from) rather than *li* (to) its meaning becomes that something different appeared to men from God. In this way *badāʾ* is interpreted as the equivalent of abrogation. Al-Mufīd also rejects any idea of the vision of God. Naturally al-Mufīd denies any idea of the Qurʾān being uncreated. However, he preserves the Shīᶜī preference for the Qurʾān being caused (*muḥdath*).

In the controversy over free-will and determinism, al-Mufīd has shifted the Shīᶜī position into agreement with the Muᶜtazilah. He follows the Muᶜtazilites of Baghdad in regarding ability to act as merely physical soundness and then with them he regards man as producing his own acts, but he will not go as far as saying that man created his own acts. He more or less continues the doctrine of the distinction between faith (*īmān*) and Islam.

Naturally al-Mufīd took part in the controversy over the occultation. In his work *al-Fuṣūl al-ᶜasharah fīʾl-ghaybah* ("Ten Chapters on Occultation"), he attempts to justify the occultation on the basis of reason. He argues that men have been known to live for very long periods and cites examples of Biblical figures for whom such claims have been made. He accepts the Traditions of the miraculous nature of the imams. With the belief in the occultation of the twelfth imam, it was impossible to accept anything else. Al-Mufīd enters the controversy that had been going on for some time outside the Shīᶜah over whether the imam (here used in the theological sense of "the caliph") was necessary by virtue of revelation or reason. He maintains that the imamate is necessary for both these reasons. There is a revelation for the necessity of the imamate, but men could arrive at the imamate by using reason. Al-Mufīd, also following the Nawbakhtīs, brings in the idea of God's bestowal of the imamate on the imams as an act of divine favour (*luṭf*).

The leadership of Shīᶜī theology after al-Mufīd was taken over by his brilliant pupil ᶜAlī b. al-Ḥusayn al-Sharīf al-Murtaḍā (d. 436/1044).[28] In his development of Shīᶜī theology al-Murtaḍā lays much greater emphasis on reason. In this he seems to be influenced by the Muᶜtazilah of Basra. One of his most important works was *al-Kitāb al-Shāfī fī ᵓl-imāmah* ("The Clear Book on the Imamate"). While this work is essentially a refutation of Qāḍī ᶜAbd al-Jabbār's section on the imamate in his *al-Mughnī*, it is wide-ranging and touches on a great number of theological points. He also has other briefer works on theological matters. He generally follows the theology of al-Mufīd, though differing with him on minor points. In particular al-Murtaḍā feels that reason is the starting-point to arrive at a knowledge of God. He also develops the doctrine of divine favour (*luṭf*) and the imamate. The institution of the imamate is not only an act of divine favour to the imams, but is also a rationally necessary act of divine favour to mankind. This was perhaps implicit in the doctrine of the imam as God's proof on earth. He is far more concerned to demonstrate that the imamate is rationally necessary, and attempts to demonstrate that mankind can never survive without leadership so that, as the need for leadership is necessary for man, it is necessary for God to provide it.

When al-Murtaḍā died, he was succeeded by another great pupil of al-Mufīd, Abū Jaᶜfar Muḥammad b. al-Ḥasan al-Ṭūsī (d. 460/1067).[29] He was just as much a Traditionist as a theologian, and his production of works on religious subjects was prolific. He wrote a summary of al-Murtaḍā's *al-Shāfī* called *Talkhīs al-Shāfī*. It is, however, much more than a summary and in it he shows himself to be very much influenced by al-Murtaḍā's rationalistic approach. On the other hand, in his work on the occultation, *Kitāb al-Ghaybah*, he uses both Traditions and reason to defend the doctrine. In his theological work *al-Iqtiṣād al-hādī ilā ṭarīq al-rashād*, he follows the theological doctrines of his two predecessors, al-Mufīd and al-Murtaḍā.

Before the death of al-Ṭūsī, the Buwayhids lost their authority in Baghdad to the Saljūqs in 447/1055. During the following 200 years the Shīᶜah became once again a persecuted sect. There is very little Shīᶜī

[28] Ibid. [29] Ibid.; and see below, ch. 4, 48.

theological literature during this time. It seems that the Shīᶜī Traditionists were still able to preserve some of the views that the Shīᶜī theologians had tried to repudiate, but their main concern was to defend the authority of Tradition in the law. This authority gradually gave ground to the demands for a greater use of reason.

Towards the end of the ᶜAbbasid caliphate in Baghdad, Shīᶜī theology received renewed impetus with the emergence of two distinguished theologians, Naṣīr al-Dīn al-Ṭūsī (d. 672/1274)[30] and his disciple Ibn Muṭahhar al-Ḥillī (d. 726/1325). Naṣīr al-Dīn al-Ṭūsī wrote a commentary on the work *Muḥaṣṣal afkār al-mutaqaddimīn wa-ʾl-mutaʾakhkhirīn min al-falāsifah wa-ʾl-mutakallamīn* by Fakhr al-Dīn al-Rāzī. In this commentary, Naṣīr al-Dīn al-Ṭūsī firmly rejects the doctrines of *badāʾ* and only accepts *taqiyyah* on the basis of fear. In his own work on theology, *Tajrīd al-iᶜtiqād*, reason is given a paramount place and such subjects as *rajᶜah* are ignored. His approach is similar to the approach set out by al-Murtaḍā. This approach is followed by al-Ḥillī in his commentary on *Tajrīd al-iᶜtiqād* called *Kashf al-murād fī sharḥ Tajrīd al-iᶜtiqād*, and in his own work *al-Bāb al-hādī ᶜashar*. These two men established an important place in Shīᶜī doctrine and their works are still part of the required study for Shīᶜī students of theology. Despite this, the doctrines of *rajᶜah*, *taqiyyah* and *badāʾ* have continued to have a place in Shīᶜī thought.

[30] For al-Ṭūsī's contribution to astronomy, see below, ch. 15.

CHAPTER 3

IBĀḌĪ THEOLOGICAL LITERATURE

ẒUHŪR: THE EXPANSION OF IBAḌISM

The same general conditions which allowed the ᶜAbbasids to establish their power in the core of the Islamic world were also exploited by the Ibāḍīs (the chief sect of the Kharijites[1]) to establish states in parts of its periphery. During the last decade of Umayyad rule their movement in Basra had been transformed into a full-scale *daᶜwah* under the guidance of Abū ᶜUbaydah Muslim b. abī Karīmah, propagating its ideology among two major disaffected groups, the Berbers of North Africa and the Yamanī tribes in southern Arabia (notably the Azd). Basran political and social networks were also exploited, particularly those of the merchants of the old Sasanid *Arḍ al-Hind*, so that cells of Ibaḍism came into being in parts of Khurāsān, Kirmān, Sijistān and al-Baḥrayn. Lesser colonies also existed in other parts of Iraq and even in Egypt: but Syria seems to have been barren ground.

Political activation of the movement in the Maghrib appears to have been precipitated by the rival propaganda of the Ṣufrīs (another Kharijite sect) in about 126/743–4, but the first full realization (*ẓuhūr*) of an Ibāḍī state resulted from a joint ᶜUmānī-Ḥaḍramī-Yamanī expedition which established ᶜAbdullāh b. Yaḥyā al-Kindī (*Ṭālib al-Ḥaqq*) in Yemen and took the Holy Cities of Mecca and Medina in the *ḥajj* of 129/747. ᶜAbdullāh was killed shortly afterwards. Following the suppression of this uprising, a rump imamate survived for a while in the Ḥaḍramawt and a weak (*ḍaᶜīf*) imam, al-Julandā b. Masᶜūd, was brought to power in ᶜUmān: both areas however, were early on brought under ᶜAbbasid control. In the Maghrib the fortunes of the numerous centres of Ibaḍism had a complicated history but, reputedly in 144/761–2, a new colony, remote from the main Arab centres, was founded at Tāhart, and in about 160/776–7 was sufficiently strong openly to proclaim ᶜAbd al-Raḥmān b. Rustam (d. 168/784) as the imam. A decade or so later the Mashriqī Ibāḍīs began to exploit the internal political divisions of ᶜUmān and finally overthrew Julandā rule in 177/793 to establish a century of strong (*shārī*) imamate rule. Some time in the fourth

[1] See *CHALUP*, 220–1, 413–4.

decade of the third/ninth century the old directing centre in Basra closed and its last "imam", Abū Sufyān Maḥbūb b. al-Raḥīl, returned to join his son in the new state: Abū ᶜAbdullāh Muḥammad b. abī Sufyān in turn acted as a general adviser to the other Ibāḍī communities until his death in 260/873. In Ḥaḍramawt a small (*difāᶜī*) imamate existed based on the Wādī Daᶜwān.

The Ibāḍī community, however, was by no means unified. Following the death of Abū ᶜUbaydah (shortly after the ᶜAbbasids came to power), a doctrinal dispute began to emerge amongst his followers, notably between his successor al-Rabīᶜ b. Ḥabīb al-Farāhīdī (d. 170/786) and a group which propounded views that threatened the integrity (*ijmāᶜ*) of the community. Surviving written material shows that amongst the issues involved was the attitude that communal prayer was not indispensable, and that the views of previous generations over such issues as *fitnah* were not binding: associated with this was an attempt to classify degrees of sin. Other matters at stake reflected current debate elsewhere in the Islamic community, *tashbīh*, *qadar*, *shakk*, *ᶜaql*, the "creation" of the Qurʾān, and so on. So internal divisions began to emerge and an Ibāḍī heresiography came into existence: politically the most important breakaway group were the Nukkarites, the deniers of the legitimacy of the second Rustamid imam, ᶜAbd al-Wahhāb b. ᶜAbd al-Raḥmān (168–208/784–823). In the Mashriq the community was doctrinally threatened by Hārūn b. al-Yamān, but Abū Sufyān managed to hold the "orthodox" line of what became known as Wahbiyyah Ibaḍism in ᶜUmān and Ḥaḍramawt; however, the Yamanīs (who had never re-established an imamate) broke away.

LITERATURE OF THE PERIOD

The nature of such Ibāḍī literature as exists from this period of *ẓuhūr* may only be understood in the light of the fact that the tradition remained oral. Strengthening the community was what mattered, and this came through attracting members to a leading *ᶜālim*'s *majlis*; notions concerning the resulting states of association (*wilāyah*), or dissociation (*barāʾah*) with other Muslims in due course came to cover "soundness" of legal opinions (*fatāwā*), and eventually elaborated to determine the conditions for breaking away and deposing an imam. Originally, all missionaries (*ḥamalat al-ᶜilm*) were trained in Basra, but as the imamates became established the leading ulema developed their own centres locally. In this way the true learning was expanded spatially from node to node and temporarily by a line of teachers who had inherited a communally developed *ijmāᶜ* (not *taqlīd*). Mutual debate was always preferred when resolving problems confronting the community, so that written exchanges were exceptional.

Ibāḍī theological literature therefore really only came into existence when personal communication was difficult. At one level we thus have what is little more than fragmentary correspondence, inter- and intra-community opinions and advice offered individually or collectively to imams and other ulema. Such "letters" are generally termed *sīrah*s, and a considerable quantity have survived in various recensions: perhaps the earliest is the only written work we know by Abū ʿUbaydah, a treatise on *zakāh* written to a Maghribī. Written communication with the Maghribī community, encouraged perhaps by the bibliophile tendencies of the increasingly urbane Tāhart imams, in fact resulted in the only large-scale recording of material from the early Ibāḍī period, for the Mashriq remained for some time the main advisory centre and there was no reliable contact outside the *ḥajj*: most of these works remained more or less unknown in ʿUmān for a long time. Perhaps the most important is a complex of *fatāwā* from the earliest teachers: the *Kitāb Jābir* (Abū Shaʿthāʾ Jābir b. Zayd, the supposed teaching founder of the movement who died in 93/711–12), the *Kitāb Ḍumām b. Sāʾib* (the main teacher of Abū ʿUbaydah Muslim b. abī Karīmah and the leading figure of "proto-Ibaḍism") and the *Athār* of al-Rabīʿ b. Ḥabīb al-Farāhīdī. Much of this collection, in reality, seems to have been set down by Abū Ṣufrah ʿAbd al-Malik b. Ṣufrah (the *Kitāb Abī Ṣufrah*), probably in the first third of the third/ninth century; one of his main sources was al-Haytham b. ʿAdī (d. *c.* 206/821–2). Another important source was the last Basran "imam", Abū Sufyān, who himself really began to rationalize Ibāḍī history in a biography of the early Ibāḍīs written specifically for the Maghribīs: unfortunately this *Kitāb Abī Sufyān* only appears to survive in the recensions of al-Darjīnī, al-Barrādī and al-Shammākhī (seventh to ninth/thirteenth to fifteenth centuries). The third major early work is the *Mudawwanah*,[2] reputedly written for the imam ʿAbd al-Wahhāb b. ʿAbd al-Raḥmān by Abū Ghānim Bashīr b. Ghānim al-Khurāsānī, but almost certainly, like the *Kitāb Abī Sufyān*, for his son the imam Aflaḥ: it contains the legal opinions (*fatāwā*) of seven of Abū ʿUbaydah's pupils (including the "heretical" ʿAbdullāh b. ʿAbd al-ʿAzīz and Abū ʾl-Muʿarrij). The existing form of all these early works has evidently resulted from subsequent editing, but without question forms a major corpus of genuine early material, mostly set down in the first third of the third century of the *Hijrah*. It shows us much about the early forms of Ibaḍism: amongst the important features to note is that *fatāwā* display virtually no critical apparatus justifying each opinion.

[2] Beirut, 1974.

Amongst the other more important intercommunity works to come down to us are *sīrah*s by Abū ʿAbdullāh b. abī Sufyān advising the Ḥaḍramīs and Yamanīs (virtually all his *fatāwā* have also been recorded) and a *sīrah* written by Abū ʾl-Ḥawārī Muḥammad b. al-Ḥawārī (late third/ninth century) to the Ḥaḍramī community. This contains some important information concerning early ʿUmānī history in the context of an exposé concerning the proper conduct of an expedition. This is an important theme in Ibāḍī *fiqh*, for it emerges from the attitude adopted towards other Muslims. The essential idea here is that they are *ahl al-qiblah* and that therefore their property and persons are inviolate; the only blood-letting permitted is in fighting an official war. Basically the blame for their condition is seen as coming from the political leadership which had fallen into the hands of the *ahl al-aḥdāth*, that is, innovating, unconstitutional rulers (*jabābirah*), and deviants (*min al-qiblah kuffār*), but not polytheists (*mushrikūn*).

THE FOURTH/TENTH TO SIXTH/TWELFTH CENTURIES

The collapse of the imamates in both Tāhart and ʿUmān in civil wars at the end of the third/ninth century profoundly revolutionized the Ibāḍī movement and brought to the fore the problem of how to deal with occupying powers and the application of *taqiyyah* (religious dissimulation): the main ʿUmānī treatise was the *Kitāb al-Muḥāribah* of Bashīr b. abī ʿAbdullāh Muḥammad b. abī Sufyān Maḥbūb al-Raḥīlī (late third/ninth century). In north Africa the imamate was never to revive and eventually Ibaḍism only survived in the Mzāb, Jarbah Island and the Jabal Nafūsah. Following defeat by the Faṭimids at the battle of Baghay in 358/868–9, the surviving communities passed into a state of secrecy (*kitmān*) and the imamate was replaced with the organization of the ʿ*azzābah* councils whose arrangements began to be formalized in a *sīrat al-ḥalqah* by Abū ʾl-ʿAbbās Aḥmad (d. 504/1111), who based himself on the rulings of his father (Abū ʿAbdullāh Muḥammad b. Bakr al-Nafūsī, d. 440/1048–9). Abū ʾl-ʿAbbās also wrote an important treatise on land, the *Kitāb Uṣūl al-araḍī* ("Land Principles/Rights")[3], clearly designed for the new colonies founded by the refugee Ibāḍīs.

Associated with such fundamental political changes came a rationalization of the "states" of the religion (*masālik al-dīn*) and an evolution of the ideas concerning the stages of defensiveness (*difāʿ*) and expansionism (*shirā*). In ʿUmān, where the imamate was to re-emerge in the fifth/eleventh

[3] Incorporated in *Kitāb al-Nīl* by ʿAbd al-ʿAzīz b. Ibrāhīm al-Thamīnī, Bārūn, AH 1305.

century, these categories were used to classify imams and their powers and past history was rationalized accordingly: in fact a *shārī* imam basically meant a permanent, plenipotentiary imam, whereas a *difāʿī* imam was one who was appointed provisionally, for a certain purpose (usually to conduct a war). Otherwise their powers were common. No conditions (*shurūṭ*) could be imposed on them, other than those emanating from the law of God by which they governed (*lā ḥukm illā li-llāh*). Since it was the duty of every Muslim to obey this law, the imam had no need of a standing army. However, he had no particular status in interpreting the law and was bound by the *ijmāʿ* of the community. Generally speaking, an imam could only be deposed for a major sin (*makfirah*), and then only after consultation and an opportunity to make atonement (*tawbah*). A further type of imam whose position was theoretically defined in this period was the *ḍaʿīf* imam, an appointment made for political expediency; in this case the condition (*sharṭ*) of compulsory consultation was imposed for an initial period. The idea of the *kitmān* imam however, was an *ex post facto* normalization developed in the Maghrib, and the nearest that can be traced in ʿUmān is the idea of the *imām muḥtasib* (probably a much later development).

The fifth/eleventh and sixth/twelfth centuries also saw a major emergence of Ibaḍism as a *madhhab*. In the second half of the third/ninth century, one can trace some attempt to record and structure the judgements of the early ulema, reportedly in the legal work of the Maghribī ʿAmrūs b. al-Fatḥ (d. 283/896), and certainly in the major compendium of Abū Jābir Muḥammad b. Jaʿfar al-Izkawī, the *Jāmiʿ Ibn Jaʿfar*. Works of *tafsīr* also began to appear towards the end of that century with that of the Maghribī, Hūd b. Maḥkam al-Hawwārī, preceding that of the ʿUmānī, Abū ʾl-Ḥawārī Muḥammad b. al-Ḥawārī (who also wrote a *Jāmiʿ*) by about two decades. The subsequent rapid development of the *fiqh* apparatus can be judged by examining Abū Saʿīd al-Kudamī's (late fourth/tenth century) critique (*al-Muʿtabar*) of the *Jāmiʿ Ibn Jaʿfar*, written probably about a century and a quarter later, and the final great exposé of *fiqh* principles of his quasi-contemporary and rival, Abū Muḥammad ʿAbdullāh b. Muḥammad b. Barakah al-Bahlawī (first half of fifth/eleventh century). Although the doors of *ijtihād* have never been closed, Ibn Barakah's *Jāmiʿ* was to become the standard work of reference for the great encyclopaedists of the next three-quarters of a century, notably Salamah b. Muslim al-ʿAwtabī's *al-Ḍiyyāʾ*, and the three works by members of a Kindah clan of Nizwā, the *Bayān al-Sharʿ* of Muḥammad b. Ibrāhīm (d. 508/1115), the *Kifāyah* (which seems largely to have disappeared) of Muḥammad b. Mūsā and the *Muṣannaf* of the prolific author, Aḥmad b. ʿAbdullāh (d. probably 557/1162). Another influential work from this time was the *Mukhtaṣar al-khiṣāl* of Abū Isḥāq Ibrāhīm b. Qays al-Hamdānī (first half of fifth/eleventh century), the last and only *shārī* imam in the Ḥaḍramawt (his surviving *Dīwān* records, *inter alia*, his campaigns in Yemen). The *Dīwān* of Ibn al-Naẓar al-Samʾūlī (sixth/twelfth century) was also considered an exemplary work and inspired commentaries through the centuries, rather in the same way as did Abū Naṣr Fatḥ b. Nūḥ al-Malashāwī's *Qaṣīdah nūniyyah* in the Maghrib.

Unfortunately, Ibaḍism in ʿUmān became increasingly split by a doctrinal dispute over the issues that had led to civil war and which still underlay current political alliances. The extremism of the so-called Rustāq party, which rejected in numerous treatises the moderate Nizwā party's notions about suspended judgement (*wuqūf*: cf. in particular Abū Saʿīd al-Kudamī's *Kitāb al-Istiqāmah*) finally alienated northern ʿUmān and the Ḥaḍramawt and led to the total collapse of the imamate at the end of the sixth/twelfth century in the core of the country: it was not to revive until the ninth/fifteenth century. For the movement to survive, therefore, it became essential that it acquire an impeccable "orthodoxy" which could challenge that of Sunnī groups and foster its belief that it formed the only true Islamic community. So we find an increasing tendency to calque the *madhhab* on the norms of Sunnism, but derive its teaching from only its own doctors. This meant normalizing the history of the movement and in the case of the Rustāq party, developing a true missionary teacher line (*ḥamalat al-ʿilm*) down to its final great exponents in the mid-fifth/eleventh century, Ibn Barakah al-Bahlawī and his pupil Abū ʾl-Ḥasan ʿAlī b. Muḥammad al-Bisyānī (or Bisyāwī). In the Maghrib it went even further and a *Ḥadīth* collection, reputedly originating from al-Rabīʿ b. Ḥabīb al-Farāhīdī, was realized in a *Tartīb* by Abū Yaʿqūb Yūsuf b. Ibrāhīm al-Warjalānī (d. 570/1174). Trained in part at Cordova, Abū Yaʿqub was an expert in *Ḥadīth* scholarship (cf. also his *Kitāb al-ʿAdl wa-ʾl-inṣāf*) and Quranic exegesis (his *Tafsīr* only survives fragmentarily): however, it is in his *Dalīl wa-ʾl-burhān* that he presents his ideas on the general development of Ibaḍism. In ʿUmān his equivalent was Abū ʿAbdullāh Muḥammad b. Saʿīd al-Qalhātī, writing probably about half a century later. His *al-Kashf wa-ʾl-bayān* similarly provides an exposé of the complete Ibāḍī theology through rebuttal of other doctrines and, in emulation of the *milal wa-ʾl-niḥal* literature, finishes by expounding it as the only true *firqah*: some of this is also expressed in his *Maqāmah* celebrating the reconversion of Kilwa in East Africa to Ibaḍism.

Thus Ibaḍism went into political decline in an explosion of scholarship that transformed its *fiqh* into a school comparable to the four schools of Sunnī Islam and put its theology into the strait-jacket of Islamic orthodoxy. This calquing process largely removed its originality and put in its place a corpus of material that eventually led to claims by leaders of the *nahḍah* that Ibaḍism was the first of the orthodox schools, and that their theology derived from the very fount of Sunnī Quranic learning. Some minor variations over interpretation of the law, some small differences over ritual and a few vestiges of theological debate reflecting early issues which for long had ceased to stir Muslim thought, were all that came to distinguish the Ibāḍīs from the Sunnīs, except for one vital matter: the theory and practice of political community. To have removed that would have been to extinguish Ibaḍism itself. So the Ibāḍīs entered their political twilight at the end of ʿAbbasid times with their theology refurbished but their political ideology intact.

CHAPTER 4

QURANIC EXEGESIS

Exegesis (*tafsīr*) forms one of the most extensive branches of Arabic prose literature. Developed over fourteen centuries, it provided the ideal vehicle for the expression of every shade of opinion adopted within Islam. Knowledge of the Qurʾān is indispensable for an understanding of Islam, but knowledge of the Qurʾān alone will not supply that understanding. Whereas the Qurʾān urged its first hearers to use their eyes and ears, but above all their minds in the pursuit of truth, the intellectual system that grew out of the Qurʾān was imbued with a spirit of conformity suspicious of every effort to act or think beyond the restraint of revelation. The definition of "revelation" gave Islam its distinct hue, while the identification as the source of knowledge of either Tradition, reason or intuition produced three broad exegetical approaches.

TRADITIONAL EXEGESIS

The individual pursues the right path if he adheres to "the way of the Muslims", the straight path which the Qurʾān commanded men to follow, "not separate paths lest they take you by various routes away from the path of God".[1] Muslims were forbidden to imitate those who "divided into sects, falling into disagreement".[2] The role of the Prophet was central to Muḥammad's concept of Islamic unity: "He who obeys the Prophet obeys God";[3] "He who disobeys God and His Prophet, transgressing the bounds God has set, will be cast into Hell."[4] If they disagreed on any matter the Muslims must refer it to God and the Prophet:[5] "We have sent you, Muḥammad, the Reminder so that you can make clear to men what has been revealed."[6] The Prophet's death altered the situation which the Qurʾān had created, and those who argued that these verses applied to all matters, including the Qurʾān, insisted that the Prophet had not merely received the Qurʾān. He had expounded it. That was the instruction men should seek; the Prophet's exegesis being the ideal interpretation.

[1] Qurʾān, vi. 153. [2] Ibid., iii.105. [3] Ibid., iv.80. [4] Ibid., iv.14. [5] Ibid., iv.59.
[6] Ibid., xvi.44.

The texts

For commentary to develop, the first requisite was to possess an indisputably correct text. But, since the recitation of the texts was central to the daily ritual, it is not necessary wholly to assent to Goldziher's assertion that the first stage of exegesis consisted of the "establishment of the text".[7] The historical exegesis set out from written texts and the variant readings which Goldziher analysed fall into distinct groups. Certain variants, by their very nature, are adequately explained by the deficiencies of the script used. It lacked a device for distinguishing unrelated consonants, or doubled consonants and had no means of distinguishing the short vowels in derivatives of common root but of nuanced meaning. More importantly, the final short vowels, the main index of grammatical case, hence of syntactical function, had not been distinguished. These vowels control meaning and can be significant for interpretation and for the extraction of regulations or *taʾwīl*.

Consideration of meaning affects the choice of reading, but in most cases in which only consonant values or only internal vowels are involved, the reading makes no real difference to the sense. It matters little whether one reads, "God knows what they are doing" (*yafʿalūna*) or "what you are doing" (*tafʿalūna*), although such close attention to minor detail underlines the fascination the texts held for Muslims anxious to achieve the most satisfactory reading, as the transition from oral to written tradition proceeded in advance of the exegesis.

Interpolation

In the case of a small number of disputed consonants or final vowels, Goldziher recognized the play of external factors, legal or theological, although his analyses do not go far enough. For example, the crux in *sūrah* xlviii.9, *tuʿazzizūhu/tuʿazzirūhu*, goes beyond deficiency of the script.[8] Curiously that had caused no problems in the parallel utterances of *sūrah*s v.12 and vii.157. The serious syntactical difficulties posed by *sūrah* xlviii.9 suggest ancient redactional activity akin to that of *sūrah* ix.3 which all recite, ". . . a declaration from God and His Prophet that God repudiates the unbelievers, and His Prophet . . .". Successful interpolation of a reference to the Prophet in both verses has disturbed the original underlying syntax.

From the context in which its discussion occurs, unsuccessful interpolation is also easily recognizable. This represents neither the use of different

[7] *Richtungen*, 1. [8] Ibid., 6.

texts nor the differing resolutions of a shared text. The presence or absence in *sūrah* iv.24 of one phrase marks the struggle to legitimize temporary marriage (*mutʿah*) by tracing mention of it to an undisputed source: "for the pleasure you derive from them [for a stipulated period] give women their fee." This is not an attempt to establish the text.[9] It is an attempt to exploit a hallowed document to underpin a disputed principle. An underlying disagreement as to the meaning of "fee", marriage-settlement(?)/hire(?), predated the attempt at interpolation (*taqdīr*) of the "elucidatory" phrase, showing this to be a sophisticated rather than primitive exegetical procedure and raising the question of the date of the quarrel. Similarly, dispute on *sūrah* v.6[10] arose at the secondary stage of working out the implications of the texts. When one meets the issue in the exegesis, the theorists are already divided as to whether the feet are to be washed (if the reading is *arjula*) or merely wiped (if the reading is *arjuli*) before the ritual prayer. Each side adduced as evidence a common written text, but offered either different memory of the oral tradition or differing vocalic resolutions of the consonantal tradition. Few comparable disputes impinge so directly upon everyday practice, exegesis being, for the most part, a theoretical rather than practical discipline.

Unsuccessful interpolation

A type of *tafsīr* unmentioned by Goldziher would make the Qurʾān the source of regulations nowhere referred to in the texts – indeed, contradicting regulations that are there. The most important instance concerns the general view that the Islamic penalty for adultery is death by stoning. This regulation, said to derive from the Qurʾān, is found only in exegetical narratives detailing the Prophet's discussion of this very question with the rabbis.[11] The narratives may have originated in efforts to elucidate certain passages which allude to the basis on which the Prophet might judge cases involving Jews if brought before him. Mālik b. Anas (d. 179/795) was commenting on *sūrah* ii.42 which accused the Jews of concealing (*kitmān*) the regulations of the Torah; Abū ʿAbdullāh Muḥammad b. Ismāʿīl al-Bukhārī (194–256/810–70), using the same *isnād* as Mālik, was commenting on *sūrah* iii.93 which concerns dietary law. Both share the motif of Muḥammad's challenge that the rabbis bring out the relevant Torah section as proof. There may well lurk, therefore, behind these narratives, an unwritten exegesis whose details, although obscured by the mists of pre-literary time, are nonetheless perceptible in the rulings alleged to have been

[9] Ibid., 13. [10] Ibid., 8. [11] Mālik b. Anas, *Muwaṭṭaʾ*, II, 165; Bukhārī, *Ṣaḥīḥ*, pt. 6, 37.

derived from the Qurʾān. Unable to produce a "stoning verse", the Muslims concluded that their texts of the Qurʾān reached them, not from the Prophet, but from his Companions, who had assembled them after his death, at which point the stoning verse was lost.[12] When some rejected the stoning penalty, insisting upon the Qurʾān's flogging penalty (xxiv.2), others argued that the *sunnah* "prevails over the Qurʾān but the Qurʾān does not prevail over the *sunnah*,"[13] introducing a principle of repeal (*naskh*), which was soon extended to state that certain verses of the Qurʾān "prevail over" other verses. Most interesting is that what is referred to throughout these discussions as "*sunnah*" had emerged from exegetical debate.

WRITTEN EXEGESIS

The literary stage of exegesis dates from the post-Prophetic period and was represented in local traditions attached to the names of various Companions of the Prophet, and was then first written down by the following generation. The greatest name in early exegesis is that of a cousin of the Prophet, ʿAbdullāh b. ʿAbbās (d. 68/688), in whose name reports were handed down at Mecca, Basra and Kufa on the authority of his "pupils". Whereas reports from the Companions are sporadic, touching only particular passages, those handed down in ʿAbdullāh's name extend over the entire Qurʾān whose texts they purport to elucidate word by word. The weight attached to Companion exegeses is evidenced by the multiplicity of (not always compatible) versions. This is even more the case with the statements attributed to ʿAbdullāh who, although only twelve when the Prophet died, is traditionally reckoned to be of the Companion generation.

Of the accumulated masses of exegetical materials preserved in the *tafsīr*, very little even claims to go back to the Prophet himself. His widow, ʿĀʾishah, explains that he had pronounced on very few verses whose interpretation was transmitted to him by Gabriel.[14] Exegesis thus appears to differ from the *sunnah* literature where the demand to trace statements bearing on the law and the cult to the Prophet, most consistently voiced by Muḥammad b. Idrīs al-Shāfiʿī (150–204/767–820), was to be consummated in the strict criteria applied to materials adopted into the *Ḥadīth* works compiled between *c.* 200/815 and 300/915. The contrast is heightened by the meagreness of the chapters of exegesis in the "classical collections" compiled by Muḥammad b. Ismāʿīl al-Bukhārī and by Muslim b. al-Ḥajjāj (202–61/817–75). Al-Bukhārī's *tafsīr* consists of disjointed, mainly anony-

[12] Burton, *The Collection of the Qurʾān*, 71; "Islamic penalty for adultery", 26.
[13] ʿAbdullāh b. Muslim b. Qutaybah, *Taʾwīl*, 199.
[14] Muḥammad b. Jarīr al-Ṭabarī, *Jāmiʿ al-bayān*, 1, 84ff.

mous, dictionary definitions, fragmentary exegeses and some specifically legal notes. There are also "tales of bygone peoples", for which it is unnecessary to presume any source other than paraphrases of the relevant Qurʾān passages. The nature and function of these stories is captured in the words attributed to the Prophet: "I wish Moses had shown more patience; then God would have told us more of this story."[15] Reports on variant readings with their attributions are frequent, while much effort is expended on identifying characters, places or times left unspecified in the Qurʾān. The total is less than 500 Traditions, whereas the nearly contemporary monumental exegetical opus of al-Ṭabarī (224–310/838–923) contains no fewer than 35,400 items of information organized under 13,026 *isnād*s.[16]

It seems unlikely that the texts, the readings, or the exegesis came from the Prophet, and it seems equally unlikely that they come from his cousin ʿAbdullāh. Not only do his principal pupils transmit incompatible reports; often "his views" are attributed in parallel reports to Companions (some also called ʿAbdullāh); the most prominent of his "pupils", ʿAlī b. abī Ṭalḥah (d. 120/737), did not derive his *tafsīr* directly from his "master", while another was not even born when ʿAbdullāh died.[17]

Tafsīr would appear to lag behind the development of other branches of the Tradition. Although the *isnād*s of the exegesis may not be original, neither are those of the *sunnah*. Both may have been appended at the same time: the first quarter of the second/eighth century.[18] In the case of the *tafsīr*, the reduced role of the Prophet is, however, conceded from the outset. Yet nothing disguises the fact that exegesis was being practised in the earliest times, and that the results of the labours of untold numbers of anonymous Muslims have been preserved, however formally imperfect the manner of their transmission. Their only questionable feature is their dubious attribution, but age of *tafsīr* must not be confused with age of *isnād*.

DATING (*SABAB*) AND IDENTIFICATION (*TAʿYĪN*)

While not designed as a manual of history, the Qurʾān constantly uses history as an argument. Apart from the most prominent personalities, names are seldom given and dates are more seldom given. It was less the Qurʾān's difficulty than its excessive vagueness, combined with human curiosity, that necessitated exegesis. Nor is this imprecision restricted to references to the remotest past. Revealed in the course of the Prophet's life, and alluding frequently to contemporary events and persons, the Qurʾān casts, even over these references, an impenetrable veil of anonymity. Yet

[15] Bukhārī, *Ṣaḥīḥ*, pt. 6, 89. [16] Horst, "Zur Überlieferung", 291. [17] Ibid., 306.
[18] Ibid.

the most striking feature of the exegesis is its horror of uncertainty. There is an unmistakable determination "to dot every 'i' and cross every 't'". Nothing, however minute and insignificant, must remain unknown. To name the unnamed is *taᶜyīn al-mubham*, while its concomitant, the dating of the undated (crucial for every allegation of *naskh*),[19] is *asbāb al-nuzūl*. Needful or not to our understanding of God's message, detail is relentlessly pursued. When the Qurᵓān (iii.173) states, "Those to whom the people said, 'The people have amassed their forces to attack you, so fear them', merely increased in faith and replied, 'God is our sufficiency – excellent is He in Whom we place our trust . . .'", the reader must be told the name of the informant, how he came by his information and to whom he imparted it, the route he travelled, the names of the enemy leaders, the size of their forces, the date of the proposed attack and the motives behind it.[20] We are not left in ignorance of the names of the seven sleepers, nor of the name (or the colour) of the dog lolling at the mouth of their cave;[21] nor of the variety of foodstuffs, with suitable condiments, provided on the tray sent down from heaven in response to Christ's prayer.[22]

If referring to the distant past, such stories are dubbed *isrāᵓīliyyāt*; for the details, ᶜAbdullāh b. ᶜAbbās is said to have consulted Jewish scholars. If they refer to the Prophet's time, they are called *sīrah* and *maghāzī* and are thus aspects of the *sunnah*. Such indefatigable probing explains the sheer size of some of the *tafsīr* works.

THE LINGUISTIC APPROACH

"We have sent it down as an Arabic Qurᵓān that you may understand."[23] The Qurᵓān's insistence upon its Arabic-ness, with its reiterated exhortations to the hearer to ponder, indicated a fruitful line of enquiry. The Qurᵓān expected to be understood by those familiar with Arabic. The earliest attempts to achieve correct recitation of the sacred texts had provided a powerful stimulus to the cultivation of the sciences of language: phonetics, writing-systems, morphology, lexicography, etymology, accidence, and, above, all, syntax. The amazing advances made in the first/seventh century are already apparent in the quality and detail of the work of the leading second/eighth-century linguistic specialists. The chief instrument available to these men had been the accumulated corpus of early and pre-Islamic poetry, to the collection, edition and analysis of which they were motivated by its recognized utility for the exegesis. Tradition once more attributed to Ibn ᶜAbbās the merit of initiating the linguistic method

19 Jalāl al-Dīn al-Suyūṭī, *Itqān*, pt. 1, 8; pt. 2, 24.
20 Ṭabarī, *Jāmiᶜ al-bayān*, VII, 399–413.
21 Suyūṭī, *Itqān*, pt. 2, 145, 177.
22 Zamakhsharī, *Kashshāf*, I, 491.
23 Qurᵓān, xii.2.

of exegesis and especially of exploiting the dazzling poetic treasures of the nation.[24] All exegetical works show this dependence upon "proof-verses" for the lexical and syntactical analysis of the Qurʾān texts. To parse is to understand the syntactical function (*mawḍiʿ*) of the word in Arabic utterance, which accurately identifies the final vowel (*iʿrāb*) essential for correct recitation and indispensable for correct interpretation. One may thus classify exegetical works on the basis of the "mixture" of techniques brought to the examination of the texts. That of Abū ʿUbaydah Maʿmar b. al-Muthannā (d. 210/825) is almost exclusively concerned with lexical and syntactical usage (*majāz al-Qurʾān*). Despite scattered references to contemporary theological disputes, the *tafsīr* of Abū Zakariyyāʾ Yaḥyā b. Ziyād al-Farrāʾ (d. 207/822) is primarily concerned with the *iʿrāb* and the determination of acceptable readings (*qirāʾāt*), although, to be acceptable, readings must preferably have been transmitted. He exploits syntax to settle disputes about the minutiae of the meanings (*maʿānī al-Qurʾān*).

Taʿyīn, *sabab*, *taqdīr*, *naskh*, *isrāʾīliyyāt*, all feature, although not to the exclusion of linguistic interests, in the exegeses of Muḥammad b. al-Sāʾib al-Kalbī (d. 146/763) and of Muqātil b. Sulaymān (d. 150/767), both of whom are in the line of transmission from Ibn ʿAbbās. A second *tafsīr* of Muqātil's is devoted to the specifically legal aspects of the Qurʾān which gives an opportunity to discuss *naskh*,[25] which, with *taʿyīn* and *sabab*, soon formed separate independent sub-literatures.

The highest place in the development of exegesis is occupied by Abū Jaʿfar Muḥammad b. Jarīr al-Ṭabarī, whose towering *Jāmiʿ al-bayān ʿan taʾwīl āy al-Qurʾān* ("Comprehensive Collection of Expositions of the Interpretation of the Verses of the Qurʾān") abruptly scaled heights not previously glimpsed and never subsequently approached.[26] By a signal stroke of fortune, the discovery in private hands of a complete manuscript led to the publication of this monument of exegetical science in 1903 in thirty tomes totalling 5,000 pages. Encyclopaedic in range, it covers every aspect of Qurʾān investigation: different readings; conflicting etymologies and definitions of rare or unusual words or idioms; varying interpretations of the legal and theological issues adumbrated in the texts; and exhaustive exploration of the historical and legendary background, sometimes extending over many pages and drawn from Islamic, Biblical and apocryphal sources – all repeated *in extenso* when a variant wording or a different *isnād* occurs in his sources. Working his leisurely way from verse to verse, al-Ṭabarī amasses a wealth of materials, each Tradition scrupulously prefixed

[24] Suyūṭī, *Itqān*, pt. 1, 120–33; Rippin, "Ibn ʿAbbās's al-Lughāt fī'l-Qurʾān", 15–25.
[25] *Tafsīr al-khams miʾat āyah min al-Qurʾān.*
[26] For al-Ṭabarī's contribution to historiography, see below, ch. 12, 199f.

by its *isnād* and with occasional observations on the "soundness" or otherwise of the *isnād*s, or the trustworthiness of individual transmitters. Exegesis had by now created its own tradition, and al-Ṭabarī has preserved this by subsuming whole *tafsīr* works by earlier writers,[27] while similarly appropriating *in toto* detailed passages of linguistic exposition from the works of previous grammarians. The entire enterprise is inspired by the principle that the soundest interpretation of the Qurʾān is that which conforms with what actually appears (*ẓāhir*) in the written texts of the Muslims, read at face value (*ẓāhir* as opposed to *taqdīr*), unless there is good reason for departing from the *ẓāhir*; and accords with the rules of Arabic and with *ḥadīth*s transmitted from the Companions and the Successors and acknowledged by the specialists in Islamic lore.[28] For al-Ṭabarī, the *ijmāᶜ*, or consensus, of a majority of scholars is paramount. He ignores minority views on any aspect of Qurʾān study, while conflicting reports from Successors and Companions, if unresponsive to attempts at harmonization, are shrugged off as concerning only minor matters, knowledge of which is not necessary for salvation and ignorance of which is not harmful. They must, in the absence of a report from the Prophet which would be decisive, remain in abeyance.[29] In orthodox Sunnī eyes, al-Ṭabarī's approach is admirable and his work is regarded as the very embodiment of the ideal Tradition-based exegesis. Massive as it is, the work is incomplete, in so far as al-Ṭabarī refers the reader, anxious for more detailed treatment, to his specialist works on law and *qirāʾāt*.[30] The scale was too vast to be often emulated, while the expense of reproducing copies probably accounts for the early appearance of a series of epitomes.[31] If the "elucidations" are unconvincing, it is because the process of adjusting the Qurʾān texts to the inherited exegeses is all too obvious.

Meanwhile, the linguistic, legal and theological schools matured apace and their standard works appeared. Apart from the tedium involved, the mere passage of time made insistence upon unbroken *isnād*s impracticable. Besides, the paths of *sunnah* and Qurʾān had long diverged to form separate disciplines distinct in aim and method. Law (*fiqh*) was the abiding interest of scholars; theology was developing and exegesis would be subordinated to both. Within the perspective of *tafsīr*, al-Ṭabarī's insistence upon verbatim reproduction of reports with *isnād*s can be seen as atypical. The Qurʾān would continue to provide the ideal vindication of sectional legal and theological views, while offering mature scholars a structure within which to sum up a life's work, for the compiling of a *tafsīr* came to be regarded as a work of pious preparation for the meeting with one's Maker.

27 Horst, "Zur Überlieferung",307. 28 Ṭabarī, *Jāmiᶜ al-bayān*, I, 3–93. 29 Ibid., III, 231.
30 Ibid., I, 148; II, 207. 31 Goldziher, *Richtungen*, 87, n.4.

Al-Ṭabarī had shown how few Prophetical dicta were available and the extent to which the Successors and the Companions had been divided in their exegetical views. Two principal approaches dominated the subsequent literature. Although remaining wedded to the idea of Tradition, while swinging away from reliance on or – following the appearance of the major standard works – even a need for the strict *isnād*, scholars refer more to books than to men, as the legal, linguistic or theological traditions of the school come to the fore in the shaping of the exegesis.

The Shīʿī exegesis shared this development in emphasis. Although considerably less prolix than his great Sunnī contemporary, ʿAlī b. Ibrāhīm al-Qummī (d. 307/919) skilfully arranged into smooth narrative, punctiliously prefixed by *isnād*s, the exegeses transmitted from the imams Muḥammad al-Bāqir and Jaʿfar al-Ṣādiq. Based on specially adapted Imāmī readings,[32] his texts concentrate on the legal, theological and particularly on the political doctrines of the Twelver sect, whose adepts alone he addresses. In contrast, Abū Jaʿfar Muḥammad b. al-Ḥasan al-Ṭūsī (385–460/995–1067), placing greater emphasis upon strict linguistic criteria, organizes the discussion of the traditional readings under a precise sequence of rubrics: verse – reading – etymologies – *sabab* – *iʿrāb* – meaning – *tafsīr*, giving his work a more rigid mechanical framework. Among al-Ṭūsī's numerous sources, in addition to the imams, are the Companions and the Successors and a host of well-known theologians.

The even denser concentration of linguistic analyses assembled by al-Faḍl b. al-Ḥasan al-Ṭabarsī (462–552/1069–1157) parallels the rigorously linguistic approach of the Andalusian Muḥammad b. Yūsuf b. ʿAlī b. Ḥayyān (654–745/1256–1345), who felt it necessary to justify in his introduction the conscious abandonment of the *isnād* and in whose work literary references abound.

ʿAbd al-Ḥaqq b. ʿAṭiyyah (481–542/1088–1147) and Muḥammad b. Aḥmad al-Qurṭubī (d. 671/1272) both pondered the Prophet's reported saying, "He who pronounces on the Qurʾān except on the basis of [Traditional] knowledge (*ʿilm*), and produces a correct interpretation has nevertheless erred", finally deciding that it authorized use of the findings of the established sciences.[33] The exegete must take account of the accumulated principles of linguistics and of law in wrestling with the Qurʾān texts. That is the spirit which informs al-Qurṭubī's own large work in which he analyses the readings and etymologies and, above all, the theological and legal discussions centring on the verses. His concern, and also, to an even

[32] *Tafsīr*, I, 9–12.

[33] Jeffery, *Two Muqaddimahs*, 262; cf. Qurṭubī, *al-Jāmiʿ li-aḥkām al-Qurʾān*, I, 32–3, and Ṭabarī, *Jāmiʿ al-bayān*, I, 77–9.

greater extent, that of Abū Bakr Muḥammad b. ʿAbdullāh b. al-ʿArabī (469–543/1076–1148), was to demonstrate the Quranic basis of the views taught in the Mālikī school of law. A similar office had been performed for the Ḥanafī code by Abū Bakr Aḥmad b. ʿAlī al-Jaṣṣāṣ (302–70/914–81). The particular nature of their works, written from a declared school position and reflected in their common title, *Aḥkām al-Qurʾān*, places them in a special category of *tafsīr*.

THE RATIONAL APPROACH

Linguistic expertise was among the many accomplishments brought to his analysis of the Qurʾān by Abū ʾl-Qāsim Maḥmūd b. ʿUmar al-Zamakhsharī (467–538/1074–1144). This celebrated philologist did not hesitate to adduce his proof-verses from the ʿAbbasid poets alongside references to the *Ṣaḥīḥ* of Muslim and many other literary products of the several scholarly disciplines. Although the avowed objective of his study was to bring out the signal beauties of Qurʾān style and to demonstrate by analysis of the elegance of its argumentation and effectiveness of its rhetoric the doctrine of the Qurʾān's miraculous literary inimitability (*iʿjāz*), his *tafsīr* presents in fact a model of detailed syntactical analysis directed, as usual, at the determination of the most justifiable readings and interpretations. He shows a predilection for the question-and-answer method, but his book abounds also in *ḥadīth*s (without *isnād*s). He had, however, a deeper purpose: by showing from the Qurʾān itself that God had expressed his clear divine preference for "the people of unicity and justice" – al-Zamakhsharī's own Muʿtazilite school – to demonstrate the sound Quranic basis of their theological teachings, and their exclusive title to the name of Muslim. All anthropomorphic interpretations, simplistic predestinarianism, superstitious folk-beliefs and *ḥadīth*s or opinions offensive to reason, the "dualistic" notion of the uncreated Qurʾān, had all to be eliminated from the Islamic system of ideas. Their propagation, not merely by the simple artisan class, but even by respected doctors of the Sunnī sect, proved a scandal prejudicial to the Muʿtazilite goal of re-establishing Islam's intellectual appeal. If it were alleged that such unworthy doctrines were rooted in the Qurʾān and in the Tradition, then clearly the sources called out for reinterpretation.

On Qurʾān, iii.18, for example, "God testifies that there is no god but Him alone. The angels and the possessors of knowledge also testify to this, on the basis of justice: 'there is no god but Him alone, the almighty, the all-wise'", al-Zamakhsharī comments:[34] "'the possessors of knowledge' are

[34] *Kashshāf*, I, 314.

those who, adducing the clearest arguments and most telling proofs, affirm God's unicity and His justness – i.e. the scholars of the party of justice and oneness. In Qurʾān, iii.19, God adds: 'Only Islam is the true religion in God's sight'." God declares that justice and oneness alone is the true religion in his view. In God's opinion, all other groups are no part of the religion. Thus, anyone who upholds anthropomorphic views or any notion that conduces to likening God with his creation (such as the idea that the believer will look upon God in the afterlife), or who adopts the opinion that men's ultimate fate is predestined and that their actions are predetermined – which is the very soul of injustice – is not, in God's view, an adherent of God's religion, the religion of Islam.

In discharging his duty of defining the true faith, al-Zamakhsharī neglects no opportunity to mock the opponents of his school, deploying the devastating weapons of irony and humour.[35] Doubtless it was the arrogance of his theological claims, the ferocity of his attacks on the Ṣūfī confraternities and the deep bitterness of his denunciation of slavish adherence (*taqlīd*) to Tradition which made these particular features of his work appear to be its salient characteristic. They are, in fact, outnumbered by considered paragraphs of comparative *fiqh* in which scrupulous fairness to opponents sharply differentiates these passages from his more acerbic theological comments.

Al-Zamakhsharī's book attracted super-commentaries and counter-commentaries from conservative scholars who balanced grudging admiration for the man's acute linguistic insights with vituperative denunciation of his regrettable heresies. Averting their eyes from his more scandalous jibes, the pious have admitted their dependence upon al-Zamakhsharī's signal contribution to the linguistic analysis of the texts and the readings, especially his services to the Qurʾān's literary qualities. His *Kashshāf ʿan ḥaqāʾiq al-tanzīl* ("The Discloser of the Truths of the Revelation") has continued to be studied and is regularly reprinted.

The depth of Hellenism's penetration of Islam is illustrated by the *tafsīr* of Fakhr al-Dīn abū ʿAbdullāh Muḥammad b. ʿUmar al-Rāzī (543–606/1149–1209), *Mafātīḥ al-ghayb* ("Keys of the Unseen"), which presents the response of Ashʿarite rationalism to Muʿtazilism, Shiʿism and agnosticism. Insisting upon the *iʿjāz* of the Qurʾān as Muḥammad's major evidentiary miracle, al-Rāzī developed the study of the *munāsabah* or appropriateness of the literary sequence of the verses and the *sūrah*s. An interesting, if severely technical introductory essay on the structure of the language scarcely seems necessary at this date, while his prolixity may be judged from his devoting

[35] Ibid., 320.

almost an entire volume to the brief opening *sūrah*. As against the extreme Shīʿī claim that God's existence is known only from the instruction of the Prophet and the imams, and that of the Tradition-minded that our knowledge of God derives solely from knowledge of the Qurʾān and the *Ḥadīth*, al-Rāzī argues that belief in the prophets is a consequence of belief in God, sufficient evidence of whose existence and oneness is furnished in nature. The authenticity of Muḥammad's claim to prophethood rests upon the demonstrable miraculously inimitable style of the Qurʾān.

Lengthy digressions on physics, metaphysics, astronomy, astrology, alchemy, medicine and logic, which break the continuity of the work, converge upon a central theme: the harmony of the natural and mental sciences with the chief of all sciences, theology. The Qurʾān, the word of God, and the universe, the work of God, together attest to the existence and operation of the Divine Being. The Qurʾān's mention, for example, of a thunderstorm provides the opportunity to show that natural science cannot explain all natural events. Two opposing elements, heat (lightning) and damp (rain), indisputably can occur simultaneously in one place (thundercloud). Only theology which knows of a self-subsisting creator acting under no compulsion and capable of producing trans-rational effects can satisfactorily explain such anomalies. Sometimes all that separates philosophy from theology is mere vocabulary. The higher forms of life influencing events, according to the philosophers, are none other than the angels.[36] Al-Rāzī expresses wonder that scientists and philosophers hesitate to believe when the findings of natural science and philosophy coincide with those of *tafsīr*.[37]

His familiarity with the literatures of Islamic and non-Islamic thought impresses both in its sweep and in its detail and his care to name sources brings references to *Ḥadīth*, grammar, theology and history and to the sayings of Persian, Indian, Greek and Arab sages pell-mell into his crowded pages. The infectious enthusiasm of the author propels the reader as Christ, Moses, Abraham and Muḥammad rub shoulders with Ptolemy, Socrates, Aristotle and Galen. Yet, underneath the urbanity and erudition, a traditionally inclined Muslim mind defers to a report from the Prophet, while, even in physics, questions eventually cease. Setting out details of his belief in indirect, gradual creation, when asked why God did not simply create each species directly, al-Rāzī merely replies that God does as he pleases.[38] His extreme dislike for *taqlīd* is the reflex of his impassioned defence of theology against the doubts of the first Muslims, who regarded it as little better than dabbling with divine secrets.[39] Tradition must not be

[36] Rāzī, *Mafātīḥ al-ghayb*, pt. 19, 20. [37] Ibid., 26. [38] Ibid., pt. 2, 110. [39] Ibid., 96.

pitted against reason; the original acceptance of Tradition rested upon reason and to attack it was to attack both reason and Tradition together.[40]

All human concern is present in this stimulating work, although the scholastic method adopted by the author permits too frequent interruption, with endless division into section, subsection and sub-subsection which makes it extremely difficult to retain the thread of the argument throughout a lengthy exposition. The work is more reminiscent of the *adab* literature than is normal in an exegesis, inducing one critic to dismiss it as containing everything except *tafsīr*.[41]

Anwār al-tanzīl wa-asrār al-taʾwīl ("The Lights of the Revelation and the Secrets of the Interpretation") by ʿAbdullāh b. ʿUmar al-Bayḍāwī (d. 685/1286), designed partly as an "expurgation" of al-Zamakhsharī's Muʿtazilite *tafsīr*, but based on other works, including al-Rāzī's, has proved even more to readers' tastes, probably on account of its more manageable proportions, although conciseness has been purchased at the cost of extreme compression, making for obscurity if not dullness. All pretension to literary style has been abandoned, producing what is little more than a technical manual, but the work, regarded as a classic of orthodox *tafsīr*, is among the most frequently printed.

THE ROLE OF INTUITION

The Qurʾān teaches the vanity and transience of this world and belittles preoccupation with material possessions. An other-worldly ascetic strain has, in consequence, been present in Islam since its beginnings. This too, is represented in exegesis, as in the *tafsīr* of Sahl al-Tustarī (d. 283/896), pupil of the celebrated Egyptian mystic, Dhūʾl-Nūn (d. 246/861). Sahl was familiar with the rather obscure *ḥadīth* that every Qurʾān verse has four dimensions: *ẓāhir*, *bāṭin*, *ḥadd* and *muṭṭalaʿ*, which he glossed as respectively: wording, meaning, regulation and intuition of the true import of the verse. The last (equivalent to illumination, i.e. *ilhām*), is a special gift reserved for the chosen to whom God reveals what he really intended by the revelation. Anyone familiar with Arabic can grasp the *ẓāhīr* or surface meaning. God's real purpose was, however, the *bāṭin*, and in his exegesis, Sahl proposed to interpret the Qurʾān at both levels.[42] The Ṣūfī attitude to the meanings and uses of words frequently makes their statements arcane, but Sahl's comparatively short work is reasonably unpretentious. His general purpose being ethical, he uses for illustration edifying anecdotes from the lives of

[40] Ibid., 57.
[41] Suyūṭī *Itqān*, pt. 2, 190; Ḥājjī Khalīfah, *Kashf al-ẓunūn*, ed. G. Flügel, Leipzig, II, 1837, 338.
[42] Muḥammad Ḥusayn al-Dhahabī, *al-Tafsīr wa-ʾl-mufassirūn*, II, 380ff.

the saints (*awliyāʾ*). Many Qurʾān stories are symbolic. For instance, the believer's wife, sons and property can, like the calf worshipped by the Israelites, distract him from thinking of God. The Israelites could not return to monotheism until they had abandoned worship of the calf and then, as commanded, slain themselves, that is, their souls, their appetites (vii.148). Thus the believer must strive to empty his soul of the love of all worldly things, including those most dear to him. God's command to Abraham is a favourite theme. The actual slaying of his son was not desired. What God intended was that Abraham empty his heart of all except love of God (xxxvii.107). God gives men to eat and drink – to eat of the sustenance of faith and to drink of the water of reliance upon God alone (xxvi.78–82). Yet fear must balance hope, for salvation is not automatic.

The conservative scholars were indulgent towards insights of this kind, but the exegete had to be discreet. Vilification was the reward of men like Abū ʿAbd al-Raḥmān al-Sulamī (330–412/941–1021), who openly alleged that their symbolic exegeses represented God's true intent. Despite his reputation as an expert in *Ḥadīth*, al-Sulamī was widely denounced as a forger and a liar following the appearance of a largish book, *Ḥaqāʾiq al-tafsīr* ("The Truths of Interpretation"), in which, collecting the sayings of prominent figures, he attached them to relevant verses. Confining himself to "the inner truths" and omitting to mention "the outer truths", al-Sulamī earned the wrath of the scholars. Al-Suyūṭī considered the work heretical, al-Dhahabī wished it had never been written, while al-Wāḥidī (d. 468/1075) denounced the author as an unbeliever.[43] Al-Sulamī's interpretations hardly differed from Sahl's, but his incaution was his undoing.

Bolder spirits, throwing all caution to the wind, decried the ulema who could see only the envelope, whereas the adepts could read the message within. The *tafsīr* of the Qurʾān, the bare meanings of the words, are accessible to all who read Arabic, but what has been transmitted to date cannot possibly exhaust the riches of a divine book whose depths must, by definition, be infinite. Man perhaps cannot reach them unaided.[44]

Neo-Platonic emanation theories furnished the trappings of Islamic mystical philosophy to whose practitioners God divulges the secrets of his creation and the true appreciation of his revelation. To ignore the outer meanings of the Qurʾān merely leads to esotericism, but to ignore the inner secrets is the way of the slave of Tradition who sees no further than the outer wrappings. One must strive to penetrate beyond the visible to reach the very soul of the revelation.[45] The Qurʾān itself invites reflection: "Reflect, you who have eyes" (*iʿtabirū yā ūlī ʾl-abṣār*). By clever word-play

[43] Ibid., II 386; cf. Suyūṭī, *Itqān*, pt. 2, 184. [44] Goldziher, *Richtungen*, 197. [45] Ibid., 236–7.

sūrah lix.2 becomes: pass beyond what you see with the outer eye (*abṣār*) to the meanings which the visible suggests to your inner being (*bāṭin*) and which are perceptible only to the inner eye (*baṣāʾir*).

To show contempt for this illusory world by the suppression of the human appetites in regular contemplation of the divine verses, to reject the wilful self in preparation for the annihilation of the self in the divine, is the path to selection for intimate divine encounter leading to an infusion of inspiration directly into the attentive soul. One becomes the recipient of immediate knowledge (*maʿrifah*) which is unquestionable, guaranteed by the manner of its bestowal.[46]

Subjecting selected Qurʾān passages to their particular interpretation technique (*taʾwīl*), the Ṣūfīs imparted their revelations to a close circle of disciples, preferring not to publish their secrets abroad, although much *taʾwīl* is found scattered throughout the prolific writings of the great masters, Abū Ḥāmid Muḥammad b. Muḥammad al-Ghazālī (451–505/1059–1111) and Muḥyī ʾl-Dīn Muḥammad b. ʿAlī b. al-ʿArabī (560–638/1165–1240), the latter one of the giants of Ṣufism to whom, in addition to extensive writings of an abstruse technical character, a systematic exegetical work has also (questionably) been attributed.[47]

The Ṣūfīs generally took the precaution of avoiding the term *tafsīr*, preferring to speak of hints (*ishārāt*), partly to avoid the presumption of binding the divine intent to one particular interpretation, but, more importantly, to avert the ire of conservative circles hostile to any claim to "knowledge" attained without years of sacrifice and toil. Muḥyī ʾl-Dīn b. al-ʿArabī's arrogance towards mere book-learning (*ʿilm*) and his extravagant boasts of personal meetings, not merely with prophets and angels, but even with God himself, provoked the orthodox to sarcasm. Some of his exegetical statements, which are of extreme complexity, certainly could be read as presenting grave dangers to belief.[48] A *modus vivendi* was generally, however, desired, as it was clear that considerable spiritual benefits could be derived from Ṣūfī insights. Their *taʾwīl* could be accommodated within the science of *tafsīr*, as long as it was emphasized that they claimed merely to supplement, not to replace, the massive body of interpretation built up over generations.

Muḥyī ʾl-Dīn ("Resuscitator of the Religion") b. al-ʿArabī – to the irreconcilable, Mumīt al-Dīn ("Assassin of the Religion") – thus took pains to insist that his symbolic interpretations might not be taken as other than parallel and complementary to the traditional *tafsīr* of which they offered a

46 Ibid., 246.

47 Dhahabī, *al-Tafsīr wa-ʾl-mufassirūn*, II, 400–1; cf. Gätje, *Koran und Koranexegese*, 62.

48 Goldziher, *Richtungen*, 223; Dhahabī, *al-Tafsīr wa-ʾl-mufassirūn*, II, 342.

fuller development, extending into the spiritual dimension from which the traditional *tafsīr* had fallen sadly short. Neither philosophy nor philology can lead to spiritual perfection.[49] Ibn al-ʿArabī's Ṣufism, far from antinomian, coming not to destroy the law, but to fulfil it, embraced and insisted upon the fullest implementation of the *sharīʿah* to the smallest detail. The mystic's role was to illumine, to vivify the law by unveiling its spiritual fullness and by uncovering the hidden splendours of the revelation.

[49] Ibid., 206.

CHAPTER 5

THE PROSE LITERATURE OF ṢUFISM

The prose literature of Islamic mysticism, or Ṣufism, during the ᶜAbbasid era is rich and varied. Distinct accomplishments can be credited to Ṣūfī writers who often did not shun the use of prevailing genres and styles of expression. In the face of criticism and pressures from the ulema, Ṣūfī authors often resorted to the oblique and enigmatic as tools of literary expression and ideological articulation. Beliefs were often couched in symbolical and allegorical references, and so thoroughly camouflaged at times that authors in the later centuries found it necessary to write their own commentaries.

Basically Ṣūfī writers were not particularly innovative with regard to prose categories. They favoured definitive and descriptive works, guidance and reference manuals, epistolary and instructional treatises and biographies and hagiographies. Their themes tended to explain and moralize, with heavy stress on the exemplary. Didactic techniques seem to govern most aspects of their writings, particularly in the later stages when instructing and guiding novices required much wisdom and exemplification.

On the defensive during much of the earlier centuries, Ṣufism generated a wealth of polemical and introspective literature. To enlist sympathy for their cause, Ṣūfīs developed a remarkable capacity for communication. In contriving the means, they contributed not only to literary norms but to the language as well, in the form of direct facile expressions which, in the long run, reduced the tendency toward affectation, subtlety and exaggeration. To Arabic literature they added flashes of brilliance and imagination, boldness and freedom of expression in the face of strong adversity, and with no compromising of moral and ethical standards, which made of them the spiritual teachers of the Muslims. Ibn Qutaybah (d. 276/889) complimented them on the breadth and depth of their intellectual interests and capacities. Men like Ḥārith b. Asad al-Muḥāsibī (d. 243/857) and ᶜĀṣim al-Anṭākī (d. 215/830) were sophisticated rationalists and master dialecticians, adepts at the accommodation of scholastic vocabulary to writing methods. Indeed, they and their adherents were able to harmonize the extreme positions of the

Muᶜtazilites on the one hand and the orthodox ulema on the other. Ibn Karrām (d. 241/855) of Khurāsān excelled at using analytical techniques to differentiate between matters of faith and those of gnosis.

Ṣūfī authors were also successful in assimilating literary devices used by Traditionists: classification, narration and verification. Some maintain that their literature was in reality directed against the formalism of orthodoxy and aimed at deeper probings of religious mysteries. In so doing, they achieved a sublime conception of religious devotion. Unaffected by material or intellectual pursuits, Ṣūfī writings came to embody Islam's highest ideals, and, in the later centuries of spiritual malaise, they were still able to draw on the values of everyday life in their milieus. They were in tune with their environments and mirrored the times in their writings, both spiritually and socially.

Weak and devoid of the richness of ideas and expressions of earlier centuries, the cultural and literary legacy of Ṣūfīs in the later centuries reflects degenerating times. Writers employ references and terms so rare that they cannot be found in lexicons. Grammar also suffers, and the use of incorrect sentence structures and trite expressions is frequent. This latter is not a form of literary decrepitude, but rather the conscientious efforts of Ṣūfī writers to communicate with a nearly illiterate audience at a much reduced level of comprehension. Their techniques were often affected by local usages and tended to vary from place to place. Non-Ṣūfī literature, on the other hand, was free of local and pedantic influences because authors, mostly Traditionists, were addressing a learned group. Thus the adorned and well-turned expression constituted an art with writers of the third and fourth Islamic centuries. The Ṣūfī author, however, derided such techniques and was dubbed an anti-intellectual lacking in literary graces.

The general consensus nevertheless is that he did not lack literary taste. It is he who elevated music, for example, to an art, distilling in the process the finest expressions of his world of perception and translating the sublimest sentimentality into tender words richly endowed with subtle meanings. Al-Ḥallāj, Muḥyī ʾl-Dīn b. al-ᶜArabī and ᶜUmar b. al-Fāriḍ (d. 632/1235) said it all and said it well. Nor were they inept at the use of philosophical techniques. Indeed, some critics call their writings "literature of reflection", steeped in ethical concepts. For them writing was not an end in itself, but rather the medium for stating the aspirations and endurements of the spirit and the soul yearning after its Maker, the attainment of perfection in the realization of God's presence, and the ultimate transports of the spirit when submerged in the divine.

Overall, their literature has been superb, emulated for centuries by men of literary appreciation. If Ṣūfī writers had left no other legacy, scholars of Arabic would long be indebted to them for a style of expression free from artificiality and slavish subservience to conventionalism. They did not prostitute their art in praise of the high and mighty among mortals as others did, and by placing security of soul above that of the body, they served as models of bravery and boldness. Their noble and virtuous spirit imbued Arabic literature with the moral values characterized by reflections on personal experience, not the fiat of abstract decrees issuing forth from the ulema.

While the oblique, enigmatic and allegorical left their mark on Arabic literature most conspicuously in the nineteenth century in official writings and correspondences, still the reader is indebted to Ṣūfī authors for ridding the language of story techniques. To them, if it lacks a moral basis, expository writing has no contextual or literary validity. At first their writings focused on pragmatic matters – piety, wise counsel and admonition – as they groped for cures to the "diseases of the heart"; but as they became increasingly absorbed in the meditative life, their writings acquired abstract qualities, both in the choice of topics and modes of expression.

In general, Ṣūfī authorship can be characterized as synoptic, reflecting prevalent literary trends but clothed with greater spirituality. The broadness of its appeal is the result of a variety of beliefs represented by converts to Ṣufism. Philosophers, Ashᶜarites, Muᶜtazilites, Traditionists, Shīᶜīs and a bevy of esotericists opted for the Ṣūfī way, and one can hardly expect men of such varied learning and beliefs to wipe the slate of their minds clean as they engaged in new intellectual pursuits. The theme of love, so integral to Ṣūfī literary digressions, could not be divorced from its sensuous component, however divine it became later. Rābiᶜah (d. 185/801), the epitome of pure selfless love for God, was an entertainer and singer before turning ascetic and transferring the richness of her love experiences to the Beloved. Ibn al-Fāriḍ, "the sultan of lovers", was particularly attracted to beauty and consciously sought to distil the beautiful from his environment as he expressed it in exquisite verse.

There is little that can be termed ascetic or mystical literature before the early ᶜAbbasid era. Al-Ḥasan al-Baṣrī (d. 110/728) is considered a pioneer for his wise preaching and admonitions. He generated a trend focusing on short treatises offering counsel and advice, which were ethical and instructional in aim and cited by al-Jāḥiẓ (d. 255/868–9), Abū ʾl-Faraj al-Iṣfahānī (d. 356/967), Ibn ᶜAsākir and other biographers. Asceticism was still the dominant theme in the first ᶜAbbasid century, with the Prophet and his Companions and Successors commanding the attention of authors. The earliest recordings of moral sayings with distinct traces of a mystical flavouring appear in the third/ninth century, in Basra. Some say this trend first appears with Jaᶜfar, the sixth imam, with his mystical interpretation of the Qurᵓān. But actually it was Dhū ᵓl-Nūn al-Miṣrī (d. 246/861) who was the first to develop a distinctly mystical writing in Islam, coining terms popularized by other Ṣūfīs at a later date.

The Qurᵓān inspired early Ṣūfī writing in its alleged allusion to a pre-eternal covenant between God and man, the re-enactment of which filled the mystic with extreme enthusiasm. Al-Muḥāsibī wrote a non-esoteric exegesis on the holy book entitled *Kitāb Fahm maᶜānī al-Qurᵓān*; al-Tirmidhī (d. 279/882) made a synopsis of it under the title of *Taḥṣīl naẓāᵓir al-Qurᵓān*, and Muḥyī ᵓl-Dīn abū ᶜAbdullāh Muḥammad b. ᶜAlī b. al-ᶜArabī (d. 638/1240) wrote an impressive and truly esoteric *tafsīr* in which we have the widest possible condensations in a mystical context of the full gamut of unitarian convictions.[1] The *Taysīr* of ᶜIzz al-Dīn al-Dīrīnī (d. 697/1297) is a didactic poem of 3,200 verses on Quranic exegesis. Al-Sulamī (d. 412/1021) concerned himself with the science of exegesis itself in his *Ḥaqāᵓiq al-tafsīr*.

It was in Basra, Kufa and Damascus that Ṣūfī prose had its inception in the form of sermonettes, adages and admonitions against growing worldliness under the Umayyads. Al-Ḥasan al-Baṣrī's discourses on the subject were compiled by his contemporaries and disciples and published after his death by Ḥāmid al-Khuzāᶜī (d. 142/759). His correspondence and sermons on canon law, morality and dogma survive in the works of others. He is the model author on how eloquence and intellect can be brought to bear upon reflection so as to mirror the good and God's benefactions. Al-Jāḥiẓ describes his sermons exhorting to consciousness as both penetrating and as Islam's most beautiful. He is credited with steering the caliph ᶜUmar II (reigned 99–101/717–20) toward a life of piety. Khālid b. Ṣafwān and al-Awzāᶜī (d. 157/774) also addressed correspondence and sermons to princes and caliphs, samples of which are preserved in Ibn Qutaybah's *ᶜUyūn al-akhbār*.

This type of literature remained in vogue during the second Muslim century, expressed now in the *maqāmah* style. This was later to be cultivated fully by al-Hamadhānī (d. 398/1007) and al-Ḥarīrī (d. 516/1122), thanks to its popularization by Dhū ᵓl-Nūn al-Miṣrī, who used it to good advantage in his correspondence with al-Mutawakkil (reigned 232–47/847–61), and also by al-Tujībī in his story-like adages preserved in Muḥammad b. Yūsuf al-Kindī's *Kitāb Wulāt Miṣr*. In the third/ninth century this trend in literature acquired deeper and broader forms, new trends and expressions more clearly manifest in a wider range of Ṣūfī authorship.

[1] Cf. above, ch. 4, 54.

MORALIZING LITERATURE

Works designed to instruct by moralizing took the form of testaments and brief admonitions, narratives and short accounts, problems and issues, examples of virtue, with ethics and etiquette providing a running theme. Testaments, or *waṣāyā*, are among the oldest of Ṣūfī writings. Those of ʿAlī were especially cherished, and had a remarkable tendency to fructify as *Nahj al-balāghah* ("The Path of Eloquence")[2] proves. Other renowned testaments and admonitions are those of Abū Yazīd of Bisṭām (d. 261/874 or 264/877–8) and al-Ḥallāj (executed 857/922). Al-Muḥāsibī left us his *Naṣīḥah li-ʾl-ṭālibīn*. We also have testaments from others like al-Rudhabārī (d. 369/979), al-Sulamī, and Abū Saʿīd Aḥmad b. Muḥammad b. Ziyād al-Aʿrābī (d. 341/952), who entitled his *Risālah fī ʾl-mawāʿiẓ wa-ʾl-fawāʾid*. In his *Kitāb al-Amthāl*, focusing on the exemplary as evinced in the Qurʾān and in the Traditions, al-Tirmidhī was a pioneer. A fine work that combines wise counsel with example and deed is *al-Ḥikam* of Tāj al-Dīn b. ʿAṭāʾallāh ʿAbbās al-Sakandarī (d. 709/1309). The work is relatively easy to follow, considering his depictions and metaphors could lend themselves to a number of interpretations. There is almost a deliberate interlacing of ideas with a variety of lexical significations. He appears to delight in accentuating grammatical features, as in:

> How could it be that anything can veil Him who has given form to everything, and who has appeared *in* everything, *by* everything, *before* everything, and more visible than everything . . .[3]

On the negative side, *al-Ḥikam* is deficient in terms of structure; the haphazard organization of topics strips it of harmony and continuity, and only its rich consistent rhyme holds it together.

With regard to short accounts and narratives, we have *al-Ḥadīth* of Maʿrūf al-Karkhī (d. 200/815), the *Aḥādīth* of Manṣūr b. ʿAmmār of Basra, *al-Fawāʾid wa-ʾl-ḥikāyāt wa-ʾl-akhbār* of Abū Ḥātim al-Aṣamm of Balkh (d. 237/851), *Kalimāt* from Sahl al-Tustarī, and *Kalām* from al-Nūrī (d. 295/907). The *Akhbār* of al-Ḥallāj were collected by his disciples and provide us with a sampling of what this genre contains: sayings, doings, preachings and information about the person concerned. Again there is no consistent method pursued in the organization of the work, nor any chronological ordering of the material in the edited form. The collection appears to have been gleaned from scattered unconnected sources. Another significant work in this vein is *Akhbār al-ṣāliḥīn* of ʿAlī al-Ḥamadhānī (d. 414/1023).

[2] *CHALUP*, 305. [3] *Ḥikam*, 12–13.

Examples of virtuous deeds, or *manāqib* works, aimed likewise at instructing by example. Essentially they were personal hagiographies, noteworthy among which were *Kitāb Khatm al-wilāyah* of al-Tirmidhī and *Maqāmāt al-awliyāʾ* of al-Sulamī; Muḥyī ʾl-Dīn b. al-ʿArabī depended upon both of these in his *Muḥāḍarāt al-abrār*. Dhū ʾl-Nūn penned *Risālah fī Dhikr manāqib al-ṣāliḥīn*, and those of Abū Yazīd are among the most popular. Nearly all founders of Ṣūfī orders left such works or were honoured by them. Those of ʿAbd al-Qādir al-Jīlānī (d. 564/1168) are preserved in *al-Fatḥ al-rabbānī* and *Jalāʾ al-khāṭir*, while his discourses are gathered in *Futūḥ al-ghayb*. The *Mafākhir al-ʿaliyyah* of Aḥmad al-ʿAbbād encompasses the wisdom and virtues of al-Shādhilī (d. 656/1258). An all-embracing work is *Bahjat al-asrār* of al-Shaṭṭanūfī (d. 713/1313), which concentrates on the *manāqib* of such Egyptian founders as Abū Ḥasan ʿAlī al-Shādhilī, al-Rifāʿī, al-Dasūqī and al-Ṣabbāgh. ʿAbd al-Wahhāb al-Shaʿrānī (d. 973/1565) saw fit to focus on his own virtues in *Laṭāʾif al-minan* ("Subtleties of Blessings"), wherein he points to parallelisms in the experiences of other Ṣūfī masters. Impressive works of this kind by non-order founders are *Manāqib ahl al-ḥaqq* of al-Tustarī and *Manāqib al-abrār* of Tāj al-Islām al-Mawṣilī (d. 552/1157), a disciple of al-Ghazālī.

Problems and answers (*masāʾil* and *ajwibah*) consisted of posing hypothetical questions and answering them, a technique used also to impart instruction by focusing on distinctions between right and wrong, virtue and evil, sin and righteousness. This genre is usually characterized by unusual perceptiveness expressed in curt, crisp phrases, elegant language and superb imagery, as, for example:

Q What sayest thou of consulting with others?
A Have no faith in it, save it be with a trustworthy man.
Q And what sayest thou concerning the giving of advice?
A Consider first whether thy words will save thyself; if so, thy guidance is inspired, and thou wilt be respected and trusted.[4]

Correspondence also served as a medium for imparting wise counsel. The epistles of al-Junayd (d. 297/910) are an example of the finest. Addressed to brethren, they expound nearly all his mystical and theosophical views. His style favours the tangential, abstract, complicated and ponderous yet not without impact.

As it was perhaps the most popular genre for disseminating ideas and instructing, the epistle (*risālah*) constitutes the bulk of Sūfī prose. Indeed, the tradition is imbedded in the Judaeo-Christian world. The Apostles

[4] Quoted from ʿĀṣim al-Anṭākī, trans. Arberry, *Sufism*, 43.

resorted to it, and Muslim men of piety and esteem found it a particularly effective means for inculcating disciples and companions with their wisdom. Al-Muḥāsibī pioneered with his *Risālah fī ʾl-Taṣawwuf*; al-Tustarī left a work on *ḥikam*; Ibn ʿAbbād of Ronda has a collection of epistles in his *al-Rasāʾil al-Ṣughrā*, but Dhū ʾl-Nūn was the most adept at the *risālah*:

O brother, know ye there is no honour above Islam, no generosity dearer than piety, no intelligence more fortified than Godfearingness, no cure more successful than repentance, no attire more enhancing than good health, no protection more inuring than security, no treasure richer than contentment, no passion more enriching than satisfaction with nourishment. So he who is content with attaining satiation has ordered tranquillity, for ambition is the key to exhaustion and the tool of hardship; prudence decrees assault on faults; many an ambition is a lie, an aspiration illusory, a hope leading to deprivation, and gain resulting in loss.[5]

BIOGRAPHY

Biography was a most convenient tool for exemplifying the lives and deeds of those whose emulation was desired. A most interesting early quasi-autobiographical work is *Badʾ shaʾn al-ḥakīm al-Tirmidhī*.[6] But one of the all-time classics is Abū Ḥāmid al-Ghazālī's *Bidāyat al-hidāyah*. His *al-Munqidh min al-ḍalāl* is an equally important spiritual autobiography, and perhaps the best single source on his life. In it he weighs the pros and cons of all four groups striving after the truth – theologians, philosophers, authoritarians and Ṣūfīs, opting for the ways of the latter. After ten years of withdrawal and introspective search concerning the truth of being, al-Ghazālī reached the conclusion that the real cannot be attained by sense perception but, rather, by intuitive revelation. The attainment of truth through ecstatic or experiential means is further adumbrated in his book *ʿAjāʾib al-qalb*.[7]

Personal biographies were inspired by masters of the way. On al-Jīlānī we have al-Shaṭṭanūfī's *Bahjat al-asrār*, an elaborate work which unfortunately does more to obscure than bring out his personality. For the life of Abū ʾl-Ḥasan ʿAlī al-Shādhilī and his disciple Abū ʾl-ʿAbbās al-Mursī there is Tāj al-Dīn b. ʿAṭāʾallāh's *Laṭāʾif al-minan* and Muḥammad b. al-Ṣabbāgh's *Durrat al-asrār* (compiled around 720/1320). On Aḥmad al-Rifāʿī (d. 578/1182) there is *Tiryāq al-muḥibbīn* by Taqī ʾl-Dīn al-Wāsiṭī.

Versatility is manifest in larger compendia, particularly those of the fifth-sixth/eleventh-twelfth centuries. The *Ṭabaqāt al-ṣūfiyyah* of ʿAbd al-Wāḥid al-Warathānī (d. 372/982) was al-Sulamī's main reference, as was Aḥmad al-Nasawī's (d. 396/1005) with the same title. Al-Sulamī's *Ṭabaqāt al-ṣūfiyyah*

[5] Cited by al-Sarrāj in his *al-Lumaʿ*, 265. [6] Ed. ʿUmar Yaḥyā in *al-Mashriq*, LV, 1861, 245–76.
[7] *Iḥyāʾ ʿulūm al-dīn*, III, *Sharḥ ʿAjāʾib al-qalb*, Cairo, n.d.

("Classes of the Ṣūfīs") is the oldest extant, and the model for later writers. Structured into five "layers" or "classes" comprising Ṣūfī shaykhs and ulema, each centres on about twenty people who were contemporaries. By choice, the author focuses on the essence and what best represents the subject's life and sayings. The work is deliberately concise having altogether only 105 entries: the data is compact, the *isnād*s abridged, the style is lucid, facile and flowing but with a touch of the *maqāmah*. For its streamlined features this work can be matched perhaps only by a similarly titled one of ʿAbdullāh al-Anṣārī (d. 412/1022).

The leading work in this category is the *Ḥilyat al-awliyāʾ* of Abū Nuʿaym al-Iṣfahānī (d. 430/1038). This ten-volume anthology of 689 biographies is an excellent example of the narrative-type compilation, starting with the Prophet and his wives and daughters. The main criteria for selection seem to be piety, purity and religiosity, with stress also on the miraculous. It is relatively dull, lacking in humour and colour, but the author's main concern is to encourage piety, not to entertain. All men of piety, Ṣūfī or not, are given attention. In contrast with al-Sulamī's work, Abū Nuʿaym's lacks symmetry and is uneven in space allocation, the longest entry taking up 142 pages, the shortest less than one. There is also a conspicuous lack of inner harmony of treatment. The narrative tends to be disjointed and at times inconstant. The last volume alone takes up nearly a third of the whole. Al-Tirmidhī's *Khatm al-wilāyah* contains, besides his own biography, the spiritual biography of important early mystics. In this fascinating work the author argues the case of a seal for saints as others have for prophets. Impressed by his arguments, Muḥyī ʾl-Dīn b. al-ʿArabī developed them further, adding to them his own colour and stamp.

An enjoyable and significant work in this vein is Farīd al-Dīn ʿAṭṭār's (d. before 627/1230) *Tadhkirat al-awliyāʾ*, which incorporates a vast store of information tastefully and entertainingly presented. Put together most likely in the author's lifetime, it represents a synthesis of material drawn from earlier popular or little-known works. In focusing on the "saints", he sought to strengthen spiritual resolve, heighten aspiration and destroy self-conceit. For as al-Junayd put it, "their sayings are one of the armies of Almighty God",[8] and as the Prophet said before him, "Mercy descends at the mention of the pious". The comments of saints allegedly serve to interpret better the Qurʾān and Traditions, and dispose men to renounce the world, meditate on the future life, love God and prepare themselves for the end.

8 Cited by ʿAṭṭār in Arberry's translation, *Muslim Saints and Mystics*, 11.

LITERATURE OF VENERATION

The cult of venerating the saints received an early boost in al-Tirmidhī's *Khatm al-wilāyah*. It is strongly reflected in the literature of the orders, wherein the focus is the shaykh and the *barakah* associated with him, if alive, and with his tomb, if dead. This is also the basis of *ziyārāt* and *muᶜjizāt* literature. The so-called miracles were construed as proof of the master's sanctity and the way to distinguish between the saint and the imposter. ᶜAfīf al-Dīn al-Yāfiᶜī (d. 768/1367) placed considerable stress on *karāmāt* in his *Rawḍ al-rayāḥīn fī manāqib al-ṣāliḥīn*, wherein he betrays lack of authority and credibility which in a sense points to a facet of Ṣūfī writings in the period of decline.

Concomitantly, we witness also a genre of literature designed to accommodate pseudo-sciences like astrology, divination and magic, professing not only to reveal the secrets of the unseen world, but to control them as well. Aḥmad al-Būnī (d. 623/1225) was the first to concentrate systematically on divination, astrology and magical invocation. Ṣūfī orders already were stressing the *power* of the *word* of God, and hundreds of tracts purported to show the virtues and properties of the names of God. Abū ᵓl-Qāsim ᶜAbd al-Karīm al-Qushayrī's *Taḥbīr* is a treatise on the ninety-nine names of God. Others sought to unravel the underlying mystery of the *basmalah*, and such Quranic verses as ii.255 and *sūrah*s as xxxvi. Abū ᵓl-Ḥasan ᶜAlī al-Shādhilī's *Ḥizb al-baḥr* and al-Jāzūlī's *Dalāᵓ il al-khayrāt* give such names, verses and chapters magical properties and accentuate the power of symbolism based on words. The *Alwāḥ al-ᶜimādiyyah* of Shihāb al-Dīn Yaḥyā al-Suhrawardī al-Maqtūl (executed 587/1191) deals with the absolute and divine attributes in the context of their signification.

REFERENCE LITERATURE

The main works of reference are Ṣufism's most developed literary genre, for they encompass the full range of beliefs and teachings. Since originally the intent was to explain and defend Ṣūfī theories and views, the apologetic tone is conspicuous as authors sought to show the conformity of their teachings with orthodoxy. A key major work executed in an orthodox vein is *al-Riᶜāyah li-ḥuqūq Allāh* of al-Muḥāsibī. The *Qūt al-qulūb* of Abū Ṭālib al-Makkī (d. 386/996) is an early landmark on which al-Ghazālī relies heavily in his *Iḥyāᵓ ᶜulūm al-dīn*. The *Kitāb al-Lumaᶜ* of Abū Naṣr ᶜAbdullāh b. ᶜAlī al-Sarrāj (d. 378/988) is a work of textbook proportion, treating in detail the full range of Ṣufism's fundamental beliefs and observances in a simple, straightforward, expository style. The eloquence of al-Ḥujwīrī (d. *c.* 465-69/1169–73) in his important reference text entitled *Kashf al-maḥjūb* ("Revealing the Veiled": first written in Persian) is evinced as follows:

Know [ye] that I have found the universe to be the shrine of the Divine mysteries; for to the created things has God entrusted Himself and within that which exists has He hidden Himself. Substances and accidents, elements, bodies, forms and dispositions are all veils of these mysteries.[9]

The work generally regarded as the Bible of Ṣufism is *al-Risālah al-Qushayriyyah*, of Abū ʾl-Qāsim ʿAbd al-Karīm al-Qushayrī (d. 465/1072). It is perhaps the best, all-embracing synopsis extant on the whole sweep of Ṣufism up through its classical period of development. The title, unrepresentative of its scope, is in keeping with its original form: a series of epistles to disciples in different provinces, furnishing them with precise information on the place of Ṣufism within the religion of Islam. Supporting data derives from the *manāqib* of shaykhs, and is enlisted in such a fashion so as to focus on all aspects of Ṣūfī philosophical thought. The object is to impart fresh glory to doctrines that had fallen rather out of fashion in al-Qushayrī's day. The lofty aspiration of the mystic is best epitomized in his observation: "The servant is like a body in the hands of God, plunged in the depths of the ocean of oneness, having passed away from the self and from the clutches of things created, so that in the end the servant returns to what he was before he began."[10] The additional significance of the author lies in his knowledge of *fiqh*, his great skill in calligraphy and a remarkable amount of erudition in literary matters.[11]

An earlier work in the same vein, albeit concise, is *al-Taʿarruf li-madhhab ahl al-taṣawwuf* of al-Kalābādhī (d. 380 or 384/990 or 994). Subject to numerous commentaries in the following century, the work became a reference for novices because of its capsular presentation of Ṣūfī doctrines. A later, but equally comprehensive work, is *ʿAwārif al-maʿārif* of Shihāb al-Dīn ʿUmar al-Suhrawardī (d. 632/1234), a miniature *Iḥyāʾ* in its range.

These master works of Ṣufism were heirs to the finest literary tradition, for prose writing by now had acquired the full range of technical and stylistic development, mature and expressive, varied, brilliant and imaginative. Aims were clearly and fully defined, truthfully and boldly stated, and their impact strongly felt. Having interacted courageously with the ulema, Ṣūfī writers adopted their scholastic techniques and were versatile in the philosopher's techniques as well. Their prose clearly reflects such stylistic vagaries as a heavy dependence on similes, adages, allegories, delicate portrayals and imagination.

[9] Cited by Smith, *Readings*, 55. [10] Ibid. [11] Huart, *Arabic Literature*, 271–2.

ETIQUETTE LITERATURE

Etiquette figured prominently in every phase and step of the way – from preparation, to embarkation, to arrival. Other aspects of Arabic literature reveal almost no commensurate concern for the minutiae that seem to absorb Ṣūfī attention. There are tracts on every aspect of Ṣūfī conduct in nearly all circumstances. Such works are very much in evidence during the organizational phase of the movement, when novices needed guidance and careful instruction. Being mostly withdrawn and self-centred, there was no demand for the early ascetics to share their experiences or explain the wherewithal of spiritual perfection.

For specific treatises we have *Ādāb al-nufūs* of al-Muḥāsibī, *Dawāʾ al-qulūb* of ʿĀṣim al-Anṭākī, *Kitāb al-Murīdīn* of Abū Zakariyyāʾ Yaḥyā b. Muʿādh al-Rāzī (d. 258/872), *Kitāb Adab al-nafs* of al-Tirmidhī, *Adab al-faqīr* of al-Rudhabārī, a treatise on the etiquette of prayer by al-Kharrāz (d. 286/899) and short correspondences by Dhū ʾl-Nūn al-Miṣrī and al-Junayd.

The more extensive works on the subject of etiquette appear in conjunction with the solidification of Ṣūfī orders and the need for manuals to train novices and guide shaykhs. The most comprehensive work is al-Sulamī's *Jawāmiʿ ādāb al-ṣūfiyyah*, incorporating a number of separate treatises on etiquette. Ḥusayn al-Wazzān, a contemporary, left us *Kitāb Adab al-murīd*, and *Ādāb al-murīdīn* of Ḍiyāʾ al-Dīn ʿAbd al-Qāhir al-Suhrawardī (d. 563/1168) is a landmark. The *Ghunyah* of al-Jīlānī, composed at the request of companions and followers, is both a full manual and a complete treatise on Ṣufism detailing rules of conduct for a life of virtue, and the requisite etiquette for every phase thereof. He was one of the first to stress the observance of strict and proper etiquette wherever and whenever called for.

The style is basically narrative characterized by lucidity. Some treatises however seem to favour the indirect quotation with Quranic and *Ḥadīth* support. Occasionally there is a touch of humour, a slight compensation for a serious genre:

> It is incumbent upon the novice not to speak at all except by the will of his master if he be present in the flesh; if absent, then he should seek permission through his heart if he is to progress in attaining his Lord's truth.[12]

Truthfulness and propriety receive direct attention in al-Kharrāz's *Kitāb al-Ṣidq*. Al-Qushayrī's *Tartīb al-sulūk* emphasizes the etiquette to be observed along the Ṣūfī path, as does *Adab al-sulūk* by an anonymous Andalusian

[12] Cited by al-Shaʿrānī, on the authority of al-Dasūqī, in his *Ṭabaqāt*, I, 165.

residing in Damascus in Ṣalāḥ al-Dīn's time. The *Sulūk al-ᶜārifīn* of al-Sulamī belongs to the same category, and so in some respects does the *Manāzil al-sāᵓirīn* of al-Anṣārī, executed in rhyming prose.

LITERATURE OF DIVINE CONVERSE

This genre embraces prayers, invocations and supererogations. The Prophet pointed the way with his, "Nothing is more pleasing to God than invocation". *Duᶜāᵓ* (invocation) thus elicited much literary attention, with an etiquette of its own. ᶜAli Zayn al-ᶜĀbidīn, the grandson of Alī b. abī Ṭālib, became the centre of a superb invocation literature, elegantly transcribed in gold so as to focus on the full strength of its wording. Considered privy to the innermost secrets of spirituality, addressing commoners convincingly in one tone and the elect equally so in another, Zayn was elevated by his Shīᶜah admirers to the supreme rank of spiritual embodiment.

Muḥammad al-Niffarī (*fl.* 350/961) excelled at *munājāt* or contemplative literature with his *Kitāb al-Mukhāṭabāt* and *Kitāb al-Mawāqif*. The vision technique he employed in these works might well reflect a continuation of Abū Yazīd's tradition of direct converse with the Divine, as:

> And I saw Fear holding sway over Hope; and I saw Riches turned to fire and cleaving to the fire; and I saw Poverty an adversary adducing proofs; and I saw every thing, that it had no power over any other thing; and I saw this world to be a delusion, and I saw the heavens to be a deception.[13]

Al-Shādhilī was equally effective with regard to extra-ritual prayers known as *awrād* and *aḥzāb*, incantations or litanies. He was uniquely talented in this area, and his *Ḥizb al-baḥr* ("Litany of the Sea") and *Ḥizb al-barr* ("Litany of the Land") are two fine examples. In the latter, even words seem to acquire magical properties. The formulae were reportedly communicated to him by the Prophet himself, and they so impressed globetrotting Ibn Baṭṭūṭah that he inserted them almost verbatim into his *Tuḥfat al-nuẓẓār*. They essentially consist of a mixture of Quranic verses, personal invocations and fervid religious phraseology, as, for example:

> O God, open my heart with Thy light, and with Thy mercy grant me the power to be obedient to Thee; shield me from defiance of Thee; grant me the power to know Thee; with Thy power and knowledge render mine unnecessary, and by Thy will free me from mine; through Thy attributes deliver me from mine . . . for Thou art most capable over all things.[14]

[13] Cited by Arberry, *Sufism*, 64.

[14] Cited by M. al-Khamīrī in his *Durrat al-asrār*, 61.

The *awrād*, differing only in time of application, constituted a plentiful genre, as masters and guides tailored them to every novice according to his capacity to apply them. They are to be found in nearly all manuals, together with *waṣāyā* and *manāqib*. Specifically, reference may be made to *al-Fuyūḍāt al-rabbāniyyah*, a Qādiriyyah manual; *al-Mafākhir al-ᶜaliyyah*, a Shādhiliyyah manual, and *al-Sirr al-abḥar* a manual for the Tijāniyyah. An important non-order oriented manual is al-Junayd's *Kitāb Dawāᵓ al-arwāḥ*.

THE ALLEGORICAL

Abū Yazīd inspired a number of tracts by his exaggerations (*shaṭḥiyyāt*) which were cited in al-Sarrāj's *al-Lumaᶜ*, and also in al-Jīlānī's *Sharḥ shaṭḥiyyāt Abī Yazīd.* Abū Yazīd is also responsible for introducing allegory into Ṣūfī literature by adopting the *miᶜrāj* of the Prophet to explain his own journey to God. The enticement to pursue this genre further resulted in a few masterful pieces like Jaᶜfar al-Mirghānī's *Qiṣṣat al-Miᶜrāj.*

The allegorization of mystical themes is first noted in *Qaṣīdat al-ṭayr* of Ibn Sīnā. This mode of expression was a convenient way to convey controversial arguments with minimum repercussions. Al-Ghazālī took up the method in a little-known treatise by the same title, which some authorities insist is the work of his brother Aḥmad. These in turn provided the models for ᶜAṭṭār's *Manṭiq al-ṭayr* (completed in 573/1178). The theme of Ibn Sīnā's work is the imprisonment of the soul in this world. In ᶜAṭṭār's work the soul is likened to a caged bird, and the whole path is represented by its flight over arduous valleys.

Further development of allegory in conjunction with the parable received a boost from Shihāb al-Dīn Yaḥyā al-Suhrawardī al-Maqtūl, once a rigorous philosopher turned mystic, whose talents in both fields well nourished his powers of imagination. His beautiful myths hark back to Plato via Ibn Sīnā, whose *Qaṣīdah* he recast into an impressive and graphic myth allegorizing neo-Platonist notions of the soul's descent into the body, already accepted by other Ṣūfīs as a prefiguration of the Quranic concept of the primordial covenant. The use of animals and birds to symbolize phenomena is not new; the first representative work of this technique being *Kalīlah wa-Dimnah*.

LITERATURE OF THE PATH (*ṬARĪQAH*)

Other topics broadly and specifically dealt with in Ṣūfī literature run the full gamut of their mystical strivings. Ideals of renunciation and poverty, abstinence and denial of self are dealt with at length, as are spiritual exercises, the stages and states of the Path, the struggles and attainments of the soul, and the ultimate experience of gnosis and union. Al-Muḥāsibī pioneered works on the subject as did Muḥammad al-Sammār (d. 260/873) in his *Kitāb fī Dhamm al-dunyā* and Abū Saʿīd Aḥmad b. Muḥammad b. Ziyād al-Aʿrābī in his *Kitāb fī Maʿnā ʾl-zuhd* and *Ṭabaqāt al-nussāk*. On piety, reverence and fear, there is al-Muḥāsibī's *al-Makāsib wa-ʾl-warʿ*; on patience and satisfaction, al-Tirmidhī's *Risālah . . . fī ʾl-shukr wa-ʾl-ṣabr*; on intent, his *Masāʾil fī ʾl-niyyah*; on the self's deficiencies and on treating them, Aḥmad al-Burnusī's (d. 899/1493) *al-Uns fī sharḥ ʿuyūb al-nafs*, al-Sulamī's *ʿUyūb al-nafs wa-mudāwātuhā* and also *Dawāʾ al-arwāḥ* by an unknown.[15] On the heart and its role as the seat of gnosis, there is al-Nūrī's *Maqāmāt al-qulūb*, al-Tirmidhī's *Ṣifāt al-qulūb* and his important *Bayān al-farq bayn al-ṣadr wa-ʾl-qalb . . .*; on diagnosing the secrets of and training the soul, al-Junayd's *al-Sirr fī anfās al-ṣūfiyyah*, al-Tirmidhī's *Aʿḍāʾ al-nafs* and *Riyāḍat al-nafs*; on states, al-Muḥāsibī's *al-Tawahhum bi-kashf al-aḥwāl* and al-Sulamī's *Bayān aḥwāl al-ṣūfiyyah*.

Tracts and full works on ultimate spiritual discoveries likewise abound. There is *Kitāb al-Mushāhadah* of ʿAmr al-Makkī (d. 297/909), the *Kitāb Ruʾyat Allāh* of Aḥmad b. Muḥammad al-Aʿrābī and on gnosis *Sharḥ al-maʿrifah* by an unknown, and *Bustān al-maʿrifah*, a condensation of al-Ḥallāj's views. On ecstasy we have the *Kitāb al-wajd* of Aḥmad b. Muḥammad al-Aʿrābī, among others.

The themes of unicity (*tawḥīd*) and oneness of being (*waḥdat al-wujūd*) elicited much writing. There is al-Tirmidhī's *Kitāb al-Tawḥīd*, and Ibn Sīnā's *al-Ishārāt wa-ʾl-tanbīhāt*, which reflects his and other views on the unity of all being, there being no creator or created, servant or master, only one being: God. Multiplicity represented by the external world of sense-perception simply mirrors various facets of the One. This is the theme that Muḥyī ʾl-Dīn b. al-ʿArabī fully exploited.

Ṣūfī prose in the fourth/tenth century reflects strongly these two themes, the ground having been paved by al-Junayd's work on *tawḥīd*. The abundance of related technical terms – increasing stress on the symbolical and oblique, the play on words and increase in pedantic expressions – not only evinced the growing interest in these subjects, but also had the unfortunate consequence of de-emphasizing the artistic. Not until the sixth/twelfth century is there a return to the sober assessment of the Ṣūfī search for the ultimate awareness, and to the artistic, without compromising the technical flow of meaning, clarity of purpose, sentimentality and freedom of conscience. Techniques are straightforward and modes of

15 Ed. and trans. A.J. Arberry, "The Book of the Cure of Souls", *Journal of the Royal Asiatic Society*, 1937, 219–31.

expression firm. Even allegories are brought out in tangible forms, and material personifications are relatively free of affectation and artificiality. Authors are generally more careful to select and employ terms that have a universal ring and can sensitize the heart. Peculiarly Ṣūfī terms are more frequently employed, but the liveliness of expression is not weakened and nor is the analytical approach to the subject.

APOLOGETIC LITERATURE

This genre concerned the relative merits of the *ṭarīqah vis-à-vis* the *sharīʿah*. Al-Sulamī made the distinction in his *al-Farq bayn ʿilm al-sharīʿah wa-ʾl-ḥaqīqah*; al-Kharrāz elaborated on the subject in his *al-Kashf wa-ʾl-bayān*, as did Abū Bakr Muḥammad b. ʿUmar al-Warrāq (d. 280/893) in *al-ʿĀlim wa-ʾl-mutaʿallim*. The duel was in progress before al-Ghazālī wrote *Mīzān al-iʿtidāl* and *Kīmiyāʾ al-saʿādah*, wherein he systematically and methodically endeavoured to attribute the weakening of faith to the fanciful assertions of rationalists. Al-Tirmidhī had confronted them in his *al-Raddʿalā ʾl-rāfiḍah*,[16] as did al-Sulamī in his *al-Radd ʿalā ahl al-kalām*. The *Dhamm al-kalām* of al-Harawī (d. 482/1089) was an attempt to counter the premises of dogmatic and scholastic theology. When Ibn al-Jawzī (d. 597/1200) criticized Ṣūfī practices in his *Talbīs Iblīs*, ʿIzz al-Dīn al-Maqdisī (d. 678/1279) countered with his *Taflīs Iblīs*, even imitating the style of the *Talbīs*.

Apologia of a personal nature is best exemplified by *Shakwat al-gharīb* of ʿAyn al-Quḍāt ʿAbdullāh al-Hamadhānī. In it he eloquently and movingly argues that every department of knowledge had its mutually agreed terminology, whose meaning is known only to the committed. Resort to terminological usages generated a body of literature which Massignon has surveyed up to the third/ninth century in his *Essai lexique*. Al-Muḥāsibī was among the first to concern himself with such terms as *maʿrifah*, *yaqīn*, *khawf*, *taqwā* and the like. In both *Kitāb al-Furūq wa-maʿnā al-tarāduf* and *Kitāb al-ʿUlūm* al-Tirmidhī relates lexical derivations and usages. Al-Kalābādhī and al-Qushayrī also wrote brief tracts on the subject. Muḥyī ʾl-Dīn b. al-ʿArabī put together his concise but popular *Iṣṭilāḥāt* to quiet ulema critics. The *Ḥall al-rumūz* of al-Makdisī likewise attempted to explain references and symbols used by Ṣūfīs.

Certain types of correspondence were employed to camouflage personal interpretations of doctrinal and practical points, the secrets of the Path, and sometimes the deepest esoteric meaning attached to spiritual and psychological experiences. Enigmatic and symbolic, baffling to the untrained eye, such missives were still cast in the most elegant language, not always in the

[16] Ed. A.S. Furat, *Şarkiyat Mecmuasi*, VI, 1966, 37–46.

maqāmah style, and employed to offer congratulations or condolences regarding worldly, social or familial matters. Later Ṣūfis reflected broad reading, and were not averse to mixing Persian with Arabic, Turkish with Persian. Syriac and even Kurdish would be employed in set sequences to chide lingual purists or to excite a melodic chord. By patterning sound or alphabetical letters, they tended to emulate magical techniques and those of fortune tellers.

THE *QAṢAṢ* TECHNIQUE

Genres centring on story-like accounts (*qaṣaṣ*), usually a vision, miracle or some unusual happening, with or without a basis in fact, were especially conducive to the development of this technique. The art of story-telling was one of the earliest of Ṣūfī prose. Though often illusionary, still the power and fertility of imagination left their imprint on literary expression. Proverbs, wise sayings and adages were popular in the seventh/thirteenth century. Earlier, al-Tujībī, the bard of Egypt, excelled at adapting Quranic material to suit his audience's interests. Stories served to moralize and instruct, and Dhū ʾl-Nūn al-Miṣrī was a pioneer in the transformation, given his versatility in prose techniques. His writing ranged from alchemical opuscules and cabalistic apocryphals to parables and anecdotes. He was a fearless innovator; the first, for example, to employ the theme of love and the notion of gnosis without hesitation. Stylistically, he set a precedent for "sumptuosity altogether poetic". His use of allegory, his abundant recourse to metaphor in concealing the hardiness of his theses or expressing high sentimental values made the pious wonder whether he was not a hedonist at heart.

Both from a technical and a stylistic point of view, *qaṣaṣ* accounts continued to acquire greater sophistication in the century following Dhū ʾl-Nūn, with stress on facility and clarity of expression, innovative descriptions and personification of the logical. Erudition and selectivity in use of terms was often accompanied by forthrightness. In the fourth/tenth century, the technique was misappropriated to lend credence to fables and miracles, with one consoling side effect: humour now played a greater role in instructional literature, as attested in *al-Ḥikāyāt al-ṣūfiyyah* of Abū Bakr Muḥammad b. Shādhān al-Rāzī (d. 376/986).

THE THEME OF LOVE

Love is the one theme that consumed the true mystic's spirit and aspiration. It was the alpha and omega of Ṣūfī striving for, as al-Nūrī put it, "love is the rending of the veil and the revelation of what is hidden from the eyes of men".[17] Converts to Ṣufism had known and appreciated love and its beauty, which they now transferred to the Divine. In olden times when spurned, love could sharpen the sense of yearning for the beloved, and denial of access could induce such states as abstinence and chastity, yearning and intense desire. These were simply transferred to God in a Ṣūfī context. An awareness of beauty, appreciated by both God and the Prophet, served to fuel the impulses of love. Admiration for and preoccupation with beauty graces much of Ṣūfī literature.

The transfer of the love sentiment from mortals to God is discernible in al-Niffarī's work on *maḥabbah* in the form of utterances assembled by others. Numerous tales are attributed to Dhū ᵓl-Nūn, reminiscent in part of classical love-stories like that of Qays and Laylah, except that Qays now roams in yearning after God not after Laylah; we find a similar theme in al-Khuldī's (d. 348/959) *Ḥikāyāt al-ᶜushshāq*, in the abridgement by Abū Naṣr ᶜAbdullāh b. ᶜAlī al-Sarrāj, *Maṣāriᶜ al-ᶜushshāq*.

While there are separate tracts and treatises on various facets of love, it is in the larger works that the theme receives fuller treatment. Separate works include the *Kitāb ᶜAṭf al-alif* of ᶜAlī b. Muḥammad al-Daylamī and *Manāzil al-maḥabbah* of Aḥmad al-Dānī. A contemporary, Shihāb al-Dīn Aḥmad al-Ghazālī (d. 520/1126), the brother of Abū Ḥāmid, penned the important *Sawāniḥ al-ᶜushshāq*, and the *Kitāb al-Maḥabbah* of ᶜAmr al-Makkī was a chief reference for later theorists. The *Risālah fī ᵓl-ᶜIshq* of Ibn Sīnā focuses on gnosis as the ultimate reward of love.

THE THEME OF THE LOGOS

The emergence of saintship notions was accompanied by an evolving conception of Muḥammad and greater reverence for his person. Al-Tirmidhī's writings provided much impetus for practical devotion to saints and prophets, but it was Muḥyī ᵓl-Dīn b. al-ᶜArabī's highly unitarian views that gave permanence to the Logos principle implied therein. It evolved from the conception that God communicates a portion of his divinity to the prophets and thence to the saints and poles (*quṭb*, pl. *aqṭāb*). Literature on *al-dhāt al-Muḥammadī* ("The essence or nature of Muḥammad") treats the Prophet as an eternal reality, not a human personality: a physical manifestation of that divine principle appearing in Adam as first created, Idrīs as first prophet, Noah as first saviour, Abraham, Moses, Jesus and finally Muḥammad, the seal, following whom it passed from one *quṭb* to the next.

The principle receives its fullest treatment in the *Insān al-kāmil* of al-Jīlī

[17] Cited by Smith, *Readings*, 33.

(d. 809 or 820/1406 or 1417). In it the *quṭb* is treated as the apex of saintship, manifesting himself in every epoch as a necessity for world subsistence. He has various guises, appears in diverse bodily tabernacles, and bears a name suitable to the guise in any given age. The perfect man, a microcosmos of a higher order, reflects not only the powers of nature but divine powers as well. All apparent differences are modes, aspects and manifestations of the One, the Real, with phenomenal existence being no more than the outward expression of that Real. Essence, Creator and created are three in one,

> If thou sayest it [Essence] is One, so it is; or
> If thou sayest it is two, two in fact it is; and
> If thou shouldst say: nay it is three, thou art correct, for
> The real nature of man it is![18]

In this work we have a fine example of Ṣūfī rationale; moreover it enjoys both educational and literary distinction, as "it gathers up the thread of a whole system of thought and serves as a clue to it":

> Lo, I am that whole, and that whole is my theatre:
> 'Tis I, not it, that is displayed in its reality.
> Verily, I am a Providence and Prince to mankind: the entire
> creation is a name, and my essence is the object named.[19]

This theme, so central to Muḥyī ʾl-Dīn b. al-ʿArabī's philosophical outlook, is responsible for some of the most significant writings in Ṣūfī literature. With powerful imaginative resources, Ibn al-ʿArabī expounded the depths of Ṣūfī beliefs and left his mark on nearly all who came after, notably the Persians. With 289 known works to his name, his impact on philosophy, theology and literature was bound to be felt. His *Futūḥāt*, *Fuṣūṣ*, and *Tafsīr* are of substantial size, impact and merit. Even his *Dīwān* embodies his same constant outlook. His style and technique inspired Persian poets such as Jāmī, Fakhr al-Dīn Ibrāhīm al-ʿIrāqī (d. 688/1289), Awḥad al-Dīn Ḥāmid b. abī ʾl-Fakhr al-Kirmānī (d. 635/1238) and Saʿd al-Dīn Maḥmūd al-Shabistarī (d. *c.* 720/1320).[20] In twelve volumes the *Futūḥāt* condensed Ṣufism's spiritual aspect just as al-Ghazālī's *Iḥyāʾ* distilled the essence of its intellectual side. Ibn al-ʿArabī wrote with caution and restraint and thus became the master of allegory, metaphor, the *double entente*, the oblique and enigmatic, all to escape al-Ḥallāj's fate.

The *Fuṣūṣ* in the eyes of some has had a greater impact in consolidating his credo, and is regarded by many as his greatest work. It is a mosaic of precepts centred around the twenty-seven principal prophets, revealed to him, as with other works, following a vision of the Prophet. Divine truths are best exemplified by the prophets, each epitomizing a facet thereof, for

[18] Jīlī, *al-Insān al-Kāmil*, I, 10. [19] Nicholson, *Studies*, 108.

[20] His *Gulshān-i-Rāz* expresses in "verses of celestial beauty" Ibn al-ʿArabī's Ṣūfī doctrines.

example: Adam, *successorship* (to God); Job, *suffering* – but only because he is veiled from God; Jesus, the *word*, etc.

More than any other writer he was at home with the esoteric. One has the impression he deliberately sought to complicate and conceal the obvious. His expressions bear at least two meanings, one for the benefit of the ulema, and the other the intended one. He has a marked tendency to amble, be deliberately vague in choice of terms, and to rely on the symbolical and tangential when cornered. Circuitous and evasive, highly imaginative and sentimental, scholars have been at their wits' end to decipher what he means. He drew supporting data from a variety of sources – from the Qurʾān, *Ḥadīth*, scholasticism, neo-Platonism, Ismaʿilism – adding to it his own colouring and terminological peculiarities which have served to compound the confusion. Yet still al-Fīrūzābādī, author of the lexicon, and al-Shaʿrānī insist Ibn al-ʿArabī was faithful to both Sunnī orthodoxy and the *sharīʿah*. Posterity might remember him better for his inventive facility and a unique legacy of symbolic and terminological usages.

OTHER THEMES

Other themes dwelt on by Ṣūfī authors relate to morality, ethics and virtue in all forms. *Futuwwah*, with its stress on valour, self-sacrifice, bravery and chivalry received a Ṣūfī colouring in ʿAbdullāh al-Anṣārī's *Manāzil al-sāʾirīn*. In al-Qushayrī's *Risālah*, it is defined as a sort of ethical self-offering. Aḥmad al-Rifāʿī interpreted it to signify labouring purely for God's sake, not for rewards. So affected with its merits were masters of the Way that they were often referred to as *shūyūkh 'al-ḥirfah* ("Shaykhs of the Craft"), after the guilds favouring *futuwwah*.

Virtue and courage were Ṣūfī trademarks, and Ṣūfī shaykhs lectured the mighty on them, as in Ibn Iyāḍ's address to Hārūn al-Rashīd: "If thou seekest refuge from God's torment, then let the great among Muslims be like unto thy father, their middling as thy brother, and the weakest as thy son; respect thy father, be kind to thy brother, and sympathetic to thy son." Brotherliness was an important theme of virtue to Ṣūfīs, who regarded themselves as the special guardians thereof in their writings. Celibacy was also looked upon as a virtue, although its merits over marriage were never fully convincing. Nevertheless, much polemical ink was spilled over the controversy, with those in favour of it hiding behind the need to concentrate on God, and those against it seeking refuge in Prophetic injunctions, amply attested in Muḥammad b. Qayyim al-Jawziyyah's (d. 751/1350) *Rawḍat al-muḥibbīn*.

Other themes dealt with the widest variety of topics when deemed relevant to Ṣūfī arguments: wisdom, intelligence, philosophy, science, theological issues, esoteric sciences and many other areas of knowledge, a testimony to their vast erudition and skills both in a substantive and literary context. Their learning and skills were of such strength and durability that during the centuries of intellectual decline it was largely Ṣūfī authors, like al-Shaʿrānī in the tenth/sixteenth century and ʿAbd al-Ghanī al-Nābulusī in the twelfth/eighteenth century, who kept the flickering light of writing alive, although institutionalized Ṣufism tended to stifle imagination and originality in the Arabic-speaking world of Islam, and Ṣūfī creativity henceforth was kept alive largely by the Persian masters of literature.

CHAPTER 6

PHILOSOPHICAL LITERATURE

Arabic philosophic writing is a form of Arabic literature. Like Arabic poetry and artful prose it employs generally accepted opinions, rhetorical reasoning and devices, and imaginative projections to persuade and move an audience with particular linguistic and cultural habits, traditions and inclinations, and it responds to particular questions and deals with particular problems, which in turn shape its style and manner of exposition. Unlike most other forms of Arabic literature, however, Arabic philosophic writing tends to respond to questions and deal with problems that have to do with the audience's beliefs and opinions about matters theoretical and practical, human and divine, which the philosopher and his audience take to be of paramount importance both for the conduct of everyday life and ultimate salvation. Thus it tends to be serious but not humourless, rational but not inattentive to the role of emotions, rigorous but not unplayful, harsh but not misanthropic. Its scope is universal, dealing with all branches of knowledge; and in this respect philosophy is often compared to dialectic, rhetoric and poetry. In fact Arabic philosophic writing uses most of the rules of dialectic, rhetoric and poetry to examine and clarify generally accepted opinions, and to persuade and arouse the audience to embrace and endorse certain views and courses of action or to reject and abhor others. All major Arab philosophers were assiduous students of the Arabic language; each created his own individual style of writing; and if they wrote with great care and consummate art, it was because they were aware that their success or failure as philosophers depended, not on their inventions in applied science, but on the quality of their verbal art, their similes, metaphors and analogies, and on their ability to articulate a verbal whole that imitates the structure of the human soul and of the universe within which man lives.

True, these writings include accounts of certain specialized sciences such as formal logic, geometry, astronomy and music, whose aim is to describe the properties of abstract thought, lines and figures, celestial movements, and sounds; and their authors even practised arts such as music and medicine. But both they and the specialists in those sciences and the practitioners of these arts distinguished a philosopher's interest and approach from that of a specialized scientist or practitioner of a practical art. The current view that Arabic philosophic writing was understood by its authors as "scientific" writing in a modern sense and that it should be read as such does not take this distinction into account and cannot account for the fact that, in any case, the vast majority of it is not of this type.

Nor does the view that Arabic philosophic writing is a received tradition of Greek and Syriac provenance account for, or provide a reason to dispense with, looking at Arabic philosophic writing as a form of Arabic literature. Greek and Syriac philosophy were themselves forms of Greek and Syriac literature respectively. There was a tradition of philosophic literature – especially the literary styles of Plato, Aristotle and Plotinus, but also those of the Greek commentators – that was learned and imitated by philosophers writing in Arabic. But the activity of translating, imitating and interpreting this received tradition – all the many forms of restating it, whether in translations, summaries, paraphrases, or commentaries, whether presented in prose, verse or fictional form – is a literary activity in which the imitation, unlike photographic reproduction, is an attempt to repaint the original with a new and different audience in view. What is particularly interesting about the activity of the philosophers writing in Arabic is not their recasting of earlier accounts available to them in Arabic translation, but their manner of transforming, recreating and representing the received tradition, an activity which was continued later within the Arabic philosophic tradition as subsequent authors restated the accounts of their predecessors. This type of activity is analogous to the activity of the poet or novelist who recreates a poem or a novel by an earlier author.

It is known of course that prominent Arab philosophers wrote major works on literary criticism in the form of accounts of rhetoric and poetics, elaborating the received tradition in these arts with special attention to the history of the indigenous Arabic literary tradition. Yet the misconception continues to linger that they were interested in rhetoric and poetics only as "logical" forms of argumentation, and that in the vast majority of their writings, or in their "philosophic" writings proper, they meant to present scientific demonstrations rather than make use of the questionable arts of the rhetorician or the poet. But if the reader studies the works of almost any one of these philosophers – Yaᶜqūb b. Isḥāq al-Kindī, Abū Naṣr Muḥammad al-Fārābī, Ibn Sīnā, Ibn Bājjah, Ibn Ṭufayl or Ibn Rushd – and asks what portion of them is or pretends to be in the form of scientific demonstration, he is likely to be disappointed; indeed he will not begin to understand the philosophic art of writing until he becomes aware of their almost constant use of enthymemes, examples, metaphors, analogies and imaginative representations, devices that were discussed in detail by these same authors in their works on dialectic, rhetoric and poetics.

Finally, the view that these philosophers were not rhetoricians or poets, but were *doing* philosophy makes little sense unless one understands *doing* philosophy in their case as preparing for and composing the works they left behind. For, as far as we know, their philosophic activity consisted in reading, teaching and writing such works. To *do* philosophy meant to write works in the form of: disputed questions, examinations of conflicting opinions about theoretical and practical matters, the opinions of their predecessors, histories of philosophy, encyclopaedias, divisions and organization of the branches of knowledge, real or fictive letters, real or fictive answers to questions, postscripts to real or fictive oral discussions, many levels of commentaries or multiple accounts of the same subject-matter meant for different audiences, legal opinions and legal and theological works or philosophic works concerned with legal and theological matters, commentaries on the Qurʾān and on Prophetic Traditions, histories, stories, commentaries on such stories, poems, commentaries on poems. These works were written in response to real situations in which they meant to educate (that is, examine and refine generally accepted opinions) and guide others to pursue knowledge of all things, or to persuade their audience about a practical political course of action. If they *did* philosophy in any other way, this is something no one knows anything about; what we can know is what they *did* to the extent that they communicated their activity to us in their writing, and what we can reconstruct are the situations, the questions, and the problems they responded to, answered, or tried to explain in these writings.

AL-FĀRĀBĪ ON PLATO AND ARISTOTLE

Perhaps a good illustration of these preliminary remarks is the account of rewards and punishments in al-Fārābī's *al-Jamʿ bayna raʾyay al-ḥakīmayn Aflāṭūn al-ilāhī wa-Arisṭūṭālīs* ("Harmonization of the Opinions of Plato and Aristotle").[1] The book begins by explaining that it is meant to respond to the following concrete situation: that most of his contemporaries – an oblique reference to the *kalām*-theologians – were discussing and disputing a number of questions central to both religious and philosophic convictions, and they claimed that the two most prominent philosophers of antiquity – Plato and Aristotle – disagreed on these questions or disagreed with religious convictions. Al-Fārābī responded by harmonizing or showing the agreement between the convictions of Plato and Aristotle. His goal

[1] *Jamʿ*, ed. Dieterici, 32–3.

was to show, first, that the two primary philosophic authorities did not disagree; that is, that there is a solid philosophic front which cannot be ignored by claiming that philosophers contradict one another and that the philosophic tradition does not, therefore, provide a reliable way to knowledge; and secondly, that philosophic convictions do not necessarily disagree with religious convictions and that one need not suspect philosophers of unbelief. To reach this goal, al-Fārābī goes through the disputed questions, one by one, until he reaches the question of rewards and punishments, where it appears that the difficulty is not whether Plato and Aristotle are believed to have disagreed, but whether they have agreed to reject the belief that good deeds are rewarded and evil deeds punished. This is obviously a matter of great moment, for should this charge against them go unchallenged, the suspicion that the main philosophic tradition is opposed to religious dogma will discourage believers from studying the works of Plato and Aristotle. After all, to deny the possibility of rewards and punishments is tantamount to denying revealed religion. Al-Fārābī begins his response by referring to Aristotle's "explicit statement" that recompense is necessary in nature. This ambiguous statement is then followed by a long quotation from a letter Aristotle is said to have addressed to Alexander the Great's mother, who had just received the news of her son's death and was beside herself with grief and bereavement. After elaborate praise of Alexander's achievements and fame as signs of divine election, Aristotle counsels his mother to do nothing that would estrange her from her son when the time comes "to meet in the company of those who are good". "Strive," he writes to her, "to do what will bring you close to him, and the first thing to do is to attend with your pure soul to the business of sacrifices in the temple of Zeus." This and what follows it (al-Fārābī refers to, but does not quote the rest of this document so crucial to his argument) is a plain indication, argues al-Fārābī, that Aristotle was convinced of the necessity of rewards and punishments. As for Plato, al-Fārābī refers to the end of the *Republic* and the famous "story" that speaks of resurrection, and so forth.

What al-Fārābī may or may not have believed concerning Aristotle's and Plato's convictions regarding the hereafter (we shall see that he is reported as having said in his commentary on Aristotle's *Ethics* something to the effect that all talk about the hereafter is old wives' tales) is immaterial in this context; here he is addressing a particular audience and using documentary proof (a personal letter and a story) to persuade this audience that Plato and Aristotle cannot be suspect as they are reputed to be, and that one should not listen to contentious people who charge these virtuous, wise men with things of which they are innocent.

To the same author we owe the first explicit, and perhaps the most important, discussions of the style and art of writing in Arabic philosophy, presented in the guise of accounts of the writings of the ancients and their views on the proper method of instruction. Al-Fārābī's most accessible, and therefore somewhat popular, account of the writings of Plato and Aristotle is again contained in *al-Jamᶜ bayna raʾyay al-ḥakīmayn* immediately following the account of their ways of life.[2] It concerns the different style, procedure, or method (*madhhab*) they would use in writing down (*tadwīn*) the things they knew and in composing books (*taʾlīf*).

In Plato's "early period" he used to abstain altogether from writing down the things he knew and entrusting them to the "bellies of books instead of pure hearts and congenial minds". But as time went on and he came to possess abundant knowledge and wisdom, he grew apprehensive lest he himself become negligent and forgetful, and his discoveries be lost. Therefore "he chose signs (*rumūz*) and riddles (*alghāz*) with the intention of writing down the things he knew and his philosophy" in a way that they would be found only by those who deserved them and could pursue them by their own investigation and effort. Aristotle's procedure, on the other hand, was "to make things flawlessly clear, write them down, and order them well; express them eloquently, openly, and plainly; and do all this as fully as possible". There is, then, an apparent disagreement between these two procedures.[3]

Although al-Fārābī qualifies the disagreement between the two procedures as "apparent", he does not deny the fact that they are different. He explains the genesis of Plato's procedure as a necessary compromise between his original procedure not to write at all but communicate his wisdom orally to a select group, and his fear of forgetfulness and the loss of his wisdom. The compromise consisted in devising a written form of communication that met his original objection to writing, and that could be deciphered only by investigators who possessed the qualifications that would have made them eligible for receiving his discoveries through oral communication. Plato's style of writing corresponds with his intention: it is a device invented by him for the purpose of restricting the availability of his discoveries to qualified readers only. This intention is kept behind the apparent intention of writing in signs and riddles, the surface of his writings as it first meets the reader's eye.

Al-Fārābī's account of Plato's style consists, first, of a biographical story; secondly, the assertion that the signs and riddles the reader meets on the surface of Plato's writings do not express what their author knew or his

[2] Ibid., 5–7. [3] Ibid., 5–6.

wisdom and, in particular, that they hide and protect rather than reveal their author's discoveries; thirdly, that Plato's ultimate intention was not to hide his discoveries absolutely, but to preserve and reveal them for the deserving few. We are thus led to understand Plato's choice of signs and riddles in terms of his intention to hide and reveal his discoveries at the same time. This intention itself is hidden by the apparent intention of writing nothing but signs and riddles, or of never revealing his own discoveries.

Aristotle's apparent intention in his writing is different. His procedure seems to express the intention of being always clear, orderly and plain. Yet according to al-Fārābī, this is an intention that Aristotle feigns but does not follow consistently. The inconsistency is not revealed, however, to the casual reader but only to him "who examines the Aristotelian sciences and is diligent in the study of his books", for he will not miss Aristotle's use of the various "modes of abstruseness (*ighlāq*), obscurity (*taᶜmiyah*), and complexity (*taᶜqīd*), despite his apparent intention to be plain and clear". Al-Fārābī lists six examples of this procedure:

(1) Frequent omission of the necessary premise from syllogisms dealing with natural, divine and ethical matters, as indicated by the (ancient) commentators.
(2) Frequent omission of the conclusions of arguments.
(3) The omission of one of two correlated assertions. Here al-Fārābī quotes a letter by Aristotle to Alexander the Great proposing the reward of just men and omitting to mention the punishment of the unjust.[4]
(4) Stating the two premises of a certain syllogism and presenting the conclusion of another syllogism, then stating two other premises followed by the conclusion pertaining to the first pair of premises. Al-Fārābī offers here as an example Aristotle's procedure in the *Prior Analytics* where he mentions that "the parts of substance are substances".
(5) Making a show of exhaustiveness and of having made an extreme effort to enumerate the particular instances of something that is clear in itself, and then bypassing what is ambiguous without elaborating it or giving it a full definition.
(6) The systematic order of his scientific books "to the point that you are led to think this is an unchangeable natural disposition"; but if the reader considers his "Letters", he will find them organized according to a system and order different from those of his scientific books.

[4] Ibid., 6, cf. 32.

Al-Fārābī concludes the list by quoting from an exchange of personal letters between Plato and Aristotle, which al-Fārābī says is sufficient to prove the case he is making. Plato is said to have written to Aristotle blaming him for composing systematic scientific works and publicly exposing the sciences in complete and exhaustive writings. Aristotle rejoined by declaring to Plato that, although he had written down the things he knew and the "well-guarded, esoteric (*maḍnūn bihā*) portions of wisdom", he arranged and expressed them in such a way that only those worthy of them will be able to find them. Al-Fārābī is thus able to conclude that the two apparently different procedures are in fact two surface modes expressing a single underlying intention.[5]

Al-Fārābī's harmonization of Plato's and Aristotle's style of writing is based on his accepting the popular view of the general character of their style of writing. In the case of Plato, al-Fārābī limits himself to an explanation or a justification of his use of signs and riddles that elicits its underlying intention. In the case of Aristotle, however, al-Fārābī is willing to reveal a number of his omissions, invoke the authority of the commentators and of certain "Letters" attributed to Aristotle, and remind the readers of the "Histories of the Ancients" (from which the popular view of the styles of the two philosophers is derived), all of which argue against the popular view of his style. He does not need to challenge the popular view of Aristotle's style on the basis of his own judgement or the judgement of the commentators alone or challenge the reader to investigate Aristotle's scientific investigations in case he does not accept these judgements; he resorts to documents popularly accepted as originating with Aristotle to modify the popular view of his style. Using the popular belief that these documents are genuine, he is able to force the reader to admit that Aristotle's apparent intention to be plain and clear throughout his writings is not the last word about his style, and that Aristotle's true intention (confirmed in a private letter to his master Plato) is to keep the things he knew from the many and reveal them only to those worthy of them. There is thus a single intention expressed in two different styles of writing: Plato carries it out by employing signs and riddles, Aristotle by a pretence of clarity. This is a sufficiently strong popular argument in favour of agreement in the intention underlying the different modes of expression employed by Plato and Aristotle. Both made a deliberate choice to keep their knowledge from public view and preserve it for the qualified and deserving few; they disagreed only concerning the method of effecting this concealment. Granting that they had an identical intention, on what did

[5] Ibid., 6–7.

they base their conviction that it could be carried out with equal success by means of two different, if not opposite, methods?

In al-Fārābī's introduction to his *Talkhīṣ Nawāmīs Aflāṭūn* ("Paraphrase of Plato's *Laws*"), we find a more elaborate statement of Plato's method of writing.[6] This statement follows immediately upon al-Fārābī's characterization of the natural inclination of all men to make universal judgements based on incomplete induction of particular cases; the fact that wise men are aware of this weakness in human nature and put it to use with the intention of achieving what is useful or avoiding what is harmful; and the story of the ascetic who, fearing the tyrannical sovereign whose command had gone out for his arrest, saved himself at the crucial moment by acting (contrary to his habitual manner) like a libertine. This story relates how the ascetic was able to leave the city wearing the dress of a vagabond, carrying a cymbal, pretending to be drunk and telling the city's gatekeeper, "I am So-and-so, the ascetic". Thinking the ascetic to be only a libertine making fun of him, the gatekeeper allowed him to leave the city. Al-Fārābī's intention is to justify Plato's style of writing:

> Our purpose in making this introduction is this: the wise Plato did not allow himself to reveal and uncover the things he knew to all people. Therefore he followed the method of using signs and riddles, of obscurity, and of difficulty (*taṣʿīb*), so that knowledge would not fall into the hands of those who do not deserve it, and it be debased, or into the hands of one who does not know its worth or who uses it improperly. In this he was right. Once he knew and became certain that he had become well known for this practice, and that all people had come to know that he used signs in everything he desired to say, he sometimes turned to the thing he wished to discuss and stated it openly and literally; but the one who reads or hears his discussion thinks that it is a sign and that he intended something different from what he had stated openly. This notion is one of the secrets of his books.[7]

Here we have the element lacking in the description of Plato's style in *al-Jamʿ bayna raʾyay al-ḥakīmayn*.

We have learned from *al-Jamʿ bayna raʾyay al-ḥakīmayn* that Aristotle's normal procedure, the procedure for which he is generally known, is to write clearly and systematically, but that serious students of his works detect certain ways of concealment and places where his style is unrevealing. In particular, he elaborates about things clear in themselves, but presents what is ambiguous without elaborate argument and without giving it its due. His letter to Plato, finally, states openly that this practice is intended to conceal the things he knew. Plato's normal procedure, the procedure for which he became generally known, on the other hand, is to

6 *Talkhīṣ: Compendium Legis Platonis*, ed. F. Gabrieli, London, 1952, 3–4. 7 Ibid., 4.

write ambiguously and conceal through the use of signs and riddles. But the ones trained in the pursuit of the knowledge about which he speaks find that occasionally, albeit rarely, he states what he intends to say openly. Thus while in this respect the secret of Plato's books consists in concealing his occasional clear statements by means of habitual ambiguity, that of Aristotle's consists in concealing his occasional ambiguous statements by means of habitual clarity.

Further, the introduction to the *Talkhīṣ Nawāmīs Aflāṭūn* relates Plato's style of writing to the general rule (enunciated both there and in *al-Jam*ᶜ) regarding man's disposition to make universal judgements on the basis of insufficient instances, and indicates that Plato laboured intentionally to become well known as an ambiguous writer who employed signs and riddles. *Al-Jam*ᶜ *bayna ra*ᵓ*yay al-ḥakīmayn* indicates that Aristotle laboured to make a show of clarity and arranged to conceal his ambiguous statements. The two wise men, acting on the basis of their knowledge of man's disposition, assumed a certain manner and encouraged people to judge them accordingly, with the intention of being able on certain occasions to act differently without being noticed. Plato assumed the character of an ambiguous writer and succeeded in making people believe that he always followed this style of writing. As a result, he was able occasionally to state his intention openly without being detected; his common readers continued to suppose that he must be using a symbol. Aristotle, on the other hand, assumed the character of a clear and systematic writer and was able to conceal his knowledge by occasionally omitting certain things and being ambiguous and obscure. Again, this escaped his common readers, who continued to suppose that these statements, too, must be clear and systematic. The two procedures only appear to be diametrically opposed to one another, but they are based on the same general rule regarding man's disposition, follow the same method based on man's propensity to make universal judgements, and pursue the same objective; that is, to keep and protect the writer's knowledge from the vulgar and the mischievous. The very fact that, after the passage of fourteen centuries, people continued to believe that Plato and Aristotle disagreed on fundamental issues because the one used signs and riddles while the other was clear and systematic is sufficient proof that both were wise students of human nature and equally successful in achieving the objective they pursued.

Finally, the story of the pious ascetic in the introduction to the *Talkhīṣ Nawāmīs Aflāṭūn* states the problematic character of writing to indicate what is to be learned about Plato's style of writing. This lesson is not immediately evident. The story is about a pious ascetic, not a philosopher, and it is about lying in deed, not in speech. Al-Fārābī does indeed attribute a certain asceticism to Plato in describing the generally accepted view about his deeds, but he does not apply the epithet "ascetic" (*zāhid*) to him. If Plato's general dislike for, and avoidance of, worldly things remind us nevertheless of the pious ascetic in the story, the lesson may be this: Plato's other-worldly, as well as Aristotle's worldly, deeds were studied dissimulations or habitual courses of conduct designed for the successful performance of the lie in deed; and the harmonization of the different conduct (habitual to each of them) would have to be achieved on the basis of understanding their knowledge of man's disposition, the methods they followed in writing down what they knew and their identical aim.

However, in the "Histories of the Ancients" preserved in Arabic, it is not Plato, but his master Socrates, who is known as the ascetic. Socrates is not mentioned in *al-Jamᶜ bayna raʾyay al-ḥakīmayn.* Instead, the characteristic feature of his life is attributed to Plato, and his refusal to write is said to be the position taken by the young Plato. The figure of Plato that emerges from *al-Jamᶜ* is then a synthesis of the popular accounts of Socrates and Plato. The accounts of Socrates attribute to him the things for which the ascetic of the introduction to the *Talkhīṣ Nawāmīs Aflāṭūn* had become well known: abstemiousness, probity, propriety and worship. All the reports insist, however, that Socrates worshipped, not the gods of the city, but some higher divinity, and he is even reported to have said that the idols of the city, though useful for the king, were harmful for Socrates. This is alleged to have been one of the causes of Socrates' death. Yet when in danger for his life, Socrates did not wish to escape from his city and preferred to die. Al-Fārābī's pious ascetic could only escape death because of his capacity to lie in deed, thereby persuading the gatekeeper that he could not have been the pious ascetic. According to al-Fārābī's *Falsafat Aflāṭūn* ("Philosophy of Plato"), Socrates was incapable of persuading the multitude, that is, people like the gatekeeper.[8] Plato, on the other hand, showed how to combine the art of Socrates with the art of Thrasymachus, which consisted in the capacity to persuade the multitude. In this sense, Plato incorporated Socrates into himself: his deeds, like the deeds of the pious ascetic in the introduction to the *Talkhīṣ Nawāmīs Aflāṭūn* combine Socrates' piety with the capacity to perform an impious deed; and his method of writing was a harmonization of Socrates' objections to writing and the necessity or usefulness of writing for the preservation of his wisdom.

Be this as it may, Plato's style of writing is based on the experience of the ascetic in the story – not on the ascetic's art of writing, but his mode of life, his probity and propriety, habitual truthfulness, and perhaps even his

[8] Fārābī, *Falsafat Aflāṭūn*, ed. F. Rosenthal and R. Walzer, London, 1943, 21–2.

bluntness in exposing and decrying the idolatry of his city. This brought the ascetic into conflict with the city and its tyrannical king: the habitual truthfulness of his speech forced him to flee from his city and live in exile. Although he preserved his life, his habitual conduct did not offer the best solution to the problem of his relation to the city. It forced on him a tragic choice between death and abandoning his city; the comic act of lying in deed saved him from death but not from exile. In order to draw a lesson from the fate of the pious ascetic for Plato's style of writing, we need to notice the points of resemblance between the two. Plato did not declare his meaning clearly except on rare occasions, and after having made certain that he would be detected only by the deserving few. His habitual way was not to declare his meaning clearly, but, in effect, to lie in speech. Thus in his speech Plato seems to have reversed the style of the pious ascetic. Having seen that it was habitual truthfulness that had been the source of danger to both the city and the philosopher, and that he was able both to protect the city and save himself only by concealment, Plato chose concealment as his habitual method of writing. He was able thus to avoid the conflict with the city and to save himself without resorting to the unattractive alternative of forced exile. In this manner he was also able to state the dangerous truth in written and permanent form, and to preserve it within the city without great risk. We are, then, dealing with a reversal of roles. The ascetic's primary allegiance was to the city. It was for the city that he sacrificed his safety and comfort – he was, in effect, a revolutionary. The philosopher's main allegiance is to philosophy and its survival in the city. Aristotle's case is no different, for his habitual clarity is not about crucial or dangerous things.

Although it is apparent that these and similar accounts of Plato's and Aristotle's style of writing are not meant as mere historical accounts, this fact can be seen more clearly if we listen to al-Fārābī speak in his own name, and in the name of all those whom he would characterize as "philosophers":

> We [philosophers] are political by nature. It is incumbent on us therefore to (1) live in harmony with the public, love them, and prefer doing what is useful to them and redounds to the improvement of their condition (just as it is incumbent on them to do the same in our regard). (2) Associate them in the good things the care of which is entrusted to us (just as it is incumbent on them to associate us in the good things the care of which is entrusted to them) by showing them the truth concerning the opinions they hold in their religions; for when they share with us in the truth, it will be possible for them, to the extent of their ability, to associate with philosophers in the happiness of philosophy. (3) Move them away from things – arguments, opinions, laws – in which we find they are not right. This cannot be done with them through certain demonstrations because these are not within their reach, are strange to them, and difficult for them. It is only possible through portions of knowledge that we have in common with them – that is, in that we address them

with arguments that are generally accepted among them, well known to them, and well received among them. This class of instruction results in popular (*dhāʾiʿah*) philosophy, which is known as external (*khārijah*) and exterior (*barrāniyyah*) philosophy. (Indeed Aristotle mentions in many of his books that he wrote books on external philosophy in which he sought to instruct the public through generally accepted things.) We acquire the power to practise this philosophic art only by having ready and available generally accepted opinions, and this we achieve through the art of dialectic. Through it the philosopher associates with the public and becomes well protected so that he is not found burdensome or engaged in an objectionable business; for the public is in the habit of finding what is strange to them burdensome and what is out of their reach objectionable.[9]

THE PHILOSOPHER AND THE CITY

The relation between the philosopher and the city is the theme of a series of philosophic writings in Arabic and Persian, which are literary in the strict sense – that is, stories which make use of the basic methods of poetry and rhetoric: imitation and examples. These include Ibn Sīnā's so-called "visionary recitals" *Ḥayy b. Yaqẓān* and the *Risālat al-Ṭayr* ("Epistle of the Birds"), the story of *Salāmān and Absāl* by an anonymous author, of which Naṣīr al-Dīn b. al-Ḥusayn al-Ṭūsī (d. 672/1274) gives a condensed version in his *Kitāb Sharḥay al-Ishārāt* ("Two Commentaries on Ibn Sīnā's *Hints*"), Ibn Ṭufayl's (d. 581/1185) *Ḥayy b. Yaqẓān*, Shihāb al-Dīn Yaḥyā al-Suhrawardī's *Qiṣṣat al-Ghurbah al-gharbiyyah* ("The Story of Occidental Exile"), and Ibn al-Nafīs's (d. 687/1288) *al-Risālah al-Kāmiliyyah fī ʾl-sīrah al-nabawiyyah* ("Story of the Perfect Man: On the Prophetic Life"). These stories have engaged the attention of medieval and modern students of Arabic philosophy and provided them with occasions for sundry interpretations. The stories themselves are largely re-creations and reformulations of earlier ones. Thus in *al-Ishārāt wa-ʾl-tanbīhāt* ("Hints and Indications"), Ibn Sīnā refers the reader to the "Story of Salāmān and Absāl",[10] by which he may have meant the story of these two characters as included in the story of Ḥayy b. Yaqẓān, translated from the Greek by Ḥunayn b. Isḥāq, or the story condensed by Naṣīr al-Dīn al-Ṭūsī, or both; and Ibn Ṭufayl, al-Suhrawardī and Ibn al-Nafīs elaborate on elements and motifs drawn from Ibn Sīnā or directly from earlier stories. The story of Ḥayy b. Yaqẓān tells how Ḥayy, having been left alone as an infant on an uninhabited island, and brought up by a gazelle, nevertheless gradually attains full maturity of mind and intelligence, and penetrates all the complexities of philosophy and religion. He eventually sails to an inhabited island, but soon returns to solitude.

9 Fārābī, *Kitāb al-Jadal*, Bratislava MS 231 TE 40, fol. 203.
10 Ibn Sīnā, *Ishārāt wa-ʾl-tanbīhāt* ed. J. Forget, Leiden, 1892, 199.

Ibn Ṭufayl's epistle entitled *Risālat Ḥayy b. Yaqẓān: Asrār al-ḥikmah al-mashriqiyyah* ("Ḥayy b. Yaqẓān: On the Secrets of Oriental Wisdom") is addressed to a friend who is not an initiate in what Ibn Ṭufayl would call "philosophy". It responds to a request that Ibn Ṭufayl disclose as much as he can of the secrets of the Oriental (*mashriqī*; illuministic) wisdom mentioned by the "supreme master" Ibn Sīnā. Hinting that the question is in some fashion related to the quest for immortality and eternal bliss, Ibn Ṭufayl provides the first and last *direct* disclosure of a piece of knowledge in the entire book: "Know then that he who desires the truth without concealment (*or* peril to his life) should seek and endeavour assiduously to possess these secrets (*or* this wisdom)." This piece of advice, we soon learn, is a near quotation from Ibn Sīnā, who at the beginning of his major philosophic work, the *Shifā*ʾ ("Healing"), had said that this book is composed in conformity with the doctrine of the Peripatetics, but declares that the truth in his opinion is otherwise, and "that he who desires the truth without concealment (*or* peril to his life) should turn to his book on Oriental philosophy".[11] Ibn Ṭufayl (who likes to speak of all sorts of books, whether they contain a surface or deep sense, innocent or perilous doctrines, and also of esoteric books that perhaps existed in the East but did not reach his own area, i.e., north-west Africa and Andalusia) is suspiciously secretive about Ibn Sīnā's "Oriental philosophy"; instead, he mentions Ibn Sīnā's *Shifā*ʾ repeatedly and suggests that the path to perfection leads from the surface of this book to the perception of "its secret and deep sense, as the Master Abū ʿAlī [Ibn Sīnā] hinted in the *Shifā*ʾ".[12]

The secrets of Oriental wisdom are not then available to Ibn Ṭufayl in Ibn Sīnā's book on Oriental philosophy; and even though they may be perceived in Ibn Sīnā's *Shifā*ʾ and in some other books, these secrets, or the secret of these secrets,[13] cannot be expressed in an unadulterated form in any book at all – a puzzle that Ibn Ṭufayl sets out to communicate to his friend by confessing that his request was instrumental in generating "a noble notion that led me to partake in a vision (*mushāhadah*) of a state (*ḥāl*) I had not glimpsed before". Referring again to this new experience of the state occasioned by his friend's question, Ibn Ṭufayl admits that he had only a "taste" (*dhawq*) of it or merely a "slight taste"[14]; nevertheless, he describes it as having been so extraordinary as to be inexpressible and inexplicable, yet so joyful and pleasurable that one is incapable of remaining reticent about it or "keeping its secret", but is driven to cryptic disclosure. Cryptic disclosure – speaking the unspeakable, expressing the

[11] Ibn Ṭufayl, *Ḥayy*, ed. L. Gautier, Beirut, 1936, 4, cf. 14–15; Ibn Sīnā, *al-Shifā*ʾ, ch. 1.
[12] Ibn Ṭufayl, *Ḥayy*, 15. [13] Ibid., 156. [14] Ibid., 4, cf. 6, 18.

1 Page from a seventh/thirteenth-century manuscript of Ibn Sīnā's *al-Shifāʾ* showing the beginning of the seventh *faṣl* of the first treatise: "On the Oneness of Necessary Being: we say also that Necessary Being must be one essence."

inexpressible, explaining the inexplicable, controlling one's tongue and resisting abandonment, and training oneself in the refinements and skills necessary for mastering arts of this kind is the subject of the book, and this is introduced, appropriately, with what looks like a detailed account of the failures and successes of mystics and philosophers who spoke, or pretended to speak, of their extraordinary visions.

The account begins with an examination of certain types of cryptic speech that allude to the visionary experience itself. (Though the expression "philosophy" is absent at this stage,[15] yet such expressions as "science", "theoretical science", "theoretical understanding", "syllogisms", "physics" and "metaphysics" alert the reader that this visionary experience involves, or is involved in, certain types of philosophic speech and writing.) Ibn Ṭufayl first characterizes the cryptic speeches of three mystics as amateurish owing to their authors having lacked scientific skill. He is willing to admit that there may exist a rare individual who can somehow grasp all the subjects of the theoretical sciences without theoretical enquiry, but leaves it at that. For the rest, he examines the speech of men experienced in, and made skilful through scientific pursuits. The first of these is the "master" al-Ghazālī who, upon reaching that state, uttered a line of poetry to illustrate it:

'Twas what it was, 'tis not to be expressed;
Enquire no further, but conceive the best![16]

The line (by Ibn al-Muᶜtazz) alludes to a sexual experience which the poet affirms to have taken place; he will not describe it, and the hearer should believe him and not ask for an account.

Then begins the critique of Ibn Ṭufayl's immediate predecessor, the philosopher Ibn Bājjah (d. 533/1139), in which Ibn Ṭufayl intercalates both a long quotation from Ibn Sīnā and his own parable, with the intention of clarifying the relation between the rank attained through theoretical science, and the rank attained through the vision he experienced as a result of his friend's question about the secrets of Oriental (*mashriqī*) wisdom. Although Ibn Bājjah's speech (quoted from his treatise, *Fī ˀttiṣāl al-ᶜaql bi-ˀl-insān* ("On Conjunction") refers to a state that belongs to the blessed, can be called divine, is beyond the knowledge obtained through the ordinary sciences, and so forth, Ibn Ṭufayl refuses to believe him. Instead he asserts that Ibn Bājjah is in fact speaking about a rank reached through theoretical science, and that he is certain Ibn Bājjah did not go beyond it – that is, he did not have a vision of the truly sublime state, and so his reference to it is nothing but empty words. Yet he also affirms his certainty that Ibn Bājjah

[15] Ibid., 4–10. [16] Ibid., 4. This verse is given in Ockley's translation.

was accomplished in theoretical science – something that he says neither about Ibn Sīnā nor al-Ghazālī, praised as they are in respect of their higher achievements. So far then we have (1) three anonymous mystics who apparently experienced the vision but were innocent of scientific experience; (2) al-Ghazālī whose scientific experience enabled him to keep silent about and keep the secret of his visionary experience; and (3) Ibn Bājjah who lacks the visionary experience but is accomplished in theoretical science. Ibn Ṭufayl insinuates that he is competent to judge who has, or who has not, attained theoretical knowledge and/or the visionary experience. He intimates, in other words, that he had had a visionary experience as a result of his friend's question, but had before that reached the same rank in theoretical knowledge as Ibn Bājjah: his accomplishment in theoretical knowledge permits him to assert that Ibn Bājjah was accomplished in theoretical knowledge while the mystics were not, and his recent visionary experience permits him to assert that Ibn Bājjah lacked that experience. Still, what does the visionary experience have to do with theoretical knowledge, apart perhaps from permitting someone experienced in scientific pursuits to speak about his visionary experience with professional refinement – that is, not only to speak about it cryptically, but to keep its secret completely?

These two realms are "different" even though they are the "same", says Ibn Ṭufayl: they are the same in the sense that *nothing* is unveiled in the visionary experience that has not been unveiled already in theoretical science (provided, he will add later, that what is apprehended by theoretical means in metaphysics – and logic, mathematics, and physics, we must add, since metaphysics assumes and crowns these disciplines[17] – is "true and valid", but this, we must suppose, ought to be said of the visionary experience as well). They are different in that in the visionary experience one sees those same things (1) with greater clarity; and (2) by means of something for which there is no common name or technical term, and therefore Ibn Ṭufayl is forced to designate metaphorically as a "power" or "faculty" (*quwwah*), what Ibn Sīnā had called the initiate's "secret" (*sirr*).[18]

But there seems to be yet another difference between the two realms. Theoretical science has many parts or consists of a number of disciplines that can be studied according to some accepted order, culminating in metaphysics. The visionary experience, in contrast, does not seem to have parts, but degrees: one's taste of it admits of more or less. Ibn Ṭufayl had a taste of it, or rather only "this slight taste", as he was to say with more precision.[19] Ibn Sīnā, who is now quoted at length (from *al-Ishārāt wa-ʾl-*

[17] Ibid., 12. [18] Ibid., 5, 7, 9. [19] Ibid., 6, 18.

tanbīhāt, an esoteric work written just before his death), describes, not one, but numerous states of this visionary experience. Commenting on these descriptions, Ibn Ṭufayl says that Ibn Sīnā "intended by them that they should be [acquired] by him by way of a taste",[20] but he does not venture to speculate whether Ibn Sīnā did or did not realize his intention. He has no doubt that al-Ghazālī belongs to those who "were supremely happy and reached those honourable reaches"; but he is not certain enough to affirm that he also had a taste of that thing which he himself had not tasted until a friend asked him about the secrets of Oriental wisdom. Yet he is ready to taunt Ibn Bājjah for similar doubts about al-Ghazālī by telling him: "Do not call sweet what you have not tasted."[21] Ibn Ṭufayl labours to rehabilitate Ibn Sīnā and al-Ghazālī as men who were misunderstood and misjudged by Ibn Bājjah, men who apparently belonged to a class different from and superior to that of Ibn Bājjah.

When Ibn Ṭufayl finally allows himself to overcome his reticence and secretiveness and speak in his own name about the recently experienced vision, he asks his friend to imagine an "example" (*mithāl*): like al-Ghazālī, Ibn Ṭufayl has quoted someone else – that is, Ibn Sīnā – but unlike al-Ghazālī he now invents his own fable. The example is meant to illustrate the difference between the two states of apprehension, the theoretical and the visionary. Imagine, he tells his friend, a person with good natural endowments and discernment, except that he is born blind and has to learn everything about his city – its people, animals, streets, etc., including colours – by means other than sight; then, after achieving thorough knowledge of the city in this way he opens his eyes and finds that nothing he sees is different from the way he believed it to be, only now he experiences additional clarity accompanied by great pleasure.[22] This imaginary example foreshadows in many ways the structure and conclusion of the story about Ḥayy b. Yaqẓān. The use of the city rather than the universe as the object of the blind man's enquiry may, of course, he explained by the traditional use of the city as the image of the universe. This will not, however, explain the fact that in the main story Ḥayy achieves all manners of vision; yet he is still totally blind, as far as the city is concerned, and needs to open his eyes to see the city for what it is before returning to his island and engaging in his old ways.

But this point does not concern us for the moment. As narrated, the example follows a definite order (reproduced in the main story also) that begins with the acquisition of knowledge during the state of blindness, and ends with the same things being perceived by an open eye. And it is

[20] Ibid., 7. [21] Ibid., 10. [22] Ibid., 7–8.

followed by a commentary.[23] The first state is said to be like that of those who engage in theoretical enquiry up to and including metaphysics, providing the knowledge acquired during this state is "true and valid"; and the second state is said to be like the state of these same men who have, in addition, reached the higher stage of opening their inner or secret eye. At this point the rare possibility that someone may have this eye always open and not need to engage in theoretical enquiry is admitted, but not pursued.

To pursue this question further would lead to a number of difficulties. If it is true that in the visionary experience one perceives the very same things as through the theoretical sciences, only the person with true and valid comprehensive theoretical knowledge possesses the means to test the truth and validity of his visionary experience. Only he can avoid the fate of other visionaries, who merely imagine they have experienced the ultimate truth, and feel supremely happy because of the great pleasure attending the inventions of their imaginative power, a criticism Ibn Bājjah had levelled against mystics in particular.[24] Yet, since his visionary experience cannot be expressed in intelligible terms, how can he persuade anyone else that he has had a true vision? The reliable procedure is to begin with a thorough grounding in the theoretical sciences, and then open one's inner eye, as Ibn Ṭufayl did on the occasion of considering how to respond to his friend's question about the secrets of Oriental wisdom. That this cannot be the whole story is clear from the fact that the visionary experience seems to come as an unexpected gift. It may come after one has completed one's pursuit of the theoretical sciences. But it may also come before or midway in this pursuit. How can it be tested in these cases? What is its impact upon one's future pursuit of these sciences? And what about men and women to whom it seems to have come as children or callow youths? Ibn Ṭufayl sets all these questions aside. He suggests that the proper, or safe, order is from theoretical knowledge to a taste of the visionary experience; he even suggests that those who, like Ibn Bājjah, achieve a thorough grounding in the theoretical sciences but do not receive that gift have only themselves to blame: it is because of their excessive concern with worldly things.

The examination of the types of cryptic speech has so far been concerned with cryptic speech about the visionary experience itself. It has been shown to be an impossible task to communicate this experience. The riddle of expressing what cannot be expressed in words resists solution. What is seen in a visionary experience can be seen only in a visionary experience; it does not admit of being spoken of or written about in books, at any rate as it truly is; for sound-elements (*aṣwāt*) and their written images are instruments of

[23] Ibid., 8–11. [24] Ibid., 10.

theoretical knowledge, and the attempt to speak or write about a visionary experience is bound to transform it to its theoretical counterpart. Since this will not bring out the difference between the two states of apprehension, one is tempted to try to express the particular character of the visionary experience; and here expressions, because inadequate, will vary and lead some to slip away from the "straight path" or accepted opinion, while others will be thought to have slipped away even though they have not. The visionary experience opens up a realm that is too vast for speech or writing to capture or define.

Even though none of this was what Ibn Ṭufayl's friend meant to move him to say by his question,[25] the question itself, having led Ibn Ṭufayl to a newly won visionary experience, made it necessary. But now that he has said all this, Ibn Ṭufayl voices the suspicion – which must have been more than a suspicion – that his friend's purpose may have been to move him to write about what is seen in the state of vision "as it truly is". This he refuses to do. He does not wish to run the risk of slipping, or opening himself to the accusation of having slipped away from the straight path, not even to satisfy the desire of a friend without whose question he may not have come across the gift of a sublime visionary experience at all. He volunteers to answer the question in another way, and suggests that, since for the reasons given above it would have been impossible to meet his friend's request had he in fact meant to ask for a written account of the true nature of what is seen in a visionary experience, his purpose may have been to seek information about "this thing in accordance with the method of those who engage in theoretical inquiry", this being something about which it is possible to speak and write in books.[26]

Ibn Ṭufayl's friend must have been thoroughly confused and disappointed by now. He may not have initially expected that his question would generate a state of vision in Ibn Ṭufayl. But after hearing all this talk about visionary experience, its being superior to theoretical knowledge, and that it is "all-encompassing but not encompassed",[27] he is now told that he must be satisfied with an account that is bound to be limited, of a second order and unsatisfactory. Yet he need not lose heart altogether: Ibn Ṭufayl continues to hold out the possibility that he may some day receive the gift of visionary experience. The example of the blind man illustrating the relation between theoretical knowledge and visionary experience assumes that one starts with theoretical knowledge. But Ibn Ṭufayl is not now proposing that his friend should start with theoretical enquiry. He is holding out the prospect that those who engage in theoretical enquiry have a method of

[25] Ibid. [26] Ibid., 11. [27] Ibid.

providing information in writing about what is seen in a visionary experience: they do not put down what is experienced as it truly is, for that is not possible, nor do they disfigure its essence or transform it into theoretical knowledge. Ibn Ṭufayl's friend, who may have read or heard about the secrets of Oriental wisdom mentioned by Ibn Sīnā, does not know in what way that which cannot be spoken or written about as it truly is can still be spoken or written about by some other method, nor how those who pursue theoretical enquiry have found a way of expressing that which it is impossible to express. But he has now learned that this does have something to do with the very nature of sound-elements and written letters, the images of sound-elements. Sound-elements are instruments of theoretical enquiry; they cannot encompass the visionary experience, which is wider than the things encompassed by theoretical enquiry; and whenever they are used to "clothe" it,[28] they change its essence and transform it into a theoretical thing. Still, there seems to exist a method, developed by those who engage in theoretical pursuits, by which they are able to speak and write about that which transcends theoretical things, not as it truly is, but in a way that nevertheless provides information about it. Ibn Ṭufayl holds out the promise that he can provide his friend with information which is presumably more enlightening than the information provided so far by the three mystics, al-Ghazālī, and even Ibn Sīnā, and which supplements the information provided by Ibn Bājjah, which was shown not to be informative about this thing at all. Those who are engaged in theoretical pursuits, and only they, know the limits of language and writing because they reach the outer limits of what language and writing are designed to express, and some of them seem to have discovered a way of speaking and writing about what transcends these limits, without changing its very essence or transforming it into a theoretical thing; they have developed a method of speaking and not speaking, writing and not writing, about it.

Ibn Ṭufayl's account of the method of speech and writing employed by those who pursue theoretical enquiry as they try to provide this kind of information about what is seen in visionary experience begins[29] with disabusing his friend of the belief that this information is readily available or adequate for his purpose: it is extremely rare; only now and then does an individual seize upon a slight portion of it; even then, owing to religious prohibitions and warnings against delving into it, he does not communicate it to others except through signs. Although Ibn Ṭufayl is concerned with the state of affairs in north-west Africa and Andalusia ("the land we are in") in particular, his general remarks about the rarity and inadequacy of what

[28] Ibid. [29] Ibid., 11–12.

has been written on the subject apply to the entire body of Arabic philosophic literature: the philosophic works of Aristotle (in Arabic translation), al-Fārābī, and Ibn Sīnā, as well as what was produced in Andalusia down to his own time.

Unlike many Andalusians who were wont to sing the praises of their country, its refinement and its culture, Ibn Ṭufayl's account of the development of Andalusian philosophic culture is sober if not harsh.[30] He distinguishes four groups:

(1) The group that wrote before the diffusion of logic and philosophy from the East: these Andalusian thinkers were occupied with the mathematical sciences and could go no further.

(2) The group that added to mathematics a certain amount of logic, but this did not conduct them to true human perfection either.

(3) These were followed in turn by a generation both more skilful and nearer to true perfection. From among these Ibn Bājjah is singled out for his mental sharpness, understanding and insight, "yet the things of this world kept him busy until death overtook him before bringing to light the treasures of his knowledge or disclosing the deep recesses of his wisdom", hence the imperfect summary and incomplete character of his writings. He is quoted as confessing that his major work, the treatise *Fīʾttiṣāl al-ʿaql bi-ʾl-insān*, does not clearly express his intention, that it is difficult to understand, that in many places he did not arrange his expressions in the most adequate way, and that he would have changed them had he had the time. However this may be, Ibn Bājjah's generation includes other persons reported to have been his equals, who, unlike Ibn Bājjah, refrained from writing down anything at all, or at least Ibn Ṭufayl could find nothing written by any of them.

(4) Finally, Ibn Ṭufayl speaks of his own contemporaries: they are either still maturing, have stopped short of perfecting themselves, or else he has insufficient information about them.

Throughout this discussion Ibn Ṭufayl neglects to elaborate on the impact of religious opposition to philosophic learning in Andalusia and to Ibn Bājjah in particular, the fact that Ibn Bājjah was persecuted and accused of heresy, and the possibility that he was poisoned. This is all the more curious since he emphasizes the importance of religious strictures against philosophy in general. Nor, unless he sees a connection between Ibn Bājjah's criticism of Ibn Sīnā and al-Ghazālī (and of mysticism in general) and a certain this-worldly attitude, is it clear why he repeatedly accuses Ibn

[30] Ibid., 12–13.

Bājjah of being too concerned with the things of this world or how this accusation is relevant to Ibn Bājjah's philosophic position. It is easy to understand why Ibn Ṭufayl respects the desire for anonymity of the Andalusian thinkers (mystics, theologians and many who engaged in the "hidden" sciences), who chose to accommodate the religious prohibition against delving into the philosophic sciences and presented their views in other garbs, and others who did not write books at all but spoke to people in signs. What is not so easy to understand is his treatment of Ibn Bājjah, the central figure in the history of Andalusian philosophy and in Ibn Ṭufayl's entire account of the ultimate secret of Oriental wisdom.

Since we do not know what evidence Ibn Ṭufayl had for saying that Ibn Bājjah failed to arrive at a visionary experience, nor for that matter what Ibn Ṭufayl's own visionary experience consisted in, we should perhaps set this question aside for the moment. The central theme of Ibn Bājjah's *Fī ᶜttiṣāl al-ᶜaql bi-ᵓl-insān* is that physics and metaphysics culminate, or ought to culminate, in the experience of "lightning flashes", an intuitive kind of knowledge different from and superior to discursive knowledge, and that the philosopher can in principle proceed beyond dianoetic knowledge to noetic experience. To this extent, Ibn Bājjah and Ibn Ṭufayl are in essential, though perhaps not verbal, agreement. But Ibn Bājjah goes further: noetic experience, if genuine, must be identical for all those who experience it; hence the noetic experience of Aristotle and anyone else is the same in this life. And since only this highest form of knowledge survives after death, what survives of Aristotle and any other human being with a genuine noetic experience after death is identically the same – neither the corporeal nor natural structure of the individual, but only the divine part, which is pure intelligence, survives his death. Again, Ibn Ṭufayl nowhere explicitly disagrees with Ibn Bājjah on this issue, and the story of Ḥayy b. Yaqẓān contains many indications that he follows in Ibn Bājjah's footsteps. Finally, Ibn Bājjah is known to have despaired of the possibility of establishing a philosophic city, and of the philosophers' ever having a pivotal role in reforming existing cities. If we are to take seriously the lesson of Ibn Ṭufayl's story – Ḥayy's regret that, in his ignorance, he tried to reform the religious city in the neighbouring island and his departure to his own island to meditate in isolation – Ibn Ṭufayl seems to accept Ibn Bājjah's position on this question also. Why, then, does he engage in such polemic against him? Is it that he objects not to the substance of Ibn Bājjah's views but to his manner of expressing them, to his exposing instead of hiding them in theoretical works, and to his unnecessary and dangerous outspokenness? On the other hand, Ibn Ṭufayl's suggestions that Ibn Bājjah was too concerned with the things of this world to go beyond theoretical knowledge, his reference to the summary and unfinished character of his writings, the quotation that proves that Ibn Bājjah himself admitted that what he intended to prove in *Fī ʾttiṣāl al-ʿaql bi-ʾl-insān* is not clearly or well expressed, and his assertion that the deep recesses of Ibn Bājjah's "wisdom" were not disclosed owing to his early death – all this amounts to a public defence of a philosopher accused of heresy and to a public defence of philosophy in a land where religious strictures against philosophy made it impossible for it to survive unless it resorted to coded language.

IBN ṬUFAYL ON AL-FĀRĀBĪ

For further confirmation of this thesis we turn now to Ibn Ṭufayl's account of the works of al-Fārābī who, next to Aristotle, was Ibn Bājjah's favourite philosopher; Ibn Sīnā (Ibn Ṭufayl was to discuss Aristotle together with Ibn Sīnā, as al-Ghazālī had done before), whose doctrine of "disembodied souls" and individual survival through the imaginative power was rejected by Ibn Bājjah; and al-Ghazālī, whose pleasure in his visionary experience was criticized by Ibn Bājjah as the product of his own imagination.

Ibn Ṭufayl sets aside al-Fārābī's writings on logic and concentrates on his "philosophic" writings,[31] which he describes as "plagued with doubts". He offers three examples: (1) in *al-Madīnah al-fāḍilah* ("The Virtuous City"), he affirms that the souls of the wicked survive death and suffer infinite punishment for eternity; (2) in *al-Siyāsah al-madaniyyah* ("Political Regime"), he declares that the souls of the wicked do not survive death and only virtuous and perfect souls survive; and (3) in his *Commentary* on Aristotle's *Ethics* (a work of which no copy is known today), he describes human happiness as something that is achieved in this life only, adding words to the effect that "everything mentioned beyond this is senseless jabber and tales told by old women". On the question of the immortality of the soul then al-Fārābī says different things in different books and contradicts himself. Ibn Ṭufayl does not comment on the first two views. Though he admits, with respect to the third, that he is paraphrasing or presenting al-Fārābī's view in his own words, he does not say that it is a false view or that he himself holds another or contrary view, but only that al-Fārābī "makes all people despair of God's mercy and places the wicked and the virtuous on the same level, since all are destined for nothingness".

Ibn Ṭufayl's main concern is not with the truth or validity of al-Fārābī's radical position as he formulated it, but with its moral, political and religious implications in this life: this is why he characterizes it as serious

[31] Ibid., 13–14.

"slipping" and "tripping".[32] In addition, there is al-Fārābī's declared ill-conceived doctrine about prophecy: that it has to do with the imaginative faculty in particular, and that philosophy is to be held in higher esteem than prophecy. Ibn Ṭufayl does not comment on al-Fārābī's view of prophecy, which he radicalizes even further than he did his view of immortality (al-Fārābī nowhere declared what Ibn Ṭufayl attributes to him). He remains silent about al-Fārābī's constant association of philosophy with prophecy, and his arguments that prophecy is a stage beyond, and a neccessary accompaniment of, perfect philosophy and a necessary accomplishment for the founder of a religious community. Nor does he mention al-Fārābī's paramount interest in the active role philosophy must play in the religious community.

Ibn Ṭufayl's criticism of al-Fārābī's philosophy in terms of its possible subversion of commonly held opinions regarding immortality and prophecy makes sense only if the philosopher is viewed as considering the religious community to be impervious to philosophic teaching by nature and that he must do nothing to disturb its traditional belief, the final lesson of the story of Ḥayy b. Yaqẓān. In this, as we saw, Ibn Ṭufayl follows Ibn Bājjah, who despaired of the establishment of a philosophic city. But he goes beyond Ibn Bājjah in trying to insulate the religious community from philosophy and to insulate philosophy from the religious community: in the story of Ḥayy b. Yaqẓān the two exist each on its separate island, and a member of the religious community who feels the need for deeper things must make the journey to the philosopher's island on his own; in real life, philosophic writing must be so secretive that no prosecutor could find anything even remotely suggesting that the writer holds offensive doctrines, such as Ibn Bājjah's and al-Fārābī's views on immortality or al-Fārābī's views on prophecy.

But we must pay special attention to the manner in which Ibn Ṭufayl reads al-Fārābī's philosophic works and instructs his friend in reading them. He looks for "doubtful" passages, compares them, and arranges them in a sequence that begins with the least doubtful passage and ends with the most doubtful. When he finds that the most doubtful passage contradicts the less doubtful passages, he assumes that the most doubtful passage represents al-Fārābī's genuine opinion and comments on this passage rather than the less doubtful ones – that is, he dismisses what al-Fārābī's says about the survival of and suffering of the souls of the wicked and about the survival of the souls of the virtuous as exoteric or politically useful statements, and criticizes as politically harmful al-Fārābī's statement

[32] Ibid., 14; cf. 11.

which seems to say that survival of any kind is a myth. Finally, Ibn Ṭufayl refuses to interpret these statements so as to make them agree with common opinion: for example, that al-Fārābī's most doubtful statement occurs in a commentary on Aristotle's *Ethics* and may reflect Aristotle's view rather than his own; or that al-Fārābī commonly distinguishes between "human" or "political" and "divine" happiness, or between the happiness of this world and the happiness of the other world, so that in his commentary on Aristotle's *Ethics* he could have been speaking of "human happiness" which is possible in this world only.

IBN ṬUFAYL ON IBN SĪNĀ

The account of Ibn Sīnā[33] presents him as the only writer who has succeeded in avoiding slipping or tripping, and the only philosopher with whom Ibn Ṭufayl can find no fault. He is a writer who is able to rewrite Aristotle's books and follow his doctrine and philosophic method in the *Shifāʾ*, declare at the same time that in his opinion the truth is otherwise, and send the reader who is after the unconcealed truth to another book of his, on Oriental (*mashriqī*) philosophy, which is nowhere to be found. Ibn Ṭufayl understands all this to mean that one needs to engage in a "careful" reading of the *Shifāʾ* and Aristotle's writings. Having done so, he finds that even though the two agree for the most part, the *Shifāʾ* contains certain things that are not Aristotelian. Following a hint by Ibn Sīnā in the *Shifāʾ*, he reaches the conclusion that the surface sense of everything given in Aristotle's works and in the *Shifāʾ* does not enable one to attain perfection: for this one needs to perceive its "secret and deep sense".

Ibn Ṭufayl does not speak of a single philosophic issue in connection with Aristotle or Ibn Sīnā, giving the impression that their doctrines are blameless or rather have every appearance of being blameless. Yet Ibn Ṭufayl does not fully trust what Ibn Sīnā declares in the *Shifāʾ*. This becomes clear from the way he attempts to introduce and dispose of the works of Aristotle (none is mentioned by name) and of Ibn Sīnā without having to mention any of the issues on which al-Ghazālī had accused Ibn Sīnā of unbelief: the pre-eternity of the world, God's knowledge of particulars, and rewards and punishment in the next world. Like al-Ghazālī, he declares that, as for Aristotle's books, Ibn Sīnā took it upon himself "to express their content". Al-Ghazālī understood this to mean that one need no longer go back to Aristotle's books and could thus speak of what the philosophers thought on the basis of what is found in the *Shifāʾ*. Ibn Ṭufayl,

33 Ibid., 14–15.

on the other hand, does not trust Ibn Sīnā's claims that he is giving the contents of Aristotle's books, nor does he follow Ibn Sīnā's suggestion that the reader who is after the unconcealed truth should go to his book on Oriental philosophy. He understands Ibn Sīnā to mean that one needs to engage not only in a careful reading of the *Shifā*ᵓ, but of Aristotle's books as well. He goes through everything given both in Aristotle's books and in the *Shifā*ᵓ and warns against accepting its surface sense as insufficient, without telling us whether such doctrines as the pre-eternity of the world is one of the surface or deep senses of these works. He is thus using the distinction between the surface and deep senses of these works to avoid having to deal explicitly with any of the issues raised by al-Ghazālī in his *Tahāfut al-falāsifah* ("Incoherence of the Philosophers") and to hint that it may well turn out that al-Ghazālī dealt with the surface sense of Ibn Sīnā's *Shifā*ᵓ rather than its deep or secret sense.[34] It is perhaps characteristic of Ibn Ṭufayl's style of writing that in the only place where he speaks explicitly of the surface/deep sense distinction, he employs it to protect philosophic writings against the prying eyes of a man like al-Ghazālī rather than to reveal any deep sense in particular.

IBN ṬUFAYL ON AL-GHAZĀLĪ

The account of al-Ghazālī's writings[35] has the dubious distinction of being longer (thirty-eight lines) than the accounts of the writings of Ibn Bājjah (eleven lines), al-Fārābī (fourteen lines) and Ibn Sīnā-Aristotle (eleven lines), together. Like al-Fārābī, al-Ghazālī contradicts himself and says different things in different books. But he is not blamed as harshly as al-Fārābī. He is accused of engaging in this practice in order to court public approval, to the point that he is willing to charge others with unbelief for doctrines he himself embraces. The example chosen by Ibn Ṭufayl is again the question of survival after death: (1) in the *Tahāfut al-falāsifah* al-Ghazālī charges the philosophers (i.e. Ibn Sīnā) with unbelief because they deny the resurrection of the body and affirm that only souls are rewarded and punished; (2) in the beginning of the *Mīzān al-ᶜamal* ("Criterion of Action") he says this is definitely the doctrine held by Ṣūfī "masters"; and (3) in *al-Munqidh min al-ḍalāl* ("Deliverer from Error") he says that his own doctrine is that of the Ṣūfīs, adding that he arrived at this after "extended search". Ṣūfīs are now mentioned by name for the first time and so is al-Ghazālī's claim that he follows Ṣūfī doctrines. Since his books are said to reveal to whoever takes the trouble to consider and examine them thoroughly

[34] Ibid., 15. [35] Ibid., 15–18.

numerous things of this sort,[36] we must wonder how Ibn Ṭufayl wishes his friend to judge al-Ghazālī's skilful journey (in the *Munqidh*) from philosophy to Ṣufism, in the course of which he finds a philosophic doctrine the holders of which he had accused of unbelief, attributes the same doctrine to the Ṣūfīs, and finally says that he holds this "Ṣūfī" doctrine but arrived at it only after extended personal search, when in fact he had already found it in Ibn Sīnā.

Al-Ghazālī is not presented by Ibn Ṭufayl as a philosopher or included among the authors (Aristotle, al-Fārābī and Ibn Sīnā) whose works on philosophy arrived in Andalusia;[37] yet he is not an ordinary Ṣūfī, but a man made skilful through the pursuit of the sciences. His skilful apology for what he does in his books is that there are three classes of opinions: (1) one in which he agrees with the public; (2) another commensurate with the questioner and seeker he addresses; and (3) a third he keeps to himself and discloses only to those who share his doctrine. He is then quoted addressing his reader as follows: "Even if these utterances have no other effect than to make you doubt your inherited beliefs, they are useful enough. For he who does not doubt does not look, he who does not look does not see, and he who does not see remains blind and perplexed."[38] This is perhaps an adequate apology for the practice al-Ghazālī followed in his writings, for it enabled him to be all things to all men: to present himself as the defender of "seeing" with one's own eyes rather than accepting what one "hears" (he is quoting a second time, with his use of a line of poetry by the Toledan poet al-Waqqāshī, when expressing a delicate matter[39]), and the defender of religious orthodoxy at the same time. Ibn Ṭufayl's comment on all this is that a reader does not learn anything from this kind of instruction, which employs signs and hints for the most part, unless he already knows or is so well endowed that the slightest hint is all he needs.[40]

Al-Ghazālī's statement in the *Jawāhir al-Qurʾān* ("Jewels of the Qurʾān") that he has written esoteric books in which he incorporated the "plain truth" is treated at some length, which is curious given that Ibn Sīnā's statement to the same effect was not elaborated at all. Ibn Ṭufayl asserts that no such books reached Andalusia and refutes those who claim that one or another of al-Ghazālī's available books are esoteric. His argument is based on the notion that the more esoteric a book, the more ambiguous (*aghmaḍ*) it ought to be. But if this is the case, then either al-Ghazālī was mistaken in incorporating the plain truth in esoteric books, or else a book such as *al-Maqṣad al-asnā* ("The Supreme Purpose") is in fact an esoteric book because it contains more ambiguous things than the other works that are claimed to

[36] Ibid., 16. [37] Ibid., 11–12. [38] Ibid., 16. [39] Ibid. [40] Ibid.

be esoteric. Yet al-Ghazālī himself declared that *al-Maqṣad al-asnā* is not an esoteric book. The question then is what al-Ghazālī meant by the statement that he has written esoteric books which contain the plain truth. Given the opinion that one keeps to oneself and discloses only to those who share one's beliefs, is this another hint that books designated as, or suspected to be, esoteric are not in fact esoteric, while books that are declared not to be esoteric are in fact more esoteric than the rest?

Finally (and in the guise of reporting what was thought by a recent but anonymous person), Ibn Ṭufayl registers an interpretation of what is said by al-Ghazālī at the end of one of his more esoteric books, the *Mishkāt al-anwār* ("Niche of Lights"), that is, that those who arrive at the Divine Presence "have learned that this Being is characterized by an attribute that negates pure Unity": this passage, it was thought, shows that al-Ghazālī must have held the doctrine that there is "a certain multiplicity in the First Truth".[41] Ibn Ṭufayl defends God, but not al-Ghazālī, against what the "unjust" say of him, and then concludes by saying he has no doubt that the "master" achieved supreme happiness and reached the "most honourable reaches", without saying what he reached. Ibn Ṭufayl has now arrived at the high point of al-Ghazālī's "science of unveiling" (*ʿilm al-mukāshafah*). Al-Ghazālī thought that the experience of "unveiling", the counterpart of Ibn Ṭufayl's "vision" (*mushāhadah*), can be the subject of a scientific account and that the knowledge obtained through it can be incorporated in books. But this is an experience that Ibn Ṭufayl had declared impossible to speak or write about – one that attempts to do so would transform the experience into something else, disfigure it, and subject it to types of expressions that lead to slipping or to being thought to have slipped from the straight path. The long account of al-Ghazālī presents him as having done everything Ibn Ṭufayl insisted should not be done. Unlike the books of the philosophers (Aristotle and Ibn Sīnā, whom he maligned), which contain a surface sense the student can pursue step by step and learn from until he reaches the point where, if he can, he perceives their deep and secret sense, al-Ghazālī's books ultimately bring him through signs and hints to doubt inherited beliefs; they lack the solid surface on which the student can walk without slipping and losing inherited beliefs until he is ready to see for himself.

IBN ṬUFAYL'S PATH TO TRUTH

Ibn Ṭufayl is now ready to speak of the path he himself followed in arriving at the truth: he scrutinized and compared what was said by al-Ghazālī and

[41] Ibid., 17–18.

Ibn Sīnā, then set it against the novel opinions professed in his own time by people who claimed to philosophize, i.e., followers of al-Ghazālī who thought they had found his esoteric opinions.[42] He is also ready to declare that, up to the point when his friend's question led him to a slight taste of the truth through a visionary experience, he had pursued the path of theoretical enquiry until he arrived at the clear truth. He does not therefore consider himself one of those very rare people who possess ever-open eyes and may not need to pursue theoretical enquiry;[43] if he was able to benefit from "hearing" al-Ghazālī's signs and hints, it was because he had already acquired an insight into what they point to.[44] Nor does the friend who asked about the secrets of Oriental wisdom belong to that exceptional class of people; unlike Ibn Ṭufayl, however, he has not as yet engaged in theoretical enquiry. Because Ibn Ṭufayl thinks his friend capable of higher achievements, he refuses to convey to him the conclusions at which he has arrived, for even if his friend were to accept them, trusting in Ibn Ṭufayl's judgement, such conclusions convey no more than cryptic conventional statements. The only path leading to true knowledge is the long path followed by Ibn Ṭufayl, in which one must be sure to acquire a firm grasp of the principles, moving step by step until one arrives at and ascertains the conclusions through one's own insight – that is, probe through the surface meaning of everything found in Aristotle's books and in Ibn Sīnā's *Shifā'* to perceive their deep and secret sense,[45] and then discern what Ibn Ṭufayl has discerned in them. The secrets of Oriental wisdom are not available in the writings of Ṣūfīs like al-Ghazālī. The philosophy found in the writings of Aristotle, al-Fārābī and Ibn Sīnā, on the other hand, requires a guide, a living teacher and oral instruction. And Ibn Ṭufayl offers to guide his friend along the shortest and safest path, if he is willing to dedicate himself to the task. But he warns him of the fate of Ibn Bājjah: "This requires an appreciable length of time, freedom from all concerns, and wholehearted dedication to this art."[46] The story of Ḥayy b. Yaqẓān is neither a substitute for living instruction, nor is it meant as a short cut for the long and arduous journey. It is "a little glimpse as stimulation and encouragement for entering upon the path".[47]

All this, it must be admitted, is a very curious means of introducing a story "In which is demonstrated," to quote Simon Ockley's subtitle to his translation, "by what Methods one may, by the meer *Light of Nature*, attain the Knowledge of things *Natural* and *Supernatural*". It contradicts the impression given by the story of Ḥayy b. Yaqẓān that it is possible for man to attain "True Knowledge of God, and Things necessary to Salvation,

[42] Ibid., cf. 155–6. [43] Ibid., 9. [44] Ibid., 16. [45] Ibid., 15. [46] Ibid., 19.
[47] Ibid., 20.

without the Use of external means [*Instruction*]". Ibn Ṭufayl examines and discusses the different forms of instruction, oral and written, and instructs his friend in how one must understand what is said as well as read what is written. He indicates that the only writing which bears fruit and leads the reader to perfection is the writing which means more and other than what it says and presents on the surface, necessary and indispensable as the surface meaning is; and that the deep and secret sense of such writing is frequently marked by what, to the uninitiated eye, looks like a muddled surface, full of gaps, contradictions and inconsistencies. The story of Ḥayy b. Yaqẓān does not illustrate the point, let alone demonstrate that one can attain the highest knowledge without instruction; it is not meant to please and assure those who have difficulty with theoretical enquiry (with so-called abstractions or rationalism); nor is it written to inspire the "Enthusiasts of these present Times", as Ockley suggested in an appendix to his translation. On the other hand, the weight of its religious (Quranic), ascetic and Ṣūfī testimonies in the foreground is commensurate with the weight of the background from which Ibn Ṭufayl's friend emerged to ask about the secrets of Oriental wisdom. Ibn Ṭufayl's *Ḥayy b. Yaqẓān* is a narrative elaboration of Ibn Sīnā's story and the story of Absāl and Salāmān is a narrative interpretation of another story mentioned by Ibn Sīnā who had challenged the reader of his *al-Ishārāt wa-ᵓl-tanbīhāt* to "Interpret the sign, if you can!" Ibn Ṭufayl presents his own story as a lesson and reminder, not for those who merely listen to his words, but for those who listen to them with the kind of understanding that grasps what is beyond them. He commences his story as, and maintains the fiction that it is, merely a report transmitted from "our pious ancestors".[48] But as the story commences it becomes clear that the pious ancestors do not always speak with a single voice.[49] And as it concludes Ibn Ṭufayl confesses: "we have departed in it from the path of the pious ancestors."[50]

[48] Ibid. [49] Ibid., 24. [50] Ibid., 155.

CHAPTER 7

ARABIC LEXICOGRAPHY

"Copious without order, energetic without rules": this is how the English language appeared to Samuel Johnson in the eighteenth century and so, too, must Arabic have seemed to its first lexicographers some thousand years earlier. It was at this time that Sībawayhi (d. *c.* 183/799) created the grammar which would henceforth rule the energy of Arabic, while his master al-Khalīl b. Aḥmad (d. 175/791) brought order to its copiousness by laying the foundations of lexicography (*ᶜilm al-lughah*, "the science of language"). Just a few years after the publication of Johnson's *Dictionary of the English Language* (1755), the Arab lexicographical tradition reached its peak in the gigantic *Tāj al-ᶜarūs min jawāhir al-qāmūs* (begun in 1174/1760, finished 1188/1774) of al-Zabīdī (d. 1205/1791), which is a summation of the entire heritage, a triumph of cumulation incorporating every significant work directly or indirectly, from al-Khalīl onwards. There is hardly an item in the following sketch of the evolution of the classic dictionaries which has not found its way into the *Tāj*.

The formal lexicon is not the only product of the Arabs' interest in their language, however, and, before dealing with the standard dictionaries, some attention must be given to the other kinds of word-lists and alphabetically arranged reference works which emerged at the same time. These, though often subsumed in later dictionaries, are in no way their ancestors but had a separate existence and continued to appear side by side with them. Under pressure of rivalry from Muslims of a non-Arab background, and with the realization that Muḥammad's diction had to be interpreted through its pre-Islamic context, a knowledge of the linguistic habits of the true "Arabs" (always meaning the bedouin Arabs) had become indispensable for the construction of an Arab-Islamic civilization. Early philologists such as Abū Saᶜīd ᶜAbd al-Malik b. Qurayb al- Aṣmaᶜī (d. *c.* 216/831), Abū ᶜUbaydah Maᶜmar b. al-Muthannā (d. 210/825) and Abū ᶜUbayd al-Qāsim b. Sallām (d. 224/838) responded by compiling classified word-lists ranging over all aspects of bedouin life, activities, topography, animal husbandry, etc., providing the urban scholar with the necessary material to promote the myth of the *ᶜarabiyyah*, the pure and idealized form of Arabic alleged to have been spoken by the bedouin and in which, as the dogma had it, Muḥammad delivered the Revelation.

These vocabulary lists went on being produced, giving rise to larger and more comprehensive works. As well as specific topics (more than a score of authors, for example, wrote a "Book of the Horse"), we find general treatments such as the *Fiqh al-lughah* of al-Thaʿālibī (d. 429/1038), in which the words are grouped semantically in a manner that is presumably intended to be exhaustive and remarkably prefigures the *Thesaurus* of Peter Roget (first published in 1852). By its title (lit. "The Jurisprudence of Language"), al-Thaʿālibī affirms the close relationship between law and language which had by his time become institutionalized. The most complete example of this kind of dictionary of synonyms is the massive *al-Mukhaṣṣaṣ fīʾl-lughah* of Ibn Sīdah (d. 458/1066). Ibn Sīdah, whose other lexicon, *al-Muḥkam wa-ʾl-muḥīṭ al-aʿẓam*, will be dealt with in due course, certainly achieved his stated purpose of making all similar works redundant, and nothing has superseded it. *Al-Mukhaṣṣaṣ* is a compendium of previous word-lists arranged by subject, each entry scrupulously assigned to its source with little or no critical comment; perhaps more consciously than any other such reference work it is expressly designed to help poets, writers and bureaucrats to find the *mot juste*. An entirely different kind of thesaurus is the *Shajar al-durr* ("Trees of Pearls") of Abū al-Ṭayyib al-Lughawī (d. 381/991), which disposes the vocabulary into symmetrical groups of "trees" of 100 words, each a synonym of its neighbours, with "branches" developing further synonyms within each "tree". This virtuosity, of which Abū al-Ṭayyib provides by no means the first instance, simply demonstrates the possibilities for word games that the very wealth of the Arabic language affords.

In the process of sifting and classifying the vocabulary of Arabic, all kinds of lists were drawn up which have been detailed in Sezgin's *Geschichte des arabischen Schrifttums*. In addition to the specialist glossaries already mentioned, we find compilations of the rare words in the Qurʾān and *Ḥadīth*, technical dictionaries of the various sciences (among which we should include genealogical, biographical and geographical dictionaries), lists of words which bear simultaneously opposite meanings, inventories based on morphological or grammatical categories; in short, anything which could contribute to the organizing and mastery of the huge Arabic vocabulary. Not surprisingly there are also dictionaries of errors, which unintentionally provide the modern Arabist with valuable evidence of colloquial or dialect forms whose penetration into the classical language was resented and resisted.

Polyglot dictionaries are by no means common – the Arabs themselves can scarcely have seen the need for them. The *Muqaddimat al-adab* of al-Zamakhsharī (d. 538/1144), a monoglot grouping of nouns and verbs arranged thematically, supplemented by sections on particles and inflections, is a rare exception to the extent that it became a basis for glosses into Persian, Khwarazmian, various Turkish dialects and Mongolian. Arabic-Persian glossaries are known, for example, by al-Zawzanī (d. 486/1093) and al-Maydānī (d. 518/1124), and an Arabic-Mongolian glossary by Ibn al-Muhannā (early eighth/fourteenth century), while, in the West, al-Ghāfiqī (d. 560/1165) is credited with a version of a *Book of Simples* (*Kitāb al-Mufradāt*) which gives plant names in Arabic, Greek, Syriac, Latin, Castilian, Berber and Persian. We should probably exclude here word-lists compiled by non-Arabs, such as the twelfth-century Leiden glossary, the *Vocabulary* attributed to Ramón Martín (*fl.* AD 1250) and the Syriac-Arabic dictionaries, but the Yemeni prince al-Afḍal (reigned 764-78/1363–77) deserves attention for commissioning a list of Arabic words with equivalents in Turkish, Persian, Mongolian, Greek and Armenian. Yemen's position on the trade routes may have inspired this interest in language, which seems to have become something of a family tradition, as al-Afḍal's son al-Ashraf (reigned 778–803/1377–1400) gave his daughter in marriage to the famous lexicographer al-Fīrūzābādī (d. 817/1415), whose *Qāmūs* will be discussed below. Enthusiasm for foreign languages was undoubtedly kept low by the circumstances and doctrine of the Quranic Revelation, but, within this limitation, the Arabs showed considerable sensitivity to words of foreign origin and were able to distinguish native from introduced words systematically by applying phonological and morphological criteria identical to those of modern linguistics.

Before turning to the dictionaries proper, it is necessary to explain the complex and intriguing ways in which entries are arranged. For alphabetical ordering, three alphabets were available:

1 ʾ b j d h w z ḥ ṭ y k l m n s ʿ f ṣ q r sh t th kh dh ḍ ẓ gh
2 ʿ ḥ h kh gh q k j sh ḍ ṣ s z ṭ d t ẓ dh th r l n f b m w ʾ y
3 ʾ b t th j ḥ kh d dh r z s sh ṣ ḍ ṭ ẓ ʿ gh f q k l m n h w y

Number 1 is the ancient Semitic alphabet, never used by lexicographers, but included here for several reasons: it provides the word *abjad* (its first four letters) for "alphabet" (also termed *al-muʿjam*, lit. "the thing with the dots", referring to the diacriticals of the writing), it retains its ancient numerical values even today (roughly equivalent to our Roman numerals), and it forms the basis of the standard alphabet number 3, which was constructed broadly by bringing together letters of a similar written shape (thus ʾ, *b* [+ *t*, *th*], *j* (+ *ḥ*, *kh*], *d*[+ *dh*], etc.).

Alphabet number 2 represents an altogether different principle: the letters are ordered phonologically, beginning with the pharyngeals and laryngeals and ascending to the labials, with the semi-vowels *w*, ʾ, *y* last because of their ambiguous consonantal status. There seems no reason to doubt that this particular arrangement is ultimately connected with Indian phonetic theory, but in what way and by what means may never be precisely known, as all documentary evidence is lacking. The system emerges fully developed and linked with the name of al-Khalīl b. Aḥmad (d. 175/791), but its origins remain impenetrably obscure. The same can be said about the initial impetus to compile dictionaries at all: the assumption of a Greek model has been made but cannot be textually substantiated, nor does this hypothesis help much in understanding the dictionaries as we have them.

Whichever alphabet is used, there are still further difficulties to be overcome before an individual word can actually be tracked down. First, only the root consonants of a word are taken into account in determining its place, so that every dictionary is automatically an etymological dictionary. This needs some slight qualification, in that "etymology" here means only that the word is assigned to its putative Arabic root, regardless of its true origins: thus *sarj* (saddle) and *sirāj* (lamp) are assigned to the native root *s-r-j* (as in *saraj*, "he lied") even though both are loan words. To locate *musarraj* (saddled), we must therefore find the root *s-r-j*; a few modern dictionaries, and those of non-Arab Muslim languages such as Turkish and Persian, observe a strict alphabetical order which places *musarraj* under *m*, but *m* is such a common prefix that the result is, in the end, far less convenient than the etymologizing method. Secondly, the exact location of the root depends on the manner in which the dictionary is alphabetically arranged, namely:

A *Permutative.* All known permutations of radicals are listed together in order of the highest letter of the alphabet:

either (i) the phonological alphabet (no. 2), thus *miftāḥ* (key), radicals *f-t-ḥ*, is under *ḥ* along with all the other permutations of *ḥ*, *t* and *f*,

or (ii) the standard alphabet (no. 3), where *miftāḥ* is under *t* with all the other permutations of *t*, *ḥ* and *f*.

B *Alphabetical.* Each root is located in standard alphabetical order (no. 3):

either (i) by its *first* letter, thus *miftāḥ* is under *f*, followed by roots *f-t-kh*, *f-t-r*, *f-t-sh*, and so on,

or (ii) by its *last* letter, thus *miftāḥ* is under *ḥ*, followed by roots *f-d-ḥ*, *f-r-ḥ*, *f-s-ḥ*, and so on.

This last method produces in effect a rhyming dictionary, though there is little reason to believe that this is the true purpose of the arrangement. A more plausible explanation might be that many near-synonymous roots are distinguished only by their third radical (e.g. *n-b-j*, *n-b-ḍ*, *n-b-ṭ*, *n-b-ᶜ*, *n-b-gh*, *n-b-q*, all related to the gushing of water), which thus assumes a significance the other radicals do not have. It is worth observing (although this may be a result rather than a cause) that abbreviations often select the *last* important consonant, e.g. *q* for "folio" (*waraqah*), *ḍ* for "al-Ḥāmiḍ" (proper name), etc.

After these preliminaries it is time to look at the dictionaries themselves, which for convenience will be grouped methodologically, namely: A (i) Permutative/phonological; A (ii) Permutative/alphabetical; B (i) Alphabetical by first radical; and B (ii) Alphabetical by last radical. Names and titles are given in the short forms by which they are usually known.

A (i) *Permutative/phonological.* The first dictionary of Arabic is attributed to al-Khalīl b. Aḥmad, though it survives only in a version prepared by a younger contemporary, al-Layth b. al-Muẓaffar (active before 200/815). It is generally accepted that al-Khalīl provided the inspiration and overall plan for the work, even if he did not personally complete it; its title, *Kitāb al-ᶜAyn*, ("The Book of the Letter *ᶜAyn*") is taken from the name of the first letter in the phonological alphabet said to have been invented by al-Khalīl. Many features of the *ᶜAyn* are retained in subsequent dictionaries: liberal quotation of poetry as evidence of usage, citation of verbs in paradigmatic form (perfect and imperfect tenses, verbal noun, adjectival and nominal derivatives), extracts from the Qurʾān, occasional proverbs, random mention of place names, and a lack of obvious order in the interior arrangement of the entries (though research might reveal one). Being permutative, the dictionary has to state which combinations of radicals are in use (*mustaᶜmal*) and which are not (*muhmal*, lit. "neglected"), and, in this, apart from relying on his own *Sprachgefühl*, al-Khalīl also recognizes the principle that there are limitations on the co-occurrence of phonemes in the same root. He furthermore observes that every native Arabic root comprising four or more consonants includes at least one radical from the group r, l, n, f, b, m, an intuitively attractive proposition which his critics and successors gleefully sought to refute with counter-examples. In dividing the *ᶜAyn* into several self-contained sections, dealing separately with biliteral, triliteral, quadriliteral roots and roots containing w, ʾ, y, al-Khalīl introduced a degree of complexity which was not eliminated until al-Jawharī (d. between 393/1003 and 400/1009, see below) subsumed all types of roots under the one alphabetical series.

A number of abridgements and supplements were inspired by the *ᶜAyn*, of which that by al-Zubaydī (d. 379/989), entitled *Mukhtaṣar Kitāb al-ᶜAyn*, was reputed to be superior to the original. A larger and evidently tidier version of the ʿ*Ayn* was produced by the Buwayhid vizier al-Ṣāḥib Ibn ʿAbbād (d. 385/995) under the title *al-Muḥīṭ*, though its author relies heavily on a supplement, *al-Takmilah*, by al-Khārzanjī (d. 348/959), which survives now only through quotations. Extremely dependent on al-Khalīl's work is the *Bāriʿ* of al-Qālī (d. 356/965), a pioneer of philology in Arab Spain. While he faithfully reproduces the contents of the ʿ*Ayn*, al-Qālī follows a slightly different phonological order, which may represent a parallel tradition transmitted perhaps through al-Khalīl's pupil Sībawayhi. A curiosity of the *Bāriʿ* is the way it deals with onomatopoeic words, for example, *tigh-tigh* ("tee-hee"), *qah-qah* ("ha-ha"): al-Qālī brands these intractable fellows *awshāb* (lit. "rabble, social misfits"), a result, perhaps, of equating the perfect language with the perfect society!

The most thorough and durable reworking of the ʿ*Ayn* is *al-Tahdhīb* ("Correction") of al-Azharī (d. 370/980), which represents the first mature and fully developed dictionary. In his long preface, al-Azharī confirms that lexicography has come of age: his list of authorities, sources and teachers is a virtual history of the discipline, accompanied by some devastating criticisms of his predecessors. In substance the *Tahdhīb* is a greatly enlarged version of the ʿ*Ayn*, following the same order and reproducing it with extreme accuracy, with the addition of large amounts of material from the lists and glossaries mentioned above. Of great significance for the history of lexicography is the fact that al-Azharī clearly regarded al-Layth b. al-Muẓaffar as the author of the ʿ*Ayn*, and not al-Khalīl.

The last great lexicon on the pattern of the ʿ*Ayn* is *al-Muḥkam*, by the Andalusian scholar Ibn Sīdah. Like the *Tahdhīb*, which is one of its sources, *al-Muḥkam* is essentially another reworking of the ʿ*Ayn*, which Ibn Sīdah claims to have expanded and systematized in an unprecedented way. There are indeed many innovations in the presentation: economies are made by omitting forms which are obvious or which can easily be inferred by an expert in *ṣināʿat al-iʿrāb* (lit. "the art of inflection", but used in a peculiarly narrow sense by Ibn Sīdah to mean morphology). By expressly interrelating lexicography with grammar, prosody, logic and rhetoric, Ibn Sīdah may have been the first to compile a dictionary within the framework of a unified semantic theory. Notable among his authorities (also in his thematically arranged thesaurus *al-Mukhaṣṣaṣ*) are the highly original and inquisitive grammarians Ibn Jinnī (d. 392/1002) and al-Rummānī (d. 384/994), both of whom have made great contributions to Arabic semantics which have yet to be properly evaluated.

A (ii) *Permutative/alphabetical.* Only one dictionary, *al-Jamharah* of Ibn Durayd (d. 321/933), stands as an example of this method. Though drawing heavily on the ʿ*Ayn*, it does contain original material, and certainly does not deserve the slanderous criticism made by Nifṭawayhi (d. 323/935) that Ibn Durayd did nothing more than "rearrange the *ᶜAyn*".[1] On the other hand, there are enough well-intentioned idiosyncrasies in the *Jamharah* to account for its failure to engender a new lexicographical tradition: it retains the separation into biliteral, triliteral, quadriliteral stems, etc., is repetitive and quixotic (roots where identical radicals occur adjacently, like *fakk*, are in one place, while words in which the same radicals occur apart, for example, *fikak*, are in a different and remote section), and much of the contents are dispersed into individual monographs at the end rather than in the body of the work. To his credit Ibn Durayd furnishes, possibly for the first time in the history of linguistics, a partial frequency list of phonemes, starting with *w*, *y*, ᵓ, and finishing with (in descending order) *m*, *b*, *r*, *l*, *n*, *gh*, *kh*, *q*, *sh*, *th*, *dh*, *ẓ*. He also calculates the number of possible biliteral roots as 784 and of triliterals as 15,625 at the theoretical maximum, and gives the equation for a huge number of potential quadriliterals. His circular diagram for the permutation of roots from given radicals is directly inspired by al-Khalīl's circles of overlapping metrical schemes.

B (i) *Alphabetical by first radical.* Ibn Durayd had no successors, though his pupil al-Qālī distinguished himself with the permutative/phonological *al-Bāriᶜ* (see above). Another ordering, alphabetical by first radical, found favour at a relatively early date, but always remained limited in its appeal to the general lexicographer. The first dictionary of this type is the *Kitāb al-Jīm* of Abū ᶜAmr Isḥāq b. Mirār al-Shaybānī (d. 213/828). In the overwhelming preponderance of poetic vocabulary (some 4,300 verses as against only three quotations from the Qurᵓān and one possible *ḥadīth* in the surviving portion), the *Jīm* reflects the priorities of the period: only later did scriptural language achieve equality with pre-Islamic usage as a concern of general lexicography. Where the title of al-Shaybānī's dictionary comes from is uncertain. It is named "The Book of *J*" after the third letter of the standard alphabet, but unlike al-Khalīl's rather obvious "The Book of *ᶜAyn*" (the first letter of the phonological alphabet), the "*J*" of al-Shaybānī will always remain an enigma.

The tradition of alphabetical order by first radical is continued in *al-Maqāyīs* and its shorter version *al-Mujmal*, both by Aḥmad b. Fāris (d. 395/1005). Ibn Fāris added a complication of his own, however, by adopting a strictly cyclic arrangement in the second and third radicals, so that the first entry under each letter is the root whose second and third radicals are next

[1] Yāqūt, *Irshād al-arīb*, VI, 490; cf. also Ibn Durayd, *Jamharat al-lughah*, ed. R. Baalbaki, I, Beirut, 1987–8, 20.

in alphabetical order, and the alphabet is then completed and restarted in order to reach the radicals higher in the order. Hence *miftāḥ* (key), to use our earlier example, is under *f*, whose first entry happens to be *f-q-m*, with *f-t-ḥ* held back until the alphabet has begun again in the second and third positions with *f-ʾ-*, *f-b-*, etc. Another peculiarity of the *Maqāyīs* is that it assigns to each root a general meaning or range of meanings. This is partly explained as a response of Ibn Fāris to accusations by opponents of the Arab cultural tradition (the Shuʿūbiyyah) that Arabic was self-contradictory and irrational, and may also reflect some underlying semantic theory of his own. If so, it conflicts strikingly with the theory of his contemporary, Ibn Jinnī, that roots containing the same radicals in any order are fundamentally synonymous, a notion which found no resonance in lexicography. Another opponent of the Shuʿūbiyyah, al-Zamakhsharī, composed a dictionary arranged alphabetically by first radical which is unique in the genre: his *Asās al-balāghah* has as its only purpose the elucidation of metaphorical and extended meanings. A somewhat more ancient conflict is probably to be glimpsed at in an unusual dictionary, the *Shams al-ʿulūm* of Nashwān b. Saʿīd (d. 573/1178), also arranged alphabetically, which is remarkable not only for subdividing the entries into grammatical categories within each letter, but also for its bias towards Yemeni material, an echo of the age-old hostility between northern and southern Arab tribes.

While the permutative arrangement fell into disuse after the fifth/eleventh century, both alphabetical systems continued side by side until, under European influence, ordering by first radical has come to predominate in modern times. But it was not the method preferred in the classic dictionaries about to be described, which, as well as being formally different in their ordering by last radical, are also in their contents qualitatively different from most of the dictionaries arranged by first radical. The latter are nearly all selective in one way or another, as specific glossaries and vocabularies or purely technical reference works. They appear, therefore, to reduce the language to discrete terminologial bundles, whereas the comprehensive end-radical dictionaries express the cultural ideal of the whole of bedouin Arabic in its full breadth and depth. That they are, fortuitously, also rhyming dictionaries can be seen as a happy reflection of the supreme importance of poetry as the medium of bedouin expressivity.

B (ii) *Alphabetical by last radical.* The credit for establishing what was to become the standard arrangement goes to Abū Naṣr Ismāʿīl b. Ḥammād al-Jawharī, author of a dictionary entitled *al-Ṣiḥāḥ*. Even if, as seems likely, the idea came to al-Jawharī from an earlier dictionary, the *Dīwān al-adab* of his uncle Abū Ibrāhīm Isḥāq b. Ibrāhīm al-Fārābī (d. 350/961), the *Ṣiḥāḥ* (which al-Jawharī did not live to complete[2]) remains the pioneer of this type of work, in so far as he abolished the various morphophonological subdivisions of earlier works and listed all roots consecutively regardless of the number or type of radicals. For this, undoubtedly, al-Jawharī deserves the enormous esteem in which he is held by western critics, though since the contents of the *Ṣiḥāḥ* were totally subsumed in later works it has become less important lexically than historically. About his sources al-Jawharī is rather reticent, but he was original enough not to be entirely derivative, and the *Ṣiḥāḥ* has directly inspired a number of glosses, abridgements and reworkings. The two supplements by al-Ṣaghānī (d. 650/1252), *al-Takmilah* and *al-Dhayl*, are especially important since their author was a most meticulous scholar (he tells us he consulted over a thousand sources in compiling the *Takmilah*), whose misfortune it was to be completely overshadowed by later authors who absorbed his work into their own. Through another of his dictionaries, *al-ᶜUbāb* (praised as the best of its kind since the *Ṣiḥāḥ* itself), al-Ṣaghānī provided his successors with indirect access to many earlier works which they probably never studied at first hand.

With the *Lisān al-ᶜArab* (completed 689/1290) of Ibn Manẓūr (d. 711/1311), we reach the end of lexicographical progress. The *Lisān* (note how the work's title, "The Tongue of the Bedouin Arabs", perpetuates even at this late date the myth of the pure, spoken desert language) is wholly derivative in content, although Ibn Manẓūr scrupulously acknowledges all his sources. His achievement, however, is genuine enough, in that he took the *Ṣiḥāḥ* as his framework and extended it to a vast size by incorporating the more exhaustive but far less convenient *Tahdhīb* of al-Azharī and the *Muḥkam* of Ibn Sīdah. In this way, the *Lisān* set a standard of comprehensiveness and systematic arrangement which was not surpassed for more than four centuries.

In the meantime al-Fīrūzābādī produced his *Qāmūs* ("The Ocean"), a dense and compact work which was so popular that, in the end, *qāmūs* became the accepted term for "dictionary" itself. Taking as his starting-point the *Muḥkam* of Ibn Sīdah and the *ᶜUbāb* of al-Ṣaghānī, al-Fīrūzābādī set about eliminating all extraneous matter in the way of references, illustration and comment, and made further economies by using abbreviations to mark proper names, plurals etc., together with a method of ensuring correct vocalization (ultimately taken from al-Jawharī) by citing well-known key-words, thus "*k-b-r* like *karuma*" means that the root *k-b-r*

[2] For an account of the untimely end of al-Jawharī, see below, ch. 11, 180.

is vocalized as *kabura* (the procedure is somewhat otiose as all printed editions are fully vowelled anyway!). The result, as one might have foreseen, was not so much a dictionary as "an enormous vocabulary", as it has been called, and it was only a matter of time before it became the subject of expansion by commentary. This task was carried out by al-Zabīdī, whose enormous *Tāj al-ᶜarūs* marks the limit of development in indigenous lexicography, and was to pass into the western tradition as the basis of Lane's great unfinished dictionary. What the *Tāj* does is to restore all the information discarded by al-Fīrūzābādī, while adding a huge amount of extra material from the 113 sources which al-Zabīdī acknowledges in his preface. Among these is the *Lisān* of Ibn Manẓūr, whose entire contents are reproduced in the *Tāj*. This is enough to give an idea of the originality of al-Zabīdī; the merit of his work (apart from his reliability as a copier) is that he was able to supplement the stock of roots in the *Lisān* from his other sources, thereby coming as close as any individual ever has done to confining the copiousness of Arabic within a single work.

Al-Zabīdī himself set the number of words in the *Tāj* at 120,000 compared with 80,000 in the *Lisān*, 60,000 in the *Qāmūs* and 40,000 in the *Ṣiḥāḥ*. Correct or not, these figures can only refer to the total of words derived from all the roots rather than the actual number of roots themselves. The latter probably amount to about 6,000 (a random 10 per cent sample of Hava's dictionary, which is based on the *Qāmūs*, yielded some 5,800 roots). Thus when Ibn Sīdah claims to have gathered 5,000 "cases" (*qaḍiyyah*) in his *Muḥkam* he is probably referring to the number of roots in that work. Since there are scores of possible derivatives from any root, none of al-Zabīdī's figures is at all implausible.

In spite of their wide formal variations, the dictionaries themselves differ only superficially from each other in content and method, almost the only observable development (apart from the increasing root-stock) being the gradual introduction of more and more Quranic and Islamic material. One seeks mostly in vain in the early dictionaries for such Islamic neologisms as *dīwān*, *wazīr*, *falsafah*, *jihād*, *qānūn*, etc., or technical terms of the new sciences, and it is not until the *Lisān*, which incorporated whole specialist vocabularies, that one may rely on finding them listed and properly defined. As for the definitions themselves, they may be as short as a single synonym, or consist of a minor anthropological monograph if the word in question involves some particularly fascinating aspect of bedouin life. Sometimes a word is dismissed as "well-known" when it is frustratingly no longer so, and there is a great risk of circularity when rare words are defined in terms of their only known occurrence in the very line of verse quoted as evidence of their meaning! Levels of usage are not distinguished, though when a word is branded as "wrong", we may well be looking at a post-classical or colloquial form that has crept in. Foreign origins are sporadically mentioned, but only Ibn Durayd in his *Jamharah* shows any systematic interest in this topic, with chapters on words borrowed from Persian, Syriac, Greek and "Nabatean" (i.e. Aramaic).

The place of lexicography in Islamic culture as a whole has yet to be adequately studied. There are certain similarities in motivation, which might repay investigation, between Islam, as a kind of supranationalism, and the nationalism which is known to have stimulated the creation of European dictionaries. In both cases, the mere activity of collecting together the entire word-stock and defining it in terms of itself (intralingually) had the same effect: that of making language, and hence the power structure of which it is the source and medium (especially in "logocentric" Islam), independent of the outside world, since it was no longer necessary to refer to real objects to know the "meaning" of a word. It might even be supposed that Islam itself provided the cognitive basis for the semantics of Arabic. Moreover, the obvious effect of the dictionaries in both cases was to convert language from a process to a state, an archival inventory which could be used to define what was acceptable and to retard conceptual innovation. It is no criticism of Islam or the Arabs to say that their dictionaries were deliberate instruments of conservatism. That pre-Islamic Arabic should become the reference point of all exegesis was inevitable, and it is both natural and necessary that the products of pre-Islamic bedouin rhetoric should be zealously preserved and elaborated *in tandem with* (but *never* in competition with) the sublime and inimitable language of the Qurʾān. Secular eloquence parallels and potentiates the miracle of divine eloquence and each is indispensable to the other. One word symbolizes this fusion of language and religion: when pagan bedouin verses are adduced as linguistic evidence, they are called *shawāhid*, literally Islamic legal "witnesses".

Remembering that the transmission of knowledge, as far as possible without alteration, is not plagiarism, but a sacred duty of the Muslim scholar, we must admire the thoroughness with which the heritage of al-Khalīl, Ibn Durayd, al-Jawharī, al-Azharī and other pioneers was accumulated and passed on. But the obvious dependence of one dictionary upon another should not obscure the genuine originality of individual lexicographers, whose products will stand comparison with those of any other language or culture. Without them the allusiveness and detail of bedouin vocabulary would be lost to us. Although the rules of derivation often allow the meaning of a word to be inferred with complete accuracy if the root be known, not even a guess is possible with an unknown root: then we turn with gratitude to the dictionary to find, for example, that *baḥlasa* means "he arrived suddenly from another country without any luggage". Ignorance of the meaning of *baḥlasa* (surely the ancestor of all portmanteau words) is probably harmless, but it was always an article of faith that the well-being of Islam at large depended on a thorough knowledge of bedouin linguistic conventions. The dictionaries are thus more than mere repositories of information in a certain order: rather they are alphabetical lists of the ingredients of an entire civilization.

CHAPTER 8

ARABIC GRAMMAR

Having reached its peak of descriptive adequacy virtually at birth, Arabic grammar often seems little more than an endless discussion and restatement of the same immutable facts. This superficially stagnant aspect of Arabic grammar has provoked the no less superficial criticism that it is "a somewhat dismal science", while even the medieval Arabs complained that too much study of grammar could lead to madness. This brief historical outline will therefore emphasize the variety and flexibility of grammar as it responded to social pressures and the influence of other disciplines, in order to show that it is not the monolithic and fruitlessly abstract science it has sometimes been made to appear. For convenience, the terms *naḥw* and *naḥwī* are arbitrarily rendered "grammar" and "grammarian" throughout, but it cannot be stated too firmly that the equivalence is only partial, for neither *naḥw* nor "grammar" have remained stable in meaning over the centuries.

To keep the topic within bounds, two limitations are imposed: as far as possible only extant works are considered, and almost exclusively from the domain of syntax. The restriction to extant works ensures greater objectivity than is achieved by relying on the copious biographical literature, which provides abundant anecdotal material but seldom anything of technical value. Moreover, even the specialized grammatical biographies include many "grammarians" who have no real claim to the title – polymaths, amateur philologists, dilettanti and others who, in the absence of any surviving texts to judge them by, are no more than names. The restriction to syntax was determined by its strong links with two other disciplines similarly preoccupied with the control of human behaviour, namely law and philosophy. The aims and methods of all three frequently overlap, and to the extent that syntax is sometimes a special application of general principles of law or philosophy, it can be studied both for its own sake and as evidence of broader intellectual processes in Islam. But it is far from being the only field of Arab linguistic interest: there is a rich literature also in phonetics, morphology, lexicography, dialectology, semantics and rhetoric.

THE ORIGINS OF GRAMMAR

It has been suggested that Arabic grammar arose from the need to establish a definitive text of the Qurʾān, and to preserve the language as a whole from the corrupting influence of an ever-increasing number of non-Arabic-speaking Muslims. The biographies usually connect the birth of grammar with one Abū ʾl-Aswad al-Duʾalī (d. 69/688), an insignificant poet and sometime secretary to the Prophet's cousin ʿAlī (d. 40/661), but this and other legends must be treated with caution. What did occur towards the end of the first/early eighth century is that ambiguities[1] in Quranic spelling were removed by the introduction of certain orthographical devices, namely dots to distinguish otherwise identical consonantal shapes, diacritical marks to indicate short vowels, and various other signs marking long vowels, doubled consonants, etc. They did not all appear at once or uniformly (for a while vowels were indicated by coloured dots, later by the diacriticals now in use), but the whole operation is traditionally associated with the energetic and talented governor of Iraq, al-Ḥajjāj b. Yūsuf (*reg.* 75–95/694–714). The model for these orthographical improvements was the Syriac script (already familiar to the pre-Islamic Arabs, in whose time the first borrowings might well have been made); compare the technical term *iʿjām* (adding dots), which means literally, "making foreign".

Also to be taken into account is the possibility that Arabic grammar may owe something of its origins and methods to Greek, either directly or through Syriac intermediaries. All arguments for Greek influence are seriously weakened by the total lack of documentary evidence, while theories based on a *voie diffuse*, through which the Arabs may have acquainted themselves informally with Greek techniques, are by their nature inconclusive, however plausible they may appear. The opportunities were certainly there: the grammar of Dionysius Thrax, for instance, had already been translated into Syriac by the first/seventh century, and other relevant source material, logical as well as grammatical, was easily available. That something filtered through is not denied: it is probably no coincidence that "man", "horse" and "to strike" are standard examples in both Greek and Arabic grammar, and some terminological and hierarchical features of the earliest grammar may also have been inspired by Greek. But when elements with assumed Greek or Syriac provenance are compared directly with the fully developed grammar in the *Kitāb* of Sībawayhi, the former are seen to be either so marginal or so vague that it is difficult to imagine what contribution they could have made to the latter.

[1] See *CHALUP*, 242.

There must be a more compelling and substantial impetus for the emergence of true scientific grammar, that is, an exhaustive and coherent description of correct Arabic. Such a grammatical system is not an inevitable by-product of casual contact with other cultures, nor the natural outcome of fixing the Quranic text, which required only enough linguistic sensitivity to select from a pool of traditionally preserved variants on personal or doctrinal rather than grammatical grounds. Scientific grammar, moreover, cannot spring from mere purism, which is reactionary, authoritarian, intellectually barren and incapable of constructing any theoretical basis for its prescriptiveness. By contrast, a genuinely systematic grammar rationalizes a body of arbitrary rules of behaviour and validates them through the power of reason itself. The obvious parallel is jurisprudence, which does exactly the same thing, and it is here that the origins of Arabic grammar are to be sought. The early judges had found that they could no longer depend for their authority upon the memory of past practices or the persuasiveness of respected individuals, and had already begun to develop ways of supporting their judgements by argument early in the second/eighth century. When grammar eventually came into being, it was created by a simple transfer of the still-evolving methods of legal reasoning *en bloc* to the domain of speech acts. Paradoxically, grammar thereby achieved a systematic perfection which was not reached in law until a century later.

PRIMITIVE GRAMMAR

That grammatical speculation went on before Sībawayhi is obvious, but our only evidence for it is in the *Kitāb* itself. Sībawayhi often refers to earlier authorities, both by name and as an anonymous group whom he sometimes calls *naḥwiyyūn*. Although it is tempting to assume that this word simply means "grammarians", this is not necessarily so, and the name may be simply a natural and non-technical expression for "those concerned with the way people speak", formed from the only sense that the word *naḥw* had at this period. It was some time, probably not until late in the third/ninth century, before *naḥw* first acquired its technical meaning of "grammar", "syntax", as a back-formation from the word *naḥwiyyūn* and calque of *tekhnē grammatikē*. It is impossible to say with certainty what kind of linguistic activity was practised by the earliest *naḥwiyyūn*, though, since Sībawayhi invariably quotes them in order to refute them, we may conclude that they represent a stage in the evolution of grammar which the *Kitāb* was intended to supersede; their relatively crude reasoning is characterized by an over-rigid and unrealistic application of the principle of analogy, *qiyās*. Similar criticisms have been made of the methods of the early jurists, who would have been colleagues of *naḥwiyyūn* in the period when the Islamic sciences had not yet emerged as separate disciplines.

If we assume that the seven introductory chapters of the *Kitāb* (which circulated independently as a *risālah* or "epistle") containing Sībawayhi's preliminaries also embody most of the grammatical knowledge he inherited from his predecessors, we may form a tentative impression of pre-Sībawayhian grammar. Since, for example, he can hardly have invented it, an entire descriptive vocabulary must have been at Sībawayhi's disposal already (though the term *ḥāl* for "circumstantial qualifier" may be a neologism of Sībawayhi's own, judging by the confusion it caused his successor al-Mubarrad). Likewise, such hierarchical notions as the priority of nouns over verbs, masculine over feminine, singular over plural and indefinition over definition (the "unmarked" versus "marked" distinction in today's terminology), may be part of this inherited corpus. The awareness that nouns and verbs have a fundamentally different morphology (verbs being termed "heavier" than nouns, i.e. formally less flexible and varied) is certainly not Sībawayhi's own perception and could easily have come to him from his master al-Khalīl (d. 175/791).

The 608 references to al-Khalīl in the *Kitāb* are an acknowledgement of Sībawayhi's debt to him; in addition to an enormous mass of data, he also provided Sībawayhi with many important methodological principles. We can take it that Sībawayhi's knowledge of phonetics was gained largely from al-Khalīl, including recognition of the role of environment, ease of articulation and frequency in conditioning sound changes. In morphology, al-Khalīl, as a pioneer lexicographer, was a prolific source for Sībawayhi, and two fundamental principles of syntax can also be traced directly to him: first, the concept of speech as a social act in which linguistic form is partly determined by the listener's expectations, and, second, the criterion of substitutability, i.e. the treatment of compound elements as expansions of simple elements. It might seem from all this as if the *Kitāb* is little more than a record of al-Khalīl's teaching, but this is a false impression. Al-Khalīl was primarily a phonetician whose interest extended to lexicography and prosody, but did not take him as far as a general theory of language which it was Sībawayhi's personal achievement to construct. A sizeable body of al-Khalīl's phonetic terminology actually seems to have been discarded by Sībawayhi, presumably as irrelevant to his structural grammar, and it is surely significant that later writers, even quite close to al-Khalīl in time, identify him simply as "the prosodist" (*ṣāḥib al-ʿarūḍ*) without mentioning grammar.

THE CREATION OF GRAMMAR

It is permissible to speak of the "creation" of grammar because grammatical speculation before Sībawayhi was not coherent, exhaustive or authoritative. He was the first to undertake a complete description of Arabic at all three levels of syntax, morphology and phonology (note this order, which reveals his priorities) in the framework of a unified grammatical model based on the methods of legal reasoning. The result is embodied in a large work which never received a formal title and is known only as *Kitāb Sībawayhi* ("Sībawayhi's Book") or simply *al-Kitāb* ("The Book"). The authority of the *Kitāb* is such that it has been called "the Qurʾān of grammar" and set alongside works of Aristotle and Ptolemy as one of the three most important books ever written.

There are no sure facts to be elicited from the contradictory accounts of ʿAmr b. ʿUthmān Sībawayhi's life: we can only surmise that he died not later than 183/799 aged between thirty-two and "forty odd", having come to study in Basra from his native Shīrāz. What is interesting (because it is the kind of detail it benefits nobody to invent) is that he came to Basra to study traditions (*āthār*) and law. The story that he was driven to study grammar by his shame at mistakes made in a law class (a tale which is told in reverse about Servius Sulpicius, the Roman orator turned jurist) only confirms what is obvious in the *Kitāb*, namely, that Sībawayhi did in fact receive a legal education. The terminology and the methods of the *Kitāb* are identical with those of the law, and there is a liberal sprinkling of legal maxims and catch-phrases which leave no doubt of Sībawayhi's grounding in law.

Sībawayhi analyses Arabic as a form of social behaviour, treating language as a set of speech acts (*kalām*, "utterance", never *jumlah*, "sentence", cf. al-Mubarrad, below) occurring in a minimum context of a speaker (*mutakallim*) and a listener (*mukhāṭab*). These acts are regulated by criteria of correctness whose original ethico-legal sense (in law doubtless traceable to Aristotle's triad of the just, the lawful and the fair) had been assigned a precise linguistic value; thus *ḥasan*, "fair, good" = structurally correct, *qabīḥ*, "ugly, bad" = structurally incorrect, *mustaqīm*, "straight, right" = making sense, meaningful, and *muḥāl*, "wrong, perverted" = intrinsically meaningless. Normally only that which is both "good" and "right", i.e. formally and semantically correct, is *jāʾiz*, "permissible", though, as a good descriptive grammarian, Sībawayhi accepts formally incorrect utterances (in poetic licence) as long as they are comprehensible. The classification of speech elements into only three (!) categories (*ism*, "noun", *fiʿl*, "verb" and *ḥarf*, "particle") is disposed of in the first few lines of the *Kitāb* and half of the work is taken up with the functions of these elements, numbering more than seventy (the second half deals with morphology and phonology, a total of about 900 pages in the printed editions). Function is defined environmentally as the "place" (*mawḍiᶜ*) in which it is structurally correct (*ḥasan*) for an element to occur. Regardless of form-class, elements with the same function also have the same status (*manzilah*) and are therefore substitutable for one another; for example, the final *n* of *farasun*, "a horse", and the second noun in *farasu ᵓl-maliki*, "the horse of the king", both being regarded as functionally (i.e. distributionally) equivalent in closing off a noun phrase. In all this the determining principle is analogy, *qiyās*, exactly as in law, a methodology which Sībawayhi refined far beyond the simple fumblings of the *naḥwiyyūn* before him, to a degree which is only now becoming appreciated. Like members of human society, elements in an utterance affect their neighbours according to status and function, this effect being termed *ᶜamal*, "operation": thus every element is normally either an *ᶜāmil*, "operator", on another or is a *maᶜmūl fīh*, "operated upon", by another, the two usually combining to form a binary unit which may itself be part of a larger binary unit, and so on. This analysis is applied at every level, from complex sentences down to individual phonemes, and it is this unified treatment of Arabic, coupled with a truly astonishing comprehensiveness, which gives the *Kitāb* its undisputed authority. Even though Sībawayhi himself established no circle of disciples to speak of, evidently because he died before he could achieve the necessary eminence and reputation, the *Kitāb* became and remained the inspiration for all subsequent developments in grammar.

THE EMERGENCE OF PEDAGOGIGAL GRAMMAR

Under the patronage of the ᶜAbbasid caliphs Arabic grammar soon acquired a pedagogical character it was never to shake off. Classical Arabic having ceased to be a mother tongue (if it ever had been), the sons of Hārūn al-Rashīd (reigned 170–193/786–809), for example, could not learn it in the cradle and had instead to be taught by royal tutors such as al-Kisāᵓī and Abū Muḥammad al-Yazīdī. Al-Yazīdī (d. 202/817) was a member of a minor dynasty of grammarians and poets who served the ᶜAbbasid court for several generations, though none of their grammatical works is extant. Al-Kisāᵓī (d. 189/805) is a much more substantial figure, one of the seven "Readers" whose version of the Quranic text was accepted as authoritative, and generally acknowledged as the leading grammarian of his era until supplanted by his pupil Abū Zakariyyāᵓ Yaḥyā b. Ziyād al-Farrāᵓ (d. 207/822). However, to judge by his one surviving work, a small anthology of common formal errors, and by the many quotations in al-Farrāʾ, it seems that al-Kisāʾī was more of a professional pedant than a systematic grammarian of the calibre of Sībawayhi, standing closer to the primitive *naḥwiyyūn* in his achievement. Nevertheless Ibn al-Muʿtazz (d. 296/908), whose opinion we must respect, declares al-Kisāʾī the equal in grammar of al-Khalīl in prosody.

Already by the time of al-Farrāʾ, the emergent pedagogical trend is unmistakable. Al-Farrāʾ himself talks of "the novice in instruction" and subsequent grammarians are even more explicit. Al-Akhfash al-Awsaṭ (d. *c.* 215–21/830–6), a pupil of no less than Sībawayhi, observes that verses of poetry were sometimes made up with deliberate mistakes in them to trap the unwary student, and the same al-Akhfash is also quoted in connection with a whole set of syntactical tests which became a regular feature of later grammars. And we know from Ibn Saḥnūn (d. 256/870) that by his time there was a fully fledged curriculum for grammar and other subjects, complete with textbooks. Competitiveness among the new professionals in search of patronage and prestige is especially obvious in the many grammatical debates recorded in the literature of literary gatherings.

Al-Farrāʾ, like his master al-Kisāʾī, came originally from Kufa and held an official position at the ʿAbbasid court. He was one of the first to maintain that the language of the Qurʾān is grammatically perfect Arabic, an assertion which conforms gratifyingly with the political pretensions of his employers and also reflects the growing identification of grammar with the institution of Islam. Certainly al-Farrāʾ was an expert in this field: his *Maʿānī al-Qurʾān*, an important source for Muḥammad b. Jarīr al-Ṭabarī, is a grammatical commentary on the Qurʾān which reveals a scholarly capacity as profound as that of Sībawayhi, if not quite so developed. In view of al-Farrāʾ's role as the "Kufan" antagonist of the "Basran" Sībawayhi (see below), it is essential to point out that *Maʿānī al-Qurʾān* shares exactly the same methodology and criteria as the *Kitāb*, of which, incidentally, al-Farrāʾ is said to have possessed a copy. Although the terminology of *Maʿānī al-Qurʾān* differs in places from that of Sībawayhi, this is by no means evidence of the fundamental difference of approach traditionally attributed to the Kufan grammarians. A charge of "philosophizing" against al-Farrāʾ is difficult to prove from his extant works; the lost *Kitāb al-Ḥudūd* ascribed to him might confirm the accusation if the title means "Book of (Logical) Definitions", but *ḥudūd* can equally well mean "(grammatical) rules", retaining the quasi-legal sense it already had for Sībawayhi. On the other hand, al-Farrāʾ does show in *Maʿānī al-Qurʾān* an awareness of some issues in the rationalist theology of the time, and certainly he could not have had a more sympathetic patron in this regard than the enthusiastic philhellene al-Maᵓmūn.

Between the death of al-Farrāᵓ in 207/822 and the arrival in Baghdad of al-Mubarrad in 247/861, there must have been considerable progress in grammatical science, although there is little direct evidence, since most of al-Mubarrad's teachers were eclipsed by him, and their works, if any, do not survive. An exception is Abū ᶜUthmān Bakr b. Muḥammad al-Māzinī (d. 249/863), whose *Kitāb al-Taṣrīf* has been preserved with a commentary by Ibn Jinnī. But this "Book of Conjugation" is a morphological treatise, and although al-Māzinī is quoted often enough by others for us to deduce that he was a competent and respected grammarian (the greatest since Sībawayhi, according to Ibn Jinnī), we cannot add any substance to his reputation. His grammatical output has been described as modest, and his pre-eminence in morphology probably reflects a hardening separation of *naḥw*, "grammar in general", into *naḥw*, "syntax in particular", and *ṣarf*, "morphology", as professional scholars became increasingly specialized.

Al-Māzinī's pupil Abū ᵓl-ᶜAbbās Muḥammad b. Yazīd al-Mubarrad (d. 285/898) is without doubt the most significant grammarian of the third/ninth century. He is best known as the author of *al-Kāmil*, a thesaurus of traditional Arab rhetoric with an erudite literary, historical and linguistic commentary, but his accomplishment as a grammarian is most conspicuous in his *al-Muqtaḍab*. This is a large-scale revision and paraphrase of Sībawayhi's *Kitāb*, differing from the latter, however, in displaying an unprecedented degree of self-conscious pedagogy and authoritarianism. Whole chapters are given over to exercises and tests; the essential terms, *ḥasan*, *qabīḥ*, *mustaqīm* and *muḥāl*, which validated Sībawayhi's descriptions of normal Arabic, have been largely abandoned in favour of the peremptory *yajūz*, "it is allowed", and *lā yajūz*, "it is not allowed", and a number of new technical terms make their appearance, perhaps for the first time. Of these, *jumlah*, "sentence", *fāᵓidah*, "information", and the statement that a predicate (*khabar*) is that which can be said to be true or false, must be direct borrowings from logic, and are all the more striking because of their total absence in Sībawayhi. The tendency towards abstraction is obvious: categories which Sībawayhi had left vague have acquired names, for example, *tamyīz*, "specifying element", *afᶜāl al-muqārabah*, "verbs of appropinquation" (in Wright's aptly pedantic rendering), and terms such as *ismiyyah*, "nominality", begin to appear. Characteristic of the change of emphasis are an increasing concern with *ᶜillah*, abstract grammatical "cause" at the expense of *ᶜamal*, concrete grammatical "operation", and the ever-growing importance of *taqdīr*, the paraphrasing of unexpressed forms or meanings, a term hardly ever used by Sībawayhi and then only in phonology. This twofold development, pedagogical and philosophical, which altered the nature of grammar during the third/ninth century, stands out clearly in the *Muqtaḍab*, and here, if anywhere, the informal penetration of Greek ideas into grammar can be strongly suspected.

BASRANS AND KUFANS

Soon after the foundation of Baghdad in 145/762, the cities of Basra and Kufa were thrust into the background by the cultural prestige of the new imperial capital. In the resulting competition between grammarians at the Baghdad court, two rival "schools" evolved, labelled "Basran" and "Kufan". At first the antipathy was purely personal: in its earliest phase, for example, al-Yazīdī merely declaimed abusive poetry against his rival al-Kisāʾī even though both were born in Kufa, but under the malevolent prompting of al-Mubarrad and his arch-enemy Thaʿlab (d. 291/904), the hostility quickly developed into an irreconcilable methodological polarization. As the animosity between the two factions intensified, their origins were artificially projected back to the grammarians of the second/eighth century, principally Sībawayhi in Basra and al-Farrāʾ in Kufa, between whom there certainly were superficial terminological differences, though no conscious or systematic opposition existed at that time. This only surfaced posthumously, as is proved by the complaint of one of al-Farrāʾ's pupils that words he could not recognize were being put into his late master's mouth. From then on the two schools generated a large quantity of polemical literature, often in the form of grammatical disputes, one collection of which is attributed to Thaʿlab himself.

The substantive differences between the Basrans and Kufans are impossible to state precisely, since allegiance to the distinctive doctrines of either is hopelessly inconsistent. Some grammarians, such as Ibn Kaysān (d. 299/912) are even credited with belonging to both, and later a so-called "Baghdad" or "mixed" school is said to have evolved, though this, too, seems largely a figment of the historical imagination. The two "schools" may best be interpreted simply as the embodiment of two opposing attitudes to language, the Basrans representing the ideal of reducing Arabic to the least number of rules, while the Kufans were prepared to admit any number of anomalies into their system. The antithesis arose naturally as a reaction to the establishment of an "orthodox" grammar (the Basran one), and exactly parallels what happened in law, where four schools emerged to accommodate various levels of strictness and tolerance (from Ḥanbalī to Ḥanafī, it might crudely be said). In this process al-Mubarrad, who converted Sībawayhi's wholly descriptive, and therefore pedagogically useless *Kitāb* into a prescriptive, Basran grammar, played a role similar to that of al-Shāfiʿī in law before him, by perfecting a system which served the normative purposes now self-consciously striven after by the Islamic community. It is a coincidence that the new "orthodox" grammar is named after Basra (Sībawayhi only studied there because it was nearest to his birthplace), and it is inevitable that Kufa, as the traditional cultural rival of Basra, would become the focus of dissenting opinion. With their insistence on the right to generalize from isolated data, the Kufans were ultimately rejecting the Basran presumption of total systematic regularity, though when pedantry is measured against pedantry in their debates, the pot often calls the kettle black. In practical terms the conflict was in any case largely fictitious, and may be seen either as an important demonstration of the indestructability of nonconformism and need for slippage in any human organization, or else as a petty power struggle, rather like the big-endians and little-endians in *Gulliver's Travels*.

THE PERFECTION OF METHOD

The professionalism of the third/ninth century brought with it a questioning of the basic assumptions of grammar and, continuing on into the fourth/tenth century, a conscious striving to assert the place of grammar among the newly independent sciences. The stakes were high indeed: now that Islam had grown into an institution based on a huge volume of records of its own past (the Traditions of the Prophet having achieved canonical status equivalent to the Qurʾān itself by this time), the right to interpret this past, or rather the verbal construct it had become, brought with it great power and influence. A common accusation of this period is *ṭalab al-riʾāsah* (the pursuit of leadership), and there is no doubt that this was a dominant consideration in the rivalries between grammarians, philosophers, lawyers and theologians. External influences are very noticeable during this phase as grammarians, on the one hand, eagerly assimilate new ideas and, on the other hand, vigorously defend themselves against outsiders, especially logicians, who meddled in grammar. Logicians, with their claim to superior expertise in linguistic analysis, were a particular threat to the grammarians, and several clashes between the two are recorded in detail. Generally the winner depends on who is telling the story: the Christian logician Abū Bishr Mattā b. Yūnus (d. 329/940) is easily defeated by the grammarian al-Ḥasan al-Sīrāfī (d. 368/979) in a face-to-face confrontation before the vizier Ibn al-Furāt in 320/932, but the Christian philosopher Abū Zakariyyāʾ Yaḥyā b. ʿAdī (d. 364/975) makes a much better showing when he conducts the argument in a literary form, where he can confidently assert with seeming impartiality that grammar is confined to the study of linguistic forms, while meaning is the logician's preserve entirely.

By the fourth/tenth century the penetration of logical concepts into grammar is unmistakable, though still limited, or better, controlled by the needs of the grammarians. A good example is the very influential figure of Ibn al-Sarrāj (d. 316/928), who was both a pupil of al-Mubarrad and friend of the great philosopher Abū Naṣr Muḥammad b. Muḥammad al-Fārābī, and thus stands as a bridge between the native tradition of grammar and the foreign science of logic. General influence from recently translated Greek texts is visible in the ubiquitous use of dichotomous classification (*taqsīm*) in Ibn al-Sarrāj's *al-Uṣūl fī ʾl-naḥw*, which gives the impression of being more "organized" (in the manner of the *Organon*) than earlier works such as the *Muqtaḍab* of al-Mubarrad, whose principle of internal arrangement, if any, is not transparent. Ibn al-Sarrāj also incorporates the Aristotelian definitions of the parts of speech into his own preamble, but eclectically and without in any way allowing them to dominate the presentation, suggesting very strongly that Ibn al-Sarrāj took only what he regarded as relevant to his purpose without being unduly influenced by it. The *Uṣūl* is probably the first work to state the facts of Arabic grammar in this new framework and to undertake a systematic statement of the *reasons* for grammatical rules (which is what *uṣūl* in the book's title means), proceeding from the assumption that the bedouin language had a rationale, a *ḥikmah* (not at this stage to be equated automatically with "pure reason" as was done by later grammarians; see al-Rummānī, below).

Indeed grammarians always refused to concede that language was simply verbalized logic, and one of Ibn al-Sarrāj's greatest pupils, al-Zajjājī (d. 337/949) makes it quite clear that the purposes of grammar and philosophy were quite unrelated. It is al-Zajjājī (incidently the earliest grammarian to make explicit reference to the Greek philosophers) who claims to have been the first to examine systematically the basic presuppositions of grammar. In his *Īḍāḥ* (virtually a commentary on the introductory chapters of Sībawayhi's *Kitāb*) he asks, for example, how it is known that there are exactly three parts of speech, what are their definitions, what is grammatical causality, how did inflection originate, why is grammar necessary at all when people speak quite naturally without inflection (!), why is inflection not distributed evenly over all word-classes, and so on. It is most instructive to compare this approach with that of al-Zajjājī's exact contemporary Abū Naṣr Muḥammad b. Muḥammad al-Fārābī (we do not know whether they ever met): for al-Zajjājī logic was available as a tool of analysis and servant of grammar, grammar in turn being a servant of theology; while for al-Fārābī logic was supreme and language not only subordinate but merely a local manifestation of universal logical principles, an attitude totally abhorrent to the Muslim grammarian, committed as he was to the uniqueness and specificity of the Arabic revelation. For al-Fārābī, in contrast, truth was not revealed in any one language but was accessible through logic alone, and language merely had to be formally correct in deriving the truth by logical means and expressing it.

An extreme manifestation of the philosophical approach to language is seen in al-Rummānī (d. 384/994), a member of a small group of Muᶜtazilite grammarians who flourished in this period but about whom little is as yet known. Al-Rummānī himself left enough material for us to infer that he favoured a wholesale application of logical methods to grammar in the sincere belief that language itself was ultimately logical. This affected both the form and the content of his works: a large commentary on Sībawayhi's *Kitāb*, for example, is probably unique in grammatical writings in the way it presents first the general purpose of each chapter, then all the problems raised by the chapter (listed as *masāʾil*, i.e. *quaestiones*, in the pure scholastic manner), and finally a discussion of each question in turn. It is clear from the text of this work that al-Rummānī was consciously striving to synthesize the structuralism of Sībawayhi with contemporary logic, an impression which is reinforced in other works by al-Rummānī such as his *Kitāb al-Ḥudūd*, where we can be quite certain that the title means "Book of Logical Definitions", unlike the same title in al-Farrāʾ. The *Ḥudūd* actually prefers logical terms over the well-established grammatical terminology in such cases as *mawḍūᶜ* and *maḥmūl* for "subject" and "predicate" (in grammar *mubtadaʾ* and *khabar*); *salb* for "negation" (in grammar always *nafy*), gives *iḍāfah* its logical meaning of "relationship" as well as its grammatical sense of "annexation", and employs exclusively the Aristotelian definitions of the parts of speech, to mention only the most obvious examples. As if to leave us in no doubt of his Muᶜtazilite sympathies, al-Rummānī does not miss the chance to use that veritable shibboleth, the phrase *al-manzilah bayn al-manzilatayn*, to describe the structural ambiguity of elements which may be either predicates or adverbial phrases, for example, *huwa minnī yawmāni/yawmayni*, "he is *two days* away from me". Small wonder that his master Abū ᶜAlī al-Ḥasan b. Aḥmad al-Fārisī (d. 377/987; both were apparently pupils of Ibn al-Sarrāj at one time) is said to have disowned him for confounding logic and grammar.

The law, too, played an important role in shaping an "orthodox" grammar. Its original contribution to Sībawayhi's basic method was now reinforced by an open exchange of ideas and technicalities between adepts of both disciplines: the lawyers, for example, found grammar indispensable in handling the language of contracts and agreements (witness the emergence of *ḥiyal* (sing. *ḥīlah*) literature, with its use of linguistic ambiguities, *maᶜārīḍ al-kalām* "the vagaries of speech", to evade legal responsibilities), while the grammarians, recognizing that their aims of controlling language were essentially identical with those of the lawyers in controlling behaviour, gave their grammars an increasingly legalistic flavour. Not surprisingly, many grammarians were also practising judges.

This common preoccupation of grammar and law is explicit from the third/ninth century onwards: from Thaᶜlab's observation that "language is determined by the *sunnah*, not the *sunnah* by language",[2] we may deduce that grammar was beginning to be aware of its place in the Islamic scheme. Al-Zajjājī notes in his *Kitāb al-Lāmāt* that certain words have acquired under Islam a meaning and status they did not have before, for example, *muʾmin*, formerly "believer in anything", then "believer in Islam". He calls these terms *ṣifāt sharᶜiyyah* "legal epithets" (cf. the English expression "term of art"). One grammarian of markedly juridical tone is Ibn Fāris, whose *Kitāb al-Ṣāḥibī* is actually subtitled (the first to be so, according to the editor) *Fī Fiqh al-lughah wa-sunan al-ᶜarab fī kalāmihā* ("On the Law of Language and the Traditional Speech Habits of the Bedouin Arabs"). It is indeed a manual for lawyers: Ibn Fāris cannot conceal his dismay at their ignorance of grammar, and he offers them in the *Ṣāḥibī* a highly original survey of Arabic, its history, virtues and peculiarities, its main syntactical features, an alphabetical list of important words and their various meanings, and some guidance on Quranic, poetic and bedouin rhetoric, all with the aim of rectifying the linguistic incompetence of the jurists.

For two centuries at least grammar has a somewhat experimental appearance. During this time grammar took from logic the criteria of truth and falsehood in defining sentences, the classification of sentence types according to meaning, the arrangement of elements in hierarchies (a latent but unexploited feature of Sībawayhi's system) and an increasing number of abstract terms. There were further borrowings from law (e.g. the concept of *istiḥsān*, defined as "a rational method for the determination of decisions when conflicting principles compete for consideration"), and the tendency to adduce sayings of the Prophet (*Ḥadīth*) imposing correct Arabic as a religious obligation is a clear symptom of the gradual integration of grammar with the *sunnah*, the orthodox way of life.

The most brilliant representative of this grammatical syncretism is Ibn Jinnī (d. 392/1002). Outstanding among his surviving works is *Khaṣāʾiṣ al-ᶜarabiyyah*, a wide-ranging investigation of all aspects of Arabic covering

[2] *Majālis Thaᶜlab*, ed. A. S. M. Hārūn, Cairo, 1960, 179.

much the same ground as the *Ṣāḥibī* of his exact contemporary Ibn Fāris (they seem inexplicably unaware of each other), but in far greater depth and detail. The *Khaṣāʾiṣ*, in which Ibn Jinnī freely acknowledges an enormous debt to his master al-Fārisī, scintillates with provocative and stimulating notions, and the character of the book cannot be conveyed adequately in a few lines. It may best be described as a search for a uniform organizing principle of Arabic at all levels from phonology to syntax, from a semantic and psychological standpoint. A few examples must suffice: one chapter is entitled, "Occasions when you have to use the form you do but it is not the one you think it is", i.e. in *fī amsi* "yesterday", where the ending of *amsi* looks like the required case ending after a preposition, but cannot be so because the word *amsi* is invariable and uninflected. The *Khaṣāʾiṣ* abounds in such subtleties: another chapter reveals how a complete sentence can become incomplete by adding something to it, an apparent contradiction which arises when *anna*, "that", is prefixed to a sentence and converts it into a subordinate clause. A remark of one of Ibn Jinnī's teachers that he did not like talking to people in the dark is quoted in support of the perceptive assertion that full communication occurs only face to face. There is a running battle between Ibn Jinnī and the scholastic theologians, even though he does not scruple to apply logical analysis to language, and on one occasion goes so far as to use the famous phrase *al-manzilah bayn al-manzilatayn* (cf. al-Rummānī, above).

Prominent in Ibn Jinnī's period is the emergence of the first purely pedagogical grammars for beginners, of which half a dozen good specimens have been published. Ibn al-Sarrāj's *Mūjaz* (the title, "The Epitome", is significant) is one of the earliest, and others are by Ibn Kaysān and Lughdah al-Iṣfahānī (d. 312/924). The *Īḍāḥ* of al-Fārisī, the *Jumal* of al-Zajjājī and the *Lumaʿ* of Ibn Jinnī should also be mentioned. All these works follow the same pattern, of being simplified presentations of the entire field of language, syntax, morphology and phonology (still following the order laid down in the *Kitāb* of Sībawayhi). As one might expect, it is during this phase that grammar becomes self-conscious: there are critical backward glances at the inadequacies of earlier grammarians (even Sībawayhi is branded as archaic and obscure), and for the first time we find definitions of grammar under the influence of the recently translated *Isagoge*, for example, in the *Uṣūl* of Ibn al-Sarrāj, and in a more expanded form in the *Īḍāḥ* of al-Fārisī: "grammar is the science of analogical patterns (*maqāyīs*) derived inductively from the speech of the bedouin Arabs."[3] The separate existence of grammar (it had been called a science already by al-Jāḥiẓ in the

[3] *Īḍāḥ*, MS Brit. Mus. Or. 58, fol. 3r.

third/ninth century) is reinforced by the Greek-based classification of sciences in circulation at this time, and it is no surprise to find Qudāmah b. Jaᶜfar (d. 326/938) referring to "the two arts of grammar and logic" (*ṣināᶜatay al-naḥw wa-ʾl-manṭiq*)[4] as if they were now fully fledged disciplines. However, there are still changes ahead before grammar can be regarded as having reached its formal perfection.

THE SEARCH FOR FORM

Although it has been remarked that the grammarians of the fifth/eleventh century give the impression of having "run out of breath", the scholars of this period deserve credit for ingenuity in two areas at least. One of these is commentary. Although formal commentaries (i.e. more than haphazard marginal annotations) began to be written on the major works as early as the third/ninth century (none survive from this date, however, except a small treatise on rare word patterns in Sībawayhi by Abū Ḥātim Sahl b. Muḥammad al-Sijistānī, d. 255/869), it is obvious that full-scale commentary, supercommentary, gloss and supergloss could not flourish until there were enough basic texts (*mutūn*, lit. "backbones") to support such an activity. The short pedagogical grammars which appeared in the fourth/tenth century were just what was needed, and nearly all those mentioned above had acquired commentaries by the fifth/eleventh century. Eventually it became a regular practice for grammarians to provide commentaries themselves on their own original works.

The other contribution of the fifth/eleventh-century grammarians is more substantial and perhaps not sufficiently appreciated, namely, the reduction of the material to an ordered corpus of essential facts suitable for the curriculum of the newly established *madrasah* or "institute of higher learning". An outstanding example is the *Muqaddimah* of Ibn Bābashādh (d. 469/1077), himself the author of a commentary on al-Zajjājī's *Jumal* and not too insignificant a figure to be quoted by later grammarians.[5] His *Muqaddimah* ("Introduction", a direct calque of *Isagoge*, and a favourite title for elementary works since the early fourth/tenth century) is a radical rearrangement of the grammatical syllabus, evidently on his own initiative. It begins with the now obligatory definition of grammar, with the interesting distinction between a "higher" purpose, i.e. the understanding of God's revelation, and a "lower", i.e. correct speech. The subject-matter is arbitrarily distributed into ten chapters: three for the parts of speech, four for the case and mood inflections and one each for the operations of parts of

[4] *Naqd al-shiᶜr*, ed. S. A. Bonebakker, Leiden, 1956, 95.
[5] For the strange story of the later part of his career, see below, ch. 11, 182.

speech upon each other, concord and orthography. This presentation is completely divorced from any natural linguistic relationships between topics and is entirely dictated by pedagogical convenience; significantly, it supplied a model for later grammarians who chose to write in what they called "the Bābashādhī style". A feature of the *Muqaddimah*, which eventually became an obsession, is the permutation of forms, for example, multiplying the five classes of pronouns by the twelve categories of person to calculate that Arabic has a total of sixty pronouns. It would be valuable to know whether any grammarian before Ibn Bābashādh made use of this device, which has obvious advantages for the pedagogue.

An extreme, and possibly for that reason most durable example of the new methodology is the *Miʾat ʿāmil* of the great semanticist and rhetorician al-Jurjānī (d. 471/1078). As its name implies, "The Hundred Operators" simply reduces the entire language to exactly 100 grammatical categories, making it ideal for rote learning in the schools. Now that the facts of Arabic were no longer in dispute, only their organization could vary, and the *Miʾat ʿāmil* reveals just what a paring down of the material could be achieved by a rigorous application of dichotomous classification (*taqsīm*) and a bold pedagogical instinct for simplification.

THE GREAT MASTERS

All the tendencies outlined above converged in the sixth/twelfth century to produce the most renowned and influential grammars. These are the works which have come to be regarded as typical of the whole discipline, with occasionally disastrous results for our understanding of the early grammarians. The four greatest figures of this period are al-Zamakhsharī, Ibn al-Ḥājib, Ibn Mālik and Ibn Hishām. All of them wrote a variety of works which show a clear stratification into levels of difficulty (from the juvenile to the adult), and they would sometimes produce elementary and advanced versions of the same text. Likewise a sharp separation is now discernible between the various purposes of each work, whether pedagogical, theoretical or polemical.

Abū ʾl-Qāsim Maḥmūd b. ʿUmar al-Zamakhsharī is an author whose writings have found particular favour in East and West alike, possibly (in the latter case at least) because his arrangement of material is sympathetic to western notions of orderliness. A polymath with Muʿtazilite leanings, he was nevertheless a loyal Arabophone in spite of his Khwarazmian provenance, and scorns the Persophile partisans of the Shuʿūbiyyah in the preface to his justly famous *Mufaṣṣal*. In it he disposes the material under four headings: nouns, verbs, particles and the phonological processes common to all three. The morphology of verbs is included in their respective chapters, so that the *Mufaṣṣal* comprises all the essential contents of Sībawayhi's *Kitāb*. As the name of the work implies, the topics are subdivided into *fuṣūl* (sections), which al-Zamakhsharī has chosen with such care and linked so well that they provide a natural framework for what is probably the most massive Arabic grammar of all time: M. S. Howell's *Grammar of the Classical Arabic Language*, which runs to well over 5,000 pages. Testimony to the importance of the *Mufaṣṣal* is the number of commentaries it generated, among which that of Ibn Yaʿīsh (d. 643/1245) is the best known.

As was the fashion, al-Zamakhsharī wrote his own commentary on the *Mufaṣṣal*, as well as a starkly abridged version, presumably for children. This latter, bearing with perhaps deliberate irony a Persian word for its title, *al-Unmūdhaj* ("The Model"), gives only the bare facts unadorned by analysis and omits altogether the fourth section on the common phonological processes. About al-Zamakhsharī's grammatical opinions there is not much to say: this was not an era for innovation or renewed speculation about matters already resolved by centuries of debate. While he does give space to "Kufan" views (see above), he is clearly a "Basran" by allegiance. That he was a dyed-in-the-wool Muʿtazilite is obvious from his assertion that *lan*, "not", denotes perpetual negation (*taʾbīd*, but easily converted into the innocent *taʾyīd*, "reinforcement"), as in Qurʾān, vii.143, *lan tarānī*, "you [Moses] will not see me", interpreted as denying the beatific vision. But this is easily refuted by comparing it with the occurrence of *lan* elsewhere in the Qurʾān and, needless to say, the "Zamakhsharian *lan*" never found acceptance among the orthodox.

The next outstanding master grammarian, Ibn al-Ḥājib (d. 646/1249, active in Damascus though born and educated in Egypt) was wholly dedicated to philology, unlike most of his colleagues who usually had other livelihoods. One of his numerous works, *al-Kāfiyah* ("The Adequate"), a concise elementary syntax (morphology is dealt with in a sister work entitled *al-Shāfiyah*, "The Satisfier"), became more popular than any other of its kind except the *Ājurrūmiyyah* of Ibn Ājurrūm (d. 723/1323). The latter was a teacher in Fez, and his little book was so widely used that in Egypt *agrumiya* has come to mean "grammar" itself, and there are literally hundreds of commentaries and glosses on it. It must be admitted that the *Ājurrūmiyyah*, which was aimed at infants, has been treated with far more reverence and attention than it is worth by western scholars! The *Kāfiyah*, though in itself entirely unoriginal (being in fact simply an abridgement of al-Zamakhsharī's *Mufaṣṣal*), succeeds in reducing Arabic to a set of short and reliable definitions which can at the same time serve as the basis for more advanced and detailed discussion. Ibn al-Ḥājib thus displays a fine pedagogical instinct for the style and presentation most appropriate for his students. This is an achievement in its own right, and the huge nexus of commentary and supercommentary which developed out of the *Kāfiyah* confirms that Ibn al-Ḥājib fully deserves his place among the great masters. Notable among the commentaries is that of al-Astarābādhī (d. 686/1288), *Sharḥ Kāfiyat Ibn al-Ḥājib*, a profound but neglected work by an author about whom almost nothing is known. His commentary still needs to be studied in depth: at this stage all that can be said about it is that it is heavily oriented towards semantics with a strong logical underpinning, somewhat akin to al-Rummānī's highly structured system. Like all such commentaries by this time, the form of al-Astarābādhī's work is a typical product of elaborate and fully developed scholasticism: in the text, exactly as in the *madrasah*, each statement of the master was scrutinized, tested, expanded, dissected, objected to, refuted and counter-refuted to the limits of the participants' capacity. The limits of al-Astarābādhī have yet to be ascertained.

Ibn al-Ḥājib's place as the leading grammarian of the age was soon taken by Jamāl al-Dīn Muḥammad b. Mālik (d. 672/1274), an Andalusian by birth who travelled East to study under Ibn Yaᶜīsh in Aleppo and eventually settled in Damascus. Like Ibn al-Ḥājib, his greatness lies not in scientific innovation but in pedagogical technique. Ibn Mālik's peculiar talent (perhaps obsession would be a better word) was for versification, and several thousand doggerel verses on most aspects of grammar are the monument of this tireless pedagogical poetaster. Even here, however, he was not original: versified grammars in Arabic date back at least to the fourth/tenth century (if we exclude a grammatical verse attributed to al-Khalīl in the *Muqaddimah* spuriously ascribed to Khalaf al-Aḥmar, d. *c.* 180/796), and Ibn Mālik's most famous poem, *al-Khulāṣah fī ʾl-naḥw* ("The Epitome on Grammar"), known as the *Alfiyyah* ("The 1,000-Liner") for short, itself seems to have been inspired by the urge to outdo Yaḥyā b. ᶜAbd al-Muᶜṭī (d. 628/1231), composer of a similar 1,000-line grammatical poem which was entirely overshadowed by the enormous success of Ibn Mālik's creation. We should here mention in passing the grammatical poem *Mulḥat al-iᶜrāb* by the famous al-Ḥarīrī (d. 516/1122, better known for his emulation of al-Hamadhānī's *Maqāmāt*), reputedly one of the few Arabic poems in the couplets of the *mathnawī* metre so popular in Persia.

Ibn Mālik's *Alfiyyah* is a fairly advanced textbook embracing consecutively syntax, morphology and phonology, thus recombining the topics which had been separated in Ibn al-Ḥājib's *Kāfiyah* and *Shāfiyah*. The arrangement is into convenient stanza-like units of about forty lines for ease of memorization. Here are two typical verses comparing the modal verbs *kāda* (almost) and ᶜ*asā* (maybe) with the syntax of *kāna* (to be), translated to show the verve, lucidity and elegance of Ibn Mālik's original:[6]

> Like *kāna* are *kāda* and ᶜ*asā*; however with both of the latter
> A predicate not in imperfect tense is a most unusual matter.
> Though predicates after ᶜ*asā* without *an* are exceedingly scarce,
> The situation with *kāda* is actually quite the reverse.

A far more challenging work than the *Alfiyyah* is Ibn Mālik's whimsically titled *Tashīl al-fawāʾid* ("Simplification of the Facts"), a prose text in which he displays the highest degree of abstraction, leaving no doubt that he was an extremely accomplished grammarian as well as a facile versifier. The *Tashīl* is a difficult work, uncompromisingly terse and so far removed from the everyday use of language that only the technical terms are felt to be real – the metalanguage has now become the topic as well as the medium of discussion.

Surprisingly at this late stage the grammatical system was still capable of minor improvements, and several of these are associated with Ibn Mālik. He is said to have coined the term *al-nāʾib* ᶜ*an al-fā*ᶜ*il*, "the substitute agent", for the agent of the passive verb, hitherto expressed only periphrastically, and the nomenclature of exceptive sentences, somewhat inconsistent before Ibn Mālik, may have been stabilized by him. The acceptance of the *Ḥadīth* as linguistic evidence on equal footing with the Qurʾān is said to be another of Ibn Mālik's innovations, though in fact they are commonly cited by grammarians as far back as Sībawayhi himself.[7]

The fourth great master, Jamāl al-Dīn ᶜAbdullāh b. Yūsuf b. Hishām (d. 761/1360) enjoys the reputation of being an even better grammarian than Sībawayhi, which amounts to saying that Ibn Hishām's practical grammar was felt to be more applicable to the needs of Islam than Sībawayhi's pedagogically unusable *Kitāb*. He was indeed an effective compiler of instructional manuals which are clear, precise and interesting, such as his *Qaṭr al-nadā* ("The Dewdrop": intermediate level) and *al-I*ᶜ*rāb* ᶜ*an al-i*ᶜ*rāb* ("Expressing Desinential Inflection": juvenile). In his *Mughnī al-labīb* ("All the Intelligent Man Needs"), he attempts something new and valuable, namely an alphabetical list of the most important words in Arabic (mainly particles) with an analysis of their semantics, which would repay a deeper study.

These four are far from being the only prominent grammarians of this

[6] Ibn Mālik, *Alfiyyah*, vv. 165–6.

[7] For other works by Ibn Mālik, see below, ch. 29, 501.

period, but space permits only a brief mention of some of the lesser lights. Ibn al-Anbārī (d. 577/1181) deserves attention for his particular interest in the historical and theoretical aspects of his profession. His *Nuzhat al-alibbā*ʾ contains biographies of the grammarians from the beginnings to his own day, and in *al-Inṣāf fī masāʾil al-khilāf* he conscientiously reports in detail the grammatical disputes between the Basrans and Kufans. His *Asrār al-ʿarabiyyah* is an exposition of the reasons for grammatical phenomena presented dialectically, while *Lumaʿ al-adillah* analyses from a strictly legal perspective the nature of linguistic evidence, its transmission, the rules of inference and grammatical causality, claiming to be the first to deal with these topics in such a way. The philosophical investigation of grammatical causality had after several centuries reached a predictably high level of abstraction (already in the time of Ibn al-Sarrāj the notion of the "cause of the cause", *ʿillat al-ʿillah*, was in circulation), and the seeming artificiality of the exercise moved the Andalusian Ibn Maḍāʾ (d. 592/1196) to attack the futility of his colleagues' excessive subtlety in his *Radd ʿalā al-nuḥāt*. True to his Ẓāhirī principles, Ibn Maḍāʾ admonishes the grammarians for turning away from the simple formalities of language towards theoretical secondary or even tertiary levels of causality which are of no help to the ordinary speaker.

In the search for pedagogical concision, sundry attempts were made to equal the kind of condensed grammar achieved by Ibn al-Ḥājib's *Kāfiyah*, notably by al-Muṭarrizī (d. 610/1213), who wrote his *al-Miṣbāḥ fī ʾl-naḥw* for his own son, and by al-Quhandizī (d. 666/1267), author of *Muqaddimat al-Ḍarīrī*. This latter, also known as *Mukhtaṣar al-naḥw*, suffers from a misleading oversimplification in the interest of brevity. A fragment by al-ʿUkbarī (d. 616/1219) is noteworthy, not so much for its infantile contents as for its title, *al-Talqīn* ("Rote Learning"), the universal method of education in classical Islam. The same word, *talqīn*, occurs in the title of an amazing textbook which is almost certainly outside our period, though attributed (falsely) to Ibn Qutaybah (d. 276/889), which is unusual in being a pure catechism of the type more likely to have been in use among Christian missionaries. But it is even more spectacular in that it teaches errors, and can thus hardly have been composed by a Muslim. At the other end of the intellectual scale, grammarians such as Ibn Ṭarāwah (d. 528/1134) seem to have delighted in the most abstruse experiments, for example, an ontological classification of words and constructions into "necessary", "contingent" and "impossible"![8] In short, there was still scope for innovation and development even after six centuries, and while

[8] See al-Suyūṭī, *al-Iqtirāḥ*, Hyderabad, AH 1359, 14.

not everyone went as far as Muḥammad b. ʿAbdullāh al-Anṣārī (?twelfth/eighteenth century) in undertaking to teach Arabic in a single day (like the famous Nuremberg Funnel), the process of sifting, revising, expounding and reformulating has never ceased.

In spite of the obscurity of its beginnings, its borrowings from other cultures and fields both native and foreign, and what may seem to us its occasional stupefying triviality and speciousness, Arabic grammar remains the purest and least derivative product of the Arab-Islamic mind. A sufficient tribute to this achievement is the fact that modern linguistics, which once considered itself a science without a past, now recognizes that many of its insights into the working of language have been part of the grammatical tradition of Arabic for centuries.

CHAPTER 9

ISLAMIC LEGAL LITERATURE

The earliest juristic writings on Islamic law we possess date from the beginning of the second/eighth century. There exists little or no contemporary writing concerning the laws or customs of Arabia in the pre-Islamic era, except for some minor references in the historical works of classical authors. What we know of the pre-Islamic period is therefore gleaned from information appearing in the works of Islamic writers and later oral traditions.[1]

The number of early Islamic legal works lost or suppressed must be considerable. Early Arabic bibliographies, such as Ibn al-Nadīm's *Fihrist*, list many hundreds of early works by jurists whose names are now only encountered in the works of their pupils. From time to time a new book or document, a fragment or minor text is discovered in the archives of the great libraries of Damascus, Baghdad, Istanbul or north Africa, and it is likely that much more remains to be discovered.

The writings on law in the first two centuries of Islam fall into the following categories:

1 The Qurʾān and the immense number of commentaries (*tafsīr*) that it generated.
2 Collections of Traditions (*Ḥadīth* and books of *āthār*) concerning the behaviour of Muḥammad and his Companions.
3 Books by the principal founders of the early schools of law, which deal in the main with sources of law (*uṣūl al-fiqh*), but particularly with the recognition given to subsidiary sources of law and the relation of the sources in cases of inherent conflict.

THE QURʾĀN AND BOOKS OF *TAFSĪR*

The Qurʾān is the most important original source of Islamic law. It achieved pre-eminence as a source of the general principles of law of

[1] See *CHALUP*, 122–7. For Christian legal literature in Arabic see below, ch. 26, 449–50; for Jewish legal literature in Arabic, see below, ch. 27, 470.

accepted divine origin from the earliest times, and there are numerous *ḥadīth* which affirm its importance and show its use in legal settlement in Muḥammad's lifetime. Strictly speaking, the whole of the Qurʾān is law, in the Islamic sense of law as obligations on the individual (if only of belief and daily conduct) required by God. Little distinction is made between the moral and the legal as in the western sense. The Qurʾān, the word of God, attempts to regulate the whole of a man's life. The Qurʾān contains specific exhortations to pray, fast, give alms and other similar "moral" obligations, alongside "legal" rules. Most of the legal rules concern family law (marriage, divorce and succession), but there are a few references to criminal law (the naming of the *ḥadd* crimes), to evidence (credibility of witnesses: *ʿadl*) and commercial matters (the making of contracts: *ʿaqd*, and the taking of interest: *ribā*). However, for the most part, the Qurʾān contains only general principles which are of limited use to the lawyer interested in the day-to-day detail of practical transactions.

THE *SUNNAH* AND BOOKS OF TRADITION

The *sunnah* (practice, tradition, precedent), derived from the behaviour of Muḥammad and of his Companions, is the second original source of Islamic law. The Qurʾān does not have sufficient legal content to maintain a completely new Islamic system of law. A second and complementary source of law became necessary if only to interpret the Quranic provisions, and it was inevitable that the earliest Islamic jurists turned to the life of Muḥammad by way of example. A new system of laws requires new norms of behaviour. The life of Muḥammad was seen as one of exemplary behaviour, influenced by his closeness to God, such that his behaviour served as a pattern for the behaviour of all men. The Traditions relating to the Prophet's sayings and actions (*sunnah*) were recalled, recited and recorded: at first orally and later collected together into books.[2] Furthermore, Traditions relating to the behaviour of the Companions of the Prophet (*āthār*) were also collected, since the Companions were considered to have been influenced in their behaviour by the inspiration of Muḥammad's presence.

THE EARLY JURISTS AND THE DEVELOPMENT OF THE SCHOOLS OF LAW

In the early years of the Islamic empire after Muḥammad's death the first legal specialists accepted the Qurʾān and the *sunnah* as the "roots" (*uṣūl*)

[2] See *CHALUP*, ch. 10.

from which Islamic law was to be derived, and to these two further roots were added: consensus (*ijmāᶜ*) and reasoning by analogy (*qiyās*). The four classical *uṣūl al-fiqh* were therefore two material sources, a declaratory authority and a method. The Ḥanafites however continued to recognize the use of "reasoned opinion" (*raʾy*) under the name of "approval" or "preference" (*istiḥsān*), and the principle of "judicial practice" (*ᶜamal*) played some part in Medinan and Malikite jurisprudence. This *ᶜamal* was not the same as customary law, but an attempt to bring custom within the orbit of the *sharīᶜah*. Customary law (*ᶜurf*, *ᶜādah*) has however existed alongside the theory of Islamic law, while remaining ignored by the official system, in the whole of the Islamic world.

The capital cities of each region produced eminent jurists who influenced the development of law in that region, and created focal points for the teaching of their ideas to pupils who would perpetuate them. Not all the differences which arose were what would now be considered purely legal ones. The main difference between the Shīᶜīs and the Sunnīs was the political argument of who should succeed Muḥammad as head of the Islamic community. The Shīᶜīs insisted on the primacy of the caliph ᶜAlī, and his successors were considered by the Shīᶜīs to be the only proper interpreters of Muḥammad's message. Within the Sunnī community a number of different schools of law arose. Today, however, only four Sunnī schools of law remain, namely the Ḥanafite (originally based in Kufa), the Malikite (originally based in Medina), the Ḥanbalite and the Shafiᶜite schools. Apart from those of the Shīᶜīs and the Sunnīs there is the legal system of the Ibāḍīs.

In some cases our only knowledge of early jurists comes from their appearance in the *isnād*s of later books of Traditions; for example, Ibrāhīm al-Nakhaᶜī of Kufa (d. 95–6/713–15) is the main transmitter in two books of *āthār* of the Ḥanafite school, along with al-Shaᶜbī (d. 104/723) and Ḥammād b. abī Sulaymān (d. 120/738). We possess none of their writings, although it is clear that they had an influential role in the development of the Kufan school. Indeed the most frequent *isnād* of the Kufan Traditions is that transmitted from Ibrāhīm al-Nakhaᶜī to Ḥammād to Abū Ḥanīfah. Or again we have the names of the so-called seven lawyers of Medina (Abū Bakr b. ᶜAbd al-Raḥmān, ᶜUbaydullāh b. ᶜAbdullāh b. ᶜUtbah, ᶜUrwah b. al-Zubayr, Qāsim b. Muḥammad, Saᶜīd b. al-Musayyib, Sulaymān b. Yasār, and Khārijah b. Zayd b. Thābit), whose interpretations of the Qurʾān and *sunnah* were accepted as authoritative, but little or none of their early work survives.

The earliest legal manuscript in existence is supposedly the *Majmūᶜ al-fiqh* attributed to Zayd b. ᶜAlī (d. 122/740). This is a complete compendium of *fiqh* of the Zaydī Shīʿī school, but the modern scholarship of G. Bergsträsser and E. Griffini[3] has shown that it is not in its original form and is in fact of later origin, being based on Ḥanafite doctrines.

In the *Risālah fī ʾl-Ṣaḥābah* of Ibn al-Muqaffaʿ (d. *c.* 139/757), there is information on court ceremonial and some discussion of the position of the caliph *vis-à-vis* the *sharīʿah*, but this is more a work of literature than of law.

Abū Ḥanīfah (d. 150/767) is the earliest of the major jurists and, although he gave his name to an important school of law, almost none of his writings have survived. The only authentic document we have of his is a letter. The *Musnad Abī Ḥanīfah* is a collection of Traditions compiled by his disciples from his teaching. Two books called *al-Fiqh al-akbār* (mainly consisting of articles of faith) are attributed to him, as well as a manuscript purporting to be his will, *Waṣiyyat Abī Ḥanīfah*, which takes the form of an exhortation to his disciples on points of dogma. All of these, however, are of much later origin and are again the work of his disciples to which the name of Abū Ḥanīfah has been appended.

Abū Yūsuf (d. 182/798) and Muḥammad al-Shaybānī (d. 189/804) are the real creators of the Ḥanafite school of law. They were the disciples of Abū Ḥanīfah and they recorded his teachings in their own works, adding a commentary in which they sometimes register disagreement with their master. Abū Yūsuf became the chief *qāḍī* of Baghdad in the time of Hārūn al-Rashīd (reigned 170–193/786–809) and his most famous work, the *Kitāb al-Kharāj*, is said to have been written at the request of that ruler. It is an important work on taxation, explaining the different taxes in Islam, including the *zakāh* payable by Muslims and the taxes payable by the non-Muslims, the *jizyah* and the *kharāj*. It also contains a valuable exposition of the relationship of the caliph and of the administration to Islamic law. Again, Abū Yūsuf is said to have written many more works but few of them remain. These are: a polemical work, the *Kitāb Ikhtilāf Abī Ḥanīfah wa-ʾbn abī Laylā* on the differences between those two early jurists, a *Kitāb al-Radd ʿalā siyar al-Awzāʿī* which is a commentary on a book of al-Awzāʿī (now lost) and finally a *Kitāb al-Āthār* (a small collection of Traditions).

Al-Awzāʿī (d. 157/774) was an early jurist who, by his writings, is said to have created a separate school of *fiqh* in Syria. This school is now extinct and his writings lost. The only authentic information we have of him is as a transmitter of Traditions in the ninth book of the *Kitāb al-Umm* of al-Shāfiʿī, and he is also mentioned in the works of al-Ṭabarī. These Traditions are concerned almost exclusively with the laws of war derived from information concerning the military expeditions of the Prophet.

[3] *Corpus Iuris di Zayd ibn ʿAlī*, Milan, 1919.

Sufyān al-Thawrī (d. 161/778) was an early jurist who is said to have created a separate school of law at Basra, but today his name survives only as a transmitter of Traditions in the writings of other jurists.

With Mālik b. Anas of Medina (d. 179/795) begins a century of the most important writings on the *sharīᶜah*. Mālik's *Kitāb al-Muwaṭṭaᵓ*[4] is the earliest surviving authentic Islamic law textbook. The two standard and complete versions of this work are that of Yaḥyā b. Yaḥyā al-Laythī of Cordova (d. 234/848), often reproduced with the commentary of al-Zurqānī (d. 1122/1710), and the version of Muḥammad al-Shaybānī. The title of the book means "The Smoothed Path", which admirably describes the middle way which Mālik takes on any disputed points.

Al-Muwaṭṭaᵓ is both a book of law (*fiqh*) and a collection of Traditions (*ḥadīth*). It is arranged in books dealing with different legal topics starting with the obligations of ritual purity and fasting and giving alms and ending with books on sale and credit. Each book contains a number of chapters, the headings of which announce the legal subject to be discussed, first by mentioning a relevant Tradition or Traditions (with the *isnād*), then the commentary of Abū Ḥanīfah or al-Shaybānī is quoted, and finally Mālik's own opinion is given. Mālik quotes from only approximately 2,000 Traditions, in some of which the *isnād*s are clearly faulty. However *al-Muwaṭṭaᵓ* is a cornerstone of early Islamic law. It refers frequently to the Qurᵓān and *sunnah* of the Prophet, but also includes discussions of local Medinan practice and admits the possibility of *qiyās* and *raᵓy* to solve a problem. Because of this it is seen as a development from the rigidity of the early Traditionists (*ahl al-ḥadīth*). All the later jurists – even those who were to be the creators of new schools of law – knew of the *Muwaṭṭaᵓ* and were influenced by it. Today it is still the most important Mālikite text and is used particularly in north Africa. Mālik is said to have written many other works but none of these seem to have survived.

The writings of Muḥammad al-Shaybānī have fared better. An early but incomplete work is his *Kitāb al-Āthār*, which is a small collection of Traditions, mainly transmitted from Ibrāhīm al-Nakhaᶜī, together with the purported opinion of Abū Ḥanīfah. His early writings on *siyar* ("laws of war" – the nearest the early jurists came to discussing international law)[5] have been lost: the *Kitāb al-Siyar al-ṣaghīr* ("Abū Ḥanīfah's Laws of War") is said to have prompted a reply by al-Awzāᶜī which was then annotated by Abū Yūsuf – thus his *Kitāb al-Radd* contains a text of al-Awzāᶜī's reply though the original is lost. We know of the *Kitāb al-Siyar al-kabīr* of al-

[4] See *CHALUP*, ch. 10, 272–3.

[5] For *siyar* in this sense, see M. Muranyi, "Das Kitāb al-Siyar von Abū Isḥāq al-Fazārī", *Jerusalem Studies in Arabic and Islam*, VI, 1985, 85.

Shaybānī through the long commentary on it by Muḥammad al-Sarakhsī (d. 495/1101). Al-Sarakhsī does not give al-Shaybānī's original text. This is said to be because the commentary was written during al-Sarakhsī's time in prison from his memory of the original text.

Three books of al-Shaybānī are known together as the *Kutub Ẓāhir al-riwāyah* ("Books of Clear Transmission") because they are considered as authentic, and were transmitted by his disciples. These are the *Kitāb al-Aṣl fī ʾl-furūʿ* (or the *Kitāb al-Mabsūṭ*), the *Kitāb al-Jāmiʿ al-ṣaghīr* and the *Kitāb al-Jāmiʿ al-kabīr*. The *Kitāb al-Aṣl* is a very important work. It takes the form of a discourse between Abū Yūsuf and Abū Ḥanīfah dictated to al-Shaybānī. It includes a discussion of the relationship of the caliph to his subjects and their rights of usurpation in the event of a bad caliph; it has an important set of chapters on *siyar* (which have been translated into English by Majid Khadduri[6]), and also chapters on sale and contract and legal devices (*ḥiyal*). The *Kitāb al-Jāmiʿ al-ṣaghīr* is said to have been dictated by Abū Yūsuf and is only known as a commentary written into the margin of Abū Yūsuf's *Kitāb al-Kharāj*. The *Kitāb al-Jāmiʿ al-kabīr* is al-Shaybānī's own work. These later two books again concentrate on aspects of *siyar*. Finally there are two smaller works: the *Kitāb al-Makhārij fī ʾl-ḥiyal* (although the authorship of this is contested) and a *Kitāb al-Ziyādāt*. Al-Shaybānī's recension of Mālik's *al-Muwaṭṭaʾ* is also important. It differs in its layout from the recension of Yaḥyā al-Laythī and contains extra commentary by Abū Ḥanīfah and al-Shaybānī himself. Two other books by al-Shaybānī, the *Kitāb al-Ḥujaj* and the *Kitāb al-Radd ʿalā ahl al-Madīnah* are commented on in the *Kitāb al-Umm* of al-Shāfiʿī. Al-Shaybānī's works are the most comprehensive of any early jurist to have come down to us. Frequent commentaries have been made on them and the growth of the Ḥanafite school (having today the greatest number of adherents) owes a great deal to his teachings.

The writings of al-Shāfiʿī (d. 204/820) are extensive also but are more systematic. He is said to have written over 100 books on law. His single most important work is the *Kitāb al-Risālah fī uṣūl al-fiqh* (or simply *al-Risālah*). It is the first legal work to produce a comprehensive system of law based upon the four sources of the Qurʾān, the *sunnah*, *qiyās* and *ijmāʿ*, which he called the *uṣūl*, and it had a far-reaching effect on the development of Islamic law. Thereafter, jurists argued the details of the theoretical framework he had devised, but very few disagreed with its general thesis. He laid down rigid guidelines for the operation of *qiyās* and *raʾy* and rejected *istiḥsān* (approval, or discretionary opinion in breach of strict analogy), thus

[6] *War and Peace in the Law of Islam*, Baltimore, 1955.

limiting the scope for speculative deduction and paving the way for the rigidity and stasis of Islamic law into which it slipped in the later medieval period. Another important work of legal theory is his *Kitāb Ikhtilāf al-ḥadīth* on the juristic reasons for the possibility of differences of interpretation between schools of law. The majority of his later writings and lectures are collected in nine books which together compose his *magnum opus*: the *Kitāb al-Umm*. The nine books of this are:

1 *Ikhtilāf al-ʿIrāqiyyīn* ("Disagreement of the Iraqis")
2 *Ikhtilāf ʿAlī wa-ʿAbdullāh b. Masʿūd* ("The Disagreement of ʿAlī and ʿAbdullāh b. Masʿūd")
3 *Ikhtilāf Mālik wa-ʾl-Shāfiʿī* ("The Disagreement of Mālik and al-Shāfiʿī")
4 *Jimāʿ al-ʿilm* ("The Sum of Knowledge")
5 *Bayān al-farḍ* ("Exposition of Duty")
6 *Ṣifat al-amr wa-ʾl-nahy* ("Quality of Command and Prohibition")
7 *Ibṭāl al-istiḥsān* ("Invalidation of Discretionary Opinion")
8 *al-Radd ʿalā Muḥammad b. Ḥasan* ("Refutation of Muḥammad b. Ḥasan al-Shaybānī")
9 *Siyar al-Awzāʿī* ("Laws of War of al-Awzāʿī")

Most of these treatises are polemical in nature. The most important treatise (because the least polemical) is perhaps treatise 7. The *Ikhtilāf al-ḥadīth* is frequently printed in its margins. A book of Traditions of al-Shāfiʿī, the *Musnad*, is frequently printed in the margin of treatise 6.

Aḥmad ibn Ḥanbal (d. 241/855) is the last of the founders of the four main schools and is also the most conservative. Most of his works are collections of Traditions. His *Musnad* contains about 30,000 Traditions. Also by him are a *Kitāb al-Masāʾīl*, a *Kitāb al-Wurūʿ* and *Kitāb al-Zuhd*.

Only very few of the works of other early jurists remain and of what remains little possesses any originality. However, there is *al-Mudawwanah al-Kubrā* of Saḥnūn (d. 240/854) which is an immense early Mālikite work frequently read together with the *Muwaṭṭaʾ*, being a collection of opinions and Traditions of Mālik and Ibn al-Qāsim (d. 191/806) in answer to questions put by Saḥnūn. Also, there is the work of al-Musanī (d. 248/878), the pupil of al-Shāfiʿī who helped to popularize and spread his teacher's ideas and to create a separate school of law based on them (against the express wishes of al-Shāfiʿī). He wrote the *Mukhtaṣar*, an important Shāfiʿī compendium of law. Finally there is Muḥammad b. Jarīr al-Ṭabarī, whose immense works on *tafsīr* and *ikhtilāf* mark the end of originality in the theory of the development of Islamic law. After this there were only secondary works of compilation and commentary based on these early writings.

THE MAJOR LEGAL WORKS OF THE DIFFERENT SCHOOLS OF LAW

The writings of the early jurists and founders of the schools of *fiqh* represent diffuse collections of Tradition and the independent opinions (*raʾy*) of the authors. From this mixed collection of materials, it is difficult in practice to determine precise rules of law. The task fell to the later schools of law to analyse the sources, apply a greater degree of formalism, and produce the various texts necessary for the practical operation of the legal system. This production of texts represented a continuous process; the earlier texts became the subject-matter for commentaries, supercommentaries and glosses. Later texts built upon the foundations laid by the earlier texts. Thus a complete system of legal literature was built up for each of the schools of law.

The different books of the legal schools can be divided into various categories. It is proposed to examine each of these categories, explain the nature of each type of work, and give the best-known examples of each type. The books mentioned below are with very few exceptions chosen from the ʿAbbasid period. There is obviously a great wealth of legal material from the post-ʿAbbasid period; the different categories mentioned here also apply to these later works, and in general the categories applied here conform to those adopted by the Islamic jurists themselves.

Most of the Islamic legal works adopt a rule-by-rule approach, taking individual legal problems, discussing the different sources and arguments involved, and then explaining the opinion of the author's particular school. This rule-by-rule approach is one of the general criticisms that one can level at Islamic legal writing. In nearly all the different types of work mentioned here the tendency is to categorize and set in order individual legal rules with very little attempt to analyse the underlying principles or to discuss any issue of policy behind the law. There are a few works which attempt to analyse the law as a whole and to impose a structure on the legal system. Most such works date from the post-ʿAbbasid period. As examples of these analytical works we may cite *al-Ashbāh wa-naẓāʾir* by Zayn al-ʿĀbidīn b. Nujaym (d. 970/1563), a Ḥanafite jurist, as well as a similarly titled book by the Shafiʿite lawyer al-Suyūṭī (d. 911/1505).

Compendia of the schools

Because of the diffuse nature of the writings of the early founders of the schools, which made it difficult to extract general rules of law for that school, the initial task for the later jurists was to prepare compendia of the legal rules of each school. For many of the schools these compendia are known simply as *al-Mukhtaṣar* ("The Compendium"). The compendia of the schools follow a relatively standard pattern. They begin by discussing the rules connected with the major religious duties of prayer, alms, pilgrimage, ritual purity and fasting. Then they turn to legal material in the western sense of the term, discussing matters such as marriage, divorce, *waqf*, wills, succession, court procedure and evidence.

The compendia vary greatly in length. At one extreme is the *Mukhtaṣar* of Khalīl b. Isḥāq al-Jundi (d. 767/1365). This compendium of Malikite law by a leading Egyptian jurist is often referred to simply as *al-Kitāb*. It is said to contain over 100,000 different legal rules divided into some sixty-one chapters. It deals with all aspects of religious and personal law and has attracted more than twelve major commentaries. In fact, the text of the work is unusually concise and is almost incomprehensible without the aid of the commentaries. At the other extreme is the *Risālah* of Ibn abī Zayd al-Qayrawānī (d. 386/996). This work, also known as *Bākūrat al-saᶜd* ("The First Fruit of Happiness"), is a very short compendium of Malikite law. It consists of brief statements of legal rules arranged in chapters and designed to be easily memorized. The book is particularly popular in west Africa and has attracted a number of commentaries.

The leading compendium of the Ḥanafite school is the *Mukhtaṣar* of the Baghdādī jurist, al-Qudūrī (d. 428/1037). This compendium is said to contain some 12,500 legal decisions; it was apparently composed for the author's son. Another compendium (of particular importance for the Ḥanafites of the Indian subcontinent) is the *Hidāyah* of Burhān al-Dīn al-Marghīnānī (d. 593/1196). The *Hidāyah* was originally prepared as a commentary to an eight-volume work by the same author, the *Bidāyat al-mubtadiᵓ*, which was itself based on al-Qudūrī's *Mukhtaṣar*. Al-Marghīnānī is reported to have prepared one commentary originally, and then, before that was completed, he decided it was too diffuse and therefore he prepared the *Hidāyah* as his second commentary. Translated into English, the *Hidāyah* became the basis of many of the judgements on Islamic law delivered by the courts of British India.

The earliest *Mukhtaṣar* of the Shafiᶜites, though little known today, is by Abū Shujāᶜ Aḥmad al-Iṣfahānī (d. *c.* 500/1106). However, by far and away the best-known compendium of Shafiᶜite law is the *Minhāj al-ṭālibīn*, completed in 669/1270 by Yaḥyā al-Nawawī (d. 676/1278). This book, translated first into French, and from the French into English, has become particularly important in the courts of south-east Asia where the majority of Muslims are adherents of the Shafiᶜite school.

Turning to the last of the four Sunnī schools, the Ḥanbalites also have a *Mukhtaṣar*, prepared by ᶜUmar al-Khiraqī (d. 334/945), but a more important source of Ḥanbalite practice is *al-Mughnī* by Ibn Qudāmah (d. 620/1223), which is in format a commentary on al-Khiraqī's *Mukhtaṣar*.

Compendia of legal rules are not restricted to the four Sunnī schools alone. The various branches of the Shīᶜīs also have major compendia. Undoubtedly the single most important source for the Twelver Shīᶜīs is the *Sharāᵓiᶜ al-Islām* by Najm al-Dīn al-Ḥillī (d. 676/1277). There is an early compendium of the Zaydī Shīᶜīs, the *Majmūᶜ al-fiqh*, attributed to Zayd b. ᶜAlī.[7] For the Ismāᶜīlī Shīᶜīs the chief legal text is *Daᶜāᵓim al-Islām* by al-Qāḍī al-Nuᶜmān (d. 363/974). Al-Nuᶜmān is supposed to have consulted other jurists in preparing this work so that it represents the views of a number of scholars. The *Mukhtaṣar* of the Ibāḍīs is by Abū ᵓl-Ḥasan ᶜAlī Muḥammad al-Bisyāni (mid-fifth/eleventh century). The Ẓāhirīs also possessed a compendium of law, the *Muḥallā* of Ibn Ḥazm (d. 456/1064).

Each of the schools of Islamic law has, therefore, its own authoritative compendium setting out the rules of that school relevant both to religious practice and to law in the western sense.

Works on uṣūl al-fiqh

Classical Islamic law divides jurisprudence into the study of *uṣūl* (the sources of law) and of *furūᶜ al-fiqh* (the branches or applications of law). Works on *uṣūl* discuss the major sources, the Qurᵓān, the *sunnah*, *qiyās* and *ijmāᶜ*, as well as the other minor sources recognized by certain schools only. For example, the Ḥanafite school recognizes the subsidiary method of *istiḥsān*. For the Ḥanafites, where the result of the application of the rules of analogy (*qiyās*) would lead to an unacceptable result, the principle of *istiḥsān* is applied to choose a preferable result. The Malikites, on the other hand, recognize the subsidiary method of *istiṣlāḥ* (taking the public interest into account), as well as local practice (ᶜ*amal*) as a subsidiary source. Acceptance of these subsidiary sources was a matter of controversy. The works on *uṣūl* rehearse the various arguments in favour of the subsidiary sources. Works on *uṣūl* also discuss such issues as the abrogation of Quranic verses by later verses (*naskh*), and the relationship between Quranic verses and *Ḥadīth*

[7] But see above, 141–2.

material. They discuss the textual criticism of *Ḥadīth*, and the methods for establishing whether a *ḥadīth* is valid or not.

The most important work on *uṣūl* remains al-Shāfiʿī's *Risālah*. Later Shafiʿite jurists also produced some leading works on *uṣūl*. Among the most important are *al-Burhān* and the *Kitāb al-Waraqāt* by Abū ʾl-Maʿālī ʿAbd al-Malik b. ʿAbdullāh b. Yūsuf al-Juwaynī, Imām al-Ḥaramayn (d. 478/1085). The *Kitāb al-Waraqāt* is brief, but has attracted commentaries from several authors. Al-Ghazālī, who was a pupil of Imām al-Ḥaramayn, also wrote a work on *uṣūl* entitled *al-Mustaṣfā*.[8] For the Ḥanafites, the leading work on *uṣūl* of the ʿAbbasid period is the *Kanz al-wuṣūl ilā maʿrifat al-uṣūl* by ʿAbdullāh b. Muḥammad al-Pazdawī (d. 482/1089). There are also works on *uṣūl* written from the point of view of several of the minority religious movements within Islam.

Works on furūʿ al-fiqh

There are many books from the different schools of law which analyse a particular branch of Islamic *fiqh*. Again, however, most of the books take a case-by-case approach, discussing individual problems in that field of law in isolation. Not all areas of law have attracted the equal attention of jurists. It is possible to isolate the major branches of *fiqh* on which works have been written:

1 *ʿIlm al-farāʾiḍ*

ʿIlm al-farāʾiḍ (law of succession) is concerned with the Islamic law of succession under which fixed shares of the estate devolve upon the heirs of the deceased. Because of its complexity and the relatively large number of Quranic verses associated with the topic, this field has always been regarded as particularly rewarding by Islamic jurists. Not surprisingly, it has attracted much literary attention. The leading Ḥanafite works in this area are *al-Urjūzah al-Raḥbiyyah* by al-Raḥbī Muwaffaq al-Dīn ibn al-Mutaqqinah (d. 579/1183) and *al-Farāʾiḍ al-Sirājiyyah* by Sirāj al-Dīn abū Ṭāhir Muḥammad al-Sajāwandī (fl. end of sixth century of the *Hijrah*). Both of these texts were translated into English for use by the courts of British India.

2 *Waqf*

A *waqf* is a form of religious endowment under which property is rendered inalienable and its income or use is devoted, ultimately at least, to charitable

[8] See below, ch. 25, 425.

purposes. There are a number of important early Ḥanafite works on *waqf* under the title *Aḥkām al-waqf*, for example the work with this title by Abū Bakr Aḥmad b. ʿUmar al-Khaṣṣāf (d. 261/874).

3 Works on public law

Public law is one of the least well-developed areas of Islamic law. There are, however, a few well-known books from the late ʿAbbasid period on public-law matters. The authors of these books had to face a political situation very different from the ideals of *sharīʿah* government. Their works end up, therefore, concentrating on the ideal requirements of the government, but frequently go on to justify a reality far from the ideal described. There are two such works from the ʿAbbasid period, both entitled *al-Aḥkām al-sulṭāniyyah*, the first by Abū Yaʿlā Muḥammad b. al-Ḥusayn b. al-Farrāʾ (d. 458/1065), and the second by al-Māwardī (d. 450/1058), a Shafiʿite jurist who became *qāḍī* of Baghdad.[9]

4 Works on *furūq*

The subject of *furūq* is concerned with distinguishing between parallel and similar cases. As such, it represents a departure from the normal style of Islamic legal texts which, as has been remarked, are concerned with cataloguing individual legal rules. One of the few ʿAbbasid texts on *furūq* which has survived is *Anwār al-burūq fī anwāʿ al-furūq* by the Malikite jurist Aḥmad b. Idrīs al-Qarāfī (d. 684/1285).

5 Works on *ḥisbah*

The technical use of the term *ḥisbah* refers to the duties of the *muḥtasib*, or market inspector, although his jurisdiction was wider than this term might imply. His responsibilities extended to general control of morals, such as the enforcement of public fasts and the separation of the sexes, and he had the power to inflict minor punishments without having to refer to any other judicial authority. Works on *ḥisbah* discuss the general moral duties of Muslims, as well as the more technical legal aspects of the functions of the *muḥtasib*[10].

Miscellaneous practical works

There are various types of legal texts written on the law in practice. Many of them were designed for the guidance of *qāḍī*s or jurists. Because of differing attitudes between the schools of law, some of the categories of texts apply to

[9] See below, ch. 10, 157. [10] See below, ch. 10, 160–1.

certain schools of law only. These different categories of miscellaneous texts are as follows:

1 Handbooks for *qāḍī*s

Closely linked with the compendia of the different schools are practical books prepared for the guidance of *qāḍī*s. These books deal with the preparation of the *qāḍī*'s judgement (*sijill*) and the duties of *qāḍī*s (*adab al-qāḍī*). Each *qāḍī* usually renders judgement according to the law of the school to which he belongs. Each of the major schools, therefore, possess books of this category. Most of the leading works, however, date from the post-ᶜAbbasid period.

2 Works on *ᶜamal*

These works are limited to the Malikite school. As has been seen, the Malikites accepted as a subsidiary source of law the *ᶜamal* (judicial practice), which took official notice of local usage. The Malikite school originated in Mecca and Medina. Because of this, the Malikites argue that the local practice of Medina had a special validity. From this starting-point, by the fourth/tenth century, Malikite courts in north Africa had come to accept local practice as a source of law. The subject is first mentioned in the *Lāmiyyah* by ᶜAlī al-Zaqqāq (d. 912/1507). The Malikites have a number of books setting out the terms of local practice. Because of the late acceptance of *ᶜamal* as binding, these works largely date from the post-ᶜAbbasid period. The best-known of these texts is the work *al-ᶜAmal al-Fāsī* by ᶜAbd al-Raḥmān al-Fāsī (d. 1096/1695).

3 Works on *ḥiyal*

Ḥiyal (sing. *ḥīlah*) or legal devices (sometimes, incorrectly, translated as "legal fictions") are methods employed to achieve, usually by a series of transactions, a result which if achieved directly would have been contrary to the *sharīᶜah*. Perhaps the nearest Western equivalent today would be methods employed for the avoidance of tax. The attitude of the different schools towards *ḥiyal* varied greatly. Ḥanafite scholars were the most willing to accept and exploit them. After initial rejection of *ḥiyal*, the Shafiᶜites came to accept and develop their use. The Malikites generally rejected the use of *ḥiyal* because of their insistence upon looking at the intention behind the transaction rather than its mere form. The Ḥanbalites are amongst the strongest in their condemnation of the use of *ḥiyal*. They were strongly attacked by the Ḥanbalite jurist Ibn Taymiyyah.

There are a number of Ḥanafite and Shafiᶜite texts on the details of various *ḥiyal*. These works explain the various strategems employed and then distinguish between those strategems regarded as lawful and those which are regarded as unlawful. The chief Ḥanafite work is *Kitāb al-Ḥiyal al-sharʿiyyah* by Aḥmad b. ʿUmar al-Khaṣṣāf, which draws heavily on the work on *ḥiyal* by al-Shaybānī. For the Shafiʿites, there is *Kitāb al-Ḥiyal fīʾl-fiqh* by Maḥmūd al-Qazwīnī (d. 440/1048).

4 Works on *shurūṭ*

The subject of *shurūṭ* (sing. *sharṭ*) covers the whole field of legal documents. Whilst the *sharīʿah*, in theory, rejects the use of written evidence, and relies instead upon the oral testimony of two valid witnesses, documents were used in practice to record many transactions. The schools later came to accept this and admitted documents if attested by valid witnesses. Many books on legal documents were written from the second/eighth century onwards. Few of these works, however, have survived. A Ḥanafite work which has survived in fragments is by al-Ṭaḥāwī (d. 321/933), and there is an important Malikite work, *al-Muqniʿ*, by Ibn Mughīth (d. 459/1067).

Works on ikhtilāf al-madhāhib

Works on *ikhtilāf* (lit. "disagreement") discuss the differences between the various schools of law. The doctrine of *ikhtilāf* itself came, over time, to represent the mutual tolerance which each of the Sunnī schools showed to one another. The earlier works on *ikhtilāf* are comparative works which contrast the rules of the different schools and, in some cases, shade into polemic. Later books are less concerned with the differences between the schools and are closer in format to handbooks of the particular author's own school. There are early works on *ikhtilāf* by the two disciples of Abū Ḥanīfah, Abū Yūsuf (*Ikhtilāf Abī Ḥanīfah wa-ʾbn abī Laylā*) and by al-Shaybānī (*Kitāb al-Ḥujaj*: see above).

From the fourth/tenth century, there are two works entitled *Ikhtilāf al-fuqahāʾ*, one by Muḥammad b. Jarīr al-Ṭabarī – of which only two sections have survived but which contains much information on the early jurists – and the other by al-Ṭaḥāwī.

In the later ʿAbbasid period, the philosopher Ibn Rushd (d. 595/1198) also composed a book, *Bidāyat al-mujtahid*, which treats a wide variety of matters from the Malikite point of view. Apart from including discussions of *uṣūl* and *furūʿ al-fiqh*, the book also draws comparisons between the different schools. On these differences, Ibn Rushd focuses on the reasons behind the divergences, stressing the different texts relied upon or the different analogies applied. This is probably the best-known text on *ikhtilāf*.

Works on ṭabaqāt*: biographies of the* qāḍīs

Works of *ṭabaqāt* set out the generations of lawyers together with brief biographies for each one. Most of the main works are from the post-ᶜAbbasid period. One important early source for the works of early jurists, however, is the *Fihrist* of Ibn al-Nadīm (completed in 337/989); the sixth section of this work discusses the writings of the early jurists. Also from the ᶜAbbasid period is a Ḥanbalite work on *ṭabaqāt*, the *Ṭabaqāt al-Ḥanābilah* by Abūʾl-Ḥusayn Muḥammad b. abī Yaᶜlā al-Farrāʾ (d. 526/1133). There are also a number of collections of biographies of the *qāḍīs* of the different regions. Early sources include, for example, the *Akhbār al-quḍāt wa-taʾrīkhuhum wa-aḥkāmuhum* ("Annals, History and Decisions of the Judges") by Abū Muḥammad Bakr b. Ḥayyān Wakīᶜ (d. 330/941).[11]

COLLECTIONS OF *FATĀWĀ*

A *fatwā* (pl. *fatāwā*) is a legal response given by a *muftī* to a question on *fiqh* addressed to him. The question follows a standard form, setting out the assumed facts, and using standard fictitious names (e.g. Zayd, ᶜAmr, etc.). The response might be very brief – a mere statement that a particular action is permitted or forbidden, for example – or it may contain detailed reasoning. The institution of the *fatwā* can be traced back to similar institutions in Jewish law (*sheʾelot u-teshuvot*) and in Roman law (the *responsa prudentium*). *Fatāwā* represent a statement of the law on matters not covered by the compendia and, in particular, relate to new situations that have arisen. Not surprisingly, the *fatāwā* of renowned *muftīs* were collected and published. These collections represent an excellent indication of how Islamic law met new challenges and changing conditions.

Since each *muftī* gave his response according to the law of his own school, each of the schools had its own collections of *fatāwā*. The largest number of collections are from the Ḥanafites. The earliest collection of *fatāwā* from the Ḥanafites is the *Kitāb al-Nawāzil* by Abū Layth Naṣr b. Muḥammad al-Samarqandī (d. 373/983), which contains opinions from a wide selection of early jurists. Another early Ḥanafite work is *Majmaᶜ al-nawāzil wa-ʾl-waqaᶜāt* by Aḥmad al-Nāṭifī (d. 444/1054). Of the later *fatāwā* collections of the Ḥanafites, perhaps the best-known, especially in the Indian subcontinent, is the *Fatāwā Qāḍikhān* by Fakhr al-Dīn Qāḍikhān (d. 592/1195). On a number of questions, this collection reports differing

[11] For legal biography, see also below, ch. 11.

opinions of various jurists, but always giving the preferred opinion of the author first. Whilst strictly outside a chapter on ʿAbbasid legal writings, one collection of *fatāwā* from the Indian subcontinent deserves mention because it is without doubt the best-known. This is *al-Fatāwā al-ʿĀlamgīriyyah* which was prepared between 1075 and 1083 (1664–72) by order of the Moghul sultan Muḥyī ʾl-Dīn Aurangzīb ʿĀlamgīr. The collection was compiled by a commission headed by Shaykh Niẓām of Burhānpur aided by four superintendents, each of whom had the assistance of ten ulema. The collection remains one of the most important and is still used in south Asia today.

CHAPTER 10

ADMINISTRATIVE LITERATURE

By the end of the Umayyad period, the government bureaucracy, organized as a group of *dīwān*s or government departments concerned with finance, official correspondence and the mustering and payment of the army, was already well formed. Under the ᶜAbbasids, the existing *dīwān*s increased in size and complexity and were complemented by new ones with more specialized functions, such as confiscations (the *dīwān al-muṣādarāt*) and financial control and accounting (the *dīwān al-zimām wa-ʾl-istīfāʾ*). The role of the secretaries (*kuttāb*, sing. *kātib*), whose function had been of comparatively low standing under the Umayyads, now grew, possibly stimulated by the importance of the personal secretary to the last Umayyad caliph Marwān II (reigned 127–32/744–50), ᶜAbd al-Ḥamīd b. Yaḥyā.[1] This *kātib* class acquired a prestige in the ᶜAbbasid state similar to that of its pre-Islamic predecessors in Persia and Iraq, the Sasanid *dibhērān*, whilst the coming to full form of the office of vizier or chief executive for the caliph, achieved under the originally eastern Iranian Barmakī family in the second half of the second/eighth century, allowed the secretaries to aspire to the highest position in the state beneath the ruler himself, and to give the central administration a distinct bias towards long-established Persian traditions of statecraft.[2]

Despite this increased administrative proliferation and complexity, the positions of the exchequer, dealing with finance and taxation, and of the chancery, dealing with correspondence, remained pre-eminent. The training of secretaries to staff the bureaucracy, whilst not neglecting mathematical and accounting skills, involved also an acquisition of the body of knowledge known as *adab*, and especially, its aspect which was concerned with the so-called "Arabic" sciences, theological, legal, philological and literary; for all *dīwān*s, whatever their practical functions, required highly literate personnel. Whence the development, as an increasingly general

[1] See *CHALUP*, 164–79.

[2] See on the ᶜAbbasid *dīwān*s, Mez, *Renaissance*, Eng. trans., 76–88, and *EI*², "Dīwān. i. The caliphate"; and for Persian influence on early Arabic literature and culture in general, *CHALUP*, 483–96.

feature of the *dīwān*s, of a distinct chancery style, the art of inditing official documents, later called *inshā*ʾ (lit. "origination", reflecting a primary meaning of "producing a draft", on which was made the fair copy of the final document to be issued). The characteristic features of *inshā*ʾ style – subsequently carried over from Arabic into the Persian and Ottoman Turkish equivalents – were a use of parallel and balanced phrasing and then of rhymed prose, *saj*ʿ. The use of parallelism and assonance went back to the utterances of the pre-Islamic *kāhin*s (soothsayers) and to Quranic style, but the full *musajja*ʿ epistolary style only blossoms in the chanceries of the Buyid (or Buwayhid) period with such outstanding figures as Abū Isḥāq Ibrāhīm b. Hilāl al-Ṣābiʾ (d. 384/994), Abūʾl-Fatḥ ʿAlī b. Muḥammad al-Bustī (d. 400/1010 or 401/1011) and the other three stylists mentioned below (p. 163). Even then, some writers clung to the older simplicity, and Ḍiyāʾ al-Dīn b. al-Athīr (d. 637/1239) had still, in his influential *al-Mathal al-sāʾir fī adab al-kātib wa-ʾl-shāʿir* (as its name implies, on the stylistic methods and models required for secretaries and poets), to defend the exponents of the new elaborateness against conservative conceptions of official style.[3]

This elaboration of the machinery of government early evoked a specialist literature embracing both descriptive, practical manuals on administrative procedure, and also didactic treatises on the education and training of secretaries and on the literary forms of the documents to be drawn up. The fairly extensive body of Arabic literature falling under these two headings and that of further, associated genres to be mentioned later, is a rich and varied one, whose study provides us not only with specific historical information on the running of the ʿAbbasid caliphate and its successor states, but also with material which illuminates the general ideals of Islamic education for those members of the civilian ruling élite outside the circumscribed limits of the religious institution of the ulema and *fuqahā*ʾ.

DESCRIPTIVE, PRACTICAL MANUALS ON ADMINISTRATIVE PROCEDURE

Works on the taxation of land and other dutiable sources of income

Since the original basis of taxation in the conquered lands was at least in part Quranic, involving a poll-tax on non-Muslim cultivators and artisans and the exaction of a land-tax on agricultural land and mineral resources in those lands (*jizyah* and *kharāj* – without, however, precise delimitation of

[3] I. Goldziher, *Abhandlungen zur arabischen Philologie*, Leiden, 1896–9, I, 67; Mez, *Renaissance*, Eng. trans., 240–2; *CHALUP*, 175–6, 180–5, 196–8.

these terms, at least in the early period), financial manuals dealing with these, and also with the collection of ᶜ*ushr* or tithe as *zakāh* on lands specifically acquired by the Muslims, were closely connected with *fiqh*. Hence the earliest treatises – whose titles reflect their subject-matter – were composed by scholars whose prime training was in the religious sciences, such as the *Kitāb al-Amwāl* of the Traditionist Yaḥyā b. Ādam (d. 203/818) and the *Kitāb al-Kharāj* of the judge and co-founder of the Ḥanafite law-school Abū Yūsuf (d. 182/798); whereas, in the early fourth/tenth century, we find the only partially preserved *Kitāb al-Kharāj* of Qudāmah b. Jaᶜfar composed by one who was essentially a philologist and *adīb*.[4] It should likewise be noted that the treatises on constitutional law of one or two centuries later continue the legal approach, for example in the sections of the *Aḥkām al-sulṭāniyyah* of the Shafiᶜite scholar al-Māwardī (d. 450/1058) on the basic taxes, the division of captured plunder, the "revivification" of waste land through cultivation and irrigation, the organization of the *dīwān*s and the problems arising from the state's alienation of land in grants or *iqṭā*ᶜs (a form of tenure increasingly common in Iraq and western Persia under the Buyids and Saljūqs). Nevertheless, we can by no means consider treatises like that of al-Māwardī and that of the same name by his slightly younger Ḥanbalī contemporary Abū Yaᶜlā Muḥammad b. al-Ḥusayn b. al-Farrāᵓ (d. 458/1065) as purely theoretical, as has sometimes been asserted.

For all these authors, the focus of attention was on the Sawād of Iraq, the highly fertile, irrigated agricultural region through which ran the middle reaches of the Euphrates and Tigris, and whose financial administration had become so complex by the fourth/tenth century that it was regarded as the training-ground *par excellence* for secretaries who wished to specialize in financial affairs.[5] But manuals apparently existed – now largely lost – which dealt with conditions in the more distant provinces, such as a certain *Kitāb Kharāj Khurāsān* composed by the secretary Ḥafṣ b. ᶜUmar al-Marwazī for Hārūn al-Rashīd's representative in Khurāsān, ᶜAlī b. ᶜĪsā b. Māhān (governor there 180–91/796–807).[6] It was likewise from the far eastern fringes of the Islamic world, from the Samanid amirate in Transoxiana and Khurāsān, that there emanated in the later fourth/tenth century a concise encyclopaedia of the sciences, the *Mafātīḥ al-ᶜulūm*, written by Abū ᶜAbdullāh Muḥammad b. Aḥmad al-Khwārazmī (fourth/tenth century), a secretary who seems to have worked in the central bureaucracy in the capital Bukhārā. One section of his book deals with *kitābah*, the secretary's art, and is mainly devoted to an exposition of the technical terminology of

4 Relevant passages on taxation from these three early treatises are translated by Ben Shemesh, *Taxation in Islam*. 5 See Løkkegaard, *Islamic Taxation*, 143–91.

6 ᶜAbd al-Ḥayy Gardīzī, *Kitāb Zayn al-akhbār*, Tehran 1347 sh./1968, 131.

administrative procedures, their registers and documents, together with the technical terms of the irrigation system and postal and intelligence services.[7] The fact that some of the registers described are directly attributed to the *dīwān*s of Iraq shows that the administrative system being described was not peculiar to the Islamic East but that it included elements from the caliphal heartland, whose institutions had become normative for much of the remaining Islamic world. Of note is a distinct Persian strain in nomenclature, like the apparently Middle Persian origin of the names of certain of the registers of the secretaries of Iraq;[8] and there are other terms which go back to the former Byzantine administrative system of lands which had passed to the Arabs, like *barīd*, "postal service" (Greek, originally Latin, *veredus*, "post-horse") and *askudār*, "scroll on which are recorded details of incoming and outgoing mail" (possibly from Greek *skoutarios*, "shield-maker").[9]

Geographical literature and road-books

A contributory strand in the development of Islamic geographical writing – which began essentially in the third/ninth century – was that of the road-book or gazetteer, a topographical survey of the main routes of the empire with details of the staging-posts and rest-houses along them and of actual distances. The aim here was strictly practical: to provide information for the couriers and agents of the state postal and intelligence services (*barīd*, *khabar*), these being of premier importance in a far-flung empire such as the ʿAbbasid caliphate was in its heyday, when an efficient network of postmasters and spies was one of the few checks on ambitious, potentially rebellious provincial governors and officials. Hence it is not surprising that geographical works covering such topics were frequently called *Kitāb al-Masālik wa-ʾl-mamālik* ("Book of Routes and Realms"), exemplified in the name of the first surviving book of this genre, that of Ibn Khurradādhbih (d. *c.* 272/885).[10] The value of these surveys was shortly afterwards emphasized by Qudāmah b. Jaʿfar, who asserted that the *ʿilm al-ṭuruq*, "science or the knowledge of the roads", should not only be part of the stock of information available in the *dīwān*s, but could be especially useful to the caliph for his own journeyings to outlying regions and his despatching thither of armies.[11]

[7] Ed. G. van Vloten, Leiden 1895, 54–79; Eng. trans. Bosworth, "Abū ʿAbdallāh al-Khwārazmī on... the secretary's art", 120–64. [8] Ibid., 129. [9] Ibid., 141–3.

[10] See below, ch. 17, 308.

[11] *Kitāb al-Kharāj*, ed. M. J. de Goeje, *Bibliotheca Geographorum Arabicorum* VI, Leiden, 1889, 185.

Technical aspects of land management and fiscal assessment: irrigation and mensuration

Given the supreme importance of water-supplies for the maintenance of agriculture over much of the Middle East and the expectation by government that crops grown on the irrigated lands of regions like the Nile valley, Mesopotamia, Ahwāz and the oases of Khurāsān, Soghdia and Khwārazm should yield a high level of taxation, these were necessarily concerns of the administrator and financial official. The general works on land tenure of Yaḥyā b. Ādam, Abū Yūsuf, etc. (see above) advert to the complex legal and technological questions involved in the repartition of rights in irrigation water among cultivators; and it is again mentioned in regard to Khurāsān that the Ṭahirid governor there, ᶜAbdullāh b. Ṭāhir (in charge of the province 214–30/829–44), summoned the legal scholars of Khurāsān and Iraq to compose a work on irrigation (possibly dealing with both legal and practical aspects), the *Kitāb al-Qunī* (*qunī*, sing. *qanāh*, "subterranean irrigation channel or conduit"), a book which remained authoritative and in use in the East for at least two centuries.[12]

Abū ᶜAbdullāh Muḥammad b. Aḥmad al-Khwārazmī (see above) has sections on the technical terms of the department of state lands and resources, the *dīwān al-ḍiyāᶜ wa-ᵓl-nafaqāt*, namely, those used by the surveyors (*mussāḥ*) of land for taxation purposes, and of that of water regulation, the *dīwān al-māᵓ*. Some of the expressions of the *dīwān al-māᵓ* which are defined are specifically related to the Marw oasis and to Transoxiana and are not surprisingly Persian, such as the *dīwān al-kastabzūd* (New Persian *kāst va afzūd*, "decrease and increase [of water]"), the register used at Marw to record the tax liabilities of those with water rights; but others relate to the well-watered plains of Mesopotamia and attest the ancientness of irrigation practices and their terminology there, for not a few terms can be traced back to the Babylonians of one or two millennia previously, such as *musannāt*, "dam with sluices" (Akkadian *musannītu*, "dam, embankment") and the names of some of the weights and measures used by land surveyors and collectors of taxation in kind.[13]

The legal and administrative aspects of land measurement and of irrigation cannot easily be separated from the actual science and technology involved; land areas and crop yields had to be calculated or estimated for fiscal purposes, and irrigation water had to be raised or collected and then channelled. Hence there is not infrequently in the administrative literature an overlapping of all these aspects, the latter ones involving the sciences of

[12] Gardīzī, *Zayn al-akhbār*, 137.

[13] Eng. trans. Bosworth, "Abū ᶜAbdallāh al-Khwārazmī", 152, 154.

arithmetical and trigonometrical calculation, the *ᶜilm al-ḥisāb*, and of technical devices, the *ᶜilm al-ḥiyal*. The close connections here emerge from certain works of the later ᶜAbbasid period, for example, the *Kitāb al-Manāzil . . . min ᶜilm al-ḥisāb*, of the great mathematician of Khurāsān and Iraq Abū ᵓl-Wafāᵓ al-Būzajānī (d. 388/998), which A.S. Ehrenkreutz has used for its material on the customs and toll system of Mesopotamia,[14] and the *Kitāb al-Hāwī* of an anonymous author of late Buyid Iraq (first quarter of fifth century/second quarter of eleventh century), which Claude Cahen has utilized for its information on the trigonometrical problems involved in laying-out and excavating canals, the calculation of volumes of earth required to be moved for the construction of embankments, etc.[15] The full titles of these two treatises, "The Book of the Stages concerning what Secretaries and Tax-Collectors Need of the Science of Calculation" and "The Compendious Book for Governmental Practices and the Procedures of the *Dīwān*s Involving Calculation", explain clearly the practical nature of such manuals.

Manuals of ḥisbah

Supervision of the markets and of the wares and foodstuffs sold there was held to be a duty of the ruling power in Islam as it had been in the cities of the Hellenistic Near East, where the *agoranomos* had exercised these functions. His Islamic equivalent was at first simply known as the *ṣāḥib al-sūq*, but in the early third/ninth century he evolved into the *muḥtasib* or censor of morals and maintainer of standards of purity and probity in the markets.[16] At first, this duty of *ḥisbah* is only incidentally noted, with emphasis more on the moral than the practical side, in works primarily concerned with other matters (e.g. in al-Māwardī's treatise, mentioned above);[17] but then we find special books on *ḥisbah* appearing, for no obvious reason, in the Muslim West and particularly Spain, for we possess an epistle on this by a Cordovan author, Ibn ᶜAbd al-Raᵓūf, from the second half of the fourth/tenth century. Two or three centuries later, full-scale manuals are composed both in Spain and in the East, like the *Kitāb fī Adab al-ḥisbah* of the Malagan writer al-Saqaṭī (wrote at the end of the sixth/twelfth century

[14] "Al-Būzajānī (AD 939–997) on the 'Māᵓṣir'", *Journal of the Economic and Social History of the Orient*, VIII, 1965, 90–2.

[15] "Le service de l'irrigation en Iraq au début du XIᵉ siècle", *Bulletin d'Études Orientales*, XIII, 1949–50, 117–43; "Quelques problèmes economiques et fiscaux de l'Irâq Buyide d'après un traité de mathématiques", *Annales de l'Institut des Études Orientales de l'Université d'Alger*, X, 1952, 326–63.

[16] See *EI²*, "Ḥisba. 1. General: sources, origins, duties".

[17] See H. F. Amedroz, "The Hisba jurisdiction in the Ahkam Sultaniyya of Mawardi", *Journal of the Royal Asiatic Society*, 1916, 77–101, 287–314.

or beginning of the seventh/thirteenth century), himself a *muḥtasib*, and the *Maᶜālim al-qurbah fī aḥkām al-ḥisbah* ("Characteristics of the Pious Deed in regard to the Regulations of the *Ḥisbah*"), full of fascinating detail, of the Egyptian Muḥammad b. al-Ukhuwwah (d. 729/1329). These books, and the many imitations which they spawned, are eminently practical in aim and provide much light on social and economic conditions; thus J. D. Latham has derived information from al-Saqaṭī's manual to demonstrate how the public baker of the market, the *khabbāz*, baked his loaves from various farinaceous materials and how different extraction-rates of wheat were distinguished by the market inspector.[18]

DIDACTIC TREATISES FOR THE TRAINING AND GUIDANCE OF SECRETARIES

Already in the epistles of ᶜAbd al-Ḥamīd, several of the themes within official prose writing are apparent, for example *taḥmīd*, "eulogy"; *fī fatḥ*, "announcement of a victory"; *ikhāᵓ*, "friendship"; *taᶜziyah*, "consolation on bereavement"; *tawṣiyah*, "the enjoining of good counsels", etc., but these are not systematically distinguished. It is in the *Risālat al-ᶜAdhrāᵓ fī mawāzīn al-balāghah wa-adawāt al-kitābah* (probably by a certain Ibrāhīm b. Muḥammad al-Shaybānī of the mid-third/ninth century rather than by the official Ibrāhīm b. Muḥammad b. Mudabbir, as was earlier thought[19]) that we find a classification of types of document set forth as a guide for secretaries (*tawqīᶜāt*, *sijillāt*, *amānāt*, *ᶜuhūd*, etc.), and the author himself boasted that his epistle was a "virgin" one (*ᶜadhrāᵓ*) because it treated of topics never before handled. Thereafter, manuals of epistolary style for the would-be perfect secretary – whether concerned primarily with finance, as a *kātib al-amwāl*, or with correspondence, as a *kātib al-inshāᵓ* – follow in succession, although different works had different emphases. Thus the *Adab al-kātib* of the philologist and littérateur Ibn Qutaybah (d. 276/889) concentrates, as one might expect from an author without practical experience as a *dīwān* official, on correct grammatical and linguistic usage for the secretary. With the *Adab al-kuttāb* of Abū Bakr Muḥammad b. Yaḥyā al-Ṣūlī (d. 335 or 336/946–8), we have what Björkman has called the most important source in this field for the whole ᶜAbbasid period. Whilst not neglecting linguistic topics, it concentrates on practicalities: the use of introductory formulae in correspondence; the descriptive titles (*nuᶜūt*) of persons of rank, such as

18 "Towards the interpretation of al-Saqaṭī's observations on grain and flour-milling", *Journal of Semitic Studies*, XXIII, 1978, 283–97; "Some observations on the bread trade in Muslim Málaga (*ca.* AD 1200)", *Journal of Semitic Studies*, XXIX, 1984, 111–22.

19 D. Sourdel, "Le 'livre des secrétaires de ᶜAbdallāh al-Baġdādī'", *Bulletin d'Etudes Orientales*, XIV, 1952–4, 116, n. 2.

caliphs, amirs and viziers; the use of seals; the various sizes of paper used for letters; types of script to be employed according to occasion, like the *qalam daqīq*, "fine hand", and the *qalam jalīl*, "thick hand", etc. Questions of script and penmanship were indeed at the heart of the secretary's expertise, and some authors devoted complete treatises to calligraphy, like the vizier Ibn Muqlah (d. 328/940), to whom is credited the invention of a special hand, the *khaṭṭ al-mansūb*, "well-proportioned" one.[20]

The duties specifically appertaining to the vizier were less extensively surveyed by authors, although since every vizier had a secretarial training behind him, all the manuals of secretaryship have relevance here also. Some treatises on the *adab al-wazīr* were however composed, and two have survived: the *Qawānīn al-wizārah* of al-Māwardī and the *Tuḥfat al-wuzarāʾ* attributed to the philologist and *adīb* of Naysābūr, al-Thaʿālibī (d. 429/1038), but in reality of nearly two centuries later. These deal, in a somewhat theoretical manner, with the moral and intellectual qualities required of a vizier.[21]

These topics of *kitābah* and *wizārah* comprise the subject-matter of the fairly numerous subsequent manuals of official procedure, even though the institutions and administrative techniques involved became more complex as time went on. Lines of governors and, in some cases, completely independent dynasties which assumed control in the provinces of the caliphate modelled their own administrative institutions on those of Baghdad, whilst naturally modifying them to suit local circumstances. We see this process at work in Egypt with particular clarity, for there the lives of the cultivators and the agricultural lands themselves had been controlled by a sophisticated bureaucracy since Pharaonic times; moreover, from 358/969 onwards, it was under the dominion of the Faṭimid caliphs for two centuries, and these rulers came to outshine the ʿAbbasids of Iraq in the extensiveness of the sphere of operations of their bureaucracy. Hence it is not surprising that, from now onwards, the genre of manuals of *kitābah* finds its finest flowering within the Egyptian context. This succession passes through an author like the late Faṭimid ʿAlī b. al-Ṣayrafī (d. 542/1147) in his *Qānūn dīwān al-rasāʾil*, specifically on the correspondence department, which was now – despite the book's title – increasingly styled the *dīwān al-inshāʾ*, to the apogee of the tradition, the stupendous, all-embracing *Ṣubḥ al-aʿshā fī ṣināʿat al-inshāʾ* of the Mamlūk author Aḥmad al-Qalqashandī (d. 821/1418). The scale of this last work, comprising fourteen large volumes

[20] Björkman, *Beiträge*, 4–12; Sourdel, *Le Vizirat ʿabbāside*, I, 14–16; *EI*², "Kātib. i. In the caliphate".
[21] Sourdel, *Vizirat*, I, 6–14.

in the modern printed edition, allowed the author to pass in review such aspects of theoretical knowledge required by a secretary as law, grammar, rhetoric and geography, in addition to the more strictly technical information needed, including forms of address; the correct use of honorific titles (*alqāb*); types of script, ink and paper; the use of secret codes,[22] etc. Furthermore, al-Qalqashandī's work is rendered particularly valuable, as much for the general historian of Islam as for the specialist on administration, by the large number of original documents – most numerous for the Faṭimid, Ayyubid and Mamlūk periods – which he sets forth as models for secretaries to copy.[23] The preservation in this way of the texts of a considerable number of administrative decrees and diplomatic documents – including letters to non-Muslim potentates like the Christian kings of Spain, the Pope in Rome, the Byzantine emperor in Constantinople and the Mongol khans of central Asia – compensates in some measure for the almost total dearth of actual documents physically surviving from Islamic chanceries of these earlier centuries, a situation in sharp contrast to the wealth of original documentation, both secular and ecclesiastical, available to the historian of medieval Europe. In fact, collections of model letters of all kinds – treaties, grants of office, safe-conducts, etc. – had already been made in various parts of the Islamic world, the Persian as well as the Arabic ones, and the collected epistles of great stylists of the past, like those of the outstanding quartet of ministers and secretaries from the Buyid period, the Ṣāḥib Ismāʿīl b. ʿAbbād (d. 385/995), Abū Isḥāq al-Ṣābiʾ, ʿAbd al-ʿAzīz b. Yūsuf (d. 388/998) and Abūʾl-Faḍl b. al-ʿAmīd (d. 360/970), were eagerly studied by budding secretaries; this material is naturally much cited by al-Qalqashandī.[24]

BIOGRAPHICAL MATERIAL AND COLLECTIONS OF ANECDOTES ON VIZIERS AND SECRETARIES

The century *c.* AD 850–950 saw the particular florescence of the composition of works on the careers and lives of the great viziers and their secretaries, treated from a historical point of view and therefore valuable for their general historical information, as well as for the light which they throw on the working of the *dīwān*s. We know from sources like Ibn al-Nadīm's *Fihrist* of several works with titles such as *Kitāb al-Wuzarāʾ* or *Kitāb Akhbār*

[22] See C. E. Bosworth, "The section on codes and their decipherment in Qalqashandī's *Ṣubḥ al-aʿshā*", *Journal of Semitic Studies*, VIII, 1963, 17–33. [23] Björkman, *Beiträge*, 19ff; *EI*[2], "al-Ḳalḳashandī".
[24] Mez, *Renaissance*, Eng. trans., 242–9.

al-wuzarāʾ, but the passage of time has been regrettably hard on them. Thus all early works on the Barmakī family of viziers, whose spectacular fall in 187/203 at the hands of a resentful and vindictive Hārūn al-Rashīd excited the pity and wonder of contemporaries to an unparalleled degree, have been lost, and the ones that remain in Arabic and Persian with titles like *Akhbār al-Barāmikah* are of a late date and lack any original material not already found in earlier historical and *adab* collections.[25] Among the few biographical works which have survived, in reasonable part at least, is the *Kitāb al-Wuzarāʾ wa-ʾl-kuttāb* of Ibn ʿAbdūs al-Jahshiyārī (d. 331/942), himself of secretarial family and chamberlain to the "Good Vizier", ʿAlī b. ʿĪsā b. Dāwūd. This is of first-rate significance, above all for the early ʿAbbasid period up to al-Maʾmūn's reign, and is full of intriguing items of information, for example about the neglect of the postal and intelligence services under al-Rashīd after the fall of the Barmakīs, so that when the caliph died, 4,000 unopened despatch bags were found.[26] Al-Ṣūlī too wrote a work on the viziers, known to us only fragmentarily, but rather more survives of Hilāl b. al-Muḥassin al-Ṣābiʾ's (d. 448/1056) continuation of the earlier works, his own *Tuḥfat al-umarāʾ fī taʾrīkh al-wuzarāʾ*, notable for the chancery documents of the early fourth/tenth century which it reproduces.

Virtually all the biographical works were written by secretaries themselves and tend, implicitly or explicitly, to extol the nobility and worth of the secretarial calling; and it is relevant to note that, at this time, the secretaries were acquiring a distinct *esprit de corps*, with their own distinctive garb, the *durrāʿah* or sleeved coat, and a consciousness of their importance in the state. However, there were some who viewed these trends with less favour, these critics being in the main representatives of what might be called the Arab traditionalist party in the Shuʿūbiyyah controversies (see *CHAL/ABL*, ch. 2). Al-Jāḥiẓ of Basra (d. 255/868–9) in his *Risālah fī Dhamm akhlāq al-kuttāb* (preserved only in an excerpted form) denounces the secretaries for their pride and arrogance, their vaunting of the political and administrative achievements of the Sasanid rulers of Persia, and their depreciation of the Qurʾān and the great doctors of Islam in favour of rationalizing philosophers;[27] exaggerated charges, no doubt, for many secretaries remained perfectly good Muslims, but with a modicum of truth to them in that the secretarial tradition did tend to absorb extraneous elements and many of its exponents were indeed opposed to Arab exclusivism.

[25] L. Bouvat, *Les Barmécides d'après les historiens arabes et persans*, Paris, 1912, 5–23.
[26] Ed. M. al-Saqqāʾ, Cairo, 1357/1938, 214.
[27] Excerpts trans. into English by C. Pellat, *The Life and Works of Jāḥiẓ. Translations of Selected Texts*, London 1969, 273–5.

MIRRORS FOR PRINCES AND MANUALS OF STATECRAFT

This genre of medieval Arabic literature, although limited in its surviving extent and fated to have a subsequent development more in Persian and Turkish literature, can legitimately be included in a survey of administrative literature. At first sight, works which treat of the moral and ethical bases of kingship and of statecraft (*siyāsah*, *tadbīr al-mulk*) would appear to reflect theoretical rather than practical considerations. Yet, apart from what they reveal of contemporary attitudes towards authority, these works usually have a grounding in practical affairs, and the anecdotes which many of them contain supply what may be termed at least para-historical material for the student of Islamic administration. Occasionally, an item of information which seems vague and impersonal can be pinned down into what seems to be a genuine historical context. Thus when Ṭāhir Dhūʾl-Yamīnayn (reigned 205–7/821–2) (see below) warns his son against neglecting the daily round of administrative chores lest a backlog of unfinished work result,[28] we are reminded of a passage in al-Ṭabarī's *Taʾrīkh*, related on the authority of the great-grandson of the caliph involved, where al-Hādī (reigned 169–70/785–6) is criticized by his minister for not receiving petitions and hearing complaints (*maẓālim*) for three whole days.[29]

The genre has a further significance in that it constitutes a meeting-place for several influences on Islamic ethics and traditions of government, some of these influences being non-Islamic. The purely Islamic conception of the caliph-imam was that he held his power from God and exercised it only in conformity with the *sharīʿah*. But it has already been noted above that the ʿAbbasid secretarial class was associated, in the suspicious minds of conservative, rigidly orthodox Muslims, with Persian traditions of royal authority and statecraft, and it is indisputable that a knowledge of the Sasanid empire and its rulers is a very noticeable element in the "Mirrors for Princes" genre, as the numerous anecdotes citing with approval the policies of rulers like Bahrām Chūbīn, Khusraw Anūshirvān (reigned AD 531–79) and Khusraw Aparvīz (reigned AD 591–628) and of the wise minister Buzurgmihr, and the organization of the Persian bureaucracy and court circle, demonstrate. One can also detect a lesser influence from India in the material comprising animal fables which came into the Middle East in pre-Islamic times as the fables of Bidpay, the later Arabic *Kalīlah wa-Dimnah*, going back to the Sanskrit *Panchatantra*; whilst an important Graeco-Hellenistic component is visible in the prominent role accorded to Alexander the Great as the exemplar of wise rule (Arabic translations of the

[28] Ibn Abī Ṭāhir Ṭayfūr, *Kitāb Baghdād*, Eng. trans. Bosworth, "An early Arabic Mirror for Princes", 39.

[29] *Taʾrīkh al-rusul wa-ʾl-mulūk*, ed. Leiden, 1964, III, 581–2.

alleged letters to Alexander from his tutor Aristotle go back to the later Umayyad period, and must be considered as among the earliest examples of the epistolary genre in Arabic) and in such a counsel as that of Ṭāhir Dhū ʾl-Yamīnayn, again to his son, that the latter should practise the virtue of moderation and circumspection (*iqtiṣād*), the golden mean or *mesotes* of Aristotelian ethics.[30]

Early authors in Arabic in this genre often wrote on a limited scale, in epistles or as component parts of larger *adab* collections. The noted translator Ibn al-Muqaffaʿ (d. *c.* 139/757) is said to have translated from the Pahlavi at least three works on Sasanid imperial traditions: the royal chronicle or *Khudāy-nāmah*, the *Āyīn-nāmah* on the hierarchy and organization of the court and the *Tāj-nāmah* on the life of Khusraw Anūshirvān. Of his own original work, however, we have two epistles, the *Adab kabīr* on practical and theoretical considerations of rule, and the *Risālah fī ʾl-Ṣaḥābah* on the topic of the ruler's relationship to his civil and military entourage. From the caliphate of al-Maʾmūn, notable for his interest in the mediation of the philosophical and scientific heritage of the ancient world to the Arabs, comes the terse but meaty epistle of the general Ṭāhir Dhū ʾl-Yamīnayn addressed in 206/821 to his son ʿAbdullāh when the latter was about to take up a provincial governorship, an exposition of the duties and responsibilities which power brings and of the qualities of the perfect ruler.[31] The more extended treatise from the mid-third/ninth century, the *Kitāb al-Tāj*, like several other works attributed – but almost certain falsely – to al-Jāḥiẓ, has proved to be a rich mine of information both on the organization of the Sasanid court and the ethics of the ruler and also on Islamic history, and its title is certainly reminiscent of the Middle Persian work said to have been translated by Ibn al-Muqaffaʿ, the *Tāj-nāmah* (see above).

In the ensuing decades, works like the *ʿUyūn al-akhbār* of Ibn Qutaybah and the *ʿIqd al-farīd* of Ibn ʿAbd Rabbihi (d. 328/940) incorporate material of the "Mirrors for Princes" type. Al-Māwardī wrote a *Naṣīḥat al-mulūk* and a further work in the same vein, both of which are extant; but the title of the first one is better known as that of the Persian treatise on the Islamic religious beliefs required in a ruler and on practical statecraft commonly attributed to Abū Ḥāmid al-Ghazālī. The first part, at least, was originally composed, almost certainly by al-Ghazālī, in Persian for a Saljūq prince (who would doubtless have been unable to read it in either Persian or

[30] Richter, *Studien*, 93–10; Ibn Abī Ṭāhir Ṭayfūr, *Kitāb Baghdād*, Eng. trans. Bosworth, "An early Arabic Mirror for Princes", 32; *CHALUP*, 155–9.

[31] Ibn Abī Ṭāhir Ṭayfūr, *Kitāb Baghdād*, Eng. trans. Bosworth "An early Arabic Mirror for Princes", 25–41.

Arabic!); the second part, however, is more probably to be attributed to some unknown Persian writer working very much in the Persian ethical and political tradition.[32] Both parts achieved much wider diffusion in the Arabic version made after the authors' time, *al-Tibr al-masbūk fī naṣīḥat al-mulūk*.[33] Various other "Mirrors for Princes" in Arabic are known, some from the Muslim West like those of Ibn abī Randaqah al-Ṭurṭūshī (d. 520/1126 or 526/1132) and of the Sicilian Muḥammad b. ᶜAbdullāh b. Ẓafar (d. 565/1169 or 568/1172–3), others from the central or eastern lands like those of al-Thaᶜālibī and Sibṭ Ibn al-Jawzī (d. 654/1257), all of a predominantly literary cast. Although the literary, idealizing element remains strong in them, practical considerations obtrude to a more perceptible extent in the well-known Persian treatises, the *Qābūs-nāmah* of the Ziyarid prince of Gurgān and Ṭabaristān Kay Kāwūs b. Iskandar (wrote in 475/1082–3), and the *Siyāsat-nāmah* or *Siyar al-mulūk* of the great Saljūq vizier Niẓām al-Mulk (d. 485/1092), concerning both of which it could be said that the authors were themselves practical men of affairs.[34]

32 Cf. Patricia Crone, "Did al-Ghazālī write a Mirror for Princes? On the authorship of *Naṣīḥat al-mulūk*", *Jerusalem Studies in Arabic and Islam*, x, 1987, 167–91.

33 See below, ch. 25, 442–3; Richter, *Studien*, 4–110; Eng. trans. Bagley, *Ghazālī's Book of Counsel for Kings*.

34 E. G. Browne *A Literary History of Persia*, London and Cambridge, 1902–24, II, 212–17, 276–87; Rosenthal, *Political Thought in Medieval Islam*, 67–83.

CHAPTER 11

ARABIC BIOGRAPHICAL WRITING

Biography is one of the most extensive areas of Arabic literature. Its earliest, and characteristic form, is the biographical dictionary, although biographical writing early developed a variety of other forms.

Arabic has no single term for biography. The most widely used terms are *sīrah* (pl. *siyar*) and *tarjamah* (pl. *tarājim*). The use of *tarjamah* tends to be restricted to shorter biographical notices, while *sīrah* usually refers to biographies of substantial length.[1] The term *sīrah* was first used in literature for the biography of the Prophet Muḥammad,[2] but this did not preclude its use for the biographies of less eminent figures.[3] In both modern and medieval Arabic *sīrah* may also be found in the titles of works which are not strictly biographies at all, such as the traditional story *Sīrat ᶜAntar* and Muḥammad al-Maṭwī's history of the city of al-Qayrawān entitled *Sīrat al-Qayrawān*.[4] A less common term for biography is *taᶜrīf* (lit. "definition"), which makes its appearance in literary usage after the end of the ᶜAbbasid period. In addition there are a number of terms which are used for laudatory biography or hagiography. The most widely used of these is *manāqib* (virtues, feats, exploits), a word which frequently appears in the titles of biographies which are intended to present a portrait of a morally admirable person, together with a recital of his outstanding actions and achievements. This kind of laudatory biography early took on the character of hagiography.[5]

Concern for the details of the biography of the Prophet led to the collecting by his followers of all available traditions about him and his Companions,[6] and this naturally led on to an interest in the *muḥaddithūn*, i.e. the transmitters of *Ḥadīth*, or Traditions, which resulted in biographical material on them being collected and used to assess their reliability, this area of study being known as *ᶜilm al-rijāl* ("science of trustworthy authorities").

[1] Muḥammad ᶜAbd al-Ghanī Ḥasan, *al-Tarājim wa-ʾl-siyar*, 6, 27. [2] Cf. *CHALUP*, ch. 17.

[3] *Shorter EI*, "Sīra"; for the Ibāḍī use of *sīrah*, see above ch. 3, 35f; for the meaning of *siyar* as a technical term of Islamic law, see above, ch. 9, 143f.

[4] In the opinion of Sayyid Quṭb the use of the term *tarjamah* is also justifiable as the designation of the history of a city; see his *al-Naqd al-adabī: uṣūluh wa-manāhijuh*, Beirut and Cairo, 1980, 89.

[5] *EI*², "Manāḳib"; see also below ch. 12, 216. [6] Cf. *CHALUP*, chs. 10, 11.

In turn this led to the collection of biographical material on other classes of persons important to the development of Islamic theology and law, and later to the collection of material on other categories of persons, such as philologists, poets and judges, and so on, but even when biography became a distinct genre in Arabic literature it never completely lost the characteristics linking it with the science of *Ḥadīth*.

The predominant form of biographical writing in Arabic became the biographical dictionary, but, as well as the *Sīrah* of the Prophet, other full-length biographies of prominent individuals came to be written in the ᶜAbbasid period. Autobiographies were also composed, although these are comparatively few in number.

BIOGRAPHICAL DICTIONARIES

Greek and Roman biographers wrote collections of biographies of men belonging to the same category, but their scope and method were quite different from later Arabic works, and the genre of the biographical dictionary must be regarded as an original contribution of Islamic literature. It made its appearance some two centuries after the death of the Prophet, and has continued to flourish up to the present day.[7] It developed in close association with the study of *Ḥadīth*, because it was important to Muslims to know who the transmitters of *Ḥadīth* were, and the study of the details of their lives would provide evidence of their degrees of trustworthiness. There was, more generally, a desire to gather and record as much as possible about the lives of men and women who had known, or at least met, the Prophet (i.e. al-Ṣaḥābah), and the succeeding generation who had in turn known them (al-Tābiᶜūn). The personal details regarding such men and women were the materials for the biographical notices brought together into biographical dictionaries.

The numbers of biographical notices included in these works are often very large: Ibn Khallikān in his *Wafayāt al-aᶜyān* has over 800; Ibn Ḥajar al-ᶜAsqalānī, in his *al-Durar al-kāminah*, has over 5,000, while ᶜIzz al-Dīn b. al-Athīr (d. 630/1233) in his *Usd al-ghābah fī maᶜrifat al-Ṣaḥābah* ("Lions of the Forest regarding Knowledge of the Companions") has over 7,000, and some are even larger than this. Most of these biographies are of Muslims, but notices of non-Muslims are to be found in some dictionaries, such as those of persons from classical antiquity which are to be found in the works of ᶜAlī b. Yūsuf al-Qifṭī and Ibn abī Uṣaybiᶜah, and notices of Christian,

7 Modern examples of the genre include such works as *Taʾrīkh ᶜulamāʾ Baghdād fī ʾl-qarn al-rābiᶜ ᶜashar* (Baghdad, 1982) by Yūnus al-Shaykh Ibrāhīm al-Sāmarrāʾī, and *Tarājim al-muʾallifīn al-Tūnisiyyīn* (Beirut, 1982) by Muḥammad Maḥfūẓ.

Jewish, Ṣabian and Zoroastrian persons may be found scattered in other collected biographies.

As regards the sources of this abundant biographical material, it is obvious that in the earlier stages it was compiled from oral sources like the *Ḥadīth*, and it is presented as such, being provided with full chains of transmitters (*isnād*s). With the passage of time biographers came to rely more on written evidence, but this might still be combined with information obtained orally.

The length of notices varies widely. Some are very brief. ʿIyāḍ b. Mūsā al-Yaḥsūbī (d. 544/1149) in his *Tartīb al-madārik wa-taqrīb al-masālik li-maʿrifat aʿlām madhhab Mālik* ("Regulation of the Perception and Clarification of Procedures for the Knowledge of the Leading Adherents of the School of Mālik") has the following notice on ʿAbd al-Ḥamīd al-Sindī: "He was well known among the companions of Saḥnūn. He was an upright man. He passed away in al-Qayrawān, 253 H."

Slightly longer notices may give some brief appreciation of their subject. ʿAbd al-Raḥmān b. Muḥammad b. al-Anbārī (d. 577/1181) in his *Nuzhat al-alibbāʾ fī ṭabaqāt al-udabāʾ* ("Recreation of the Intelligent regarding the Classes of Authors") has the following concerning Abū ʾl-Haytham al-Rāzī:

> Abū ʾl-Haytham al-Rāzī was learned in the Arabic language, of attractive speech and a person of great discernment. Abū ʾl-Mufaḍḍal al-Mundaribī said: "I was constantly in Abū ʾl-Haytham's company, and I found him an outstanding person, with a retentive memory, a sound knowledge of belles-lettres, a godfearing scholar, a frequent attender at prayers and of sound religious practice; and he was not mean with his learning and literary knowledge." He passed away in 226 H, in the caliphate of al-Muʿtaṣim billāh.

In contrast to these entries others are of considerable length: Yāqūt in his *Irshād al-arīb* devotes twenty-five pages to ʿAmr b. Baḥr al-Jāḥiẓ, and over fifty to Abūʾl-ʿAlāʾ al-Maʿarrī (edition of D. S. Margoliouth).

In spite of such longer entries the Arabic biographical dictionaries are, in general, examples of prosopography, rather than biography in the strict sense. Biography seeks to understand the individual and those features of character which make him or her unique; prosopography seeks to record a group of individuals having certain features in common, and these individuals are viewed in relationship to the prevailing characteristics of the group. In their general scope the Arabic biographical dictionaries combine (and anticipate) the features of both *Who's Who* and works such as the *Dictionary of National Biography*. The most frequent matters included in the entries are the subject's date of death, his lineage, his education and travels, his appointments, descriptions of his intellectual and moral qualities and interesting anecdotes recorded about him. In addition one often finds philological notes on the form of the subject's name, a brief description of his physical appearance and, in the case of authors, a list of his books.

The earliest method of arrangement of biographical material was according to *ṭabaqāt*.[8] The term *ṭabaqah* originally meant "layer", but developed a technical meaning of "generation" or "class" to denote a group of persons who had played some role in history of significance from a religious, scientific, military, artistic or other point of view. There was no general agreement on the exact length of a generation, and consequently no agreement among biographers on which persons belonged to a particular *ṭabaqah*: Ibn Saᶜd, for example, divides the Companions and Successors into five *ṭabaqāt*, whereas al-Ḥākim al-Naysābūrī (d. 405/1014) divides them into twelve.[9] The *ṭabaqāt* arrangement did however produce a broadly chronological ordering of the material. With the increasing bulk of recorded biographies the *ṭabaqāt* arrangement was to some extent replaced by an alphabetic arrangement, although this never entirely superseded the earlier one.

In regard to the principles of selection on which the Arabic biographical dictionaries are compiled, three main groups may be distinguished: dictionaries which are devoted to persons notable in a particular field, such as Traditionists, rulers, jurists, poets, philosophers or physicians; dictionaries which are devoted to eminent persons resident in a particular city or country; and general dictionaries which do not confine themselves to any particular place or occupation, but take in eminent people from many different walks of life. A later development of the latter group is the centennial dictionary, which treats of different classes of persons who lived in a particular century of the *Hijrah*.

Some biographical dictionaries may however fall within more than one of the above groups, as for example *Ṭabaqāt fuqahāᵓ jibāl al-Yaman* ("Classes of the Jurists of the Mountains of the Yemen") by ᶜUmar b. ᶜAlī al-Jaᶜdī (d. 586/1190), while within a particular group a dictionary may be limited in its scope by some arbitrary principle of selection, as with *al-Muḥammadūn min al-shuᶜarāᵓ wa-ashᶜāruhum* ("Poets whose Name was Muḥammad and their Poems") by ᶜAlī b. Yūsuf al-Qifṭī.

The above classification is perhaps the most convenient one, but it is not followed by all literary historians; ᶜAbd al-Raḥmān ᶜUṭbah, for instance, in his survey of the classic works of Arabic literature, *Maᶜa al-maktabah al-*

8 Hafsi, "Le genre 'Ṭabaqāt'", 229f.

9 Ibid., 237. For an example of the continuing use of this term in this sense, see Ḥ. Muᵓnis, *Maᶜālim taᵓrīkh al-Maghrib*, Cairo, 1980, 216, where reference is made to the two Spanish Orientalists "F. Codera and J. Ribera and those in their *ṭabaqah*".

ʿ*Arabiyyah*, divides the biographical dictionaries into those which are "perpendicular" (i.e. arranged alphabetically), those which are "horizontal" (i.e. arranged according to centuries or *ṭabaqāt*) and those which are "local".

The biographical dictionaries devoted to particular subjects fall into several broad categories: those concerned with persons who received, preserved and interpreted the message of Islam (such as the Companions of the Prophet, transmitters of *Ḥadīth*, Qurʾān reciters and exegetes); those representing the mystical or Ṣūfī tradition in Islam;[10] adherents of non-Sunnī sects; jurists and judges; Islamic rulers; literary figures (poets and philologists); scientists, physicians and philosophers.

In the first category is the *Kitāb al-Ṭabaqāt al-kabīr* of Muḥammad b. Saʿd (d. 230/845), which has already been noted in this *History*[11] from the point of view of its importance in the development of the study of Tradition; here it is considered from the point of view of its being the earliest extant Arabic biographical dictionary (the earliest biographical dictionary in Arabic was the *Kitāb Ṭabaqāt al-muḥaddithīn* of al-Muʿāfā b. ʿImrān al-Mawṣilī, who died in 184/800, but no copy is known to have survived). Ibn Saʿd's book contains 4,250 biographical notices, 600 of them of women. The purpose of all these biographies was to provide information on people who were important for the transmission of *Ḥadīth*, and who had contributed to, or taken part in, the development of Islam during its first two centuries. The space devoted to each person is broadly proportional to his or her importance in this latter regard. Thus over eighty pages are devoted to the famous ʿUmar b. al-Khaṭṭāb, eight pages to the venerated Fāṭimah, daughter of the Prophet, and eight words to the obscure Muḥammad b. Aflaḥ (Leiden edition).

Most of the basic features of the Arabic biographical dictionary, as they have continued from the third/ninth century to the fourteenth/twentieth century are already to be found in the work of Ibn Saʿd. Among these may be noted, as especially characteristic, the interest in the descent of each individual, and the emphasis on the outer events, rather than the mental development, of a person's life. Thus two-thirds of Ibn Saʿd's short notice of Thaʿlabah b. Ḥāṭib is devoted to his descent, and to descents from him:

> Thaʿlabah was the son of Ḥāṭib, the son of ʿAmr, the son of ʿUbayd, the son of Umayyah, the son of Zayd, and his mother was Umāmah, the daughter of Ṣāmit, the son of Khālid, the son of ʿAṭiyyah, the son of Ḥawṭ, the son of Ḥabīb, the son of ʿAmr, the son of ʿAwf. Thaʿlabah's children were ʿUbaydullāh, ʿAbdullāh and ʿUmayr (their mother being from the Banū Wāqif); Rifāʿah, ʿAbd al-Raḥmān, ʿIyāḍ and ʿAmīrah (their mother being Lubābah, the daughter of ʿUqbah, the son of

[10] For Ṣūfī biographies see ch. 5, above, 62–3. [11] *CHALUP*, 278.

Bashīr of Ghaṭafān). Today Thaʿlabah b. Ḥāṭib has descendants in Medina and Baghdad. The Messenger of God (may God bless him and give him peace) pronounced a bond of brotherhood between Thaʿlabah b. Ḥāṭib and Muʿattib b. al-Ḥamrāʾ of Khuzāʿah, the ally of the Banū Makhzūm. Thaʿlabah b. Ḥāṭib was present at the battles of Badr and Uḥud.

In his notice of Rayṭah bint al-Ḥārith, Ibn Saʿd gives, in a few lines, the outer events of a life of religious conversion, exile and suffering:

Rayṭah was the daughter of al-Ḥārith, the son of Jubaylah, the son of ʿĀmir, the son of Kaʿb, the son of Saʿd, the son of Taym, and her mother was Zaynab the daughter of ʿAbdullāh, the son of Sāʿidah, the son of Mashnūʿ, the son of ʿAbd, the son of Ḥabtar of Khuzāʿah. She was the sister of Ṣubayḥah b. al-Ḥārith. She was an early convert to Islam at Mecca. She gave her allegiance to the Prophet, and was in the second wave of emigration to Abyssinia, with her husband al-Ḥārith, the son of Khālid, the son of Ṣakhr, the son of ʿAmir, the son of Kaʿb, the son of Saʿd, the son of Taym. There she bore him Mūsā, ʿĀʾishah and Zaynab. Mūsā died in Abyssinia, and Rayṭah bint al-Ḥārith perished on the return voyage [to the Ḥijāz].

The ʿAbbasid period saw the compilation of a large number of biographical dictionaries, some of the most important of which may be noted here. Abū ʿAbdullāh Muḥammad b. Ismāʿīl al-Bukhārī (d. 256/870), the author of *al-Jāmiʿ al-ṣaḥīḥ*, produced his *Kitāb al-Rijāl al-kabīr* containing biographies of all those persons known to the author whose names appear in the *isnād*s of the Prophetical *Ḥadīth*.[12] In the following century another important work on *Ḥadīth* criticism was the *Kitāb al-Jarḥ wa-ʾl-taʿdīl* ("Book of Impugning or Confirming", i.e. the evidence of transmitters of *Ḥadīth*) of Abū Muḥammad ʿAbd al-Raḥmān b. abī Ḥātim al-Rāzī (d. 327/938).

The genre of the biographical dictionary proceeded to extend to other classes of notable people, as in such works as *Kitāb Wulāt Miṣr wa-quḍātihā* ("Book of the Governors and Judges of Egypt") by Muḥammad b. Yūsuf al-Kindī (d. 350/961), and *Quḍāt Qurṭubah* ("The Judges of Cordova") by Muḥammad b. al-Ḥārith al-Khushanī (d. 371/981).[13]

Among dictionaries of jurists are the *Ṭabaqāt al-fuqahāʾ al-Shāfiʿiyyah* ("The Classes of Shafiʿite Jurists") of Muḥammad b. Aḥmad al-ʿAbbādī (d. 458/1066), the *Ṭabaqāt al-Ḥanābilah* ("Classes of the Ḥanbalites") of Abū ʾl-Ḥusayn Muḥammad b. abī Yaʿlā al-Farrāʾ (d. 526/1133), and the *Tartīb al-madārik* of al-Yaḥsūbī (see above).

Works on literary figures include the *Yatīmat al-dahr fī maḥāsin ahl al-ʿaṣr fī shuʿarāʾ ahl al-ʿaṣr* ("The Unique Pearl of the Age on the Beauties of the People of the Time regarding the Poets of the Time") of ʿAbd al-Malik b. Muḥammad al-Thaʿālibī, a biographical anthology of poets, the dictionary of philologists by Ibn al-Anbārī entitled *Nuzhat al-alibbāʾ* (see above), and

[12] Ibid.
[13] For biographies of viziers and civil servants, see above, ch. 10, 163–4.

the *Irshād al-arīb ilā maʿrifat al-adīb* ("Guide of the Intelligent towards the Knowledge of the Man of Letters") of Yāqūt b. ʿAbdullāh al-Ḥamawī (d. 626/1229).

The first dictionary to deal with physicians and philosophers was the *Ṭabaqāt al-aṭibbāʾ wa-ʾl-ḥukamāʾ* ("Classes of Physicians and Philosophers") by Abū Dāwūd Sulaymān b. Ḥassān b. Juljul of Cordova (d. 399/1009); this was followed much later by two important works in the same field in the seventh/thirteenth century, the *Ikhbār al-ʿulamāʾ bi-akhbār al-ḥukamāʾ* ("Informing the Learned of the Accounts of the Philosophers") by Jamāl al-Dīn abū ʾl-Ḥasan ʿAlī b. Yūsuf al-Qifṭī (d. 646/1248), and the *ʿUyūn al-anbāʾ fī ṭabaqāt al-aṭibbāʾ* ("Sources of Information regarding the Classes of Physicians") of Muwaffaq al-Dīn abū ʾl-ʿAbbās Aḥmad b. abī Uṣaybiʿah (d. 668/1270). Ibn abī Uṣaybiʿah was a practising physician who had studied in Damascus, and, in writing his *ʿUyūn al-anbāʾ*, he drew on earlier writers such as Ibn Juljul and al-Qifṭī, as well as information gathered from his personal acquaintances. *ʿUyūn al-anbāʾ* contains some 400 biographies organized into fifteen chapters. It abounds in information regarding the teaching and practice of medicine and the various appointments enjoyed by medical men.

Biographical dictionaries were also devoted to more unusual groups than the foregoing: an example is the as yet unpublished work *Ṭabaqāt al-muʿabbirīn* ("Classes of Oneirocritics") by al-Ḥasan b. al-Ḥusayn al-Khallāl (d. 532/1137), in which the author manages to bring together biographical notices of 600 exponents of the science of dream interpretation which, according to Ibn Khaldūn, is one of the sciences of the religious law.[14]

The urban-centred nature of Islam gave rise to a widespread interest in local history, and this led to the compilation of dictionaries containing life-notices of the worthies of particular cities, such worthies being mainly confined to the ranks of the religious scholars, jurists and poets. One of the earliest works of this type was written in the fifth/eleventh century, the *Taʾrīkh Baghdād* of Abū Bakr Aḥmad b. ʿAlī (d. 463/1071), known as al-Khaṭīb al-Baghdādī ("the Preacher of Baghdad"). This multivolume work consists of a topographical and cultural introduction to the city of Baghdad, followed by biographies of scholars who grew up in the city or settled there from elsewhere. This book was the model for most later biographical dictionaries based on a particular city, such as the even larger work of Abū ʾl-Qāsim ʿAlī b. al-Ḥasan b. ʿAsākir (d. 571/1176), entitled *Taʾrīkh Dimashq* ("History of Damascus").

Examples of this type of work from the Maghrib and Spain are the *Ṭabaqāt ʿulamāʾ Ifrīqiyah wa-Tūnis* ("Classes of the Scholars of Ifrīqiyah and

[14] *Muqaddimah*, trans. Rosenthal, III, 103.

Tunis") by Abū ʾl-ʿArab Muḥammad b. Aḥmad b. Tamīm (d. 333/945), and *al-Iḥāṭah fī akhbār Gharnāṭah* ("Cognizance of the History of Granada") by Lisān al-Dīn b. al-Khaṭīb (d. 776/1374). In the latter book Lisān al-Dīn adopts a method of procedure somewhat different from his predecessors, in that, while he uses an alphabetic order for his biographical notices, he puts rulers first, then military commanders and nobles, then judges, Qurʾān readers and ulema, then writers and poets, and so on, concluding with notices of mystics, "in order that the beginning should be monarchy, and the ending musk", as he puts it.[15]

The first general biographical dictionary which includes people of eminence in every branch of life and from every country after the age of the Companions and the Successors is the *Wafayāt al-aʿyān wa-anbāʾ abnāʾ al-zamān* ("Obituaries of Eminent Men and Notices of the Sons of the Epoch") by Shams al-Dīn abū ʾl-ʿAbbās Aḥmad b. Muḥammad b. Khallikān (d. 681/1282). It is arranged alphabetically, and includes over 800 biographies. This celebrated work has received high praise from both eastern and western critics. Abū ʾl-Maḥāsin Yūsuf b. Taghribirdī (d. 874/1469) in his *al-Manhal al-Ṣāfī* called Ibn Khallikān's book "the acme of excellence" (*ghāyat al-ḥusn*).[16] Sir William Jones asserted: "Est certe copiosior Nepote, elegantior Plutarcho, Laertio iucundior: et dignus est profecto liber qui in omnes Europae linguas conversus prodeat."[17] Among modern critics Muḥammad ʿAbd al-Ghanī Ḥasan refers to Ibn Khallikān's "splendid historical work" (*taʾrīkhuh al-jalīl*),[18] and Reynold Alleyne Nicholson characterizes it as follows: "It is composed in simple and elegant language, it is extremely accurate, and it contains an astonishing quantity of miscellaneous historical and literary information, not drily catalogued but conveyed in the most pleasing fashion by anecdotes and excerpts which illustrate every department of Moslem life."[19]

Nicholson compares the *Wafayāt al-aʿyān* with Boswell's *Life of Samuel Johnson*, but a more striking comparison might be drawn between Ibn Khallikān's book and the *Brief Lives* of John Aubrey (d. 1108/1697). The resemblances between the two works are remarkable: both evidence the same indefatigable zeal in the collection of genealogical facts, personal details and telling anecdotes, and both have the ability to sum up the essentials of a person's character in a few words – although Ibn Khallikān nowhere quite reaches the brevity of Aubrey's notice of Abraham Wheelock, one of the pioneers of Arabic studies in the University of Cambridge: "Abraham Wheelock – simple man."

15 Cf. Qurʾān, lxxxiii.26.
16 Cited by MacGuckin de Slane, introduction to Ibn Khallikān's *Wafayāt*, I, xi.
17 Ibid., iv. 18 *al-Tarājim wa-ʾl-siyar*, 43. 19 *Literary History*, 452.

A continuation to Ibn Khallikān's book, entitled *Fawāt al-Wafayāt*, was written by Muḥammad b. Shākir b. Aḥmad al-Kutubī (d. 764/1363), and this in turn was followed by *al-Wāfī bi-ʾl-Wafayāt* by Khalīl b. Aybak al-Ṣafadī. The series was concluded with the book of Ibn Taghribirdī, *al-Manhal al-ṣāfī wa-ʾl-mustawfī baʿd al-Wāfī* (see above).

The increasing abundance of biographical material led, after the ʿAbbasid age, to the production of general biographical dictionaries which were devoted to the lives of persons dying in a particular century, the first such centennial dictionary[20] being *al-Durar al-kāminah fī aʿyān al-miʾah al-thāminah* ("Hidden Pearls on the Notables of the Eighth Century") by Aḥmad b. ʿAlī b. Ḥajar al-ʿAsqalānī (d. 852/1449); this work contains over 5,000 biographical notices of persons who lived in the eighth century of the *Hijrah*.

THE BIOGRAPHICAL DICTIONARIES AS REGISTERS OF VITAL DATA

The Arabic biographical dictionaries are essential for the study of Islamic civilization; they represent in fact the "greatest untapped source of information on the medieval Middle East".[21] Their potential contribution to narrative history is clear, but perhaps more important is the cumulative value of these thousands of life histories in reconstructing a picture of Islamic medieval society.

During recent years the biographical dictionaries have attracted an increasing scholarly interest for the new light they can be made to throw on the economic, social and demographic history of the lands of Islam, by using the facts they provide on each individual's family connections, his occupations, his place of residence, his age at death, and so on, to reconstitute families, to trace the effects of epidemics and the fluctuations in the price of grain, population mobility (or lack of it), the average size of families, etc. In all this it is a question of using the biographical dictionaries, quite irrespective of their literary value, as though they were registers of vital data, and in this way they can be made to yield valuable information about the development of Islamic society in a way which would have been impossible to foresee by their authors.

The work of, among others, Richard W. Bulliet, Carl F. Petry and Charles Pellat illustrates the valuable results that can accrue from the analysis of the data of the biographical dictionaries. Studies of this kind are being furthered by the Onomasticon Arabicum, the international project

[20] *EI*², "Ibn Ḥadjar al-ʿAsḳalānī". [21] Bulliet, "A quantitive approach", 195.

based in Paris which has as its aim the classification and indexing, from the prosopographical and biographical literature, of all known persons in medieval Islam.[22]

INDIVIDUAL BIOGRAPHIES

The earliest Arabic works devoted to individual biographies are of the *manāqib* type, that is they are laudatory or hagiographical, and seek to give prominence to the merits, virtues and remarkable deeds of the individual concerned.[23] These biographies are concerned with scholars and mystics, rulers and war leaders.

An early example of an individual biography other than that of the Prophet is the life of Yamīn al-Dawlah Maḥmūd of Ghaznah (reigned 388–421/998–1030), entitled *al-Kitāb al-Yamīnī*, by Abū'l-Naṣr Muḥammad al-ʿUtbī (d. 427/1036). The conquests of Maḥmūd of Ghaznah were comparable with those of the celebrated commanders in the days of the first Islamic conquests, and al-ʿUtbī, who witnessed Maḥmūd's campaigns, glorified the great *ghāzī* in his book.

Royal biographies were an important part of historical writing in the Ayyubid and early Mamlūk periods.[24] Ṣalāḥ al-Dīn Yūsuf al-Ayyūbī (d. 589/1193) was the subject of several such biographies, which were devoted to describing his military campaigns and political triumphs, together with a presentation of his outstanding virtues. Among these biographers was Bahāʾ al-Dīn Yūsuf b. Rāfiʿ b. Shaddād (d. 632/1234), Ṣalāḥ al-Dīn's judge of the army, whose *al-Nawādir al-sulṭāniyyah wa-'l-maḥāsin al-Yūsufiyyah* chronicles the career of Ṣalāḥ al-Dīn at its height: "In his account of Saladin, written in a simple and straightforward style, he presents Saladin to us as no ordinary chronicle can . . . Bahāʾ al-Dīn may perhaps be called uncritical, but he was no deluded hero-worshipper."[25] His admiration is more often expressed by a telling observation of Ṣalāḥ al-Dīn's habitual actions than by unsubtle panegyric, as in the following comment:

> [Ṣalāḥ al-Dīn] – may God have mercy on him – used to give freely in times of hardship just as he did in times of abundance, and the officials in charge of his treasury coffers used to take the precaution of concealing a portion of the money from him so that they should not be caught unprepared by a sudden call on the funds, being aware that if he knew the money was there he would give it away.[26]

22 Fedwa M. Douglas and Geneviève Fourcade, *The Treatment by Computer of Medieval Arabic Biographical Data: an introduction and guide to the Onomasticon Arabicum*, Paris, 1976.

23 See above, ch. 5, 60f.

24 Cf. Holt, "Three biographies".

25 H. A. R. Gibb, *The Life of Saladin*, Oxford, 1973, 2.

26 Ibn Shaddād, *al-Sīrat al-Yūsufiyyah*, Cairo, 1962, 17; for another biography of Ṣalāḥ al-Dīn, see below, ch. 12, 222–3.

Of the Mamlūk sultan al-Ẓāhir Baybars (reigned 658–676/1260–1277) several contemporary or near-contemporary biographies have survived: those by Muḥyī ʾl-Dīn b. ʿAbd al-Ẓāhir (d. 692/1293), Shāfiʿ b. ʿAlī (d. 730/1330) and ʿIzz al-Dīn b. Shaddād (d. 684/1285).[27] ʿIzz al-Dīn's arrangement of his biographical work *al-Rawḍ al-ẓāhir fī sīrat al-malik al-Ẓāhir* ("The Brilliant Garden on the Biography of the Victorious King") resembles that of Xenophon's *Agesilaus*, in that the outer events of the hero's life are described first, while his virtues and exemplary traits of character are described in a separate section at the end of the book. In ʿIzz al-Dīn's work each part of the final section is introduced by a passage in rhymed prose, a form often characteristic of Islamic laudatory biography.

CHARACTERISTICS OF ARABIC BIOGRAPHY

"Any biography is inextricably linked with the priorities and assumptions of the age which produced it";[28] the priorities in Islamic culture were theological, legal and literary, whilst among its chief assumptions was that the history of the Islamic community was "essentially the contribution of individual men and women to the building up and transmission of its specific culture . . . and that their individual contributions [were] worthy of being recorded for future generations".[29]

Biographers went to great pains to achieve accuracy in the information they recorded. The problems connected with identifying people in the past arising through names written in an unvowelled script, or through different persons bearing the same name, had whole books devoted to them, such as the *Kitāb al-Mushtabih fī asmāʾ al-rijāl* ("Book of Names of Authorities Resembling Each Other") by Muḥammad b. Aḥmad al-Dhahabī (d. 748/1348), the author of the biographical work *Taʾrīkh al-Islām wa-ṭabaqāt al-mashāhīr wa-ʾl-aʿlām* ("History of Islam and Classes of Famous and Eminent Persons"). Biographers often went to great lengths to differentiate between degrees of certainty, near certainty and doubt. As an example of this Muḥammad ʿAbd al-Ghanī Ḥasan mentions the method of Yāqūt al-Ḥamawī in his *Irshād al-arīb*: "He does not state something positively when he is not certain; in such cases he uses phrases such as 'I think', 'I reckon', and similar expressions indicative of mere supposition. If he is confident of some matter he says: 'That which I know is', 'That with which I am acquainted is' and similar phrases indicative of certainty."[30]

[27] On ʿIzz al-Dīn see also below, ch. 12, 228–30. [28] A. Shelston, *Biography*, London, 1977, 15.

[29] H. A. R. Gibb "Islamic biographical literature" in B. Lewis and P. M. Holt (eds.), *Historians of the Middle East*, London, 1962, 54.

[30] *Al-Tarājim wa-ʾl-siyar*, 84; where accuracy in numbers is concerned, a cautionary note has however been sounded by L.I. Conrad, "Seven and the *Tasbīʿ*", *Journal of the Economic and Social History of the Orient*, XXXI, 1988, 42–73.

Here one may note the contrast between the precision achieved in biographies of Muslims with a certain degree of vagueness which characterizes many of the biographies of non-Muslim figures (as in the dictionaries of scientists and physicians), separated as they were from Islamic scholars by barriers of language and remoteness in time and place. This is how al-Qifṭī begins his notice of Pythagoras:

Pythagoras: the famous and celebrated Greek sage and philosopher. He lived some time later than Empedocles, and studied wisdom under the disciples of Solomon son of David the Prophet in Egypt, after they had emigrated there from Syria. Before that he had studied geometry under the Egyptians. Then he returned to the land of the Greeks and introduced geometry to them, a subject with which they had not previously been acquainted. He also introduced them to physics and theology. Through his own mental acuteness he worked out the science of harmony and the composition of musical sounds, and he arranged them according to numerical proportions. He claimed that he derived this from the lamp of Prophecy . . .

This may be contrasted with al-Qifṭī's account of an eminent Spanish surgeon:

ᶜUmar b. ᶜAbd al-Raḥmān b. Aḥmad b. ᶜAlī al-Kirmānī al-Qurṭubī al-Andalusī, Abūʾl-Ḥakam, who was well versed in mathematics and geometry, travelled to the East, where he stayed in Ḥarrān, in the Jazīrah, studying geometry and medicine. Subsequently he returned to Spain and settled in the frontier town of Saragossa. He took with him the epistles known as the *Epistles of the Brethren of Purity* (*Rasāʾil Ikhwān al-Ṣafāʾ*). It is not known that anyone brought them into Spain before him. His interest was in medicine, in which he had considerable experience and influence. He was famous for his skill in cautery, amputation, dissection, abscission and other operations of the medical art. He died in Saragossa in the year 458 H, having reached the age of ninety years or a little more.

Another aspect of accuracy in Arabic biographical writing is the universal interest in genealogy: a person whose family connections are known can be more readily identified, and his social status appreciated, than one whose family background is unknown or obscure. Nearly every Arab biographer is a genealogist, although some may emphasize a person's lineage more than others. Ibn Saᶜd, as noted above, on occasion gives a man's agnate and cognate ancestry, together with that of his wives, as well as information regarding his descendants. Writers such as Ibn al-Anbārī may pay rather less attention to pedigree than this, but others may go considerably further: in his notice of Isḥāq b. Rāhwayh (d. 238/853), a Traditionist remarkable for his powers of memory, Ibn Khallikān gives twenty-one generations of his ascendants; in the case of the centenarian Abū Umayyah Shurayḥ b. al-Ḥārith al-Kindī (d. 87/706), a man who was born before the days of Islam, he gives ten generations of his ascendants.

Biographical notices preserve much miscellaneous historical information. From Ibn abī Uṣaybiᶜah's notice of the physician Aḥmad b.

Ibrāhīm b. al-Jazzār, for instance, we learn how much money could be made from the practice of medicine in the fourth/tenth century: Ibn al-Jazzār's biographer records that when he died, over eighty years old, he left 24,000 dinars and twenty-five *qinṭārs* of medical and other books. In the short biographical notice of the lexicographer Abū Naṣr Ismāᶜīl b. Ḥammād al-Jawharī (d. between 393/1003 and 400/1009) provided by Ibn al-Anbārī in his *Nuzhat al-alibbāᵓ*, we have a record of an early attempt at flying: Abū Naṣr climbed up to the roof of the Old Mosque in Naysābūr, tied two panels on himself and announced that he was going to fly. He launched himself into the air, but hurtled to the ground and was killed. Other writers claim that al-Jawharī[31] simply fell from the roof of his own house by accident, but one wonders whether he had been inspired by earlier attempts to fly, such as the allegedly partially successful one in the third/ninth century mentioned in the biography of ᶜAbbās b. Firnās (recorded much later, in the eleventh/seventeenth century, by Aḥmad b. Muḥammad al-Maqqarī in his *Nafḥ al-ṭīb min ghuṣn al-Andalus al-raṭīb*).

As already remarked, one of the characteristics of medieval Arabic biography is its emphasis on the outer events of a person's life. This concentration on names, dates, education, writings and assessments of orthodoxy and reliability as a witness tended to narrow the biographer's view of his subject, and to lessen the possibilities for describing the development of personality. Nevertheless this shortcoming must not be overemphasized. Effective characterization of the subjects of biography often emerges from the recorded incidents in which they play a part, and clear pictures of personalities can often be discerned by implication from the anecdotal information which the biographer provides.

From the time of Aristoxenus, as Arnaldo Momigliano points out,[32] anecdotes have been considered the "natural condiment of biography", and Arabic biography has agreed both with ancient Greek and later western opinion in believing that a good biography is full of good anecdotes. Anecdotes may be used by the Arab biographer to show up the weaknesses as well as the strengths of a person's character. Ibn Khallikān writes of Rabīᶜat al-Raᵓy:

> [He] was the great jurisconsult of Medina [and] in his youth he met a number of the Prophet's Companions . . . Rabīᶜah was a great talker, and he used to say that he who keeps silent should be classed between him who is asleep and him who is dumb. Whilst he was one day speaking at one of his public conferences, an Arab, fresh from the desert, came in and stood for a long time before him, listening to his words; Rabīᶜah, who thought that the stranger was struck by admiration at what he

[31] *EI*², "al-Djawharī".

[32] *The Development of Greek Biography*, Cambridge, Mass., 1971, 76.

heard, said to him: "O Arab! How do your people define eloquence?" The other answered: "Brevity combined with precision." "And what is faulty speaking?" "That which thou hast been engaged in all day." This answer covered Rabīʿah with confusion.

(De Slane, adapted)

In the *Irshād al-arīb*, a more spirited reaction to a verbal assault is recorded by Yāqūt in his notice of the author Abū ʾl-ʿAlāʾ Ṣāʿid b. al-Ḥasan b. ʿĪsā (d. in Sicily in 417/1026):

He migrated to Andalusia and became acquainted with al-Manṣūr b. abī ʿĀmir, who honoured him and treated him with excessive kindness, and eventually appointed him vizier. He composed a number of books for al-Manṣūr, among them a book which he entitled *al-Fuṣūṣ*, after the manner of the *Kitāb al-Nawādir* of Abū ʿAlī al-Qālī. This book suffered a strange accident. When Abū ʾl-ʿAlāʾ had completed it he gave it to one of his servants to forward it by hand, but the latter's foot slipped as he was going over the bridge across the Guadalquivir, and he fell into the river together with the book. Ibn al-ʿArīf, who had had a number of rancorous disputes with Abū ʾl-ʿAlāʾ, commented on this with the following verse:

The *Kitāb al-Fuṣūṣ* has been submerged in the sea; thus is every heavy thing submerged!

Al-Manṣūr and those present laughed at this, which did not please Abū ʾl-ʿAlāʾ, and he uttered the spontaneous retort:

It has returned to its source; pearls are only found at the bottom of the seas!

Other examples of the apt retort are recorded by Ibn Khallikān of Ibn Mihrān al-Aʿmash (d. 148/765), a learned and somewhat irascible Traditionist of Kufa:

Some students having gone to him one day to learn Traditions, he said to them on coming out of his house: "Were there not in the house a person [meaning his wife] whom I detest more than I do you, I should not have come out to you." . . . It is said that the Imam Abū Ḥanīfah went to see him during a fit of illness, and having sat by him for a long time, he said, when about to retire: "It seems to me that my presence is irksome to you." "By Allāh!" replied the other, "you are irksome to me even when you are in your own house." . . . [the caliph] Hishām b. ʿAbd al-Malik wrote to al-Aʿmash requiring him to compose a book on the virtues of ʿUthmān and the crimes of ʿAlī. When al-Aʿmash had read the letter, he put it into the mouth of a sheep, which ate it up, and he then said to the bearer: "Tell him that I answer it thus."

(De Slane)

One of the least-noticed areas of biographical writing generally is the relationship between men and animals, a relationship which often throws light on human personality (cf. the very different attitudes of Johnson and Boswell towards Hodge). Arabic biographical literature contains many animal anecdotes, and as in other literatures these show up interesting facets of man's ambivalent attitude towards the animal kingdom, now seeing non-human creatures as something to hunt and herd and eat, now seeing them as companions and friends. A remarkable incident in the life of the grammarian Abū ʾl-Ḥasan Ṭāhir b. Aḥmad b. Bābashādh, recorded by Ibn Khallikān, shows that an animal might provide a moral example to a Muslim:

Being one day on the roof of the mosque at Old Cairo with some other persons, eating a collation, a cat went over to them and they gave it a bit of meat. The animal took it into its mouth and went off, but soon returned again, on which they threw another morsel to it. This it carried off also, and it kept going and coming a great number of times, at each of which it received from them another bit. Struck with this singularity, and knowing that no single cat could eat all that they had given, they suspected something extraordinary, and followed the animal. They then saw it clamber over a wall on the roof and go down into an empty place like an abandoned room. There they found another cat, but blind, eating of the food which had been brought to it and set before it by its companion. They were much struck with this, and Ibn Bābashādh said: "Since God has caused this dumb animal to be served and fed by another cat, and has not withheld from it its nourishment, how could he let a human being such as I am perish of hunger?" He immediately broke off all the ties which bound him to the world; he gave up his place, renounced his salary and shut himself up in a chamber, where he pursued his studies in the full confidence that God would provide for him. His friends then took care of him and supported him till he died.

(De Slane)

Love for a domestic creature might even ensure for it a Muslim funeral. In his little biography of al-Yaḥshūr, his father's falcon, Usāmah b. Munqidh tells us that this bird was given its own coffin and that its obsequies were attended by Qurʾān readers and *mukabbirūn*.[33]

Legal biographical anecdotes fall into a class of their own, since here the interaction of personalities must develop within the artificial constraints of the juridical situation. Works such as *Quḍāt Qurṭubah* by Muḥammad b. al-Ḥārith al-Khushanī are rich in legal anecdotes, and have much to say regarding the reactions of different characters faced with the responsibilities of judicial office. The reader is able to compare the reaction of such jurists as Muṣʿab b. ʿImrān, who defied the wrath of ʿAbd al-Raḥmān b. Muʿāwiyah in persisting in his refusal to accept the judgeship of Cordova, with the unruffled demeanour of such judges as ʿAmr b. ʿAbdullāh b. Layth al-Qabʿah. Two litigants once appeared before the latter, one of them flourishing a document which he then proceeded to conceal on his person:

ʿAmr told him: "Produce the document." The man refused. ʿAmr insisted sharply that he should produce it. Eventually the man angrily extracted it from his sleeve and threw it at the judge, hitting him in the face. ʿAmr's face turned so pale it was

[33] *Memoirs of an Arab-Syrian Gentleman* (trans. by P.K. Hitti of *Kitāb al-Iʿtibār*), Beirut, 1964, 232–5 (for al-Yaḥshūr's biography); 235–6 (for the funeral).

drained of all colour. Everyone thought he was going to give an order concerning the man, but his self-control asserted itself and he refrained from doing so. He examined the document, and then said to the litigant: "Is it not preferable to do things like this?"[34]

MEDIEVAL ARABIC AUTOBIOGRAPHY

Although there exists a fair number of medieval autobiographies (classical Ar. *sīrah*; modern Ar. *tarjamah dhātiyyah*) in Arabic, when measured against other areas of Arabic literature their number appears small. A certain degree of Greek and Persian influence may be detected in the beginnings of Arabic autobiography.[35] The two bibliographical works of Galen (AD 130–200 or 201) listing his compositions (written in Greek but known in Latin as *De libris propriis* and *De ordine librorum suorum ad Eugenianum*) contain much autobiographical matter, and these were well known to Ḥunayn b. Isḥāq,[36] who himself compiled a list of his own (translated) books. He did this in response to a request for details about his works, and like Galen he included information about himself.

The scientist Abū ᶜAlī al-Ḥasan b. al-Haytham (d. *c.* 430/1039) was certainly influenced by Galen, as he makes clear in his autobiography which Ibn abī Uṣaybiᶜah inserted in *ᶜUyūn al-anbāᵓ*. Ibn al-Haytham remarks on the similarity of his experience to that of Galen, and in this it is evident that he is referring to Galen's *De libris propriis*. Truth, for Ibn al-Haytham, lay in the study of Aristotelian philosophy; truth was the supreme aim of scientific endeavour, and was attainable by only a few of mankind, a view to be found in Galen's *De pulsibus dignoscendis*.

A Persian work composed in the time of Khusraw Anūshirvān also had some influence on Arabic autobiography. This work was the pessimistic personal record which the physician Burzōē attached to his Pahlavi translation of the Sanskrit *Panchatantra*, and which Ibn al-Muqaffaᶜ included in his Arabic translation of the same work, the celebrated book *Kalīlah wa-Dimnah*.[37]

It is true of Arabic autobiography, as of Arabic biography, that the outer events of the subject's life stand in the foreground; there is less concern with the personality than with the external circumstances in which the person finds himself and his interaction with them, and many a surviving Arabic autobiography is little more than an extended *curriculum vitae*.

A number of autobiographies have been preserved in the biographical dictionaries, the compilers having obtained such personal records from

34 *Quḍāt Qurṭubah*, Beirut, 1982, 150–1. 35 Rosenthal, "Arabische Autobiographie", 5–8, 10–11.
36 Ibid., 5. 37 Ibid., 10, and see also *CHAL/ABL*, 50–2.

various sources and inserted them in their own work in the form in which they found them. Thus in the *ʿUyūn al-anbāʾ* of Ibn abī Uṣaybiʿah we find autobiographies of Abū ʿAlī al-Ḥasan b. al-Haytham, as already mentioned, and also of ʿAbd al-Laṭīf al-Baghdādī (d. 629/1231)[38] and Ibn Sīnā. In Yāqūt's *Irshād al-arīb* there are also a number of autobiographies, including the short summary of his life and career by ʿUthmān b. Saʿīd al-Dānī (d. 444/1053), and the longer autobiographical account of a philologist who was descended from the caliph al-Maʾmūn, Aḥmad b. ʿAlī b. Maʾmūn (d. 586/1190). Not content with his caliphal lineage, Aḥmad traces his descent from Adam. Yāqūt states that he obtained this autobiographical notice from the subject's son. It records the main outlines of the career of Aḥmad b. ʿAlī, including a discreditable episode in which, in order to establish his claim to the post of *qāḍī* of Dujayl, Aḥmad wrote a letter emphasizing his own qualifications and denouncing as stupid and immature his own nephew, who had claims to the same post.

Occasionally authors add their own autobiography to one of their own books, either as a preface or as an insertion within the book. Thus Ẓahīr al-Dīn abū ʾl-Ḥasan ʿAlī b. al-Qāsim Zayd b. Funduq al-Bayhaqī (d. 565/1169) included his autobiography in his work *Mashārib al-Tajārib*. This was later included by Yāqūt in his *Irshād al-arīb*, and begins with the subject's lineage, after which al-Bayhaqī continues:

> I was born on Saturday, the 27th Shaʿbān, 499, in the city of Sabzawar in the district of Bayhaq, a town built by Sāsān b. Sāsān b. Bābak b. Sāsān. My father sent me to the elementary school. Then I travelled to Shashtamadh, one of the towns of that region where my father had estates. As a boy I learned by heart the *Kitāb al-Hādī li-ʾl-shādī* [here there follows a list of books memorized]. In the course of the year 514 I came to the school of Abū Jaʿfar al-Muqriʾ, imam of the Old Mosque in Naysābūr . . .

Some years later he was troubled by gaps in his knowledge of philosophy, and dreamed that he should betake himself to Quṭb al-Dīn Muḥammad al-Marwazī al-Naṣīrī. This he did, and studied under this scholar for two years, "and I expended the dinars and dirhams I possessed, and with this ointment healed the wounds of longing".

The Yemeni poet and *faqīh* ʿUmārah b. abī ʾl-Ḥasan al-Ḥakamī (d. 569/1175) put his autobiography at the beginning of his book *al-Nukat al-ʿaṣriyyah fī akhbār al-wuzarāʾ al-Miṣriyyah* ("Contemporary Details in regard to Accounts of the Egyptian Ministers"), with the justification, "Perhaps some person into whose hands this book comes will say: 'You have reported on others, but who are you yourself? And to which nest do you

[38] Cf. below, ch. 12, 231, where autobiographical writings by al-Malik al-Nāṣir Dāwūd and Saʿīd al-Dīn Juwaynī are also mentioned.

return for rest?'". He gives an account of his forbears, his early studies in Zabīd, his adroit seizing of commercial opportunities to make himself a wealthy man, and then his entry into diplomatic employment, when he was sent as an envoy to the Faṭimid ruler of Egypt, al-Fāʾiz.[39]

Shihāb al-Dīn abū ʾl-Qāsim ʿAbd al-Raḥmān abū Shāmah (d. 665/1268) included an autobiographical notice in his *Kitāb Dhayl al-Rawḍatayn* ("Book of the Supplement to 'The Two Gardens'") under the year of his birth; this autobiography is the first example in Arabic of one written in the third person.[40]

Samawʾal b. Yaḥyā al-Maghribī (d. 570/1174), a Jew who was converted to Islam, included an autobiographical memoir in his polemical work written against Judaism, the *Ifhām al-Yahūd*.

Lisān al-Dīn b. al-Khaṭīb added his autobiography to *al-Iḥāṭah fī taʾrīkh Gharnāṭah* (see above), and Ibn Khaldūn included an autobiography in his *Kitāb al-ʿIbar*.

Medieval Arabic autobiographies written as independent works include several of a confessional type, which seek to record the writer's spiritual struggles, the process of conversion and the deepening of religious faith. An early example is the account of his spiritual experiences given by Ḥārith b. Asad al-Muḥāsibī (d. 243/857) in his *Kitāb al-Waṣāyā* or *Naṣāʾiḥ dīniyyah*:

> I began by casting passion out of my heart, and I considered the schisms in the community . . . and I was careful not to come to a hasty conclusion without proof, and thus I sought the way of salvation for my own soul. Then I found that the way of salvation consists in cleaving to the fear of God, and the fulfilment of what he has ordained . . . and the service of God for his own sake alone, and in taking his Apostle as a model.[41]

Abū Ḥāmid al-Ghazālī made a close study of the *Waṣāyā* of al-Muḥāsibī, and in his autobiographical work *al-Munqidh min al-ḍalāl*[42] he uses similar phrases to those of al-Muḥāsibī in describing some of his own spiritual difficulties and experiences.[43]

An example of a didactic *apologia pro vita sua* is the short work *Kitāb al-Sīrah al-falsafiyyah* ("Book of the Philosophic Life")[44] of Muḥammad b. Zakariyyāʾ al-Rāzī. Some unnamed persons had reproached al-Rāzī with not living up to the philosophical conduct of his mentor Socrates. He commented on this:

> We ourselves fall far short of him . . . and readily confess our failure perfectly to practise the just life, to suppress passion, and to be in love with and eager for

39 Rosenthal, "Arabische Autobiographie", 28–9. 40 Ibid., 32.
41 Cited in Margaret Smith, *An Early Mystic of Baghdad*, London, 1977, 19.
42 See below, ch. 25, 424. 43 Smith, *Early Mystic of Baghdad*, 70.
44 See also below, ch. 21, 370–1.

knowledge . . . and if we confess ourselves his inferior we do not thereby demean ourselves; for that is the plain truth, and it is always nobler and more honourable to acknowledge the truth.[45]

Travel literature inevitably has a strong autobiographical element, and this applies to the books of celebrated medieval travellers such as the *Riḥlat al-Kinānī* of Muḥammad b. Jubayr al-Kinānī (d. 614/1217) and the *Tuḥfat al-nuẓẓār fī gharāʾib al-amṣār wa-ʿajāʾib al-asfār* of Muḥammad b. ʿAbdullāh b. Baṭṭūṭah.[46]

The most remarkable autobiographical work in medieval Arabic literature is generally allowed to be the *Kitāb al-Iʿtibār* ("Book of Learning by Example") by Abū ʾl-Muẓaffar Usāmah b. Murshid b. Munqidh (d. 584/1188). Usāmah's life was centred on his ancestral castle of Shayzar on the river Orontes, which he was obliged to defend against both the Assassins and the Crusaders, and his autobiography was written at the end of a long life when he was nearly ninety. The author intended his book to present a series of exempla, as is indicated by his title, and he reiterates time and again that whatever vicissitudes to which a man's life is subject, whatever plans he makes, whatever the height of his hope or the depth of his despair, all is predestined and predetermined. This message provides a connecting thread for a book which is otherwise loosely organized, and where reminiscence is mixed with reflections and anecdotes reported by others. Usāmah's main occupations throughout his life were intermittent war and incessant hunting – in this he was perhaps not so very different from the European nobility of the same period – and his pages are frequently spattered with bloodshed – beasts, birds, Franks and francolins, all are to be hunted down and slain.

There was, however, a more attractive side to Usāmah, who apart from venery was devoted to poetry and the delights of literature. In relating how his family *en route* from Egypt to Syria had been robbed of their money and valuables and Usāmah's library, he recalls:

The safety of my children, my brother's children and our harem made the loss of money which we suffered a comparatively easy matter to endure – with the exception of the books, which were four thousand volumes, all of the most valuable kind. Their loss has left a heartsore that will stay with me to the last day of my life.[47]

Usāmah greatly admired his father, Majd al-Dīn abū Salamah Murshid, who renounced the lordship of Shayzar in favour of a younger brother, and in the course of incidental references Usāmah gives a memorable biographical sketch of his father's extraordinary character. Majd al-Dīn spent his days

[45] *al-Sīrah al-falsafiyyah*, trans. A. J. Arberry, *Asiatic Review*, XLV, 1949, 704.
[46] See below, ch. 17, 323–4. [47] *Arab-Syrian Gentleman*, 61.

in killing animals in innumerable hunting expeditions, or in fasting, and in the evenings when it was too dark to hunt, he copied out the Qurʾān, of which he transcribed forty-six complete copies. Yet the patience required by this exacting task did not extend to other spheres of his life. He was a man of foul temper who could not brook tardiness in his servants. Usāmah describes how once when his father's groom was slow in bringing his father his horse, Majd al-Dīn hit out at the unfortunate servant with his sword, which was still in its scabbard:

> The sword cut through the outfit . . . which the groom had on, and then cut through the bone of his elbow. The whole forearm fell off. After this he (may God's mercy rest upon his soul!) used to support him, and his children after him, because of that blow.[48]

Usāmah records many extraordinary events, not only from his own experiences, but also from those of his contemporaries. Among these is his account of the astonishing escape from a dungeon in Cairo of Riḍwān b. al-Walakhshī, who dug a tunnel fourteen cubits long armed only with an iron nail.

Biography not only attained a prominent position in Islamic historiography as a whole, but eventually became so extensive that Arabic biographical literature exceeds that of any other culture in the ancient and medieval periods. Moreover in a number of ways, as in the cases of the prosopographical reference work and the biographical dictionary, it anticipated by many centuries similar developments in western biography.

[48] Ibid., 147.

CHAPTER 12

HISTORY AND HISTORIANS

There are civilizations which have no history, or which, at any rate, are as little interested in commemorating the exploits of their ancestors as they are in bequeathing an account of their own to posterity. The reverse is true of those civilizations which, since antiquity, have succeeded one another on the shores of the Mediterranean and in western Asia, whether Semitic or otherwise. Writing, which made its appearance relatively early, obviously facilitated the recording of deeds or customs. Ruins of ancient monuments remind us of the passage of time and of successive peoples. The Qurʾān is full of allusions to this past and, within the framework of a divine plan, presents in its own way an historical view of the world. Arabic poetry, as has been observed elsewhere, preserves and glorifies the memory of the exploits of various small social groups. Arabs who had become Muslims could not but reveal some sense of history, even though at the outset they did not yet write works which could be called historical.

It is not claimed, of course, that a complete catalogue can be given of historiographical literature, of which, in any case, our knowledge is variable in relation to different periods and regions. At the start it is only necessary to emphasize that in the selection of works for mention – and *a fortiori*, if such be the case, for publication, the criteria are not quite the same as for purely literary works. Although in each instance the intellectual or artistic value of the work must of course be considered, and although the documentary importance of some work or other may be of special concern, it goes without saying that the chief interest of an historical work lies in the evidence which it affords for reconstituting the past. This qualification means that a work which is in itself mediocre can be of great interest; pride of place must always be given to writings which embody direct evidence and not to latter-day compilations (subject to the proviso that these latter may contain original evidence otherwise lost).

The Arabic word which is usually considered to be the best translation of "history" is *taʾrīkh*. Its etymology is obscure, but the word is applied to historical narratives and to biographical dictionaries alike. Conversely there exist works in both these categories which are not described as *taʾrīkh*.

Other words which will be encountered include *akhbār*, *sīrah* and *ṭabaqāt*, and these are used to represent works analogous to others defined as *taʾrīkh*, which itself does not seem to appear until the period when history became a properly constituted science, that is to say in the third century of the *Hijrah*. Several earlier manuscripts have titles beginning with "*taʾrīkh*", but these are probably designations added by later copyists.

FROM THE BEGINNINGS TO THE TIME OF AL-ṬABARĪ

The origins of Arab–Muslim historiography are difficult to date exactly; it is evident only that they cannot be separated from those of the other literary and cultural genres of the first two centuries of Islam. In previous chapters of this *History*, there has been a review of the *Ḥadīth*, the *maghāzī* and the *Sīrah*.[1] Although the *Ḥadīth* may occasionally provide material for the writing of history, the inspiration behind it is obviously very different. It is another matter with *maghāzī* and with the *Sīrah*: Sezgin has shown that *maghāzī* are the Islamicized sequel to the *ayyām al-ʿArab*: in each case there is apparent a desire to transmit to posterity the memory of a glorious or important episode; in both alike this concern is bound up with the need to know or to reconstitute the family and tribal genealogies which since the advent of Islam could be of practical advantage in conferring the right to a pension or other benefits. Although the *maghāzī* and the *Sīrah* were still related exclusively to the life and times of the Prophet, it is easy to see how they might, in a subsequent age, awaken the desire for a similar record of such events as might be likely to have the same consequences or to promote an understanding of the problems then facing the emergent community (*ummah*). In this connection particular mention must be made of certain minor works recently brought to light by enquirers concerned with reconstructing the original development of Islamic ideas.[2] As is well known, the early disputes between Muslims were inextricably political and religious and consequently the first writings on the subject frequently contain historical observations, as, for example, on the struggles between ʿAlī and Muʿāwiyah. In fact, historiography was to develop gradually towards greater independence, but it can hardly be denied that for a long time it was still to encounter various preoccupations of this kind.

It is unlikely that at the start, when writing in Arabic was still at an elementary stage, revered traditions should have been passed on otherwise than by word of mouth, or by a few brief notes at most. The decisive period for the development of a true literary genre must surely have been, as it was

[1] *CHALUP*, chs. 10–18. [2] In particular M. Cook, *Early Muslim Dogma*, Cambridge, 1981.

with the *Ḥadīth*, the caliphate of ʿAbd al-Malik (reigned 65–88/685/705). However this may be, the means of conveying information at that stage can only have been the *Ḥadīth*, and also the *maghāzī*, that is to say, miscellaneous accounts gathered from individuals who had either witnessed the events themselves or were intermediaries who related what they had learned from such witnesses. In relation to the length of time throughout which it was to persist in certain departments of history, this came to be called the Traditionist method, the method of the *muḥaddithūn*. In any case it may be assumed that a writer will question first, for reasons of convenience and preference, those sources who belong to his own social-political group, and here it is possible for discrepancies to arise between written accounts produced in the environment of Medina or Damascus, centred on the Umayyads, or in Iraq in the cantonment cities (*amṣār*) of Basra and of Kufa. In Iraq, there were to be found numerous tribal groups relatively remote from the central power, and writers attaching themselves to one or other of these groups would thus reproduce their respective versions of events. There has been an attempt to detect in this or that version the interpreter of the Azd, the Tamīm, etc.[3] Such possibilities must not however be exaggerated: the tribes were in close proximity to one another and sometimes intermingled; it would be difficult, if not for the fairly primitive narrator, at least for his immediate successors not to add anything, or even on occasions not to combine with the version of their own group that of other groups near at hand.

What was written in these conditions can be roughly divided into two classes, which are not mutually exclusive. We are dealing with minor works of still very limited scope, some of them relating to particular episodes (*akhbār*), others to subjects which could well be linked to the episodes. No attempt is made, save quite exceptionally, to weave together such accounts into any kind of chronological backcloth. The reconstitution of these early minor works, limited more or less to the Umayyad period and the very beginning of the ʿAbbasid period, is difficult because they have been absorbed into larger and better-written works and it is these latter which have been recopied; the earlier works have thus been forgotten and have gradually disappeared. Many of them must have been produced in only a single exemplar, for the use of the prince or the group for which they were intended, or on fragile pieces of papyrus. Additional difficulty is often caused by authors not always giving precise titles to their minor works, or by copyists altering them or using the same title indiscriminately for a complete work or a single chapter of it. However, here again the

[3] This idea was developed by J. Wellhausen in his *Prolegomena*, 1899.

responsibility for certain gaps in our knowledge must fall to some extent on modern negligence. At the close of the Middle Ages in Egypt the attitude of mind which then developed in favour of authenticity of research by means of a return to original sources was to reveal, particularly in the case of Ibn Ḥajar al-ʿAsqalānī, the author of *al-Iṣābah fī tamyīz al-Ṣaḥābah* ("Achieving the Aim in Distinguishing the Companions"), that it was still possible for some ancient works to be recovered, and it would seem that in the intermediate periods Syrian historiography was sometimes to turn such possibilities to account.

For us, however, the corner-stones of our knowledge are the citations made, chiefly by al-Ṭabarī, but occasionally by other writers of the same century, of the works from which they had drawn their evidence. We are dealing of course with writers who make quotations which are both attributed and are more or less textually accurate, rather than those who give a summarized account without as a rule including any attribution. The main problem encountered is thus to decide whether the quotations are faithful and, in particular, how the extracts were selected. Some idea of validity may be gained by comparing the quotations from the same original work given by various writers and, in exceptional cases, by comparison with the original passage itself where it has by chance survived.[4]

It is characteristic of the early historical writings, without ever being expressly stated, to regard history as one of the principal forms by means of which not only small regional or confessional groups, but even the Community, itself, acquired consciousness of identity as a whole. Hence there is insistence on the obligation not to regard the writing of history as a genre in itself, separated from others by a line of demarcation. This was an attitude which was in certain cases to be modified in time, so that historians might acquire a degree of independence; the apparently detached tone of the writer might conceal it to some extent, but it must never be forgotten. It is also reinforced, for Islam and Christianity alike, by the tendency of many scholars to practise several disciplines simultaneously, even though posterity does not commemorate them all equally. Even when there is a division of labour, it is not difficult to recognize, in the case of a man like al-Ṭabarī for example, that the author of the "History" and the author of the "Commentary" on the Qurʾān are one and the same person. Moreover, the methods of work distinguishing the various disciplines were less divergent then than they would be today.

It was towards the middle of the second/eighth century that the first great works of *fiqh* (usually rendered "jurisprudence") were accomplished.

[4] There are several references in *GAS*, I; see especially pp. 30f.

Alongside writers who proceeded systematically by means of question and answer, there were others, particularly those with a more or less definite administrative objective, like Abū Yūsuf with his *Kitāb al-Kharāj*, who inserted into their narrative some traditions relating to the behaviour of this or that caliph or governor, especially, of course, to the behaviour of ᶜUmar b. al-Khaṭṭāb (reigned 13–23/634–44), essentially the first administrator of the Muslim state. Thus there were in circulation from that period a certain number of traditions of the kind at the same time as the Prophetic *ḥadīth*s. From these more or less authentic traditions, other writers, of a different turn of mind but not unfamiliar with juridical matters, were able to put together small concentrations of data relating to one single event or subject. The first two which have come down to us are the *Kitāb al-Riddah* of Wathīmah (who may have been a Persian – at any rate he was a cloth merchant who was born at Fasā), and the *Waqᶜat Ṣiffīn* of Naṣr b. Muzāḥim al-Minqarī. It is possible that several caliphs were dealt with in this way, as was soon to be done in any case more specifically for ᶜUmar b. ᶜAbd al-ᶜAzīz by Ibn ᶜAbd al-Ḥakam, in an anti-ᶜAbbasid and pro-Umayyad spirit. The choice itself of these subjects makes the intrusion of politico-religious interests a possibility; it is not surprising that in a Shīᶜah environment descriptions should have been written about the person of al-Ḥusayn and the drama of his death;[5] there were also brief accounts of the revolt of al-Mukhtār b. abī ᶜUbayd al-Thaqafī. More often a writer would apply himself to recounting the stories of various *fitnah*s from early times. It is possible – but this is, for the moment, pure conjecture – that these writings may have had some connection with the ferment associated with the coming of the ᶜAbbasids.

At about the same time the literature of the conquests (*futūḥ*) was reaching perfection and completion. Here the most important name is that of al-Wāqidī, who had compiled a collection of *Maghāzī*, to which the *Futūḥ* were a kind of sequel. Not much is known about this second work of al-Wāqidī, which exists only in separate minor pieces on some of the conquests. All the evidence goes to show that the accounts which have reached us are imaginative reconstructions of a later date, but the fact that they have no attributions indicates that he was considered to be the chief authority in this respect. The study of the history of the conquests was not motivated only by an interest in curious anecdotes or by pride in the Community or in one of its groups shown there in a good light; it had also the objective of establishing precisely the practical consequences, so as to deduce from them, one at a time, the juridical modalities of the constitution

[5] See the short treatises of al-Madāʾinī, *GAS*, I, 314; Abū Miḥnaf, *GAS*, I, 308.

of the empire. This aspect is clearly related to the fact that many of the traditions to be found in historical works also occur in the juridical treatises. It is quite definitely characteristic of the work of Ibn ʿAbd al-Ḥakam on the conquest of Egypt and, secondarily, on that of the Maghrib and of al-Andalus.[6] The same is also true, later and more generally, of the celebrated treatise of al-Balādhurī on the conquests (*Futūḥ al-buldān*) and even, at the end, on certain of the institutions that subsequently developed: the famous chapter on the origins of Muslim coinage, almost the only information available on the subject, must have been in use from century to century until the present day.

Not long before the mid-second century of the *Hijrah* several important works made their appearance; it was at about that time that the *Sīrah* (the biography of Muḥammad) was being perfected and that the first juridical miscellanies were being compiled, the relationship of which to history will be examined. Shortly before the fall of the Umayyads al-Zuhrī,[7] a Traditionist who made excursions into history, was at work, while in Iraq ʿAwānah and Abū Mikhnaf were writing at about the time of the ʿAbbasid accession. Simultaneously several writers were beginning to occupy themselves with linking together various episodes into a continuous narrative, of necessity paying a little more attention to chronology, not to mention interpolating the beginnings of Muslim history into the general evolution of the history of the human race. In particular they described the series of prophets mentioned in the Qurʾān which culminated ultimately in Muḥammad. Ibn Isḥāq, to judge from the scant quotations available, may possibly also have been working on these lines.

For pre-Islamic history, the starting-point was of course to be found in the Qurʾān, but it did not provide the material for a full exposition of what was regarded as more or less common knowledge. It was necessary to obtain information on the traditions and the writings of the non-Muslim peoples concerned with earlier revelations. It was of course unlikely that any Arab–Muslim writer would ever have read the Old or the New Testament in the original or would have known the general Christian histories compiled during the centuries prior to Islam; there were some local converts who were able to make translations, as indeed they could do for philosophical and scientific literature. In the field of history, however, it does not seem that a need existed which was either as widespread or as demanding. Generally speaking, writers had to be content with accounts conveyed orally by converts of their own race who had not necessarily themselves had direct access to the sacred books, and in any case could

[6] See R. Brunschvig, "Ibn ʿAbdalḥakam et la conquête de l'Afrique du Nord", *Annales de l'Institut des Études Orientales*, VI, 1942. [7] *GAS*, I, 280–3.

scarcely distinguish between them and the apocryphal works circulating at that time in the Orient. Thus there came to be formed a whole literature of *isrāʾīliyyāt* ("Israelite stories")[8] and of *qiṣaṣ al-anbiyāʾ* ("tales of the prophets").[9]

The Arabs were no less interested in their ancestors of the period of the Jāhiliyyah, who had moreover been in touch with other peoples descended from Abraham. Hence there came into being a double literature, partly devoted to ancient beliefs and partly to tribal genealogies, and the most illustrious name associated with it was that of Hishām al-Kalbī.

Finally the Persians, who remembered their forefathers and naturally sought to exalt them in the eyes of their new masters, translated, especially for the use of the latter, their ancient "Book of Kings". It was a work probably initiated after the accession of the ʿAbbasids by Ibn al-Muqaffaʿ.

Henceforth writers in Arabic compiled histories in which the Islamic period was preceded for some by Biblical history and for others by Persian history. It was naturally only a short step further to the idea of presenting these two histories in conjunction, involving the difficult task of establishing a broad chronological concordance. There seems no need to assume from all this that a definite influence was exercised by non-Arab literature, though it may have resulted in a sympathetic atmosphere. Any progress came as the direct result of demands made by the Arab–Muslim world itself. (It will be noted that the legacies of researchers and compilers are almost completely oblivious of Greek history, though not of Greek science, and by extension, *a fortiori*, of Roman history.)

From what has just been said it follows naturally that almost the entire body of writers of early history consisted of Arabs, more particularly *mawālī*, that is to say, Arabic-speaking Iraqis. The arrival on the scene of an important civil and military Khurasanian element, which rapidly became Arabicized, resulted under the ʿAbbasids in an outcrop of Iranian authors from the third/ninth century onwards. They were able, however, to preserve or develop certain specific customs, and so the various trends, which will be discussed later, were able to coexist.

It was at the junction of these periods that there appeared a new genre which was immediately highlighted by a masterpiece. It was convenient for an enquiring public to be able to find out all possible information on leading personalities of the two past centuries of Islam, both to determine their place in history and to assess their authority in the transmission of Tradition. Such was the need felt by Ibn Saʿd, whose work in which the personages studied were arranged in classes according to their generations

[8] *EI*[2], "Isrāʾīliyyāt". [9] *EI*[2], "Ḳiṣaṣ".

was for this reason called *Ṭabaqāt* ("Classes"). This voluminous collection is of untold value to us, not only for its intrinsic merit but because it is often the only source to provide us with information before such information has been modified by a change of outlook in later works.[10] Two generations later another work, in some respects comparable with it, was to be compiled by al-Balādhurī, a writer who will be considered in due course. In contrast to the *Ṭabaqāt* of Ibn Saᶜd, the *Kitāb Ansāb al-ashrāf* ("Book of the Genealogies of the Nobles") is characterized by its essential preoccupation with the personalities of the Umayyad caliphs and of their entourage.

We have little knowledge of when and how the idea of compiling a consecutive history first saw the light. It is possible that this type of history was known to be possessed by other peoples, but the need must also have been felt independently. In any case, it presented a delicate problem, for it was necessary to interpose, among the *akhbār* on which there was ample information, explanatory passages for which no material yet existed. Probably the procedure was still to interrogate surviving witnesses when these were available, but only the closest study of later chronicles still extant, and in particular those of al-Ṭabarī, would make it possible to distinguish between the oral and the written sources utilized by the early writers. The most ancient chronicle preserved to the present day is that of Khalīfah b. Khayyāṭ, whom we shall discuss, but he had apparently several predecessors.

The early writers could naturally concern themselves only with early events, and their successors in turn recorded the events which followed. It is, however, typical that priority was almost always given, in respect of historical importance, to events of the early decades of Islam. By reason of the mass of tradition collected about them, they must have occupied in written works a disproportionately greater space than did subsequent periods. The main cause of this preference is of course implicit in the fact that for the formation and life of the Muslim community, it was these early events which presented the fundamental politico-religious problems; the solution of them was still a factor in its subsequent development.

It is a commonplace to say that, in most civilizations endowed with historical literature, such literature is most frequently concerned only with "wars and kings". This is indeed true, though with important reservations in Arab–Muslim historical literature, most works being preoccupied almost exclusively with external wars and internal dissension. However this dictum has a particular significance inasmuch as many of these dissensions had in fact a lasting politico-religious effect.

[10] Cf. above, ch. 11.

To sum up, if we consider the whole course of history as presented to us in the later chronicles, we are obliged to conclude that certain events, even among the most important, have failed to find an historian. Such, most surprisingly, is the case with the ᶜAbbasid revolution. Certainly there were polemical writings, but it seems that the first comprehensive account was that of a certain Ibn Naṭṭāḥ, some three-quarters of a century after the event. It has been supposed that this work reached us in the anonymous manuscript discovered and published under the title of *Akhbār Āl ᶜAbbās* or *Akhbār al-Dawlah al-ᶜAbbāsiyyah*.[11] This may be so, but it must be stressed that this work, which must be regarded as original, appears to be based on a documentation which is in the main not different from that which the Iraqi writers have handed down to us and which, hitherto, seems to have served only one subsequent author, an anonymous Khurasanian two centuries later in date (see below). The anonymous work discovered by al-Dūrī attributes the claim of the ᶜAbbasids to the caliphate to the fact that they were heirs of the movement of Muḥammad b. al-Ḥanafiyyah and Abū Hāshim – a statement which appears to be true of the first ᶜAbbasids, but which the third, al-Mahdī (reigned 158–69/775–85), contested, proclaiming the entitlement of the family in its own right.

The writers of *akhbār*, like the collectors of *Ḥadīth* – in fact they are often one and the same – belonged to various persuasions and parties, which is probably the reason why they chose to write about episodes in which such persuasions and parties took opposing sides. It also explains why they regard the others within their number as being of greater or lesser value. This aspect of their work must not however be exaggerated. Lively as their quarrels may have been, they did not at this time result in the creation of widely divided sects, as was to happen later. It is well known that those who were afterwards to be called Sunnī accepted Traditions based on the authority of personages classed as Shīᶜīs, and *vice versa*. This means that there was no fundamental distinction between the documentary evidence used by the adherents of the Umayyads, those of the ᶜAbbasids and the early Shīᶜīs. Only gradually, as works were produced which were of wider scope and greater complexity, did they begin to seem intended more specifically for one set of people or another.

The chronological presentation of historical material soon led to its rearrangement in the form of annals, that is to say the enumeration of events year by year. It was a system which existed in pre-Islamic literature and in the literature of medieval Europe. Perhaps it would be paradoxical to say that Arab writers – in any case it never applied to all of them – did not arrive

[11] Ed. A. Duri, Beirut, 1971.

at this formula without some vague awareness of its prevalence, but it does not seem that this is essential to explain the course of development. The first point to be noted is of course that we are now dealing with lunar, not solar, years. In point of fact the Arab Muslims, as is well known, adopted very early on dating by the period of the *Hijrah* for administrative purposes. The most ancient papyri of the Islamic period prove it. Accordingly, even though a large part of the information provided by historians was originally obtained orally without precise dating, whenever they came upon official written documents, these would already be dated and they would naturally make use of them in their text under that date. The two most ancient examples which we have of exposition in the form of annals date from the middle of the third/ninth century; they consist of a part of the chronicle of Khalīfah b. Khayyāṭ, recently recovered and published, and of the lost chronicle of Abū Ḥassān al-Ziyādī. The work was called *Taʾrīkh ʿalā ʾl-sinīn* ("History Year by Year") which is indicative of its being regarded as a novelty. Henceforward, the annalistic form of presentation was to be applied to the major part of historiography, even in the case of works where the type of documentation did not so plainly demand it. Annals, moreover, did not exclude other chronological divisions, by reigns or by *duwal* (pl. of *dawlah*, i.e. "cycles" hence, "dynasty"). It was an arrangement which facilitated cross-references between works, making it easy to find in each the same events. In certain countries, however, such as Iran and Egypt, a preference remained for dealing with history more comprehensively by reigns without any other chronological distinction.

It may be said that by now the writing of history constituted an independent genre, even when it was practised by authors who also wrote works of a different kind. Quite soon it became customary to designate this genre by the term *taʾrīkh*, but this word, the etymology of which is probably related to lunar dating and which does not seem to be connected with any pre-Islamic Semitic language, has no precise definition to correspond with the European word "history". It will be seen that it can be applied to works in very different categories; its first appearance is hard to date, but one of the earliest properly attested instances is the *Taʾrīkh* of al-Bukhārī, which is a list of the original sources and the transmitters of *Ḥadīth*. Conversely, it can also happen that certain works are designated indiscriminately as *taʾrīkh*, *akhbār* and even other terms are used.

It was in any case during this period that works were being produced by the leading writers who were subsequently to be made use of by al-Ṭabarī and others, culminating in al-Madāʾinī, through whom many of his predecessors came to be known. In general it was Iraqis who were involved, for the fall of the Umayyads had compromised the passing on of

Syrian tradition. This was the era of the first urban histories, which will be discussed later.

Somewhat paradoxically, although this period of historical writing culminated in about the year 300/912–3 with al-Ṭabarī, he had been preceded by several writers (in fact unknown to him), who had sought to provide their respective circles with general expositions which were more cursory and more composite, but of which the sources must have been in general the same – Ibn Qutaybah, al-Yaʿqūbī, Abū Ḥanīfah al-Dīnawārī, etc. Ibn Qutaybah, whose fame among posterity rests chiefly on his small historical work the *Kitāb al-Maʿārif*, but whose other activities, including theology, have been brought to light in our time, was chiefly concerned with imparting both to the educated public of Baghdad and to the government secretaries a general outline of what they ought to know. He is thus one of those who contributed to the institution, on the various planes of knowledge, of a sort of average orthodoxy as it might have been conceived according to al-Mutawakkil. He was not a scholar and his work implies that he was dealing with some miscellaneous collections of information, including those already noted and others.

Abū Ḥanīfah al-Dīnawarī and al-Yaʿqūbī are quite different. Both of them were Shīʿīs at a time when, in fact, Shiʿism had not yet been clearly defined for ordinary purposes and Shīʿīs filled the offices of the caliphate itself. Abū Ḥanīfah al-Dīnawārī was a Persian of liberal outlook, who took an interest in botany among other sciences. His short historical work, *al-Akhbār al-ṭiwāl* ("The Long Accounts") is characteristic of a trend which is to be found throughout Iranian historiography, whether written in Persian or Arabic: interest is confined almost exclusively to Iranian history, both pre-Islamic and Islamic. This Muslim passes over in almost complete silence the history of the Prophet of Islam and that of the Arab conquests.

Al-Yaʿqūbī, an Arab (although a part of his working life was spent in Iran), was on the other hand of an oecumenical turn of mind. Although it was not until the end of his life that he wrote his *Kitāb al-Buldān*, in which he dealt with all those regions of the Muslim world which he had not found possible to describe in his *Taʾrīkh*, the first volume of this work, covering the pre-Islamic period without any precise chronology, enumerates all the peoples who by that time could claim to be called civilized. The author lists the Israelites, the early Christians, Syrians, Assyrians, Babylonians, Indians, Greeks, Romans, Persians, the peoples of the North including the Turks, Chinese, Egyptians, Berbers, Abyssinians, the Bedja, the black Sudanese and finally the Arabs of pre-Islamic Arabia (with no mention of Western Europeans). He also wrote a small work dealing with the effect of the weather on men. The second volume of his history gives the history of the caliphate up to 259/872.

It must be remembered that al-Balādhurī was also writing at this period. He too was unknown to al-Ṭabarī, but worked on the same lines, using in general the same sources.

The importance of Abū Jaʿfar Muḥammad b. Jarīr al-Ṭabarī (d. 310/923) and his great history *Taʾrīkh al-rusul wa-ʾl-mulūk* mark a turning-point between the old style of historiography and the new historiography which was to follow, though actually it is more a case of one or two generations overlapping than of a clear line of chronological demarcation. With al-Ṭabarī the Traditionist method reached its zenith and at the same time its swan-song, since it was impossible for it to be pursued further. It was in one sense slightly anachronistic, if the work of al-Ṭabarī be compared with that of Ibn Qutaybah, al-Yaʿqūbī or Abū Ḥanīfah al-Dīnawarī.

Strange as it may seem, although al-Ṭabarī has been regarded for generations and, to a certain extent, up to the present time as embodying in himself the whole of history, at least for the centuries preceding him, no monograph has survived on the man himself. Although history constitutes his chief claim to fame for posterity, he is no less distinguished as the author of the first great *Tafsīr* (Quranic commentary), and as a jurist. Although a writer when moving from one genre to another may change his style and method of documentation in some degree, it would be paradoxical to pretend that he is no longer the same man, particularly when what he writes can have far-reaching significance in the eyes of the Community. It is indisputably in this spirit that al-Ṭabarī should be studied and, in the absence of any earlier study on these lines, the little that we can say must necessarily be inadequate.[12]

The reputation of al-Ṭabarī has given rise to some misinterpretation. The Traditionist method which he used takes as its starting-point the collection of individual pieces of evidence on particular events. By the time of al-Ṭabarī, however, it was obviously not possible for him to undertake personal interrogations himself when he was dealing with ancient times; he could do so only for recent events. Oddly enough, however, as it seems at first sight, it is precisely with regard to his own period that al-Ṭabarī is most cautious in his expositions, because in accordance with his method he is not faced with the comparison of sources necessary in dealing with material from earlier times, in relation to which he might be thought of as the last link in a chain of oral transmission. But this is quite exceptional. Although

[12] See *EI*¹, "Ṭabarī"; *GAL*, I, 148ff; *GAS*, I, 323f; *The History of al-Ṭabarī*, XXXVIII, *The Return of the Caliphate to Baghdad*, trans. F. Rosenthal, 1986.

no writer before him had made a comparable effort to obtain documentation, several, as noted, had already achieved written compilations and it was thus essentially on the basis of written evidence that al-Ṭabarī was working. The chains of transmitters (*isnād*) are genuine, but they reproduce, apart from the last link, virtually the *isnād*s of his predecessors. In certain cases he acquires from the last one whose readings he has heard a formal authorization (*ijāzah*) for transmission, while in other cases he reproduces information from works available to the public. In any case the list of transmitters begins with the last and most recent one and then goes back to his predecessors, and it is sometimes difficult to distinguish the compilation written first from the individual pieces of evidence of which it is composed. For this purpose it is possible to rely, as several modern authors have discovered,[13] on what the precursors of al-Ṭabarī already knew, medieval men of learning like Ibn al-Nadīm in his *Fihrist* or even much later Ibn Ḥajar al-ᶜAsqalānī, especially in his *al-Iṣābah*. What has been said above on the first writers of *akhbār* or of *taʾrīkh* rests essentially on investigations of this kind, though it cannot be said that any of them are as yet complete and finished.

It will be noted that al-Ṭabarī appears to have been unaware or, perhaps, neglectful of certain of his contemporaries or immediate predecessors. In the case of al-Yaᶜqūbī or of Abū Ḥanīfah al-Dīnawārī, the omission might be due to their opinions and also to the fact that the composite form of their expositions ruled out his own method of setting to work. It is a little more surprising in relation to a writer like al-Balādhurī, who worked in the same way as he did himself, but in general using the same sources of which he had direct knowledge.

One fundamental problem obviously is to determine whether the quotations made by al-Ṭabarī are completely reliable. Where it has been possible to make comparisons with other writers of compilations or with some original material, the result has been affirmative, but this does not mean that these quotations are necessarily complete: some passages could have been omitted because they were repetitive or because they expressed opinions of which he did not approve. Al-Ṭabarī was a loyal subject of the ᶜAbbasids and, although he felt able to use sources of other persuasions when they did not contradict the versions accepted by the Sunnī community, he refrained when this was not the case.

What posterity up to the present day has seen in the work of al-Ṭabarī is a monumental corpus of everything which could be known in the light of the second/eighth century under the ᶜAbbasids. It was a labour which

[13] *GAS*, I, 324.

obviously relieved his successors of making a similar effort, a fact which may explain the gradual disappearance of most of the earlier works. There is, however, one important reservation to be made. Al-Ṭabarī dealt with the whole of Muslim history in good faith, or at least believed that he did. In fact, although he had travelled a little in Syria and in Egypt, he has very much less to say about these countries than about the eastern half of the empire. Above all, and this is remarkable, he effectively disregards the whole of the Muslim West, an aspect which did not escape the notice of readers like ᶜArīb b. Saᶜd al-Qurṭubī (see below), to whom the fame of al-Ṭabarī was well known in spite of the immense distances between them. For the modern historian, it is obvious that al-Ṭabarī affords the basis of all research for the three centuries reviewed by him, but he needs to be supplemented by all that can be discovered in authors who are wholly or partly independent of him.

THE CLASSICAL PERIOD

The reputation of al-Ṭabarī was such that henceforward many other historians were to be assessed by comparison with him; he marks, however, as has been noted, the end of a genre which various writers over the centuries were to seek to revive. Some again, on occasion, attempted to supplement his work with direct extracts from ancient sources, but as a whole they took shelter under his authority. Those who wrote the history of subsequent periods often took as their starting-point the end of al-Ṭabarī, subject to the reservation that, as has been seen, the last few years had been insufficiently examined. For these new periods they had recourse, among other sources of information, to the accounts of surviving witnesses or to personal recollections, and it may be said that in this way they continued the method of the *muḥaddithūn*. In essentials, however, the approach was now different. Muslim administrative bodies were very bureaucratic and addicted to red tape. In particular they kept copies of the correspondence of caliphs and rulers, as well as letters addressed to them and, especially, of communiqués sent through the official postal service (*barīd*) by provincial officials and informants. All this material made it possible to compile a sort of chancery journal, in which events were recorded in chronological order, or at least in the order of arrival of the communiqués concerning them.

Inconsistencies sometimes arose in relation to the beginning and the end of the year; sometimes communiqués belonging to the beginning of the year were carelessly inserted into the previous file. Indeed, an event in Dhū ʾl-Ḥijjah might only have come to the knowledge of the addressee in

Muḥarram, and the historian consigned it to the following year, or sometimes, in the belief that there had been an error in classification, he referred it back to the preceding Muḥarram. Sometimes if he drew his inspiration from earlier sources, he might even report the same event twice without being aware of it. Also, as between two separate works, there might be discrepancies in dating (not to mention errors in transcription). Although no definite information can be given on this subject, it is certain that historians had access to archives and were able to make transcriptions of whatever they liked – especially if their work was of a semi-official nature or had the approval of the prince or the vizier. It is true that al-Ṭabarī or the writers to whom he owed his information had had access to documents, but the situation was now reversed: hitherto such documents had been inserted into a comprehensive scheme which owed nothing to them, whereas now the occasional eye-witness accounts were interpolated into a scheme based on the archives. The good state of preservation of at least a part of such archives is illustrated by the use which was still to be made of them, at the beginning of the ninth/fifteenth century, by al-Qalqashandī in his *Ṣubḥ al-aʿshā*.

Although al-Ṭabarī was a private individual, he acquired official status on account of his writings. His successors in Baghdad held similar status and were regarded with sufficient esteem for there to be no need of associates or of rivals in their fields. When other works materialized they were to come from other regions or other sections of society. One remarkable fact was that the craft of historian should have been practised for more than a century and a half by members of one family from Ḥarrān – they were, in fact, non-Muslims belonging as they did to the Sabian sect (Ṣābiʾah); their conversion to Islam did not occur until the end of the fourth generation. The first of them was a mathematician, Thābit b. Sinān, who lived until at least 360/970. Nothing of his original work has reached us directly, apart from a compilation relating to the Qarāmiṭah (Carmathians), which was probably made up of excerpts from the original. There is no doubt, however, that this compilation was almost the sole source of the whole of Iraqi historiography, give or take an occasional Christian author writing in Arabic. It seems to have consisted of a combination of two kinds of material, probably derived from various communiqués, one providing an exposition followed by a list of events and the other giving an account of events from day to day, of which latter we may well have virtually a copy in the surviving portion of the chronicle of Muḥammad b. ʿAbd al-Malik al-Ḥamadhānī, to be considered shortly. It is not known exactly to what extent the nephew of Thābit, Abū Isḥāq Ibrāhīm b. Hilāl al-Ṣābiʾ, continued the work of his uncle. Abū Isḥāq was in any case well placed to undertake such a task, in his capacity as secretary to the caliph. Miskawayh (d. 421/1030) refers to them indiscriminately as "the chronicler", but his contribution was incorporated in the general work of his grandson Hilāl b. al-Muḥassin b. Ibrāhīm al-Ṣābiʾ. However, this was in the period of the Buwayhid domination and Abū Isḥāq, who had been cast into prison by ʿAḍud al-Dawlah (reigned 338–72/949–83), obtained his pardon only on condition that he compiled a history of the dynasty, adorned, of necessity, with a number of prevarications. It seems likely that a recently discovered work on the complex regional history of the south Caspian provinces during the first half of the fourth/tenth century may be more or less identical with the first volume of this *Kitāb al-Tājī* ("Tājī" from one of the titles of ʿAḍud al-Dawlah, "Tāj al-Millah"), which must also have been used later on by the Persian Ibn Isfandiyār for his history of Ṭabaristan. The accuracy and the importance of the information to be found in it must alert us to the danger of forming, *a priori*, too unfavourable an opinion of the work of Abū Isḥāq.

However that may be, the chronicle was continued by Hilāl al-Ṣābiʾ up to 447/1055–6, just before his death. A three-year section of it has survived, consisting of a chancery record of the type defined above, but some extracts which have been preserved, especially it would seem on non-Iraqi events, in the *Mirʾāt al-zamān* of Sibṭ Ibn al-Jawzī, show that it also contained more detailed and consecutive accounts. Then the chronicle was continued up to 479/1086–87 by the son of Hilāl, Ghars al-Niʿmah Muḥammad, who must have died without issue: this part, which is particularly significant, has been effectively reproduced in the corresponding section of the *Mirʾāt*. It disregards the small, piecemeal events of day-to-day existence but provides, in the order in which the relevant communiqués were received, reports of exceptional value. Finally, although not belonging to the same family, Muḥammad b. ʿAbd al-Malik al-Hamadhānī (beginning of the sixth/twelfth century) may be regarded as having undertaken a general readoption of the chronicle, which he continued up to his own times. Strange to say, so far only the first part has reached us, and that in a Maghribī manuscript, which shows how widely it was distributed. However, other continuations of al-Ṭabarī had been produced elsewhere: mention will be made of that of ʿArīb b. Saʿd al-Qurṭubī in Spain and that of Abū Muḥammad ʿAbdullāh b. Aḥmad b. Jaʿfar al-Farghānī (d. 362/973), a Turk from Central Asia transferred to Egypt by the Ikhshidids. In fact it was on the basis of al-Ṭabarī, and then of the chronicle, that Miskawayh compiled his *Tajārib al-umam*, covering the years up to 373/983–84.

Miskawayh was essentially a philosopher, or more widely a devotee of culture in all its forms at that time. So far as concerns us, he was an historian, who from the point of view of documentation is to be classed with the Ṣābiʾ

family. The chronicle was still the basis of information, but he amplified it by research in the archives and by conversations with his friends in Baghdad. He was, however, more than an ordinary historian, asking himself, as others did, but more plainly, what useful purpose was served by history, a subject to which he ascribes the function of a kind of vast *Fürstenspiegel*, both actual and experimental. It was in fact the standpoint of the princes which he adopted, since it was they who had to learn from history the lessons on good and bad government; however he was carried along by his narrative beyond the range of such precepts. He seems to have been above all a man who found himself confronted by the problems of sound government and the pages which he devoted to the regime of the *iqṭāʿ* rank amongst the most enlightened of the whole of medieval historiography. His long life must have brought him nearly to 430/1038–9, but the *Tajārib* had been compiled in about 380/990–91, in the particular atmosphere of the Buwayhid era when men like himself or Abū Ḥayyān al-Tawḥīdī (d. after 400/1009) could talk freely on almost everything in the cultivated circles of the court. Whatever his subject, the method of presentation of Miskawayh is distinguished by an effort towards synthesis and explanation, which was indispensable to the use of the rough and fragmented data of the chronicle. It has to be believed that the value of the completed work made itself known to a wide public, since a century later a man as different from Miskawayh as the caliph's vizier, Abū Shujāʿ Ẓāhir al-Dīn Muḥammad al-Rūdhrāwarī, under the Saljūqs, thought it worth while to continue the *Tajārib* and accomplished the task as a whole in almost the same manner. The fact that in the manuscript tradition the twofold work was thus compiled and regrafted, from the date of its interruption, to the chronicle of Hilāl al-Ṣābiʾ, demonstrates that for those who used it the whole constituted one and the same work.

The century which began with al-Ṭabarī was, if not the finest, at any rate among the two or three best periods for history writing in Iraq and elsewhere. The name which was in its own way the most celebrated, both in his own time and up to the present day, was that of Abū ʾl-Ḥasan ʿAlī al-Masʿūdī. A tireless traveller, coming from a great family, with a mind passionately interested in everything, he was, he says, also the author of three historical works: a great history (*Akhbār al-zamān*), an enormous compilation which must have served him as a mine in itself but of which he perhaps never made a fair copy for publication – the size of it has in any case discouraged both copyists and readers; an intermediate-sized history (*al-Awsaṭ*), likewise lost, and finally the *Murūj al-dhahab* ("Meadows of Gold"), which immediately and permanently established his reputation. This last work, also voluminous, comprises in the first place a long geographical introduction, in which the author combines the scientific data of the times with his own observations on phenomena of land and sea. The ensuing volumes give, caliphate by caliphate, the history of the first three Muslim centuries, without any concern for finality or strict chronological order, but with the object of highlighting, episode by episode, the history of these rulers. His sources are almost all the same as those of al-Ṭabarī and others, but the use he makes of them is far more personal. The style is simple, the narrative lively, sometimes fascinating – hence his success.

In fact, to judge from indications given by himself, al-Masᶜūdī was the author of a large number of other writings, most of which appear to have escaped the attention of medieval biographers and bibliographers. The reason was that they were most often openly Shīᶜī, although probably of the moderate Twelver tendency which predominated in Baghdad in his time, on the eve of the Buwayhid conquest. The *Murūj al-dhahab*, on the other hand, was concerned not with the imams but with the ᶜAbbasid caliphs and could be read by everyone. Al-Masᶜūdī is frequently quoted by the historians, but it cannot be said that the *Murūj al-dhahab* has exercised any influence on the structure and concept of historiography in the proper sense of the term.

Two other writers of this period were Ḥamzah b. al-Ḥasan al-Iṣfahānī (d. *c.* 360/970) and al-Ṣūlī. Al-Iṣfahānī sought to be concise in his outline of universal history embracing all peoples. The writer Abū Bakr Muḥammad b. Yaḥyā al-Ṣūlī was of a different kind. He was a courtier and tutor to caliphs and his work, under the significant title of *Kitāb al-Awrāq* ("Book of Leaves"), without any other pretensions, relates morsels of history, personal recollections and accounts of witnesses, with numerous quotations of poetry, not to mention reminiscences of chess-players. He has been compared, all allowances being made, with Saint-Simon.

The growing importance of the vizierate led to the writing of histories of the viziers. There was the work, only partially preserved, of Ibn ᶜAbdūs al-Jahshiyārī, which was to be continued in the following century by Hilāl al-Ṣābiʾ, both of them dealing with administrative details of the highest interest. Mention may also be made here of the *Rusūm dār al-khilāfah* ("Forms of the Abode of the Caliphate").[14]

The emphasis on doctrinal struggles inspired the production of works devoted to the study of sects and schisms, beginning with the *Maqālāt al-Islāmiyyīn* ("Treatises of the Adherents of Islam") of ᶜAlī b. Ismāᶜīl al-Ashᶜarī and the *Firaq al-Shīᶜah* ("Sects of the Shīᶜah") attributed to Abū

[14] See D. Sourdel, "Questions de cérémonial ᶜAbbaside", *Revue des Etudes Islamiques*, 1960.

Muḥammad al-Ḥasan b. Mūsā b. Nawbakht, which, although essentially doctrinal, naturally included some historical information. Also to be noted is the *Kitāb al-Badʾ wa-ʾl-taʾrīkh* ("The Book of the Creation and of History"), a treatise on general history in terms of comparative religions, by al-Muṭahhar al-Maqdisī.

It was at about this time that a new genre came into being unparalleled elsewhere, that of the histories of cities in the form of biographical dictionaries.[15] Histories of cities had existed earlier and were to continue for a little longer, but they were not collections of biographies. The *Kitāb Baghdād* of Ibn abī Ṭāhir Ṭayfūr was in fact, at least so far as concerns the volume preserved, a general history of the caliphate in relation to the city of Baghdad, its capital. The history of Mecca by Ibn al-Azraq al-Fāriqī, antedating al-Ṭabarī, with the other Meccan chronicles which followed it, is presented as a history of that city, while the history of Mosul of Abū Zakariyyāʾ Yazīd b. Muḥammad al-Azdī (d. 334/945–6), which owes something to al-Ṭabarī, is a general history of Upper Mesopotamia; the surviving half of the history of Qumm is a well-researched account of its administration. Al-Narshakhī's history of Bukhārā is a fairly general history of the Samanid dynasty.

We should perhaps mention at this point the so-called *faḍāʾil* literature, that is, books which discussed the merits (*faḍāʾil*) of particular cities or regions, and brought together quotations in praise of them. These were frequently more of an antiquarian than of an historical character.

Historiography in general was not intended particularly for writers; it had to lend itself to being easily consulted by readers of various disciplines and cultures. As a whole, therefore, authors adopted a simple style which set forth as clearly as possible what they thought ought to be stated; the exceptions only serve more or less to prove the rule. Prefaces and dedications tended to be expressed in terms suited to the eminence of the patron to whom they were addressed. Episodes which were particularly stirring might be given emphasis in the same way, and when they were the subject of poetry, quotations were freely made. The panegyrics of princes lent themselves to the sounding of trumpets, as in *al-Tājī* of Abū Isḥāq Ibrāhīm b. Hilāl al-Ṣābīʾ honouring ʿAḍud al-Dawlah, Tāj al-Millah (see above), and the history of Maḥmūd of Ghaznah by al-ʿUtbī. Here the author was an Iranian and it is impossible not to sense the influence of Persian literature, as flowery and poetical in historiography as it is in other fields.

[15] See above, ch. 11.

This same influence, like the personality of Ṣalāḥ al-Dīn, was probably also responsible for the style in which ʿImād al-Dīn Muḥammad b. Muḥammad al-Kātib al-Iṣfahānī (d. 597/1201) was to write at a later period. Such authors probably regarded history as a part of literature and wanted to use it as a means of displaying their virtuosity. However, this aspect should not be exaggerated: apart from the fact that they were few in number, they never used their literary acrobatics, at least before the Mamlūk era, to mask or falsify the hard facts which were the subject of their expositions. Of course in matters of detail each author had his idiosyncrasies of style which were sometimes influenced by the local speech of the day; indeed the fidelity with which he reproduced quotations and documentary evidence could in extreme cases result in a mosaic of styles rather than a single style. Indifference to literary trimmings is revealed in the simplicity of the titles, assuming the early writers were always responsible for them. Subsequently there were to be some colourful titles following current literary fashion, the most celebrated example being *Murūj al-dhahab* of al-Masʿūdī, but later on other works as important as those of ʿIzz al-Dīn b. al-Athīr or al-Dhahabī were to be called simply *al-Kāmil fī ʾl-taʾrīkh* or *Taʾrīkh al-Islām*.

As in other disciplines, one of the first concerns of the writers of history was necessarily to find at least one exemplar of a work dealing with the subjects which interested them before their time. This was somewhat easier than it would then have been in Europe, because the more general distribution of paper and the extension of a certain degree of culture to widening circles of well-to-do persons brought about an increase in the numbers of copies of works corresponding to their interests. Moreover, as in Europe, travels accomplished "in search of science" (*fī ṭalab al-ʿilm*) made it possible to fill in certain gaps. This again must not be exaggerated: it is easy to establish that, broadly speaking, even for matters of general interest like law, literature quite often tends to become fragmented into regional schools. *A fortiori* this applies even more to history, inasmuch as what is of interest to authors and readers is closely bound up with their particular region, large or small, and it is often impossible to find accounts of what has happened elsewhere, so that a disproportion arises between writings emanating from large and well-informed centres of culture and those the horizon of which is bounded by their own small territory. It is easy to understand also that works of great bulk have been much less copied, regardless of their merit, than even mediocre works of smaller size – and are consequently much harder to find. The vicissitudes of trade and of war, not to mention cases of individual dishonesty, sometimes resulted in the successive volumes of the same work not being discovered all in the same place, so that in some instances authors simply wrote what they knew about them. In these circumstances it is small wonder that the most important works may sometimes have taken the longest to find.

Writers have given little information as to how they gained access to the material which they intended to use. Some of them, the very rich, purchased large numbers of books; others most frequently had recourse to the libraries of princes, of mosques and later of *madrasah*s. It was possible for a teacher or the pupil of a teacher to enter such libraries, or they could write down in their own way what the teacher read or dictated. On occasions a prince might confer the favour of access to his private library. The result was that the texts available to such writers sometimes amounted more to a lucky dip than to a specialized selection. Nevertheless, they endeavoured to bring to the knowledge of their readers both what they ought to have provided in ideal circumstances and what was actually available to them.

After a work had been completed it necessarily required some time to become known and many never achieved more than the readership of a small circle dependent on a single manuscript. It was a question of the number of copyists, and this was conditioned by the reputation of the author and his ability to make payment. Delays in distribution and areas covered are also relevant, and one or two specific instances will be considered. An examination of the certificates of reading often affixed to a manuscript by its users or owners can be helpful in this kind of enquiry.[16]

Alongside the historian working directly with original materials, there naturally continued to be others who simply passed on stories about the past. These latter do not appear ever to have made researches into archives, even supposing that such research was possible under regimes which cannot have preserved archives for very long. Financial documents have been preserved, which may be useful for example in the histories of the viziers, but are of no interest to the writers of the chronicles. There is likewise no sign that such writers were interested in epigraphical inscriptions nor, with rare exceptions, in coinage. That is not to say that they were not concerned with monetary history , but they made use of their literary sources for it and seldom resorted to an examination of actual coinage.

Their sources thus consisted of one or more works handed down by earlier generations. Often they were satisfied with one principal guide, with or without the insertion of some additional notes. In general we have to distinguish between information obtained from an eye-witness by word of mouth, introduced by *ḥaddathanā* ("so-and-so told me"), and quotations from written works usually prefaced by *qāla* ("he said that . . ."). It is

[16] See J. Pedersen, *The Arabic Book*, Princeton, 1984, ch. 3.

important, however, to take care to avoid misunderstandings. At first glance we may be tempted to regard the author or authors so quoted as the principal source of the compiler, whereas frequently the opposite is the case. Certainly an author like al-Ṭabarī names all his sources for all the events described; other writers, using the same authority, will differentiate between the passages where they are summarizing him and those where they make a point of quoting his actual text. Very often, however, the main authority, precisely because he is unchanging, does not need to be named, or may have been named once and for all, so that when another name is encountered it is because there is either an isolated interpolation of different origin or an exceptional variant. Naturally some authors, in seeking to make their histories as general as possible, are obliged according to periods and regions to combine several principal guides.

The question of the objectivity of historians has already been raised in regard to al-Ṭabarī. His tone is always neutral, never polemical, and when it is possible to verify a citation it is found to be accurately reproduced. It is, however, difficult to believe that our historians were indifferent to the problems of their times, and, therefore, to the conclusions which their readers were liable to draw from their presentation of past events. They could, for example, omit things which seemed to them to lead the reader to an undesirable conclusion. This is not only true for the first civil wars in Islam, but is no less true of later historians, as has been shown by the comparative analysis of the histories of Damascus written by Ibn al-Qalānisī and Ibn ᶜAsākir.

Despite its primordial character, Iraqi historiography is not unique and it does not cover all related works. Political divisions, imposing more or less pressure according to circumstances, together with the desire of regional princes to be celebrated, encouraged the birth and growth of a regional or local historiography. In every way the vast dimensions of the Muslim world, in relation to the means of communication of the day, made it practical as in other disciplines to provide historical accounts which were adapted to the needs and the ideas of readers in each country. In the case of Iran, this process was to lead, in historiography as in other branches of learning, to the abandonment of Arabic in favour of Persian. It has been noted how promptly a translation of al-Ṭabarī was made into that language, but in fact it was a summary or collection of extracts from which anything of little direct interest to Iran was omitted. Certainly the histories of Qumm and of Bukhārā were written in Arabic, and it was also in Arabic that al-ᶜUtbī wrote his life, or rather his panegyric, of Maḥmūd of Ghaznah, but his was a scholastic language, artificially garlanded for a prince who did not know it well. It was, moreover, in Persian that Abū ᵓl-Faḍl Muḥammad b.

Ḥusayn Bayhaqī (d. 470/1077) was to write the history of the succeeding Ghaznavids.

Arabic, however, remained the language in which were usually written those histories of more general interest than certain Iranian circles yet required, but in which the Iranian point of view was accentuated. Such was the work of the famous writer Abū Manṣūr ʿAbd al-Malik b. Muḥammad al-Thaʿālibī, who began with ancient Persian history before dealing with the period of Islam in his *Kitāb Ghurar akhbār al-mulūk wa-siyarihim* ("Book of the Highlights of the History and Lives of Kings"). So far only volumes I[17] and III of the four volumes which made up the original work have been recovered. The authorship of the third volume, long disputed, can hardly now be regarded as open to doubt. For the period under review the account given is scarcely more than an outline of al-Ṭabarī. More important for our purposes is the anonymous work published by P.A. Gryaznevitch;[18] although what remains of it does not go beyond the beginning of the second/eighth century, its composition apparently dates from the beginning of the fifth/eleventh century. Like al-Thaʿālibī, the author was a Khurasanian, but unlike him he made use, whether directly or not, of the original ʿAbbasid history attributed to Ibn Naṭṭāḥ, or of some related work which must have survived in his region.

The writing of history in Egypt, after tentative ventures on the lines of *ḥadīth* and *akhbār*, made a good start with the brothers Ibn ʿAbd al-Ḥakam (see above), but so far dealt only with the period of the early days of Islam, or, as in the case of the *Sīrah* of ʿUmar b. ʿAbd al-ʿAzīz, with an episode which was wider in geographical terms but very limited in chronology and inspired by motives of anti-ʿAbbasid reaction. It does not seem that the idea had yet been formed of tracing the history of Egypt during the succeeding generations. The work must have appeared at the time when Egypt had acquired temporary independence under the Ṭulunids, whose history, however, was not written until the fourth/tenth century, by Abū Jaʿfar Aḥmad b. Yūsuf b. al-Dāyah (d. 340/951) and Abū Muḥammad ʿAbdullāh al-Madīnī al-Balawī, perhaps with the encouragement of the Ikhshidids.[19] This was also the period of the writers ʿAbd al-Raḥmān b. Yūnus, known to us only through quotations, and Muḥammad b. Yūsuf al-Kindī, who produced a history of the governors and the *qāḍī*s of Egypt. Straddling the close of the Ikhshidid and beginnings of Faṭimid rule was the writer Ibn Zūlāq, who will be discussed later.

It was also almost certainly in Egypt that the "Continuation" of al-Ṭabarī was compiled by Abū Muḥammad ʿAbdullāh b. Aḥmad b. Jaʿfar al-

[17] Ed. and trans. H. Zotenberg, Paris, 1900.
[18] *Arabskii Anonim*, Moscow, 1967.
[19] *GAS*, I, 357; *GAL*, I, 155.

Farghānī, under the Ikhshidids. It is known to us only from quotations, the most important to be found in the *Kitāb al-ʿUyūn wa-ʾl-ḥaqāʾiq*, produced by an anonymous writer in the following century. Only two volumes of this latter work survive, one dealing with the years 86/705 to 227/842, published a century ago, and the other covering the years 256/870 to 350/961 and recently published by O. Saïdi.[20] This latter part is made up essentially of a combination of passages borrowed from Miskawayh and from al-Farghānī. The Egyptian origin of the work in the Faṭimid era is further emphasized by the knowledge, limited, it is true, but exceptional in the Orient, shown by the author of the history of the Maghrib or at least of Ifrīqiyah.

The establishment of the Faṭimids gave to Egypt an independence which this time was total and lasting and was naturally accompanied by an autonomous historiography. It was in the time of the second caliph, al-ʿAzīz (reigned 365–86/975–96), that Ibn Zūlāq was writing his history, probably in the form of annals; although it has not reached us directly, it was the main source for later authors, up to, and especially, al-Maqrīzī. There followed al-Musabbiḥī who, as a member of the Faṭimid family and a high official under the regime, wrote the more or less official history of it, presented in the form of a journal. The same form was adopted by his contemporary Hilāl al-Ṣābiʾ and by his predecessors, not, apparently, because one influenced another but by reason of their use of the archival system. As in the case of Hilāl, the work of al-Musabbiḥī was accordingly voluminous and the difficulty of forming any idea of the whole is probably explained by the fact that only one copy may ever have existed. It is not absolutely certain that the work as a whole survived until the time of al-Maqrīzī, but it was probably used in the seventh/thirteenth century by Ibn Muyassar, whom al-Maqrīzī knew.

The volume covering the two years 417–18/1026–28 is preserved in the Escurial, but it has not yet been possible to discover whether any other volumes also existed there before the fire in the eleventh/seventeenth century. Despite its great interest the work was relatively neglected until quite recent times. It has now been edited by Thierry Bianquis and A. F. Sayyid.[21]

In the middle of the fifth/eleventh century, al-Quḍāʿī was at work in Egypt. He was Iranian by birth and of uncertain doctrinal allegiance, and his high reputation is hardly consistent with the modest little works which have come down to us under his name. However al-Maqrīzī, in his *Ittiʿāẓ*, affirms that he was much indebted to al-Quḍāʿī for his archaeological information and for the general history of Egypt at this time.

[20] Damascus, 1972 and 1973. [21] Damascus, 1980.

It has been seen that, for purposes of ancient history, historians writing in Arabic made use of several ancient Pahlavi works which were translated for them. For the first centuries of Islam, only Arabic was used and nothing is in Persian; later Arab authors were to be translated into Persian and a Persian historiography came into being and was developed. It is said that even then nothing was translated into Arabic. Writers in Arabic, Persian by birth, were to disregard historical works written in Persian, with very few exceptions, so that two parallel lines of documentation evolved which were unaware of, and completely independent of each other.

In the Semitic countries and Egypt the process was different. Although the Syriac language persisted in the field of literature, the masses adopted Arabic as their colloquial language, and the Copts, who had only the most limited literature, soon became almost completely Arabicized. In the same way Greek, reduced to small linguistic islets, disappeared even among the faithful of the Melkite church. Syriac historiography survived and even experienced a last and notable upward trend in the sixth/twelfth and seventh/thirteenth centuries among the Monophysites in the regions of Upper Mesopotamia; in Iraq, among the Nestorians, it barely lasted into the fifth/eleventh century.[22]

It is understandable that Arabia, which was almost always divided politically and even doctrinally, should not have been able to supply material for a history in the true sense of the word. On the other hand, special interest came very quickly to be taken in the history of the holy cities and also of the cities in the area of the Yemen. Mention has already been made of the histories of Mecca, by al-Azraqī and his successors;[23] we are less well informed on histories of Medina, having only extracts from them in works of later date, such as that of al-Samhūdī. For the Yemen, the most ancient work of this kind extant is that of Abū ʾl-ʿAbbās Aḥmad b. ʿAbdullāh b. Muḥammad al-Rāzī (d. *c.* 460/1068) on Ṣanʿāʾ. A special place must, however, be given to the work of Abū Muḥammad al-Ḥasan b. Aḥmad al-Hamdānī (d. 334/945), who, while first and foremost a Yemeni, was not too proud to take an interest in Arabia as a whole. He can hardly be described as an historian in the strict sense of the term, but he mingled history, geography, tribal genealogies, pre-Islamic antiquities, and so on, in a work of high quality, the essential features of which have now been reconstructed.[24] Among other topics the author strove to describe the passing of the ancient Yemen into the Yemen under Islam, although he could at best read the ancient texts imperfectly and mainly relied on the

22 For Christian historical writing in Arabic, see below, ch. 26.

23 Such as Ibn Shabbah (also author of a history of Basra), al-Faqīhī, etc.; *GAS*, I, 345–6.

24 *EI*², "al-Hamdānī".

traditions of the Islamic era, which at least were still relatively fresh in his time.

Within fluctuating frontiers a principality of the Zaydī *madhhab* was formed in the Yemen, which gave rise to a literature devoted specifically to the Imams, beginning with Abū ʾl-Ḥusayn Yaḥyā al-Hādī ilā ʾl-Ḥaqq (d. 298/911). These biographies were compiled by ʿAlī b. Muḥammad al-ʿAlawī and Abū Jaʿfar al-Kūfī.[25]

The Muslims of the West had, in relation to the East, certain specific characteristics not incompatible either with domestic differences or, notwithstanding, with a close kinship in cultural development and the creation of literary genres. Conquest having come at a later date than in the East, and having been achieved by groups of men who were separate from the ethnocultural community of the Near East, it is understandable that the beginnings of historiography should have occurred somewhat later there than in the East, which could, however, provide exemplars. Of the works produced some were peculiar to Ifrīqiyah or to Spain, others were common to Spain and to Morocco, which history has often associated together, others again dealt with the whole of the West in the period when it had been more or less completely unified by the Almoravid (al-Murābiṭ) and the Almohad (al-Muwaḥḥid) empires.

The first writers to have concerned themselves with the history of the West were the Egyptians. This is not hard to explain when it is remembered what part they (and the Syrians) played in the establishment and organization of the new regimes. Later still it was to be from them that the Muslims of the West were to seek the juridical and historical information which they found they needed. It is sufficient to recall here the work of Ibn ʿAbd al-Ḥakam. That Spain had a relationship with Syria is confirmed by the knowledge of the Orient revealed in the small Latin chronicle known as the "Anonymous Work of Cordova" (mid-eighth century AD).[26] Subsequently, the political break between East and West was to be conveyed in western historiography by an almost total disregard for the history of the Orient after the era of the Prophet; the writing of history had still been very little developed by the time of the advent of the Umayyads of Spain, who preserved only a shadow of the traditions of their ancestors in Damascus.

Abū Marwān ʿAbd al-Malik b. Ḥabīb (d. 238/853), the first historian born in Spain to interest himself in the history of that country, also worked in the Traditionist manner. In the fourth/tenth century, the golden age of the caliphate of Cordova, two other writers were also at work: Ibn al-

[25] *GAS*, I, 346.

[26] See E. Lévi-Provençal, *Histoire de l'Espagne musulmane*, I, Leiden and Paris, 1950–3, 10.

Qūṭiyyah ("son of the Gothic woman") and the anonymous author of the *Akhbār majmūʿah* ("Collected Notices"), a collection of episodes mostly relating to the distant past. The smaller sequel, centred on Spain, which ʿArīb b. Saʿd al-Qurṭubī attributed to al-Ṭabarī, is evidence of the interest also taken in the historiography of the Orient, borne out on a grander scale by *al-ʿIqd al-farīd* of Ibn ʿAbd Rabbihi. Ibn Ḥazm, the philosopher–poet, concerned himself with traditional tribal genealogies and also with the history of the sects from the Umayyad viewpoint, and ʿAbdullāh b. Buluggin b. Bādīs (reigned 469–83/1076–90), the last Zirid of Granada, composed his memoirs.[27] The fact remains, however, that according to the later Muslim historians themselves, the original founders of Spanish Arabic historiography, in the fourth/tenth century, were two Arabicized Persian immigrants, Abū Bakr Aḥmad b. Muḥammad b. Bashīr al-Rāzī, and his son ʿĪsā b. Aḥmad.[28] For us the most important author in the first half of the fifth/eleventh century is Abū Marwān Ḥayyān b. Ḥayyān, who, after having more or less completed his monumental exposition of the history of Muslim Spain, produced an abridged version of it, also large, the *Muqtabis*, five volumes of which have by degrees been recovered and published.

We have practically no means of knowing how Arab historiography began in Ifrīqiyah, or *a fortiori* in Morocco. An Aghlabid prince, Muḥammad b. Ziyādatullāh, and the son of the great jurist Saḥnūn wrote on the dynasty and its era works which have disappeared and do not seem to have been widely used by subsequent authors.[29] Probably somewhat fortuitously, the most ancient chronicle to be preserved, which in fact is rather short, is that devoted to the Kharijite Ibāḍī Rustamids of Tāhart (western Algeria) towards the end of the third/ninth century by a writer named Ibn al-Ṣaghīr,[30] who probably did not belong to their religious sect. The accession of the Faṭimids and their subsequent decline may well have accounted for the disappearance of several works of their own period or earlier. The *Kitāb Iftitāḥ al-daʿwah* by their great doctor al-Qāḍī al-Nuʿmān, is an essential work for the early days of the dynasty, but does not go further, while the *Sīrah* of al-Ustādh Jawdhar is little more than a collection, quite valuable in fact, of his official correspondence. In the eyes of posterity, including Ibn Khaldūn, the true founder of Maghribi historiography was Ibn Raqīq of al-Qayrawān, writing at the beginning of the fifth/eleventh century. Under his name there has recently been published a fragment of a work dealing with a number of the Aghlabids, the *Taʾrīkh Ifrīqiyah wa-ʾl-*

27 Memoirs of ʿAbdullāh al-Zīrī in *Andalus*, III, 1935, IV, 1936, VI, 1941.

28 *GAS*, I, 362; C. Pellat, "The origin and development of historiography in Muslim Spain" in Lewis and Holt, *Historians of the Middle East*, 119.

29 For Ziyādatullāh and the son of Saḥnūn, see Talbi, *L'Emirat Aghlabide*, 910.

30 See *GAS*, I, 356.

Maghrib;[31] even though this text is definitely connected with Ibn Raqīq, its direct authenticity has not been established. Ibn Raqīq was succeeded by Abū ᶜAbdullāh Muḥammad b. ᶜAlī b. Ḥammād and Ibn al-Abbār; Ibn Sharaf continued the work and he in turn was followed by Abū Ṣalt.[32]

It does not appear that any true historiography was produced in Sicily, although other branches of Arab–Muslim culture were to be found there. Amari has noted information in the so-called Cambridge chronicle, which still awaits identification. Somewhat later the geographer and historian Muḥammad b. Yūsuf al-Warrāq wrote on the subject of the Maghrib for one of the princes of partitioned Spain of the fifth/eleventh century. The work, now lost, was to be used shortly afterwards by al-Bakrī.

The Maghrib would appear to have been readier to attach importance to biographical literature, as is demonstrated by the *Ṭabaqāt* of Abū ᵓl-ᶜArab, at the end of the second/eighth century, and among others (under the first Zirids), a part at least of the lost work of the physician Aḥmad b. Ibrāhīm b. al-Jazzār (fourth/tenth century)[33], both of which were used by various subsequent Maghribi writers like the anonymous author of the *ᶜUyūn wa-ᵓl-ḥaqāᵓiq* mentioned above. To the mid-sixth/twelfth century, before the Almohad unification, belongs a work which must be regarded as deserving special interest, the history of al-Qayrawān by ᶜAbd al-ᶜAzīz b. Shaddād, which in fact covered the history of the whole of Ifrīqiyah, probably since the Arab conquest. So far this work has not come to light, though it is possible that it still exists somewhere in the Orient. The writer was obliged at the end of his days to emigrate to Syria; he took his manuscript with him and almost all that oriental historians were to know about Ifrīqiyah up to the beginning of the Almohad period they owed to him, from Ibn al-Athīr and his disciple Ibn Khallikān to al-Nuwayrī and even Ibn al-Furāt at the end of the eighth/fourteenth century.

From Morocco nothing has reached us which is earlier in date than the sixth/twelfth century.

If there is, in some degree, a historiography appropriate to each region, there can also be a tendency towards one peculiar to a community of a political and ideological nature. It is necessary, however, to make a distinction here. Such communities desire, as do groups of other kinds, to have their own registers of doctors and persons of authority – in other words, separate dictionaries of Ibāḍīs, Shīᶜīs, Muᶜtazilites, etc. However, so far as the true history of the community is concerned, it can only be achieved specifically if the experts are not too widely dispersed and

31 Ed. M. Kaabi, Tunis, 1968.

32 Idris, *La Berbérie orientale*, xv–xvii.

33 *GAL*, I, 274, and *GAL*, SI, 424.

intermingled with others. In the case of a political organization it operates more or less the other way round and then becomes partially confused with the regional historiography. The Faṭimids, before the formal constitution of their state, had an earlier history, described, as has been seen, by al-Qāḍī al-Nuʿmān, who appears scarcely to have been known outside Ismāʿīlī circles. On the other hand this same history had also been recounted by a certain Ibn akhī Muḥsin, whose work seems to have been used by most of the historians of the Orient (and most extensively by Abū Bakr ʿAbdullāh b. Aybak al-Dawādārī).

From the foregoing it is easy to see how far, as already suggested, historical considerations entered into numerous sectors of cultural and social life, with the inevitable result that historical expositions occur in works of very different kinds.

The adherents of the various sects naturally felt the need to know their own history or, rather, an idealized version of it, and this desire gave rise to a type of history which should be called hagiography, that of the *manāqib* (virtues, feats, exploits) which was to develop in direct proportion to the increase in congregations placed under the protection of an ancient patron saint; from classical times there existed among others the *Akhbār al-Ḥallāj* (tales of the mystic al-Ḥallāj)[34]. A comparison of the *Sīrah* of ʿUmar b. ʿAbd al-ʿAzīz, a political but also historical document discussed above, with the *manāqib* compiled three-and-a-half centuries later by Ibn al-Jawzī, shows the development of this kind of composition. In general the sects exalted their martyrs: thus Abū ʾl-Faraj al-Iṣfahānī wrote in his youth a catalogue of ʿAlids put to death, the *Maqātil al-Ṭālibiyyīn*.

THE POST-CLASSICAL PERIOD

The middle of the fifth/eleventh century is marked in historiography, as in general cultural activity, by a break in continuity owing to political upheavals, which not only altered frontiers but gave power to an aristocracy with no knowledge of tradition or even, in some cases, of the Arabic language. Historiography, however, offered a better resistance than other genres, because its materials renewed themselves naturally without the need for an effort to achieve intellectual renaissance.

The misfortunes of the caliphate of Iraq and of Baghdad explain both the mediocrity and the reduction in scope of historical output before the period of relative recovery at the end of the sixth/twelfth century. We are told[35] that Muḥammad b. ʿAbd al-Malik al-Hamadhānī (see above) was

[34] See L. Massignon, *La Passion d'al-Halladj*, Paris, 1978.
[35] Ibn Khallikān, *Wafayāt al-aʿyān*, trans. de Slane, I, 290.

followed by al-Raghūnī and then by the Ḥanbalite Ibn al-Ḥaddād, of whom we have no direct knowledge. In fact the identity of this al-Hamadhānī is uncertain. The chronicler of the ninth/fifteenth century, Badr al-Dīn al-ʿAynī, for the period which concerns us here, put side by side the concise paragraphs borrowed from the small chronicle of Muḥammad b. ʿAlī al-ʿAẓīmī (483 – after 556/1090 – after 1161) with others of the same character from Muḥammad b. ʿAbd al-Malik, which can hardly belong to the same work as the continuation of al-Ṭabarī previously noted. On the other hand, the circumstantial accounts given by Ibn al-Furāt (without – and this is exceptional – naming the author) of events in Mesopotamia from the beginning of the sixth/twelfth century, which bear a close resemblance to those of ʿIzz al-Dīn b. al-Athīr, could be better attributed to al-Hamadhānī, inasmuch as they are confined to be beginning of the century, after which as we know his "History" came to a finish. Of similar character are the various extracts preserved by Ṣibt Ibn al-Jawzī (period of Malik-Shah), Kamāl al-Dīn b. al-ʿAdīm (d. 660/1262) and others.

The fact that before long an historian of the quality of Ibn al-Athīr referred collectively to "the Iraqis" among his sources certainly implies that there were several of them, but they probably duplicated the work of one another without any single writer standing out independently. Mention must, however, be made of the encyclopaedist Ibn Ḥamdūn, belonging to the middle of the century, who, in the twelfth and last book of his *Tadhkirah*, gave a valuable and circumstantial exposition of general history, for which he may also have collected material in Syria. It was probably at the request of a Syrian prince that the exiled Iraqi Ibn al-ʿImrānī, during the same period, compiled the summarized history of the caliphate *al-Inbāʾ fī taʾrīkh al-khulafāʾ*.

At the close of the century there appeared a work of greater importance but with limitations which are all the more significant. Ibn al-Jawzī was a doctor of the Ḥanbalite school which was then coming into being in Iraq and to a small extent in Syria. He was a preacher who fired crowds with enthusiasm, the author of works of many different kinds, teeming with information and with polemical observations on religious, moral and social life. An indefatigable writer, he has given us among other things a substantial work entitled *al-Muntaẓam* ("The Well-Ordered"), a voluminous history of the Muslim world up to his own time.[36] The first half is the usual imitation of al-Ṭabarī and the remainder does the same in relation to those who continued his work. However, he adds to them, increasingly, in dealing with the life and social–religious conflicts of Baghdad, supplemen-

[36] *EI*², "Ibn al-Djawzī".

tary material borrowed from Ḥanbalite informants and drawn from his own personal experience. The extreme unevenness of the chapters and the paragraphs gives the impression of a work somewhat botched and unfinished, but in any case its main characteristic is the curtailment of the horizon to Baghdad or, even more, to such matters as were of direct interest to himself: there is scarcely a word anywhere on the struggle against the Crusaders. Such as it is, *al-Muntaẓam* has been little used by later writers except in respect of the more methodical insertions made by the author's grandson, Sibṭ Ibn al-Jawzī in his *Mirʾāt al-zamān*. From a technical point of view, *al-Muntaẓam* appears to be the first example of a type which must subsequently have been widely produced, consisting of an addition to the events of each year of obituary notices on deceased celebrities. *Al-Muntaẓam* was continued for the closing years of the century by al-Qādisī, who was known to Sibṭ Ibn al-Jawzī, but whose work has been lost.

Elsewhere the reputation of the *Taʾrīkh Baghdād* encouraged a series of writers to produce sequels to it concerning their own times: first al-Samʿānī in the sixth/twelfth century, then al-Dubaythī and, on the same lines, Ibn al-Najjār in the seventh/thirteenth century. Al-Samʿānī moreover was the author of a useful handbook; the multiplicity of names of authors known only by their *nisbah* (name derived from place of origin, etc.) made it increasingly difficult to distinguish them and to identify the places from which they took their names, and al-Samʿānī in his *Kitāb al-Ansāb* supplies a general register which can in some ways be compared with the geographical dictionaries, but with the addition, alongside each locality, of the names of the most important authors who had received their *nisbah* from it.

Surprisingly enough, the Saljūqs had in their own time no true historian writing about them specifically, either in Arabic or in Persian. Their history has become available to us only by way of extant Iraqi historiography or from works in either of these languages of later date than the middle of the sixth/twelfth century, one of which at least was produced outside their own domain at the request of a prince all the more tenacious of their traditions. The author of this last Saljūq history, ʿImād al-Dīn al-Iṣfahānī, who will be discussed later, had made his career in the Arab countries of Mesopotamia and of Syria, but he was Iranian by birth, a fact which allowed him, although he wrote only in Arabic, to make equal use of sources in both languages, an unusual occurrence. For the early times he had recourse to Iraqi literature, and for the ensuing period to the memoirs of the Persian vizier Sharaf al-Dīn abū Naṣr Anūshirwān b. Khālid (d. 532 or 533/1137–8 or 1138–9); finally he drew on contemporary information available to him in Syria. As will be seen, his over-embellished style was a deterrent to ordinary readers, while a delight to specialists, and it was for this reason that his compatriot al-Bundārī, also bilingual, produced a simplified version of the work, which is the only one to have come down to us.

The other general history of the Saljūqs which has been preserved, *Akhbār al-Saljūqiyyah* for which one, or more probably two, little-known authors were responsible,[37] came in any case in its final form from the north-west of Iran, where Arabic continued to be more in use. It must have been written by an Atābak of Adharbayjān, and certainly contains information relating to that province. It was to these two Arabic works that subsequent historians with no knowledge of Persian owed the essential features of what they knew about the Saljūqs of the sixth/twelfth century.

Mention might be made at this point of the *Mashārib al-Tajārib* which Ibn Funduq (ʿAlī b. al-Qāsim Zayd al-Bayhaqī),[38] the author of the remarkable little *Taʾrīkh-i Bayhaq* ("History of Bayhaq") in Persian, compiled, this time in Arabic, as a sequel to the *Tajārib* of Miskawayh. We know of it only from Ibn al-Athīr in whose time it was still extant.

Henceforward, although Arabic continued to be employed in Iran for religion and for law, any further historical works there were to be written in Persian. It was in Arabic, a language which he was obliged to know as a high official attending on Jalāl al-Dīn Mängübirti (reigned 617–28/1220–31), that Muḥammad b. Aḥmad b. ʿAlī al-Nasawī was to write, soon after 628/1230, the notable biography of his late master, but the adventures of the latter resulted in his meeting his death in an Arab country, where he had settled to write for Arabic-speaking readers and sponsors.

The situation in Syria was quite different. More divided politically than ever, at least in the northern half, it had, in every centre, small literary circles, where many a minor notable prided himself as a writer and often wrote history, but within a strictly local horizon. This fragmentation, and probably also elements of dialect in the style of writing, explain why posterity has retained practically nothing of these works, of which we know only the titles, mentioned rarely by later authors. The last important history produced in Syria was that of Yaḥyā b. Saʿīd al-Anṭākī ("of Antioch") (d. 458/1066), who, paradoxically, compiled it in a Byzantine Christian environment; he was by birth a Christian of Egypt and wrote in Arabic, a language which had certainly become almost as current in Antioch as in the Muslim provinces.

A century or more was to elapse before any other work of note emerged. At most a few names can be mentioned, with no claim to an exhaustive list: Abū Ghālib al-Maʿarrī,[39] for example, of the illustrious family of Maʿarrat

37 Lewis and Holt, *Historians of the Middle East*, 69–71; W. Madelung, "The identity of two Yemenite MSS", *Journal of Near Eastern Studies*, XXXII, 1973, 179.

38 Lewis and Holt, *Historians of the Middle East*, 58.

39 Cahen, *La Syrie du Nord*, 44 and n. 3.

al-Nuʿmān, which in the first half of the fifth/eleventh century had produced the great poet Abūʾl-ʿAlāʾ al-Maʿarrī; and in the first quarter of the sixth/twelfth century Hamdān b. ʿAbd al-Raḥīm, who was the author of a history of the Franks among whom he had practised medicine.[40] Somewhat later two writers are to be encountered who appear to have been more important, but whose major works have none the less also disappeared: ʿAlī b. Munqidh of the celebrated Munqidh family, to be discussed shortly, and al-ʿAẓīmī. It is likely that the chronicle of ʿAlī b. Munqidh was the source for various items of information in later chronicles[41], but it quite early acquired the reputation of having been badly done and probably savoured of Shiʿism, which may well have been why it has not been preserved. From al-ʿAẓīmī a summary chronicle has survived which is useful indeed, but he had compiled a much more substantial work often quoted in the *Bughyah* ("Object of Desire") of Kamāl al-Dīn b. al-ʿAdīm. He wrote from the standpoint of a native of Aleppo who did not bear the banner of any particular religious adherence.[42] Finally there is an exceptionally good reason for proceeding here to the end of the sixth/twelfth century, when the small chronicle known by the name of the *Bustān* appeared still to provide a link with these families of authors from Aleppo and northern Syria.

Different again was the state of affairs in central and southern Syria over the same period, probably by reason of the relative unity which Faṭimid domination had given it and which was preserved for half a century by the Atābaks of Damascus. In this realm we actually know of only one work, but one of prime importance, the *Damascus Chronicle*, in which Ibn al-Qalānisī recounts the history of his city and province from the mid-fourth/tenth century to 555/1160. The great documentary value of the work notwithstanding, the author does not scruple to overlook certain inconvenient episodes.

Finally we may consider in relation to these groups the history of Mayyāfāriqīn by Ibn al-Azraq al-Fāriqī in Diyār Bakr; this important chronicle exists in two versions which have hitherto found no editors for the last century it covers (i.e. up to 572/1176–77).

It is obvious that all these chronicles, which are confined for practical purposes to the lifetime of the author, relied essentially on oral sources or on the writer's own personal experience, and indeed this may also apply to the latest sections of those chronicles which themselves go back to a more distant past. Particularly remarkable in this respect is the *Damascus Chronicle*, with its lively narrative style often coloured by dialect. For earlier periods, on the other hand, this chronicle, like those of Ibn al-Azraq and

[40] Ibid., 41–2. [41] Probably in the case of the *Bustān*, cited below.
[42] Cahen, *La Syrie du Nord*, 42–3.

probably of al-ᶜAẓīmī also, used more or less recognizable literary sources and here and there the authors may have had access to documents from archives.

It is difficult to know how to classify the Munqidh family, several members of which, including ᶜAlī, tried their hand at writing history. Its most celebrated member, Usāmah (d. 584/1188), was the author of a work unique of its kind, famous today but ignored by the whole Arab tradition, the *Kitāb al-Iᶜtibār*.[43] In it Usāmah, with a complete disregard for chronology but with great spontaneity, scatters the recollections of a life of travel which had taken him, sometimes under romantic conditions, from his birthplace, Shayzar on the Orontes, to Diyār Bakr and to Egypt then ruled by the last of the Faṭimids, to finish eventually in the service of Ṣalāḥ al-Dīn; of particular interest are his reports of minor wars and minor friendships with the Franks of the Latin Orient in the two or three decades following the First Crusade.

In the field of biography, Ibn ᶜAsākir endowed the city of Damascus with an immense dictionary, rivalling that which al-Khaṭīb al-Baghdādī had conferred on Baghdad in the previous century and slightly more open-minded than that work on the non-religious aspects of life, a tendency which, in the following century, was to be even more marked, notably in the *Bughyah* of Kamāl al-Dīn b. al-ᶜAdīm, to which further reference will be made. Mention may also be made here of Ibn ᶜAsākir's book on the *faḍāʾil* (merits) of Jerusalem, produced against the background of its reconquest by Ṣalāḥ al-Dīn.

The historiography of the second Faṭimid century is little known to us. On the one hand it appears that the decline of the regime may have discouraged the production of major works; on the other, the catastrophe of the final Ayyubid conquest may well have brought in its train the loss, dispersal or concealment of written works, only a few of which were destined to reappear, if not for us, at least for certain authors of the late Mamlūk period. Two histories, more or less general, of the regime appear to have followed parallel but mutually independent lines. We know nothing of one which was produced towards the mid-sixth/twelfth century by an author mentioned only by his court title of al-Muḥannak, apart from the fact that it was the principal source used by Jamāl al-Dīn abū ʾl-Ḥasan ᶜAlī b. Ẓāfir al-Azdī at the close of the century and again by Muḥammad b. ᶜAlī b. Muyassar (d. 677/1278) at the beginning of the Mamlūk regime; no subsequent author makes any reference to it. The reverse is true of Ibn Ṭuwayr, whose history combined a fairly detailed account of the events of

[43] See above, ch. 11, 186–7.

the sixth/twelfth century, up to the Ayyubid conquest, with a systematic and penetrating discussion of the institutions of the defunct regime as, in his view, the new rulers must have found them, which is presumably the point of the title *Nuzhat al-muqlatayn fī akhbār al-dawlatayn* ("Recreation of the Eyes in Regard to Accounts of the Two Dynasties"). Despite its considerable interest, no subsequent author mentions the work before the end of the eighth/fourteenth century, when it seems likely that, without any explicit reference to it, Ibn Khaldūn found it of use. Ibn al-Furāt, whose range in his choice of sources was particularly wide, was also much indebted to it, deriving from it the essential features of his knowledge of the second Faṭimid century; al-Maqrīzī and Ibn Taghribirdī were to do likewise. Then, with the decline of Egyptian historiography, silence descended upon Ibn Ṭuwayr's work, to such an extent that until recent times it was not even known when the writer had lived.

The increase in power of the viziers in Egypt at the expense of the caliphs explains the burgeoning of monographs on al-Afḍal, al-Maʾmūn al-Baṭāʾiḥī and Ṭalāʾiʿ b. Ruzzīk, more or less bound up with political rivalries but rich in information on administrative life. They were still available in the time of al-Maqrīzī, but none of them appears to have been preserved in its original form until the present day. Alongside these monographs and of a more summary and general nature is deserving of mention a history of the viziers entitled *al-Ishārah ilā man nāla ʾl-wizārah* compiled by ʿAlī b. al-Ṣayrafī (d. 542/1147), a high official of the chancery at the beginning of the sixth/twelfth century.

The writing of history in Arabic was continued in Egypt both with the *Kitāb al-Siyar* of Sāwīrus b. al-Muqaffaʿ and with a special work attributable to the Armenian immigration – that of Abū Ṣāliḥ on the churches of Egypt.

The Faṭimid period corresponded in the Yemen to the domination of the Ṣulayḥids, more or less loyal vassals, but this did not exclude the continued existence of Zaydī caucuses or of a Shafiʿite community. Each of these groups had its literature; here it is enough to mention the chronicle, of ill-defined contents, by Muslim al-Laḥijī[44] and the more literary work of the poet ʿUmārah b. abī ʾl-Ḥasan al-Ḥakamī.

The fame of Ṣalāḥ al-Dīn al-Ayyūbī and the fact that, in the midst of Turkish princes, he was himself of Arab culture, led to the gathering around him of a circle of writers. Mention has already been made of ʿImād al-Dīn al-Iṣfahānī in connection with the history of the Saljūqs, which he had, in fact, written in Syria at the time when he entered the service of Ṣalāḥ

[44] Madelung, "The identity of two Yemenite MSS", 179.

al-Dīn. Otherwise almost the whole of his work aimed at producing a history of that prince. The most important part of it was the *Barq al-Shām* ("The Lightning of Syria"), an account of the career of his hero, brought up to date and continued up to the end of his reign, including a description of the reconquest of Jerusalem, the recovery of Syria and Palestine from the Franks and of the resistance to the Third Crusade. It was written in a style worthy of the celebrated Sultan, but which in fact he had also adopted for his Saljūq history, as already noted. There is no reason, however, to believe that the adornments were detrimental to the accuracy of the work, which is indisputable. Moreover the author, who was principally in charge of his master's correspondence, is obliging enough to give numerous examples from it, which for us have the value of authentic chancery documents. Posterity has regarded the *Barq* as the essential source for the history of Ṣalāḥ al-Dīn, so that subsequent writers have followed it almost to the exclusion of all others. ᶜImād al-Dīn had a considerable reputation as a stylist; nevertheless he must on this account have exhausted the copyists, for only three fragments of his original work have come down to us and an abridgement was made of it by that same al-Bundārī who already seems to have been occupied with Saljūq history. Even from the abridged version only passages covering a few years have been recovered – and that quite recently. The best-known recension is that made by Abū Shāmah in the following century.[45]

From this fundamental work ᶜImād al-Dīn detached a special portion devoted to the taking of Jerusalem, better preserved by reason of its more modest proportions and importance of the subject. Having survived his master by nine years, he also produced, in two consecutive volumes, a continuation of the *Barq*, which Abū Shāmah has preserved. In addition he compiled an anthology of the poetry of his time, in the tradition of the *Yatīmah* of al-Thaᶜālibī, with supplementary notes on the poets.[46]

Together with ᶜImād al-Dīn mention must be made of his colleague and friend ᶜAbd al-Raḥmān b. ᶜAlī known by the name of al-Qāḍī al-Fāḍil (d. 596/1200), who, although Egyptian by birth, also delighted in the acrobatics of style which must have contributed to the fame of their common master. In the *Barq* are to be found as many quotations from the official correspondence of al-Fāḍil as from that of ᶜImād al-Dīn. Moreover, al-Qāḍī al-Fāḍil, who was more particularly involved in internal administration, maintained, as was the practice in most chanceries, a journal of events and decisions that he later decided to edit for publication. In this task he was assisted by Abū Ghālib al-Shaybānī, known for his abridgement and

[45] See below, 228. [46] *EI*², "ᶜImād al-Dīn".

continuation of al-Ṭabarī. The chancery journal of al-Fāḍil was still available in the time of al-Maqrīzī[47] and some manuscripts of miscellaneous content from his correspondence are extant today.

The years under consideration correspond broadly with the peak period of the sect of the Assassins in Syria. No history emanating from them has survived, but we have at least a biography – late, it is true, and semi-legendary – of Rashīd al-Dīn Sinān, the Grand Master who was a contemporary of Ṣalāḥ al-Dīn.[48]

Just as political divisions tended to encourage local histories, so the succession of dynasties or, for certain individuals, the maintenance of interest in the Muslim community as a whole, provided encouragement for a new form of composition. In fact it was to be an attempt to combine with a chronological exposition an account of events throughout the whole Muslim world – a difficult task, to be successfully achieved in only a single instance. To the extent to which it was possible to refer to the specific histories of princes or of dynasties or even to regional histories, the most convenient method of documentation was simply to string individual histories together in a general compilation. This was done in some degree by Ibn Bābā al-Qāshī in about 500/1100 and, more obviously, by the Persian author of the *Mujmal al-tawārīkh* a little later. In the Arab domain an excellent example was provided at the end of the sixth/twelfth century by *Akhbār al-duwal al-munqaṭiʿah* by Ibn Ẓāfir al-Azdī. Further afield it was the formula later to be applied by writers as open-minded as al-Nuwayrī, Rashīd al-Dīn Ṭabīb (in Persian) and even Ibn Khaldūn.

At this point it seems appropriate to draw attention to a type of chronicle which, by analogy with its counterparts in Byzantium and the other literatures of East and West, we shall call the "abridged chronicle". It goes without saying that, somewhere between the indifferent public and the specialist, there must have been people who were interested in reading short historical accounts and scholars desirous of consulting quickly some work of ready reference. For this category of users, it was necessary to assemble collections of extracts or epitomes; these indeed could hardly be regarded as works of literature but would serve a purpose in diffusing historical culture. At least they show us what the authors deemed most useful to bring to the attention of their contemporaries. It is also evident that for the modern historian they rarely supply information not already available from elsewhere. However, cases where they may have preserved shreds from sources subsequently lost should not be overlooked. These

[47] Cahen, *La Syrie du Nord*, 52.

[48] See S. Guyard, "Un grand maître des assassins au temps de Saladin", *Journal Asiatique*, April-May-June 1877, 324–489.

abridged chronicles are not all analogous; some have the appearance of rudimentary notes and can only be properly understood in the light of other more explicit information. Others select, but maintain in what they have chosen the shape of a readable continuous narrative. The writers of these abridged chronicles are also frequently those of the more extensive works; in some cases, when the chronicle post-dates a longer work by the same author, he may expand the version of the more recent years. It cannot be said either that the abridged chronicle is always the summary of a longer chronicle; there are, up to a point, two independent lines of work and the chronicle may follow other earlier chronicles without reference to more detailed works by the same author. The chronicle may sometimes be earlier, sometimes later than the longer work. Ibn Wāṣil, for instance, wrote his *al-Taʾrīkh al-Ṣāliḥī before* his large *Mufarrij*, Ibn abī ʾl-Dam his brief chronicle *after* his long one. Ibn al-Naẓīf copied the whole of the first part of his chronicle from the *Bustān*, al-Makīn b. al-Amīn his own, as far as the death of Ṣalāḥ al-Dīn, from the *Taʾrīkh al-Ṣāliḥī* of Ibn Wāṣil. The apparent multiplication of abridged chronicles in the post-classical period may indicate a certain democratization of this form of culture.

The Ayyubid epoch was for the historiography of Syria and the Jazīrah a century of glory, which was to continue under the first of the Mamlūks but by then was running parallel with Egyptian historiography, which was ultimately to take first place. The fact was that the position of Syria in the general history of the Near East was acquiring an international significance. It was to Syria that the last Arabic-speakers of Iran turned when Baghdad was no longer their chief centre, and the same was true of those in the West, especially in Spain, after the setback of the Christian *Reconquista*. There was, of course, also Egypt, but apart from the fact that the rulers who held it in common with Syria were particularly active in that province, the fall of the Faṭimid regime and the appropriation of all high offices by the newcomers from nearby Asia, who brought different traditions with them, put a brake on the development of a common Egyptian culture, which was not to be achieved until the advent of the Mamlūks.

The first major author to be encountered is still in a sense a survivor from the previous century. Ibn abī Ṭayyiʾ was the last representative of a great Shīʿī family of Aleppo; he had, however, seen the majority of his co-religionists converted to the official Sunnism. He owed to his father an abundant supply of documentation, either original or derived from the small local histories already mentioned. His *Maʿādin al-dhahab* ("Gold Mines") constituted a general history of the Muslim world, but apart from some extracts in ʿIzz al-Dīn b. Shaddād, it is hardly known to us except for the part dealing with the sixth/twelfth century. His observations on the regions outside Syria and some outside Egypt amount to scarcely more than an indication of the usual known sources, as, for example, ʿImād al-Dīn al-Iṣfahānī for the Saljūqs and again, on an even larger scale, for the reign of Ṣalāḥ al-Dīn. On the other hand, there is considerable interest in what he tells us about the history of northern Syria (for Damascus he takes his inspiration from Ibn al-Qalānisī) and about certain phases of Egyptian history, so much so that an author like the Sunnī Shihāb al-Dīn abū Shāmah, while omitting the name of Ibn abī Ṭayyiʾ from his prefatory list of sources, cannot resist quoting him constantly in the passages devoted to the reigns of Nūr al-Dīn Maḥmūd b. Zankī and the early years of Salāḥ al-Dīn. Still more important for us is his account of the history of the first half of the sixth/twelfth century, although it has survived only through the medium of the belated chronicle of Ibn al-Furāt, for a long time disregarded and of which the awaited translation and publication have not yet appeared. Ibn abī Ṭayyiʾ followed up his great work with a biography of Ṣalāḥ al-Dīn's son and governor of Aleppo, al-Malik al-Ẓāhir, with whom he seems to have been on polite terms. He had met Yāqūt who devoted to him a note, preserved by al-Ṣafadī but missing, assuredly not by chance, from the manuscripts of the *Irshād*.[49]

The small town of Ḥamāh must have been, until the beginning of the eighth/fourteenth century, a notable centre for historians, culminating in the prince Abū ʾl-Fidāʾ. The first representative of this line, moreover, was already a prince, Muḥammad b. ʿUmar b. Shāhinshāh b. ʿUmar, nephew of Ṣalāḥ al-Dīn and ruler of the city. His *Miḍmār al-ḥaqāʾiq* is mainly, as regards the part recently recovered, an abridgement of ʿImād al-Dīn, augmented by certain family traditions and a supplementary Baghdad documentation of uncertain value.

The Qāḍī Ibn abī ʾl-Dam, whose treatise on the office of *qāḍī* has survived, also compiled a vast general history of which unfortunately we possess only odd extracts, although a complete copy of it appears to have existed in the Escurial until the fire in the eleventh/seventeenth century. He too wrote about Baghdad and apparently took a sporadic interest in Sicily. His abridged chronicle, *al-Taʾrīkh al-Muẓaffarī*, dedicated to al-Muẓaffar of Ḥamāh, has survived, but is of documentary value to us only for the very last years. It was later in date than the great History, but was not necessarily inspired by it.

There remain other authors native to Ḥamāh like Ibn al-Naẓīf and Ibn Wāṣil, of whom mention will be made later. Ibn al-Naẓīf, who pursued a career chiefly in the service of the lord of Qalʿat Jaʿbar, also produced a major and a shorter history, though the basis of his documentation is

49 See *EI*², "Ibn abī Ṭayyiʾ".

unknown. The former is lost and it is not even certain that it was ever circulated. The second, the manuscript of which was recently published in facsimile, is very concise up to the sixth/twelfth century, at which point it relies on the *Bustān*,[50] but the continuation contained original information, for example on Sicily and Turkish Asia Minor.

The most important writer of the period, however, was undeniably ᶜIzz al-Dīn b. al-Athīr, certainly one of the greater Arab–Muslim historians. He came from a well-to-do family of the Jazīrah, Ibn ᶜUmar, which produced at the same time two brothers, one the vizier of a minor Ayyubid (Majd al-Dīn), the other a well-known man of letters (Ḍiyāᵓ al-Dīn); he seems not to have needed to concern himself with earning a living, apart from such benefits as might accrue to him by favour of the Zangids of Mosul, whose loyal servant he was. He seems to have been chiefly preoccupied with providing his co-religionists with a handbook that would supply them with all the essential information they might need. Certainly this preoccupation is mingled with others in his history of the Atābaks of Mosul, which aimed at achieving a true assessment of Nūr al-Dīn in relation to Ṣalāḥ al-Dīn, but it was the actual starting-point of his *al-Kāmil fīᵓl-taᵓrīkh*, which he finished under the protection of Badr al-Dīn Luᵓluᵓ, the heir of the Zangids. One important quality of Ibn al-Athīr is his clarity of style and care in explanation, which leads him, if need be, to stretch or to overstep the rigorously annalistic framework of his exposition. What is particularly remarkable is the scope of his documentation. For the periods closest to his own, he naturally made use of the archives of Baghdad, Mosul and perhaps of Damascus and elsewhere. On the other hand, especially in dealing with Iran, he directly questioned merchants, ambassadors and the like, although he himself had no knowledge of Persian.[51] With regard to earlier centuries, he of course took al-Ṭabarī as his base, while at the same time supplementing and producing a detailed summary of him on occasion, whether with or without the help of earlier abridgements we do not know. For the period of the fourth/tenth to the sixth/twelfth centuries, he was familiar with the series of Iraqi authors previously mentioned above, as far as *al-Muntaẓam*, and himself added the Syrian Ibn al-Qalānisī. He was also remarkable as the first writer in the East to make use of western Muslim sources, not only of ᶜAbd al-ᶜAzīz b. Shaddād, who had emigrated to Damascus, but also the Spaniard Abū Bakr Aḥmad b. Muḥammad al-Rāzī. From all of them he knew how to extract what was essential in concise form and on occasion to draw the necessary comparisons.

[50] See above, 220.

[51] D. S. Richards, "Ibn al-Athīr and the later parts of the Kāmil" in D. O. Morgan (ed.), *Medieval Historical Writing in the Christian and Islamic Worlds*, London, 1982.

In the thirty odd years following Ibn al-Athīr, three major writers must be noted. Sibṭ Ibn al-Jawzī, the grandson (*sibṭ*) of Ibn al-Jawzī (whose daughter was his mother) and like him a preacher who could appeal to crowds, had settled in Syria in the service of the Ayyubids of Damascus; he belonged to the Shāfiʿī *madhhab*. In his *Mirʾāt al-zamān* there is no evidence that he drew upon information equal to that of the *Kāmil*; sometimes indeed he avoids using evidence condemned by his predecessors. He copied from his sources quite slavishly – *al-Muntaẓam* of his grandfather included – and he is particularly valuable for the period 448–79/1056–87, having transcribed verbatim the important work of the son of Hilāl al-Ṣābiʾ.[52] On the other hand, for his own lifetime, he provides detailed original information, as well as several borrowings from the memoirs of his friend Saʿd al-Dīn. The major part of his work concentrates on Iraq, where the most important historians had been operating, but in its concern with the general course of development it became increasingly a history of Syria, which he continued until 653/1256, shortly before his death. It was he who introduced into Syria the practice his grandfather had inaugurated of appending to a record of events the principal obituary notices of the year, interpolating rather awkwardly a recital of the events connected with the deaths of political leaders, with the effect of interrupting the narrative. This practice was henceforth to spread first of all to Damascus and then throughout the whole Mamlūk realm. The automatic arrangement of the information in annal form was to make the *Mirʾāt*, even more than the *Kāmil*, the favourite source of many later historians.

Shihāb al-Dīn abū Shāmah, also of Damascus, is known to us mainly for his *Kitāb al-Rawḍatayn* ("Book of the Two Gardens"), in which he sets out the history of the reigns of Nūr al-Dīn and of Ṣalāḥ al-Dīn. Its success was due to the fact that it combined the versions of ʿImād al-Dīn al-Iṣfahānī (in simplified style), ʿIzz al-Dīn b. Shaddād, sometimes Ibn abī Ṭayyiʾ and of Ibn al-Athīr, not to mention abundant extracts from the correspondence of ʿImād al-Dīn al-Iṣfahānī and his friend al-Qāḍī al-Fāḍil. Later he wrote a supplement (*dhayl*), which began by drawing its inspiration largely from Sibṭ Ibn al-Jawzī, but subsequently became much more personal.

Ibn Wāṣil was relatively and unjustly neglected until recently, despite the existence of good manuscripts which were easily accessible. A native of Ḥamāh, who settled in Egypt during the reign of the last Ayyubid, al-Ṣāliḥ, he first of all compiled for this prince a general history up to the year of his accession, 635/1237. It was an abridgement and a continuation of al-Ṭabarī, perhaps through an intermediate source. He had still no knowledge of the *Kāmil*, and it was the increasing success of this latter and the *Mirʾāt* which later caused Ibn Wāṣil's work to fall into oblivion. Ibn Wāṣil subsequently

[52] See above, 203.

set to work, shortly after the fall of the Ayyubids, to compile a detailed general history of the dynasty, the *Mufarrij al-kurūb*, which became the essential source for the history of this period. The author discusses various subjects with an open mind and does not hesitate to pass beyond the political horizon of the dynasty. His style is clear and simple and it is hard to understand why it should have been necessary to wait until the middle of the present century for an edition, which has not yet been completed, and why only extracts should so far have been translated into a western language. By the time of this later work, Ibn Wāṣil had come to know both the *Kāmil* and the *Zubdah*, but apparently owed the essential part of his documentation to his own numerous relations.

It is interesting to consider the delays which were necessarily involved in the diffusion of an historical work over a distance from the place where it was written. The continuation of al-Ṭabarī by Abū Muḥammad ʿAbdullāh b. Aḥmad al-Farghānī, now lost, was in its day known both in Egypt and in Syria, but seems never to have made an appearance in either the Maghrib or in Iraq. When, in 645/1247, Ibn Wāṣil finished *al-Taʾrīkh al-Ṣāliḥī* in Egypt, he was still unaware of the *Kāmil* of Ibn al-Athīr compiled in 626/1228–9, though he had become acquainted with it fifteen years later, in time to use it for his *Mufarrij*. At the same time, however, he appears to have been entirely ignorant of the existence of the *Mirʾāt al-zamān* of Sibṭ Ibn al-Jawzī, completed in 653/1256, whereas Sibṭ Ibn al-Jawzī for his part had known the history of the Atābaks by Ibn al-Athīr, but not the *Kāmil*. For generations, as already observed, two quite separate lines of historians were to continue even in two cities as relatively close as Damascus and Cairo.

During this period two works of equal interest were being produced in Aleppo, by Kamāl al-Dīn b. al-ʿAdīm and ʿIzz al-Dīn b. Shaddād respectively. The former, belonging to an important family formerly Shīʿī but converted to Sunnism in the previous century, was the author of two related works – the *Zubdah* and the *Bughyah*. The *Zubdah* is an episodic history of Aleppo and of its surroundings, which is developed in increasing detail as it approaches the author's own period. For the sixth/twelfth century the sources are almost the same as those of Ibn abī Ṭayyiʾ, but are differently employed; the author moreover appears to have been unaware of his Shīʿī predecessor. The style is restrained and the sources are seldom named. The *Bughyah* is much more voluminous and there is no certainty that it was ever finished; in any case, by the close of the Middle Ages no more than ten volumes existed in different places. We possess nine of them, including one in two copies, and they are still not completely published. The *Bughyah* resembles in appearance the other great dictionaries of cities, and in relation to Aleppo, it is partly a dictionary though quite different in approach and method. The writer assigns an important place to princes and to political notables, and he collects in this work, naming his sources, all the materials which he weaves together in the *Zubdah*. The first volume deals with geography and the *faḍāʾil*. The *Zubdah*, which has been known for a long time though published in full only recently, has been translated into French in a rather uneven fashion.[53]

ʿIzz al-Dīn b. Shaddād, who took refuge in Egypt after the Mongol invasion, had already put together the essential elements of his *al-Aʿlāq al-ḥaẓīrah* before his flight from Aleppo. This work which must have been continued by others but which had no predecessors, sets out to provide in three parts a historical and administrative geography of Upper Mesopotamia where the writer had exercised high office, of northern Syria, including Aleppo of which he describes all the monuments, and finally, in less detail, of southern Syria, then only recently united politically with Aleppo. For his general historical information he draws largely on the work of Ibn al-Athīr and continues it up to his own time; he also shows some knowledge of Ibn abī Ṭayyiʾ.

There is no lack of commentaries to underline the primacy of Syria at this time in the field of historiographical literature. It must be added that Syria saw the advent of a new type of biographical dictionary, exemplified in the works of Yāqūt, al-Qifṭī (an Egyptian resident in Aleppo), Ibn abī Uṣaybiʿah and Ibn Khallikān.[54]

Egypt makes a somewhat meagre showing during this period. It seems appropriate nonetheless to mention one writer who was active under the last Ayyubids and at the very beginning of the Mamlūk era, to which he makes no allusion in his writings. Ibn Muyassar, whose annals of Egypt we possess only in an incomplete form as copied by the hand of al-Maqrīzī, is valuable as the only original source for the history of the last of the Faṭimids;[55] his work was continued up to and included the Ayyubids, but the existence of better sources for this period, perhaps used by Ibn Muyassar himself, explains why we have here many fewer explicit quotations.

Christians and Muslims alike were interested in the past, which had become legendary, of Pharaonic Egypt. Here it will be sufficient to mention the work edited and translated in the eleventh/seventeenth century by P. Vattier under the title of *L'Égypte du Murtada, fils du Gaphiphe*, which owes its present reputation to the fact that the original manuscript was lost and the author remained unidentified until quite recently.[56]

[53] *Recueil des historiens des Croisades: historiens orientaux III*, Paris, 1884, 571–732.
[54] See above, ch. 11. [55] H. Massé, *Annales d'Egypte*, Cairo, 1921.
[56] The identification was supplied by Yūsuf Rajīb in *Arabica*, XXI, 1973.

Although the memoirs of Usāmah continue to be unique within their class of Arab historical literature, the Ayyubid period has bequeathed to us in a more or less complete form three other memoirs which are worthy of interest. The physician ᶜAbd al-Laṭīf al-Baghdādī, who wrote a little of everything, compiled memoirs of a kind to be used in relation to the history of his time; they have reached us only in fragments through the works of two Damascus writers, Ibn abī Uṣaybiᶜah, and al-Dhahabī. ᶜAbd al-Laṭīf had no claims to historical erudition, but he combined in his memoirs highly personal information with passages of general exposition. The prince al-Malik al-Nāṣir Dāwūd left a correspondence which his sons put together into a sort of small posthumous memoir. Saᶜd al-Dīn al-Juwaynī, of the family of the four famous "Sons of the Shaykh",[57] has left an account of his experiences under the Ayyubids and a certain number of extracts from it figure in the works of Sibṭ Ibn al-Jawzī and al-Dhahabī.

Historiography in the Yemen, which was to be developed very considerably in the following centuries, was summed up, for the Ayyubid period, in the work of Abū Muḥammad Yūsuf al-Ḥujūrī (*fl.* sixth/twelfth century).

The Mongol invasion and the fall of the caliphate of Baghdad caused the disappearance of such historical works as had existed in Baghdad before 656/1258. The principal writer there had been Tāj al-Dīn ᶜAlī b. Anjab b. al-Sāᶜī (d. 764/1275), from whom a fragment dealing with the early years of the century is all that has hitherto been recovered and published.[58] The writer appears broadly speaking to have put together general historical accounts mainly borrowed from the *Kāmil*s and a detailed chronicle dealing particularly with the domestic affairs of Baghdad. He does not appear to have gone back further than the caliphate of al-Nāṣir (reigned 575–622/1180–1225).

The establishment of the Almoravid and the Almohad empires, by giving a more or less complete unity to the Muslim West, Andalusia and the Maghrib, may perhaps have created conditions favourable to an extension of the horizon in the writing of history, although it is true that the works produced in the West showed, generally speaking, more ignorance of the affairs of the East than did those of the East regarding the West. As the area of Muslim dominion in Spain shrank, many of the cultivated elite emigrated to the Orient. Ibn Khaldūn was to do so later, and also Abū ᵓl-Ḥasan ᶜAlī b. Mūsā b. Saᶜīd al-Maghribī, the geographer, historian and man of letters, in the time of the Ayyubids. His *Kitāb al-Mughrib fī ḥulā ᵓl-Maghrib*, which has been recovered and published piecemeal, is one of the most original and open-minded of the historical works of the period.[59]

In the West the discovery was made this century of the short history of

57 *EI*², "Awlād al-Shaykh". 58 Ed. Muṣṭafā Jawād, Baghdad, 1353/1934.
59 *EI*², "Ibn Saᶜīd al-Maghribī".

the early days of the Almohads by Baydaq.[60] However, the work on which we depend for a large part of our knowledge of the sixth/twelfth and seventh/thirteenth centuries remains, both for the Maghrib and for Spain, the *Bayān* of Ibn ᶜIdhārī al-Marrākushī (late seventh/thirteenth century); which is slightly later in date than the period under consideration here. As a whole, what was written in the interval belongs rather to the class of biography or dictionary, as in the Maghrib the work of al-Malikī, in Spain of Ibn al-Faraḍī (d. 403/1012) and of his successor Ibn Bashkuwāl (d. 578/1183),[61] who came soon to be known in the East also. Much historical information is to be found in the *Dhakhīrah* of Ibn Bassām (d. probably 542/1147).[62]

From the same period the Ibāḍīs have left us a history of their past written by Abū Zakariyyāʾ Yaḥyā b. abī Bakr al-Warjalānī;[63] while Abū ʾl-ᶜAbbās Aḥmad b. Saᶜīd al-Darjīnī wrote an Ibāḍī biographical dictionary entitled *Kitāb Ṭabaqāt al-mashāyikh*.

CONCLUSION

Here and there points of comparison have been suggested, in outline, between various branches of the historiography of the Near East. It may well be useful to proceed further with the comparison between Arab and Persian historiography, which latter was revived during the last of the periods discussed here, not perhaps without the rediscovery of several traditions belonging to an earlier period than that of Arabicization. It could probably be effected more successfully in relation to subsequent periods, when it was to attain its full development. In many respects it assimilated the historiography of the Arabic language, even in the field of biographical dictionaries, just as Arab historiography had made several borrowings from Iran, such as the *Fürstenspiegel*. On the other hand, Persian historiography was most often distinguished by a tendency towards more ornate style, sometimes a little fanciful, and a less annalistic presentation, with a preference for arrangement according to reigns.

To take a broader view, as was suggested at the beginning, it might be helpful to abstract what has been said in this chapter about the elements of comparison with the historiographies of neighbouring civilizations, particularly the Byzantine: between the two were the Christian literatures of the Orient, some integrated within the Muslim domain and others, of which brief mention has been made, external to it like the Armenian and the

60 E. Lévi-Provençal (ed.), *Documents inédits d'histoire almohade*, Paris, 1928.

61 *GAL*, I, 412, 415.

62 *EI*², "Ibn Bassām, Abū ʾl-Ḥasan ᶜAlī b. Bassām al-Shantarīnī"; *GAL*, I, 414.

63 E. Masqueray (ed.), *Kitāb al-Sīrah*, Algiers and Paris, 1878.

Georgian. Further, some interest may perhaps be aroused in the contemporary historiography of the Christian West. Arab historiography, by reason of the geographical area which it covers, is superior both in volume and in diversity. Certain elements, such as biographical dictionaries, were its own independent creation. It is the function of historiography everywhere to translate into its own terms certain aspects of the world of ideas in which it takes shape and it is not possible to undertake here a comparison from this point of view; it is enough to say a word about the manner in which it expresses what it wishes to say or to imply and about its methods of obtaining information. Byzantine historiography, the heir to ancient history, did not of course pass through the youthful phase experienced by Arab historiography at its traditional stage. A broad comparison is thus to no purpose except as between classical and post-classical centuries.

The period considered here comes to an end with the rise of the Mamlūk regime and the Mongol empire. The historical works of this later period have survived in greater numbers and present certain new features, but in general they continue the historiographical tradition of the preceding period, in particular that of the Ayyubids.

CHAPTER 13

FAṬIMID HISTORY AND HISTORIANS

Although Faṭimid rule in Islamic history lasted only for about two and a half centuries (297/909 to 567/1171), it was of greater importance than any of the other provincial regimes which arose during the decline of the ᶜAbbasid caliphate, for a number of reasons. It was the product of a movement, popularly known as Ismāᶜīlī, the history of which goes back to the beginnings of the ᶜAbbasid period, that is the time of the Shīᶜī imam Jaᶜfar al-Ṣādiq. It ushered in the first serious imperial challenge to the empire of the caliphate at Baghdad. Its intellectual legacy was as brilliant as those of the most productive periods of Islam. Lastly, its impact was felt till much later times, judging by the histories of the period that continued to be written, despite the withering away of Faṭimid religious influence in Egypt and Syria.

The Faṭimid *daᶜwah* (mission), unlike any other mission, did not simply create a state, but continued to guide it throughout its existence and created an extensive literature. Never in Faṭimid history was its mission geared to mass proselytization. Its teachings were addressed to a candidate (*mustajīb*) seeking admission to the community. It aimed at creating an elite class of *dāᶜī*s (religious missionaries cum political agents) supported by a political base such as the Faṭimid caliphate. Once that base was gone, the community was destined to disappear, as the elite had been wiped out and there had in any case never been a mass following of the faith. The majority of the Muslim population in Egypt and Syria during the Faṭimid period had always been Sunnī, although not under the authority of the ᶜAbbasid caliphate. The teaching of the *daᶜwah* was described by its opponents as a graded system of intellectual seduction, leading simple unsuspecting people to heresy and immorality. In fact, there was simply a system of training for *dāᶜī*s called *tarbiyat al-ḥudūd* (*ḥadd* was an officer of the *daᶜwah* in Ismāᶜīlī terminology). This teaching and training followed a graded syllabus from elementary to more complex works of religious literature. In the latter category were the works of esoteric interpretation (*taʾwīl*) and philosophy (*ḥaqāʾiq*). Historical works, as well as those of language, grammar and law were taught at an earlier stage. The historical literature was, therefore, always available, even to an outsider, except when controversial topics were discussed such as the Faṭimid genealogy or when the identity of a hidden imam, if disclosed, would expose him to danger from a hostile administration.[1]

FAṬIMID LITERATURE

Much has been said about the secrecy of the Faṭimid literature which is not correct, particularly now, when even the most esoteric works are to be found in print and readily available. This chapter will isolate the historical literature and mention other genres when historical material is found in them. It will also include Sunnī historical sources of both the Faṭimid and later periods that have a bearing on Faṭimid history. Although there are many private Ismāᶜīlī libraries that are difficult to reach, enough Ismāᶜīlī material is available at such places as the Bombay University Library (Fyzee Collection), Tübingen University Library (almost the whole list is included in Heinz Halm's *Kosmologie und Heilslehre der Frühen Ismāᶜīlīya*, 1978); the Ambrosian Library, Milan (of which an exhaustive catalogue has been made by Löfgren and Traini); the Bibliothèque Nationale, Paris; Leiden University Library; the Library of the School of Oriental and African Studies, London; the Library of the Institute of Ismāᶜīlī Studies, London (whose manuscript collection has been catalogued by Adam Gacek[2]) and the Hamdani collection of Ismāᶜīlī manuscripts which is in the author's possession (listed in Poonawala's *Biobibliography*). Scattered material could be found elsewhere too. The library of the Bohra *dāᶜī* in Bombay is the richest, as it comprises the collection of several private *waqf*s taken over by the *daᶜwah*, but it remains inaccessible. Private collections in the Yemen should yield new material. There is some Ismāᶜīlī material in the library of the Great Mosque of Ṣanᶜāʾ. Western scholars are now able to reach the Mosque's manuscript wealth as it has been moved out of the Mosque's precincts.

The present study is restricted to the *daᶜwah* literature, general medieval standard histories and modern research into these. It only covers the Faṭimid period in north Africa, Egypt, Syria and the Yemen and the Alamut period in Iran.

[1] A. A. A. Fyzee, "The study of the literature of the Fatimid daᶜwah" in G. Makdisi (ed.), *Arabic and Islamic Studies in Honor of H. A. R. Gibb*, Leiden, 1963; S. M. Stern, "The 'Book of the Highest Initiation' and other anti-Ismāᶜīlī travesties" in S. M. Stern, *Studies in Early Ismāᶜīlism*, Jerusalem, 1983; Abbas Hamdani, "Evolution of the organizational structure of the Faṭimid Daᶜwah", *Arabian Studies*, 1976.

[2] *Catalogue of Arabic Manuscripts in the Library of the Institute of Ismāᶜīlī Studies*, London, 1984–5.

THE "PERIOD OF CONCEALMENT"

The first stage in Faṭimid history is the "Period of Concealment" (*satr*). It is so-called because the imams of that period were in hiding. It begins in 148/765, the date of the Shīʿī imam Jaʿfar al-Ṣādiq's death, and ends in 297/909, the year of the declaration of the Faṭimid caliphate in north Africa by the caliph–imam ʿUbaydullāh al-Mahdī (reigned 297–322/909–34). The understanding of this period involves certain problems. The first concerns the question of succession to Jaʿfar and the nature of the movement. The conflict for succession took place in Jaʿfar's lifetime when the imam-designate, his second son Ismāʿīl, died suddenly in 145/762 and the *daʿwah* now split between the claims of Ismāʿīl's younger brother, Mūsā, and Ismāʿīl's son Muḥammad. The conflict was temporarily patched up by the acceptance of Jaʿfar's eldest son, ʿAbdullāh, as the imam after Jaʿfar's death. ʿAbdullāh, however, soon died and the conflict surfaced again. Behind the question of succession, there appears to have been a debate among the *dāʿī*s about their policy towards the ʿAbbasid state. Those who wanted to continue a peaceful resistance supported Mūsā and his line of imams. They came to be known as the Ithnā ʿAshariyyah (Twelvers). Those who wanted either the overthrow of the ʿAbbasid regime or at least the setting up of a rival, Shīʿī regime, supported Muḥammad b. Ismāʿīl. They were seeking a *dār al-hijrah* which did not only mean a place of refuge but the foundation of a new state. Evidently such a movement had to go underground and its leaders had to remain hidden. This movement is popularly known as Ismāʿīlī, although its mission simply called itself *al-daʿwah al-hādiyah* ("the rightly guiding mission").

Another problem of the period of *satr* is genealogical. P. H. Mamour, in his *Polemics on the Origin of the Fatimi Caliphs*,[3] has pointed out that there are more than 200 versions of the line of succession between Ismāʿīl and al-Mahdī, the founder of the Faṭimid dynasty. This would make one doubt the continuity of the line. S. M. Stern, in his "Ismāʿīlīs and Qarmaṭians"[4] positively rejects such a continuity. W. Madelung in his "Das Imamat in der frühen ismailitischen Lehre"[5] is sceptical about it. In his *Origins of Ismāʿīlism*, Bernard Lewis had argued in favour of two lines of imams (one truly Ismāʿīlī and the other "trustee", Qaddaḥid), suggesting that the Faṭimid al-Mahdī had a non-Faṭimid descent from an early *dāʿī*, Maymūn al-Qaddāḥ. Wladimir Ivanow refutes Lewis's position in his *Ismāʿīlī Tradition Concerning the Rise of the Fatimids*[6] on the basis of several standard

[3] London, 1934.
[4] *L'Elaboration de l'Islam* (Colloque de Strasbourg, 12–14 June 1959), Paris, 1961.
[5] *Der Islam*, XXXVII, 1961. [6] Calcutta, 1942.

Ismāʿīlī historical sources, thus upholding the traditional version of the Faṭimid genealogy. T. Nagel, in his *Frühe Ismāʿīlīya und Fatimiden im Lichte der Risālat Iftitāḥ ad-Daʿwa*,[7] suggested a Ḥasanid background of the Faṭimids, at least in doctrine, if not in physical descent. Ḥusayn Hamdānī, on the basis of the Faṭimid al-Mahdī's statement about his own genealogy, constructed a line of imams going back, not to Ismāʿīl, but to ʿAbdullāh, the eldest son of Jaʿfar al-Ṣādiq.[8] With François de Blois the present writer contends in the paper "A re-examination of al-Mahdī's letter to the Yemenites on the genealogy of the Fatimid caliphs"[9] that during the *satr* period there was a close collaboration and even a zigzag succession between the lines of ʿAbdullāh and Ismāʿīl. Both ʿAbdullāh and Ismāʿīl were sons of the same mother, Fāṭimah bint al-Ḥusayn b. al-Ḥasan b. ʿAlī b. abī Ṭālib, as distinguished from the other sons of Jaʿfar al-Ṣādiq. Thus the Faṭimids could claim descent from two Fāṭimahs, one the mother of Ḥasan and Ḥusayn, sons of ʿAlī and grandsons of the Prophet Muḥammad, and the other, the mother of both ʿAbdullāh and Ismāʿīl, the sons of Jaʿfar al-Ṣādiq. Since the second Fāṭimah was a granddaughter of Ḥasan b. ʿAlī, the Faṭimids could claim both a Ḥasanid and Ḥusaynid origin. Once the question of this collaboration is settled, the doubts about the continuity of the movement, as well as the adoption of the name, Faṭimid, begin to disappear.

The third problem of this period is the identification, or the distinction, between Ismāʿīlīs and Qarmaṭians. Stern in his "Ismāʿīlīs and Qarmaṭians" considers the messianic return of Muḥammad b. Ismāʿīl as the original doctrine of the *daʿwah* in the late third/ninth century inherited from an earlier time. In about 286/899 the *dāʿī* Ḥamdān Qarmaṭ, from whose name the term "Qarmaṭian" is derived, defied the imam in hiding at Salamiyyah in Syria by rejecting the imam and asserting the original doctrine. Thus, according to Stern, the Qarmaṭians had a doctrinal continuity; whereas the Faṭimid Ismāʿīlī imams had neither a physical nor doctrinal continuity from the earlier imam Muḥammad b. Ismāʿīl. Madelung in his "Das Imamat" accepts this and applies the question of the return of Muḥammad b. Ismāʿīl as a litmus-test to determine not only the religious affiliation of a particular author to the Faṭimid *daʿwah* or otherwise, but also the time of the composition of an Ismāʿīlī work. The present writer has differed from this interpretation.[10] The doctrine of the return of Muḥammad b. Ismāʿīl is indeed a link between the early Ismāʿīlī *daʿwah* of the second/eighth century

[7] Bonn, 1972. [8] *On the Genealogy of the Fatimid Caliphs*, Cairo, 1958.

[9] *Journal of the Royal Asiatic Society*, 1983.

[10] "An early Faṭimid source on the time and authorship of the *Rasāʾil Ikhwān al-Ṣafāʾ*", *Arabica*, XXVI, 1979.

and that of the late third/ninth century, but it was kept up to avoid questions about the identity and whereabouts of the hidden imams. It was not so much a doctrine as a strategy, and once the Faṭimid imamate came out into the open, that doctrine had to be explained away. The dissident *dāʿīs* in Kufa, Baḥrayn and the Yemen, who had very little in common except defiance of the Faṭimids and a vague appelation "Qarmaṭian", stuck to that doctrine exclusively. We find early and later Faṭimid-Ismāʿīlī works still using the doctrine without any intention to defy the Faṭimid caliphate.

The time and authorship of the celebrated medieval Islamic encyclopaedia, the *Rasāʾil Ikhwān al-Ṣafāʾ*, are in dispute. The general consensus of scholars is that the work is Ismāʿīlī, and we should add Faṭimid, and not Qarmaṭian. The present writer also takes the view that the work was composed between 260/873 and 297/909, i.e. shortly before the establishment of the Faṭimid caliphate, rather than the later period around 373/983 as previously believed. If the earlier dating of the *Rasāʾil* is accepted it would precede the time of Muḥammad b. Muḥammad al-Fārābī (d. 339/950) and make the Ikhwān pioneers in the adaptation of neo-Platonic thought to Islamic philosophy; it would also make their writing a preparation for the new caliphate about to be established, in the same way as Muʿtazilite doctrines paved the way for the establishment of the ʿAbbasid caliphate.

The details of the factional conflicts, particularly the internal conflicts of the Shīʿah, can best be studied from a vast literature on the Muslim sects, that is the *firaq* or *milal wa-ʾl-niḥal* literature, such as *Firaq al-Shīʿah* (compiled *c.* 286/899) of Abū Muḥammad al-Ḥasan b. Mūsā b. Nawbakht al-Nawbakhtī, *Kitāb al-Maqālāt wa-ʾl-firaq* (compiled *c.* 292/905) of Saʿd b. ʿAbdullāh al-Qummī, *Uṣūl al-niḥal* and *Kitāb al-Awsaṭ* of al-Nāshiʾ al-Akbar (d. 293/906), *Maqālāt al-Islāmiyyīn* of Abūʾl-Ḥasan al-Ashʿarī (d. 324/935) *Kitāb al-Tanbīh wa-ʾl-radd* of al-Malaṭī (d. 377/987), *al-Farq bayn al-firaq* of ʿAbd al-Qāhir b. Ṭāhir al-Baghdādī (d. 429/1037), *al-Fiṣal fī ʾl-milal wa-ʾl-ahwāʾ wa-ʾl-niḥal* of Ibn Ḥazm (d. 456/1064), *Kashf asrār al-Bāṭiniyyah* of Ibn Mālik al-Ḥammādī (fifth/eleventh century), *Bayān al-adyān* (in Persian 485/1092) of Abū ʾl-Maʿālī Muḥammad b. ʿUbaydullāh, *Kitāb al-Milal wa-ʾl-niḥal* of al-Shahrastānī (d. 548/1153), *Qawāʿid ʿAqāʾid Āl Muḥammad* of Muḥammad b. al-Ḥasan al-Daylamī (d. 707/1308) and *Ifḥām al-Afʾidat al-Bāṭiniyyah al-ṭagḥām* of Yaḥyā b. Ḥamzah al-ʿAlawī (d. 745/1345). To this list can be added an important early Faṭimid source, *Kitāb al-Zīnah* (which contains a very useful section on Muslim sects) of the *dāʿī* Abū Ḥātim Aḥmad b. Ḥamdān al-Rāzī (d. 322/933–4). These sources, Twelver, Zaydī, Ismāʿīlī and Sunnī, throw ample light on the incubation of the Ismāʿīlī movement and the beginnings of the Faṭimid caliphate.

THE NORTH AFRICAN PERIOD OF THE FAṬIMID CALIPHATE

The following are the earlier Faṭimid historical sources for the north African period of the Fatimid caliphate: *Kitāb al-Munāẓarāt fī ʾl-imāmah* of Abū ʿAbdullāh Jaʿfar b. Aḥmad, describing the author's controversy with the famous *dāʿī* Abū ʿAbdullāh al-Shīʿī in 296/909, the works of the famous Faṭimid historian and jurist al-Qāḍī al-Nuʿmān (d. 363/974) such as *al-Manāqib wa-ʾl-mathālib* (history of Shiʿism up to the end of the Umayyad period), *Iftitāḥ al-daʿwah* (history of the establishment of the Faṭimid mission in the Yemen and north Africa), *Maʿālim al-Mahdī* (biography of the first Faṭimid ruler al-Mahdī, lost, but quoted in later works), *Sharḥ al-akhbār* (early Shīʿī and Ismāʿīlī history) and *al-Majālis wa-ʾl-musāyarāt* (the first in a genre of Ismāʿīlī *majālis* – séances – literature, a store of scattered historical information) and several other less important works. Al-Mahdī's letters to the Yemeni *daʿwah* and to the Qarmaṭian leader Abū Ṭāhir al-Jannābī (301–32/914–43) are also preserved.[11] *Kitāb al-ʿĀlim wa-ʾl-ghulām* is an early work by Ibn Ḥawshab (d. 302/914), the founder of the Faṭimid mission in the Yemen. His biography, *Sīrat Ibn Ḥawshab*, was written by his son Jaʿfar b. Manṣūr al-Yaman (d. *c.* 362/972). It is lost but is quoted in later works. On the principles and organization of the Faṭimid *daʿwah* he wrote an important work *Kitāb al-Farāʾiḍ wa-ḥudūd al-dīn* ("Book of Religious Duties and Ordinances"), which contains al-Mahdī's letter to Ibn Ḥawshab about the Faṭimid genealogy.

The fourth Faṭimid caliph, al-Muʿizz (reigned 341–65/953–75), addressed al-Ḥasan b. Aḥmad, the Qarmaṭian leader of Baḥrayn and the *dāʿī* Jalam b. Shaybān of Multan in letters that have been preserved and studied. The *dīwāns* of two Faṭimid poets, Ibn Hāniʾ (d. 362/973) and Amīr Tamīm b. al-Muʿizz (d. 375/985), have historical references. Two non-Ismāʿīlīs in the service of the early Faṭimid caliphs have left precious information: al-Ḥājib Jaʿfar b. ʿAlī in his *Sīrah* described the journey of al-Mahdī from Syria to north Africa, and al-Ustādh Jawdhar in his *Sīrah* gives us information on the Faṭimid preparations in north Africa for the conquest of Egypt.

On the north African period, we have standard non-Faṭimid histories of great value: the *Taʾrīkh* of Abū Zakariyyāʾ Yaḥyā b. abī Bakr al-Warjalānī (d. 471/1078), *Taʾrīkh Banī ʿUbayd* (compiled 617/1220) of Abū ʿAbdullāh Muḥammad b. ʿAlī b. Ḥammād (d. 628/1231), *al-Mughrib fī ḥulā ʾl-Maghrib* of Abū ʾl-Ḥasan ʿAlī b. Mūsā al-Maghribī (d. 685/1286), *al-Bayān al-mughrib* (compiled 706/1306) of Ibn ʿIdhārī al-Marrākushī, *Kitāb al-ʿIbar* of Ibn

[11] Ḥasan and Sharaf, *ʿUbaydullāh*.

Khaldūn (d. 808/1406) and *Kitāb al-Ittiʿāẓ* and *al-Muqaffaʿ* of al-Maqrīzī (d. 845/1442). Other sources of lesser importance are *Kanz al-durar* of Abū Bakr b. ʿAbdullāh b. Aybak al-Dawādārī (d. 732/1331), *Nihāyat al-arab* of Aḥmad al-Nuwayrī (d. 732/1332) and *al-Nujūm al-ẓāhirah* of Abū ʾl-Maḥāsin Yūsuf b. Taghribirdī (d. 874/1469). Sunnī geographical works also have historical information. Prominent among them are *Aḥsan al-taqāsīm* of al-Muqaddasī, *Ṣūrat al-arḍ* of Ibn Ḥawqal, *al-Masālik wa-ʾl-mamālik* of al-Bakrī and *Nuzhat al-mushtāq* of al-Idrīsī.

A *dāʿī* of the time of the caliph al-ʿAzīz, Aḥmad b. Ibrāhīm al-Naysābūrī, wrote his *Istitār al-imām* about the pre-caliphate *satr* period and his *al-Risālat al-Mūjizah* about the qualifications of a *dāʿī*.

PERIOD OF AL-ḤĀKIM

The time of the Faṭimid caliph al-Ḥākim (reigned 386–411/996–1021) was a turbulent one. On the one hand, the Faṭimid empire had reached its widest extent; on the other, it was the beginning of its decline. The ʿAbbasid caliphate had issued a manifesto defaming the Faṭimids. The Berber and Turkish troops of the Faṭimid state were at war with each other. The Zirids of north Africa were beginning to break loose from Faṭimid control and a new dissident sect, that of the Druzes, had made its appearance. But this was also the time of a great writer, the *dāʿī* Ḥamīd al-Dīn Aḥmad b. ʿAbdullāh al-Kirmānī (d. *c.* 411/1021). In him we find the climax of the Faṭimid doctrine and of Ismāʿīlī neo-Platonism, which had made its beginning in the *Rasāʾil Ikhwān al-Ṣafāʾ*. Al-Kirmānī's philosophic thinking is embodied in his *Kitāb Rāḥat al-ʿaql* and *Kitāb al-Riyāḍ* which is a study of the doctrinal controversy between three early Persian Ismāʿīlī *dāʿīs*, Abūʾl-Ḥasan Muḥammad b. Aḥmad al-Nasafī (killed in 332/943), his pupil Abū Yaʿqūb al-Sijistānī (d. *c.* 390/1000) and Abū Ḥātim Aḥmad b. Ḥamdān al-Rāzī. Al-Kirmānī wrote several tracts (*rasāʾil*), each concerning a specific problem that the Faṭimid *daʿwah* faced. Against the ideas of the elder *dāʿī*, Abū Yaʿqūb al-Sijistānī, contained in *Kitāb al-Maqālīd*, he wrote, for example, his *Risālat al-Muḍīʾah*; in support of the fixed Faṭimid calendar (not depending on the sighting of the crescent moon for the beginning of a month), he wrote *Risālat al-Lāzimah* and *Mabāsim al-bashārāt*; against the Druzes he wrote *Risālat al-Wāʿiẓah* and against the Zaydīs, the *Risālat al-Kāfiyah*. In refutation of the philosopher Abū Bakr Muḥammad b. Zakariyyāʾ al-Rāzī, he composed his *al-Aqwāl al-dhahabiyyah*, and against the thought of the celebrated writer al-Jāḥiẓ he wrote *Maʿāṣim al-hudā*.

Sunnī writers flourished during the reigns of al-Muʿ izz, al-ʿAzīz and al-

Ḥākim and are quoted in later works such as those of al-Maqrīzī. They are Ibn ᶜAbd al-Ẓāhir, Ibn al-Mutawwaj, al-Sharīf al-Juwwānī, al-Quḍāᶜī, Ibn Duqmāq and also Abū Ṣāliḥ the Armenian. Several works of Abū Muḥammad al-Ḥasan b. Ibrāhīm b. al-Ḥusayn b. Zūlāq (d. 386/996) are also cited, including his biographies of al-Muᶜizz, al-ᶜAzīz and the conqueror of Egypt, the *qāʾid* Jawhar al-Ṣiqillī (d. 381/992). His history of Egypt was continued by his son Abū ʾl-Ḥusayn and his grandson Ibn abī ʾl-Ḥusayn (d. 415/1024). Other writers of the period are al-Uswānī (d. *c.* 350/961) who wrote a history of Nubia, and al-ᶜUtaqī (d. 384/994) who was the astrologer of al-Muᶜizz.

The Dār al-ᶜIlm founded in the caliph al-Ḥākim's time became the centre, not only of the Faṭimid *daᶜwah*, but also of a wider literary and scientific activity. Abū Bakr al-Anṭākī, exponent of Malikite law, and the famous historian ᶜIzz al-Mulk Muḥammad b. abī ʾl-Qāsim al-Musabbiḥī (d. 420/1029) worked there. Mention should also be made of the Sunnī *muḥaddith* ᶜAbd al-Ghanī b. Saᶜīd al-Azdī (d. 409/1018); also of the Christian chronicler of the period AD 938–1034, Yaḥyā b. Saᶜīd al-Anṭākī (d. 458/1066), important for the study of Faṭimid-Byzantine relations.

Following al-Ḥākim's disappearance the Druze sect, which believed in his divinity, separated from the Faṭimid fold and took refuge in the mountains of Lebanon, where it grew and flourished. It produced an extensive literature which is described in De Sacy's *Exposé de la religion des Druzes*. Particularly noteworthy are the works of Ḥamzah b. ᶜAlī b. Aḥmad (d. after 411/1020), Ismāᶜīl al-Tamīmī and al-Muqtanaᶜ (d. after 433/1041).

THE REIGN OF AL-MUSTANṢIR

The long reign of the eighth Faṭimid caliph, Maᶜadd al-Mustanṣir (reigned 427–87/1036–94), saw many important events, including the end of the Būyids (Buwayhids) and the rise of the Saljūqs in the East, the battle of Manzikert (Malāzkird; 463/1071) and the beginning of the process of Turkicization of Asia Minor; the north African (Zirid) revolt against the Faṭimids brought about by the Saljūq–Zirid collaboration, the crushing of that revolt by the Faṭimid-sponsored Hilalian invasion and the Arabicization of Berber north Africa, the internal conflict in Egypt between the Berber, Turkish and Sūdānī factions of the army, then the introduction of the new Armenian element under Badr al-Jamālī, the great confrontation between the Faṭimids and the ᶜAbbasids resulting in the temporary occupation of Baghdad by al-Basāsīrī on behalf of the Faṭimids, the rise of the Ṣulayḥid state in the Yemen under Faṭimid suzerainty, the period of the great famine and administrative breakdowns in Egypt and, finally, the stabilizing leadership of the *daʿwah* under al-Muʾayyad fīʾl-Dīn al-Shīrāzī (d. 470/1077).

The historical and autobiographical work of al-Muʾayyad is his *Sīrah*, which gives a first-hand account of the Basāsīrī episode. Al-Muʾayyad's *Dīwān* and eight volumes of his *Majālis* also throw much light on the history of that time. Al-Muʾayyad's *Majālis* contains his *Munājāt* ("Confidential Talks") and *Khuṭab* ("Addresses"), as well as interesting controversies with the rationalist savant Abū ʾl-ʿAlāʾ al-Maʿarrī and the Muʿtazilite scholar Ibn al-Rāwandī. Al-Muʾayyad followed al-Qāḍī al-Nuʿmān's *al-Majālis wa-ʾl-musāyarāt* and was in turn followed by the *majālis* writings of Badr al-Jamālī (d. 487/1094), Abūʾl-Barakāt (d. after 560/1164–5), Ḥātim b. Ibrāhīm al-Ḥāmidī (d. 596/1199) and others, thus forming a separate genre of compendium literature.

Al-Muʾayyad was visited by the famous Central Asian Persian poet and *dāʿī* Nāṣir-i-Khusraw (d. 452 or 453/1060 or 1061), whose *Safar-Namah* and *Dīwān* are important historical sources for the description of Egypt and the Qarmaṭian state of Baḥrayn. His works are described in Ivanow's monograph on the *dāʿī*[12] and can be classified as a separate Badakhshānī school. Although they are the common heritage of both the Nizārī and Ṭayyibī branches of the Faṭimid *daʿwah*, they have been exclusively preserved by the Nizārīs, probably because they were written in Persian and the Nizārī *daʿwah* spread in the Persian region at the outset.

A valuable contemporary source for the history of the time is *Kitāb al-Dhakhāʾir wa-ʾl-tuḥaf* of Ibn al-Zubayr.[13] Exchange of gifts between states is the apparent subject of the book, but it contains more than this. It is an outstanding record of diplomatic missions and social history. Public festivals and court ceremonials can be studied through the information it provides.

With al-Muʾayyad's guidance, the old Yemeni Faṭimid base of Ibn Ḥawshab was revived under the leadership of a *dāʿī*-king, ʿAlī b. Muḥammad al-Ṣulayḥī in 439/1047. We now have a new phenomenon, the rise of a dynasty of *dāʿī*s even stronger than the imperial dynasty of Faṭimid imams. The caliph Maʿadd al-Mustanṣir kept in constant correspondence with the Ṣulayḥid ruler *dāʿī*s. These letters are collected in *al-Sijillāt al-Mustanṣiriyyah*. ʿAlī's deputy the *dāʿī* Lamak b. Mālik al-Ḥammādī became the founder of the religious organization in the Yemen, and was sent on a five-year mission (454–9/1062–8) to Cairo. A later *dāʿī*, Ḥātim b. Ibrāhīm al-Ḥāmidī, reports that this long mission sought the imam's guidance on twenty-seven

[12] *Ismāʿīlī Tradition.* [13] Ed. M. Ḥamīdullāh, Kuwait, 1959.

matters. From al-Mustanṣir's letters to the Yemeni *daᶜwah* and other evidence, we can discern some of the matters discussed in Lamak's Cairo embassy, such as the desire of ᶜAlī to come to the aid of the Faṭimid state (a role that was later filled by Badr al-Jamālī); the question of succession to ᶜAlī, the close collaboration between the Faṭimids and the Ṣulayḥids, the spread of the *daᶜwah* in Ḥaḍramawt and India and probably the transfer of the bulk of Ismāᶜīlī literature from the Dār al-ᶜIlm in Cairo to Ṣanᶜāʾ for safe-keeping with the Ṣulayḥid state. In the view of the present writer, this is the reason why much of the Ismāᶜīlī literary heritage came to be preserved in the Yemen, and then via the Yemen in India, at the time of the transfer of the *daᶜwah* headquarters to India, while it was lost in Egypt itself after the Ayyubid conquest.

In all the writings of the Yemeni *daᶜwah*, al-Muʾayyad fī ʾl-Dīn al-Shīrāzī occupies a place of the father-figure. The emphasis now is not on philosophical innovation (*ḥaqāʾiq*) but on conservation by esoteric interpretation (*taʾwīl*). The *Rasāʾil Ikhwān al-Ṣafāʾ* now becomes the Yemeni *daᶜwah*'s main doctrinal inspiration. A major historical source of the early Ṣulayḥid period is *Sīrat al-Mukarram* of the second Ṣulayḥid ruler. It has hitherto been considered lost, but a copy has recently been discovered by al-Qāḍī Ismāᶜīl al-Akwaᶜ in one of the Yemeni libraries. In any case quotations from it survive in later Yemeni historical writings. During the time of the third Yemeni ruler, the Queen (Sayyidah) Arwā, the Yemeni *daᶜwah* separated from the Faṭimid state (524/1130), thus accepting after Maᶜadd al-Mustanṣir only the caliphs al-Mustaᶜlī (reigned 487–95/1094–1101) and al-Āmir (reigned 495–524/1101–30) and the latter's son Ṭayyib as imams, but not recognizing the last four Faṭimid Caliphs al-Ḥāfiẓ (reigned 525–44/1131–49), al-Ẓāfir (reigned 544–49/1149–54), al-Fāʾiz (reigned 549–55/1154–60) and al-ᶜĀḍid (reigned 555–67/1160–71), who were upheld by a lukewarm, makeshift Ḥāfiẓī *daᶜwah*, which in the Yemen found adherents in the Zurayᶜids of ᶜAdan and the Hamdanids of Ṣanᶜāʾ, being in fact an alignment against the Ṭayyibī *daᶜwah* of the Yemen. An interesting document of the time is *al-Hidāyat al-Āmiriyyah* ("Guidance by al-Āmir"), a short tract written by the caliph al-Āmir against the Nizārī claims. He was assassinated by Nizārī agents.

THE ṬAYYIBĪ *DAᶜWAH*

The Ṭayyibī *daᶜwah* of the Yemen concentrated on the Ḥarāz region, but soon lost political power. It continued to produce literature and to preserve the literary heritage of the Faṭimid *daᶜwah* of Egypt. The great *dāᶜī*-authors of the time were Sulṭān al-Khaṭṭāb al-Hamdānī (d. 533/1138), the second *dāʿī muṭlaq* Ibrāhīm b. al-Ḥusayn al-Ḥāmidī (d. 557/1161), Muḥammad b. Ṭāhir al-Ḥārithī (d. 584/1188) and the third *dāʿī muṭlaq* Ḥātim b. Ibrāhīm al-Ḥāmidī. Al-Khaṭṭāb's *Dīwān* and *Ghāyat al-mawālīd*, al-Ḥārithī's *Majmūʿ al-tarbiyyah*, Ibrāhīm's *Kanz al-walad* and Ḥātim's *Tuḥfat al-qulūb* and *al-Majālis* are all of value to historians.

During Ḥātim's time the Faṭimid state of Egypt and Syria fell to the Ayyubids, who also occupied the Yemen. The subsequent history of the Ṭayyibī *daʿwah* in the Yemen and India is a long one, but it falls outside the scope of this chapter. Two great histories of a later period, however, must be mentioned: *Kitāb ʿUyūn al-akhbār* (seven volumes), and *Kitāb Nuzhat al-afkār* (two volumes) by the prolific writer *dāʿī* Idrīs ʿImād al-Dīn al-Anf al-Qurashī (d. 833/1428). They are not only relevant for the Faṭimid period but contain information based on earlier sources and information so intimately bound up with the *daʿwah* that it would not be possible to find it anywhere else. Another later work is also valuable for earlier Faṭimid times, namely the *Kitāb al-Azhār* ("Book of Flowers"), a chrestomathy in seven volumes by the Indian *dāʿī* Ḥasan b. Nūḥ (d. 939/1533). It preserves sections from some rare or lost works of the earlier Faṭimid period.

THE NIZĀRĪ *DAʿWAH*

In the time of the Faṭimid caliph Maʿadd al-Mustanṣir a Persian *dāʿī*, al-Ḥasan b. al-Ṣabbāḥ (d. 518/1124), had visited Egypt in 471/1078, a year after the death of the chief *dāʿī*, al-Muʾayyad fī ʾl-Dīn al-Shīrāzī. He had ambitions of becoming the saviour of the caliphate from the persistent economic and military crises in which it was engulfed, in the same way as ʿAlī b. Muḥammad al-Ṣulayḥī had wanted to do. Just a few years before al-Ḥasan's arrival Badr al-Jamālī had in fact succeeded in a similar ambition. Al-Ḥasan b. al-Ṣabbāḥ faced the hostility of Badr and returned to Persia where at Alamūt he set up his mission, first on behalf of Maʿadd al-Mustanṣir, and then on the latter's death in 487/1094 on behalf of his elder son Nizār, who was deprived of the Faṭimid succession by Badr's son al-Afḍal. Thus a new *daʿwah* was born in Persia – the Nizārī *daʿwah*, even before the birth of the Ṭayyibī *daʿwah* (524/1130) in the Yemen. Al-Ḥasan b. al-Ṣabbāḥ (d. 518/1124) is supposed to have written an autobiography called *Sarguzashti Sayyidnā*, which was used by ʿAlāʾ al-Dīn ʿAṭā-Malik b. Muḥammad al-Juwaynī (d. 681/1283) in his *Taʾrīkh-i-Jahān-Gushāy*.

A younger contemporary of al-Ḥasan was the celebrated author of *Kitāb al-Milal wa-ʾl-niḥal*, Abū ʾl-Fatḥ Muḥammad b. ʿAbd al-Karīm b. Aḥmad al-Shahrastānī. He has been shown to have been an Ismāʿīlī *dāʿī* by the researches of Danishpazuh.

Al-Ḥasan b. al-Ṣabbāḥ's two *dāʿī* successors were followed at Alamūt by the imam al-Ḥasan b. Qāhir b. Muhtadī b. Hādī b. Nizār (d. 561/1166), whose lieutenant in Syria was the famous Rashīd al-Dīn Sinān (d. 589/1193). A certain Raʾīs al-Ḥasan b. Ṣalāḥ Munshī Birjandī, who was a scribe to Shihāb al-Dīn (*c.* 621/1224), an Ismāʿīlī governor of Qūhistān, wrote a history which was used by Rashīd al-Dīn Ṭabīb in his *Jāmiʿ al-tawārīkh*.

The last Nizārī imam of the Alamūt period, Rukn al-Dīn Khurshāh (d. 654/1256), who surrendered to the Mongol invader Hūlāgū in 654/1256, was served by the well-known scientist and scholar Naṣīr al-Dīn al-Ṭūsī, who at least for part of his life embraced the Ismāʿīlī faith. During the Alamūt period we do not find any other Ismāʿīlī historical work.

Both the Ṭayyibī and Nizārī *daʿwah*s finally found headquarters in western India. There were earlier unaffiliated Ismāʿīlī periods in the history of Sind during the Sūmra dynasty (388–752/998–1351) which, however, did not produce any historical literature.

THE LAST PERIOD OF THE FAṬIMID CALIPHATE

In the last phase of the Faṭimid caliphate of Egypt (524–67/1130–71), the phase of the Ḥāfiẓī *daʿwah* (which was not supported by either the Nizārī *daʿwah* of Persia or the Ṭayyibī *daʿwah* of the Yemen), the caliphate had not only lost the organizational backing of the *dāʿī*s but was also beset by two threatening outside forces, namely the Turks (Zangids of Syria) and the Crusaders. The administrative support of some of the viziers for Twelver Shiʿism and Sunnism had already corroded the shaky edifice of the Ḥāfiẓī *daʿwah*, when the blow of the Ayyubid conquest and restoration of Sunnism descended on the Faṭimid state.

The *Dīwān* of Ẓāfir al-Ḥaddād (d. 529/1134) contains panegyrics of viziers and caliphs until the time of the caliph al-Āmir (d. 524/1130). The *Dīwān* of the vizier Ṭalāʾiʿ b. Ruzzīk (d. 556/1160) describes the happenings of the time of the caliphs al-Ḥāfiẓ and al-Ẓāfir and the encounters with the Crusaders. An important historical document of the period is *al-Ishārah ilā man nāla ʾl-wizārah* of ʿAlī b. al-Ṣayrafī (d. 542/1147). We also have *al-Nukat al-ʿaṣriyyah fī akhbār al-wuzarāʾ al-Miṣriyyah* of the *qāḍī* ʿUmārah b. abī ʾl-Ḥasan al-Ḥakamī al-Yamanī. He also wrote a well-known history of the Yemen, *al-Mufīd fī taʾrīkh Ṣanʿāʾ wa-Zabīd*, besides his *Dīwān*. The lost history *Akhbār Miṣr* of the vizier al-Maʾmūn al-Baṭāʾiḥī (d. 519/1125) has been reconstructed by Ayman Fuʾād Sayyid.[14] Jamāl al-Dīn abū ʾl-Ḥasan

[14] In "Lumières nouvelles sur quelques sources de l'histoire Fatimide en Egypte", *Annales Islamologiques*, XIII, 1977, 1–41.

ʿAlī b. Ẓāfir al-Azdī's (d. 613/1216) *Akhbār al-duwal al-munqaṭiʿah*, although concerned with the whole Faṭimid period, has more details on the last phase of the Faṭimid caliphate. Lastly Ibn Muyassar's (d. 677/1278) *Akhbār Miṣr*, although an abridgement, has very useful details on the latter half of the Faṭimid period not found elsewhere.

GENERAL HISTORIES

Some general histories, particularly those of al-Masʿūdī, al-Ṭabarī, Ibn al-Athīr, Miskawayh, Abū Shujāʿ al-Rūdhrāwarī, Hilāl al-Ṣābiʾ, Ibn al-Jawzī, Sibṭ Ibn al-Jawzī, Niẓām al-Mulk, ʿAlāʾ al-Dīn al-Juwaynī, Rashīd al-Dīn Sinān, Ibn Khallikān and historians of Syria such as Ibn al-Qalānisī and Kamāl al-Dīn b. al-ʿAdīm are also useful for some phases of Ismaʿilism. Later historians such as al-Nuwayrī, al-Qalqashandī and al-Dhahabī sometimes give useful information from earlier sources. One work that should be the constant companion of any historian of the Faṭimid period is the already mentioned *Kitāb al-Ittiʿāẓ* of Taqī ʾl-Dīn Aḥmad al-Maqrīzī.

LATER DEVELOPMENTS

We have noted how the bulk of the Faṭimid *daʿwah* literature was transferred to the Yemen, and remained monopolized by the Ṭayyibī *daʿwah*. When the headquarters of this *daʿwah* shifted to the west coast of India in 946/1539, shortly after the Ottoman conquest of Yemen in the tenth/sixteenth century, most of this literature was transferred to India. Some still remains in the Yemen and it is likely that an occasional missing volume will be discovered there. Since Surat and Bombay were the last two centres of the Ṭayyibī (Bohra) *dāʿī*s, it is there that this literature was deposited, and where it has been brought to light during the last sixty years. The Nizārī (Khoja) community of India received the works in Persian transferred there from the Badakhshānī, Alamūt and post-Alamūt periods of Ismāʿīlī history. Some still remain in Central Asia, particularly in Tajikistan and in the library of Dushanbe. In India, a special type of Khoja literature, the Islamo-Hindu mystical poetry, was developed in several Indian languages; this was known as *ginān*s.[15] The Gujarat state of India and the Sind province of Pakistan, therefore, became the sites for gathering together the various threads of Faṭimid Ismāʿīlī history and weaving the fabric together in modern research.

The journeys of the two scholars Ḥusayn Hamdānī and Wladimir Ivanow

[15] Azim Nanji, *The Nizārī Ismāʿīlī Tradition in the Indo-Pakistan Subcontinent*, Delmar, NY, 1978.

in the 1920s were of paramount importance in making known the riches of Ismāʿīlī literature. Hamdānī travelled from Bombay to London and carried with him a representative section of his family collection of manuscripts. He gave photostat copies to some European libraries and friends such as Paul Kraus, and helped identify certain works in European libraries as Faṭimid. His short bibliographical article, "Some unknown Ismāʿīlī authors and their works", opened up a new dimension in Faṭimid studies – the quest for the early works of its central *daʿwah*.

Ivanow, who was the keeper of the oriental manuscripts in the library of St Petersburg and was acquainted with that library's collection of Central Asian Badakhshānī and Nizārī material, left Russia at the time of the Revolution and joined the service of Agakhan III at Bombay. It is here that he was introduced to the treasures of the Bohra libraries, particularly those of A. A. A. Fyzee and Ḥusayn Hamdānī. Using them and certain other materials such as the *Fihrist al-Majdūʿ*, he produced his *Guide to Ismāʿīlī Literature*. It contained some errors and its sources were unacknowledged, yet it was the greatest attempt up to that time at producing a full Ismāʿīlī bibliography.

Ḥusayn Hamdānī, W. Ivanow, A. A. A. Fyzee and Zāhid ʿAlī were the first generation of scholars in the field of reconstructing Faṭimid history from the sources of its own *daʿwah*. In our generation there are many scholars active in this field, but pride of place belongs to S. M. Stern, Bernard Lewis, Kāmil Ḥusayn, W. Madelung, Ismail Poonawala, Ayman Fuʾād Sayyid, Hans Halm, Muṣṭafā Ghālib and ʿĀrif Tāmir. The Institute of Ismaili Studies in London has made a major contribution to the promotion of Faṭimid studies and to the collection of as many Faṭimid literary works and studies as possible in one place.

CHAPTER 14

MATHEMATICS AND APPLIED SCIENCE

As a result of the great conquests of the first century of Islam, the Arabs became the heirs of the ancient civilizations of western Asia and north Africa. They also inherited the links that those civilizations had maintained over the centuries with their neighbours, and thereby came into possession of a considerable corpus of written material covering a wide field of knowledge, including scientific subjects. Many Greek manuscripts were preserved in Byzantium, but the Byzantines did little more than preserve, and made few significant contributions to the progress of science. Of greater significance were the Greek schools set up in Asia Minor soon after the council of Nicaea in AD 325. The Nestorian church made one of these schools, that of Edessa, their scientific centre. In AD 489 this school was transferred to Nisibin, then under Persian rule, with its secular faculties at Jundishāpūr in Khūzistān. Here, the Nestorian scholars, together with pagan philosophers banished by Justinian from Athens, carried out important research in medicine, astronomy and mathematics. To assist in instruction a number of Greek works were translated into Syriac. At about the same time the sect of the Monophysites, who like the Nestorians were subject to persecution by the Orthodox church, were working on similar lines in Syria. They also made translations of philosophical and scientific works into Syriac. A group who were to provide some of the greatest translators and scientists of Islam were the Ṣabians of Ḥarrān in Mesopotamia. Their liturgical language was Syriac, and a number of their educated elite also knew Greek and possessed a wide knowledge of classical Greek literature.

While a great deal is known about the channels through which Greek knowledge passed into Arabic, similar transmissions from India and other cultural areas are not easy to trace, although it is beyond doubt that such transmissions occurred and were immensely fruitful, especially for astronomy and mathematics. We do know, however, that Hindu astronomical tables were translated from Sanskrit into Arabic, and that Indian ideas were an important element in the development of Arabic mathematics. Arabic writers have also recorded the existence of a considerable body of literature in Middle Persian, written during the final centuries of the Sasanid dynasty.[1] For instance, al-Masʿūdī[2] relates that in 303/915, when he was in Iṣṭakhr – the ancient Persepolis – an eminent person showed him a book said to have been composed in 113/731 from works discovered in the collections of the Iranian kings and translated from Middle Persian into Arabic for the caliph Hishām. It contained much information on Persian science, history, architecture and public institutions.

During the great conquests and their immediate aftermath, as the empire of the Arabs changed gradually into the world of Islam, men were largely preoccupied with military, political, legal, social, religious and economic matters. It was not until the ʿAbbasid assumption of power in 132/750 and the transfer of the capital from Damascus to Baghdad that the task of assimilating Greek and Indian sources began in earnest. The translators into Arabic, many of whom were eminent scholars in their own right, thus made these foreign sources accessible throughout Islam. At the same time the language was adapted to serve as a powerful and flexible instrument for expressing philosophical and scientific ideas, a purpose that it had not previously been required to fulfil. This intellectual activity was energetically supported by the great ʿAbbasid caliphs and seems to have reached its apogee in the reign of al-Maʾmūn and his immediate successors. Among the most important men of this period of creativity were the three sons of a certain Mūsā b. Shākir – Muḥammad, Aḥmad and al-Ḥasan. After the death of their father, who had been a close friend of al-Maʾmūn, they were brought up as the wards of that caliph, and afterwards became close associates of his successors. They were skilled in mathematics, astronomy, medicine and mechanics – their *Kitāb al-Ḥiyal* ("Book of Ingenious Devices") is discussed below. They are also important, however, because they were in a position to extend patronage to other scholars, notably Ḥunayn b. Isḥāq (192–260/808–73), who became the leader of a group of translators. Among his associates were his nephew Ḥubaysh b. al-Ḥasan (*fl.* end of third/ninth century) and the renowned Thābit b. Qurrah al-Ḥarrānī (211–88/836–901). Owing to the efforts of these scholars and many others the major part of surviving Greek and Indian philosophical and scientific knowledge had been assimilated into Arabic by the close of the third/ninth century. Meanwhile an independent Arabic science had developed by a synthesis of the elements taken from other sources, a science that was to prove capable thenceforward of developing along its own path. In the centuries that followed science and other forms of intellectual activity flourished in Islam whenever circumstances were propitious. The ʿAbbasid

1 Jan Rypka, *History of Iranian Literature*, Dordrecht, 1968, 55–8, 128–33.
2 *Kitāb al-Tanbīh wa-ʾl-ishrāf*, Leiden, 1894, 106.

empire broke up into self-governing provinces and principalities long before its final overthrow in 656/1258. At different times and places, centres of learning came into being either because the rulers and their courtly circles encouraged learning for its own sake, or because they were aware of the prestige brought to their courts by the presence there of eminent scholars. These centres were as likely to be in the chief cities of petty states under the control of a short-lived local dynasty, as in the capitals of empires or great provinces.

The Arabs took an encyclopaedic view of knowledge, as the Greeks had done, and in an attempt to codify contemporaneous knowledge, they composed several valuable classifications of the sciences. We have, for example, the *Kitāb Iḥṣāʾ al-ʿulūm* ("Survey of the Sciences") by Abū Naṣr Muḥammad b. Muḥammad al-Fārābī and the definitions given by Ibn Sīnā in his *Fī Aqsām al-ʿulūm al-ʿaqliyyah* ("Divisions of the Intellectual Sciences"). Perhaps the most useful of these classifications, however, is the *Mafātīḥ al-ʿulūm* ("Keys of the Sciences") compiled by Abū ʿAbdullāh Muḥammad b. Aḥmad al-Khwārazmī[3] between 365/975 and 381/991. As usual, the division is made between Islamic sciences – theology, tradition, jurisprudence, and so on – and foreign sciences, comprising philosophy, logic, medicine, mathematics, astronomy, music, mechanics and alchemy. It is essentially a vocabulary of terms used in those sciences, with brief but adequate descriptions, and some revealing remarks on etymology. It therefore provides us with a very convenient summary of the extent of scientific knowledge in Islam at the close of the fourth/tenth century. Impossible to ignore, but difficult to categorize or evaluate, are the writings of the Brethren of Purity (Ikhwān al-Ṣafāʾ), who are thought to have composed their *Rasāʾil* ("Epistles") between 350/961 and 375/986. By no means without scientific value, they are basically an attempt to fuse the teachings of Greek philosophy, especially neo-Platonism, with the developing dogmas of the Ismāʿīlī creed. This is, of course, but one example of the scholasticism that characterized intellectual life in the Middle Ages, both in Islam and in the West. For present purposes the effects of scholasticism, profound as they were, are ignored and the Arabic achievements are assessed solely upon their scientific merits. In the remainder of this chapter the contribution of the Arabs to the progress of science and technology is discussed in three sections, by a consideration of the work of a limited number of outstanding intellects. In the fields of physics and technology this method provides a fair appraisal, but in mathematics, to which so many men devoted their attention, it inevitably means that justice

[3] Not to be confused with the great mathematician Abū Jaʿfar Muḥammad b. Mūsā al-Khwārazmī.

has not been done to all. To use any other method, however, would have resulted simply in a biographical listing, with a consequent blurring of the complete picture. Up to the present time, although much work remains to be done in all fields, far more attention has been paid to Arabic science than to technology. The section on mechanical technology, which in any case embraces a good deal of physical science, is therefore considerably longer than the other two.

MATHEMATICS

Among the works that had been translated into Arabic by about the end of the third/ninth century were all the writings that were to have a decisive effect upon the origin and growth of Arabic mathematics. These included: from Greek – Euclid's *Elements*; the mathematical and physical works of Archimedes; the *Conics* of Apollonius of Perga; the *Arithmetica* of Diophantus; Pappus; the *Almagest* of Ptolemy; from Sanskrit – the astronomical work *Mahāsiddhānta* ("The Great Sindhind") and some astronomical tables (*zīj*); from Pahlavi – astronomical tables known as *Zīj al-Shāh*. We know of many other works by Greek writers, too numerous to be listed here, that were also translated into Arabic but, apart from astronomical works, no references to Indian authors or titles have yet been found in Arabic treatises on mathematics. From the frequent attribution of the place-number system to Indian sources we can, however, be sure that Indian influence was strong; the development of Arabic mathematics is therefore seen to be based largely upon Greek and Indian models, although Hebrew and Babylonian influences cannot be discounted. It would be misleading, however, to describe Arabic mathematics as a synthesis from these sources combined with original contributions from the Arabic mathematicians themselves. Misleading, because such a description implies the existence of at least one work that incorporates the complete corpus of Arabic knowledge on the subject, and no such work exists. To be sure, encyclopaedists gave classifications of the sciences including the various divisions of mathematics, with examples from each branch, but these lists cannot be considered as comprehensive manuals. Fourteen of the epistles of the Brethren of Purity, for example, deal with mathematics and logic from a gnostic viewpoint, with scant attention to practical applications. In general, Arabic mathematicians felt free to investigate the aspects of the subject that appealed to their tastes and met their requirements and to pursue their investigations in any way they chose. Their treatment might be mainly theoretical and speculative, as in the case of Ibn Sīnā, or concerned more with practical application to other sciences. Nor did they feel constrained to use any particular method of approach – no method was considered superior to all others to the extent that it became dominant. For instance, Abū Bakr Muḥammad b. al-Ḥasan al-Ḥāsib al-Karajī, one of the greatest Muslim mathematicians, who flourished in Baghdad at the start of the fifth/eleventh century, totally neglected Indian mathematics, presumably by deliberate choice. This having been said, the fact remains that mathematics was consciously divided into its various branches by Arabic scholars, and it is therefore legitimate to consider those branches separately.

In the *Mafātīḥ* geometry is given two names, *jūmatria* from the Greek, and *handasah*, said to be an Arabicized Persian word. The *muhandis* is "he who calculates the course of *qanāt*s (canals) and the places where they are to be dug".[4] The *muhandis* thus fulfils one of the functions of a civil engineer, and, indeed, the word in modern Arabic denotes an engineer. In Arabic writings, however, the meaning of *handasah* oscillates between the practical and the theoretical, depending upon the interests of the writer. Abū ʿAlī al-Ḥasan b. al-Ḥasan b. al-Haytham, for instance, wrote a treatise on surveying in which he applied geometrical results to land measurement while, on the other hand, there are many treatises, including at least one by Ibn al-Haytham himself, that are concerned solely with the elaboration of Apollonian problems. Taken as a whole, the Arab geometers equalled without surpassing the achievement of their Greek predecessors, but that achievement was of course one of the greatest in the history of mathematics. Until very recently plane geometry was almost synonymous with Euclid's name, while the work of Apollonius, Pappus and others on conic sections saw few improvements until the time of Descartes. Nowadays, very few people, except professional mathematicians, would find it easy to follow the complex reasoning of Apollonius without recourse to the aids of co-ordinate geometry and the calculus. And indeed the so-called "Method of Exhaustion" developed by Greek geometers and the "Method" of Archimedes, both of which were fully understood and appreciated by the best Arabic geometers, approach very closely the principles of integral calculus. During the long flourishing of Arabic mathematics a number of translations of Euclid, Apollonius, Pappus, Archimedes, Menelaus and other Greek writers were made, and commentaries on these works were numerous. Not infrequently, problems arising from other disciplines, particularly when these involved equations of degrees higher than the second, were satisfactorily solved by the intersection of two conic sections. The preservation, and in some cases elaboration, by the Arabs of the main corpus of

[4] See Abū ʿAbdullāh Muḥammad b. Aḥmad al-Khwārazmī, *Mafātīḥ al-ʿulūm*, ed. G. van Vloten, Leiden, 1895, 202.

Greek geometrical knowledge, was a powerful vehicle for the transmission of this knowledge into Europe.

Trigonometry is not listed in the classifications as a mathematical subject, since it was considered as a branch of astronomy; then, as now, it was impossible to obtain a full understanding of spherical astronomy without also having a good grasp of plane and spherical geometry and trigonometry. All the good Arabic astronomers were also good mathematicians. The principal sources of their knowledge were Ptolemy's *Almagest* and the Indian *Siddhānta*s. Translations and commentaries on the former were more numerous than those on the latter, and the *Almagest* was undoubtedly the most powerful single influence upon Arabic astronomy. It was probably an Indian source, however, that provided the inspiration for the most notable achievement of the Arabs in trigonometry, namely the introduction of the six basic trigonometrical ratios, and their elaboration for the solution of geometrical problems. This, the replacement of the clumsy method of chords used by Ptolemy with an essentially modern trigonometry, was a development of the greatest importance in the progress of mathematics. One of the first writers in Arabic to appreciate the value of the sine was Yaʿqūb b. Ṭāriq (second/eighth century). Abū Jaʿfar Muḥammad b. Mūsā al-Khwārazmī compiled astronomical tables (*Zīj al-Sindhind*) that contained not simply the sine but also the tangent, although the latter may be an interpolation by a later writer. It seems likely that the idea of the tangent or "shadow", was first introduced by Aḥmad b. ʿAbdullāh Ḥabash al-Ḥāsib al-Marwazī who flourished in Baghdad in the middle of the third/ninth century. The completion of the introduction of the tangent and cotangents and the compilation of a table of cotangents was due to Abū ʿAbdullāh Muḥammad b. Jābir b. Sinān al-Battānī. Of Ṣabian origin, though himself a Muslim, he flourished in Raqqah and died in 317/929 at Samarra. Al-Battānī also knew the relationship between the sides and angles of a spherical triangle which we express by the formula: $\cos a = \cos b . \cos c + \sin b . \sin c . \cos a$. Notable advances in trigonometry were made by Abū ʾl-Wafāʾ al-Būzajānī, one of the greatest Arab mathematicians, who was born in 328/940 and died in 388/998. He was probably the first to show the generality of the sine theorem to spherical triangles and gave a new method of constructing sine tables, the value of sine 30′ being correct to the eighth decimal place. Further contributions were made by ʿAlī b. Yūnus, perhaps the greatest Muslim astronomer, who died in Cairo in 399/1009. He solved many problems of spherical astronomy by means of orthogonal projections and introduced the first of those prosthapheretical formulae that were indispensable before the invention of logarithms, namely the equivalent of our formula: cos. a. cos $b = \frac{1}{2}$ [cos $(a - b)$ + cos $(a + b)$]. Inevitably, the arbitrary selection of these few examples does injustice to the many other Arab astronomer/mathematicians who laboured to improve the means for the mathematical reduction of astronomical observations. Suffice it to say that the results of their labours were to present developing European science with an organized trigonometrical system that could be applied to the solution of problems in astronomy – Copernican as well as Ptolemaic.

Although it is convenient here to treat arithmetic and algebra as separate subjects, the distinction was not clearly made by Arab mathematicians; the main distinction which they made was rather between *ᶜilm al-ᶜadad* ("the science of number") and *ᶜilm al-ḥisāb* ("the science of reckoning"), the latter embracing both arithmetic and algebra, more or less as we understand the terms. *ᶜIlm al-ᶜadad* embraces the subjects treated in books VII to IX of Euclid's *Elements*; irrational magnitudes, dealt with in book V of the *Elements*, were generally considered by Arabic scholars as belonging to geometry rather than arithmetic, although ᶜUmar al-Khayyām moved towards the position of regarding irrationals as numbers. A work on *ᶜilm al-ᶜadad* that enjoyed great popularity was Nicomachus of Gerasa's *Introduction*, translated into Arabic by Thābit b. Qurrah, himself an accomplished mathematician. Through it mathematicians became acquainted with Pythagorean arithmetical concepts, such as the special characteristics of individual numbers, perfect and amicable numbers, and so on. (A perfect number is one which is the sum of all its factors including unity, e.g. 6, 28; two numbers are said to be "amicable" when each is the sum of all the aliquot parts of the other, e.g. 220, 284.) The influence of these ideas is seen most clearly in the writings of the Ikhwān al-Ṣafāʾ, according to whom arithmetic, the first stage on the way to wisdom, is a study of the properties of things through a study of the individual numbers corresponding to those things.

ᶜIlm al-ḥisāb is concerned with the fundamental arithmetical operations– addition, subtraction, division, multiplication and the extraction of roots. Although for us the main interest of Arab writings on *ᶜilm al-ḥisāb* must lie in the introduction of the decimal place-value system of numeration and of decimal fractions, other systems of reckoning and numerical expression predated the Hindu system and continued in existence after its introduction. The oldest is the *abjad* system in which the twenty-eight letters of the Arabic alphabet represent the units, tens and hundreds up to and including 1,000. The system is named from the four letters of the mnemonic "word" for the first four numbers. *Abjad* is pre-Islamic and probably derives from similar usages in Hebrew and Aramaic numeration. It was invariably used for marking the divisions of astrolabes and is also found, though not consistently, in the treatises on machines. The sexagesimal system was not confined to astronomical and geometrical purposes but was also employed in arithmetic. For example, the remainder in a division is multiplied by powers of sixty, then divided by the divisor. Another method of calculation was known as *ḥisāb al-yad* ("hand arithmetic"). Arithmetical operations were carried out mentally and the partial results obtained in the process of reaching the final solution of a problem were "retained" by holding the fingers in certain positions.

The main achievement of the Arab arithmeticians, however, was eventually to produce an arithmetic based upon the consistent application of the decimal place-value idea and the use of Indian numerals. The first treatise on Hindu reckoning, that of Abū Jaᶜfar Muḥammad b. Mūsā al-Khwārazmī (d. *c.* 236/850), exists only in a number of Latin versions, one of these being a thirteenth-century manuscript entitled *Algoritmi de numero indorum* – hence our word "algorithm". This work explains the decimal place-value system of numeration, using a small circle for zero. In performing the arithmetical operations, the numbers are placed one above the other and the process begins on the left. Erasure and shifting of numbers is used, clearly implying that operations were carried out on a dust-board. (In the Islamic world numbers have existed and still exist in two forms, an eastern form called "Indian" and a western form, the immediate parent of modern European numerals, the *ghubār* [dust] numerals.) Much less well known than al-Khwārazmī's book, but scarcely less important, is a treatise composed by Abū ʾl-Ḥasan Aḥmad b. Ibrāhīm al-Uqlīdisī in Damascus in 341/952. The most surprising feature of this book is the explanation and application of decimal fractions, an innovation that until recently had been ascribed to al-Kāshī, some five centuries later.

The oldest, and one of the most influential works on algebra in Arabic was Abū Jaᶜfar Muḥammad b. Mūsā al-Khwārazmī's *Kitāb al-Mukhtaṣar fī ḥisāb al-jabr wa-ʾl-muqābalah* ("Abridged Book on the Calculation of Integration and Equation"). It became known in Europe through Latin translations, notably those made in the sixth/twelfth century by Robert of Ketton and Gerard of Cremona. It is usual to illustrate the concepts of Arabic algebra by examples from this book but, by way of a change, we will quote here from the admirably succinct definitions given by Abū Abdullāh Muḥammad b. Aḥmad al-Khwārazmī (fourth/tenth century), author of *Mafātīḥ al-ᶜulūm*. He says: "the *shayʾ* (thing) in the speech of the people of *al-jabr wa-ʾl-muqābalah* is the unknown root (*jidhr*). [It] is one of the methods for calculating and arrangement, with excellent results for difficult problems concerning wills, inheritances, transactions and [commercial] dealings."[5] An example of *al-jabr* is given as: "Put into the problem a capital (*māl*) minus (*illā*) three roots, equal to one root, and bring to a quantity equal to four roots. This is sixteen, because you have completed the *māl* and added to it what was omitted from it, so it has become a complete *māl*."[6] In our notation this reads $x^2 - 3x = x$, whence $x = 4$, $x^2 = 16$. Thus *al-jabr* means eliminating quantities prefixed by *illā* by adding these quantities, in the sense of "restoring". An example of *al-muqābalah* is given in similar wording, which in our notation becomes: $x^2 + 2x = 5x$, "so obtaining a *māl* equal to 3 roots, which is 9". *Al-muqābalah* is therefore the confronting of two qualities with one another in order to examine their likenesses or differences. The modern reader will notice some differences between this system and our own algebra, notably its origins in commerce and its adoption of commercial terms, its use of words instead of symbols (also applicable to Arabic trigonometry), and the somewhat artificial distinction between *al-jabr* and *al-muqābalah*. Nevertheless, building upon the foundations laid by al-Khwārazmī, later Arabic mathematicians were able to develop an algebra that became a powerful instrument for the solution of mathematical problems. Abū Kāmil Shujāᶜ, who flourished in Egypt at the beginning of the fourth/tenth century, made valuable contributions to the theory, and exercised a considerable influence on the development of Western algebra. He introduced methods for the multiplication and division of algebraic quantities and for the addition and subtraction of radicals, and discussed problems of a higher degree, but only those which could be reduced to quadratic equations. He admitted irrational quantities as solutions. The development of algebra culminated in the work of ᶜUmar Khayyām – Ghiyāth al-Dīn Abūʾl-Fatḥ ᶜUmar b. Ibrāhīm al-Khayyām (d. 526/1132) – who discussed all forms of equations up to the third degree in a systematic manner. He distinguished clearly between algebraical and geometrical proofs, considering both necessary, but stated that he was unable to give algebraical solutions of third-degree equations. He tried to give the conditions for solutions for every type of equation in his classification, but excluded negative solutions, and, by his failure to use both branches of a conic, he sometimes missed one of the positive roots.

PHYSICS

The students of the physical sciences in Islam were far fewer than the students of mathematics, astronomy, alchemy and medicine. Of the

[5] Ibid., 199–200. [6] Ibid., 200–1.

subjects usually considered as constituting the substance of classical physics – electricity and magnetism, heat, sound, optics, solid and fluid mechanics – only the last two were given much attention by Arabic writers. In two fields, however, those of statics and optics, the Arabic contribution was very important and can best be appreciated by a consideration of the achievement of a few very great scientists. Before doing this, we shall discuss briefly the work done on the other subjects, where there is anything of significance to report.

References to magnetic phenomena are to be found here and there in the works of Arabic scientists and geographers. It was known that an electric charge could be induced in amber or musk by rubbing them. Several reports say that in the mountains near Āmid in Mesopotamia there was a cleft in a rock; if a sword was drawn repeatedly through this cleft it became magnetized and would attract nails and other small objects made of iron. The invention of the floating magnetic needle as applied to the ship's compass is probably due to the Chinese, but it was certainly in use by Muslim mariners early in the sixth/twelfth century.

Heat was not studied at all as a scientific subject, since it can only be considered quantitatively with the aid of temperature scales and thermometers and, although we have a comment from al-Bīrūnī showing that he realized that the speed of light was immensely greater than the speed of sound, the study of sound was in general confined to the theory of music. Yaᶜqūb b. Isḥāq al-Kindī is the earliest Arab writer on music whose works have come down to us; they contain a notation for the determination of pitch. Abū Naṣr Muḥammad b. Muḥammad al-Fārābī wrote an important treatise on music, indicating that he had some knowledge of mensural music and recognized the major third and the minor third as consonances. The musical part of the *Kitāb al-Shifāʾ* by Ibn Sīnā marked much progress upon al-Fārābī's treatise, itself far ahead of Western knowledge on the subject. It deals with doubling with the octave and doubling with the fourth and fifth, this being a great step towards the harmonic system.

One of the most notable contributions made by Arabic writers to the progress of science was in the study of optics. Yaᶜqūb b. Isḥāq al-Kindī wrote a treatise on geometrical and physiological optics that greatly influenced European scholars. Ibn Sīnā made some penetrating comments about the nature of light, observing that if the perception of light is due to the emission of some sort of particles by the luminous source, the speed of light must be finite. The greatest student of optics in Islam, however, and one of the greatest of all times, was Abū ᶜAlī al-Ḥasan b. al-Ḥasan b. al-Haytham (d. *c.* 430/1039). He was also an astronomer, a mathematician, a physician, and wrote commentaries on Aristotle and Galen. The Latin translation of his main work on optics, *Kitāb al-Manāẓir*, exercised a great influence upon Western scientists, notably Roger Bacon and Johannes Kepler. Ibn al-Haytham (Alhazen in Latin) is remarkable for the importance he attached to the use of experimental methods in his studies of reflection (catoptrics) and refraction (dioptrics). He discovered spherical aberration, and made a special study of spherical and parabolic mirrors. His mathematical genius is best demonstrated by the problem which today bears his name: from two points in the plane of a circle to draw lines meeting at a point of the circumference and making equal angles with the normal at that point. This leads to an equation of the fourth degree, which Ibn al-Haytham solved by the intersection of a quadrilateral hyperbola with a circle. In dioptrics he established that the ratio between the angle of incidence and refraction does not remain constant, and discussed the magnifying power of a lens. He correctly explained atmospheric refraction and the apparent increase in size of the sun and moon when near the horizon. He established that twilight only ceases or begins when the sun is 19° below the horizon, and estimated the height of the atmosphere at 52,000 paces. He expounded for the first time the use of the camera obscura, in the observation of solar eclipse. Although he considered the lens as the sensitive part of the eye, Ibn al-Haytham gave a better description of the eye and of vision than any previous writer; he considered that rays of light start from the object and travel towards the eye.

In the medieval world, both East and West, a distinction must be made between those who applied the principles of hydraulics and mechanics to the construction of useful machines and ingenious devices, on the one hand, and the scientists who attempted a mathematical analysis, on the other. The writers on machines (discussed below), the millwrights, and the constructors of *qanāt*s, surface irrigation works, and water-lifting wheels – all had a good empirical grasp of hydrostatics, fluid flow, statics and dynamics. Those who committed their ideas to paper were greatly outnumbered by the countless craftsmen, most of them probably illiterate, who constructed utilitarian machines. We know the name of one of the latter, Qayṣar b. Musāfir Taʿāsīf (*c.* 574–649/1178–1251). He constructed the great waterwheels on the Orontes at Ḥamāh, the remains of which can still be seen today, and also a celestial globe, now in the Museo Nazionale of Naples.

The distinction between practical men and theorists is not total. The writers on machines had a good knowledge of applied geometry and arithmetic, and they understood the principles of the simple machines, including the correct use of gear ratios, and some of the principles of hydrostatics; for example, that the rate of discharge from an orifice depends upon the height of water above it. And the best of the scientific writers were able to verify their results experimentally. The distinction is a real one, however, and can best be expressed as follows: the engineers dealt with both the static and dynamic aspects of hydraulics and dynamics; the scientists, although they speculated about dynamics, were unable to elucidate its basic principles because they lacked the mathematical means to do so, and their significant results are therefore confined to statics. In this field the works of Archimedes, a large number of which were available in Arabic by the end of the third/ninth century, and the *Mechanics* of Hero, provided the most fertile field for study. In general the Arabs added little to the theoretical results recorded by Archimedes and Hero. In the eighth chapter of the *Mafātīḥ al-ʿulūm*, for instance, a list of simple machines – lever, pulley, wedge, screw and press – is given, with etymological information but without any mathematical analysis. Al-Bīrūnī's determinations of specific gravity, however, are of great significance because of the rigorous experimental method used. He weighed a known volume of the material, immersed it carefully in a special vessel, and measured the quantity of water that was discharged through a hole in the vessel. The results that he obtained for eighteen metals and precious stones were remarkably accurate.[7]

The summit of the Arab achievement in the physical sciences was reached in *Kitāb Mīzān al-ḥikmah* ("Book of the Balance of Wisdom"), completed in 515/1121–2 by Abūʾl-Fatḥ ʿAbd al-Raḥmān al-Manṣūr al-Khāzinī.[8] This is one of the most remarkable books on mechanics, hydrostatics and physics of the Middle Ages. In it al-Khāzinī summarizes all that was then known of these subjects, as derived from Greek and earlier Arabic writers, and makes significant contributions of his own. Following al-Bīrūnī, but using a complex balance, he derives specific weights of various substances with great accuracy and also investigates the Archimedean problem: to determine the individual weight of two substances in a body composed of a mixture of substances. If the body, of weight W and specific gravity S, is composed of substances A and B of specific gravity S_1 and S_2 respectively, and contains x units by weight of substance B then:

$$\frac{W}{S}=\frac{W-x}{S_1}+\frac{x}{S_2}$$

Al-Khāzinī gives a history of statics and hydrostatics with commentaries upon the work of Archimedes, Euclid, Menelaus, al-Bīrūnī and ʿUmar al-Khayyām. His own exposition on weighing is detailed and lucid, and shows that he fully appreciated the theory of the lever. He gives an explanation of

[7] Cf. below, ch. 24, 419–20. [8] Ed. Hāshim al-Nadwah, Hyderabad, 1940.

gravity that defines it as a universal force directed towards the centre of the earth and discusses the centres of gravity of solid bodies and the gravity of air. He makes observations on capillarity, and writes a chapter on Pappus' areometer, describing its use to measure densities and appreciate the temperature of liquids. He also mentions the application of the balance to levelling. His chapter on the "Balance of the hours" is more akin to engineering than to physics, since he gives a full description of the device together with illustrative drawings. It was a steelyard clepsydra, consisting of a lever arm balanced at a fulcrum with a vessel containing sand or water suspended close to the fulcrum at (say) the left-hand side. The vessel had an orifice at the bottom calibrated to discharge the complete contents of the vessel in twenty-four hours. To the right of the fulcrum was a graduated arm carrying a large weight and a small weight, the ratios between the weights themselves, and between the weights, the full and empty vessels, and the distances along the scale being such as to allow the elapse of minutes and hours to be determined with some degree of accuracy. When the orifice was opened the sand or water began to discharge from the vessel, and the small weight was moved along the minute scale to keep the arm in balance. When an hour had elapsed the large weight was moved to the end of the first major division, and the movement of the small weight is continued along the minute scale, and so on. The *Kitāb Mīzān al-ḥikmah* is an admirable combination of theory and experiment, and marks the summit of Arabic writing on hydrostatics and mechanics, if purely engineering aspects are excluded.

MECHANICAL TECHNOLOGY

Before modern times, and especially before the Renaissance, treatises upon technological subjects appeared only rarely. For machines in everyday use there are no full descriptions from the medieval period. The water-mill driven by a vertical paddle-wheel, for example, was first described by Vitruvius in the first century BC, but apart from isolated pictorial representations there are no further descriptions of mills until the sixteenth century. This silence should not surprise us. Mills, water-raising machines and other utilitarian devices were built by anonymous craftsmen drawing upon a fund of empirical knowledge built up over the centuries. They would have acquired this knowledge by oral and practical instruction, in many cases from their fathers, and would have had no need for instructional manuals, which in any case they would have been unable to read. Water-wheels of various types were a common sight in all agricultural areas and they were mechanically quite simple. Literate engineers had no incentive, therefore, for describing these commonplace machines. Instead, we find that the surviving treatises are all concerned with more complex devices: timepieces, astronomical instruments, automata, fountains, and so on. They also sometimes deal with larger machines, usually water-raising wheels, in which radical changes had been made to the traditional types.

We shall discuss the purposes of these treatises later, but first it must be emphasized that ingenious devices (*ḥiyal*) should not be regarded as characteristic of Arabic mechanical engineering simply because the surviving treatises deal mainly with this type of construction. They were written by practical engineers, experienced in all types of public-works undertakings, who clearly felt that the construction of ingenious devices was the most interesting and intellectually satisfying of their activities. In this type of work, however, they drew extensively upon their knowledge of more mundane engineering – milling, water-raising, irrigation, etc. They also needed an appreciation of the skills of craftsmen such as metal-workers, jewellers and cabinet-makers. It is not necessary in the present chapter to describe in detail the utilitarian mechanical engineering of medieval Islam, but a brief survey will help to put the *ḥiyal* treatises in perspective.

Although we do not have precise written descriptions of the traditional machines, the details of their construction are well known. The various types of water-mills, water-raising machines and windmills were all in use until quite recently. Some types are still giving service today and specimens of the obsolete types have been preserved in working order. There is sufficient evidence – archaeological, iconographic and literary – to confirm that they were all invented before the birth of Christ and were in widespread use in the Arab world and Europe during the Middle Ages and beyond. Their designs have not changed significantly since their introduction. Our best information about the extent of mechanical technology in Islam and its application to the needs of society is to be found in the works of Arab geographers and travellers, and to a lesser degree in the histories. Water-mills were numerous in the Muslim world from Morocco to Central Asia. To take but one example, there were many large ship-mills on the Tigris, Euphrates and Khābūr rivers in the fourth/tenth century in Upper Mesopotamia. These were used for grinding corn to supply Baghdad; each one was capable of producing about ten tonnes of flour in twenty-four hours. In the same century al-Muqaddasī saw tidal mills in the Basra area (about a century before their first appearance in Europe). Apart from grist-milling, water-power was used for many industrial purposes including: paper-making, fulling cloth, rice-husking, crushing sugar-cane, and in the processing of metallic ores. Cams attached to the extended axles of the water-wheels operated trip-hammers which pounded the materials. Dams were sometimes used to increase the power delivered to mills. In the sixth/twelfth century at Cordova in Spain, there was a dam below which were three mill-houses, each housing four mills. Windmills with vertical axles were used for grinding corn and occasionally for other industrial purposes. Extensive use was made of water-raising machines, particularly the animal-driven chain-of-pots (*sāqiyah*) and the noria, the water-driven wheel (*nāᶜūrah*). As with water-mills, dams were sometimes used to increase the head of water above norias. Both machines were very successful and have remained in use until the present day.

The engineering writers certainly drew upon the fund of knowledge embodied in these everyday machines. Another source was a centuries-old tradition for the construction of delicate mechanisms and automata. Although there are very few treatises dealing with these devices, there is good reason to believe that they were constructed for courtly circles from about 300 BC onwards. From references in literary works we know that elaborate water-clocks, for example, were constructed in Hellenistic Alexandria, the Byzantine empire, Umayyad Damascus, ᶜAbbasid Baghdad and in the Maghrib and Spain. A similar diffusion can be traced for automata, ingenious toys, fountains, and so on. If a ruler wished to have this kind of device made for his court, he would have found little difficulty in obtaining craftsmen with the requisite skills. Some of these men were simply artisans who had served an apprenticeship and could construct a variety of machines to traditional designs. Despite the reported distaste of Plato and Aristotle for manual work, however, there was no stigma attached to craftsmanship, especially in Islam, where, for example, the most highly prized astrolabes were those made by astronomers. So we have examples of scholars who were well versed in the natural sciences but were also capable of constructing, or at least supervising the construction, of a whole array of machines. Such were Hero of Alexandria in the first century AD and the Banū Mūsā b. Shākir in the third/ninth century. It is possible that scholars like these used craftsmen to construct machines to their designs; this is something like the modern engineer/technician relationship, although we should be wary of using this modern terminology for a period when specialization was unknown. The few surviving technical treatises were nearly all written by this type of scholar/engineer. There is, however, a third category, namely the literate engineer who concerned himself solely with practical matters. The one outstanding example of this type is Abūʾl-ᶜIzz Ismāᶜīl b. al-Razzāz al-Jazarī (second half of sixth/twelfth century). Although we know little about his life, it seems that he started his career as a metal-worker, became well versed in other crafts, and gained a good command of written Arabic. In his book, incidentally, he gives us valuable insights into his use of inherited knowledge. He read the works of his predecessors, or inspected their constructions. He then describes how he used them as a basis for his own improved designs. In every case except two these earlier sources were Islamic, indicating that by his time Hellenistic knowledge had been fully absorbed by Muslim engineers. There was therefore no need to refer back to the Greek treatises. In the earlier Islamic centuries, however, the Arabic writers had derived their inspiration directly from Greek works.

The great scientist Archimedes is known to have been concerned with the construction of machines, although no treatise of his on practical engineering survives. There exists, however, an Arabic treatise on the construction of water-clocks that bears his name. All the Arabic writers, from Ibn al-Nadīm to al-Jazarī, are unanimous in attributing the early chapters of this work to him, and there is no reason to doubt this attribution (later chapters are Byzantine and Islamic additions). The water-machinery in this clock was a most ingenious method of feedback control for maintaining a constant head of water above the orifice and hence a constant rate of discharge. A small vertical float-chamber was connected by a pipe to the bottom of the reservoir – both vessels were cylindrical. The end of this pipe was formed into the seat of a conical valve whose plug was on the top of a small float in the float-chamber. When the outlet from the float-chamber was opened, the water-level in the chamber fell momentarily, allowing water to enter the chamber through the valve, whereupon the float rose, closing the valve momentarily, and so on. The head in the float-chamber remained virtually constant. A heavy float in the reservoir therefore descended at constant speed throughout the day. A string attached to the top of this float activated time-recording mechanisms through a system of pulleys. This system was used in most large Hellenistic and Arabic water-clocks.

One of the most prolific inventors of Hellenistic times was an Egyptian engineer called Ctesibius (*c.* 300–230 BC). His work is known only through the writings of Vitruvius who credits him with the invention of the organ, the monumental water-clock and the force-pump. Some of his work may be incorporated in the *Pneumatics* of Philo of Byzantium, who flourished in the last quarter of the third century BC. The *Pneumatics*, which is extant only in Arabic, begins with demonstrations on the principles of aerostatics and hydrostatics and continues with descriptions of trick vessels and automata in which siphonic action is an important element. Transmission of power and motion is achieved by means of ropes and pulleys. Philo's work was continued and expanded by Hero of Alexandria (*fl.* middle of first century AD). A number of his works survive, including *Mechanics*, *Automata*,

Automatic Theatre, *Pneumatics* and treatises on surveying, war machines, mirrors and mathematics. Hero's machines are somewhat more complex than those of Philo, but they embody the same basic principles. The *Mechanics*, a largely theoretical work, is extant only in Arabic whereas the remainder, apart from one in Latin, are in Greek. Hero himself tells us that he wrote four books on water-clocks, none of which has survived. It is certain, however, that several of his works were known to the Arabs. The earliest mention we have occurs in the writings of the Egyptian historian Muḥammad b. Yūsuf al-Kindī (238–350/897–961), who says that he was a geometrician who wrote about geography and pneumatics and that he made clocks and other instruments for measuring time. We can be sure from derivations in the Banū Mūsā's work (see below) that Hero's work was known in the Arab world by the third/ninth century.

The earliest surviving Arabic treatise on machines was written by the Banū (sons of) Mūsā b. Shākir about the middle of the third/ninth century. Several Arabic biographers included articles about them, including Ibn al-Nadīm and al-Qifṭī, and there are scattered references to them in the work of the great historian al-Ṭabarī. Their father, Mūsā b. Shākir, was a close companion of al-Maʾmūn when the latter was residing in Khurāsān before he became caliph in 198/813. When Mūsā died he committed his sons to the care of al-Maʾmūn and they became influential members of his court and the courts of his successors. Their names, in order of seniority, were Abū Jaʿfar Muḥammad, Aḥmad and al-Ḥasan. We do not know their dates of birth, but Abū Jaʿfar Muḥammad died in 259/873 and could hardly have been less than seventy years old, because his youngest brother was already a brilliant geometrician in the reign of al-Maʾmūn. Their activities were manifold. They took part in the turbulent palace politics of Baghdad, undertook public works, and were patrons of renowned scientists and translators such as Ḥunayn b. Isḥāq and Thābit b. Qurrah. They were also prominent scientists in their own right and are credited with some twenty mathematical and technical treatises, only two of which have survived. One is a treatise on mensuration, extant only in a Latin translation, and the other is the *Kitāb al-Ḥiyal*[9] ("Book of Ingenious Devices"), which is our present concern.

The *Kitāb al-Ḥiyal* was probably mostly the work of Aḥmad. It contains descriptions of 100 devices, of which over eighty are trick vessels of various kinds. The remainder includes fountains, self-trimming and self-filling lamps, a clamshell grab and a "gas mask" for protecting workers in polluted wells. The trick vessels display a bewildering array of effects. To name but three:

[9] Ed. A. Y. al-Hassan, Aleppo, 1981.

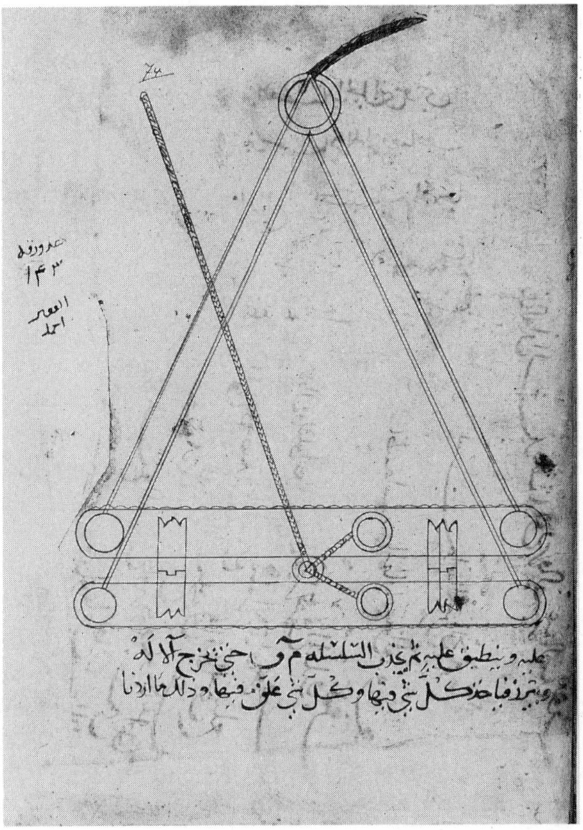

2 Design for a dredging machine from a third/ninth-century manuscript of the *Kitāb al-Ḥiyal* of the Banū Mūsā b. Shākir.

1 A jar with a tap into which three different liquids can be poured without mixing. When the tap is opened the liquids discharge in the sequence in which they were poured in.
2 A jar with an outlet pipe from which, after wine has been poured in, wine discharges as long as water is poured in, then water discharges as long as wine is poured in.
3 A trough that always replenishes itself when men draw water from it or when animals drink from it.

About twenty of these vessels are copied fairly closely from vessels described by Philo or Hero, but the remainder show radical departures from the Greek writings. The Banū Mūsā were much more concerned with automatic controls, and made subtle use of small changes in the pressures of air and liquids. For example, by using a special type of siphon, perhaps invented by themselves, they were able to produce airlocks that stopped the flow when certain conditions were met. They also made extensive use of conical valves in a remarkably advanced manner. The valves were installed as components of hydraulic systems and opened or closed automatically under predetermined impulses. Most of their components were hydraulic, although cranks appear in several of their devices – the first known use of a non-manually operated crank. They occasionally used pulley systems and gears – rack-and-pinion and worm-and-pinion. The Banū Mūsā are quite unique; no one after them attempted to emulate their grasp of pneumatic and hydraulic controls. They had exhausted the subject – five centuries later Ibn Khaldūn had this to say about their work: "There exists a book on mechanics that mentions every astonishing, remarkable and nice mechanical contrivance. It is often difficult to understand, because the geometrical proofs occurring in it are difficult. People have copies of it. They ascribe it to the Banū Shākir."[10]

Abū ᶜAbdullāh Muḥammad b. Aḥmad al-Khwārazmī's work, *Mafātīḥ al-ᶜulūm*, is the only work of any note about engineering known to us from the fourth/tenth century. The eighth treatise deals with mechanics and with ingenious devices, and lists a number of components and techniques, with etymological information, that were used by makers of these machines. This is a particularly useful work, since the author does not confine himself to definitions, but includes descriptions of manufacturing processes.

A most important treatise was written in Muslim Spain in the fifth/eleventh century by a certain al-Murādī. Unfortunately, the only known manuscript is so badly defaced that it is impossible to deduce from it precisely how any of the machines was constructed. Most of them were water-clocks, but the first five were automata machines that included several significant features. Each of these devices, for example, was driven by a full-size water-wheel, a method that was employed in China at the same period to drive the monumental water-clock of Su Sung. The automata were similar to those found in large water-clocks; for example a set of doors in a row that open at successive intervals to reveal jackwork figures. The most remarkable feature of these machines, however, is the gearing. The gear-trains used for the transmission of power were quite complex and included segmental gears, i.e. gear-wheels having teeth on only part of their perimeters; these were used to produce intermittent working. Gearing of equal complication had been known since Hellenistic times, but not for the

[10] *Muqaddimah*, trans. Rosenthal, 132.

transmission of high torque. Similar gearing did not appear in Europe until the eighth/fourteenth century.

This is an appropriate moment at which to mention briefly the treatises on astronomical instruments. Treatises on the astrolabe are quite common, one of the most comprehensive being by the great scientist al-Bīrūnī, incorporating much of the work of his predecessors. In this same treatise there occurs the description of a geared calendar which shows the moon's phases and the positions of the sun and moon in the ecliptic. Fragments of a similar device, Byzantine in origin and dated to the late fifth or early sixth century, can be inspected in the Science Museum, London. Treatises on equatoria first appear in Muslim Spain in the fifth/eleventh century. The equatorium has as its objective the determination of the longitude of any one of the planets for any given time. This was done by constructing to scale by mechanical and graphical means the Ptolemaic configuration for that particular planet at the given instant. The desired result was then simply read off a scale of the instrument. Where great accuracy was not required the equatorium relieved the tedium of numerical computation. The knowledge of astrolabes, equatoria and other instruments entered Europe from Muslim Spain in the fifth/eleventh century.

The first full description of a monumental water-clock we have is the treatise *Kitāb ᶜAmal al-saᶜāt wa-ʾl-ᶜamal bihā* ("On the Construction of Clocks and their Use") completed by Riḍwān b. al-Saᶜātī in 600/1203. This describes the reconstruction by Riḍwān of a water-clock built by his father, Muḥammad al-Saᶜātī, in the reign of Nūr al-Dīn Maḥmūd b. Zankī in Damascus (reigned 549–69/1154–74). After Muḥammad's death it fell into disrepair and several craftsmen made unsuccesful attempts to repair it before this was finally achieved by Riḍwān. The clock-face consisted of a wall of well-seasoned timber about 4.23 metres long by 2.78 metres wide, installed on a masonry lower-wall and between masonry side-walls. In this screen was a row of doors, at either end of which was the figure of a falcon. During the day a small crescent moved at constant speed in front of the doors and at every hour a door rotated to reveal a different colour, the falcons leant forward, discharged pellets on to cymbals and resumed their upright positions. Above the doors a zodiac circle rotated at constant speed. Above this was a semicircle of twelve circular holes. During the night one of these holes became fully illuminated every hour. The clock was operated by the "Archimedes" water-machinery and the motion was transmitted to the activating mechanisms by pulley-and-rope systems.

As with most large water-clocks, the hours signalled by this clock were temporal hours, i.e. the lengths of daylight and darkness were divided by twelve to give hours that varied in length from day to day throughout the year. This meant that the rate of discharge from the float-chamber also had to be varied daily. A flow-regulator was therefore fitted to the outlet from the chamber. This was a device that permitted the orifice to be rotated through 360° inside an annulus which was divided into the twelve zodiacal signs, each sign being subdivided into degrees. The orifice was placed at the appropriate degree for a given day in order to produce the correct length of temporal hours for that day. In the case of the Damascus clock, the annulus was equally divided into "signs" of 30° each, which is quite inaccurate. (In the Archimedes clock the flow-regulator was semicircular, which is even more inaccurate.) The clock also had serious structural defects, mainly owing to the fact that all the mechanisms and pulley systems were fixed directly to the wooden screen. This would have caused the timbers to distort and so lead to mechanical breakdowns. Indeed, the clock had a history of damage by fire and mechanical failure.

The only information we have about Ibn al-Razzāz al-Jazarī's life is his own brief statement at the start of his book. He tells us that at the time of writing it he was in the service of Nāṣir al-Dīn Maḥmūd (reigned 597–619/1201–22), the Artuqid king of Diyār Bakr. He had by then spent twenty-five years in the service of the family, having served the father and the brother of Nāṣir al-Dīn before him. According to al-Jazarī's own account we owe the existence of his book to Nāṣir al-Dīn, because he ordered al-Jazarī to compose it so that the things he had constructed, many of them very fragile, should not be lost. The work is called *Kitāb fī Maᶜrifat al-ḥiyal al-handasiyyah* ("The Book of Knowledge of Ingenious Mechanical Devices").[11] It is the most important work on engineering to have come down to us from pre-Renaissance times, not only for the intrinsic interest of the machines and techniques described in it, but because of the way they are described. For each machine, detailed step-by-step instructions are given for the manufacture, assembly and testing of the components. The instructions are so precise that modern craftsmen have found no difficulty in reconstructing several of the machines. We therefore know more about medieval mechanical engineering from al-Jazarī's book than from all other sources combined. The bulk of what was known on the subject in the Muslim world, together with his own innovations and improvements, is contained in his work. It is divided into six categories:

1 Water-clocks and candle-clocks
2 Trick vessels
3 Water dispensers and phlebotomy measuring devices

[11] Trans. D. R. Hill, Dordrecht, 1974.

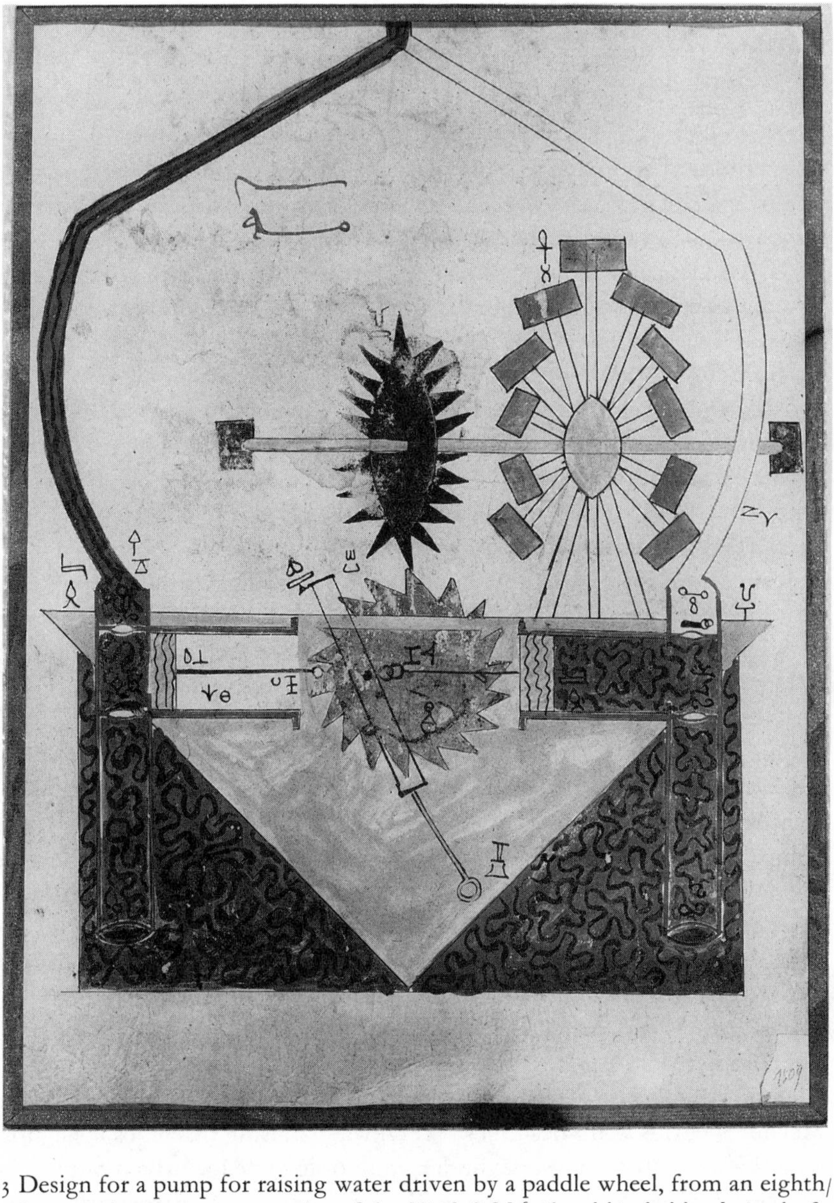

3 Design for a pump for raising water driven by a paddle wheel, from an eighth/fourteenth-century manuscript of the *Kitāb fī Maʿrifat al-ḥiyal al-handasiyyah* of Ibn al-Razzāz al-Jazarī.

4 Fountains and musical automata
5 Water-raising machines
6 Miscellaneous

His first clock, which is very similar to that of Riḍwān b. al-Saʿātī, typifies his methodical approach and his refusal to accept traditional designs. The face of the clock is narrower and is made of bronze. Most of the working parts are kept away from the face, so that it does not have to carry excessive loads. He describes how he constructed the flow-regulator, first having tested and rejected the equally divided circle and semicircle, although he retained the circular shape. He carefully calibrated the orifice for the required discharge on the longest day. He then painstakingly marked the divisions on the annulus by trial and error. Two of his water-clocks – the third and the fourth – are driven by a very ingenious hydraulic/mechanical system. One of the effects is the release of a ball on to a cymbal; this is not simply a time-recording signal, since the release of the ball automatically resets the mechanisms for the next hour. This is therefore a closed-loop system – as long as balls are loaded into the magazine the clock will continue to operate. This type of clock appears in no other treatise and may have been al-Jazarī's own invention. In his trick vessels and dispensers he does not attempt to emulate the Banū Mūsā by using small variations in pressure, but relies upon hydraulic and mechanical methods.

One of his water-raising machines is very important in the history of machine design. This is a water-driven double-acting pump with twin cylinders and true suction pipes, the first known example of this type of pump. Space does not permit discussion of any of his other machines; we can only list some of the ideas and techniques that appear for the first time in his work: static balancing of wheels; lamination of timber; the crank in a machine used to transmit power; calibration of orifices; tipping-buckets; the casting of metals in closed mould-boxes with green sand.

The last-known treatise on machines from the classical Islamic period was completed by Taqī ʾl-Dīn in the year 959/1552. Called *Kitāb al-Ṭuruq al-saniyyah fī ʾl-ālāt al-rūḥāniyyah* ("The Sublime Methods of Pneumatic Machines"), this work describes several water-raising machines. The most remarkable of these is a six-cylinder "monobloc" water-driven pump.

The *Libros del Saber de Astronomia*[12] is a compilation of translations and paraphrases from Arabic into Castilian completed in AD 1277 under the direction of Alfonso X of Castile. This large work deals mostly with astronomical treatises, but it contains descriptions of five timepieces, one of which is of great interest. This consists of a large wooden drum divided

[12] Ed. Manuel Rico y Sinobas, Madrid, 1863–7.

4 A water-raising device having an animal-powered flume-beam swape incorporating the first known use of a crank in a machine: design from a seventh/thirteenth-century manuscript of Ibn al-Razzāz al-Jazarī's *Kitāb fī Maʿrifat al-ḥiyal al-handasiyyah*.

internally into twelve compartments, with small holes between the compartments through which mercury flowed. The drum was mounted on the same axle as a large wheel powered by a weight-drive wound around the wheel and acted as an effective escapement for the descent of the weight. Clocks based on this principle had been known in Islam since the fifth/eleventh century, and were quite popular in Europe from the sixteenth century to the eighteenth.

There are many instances, some of which have been mentioned above, of ideas and techniques that were known in the Muslim world before their appearance in Europe. It is very difficult to find positive proof for diffusion, however, because none of the Arabic treatises was translated into Latin in the Middle Ages. Indeed, apart from the *Libros del Saber*, there were no translations into any European language until modern times. Making the reasonable assumption that transmission did in many cases take place, we must therefore infer that this was by non-literary means. Communications among craftsmen, travellers' reports and the inspection by Christians of Muslim constructions, above all in the Iberian peninsula, suggest themselves as the most likely channels for the passage of information. It has been shown, for example, that all the elements of the mechanical clock, except the escapement mechanism, were present in Arabic fine technology – complex gearing, weight-drive, celestial and biological automata. They were diffused to northern Europe, almost certainly from Spain, during the fifth/eleventh century, and were adopted by the makers of water-clocks, from whose ranks the inventor of the escapement probably came. We can therefore postulate an Arabic influence on the invention of the mechanical clock. Similar sequences could be constructed for the transmission of other ideas.

In considering the importance of Arabic fine technology as recorded in the treatises, we need to look beyond the "nuts-and-bolts" of the machines to the purposes of the authors. In the first place, some of the machines were utilitarian and incorporated real advances in mechanical engineering. In the case of trick vessels and automata, however, the quality of the engineering seems to be ill matched with the triviality of the end-products. (The same can be said of computer games and some television programmes.) One obvious reason for making them, of course, was that they were in demand. Patrons wished to be entertained and given aesthetic pleasure – some of the devices were very beautiful – and were interested mainly in the end results, not in the means used to achieve them. It is probable, however, that in constructing these devices and writing about them the engineers were prompted by several motives, as well as by the hope of reward.

In the first place, they believed that they were following the philosophy of Aristotle's *Mechanical Problems* in bringing forth machines "from potentiality into actuality".[13] Secondly, the Arabs were very interested in constructing machines that "moved by themselves" and therefore concerned themselves deeply with automatic control systems. Closely related to this motive was the urge to represent the universe by mechanical means. Man has a deep-rooted urge to simulate the world about him through the graphic and plastic arts, and a natural extension of this urge is to impart movement to static simulations and so create biological and celestial automata. The theme of man-made organisms, magically endowed with a life of their own, has exercised a powerful fascination from the early Greek legends, such as that of Pygmalion, to the animated beasts of the *Thousand and One Nights*, the medieval European legends that endowed the poet Virgil with magical powers, and the doll Olympia in the *Tales* of E. T. A. Hoffmann, to take but a few examples.

A key role can therefore be assigned to the makers of automata in the development of a rational mechanistic view of the universe, so providing a stimulus to the progress of mechanical technology. When the demand arose for utilitarian machines with their own internal controls, the concept of automation was already understood and accepted. Moreover, ways for achieving a large measure of control were to be found in Arabic machines: automatic switching, feed-back control, closed-loop systems, and so on. It is therefore postulated that European mechanical technology benefited from Arabic engineering in three ways: components and techniques; control systems; and the potent idea of self-regulating machinery.

13 See G. Saliba, "The function of mechanical devices in medieval Islamic society", *Annals of the New York Academy of Sciences*, XLI, 1985, 141–51.

CHAPTER 15

ASTRONOMY

During the millennium which followed the introduction of mathematical astronomy from Indian, Sasanid and Hellenistic sources to the vigorous cultural scene of ʿAbbasid Iraq in the second/eighth and third/ninth centuries, Muslim astronomers compiled a remarkably rich and varied corpus of literature relating to their subject. Some of this literature survives in about 10,000 manuscript volumes preserved in the libraries of south-western Asia, north Africa, Europe and the United States, and during the past 200 years a very small number of scholars has turned its attention to a fraction of this surviving material. Catalogues of varying quality exist for some library collections, but there are many important collections of scientific manuscripts which are not yet catalogued at all. Lists of medieval authors, titles of their works and available manuscripts thereof, have been prepared from these catalogues by H. Suter, C. Brockelmann, C. A. Storey and F. Sezgin.

No classification of the Islamic astronomical literature exists in the modern literature, and besides, the scope of this literature has only become known during the past few decades. The present chapter represents an attempt to fill this gap, and to discuss the different categories of Islamic astronomical literature, the variety of which reflects the keen interest of Muslim scholars in astronomy for over a millennium. Very little of the Islamic material was transmitted to Europe in the medieval period, and that which was transmitted was hardly representative of the whole. Thus the traditional image of the Muslims as the torchbearers of classical astronomy to Europe is to be abandoned.

The available original sources enable us to distinguish four main periods of Islamic astronomy: first, a period of assimilation and syncretization of earlier Hellenistic, Indian and Sasanid mathematical astronomy and pre-Islamic Arabian folk astronomy (*c.* 75/700 – *c.* 200/825); second, a period of vigorous investigation in which the superiority of Ptolemaic astronomy was recognized, programmes of astronomical observations were conducted, and significant contributions were made (*c.* 200/825 – *c.* 425/1025), third, a period when a distinctively Islamic astronomy flourished and in general continued to progress, if with decreasing vigour (*c.* 425/1025 – *c.* 850/1450); and, finally, a period of stagnation in which this traditional Islamic astronomy continued to be practised with enthusiasm but without innovation of any scientific consequence (*c.* 850/1450 – *c.* 1320/1900).

FOLK ASTRONOMY

We begin with the traditional folk astronomy of the Arabian peninsula, which was already well established if not documented by the time of the Prophet Muḥammad. This astronomical folklore involved a knowledge of the seasons and associated agricultural and meteorological phenomena, the fixed stars, the passage of the sun and moon through the zodiacal signs and lunar mansions, and very crude techniques for timekeeping. This folklore was eventually recorded in the *kutub al-anwāʾ*, of which over twenty examples were compiled in the third/ninth and fourth/tenth centuries alone, although only four of these survive. One of these is the *Kitāb al-Anwāʾ* of Ibn Qutaybah, which is representative of one type of *anwāʾ* book, being a collection of knowledge of celestial and meteorological phenomena as found in Arabic sources of folklore, literature and poetry. Another, representative of a second type, is arranged in the form of a calendar containing agricultural, meteorological and astronomical events of significance to farmers: such is the *Calendar of Cordova*,[1] compiled for a specific year in the fourth/tenth century. More research on this material is necessary before we can talk intelligently about pre-Islamic Arab astronomy. Most of the work so far on the available texts has been conducted by Arabists without any background in science.

RELIGIOUS ASPECTS OF ASTRONOMY

A distinct Islamic flavour was added to this pre-Islamic folk astronomy by the fact that the times of Muslim prayer were defined astronomically and the direction of Muslim prayer was defined geographically. A corpus of literature appeared in which these two subjects, the prayer-times and the *qiblah*, were discussed in terms of primitive folk astronomy. These are the *kutub al-mawāqīt* and the *kutub dalāʾil al-qiblah*, of which the earliest examples are known only by quotation in the numerous later works dealing with these subjects in a non-mathematical way. The topics discussed in these works included, for example, the regulation of the daytime prayers by shadow lengths, and of the night-time prayers by the lunar mansions, and

[1] Ed. and trans. C. Pellat, Leiden, 1961.

the determination of the *qiblah* by the direction of the wind and the risings and settings of the fixed stars. All of this material has only recently been investigated for the first time. There was a quite distinct tradition in which the same problems were solved by mathematical means: we shall return to this later.

MATHEMATICAL ASTRONOMY

Astronomical handbooks (zīj)

The earliest Islamic works relating to mathematical astronomy, that is, planetary astronomy and spherical astronomy, were based on Indian and Sasanid works. With very few exceptions these early Islamic works are lost, and our knowledge of them has been pieced together from later citations, first by C. A. Nallino and more profoundly by D. Pingree and E. S. Kennedy. Already in the second/eighth century in India and Afghanistan there were compiled a number of Arabic *zīj*s, that is, astronomical handbooks with text and tables. These earliest examples of Islamic *zīj*s, based on Indian and Sasanid works, are lost, as are the earliest examples compiled at Baghdad in the second/eighth century.

In the third/ninth century, when the *Almagest* of Ptolemy and various other Greek astronomical works were translated into Arabic, a corpus of literature arose mainly in the form of commentaries on particular sections or specific problems from these Greek works. With some notable exceptions, such as a critical edition of the recension of Menelaus' *Sphaerica* by Abū Naṣr Manṣūr b. ʿAlī b. ʿIrāq (d. *c.* 408/1018) and the non-critical editions of various recensions of minor Greek works by Naṣīr al-Dīn al-Ṭūsī, most of this material is untouched by modern scholarship. With the *zīj*s compiled in Baghdad and Damascus in the early third/ninth century under the patronage of the caliph al-Maʾmūn we are on somewhat firmer ground than we are with the second/eighth century Islamic *zīj*s. Manuscripts exist of the *Mumtaḥan zīj* of Yaḥyā b. abī Manṣūr and two *Zīj*s by Ḥabash, each of which was based on essentially Ptolemaic theory rather than Indian. The *Zīj al-Sindhind* of Abū Jaʿfar Muḥammad b. Mūsā al-Khwārazmī, based mainly on Indian planetary theory, has survived in a Latin translation of an Andalusian recension.

The Islamic *zīj*s represent the most important category of astronomical literature for the historian of science, by virtue of the diversity of the topics dealt with, and the information which can be obtained from the tables. In 1956 E. S. Kennedy published a survey of 125 Islamic *zīj*s.[2] We now know

[2] "A survey of Islamic astronomical tables", 123–77.

of close to 200, and research is currently in progress on a revised version of the *zīj* survey. To be sure, many of these works are lost, and many of those which are extant are derived from other *zīj*s by modification, borrowing or outright plagiarism. Nevertheless, there are enough *zīj*s available in manuscript form to reconstruct a reasonably accurate picture of the Islamic activity in this field. Also, since the major contributions of the Muslim astronomers were in the development of computational techniques and the compilation of tables, the *zīj*s are the category of literature in which these contributions are most clearly visible.

Most *zīj*s consist of several hundred pages of text and tables. The treatment of the material presented may vary considerably from one *zīj* to another, but most contain chapters and tables relating to the following aspects of mathematical astronomy:

1 Chronology
2 Trigonometry
3 Spherical astronomy
4 Planetary mean motions
5 Planetary equations
6 Planetary latitudes
7 Planetary stations
8 Parallax
9 Solar and lunar eclipses
10 Planetary and lunar visibility
11 Mathematical geography (lists of cities with geographical co-ordinates)
12 Uranometry (tables of fixed stars with co-ordinates)
13 Astrology

The only *zīj*s which have been published with translation and commentary are those of Abū Jaᶜfar Muḥammad b. Mūsā al-Khwārazmī (d. after 232/846) in a much modified later recension, and of Abū ᶜAbdullāh Muḥammad b. Jābir b. Sinān al-Battānī. The *zīj* of al-Bīrūnī, called *al-Qānūn al-Masᶜūdī*,[3] has been published without translation or commentary. The introductions, but not the tables, in the *Zīj*s of Ibn Bannāʾ (*fl.* Marrakesh, *c.* 700/1300) and Ulugh Beg (*fl.* Samarqand, *c.* 825/1425) have been published and translated. The observation accounts in the introduction to the *Ḥākimī zīj* of Ibn Yūnus have been published and translated. No other *zīj*s have received such attention.

Much scholarly work has been done in the past twenty-five years on the various categories of tables in Islamic *zīj*s. However, there is a great deal of

[3] See below, ch. 24, 418.

basic research waiting to be done on *zījs* of prime importance to the history of Islamic science, such as the *Zījs* of Aḥmad b. ʿAbdullāh Ḥabash al-Ḥāsib al-Marwazī, the *Ḥākimī zīj* of Ibn Yūnus mentioned above, the *Īlkhānī zīj* of Naṣīr al-Dīn al-Ṭūsī, the *Zīj al-jadīd* of Ibn al-Shāṭir (*fl.* Damascus, *c.* 750/1350) and the *Sulṭānī zīj* of Ulugh Beg already mentioned.

Numerical notation

The vast majority of Islamic astronomical tables have entries written in Arabic alphabetical notation and expressed sexagesimally, that is, to base 60. A number equivalent to 23 15 54 seconds, which in modern sexagesimal notation is 23;15,54, means:

$$23 + \frac{15}{60} + \frac{54}{3600}$$

In sexagesimal arithmetic, more so than in decimal arithmetic, it is useful to have a multiplication table at hand, and such tables are also useful for division. The astronomers of medieval Islam used sexagesimal multiplication tables displaying 3,600 products of the form $m \times n$ (m and $n = 1, 2, \ldots, 60$), such as, for example, $27 \times 51 = 22,57$ ($= 1377$). Such tables were not usually contained in *zījs*, although sometimes they were included in works on arithmetic. The surviving examples of Islamic multiplication tables all post-date the eighth/fourteenth century. Some display 216,000 products of the form $m \times n$ ($m = 0,1, 0,2, \ldots, 59,59, 60,0$, and $n = 1, 2, \ldots, 60$), such as $40,27 \times 37 = 24,56,39$. The operations of sexagesimal arithmetic are generally taken for granted by authors of *zījs*. They are spelled out in detail in certain works dealing with arithmetic.

Trigonometric tables

Most *zījs* contain tables of the sine and tangent function for each whole, or half, or quarter degree of arc. Entries are generally given to three sexagesimal digits, corresponding roughly to five decimal digits. But certain Muslim scholars compiled more extensive sets of trigonometric tables which were not included in *zījs*. Already in the early fourth/tenth century Abū ʾl-Fatḥ Saʿīd b. Khafīf al-Samarqandī prepared a set of tables of the tangent function with entries to three sexagesimal digits for each minute of arc. Again, in the late fourth/tenth century the Egyptian astronomer Ibn Yūnus tabulated the sine function to five sexagesimal digits, equivalent to about nine decimal digits, for each minute of arc, also giving the differences for each second. He also tabulated the tangent function for each minute of arc, and the solar declination for each minute of solar longitude. His trigonometric tables were not sufficiently accurate to warrant this number of significant figures, and over four centuries were to elapse before the compilation in Samarqand of the magnificent trigonometric tables which were contained in the *Zīj* of Ulugh Beg and which were later also copied separately. These display the values of the sine and tangent to five sexagesimal digits for each minute of argument, and are generally accurate in the last digit.

Computation of planetary positions

Most *zīj*s contain accounts of the computation of planetary positions using the accompanying tables, without any exposition of the underlying theory, a topic generally reserved for works on theoretical astronomy (see below). Often the parameters underlying the tables, that is, the astronomical "constants" such as solar, lunar and planetary mean motions and the oscillatory motions about the mean motions, will be new, but, with some notable exceptions, generally the observations and calculations by which these parameters were derived were not recorded. Islamic planetary tables normally followed those of Ptolemy's *Handy Tables* in their conception. However, several new varieties of tables were devised by Muslim scholars to facilitate the numerical solution of astronomical problems. Of particular interest are certain Islamic planetary equation tables which display the planetary equation directly in terms of two arguments which can be found from the mean motion tables, thus obviating the need for any calculation.

Compilation of ephemerides

All Islamic *zīj*s contained tables of mean motions and equations for computing solar, lunar and planetary positions for a given time. From the ʿAbbasid period onwards, Muslim astronomers also compiled ephemerides displaying solar, lunar and planetary positions for each day of the year. Thābit b. Qurrah called them *daftar al-sanah* ("register of the year"); in later centuries they were called *taqwīm*. Al-Bīrūnī described how to compile them in detail in his astronomical/astrological handbook, the *Tafhīm*.[4] Manuscripts of such ephemerides had a high rate of attrition since the tables could be dispensed with at the end of the year: the earliest extant examples of such ephemerides are from eighth/fourteenth century Yemen, disco-

[4] See below, 413–16.

vered in Cairo only a few years ago. On the other hand, literally hundreds of ephemerides survive from the late Ottoman period. Such ephemerides usually contain astrological predictions based on the planetary configurations revealed in the tables. Naṣīr al-Dīn al-Ṭūsī in the seventh/thirteenth century compiled a treatise on the subject of *ʿilm al-taqwīm*, and numerous other astronomers wrote treatises on this subject in the following centuries. There was also an Islamic tradition of auxiliary tables for generating annual ephemerides without using the standard Ptolemaic-type mean motion and equation tables. Apart from these auxiliary tables, no Islamic ephemerides or explanatory treatises have been studied in modern times.

Equatoria and eclipse computers

There are several Islamic treatises on eclipse computers and planetary equatoria for determining the positions of the planets for a given date, with which the standard problems of planetary astronomy dealt with in *zīj*s are solved mechanically. Such was the affection of the Muslim astronomers for tables and computing devices that one fourth/tenth-century astronomer inscribed the tables of his *zīj* on the plates of an astrolabe, which he called *Zīj al-ṣafāʾiḥ* ("*Zīj* of plates").

Crescent visibility

The subject of lunar crescent visibility was also treated in *zīj*s, and a wide variety of methods and tables were devised to facilitate the solution of this problem. The earliest Islamic works relied on a simple Indian condition for determining visibility, but already in the fourth/tenth century individuals such as Thābit b. Qurrah and Ibn Yūnus presented advanced mathematical procedures for determining visibility. There is as yet very little published material available on this very important aspect of Islamic astronomy.

Stellar co-ordinates and uranography

Most *zīj*s contain lists of stellar co-ordinates in either the ecliptic or the equatorial systems, or occasionally in both systems. A survey of the stellar co-ordinates in Islamic *zīj*s would be a valuable contribution to the history of Islamic astronomy, and could help determine the extent to which original observations were made by Muslim astronomers.

In his *Kitāb Ṣuwar al-kawākib al-thābitah* ("Book of Constellations") the Shīrāz astronomer ʿAbd al-Raḥmān b. ʿUmar al-Ṣūfī (d. 376/986) presented

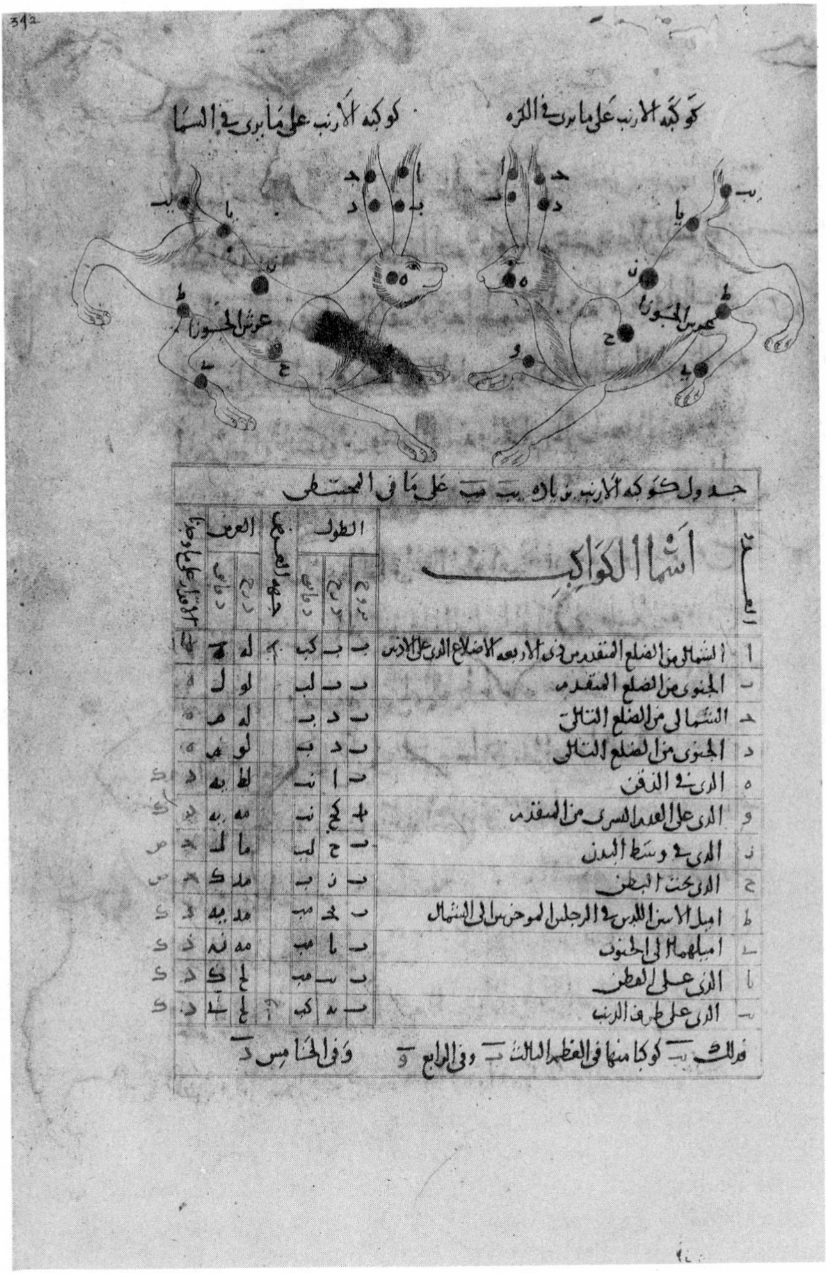

5 The southern constellation Lepus (al-Arnab), as illustrated in a manuscript (completed in 400/1009–10) of al-Ṣūfī's *Ṣuwar al-kawākib al-thābitah*. On the left the constellation is shown as seen in the sky; on the right as seen on a celestial globe. Below is a list of the stars in the constellation.

lists of stellar co-ordinates, as well as illustrations of the constellation figures from the Hellenistic tradition, and also information on the lunar mansions following the Arab tradition. The Arabic text of this important work, and also a later Persian version, have been published. The only earlier Arabic work on the constellations, written by a third/ninth-century astronomer called ᶜUṭārid b. Muḥammad al-Ḥāsib, is mentioned by al-Ṣūfī in the introduction to his own treatise but is no longer extant. Later Islamic works on uranography are mostly restricted to Persian and Turkish translations of al-Ṣūfī, although some astrological works such as the fifth/eleventh-century Persian *Rawḍat al-munajjimīn* of Shāhmardān Rāzī contain illustrations of the constellations which have only recently attracted the attention of historians of Islamic art. An impressive amount of research on Arabic star names and their later influence in Europe has been conducted in the last few years by P. Kunitzsch.

Spherical astronomy and spherical trigonometry

Most *zīj*s contain in their introductory text the solutions of the standard problems of spherical astronomy, such as, to give only one example, the determination of time from solar and stellar altitude. Rarely is any explanation given of how the formulae outlined in the text were derived. There were two main traditions involving either projection methods, in which the problems relating to the celestial sphere are reduced to geometric or trigonometric problems on a plane, or methods of spherical trigonometry. Both techniques are ultimately of Greek origin, but Muslim scholars made substantial contributions to each. There is some confusion about these contributions in the modern literature, since it has been assumed by modern writers that because a medieval writer used a medieval formula which is mathematically equivalent to the modern formula derived by a specific rule of spherical trigonometry, then the medieval scholar must have known the equivalent of the modern rule of spherical trigonometry, when, in fact, the medieval formula was derived without using spherical trigonometry at all. Likewise, it is commonly thought that the first Islamic treatise dealing with spherical trigonometry as a separate subject was the treatise *Risālah fī Shakl al-qaṭṭā*ᶜ ("On the Complete Quadrilateral") compiled by Naṣīr al-Dīn al-Ṭūsī in the mid-seventh/thirteenth century, which is available in published form. A more accurate appraisal of the situation recently published by M. T. Debarnot takes into consideration the contributions of a series of first-rate earlier scholars such as Thābit b.

Qurrah, al-Nayrīzī, Abū'l-Wafā' al-Būzajānī, al-Khujandī (*fl.* second half of fourth/tenth century), Kūshyār (d. first quarter of fifth/eleventh century), al-Sijzī, Abū Naṣr Manṣūr b. ʿAlī b. ʿIrāq, and particularly the *Maqālīd ʿilm al-hay'ah* ("Keys to Astronomy") of al-Bīrūnī (see below). From the post-classical period there are the works of the Andalusians Ibn Muʿādh and Jābir b. Aflaḥ (probably *fl.* middle of sixth/twelfth century), and from the Muslim East, two treatises on spherical trigonometry by two contemporaries of al-Ṭūsī, namely Muḥyī 'l-Dīn al-Maghribī (d. between 680 and 690/1281 and 1291) and Ḥusām al-Dīn Sālār.

Modern methodology

In recent years the electronic computer has been applied to various problems in the history of Islamic astronomy. The computer can be programmed to tabulate any mathematical function using any range of terrestrial and astronomical parameters, and computer programmes have been prepared for recomputing all of the standard tables in *zījs*, as well as the other kinds of Islamic tables, such as for co-ordinates for drawing curves on sundials or on astrolabes and quadrants, or for finding the *qiblah*, or for determining the times of prayer. To give a specific example, tables have been prepared of the standard trigonometric functions with values for each minute of argument to five sexagesimal digits: with such tables one can confirm at a glance the astounding accuracy of the trigonometric tables in the *Zīj* of Ulugh Beg. However, no comparative analysis of Islamic trigonometric tables has been conducted yet. Another example of the use of the computer is the data processing of the geographical co-ordinates in a large number of medieval Islamic astronomical works: in this case the computer was programmed to rearrange the data alphabetically according to the place-name, and according to increasing latitude and increasing longitude. The relationship between various sets of geographical tables has thus been established.

THEORETICAL ASTRONOMY

Another category of Islamic astronomical literature can be labelled *kutub al-hay'ah*, and consists of general expositions of the principles underlying astronomical theory. There were two main traditions, one eastern and the other western. The eastern tradition is exemplified in the writings of the early fifth/eleventh-century scholar Ibn al-Haytham, and of the sixth/twelfth-century astronomer al-Kharaqī. Later examples from the seventh/

thirteenth century are the *Tadhkirah* of Naṣīr al-Dīn al-Ṭūsī, and the treatises of Muʾayyad al-Dīn al-ʿUrḍī and Quṭb al-Dīn al-Shīrāzī, and from the eighth/fourteenth century, the treatise by Ibn al-Shāṭir. Some aspects of al-Ṭūsī's *Tadhkirah* were investigated by Carra de Vaux at the end of the thirteenth/nineteenth century. The most interesting aspect of this work is a device which al-Ṭūsī introduced to replace the equant in the Ptolemaic planetary model, which some medieval astronomers found objectionable for philosophical reasons. In the 1950s, E. S. Kennedy discovered that the geocentric planetary models of Ibn al-Shāṭir described in his treatise *Nihāyat al-suʾl* are mathematically identical with the heliocentric models of Copernicus. In other words, the modifications to the Ptolemaic models introduced by Ibn al-Shāṭir and Copernicus are the same. It later proved possible to outline an eastern Islamic tradition of modifications to Ptolemy's models (based on philosophical speculation rather than observation) from al-Ṭūsī to al-Shīrāzī and Ibn al-Shāṭir.[5] None of these texts by al-Ṭūsī, al-Shīrāzī, or Ibn al-Shāṭir has been published. Recently a work on planetary theory by Ibn al-Haytham was discovered in the USSR, and using it we may be able to achieve a deeper understanding of these Islamic modifications to Ptolemaic planetary theory.

The western tradition of *ʿilm al-hayʾah* is characterized by the works of Jābir b. Aflaḥ and al-Biṭrūjī, both of whom flourished at the end of the sixth/twelfth century. The *Iṣlāḥ al-Majisṭī* of Jābir is a new version of the *Almagest* simplifying the trigonometric procedures, but leaving out tables and technicalities. The *Kitāb fī ʾl-Hayʾah* of al-Biṭrūjī represents an attempt to put the model for a planet on the surface of its sphere, so that the distance of the planet from the centre of the universe would not vary. Al-Biṭrūjī's work has been published and analysed by B. R. Goldstein. The writings of Andalusian philosophers who dabbled in planetary theory, such as Ibn Bājjah (d. 533/1139) and Ibn Rushd (d. 595/1198), are either lost or have survived only in Latin.

ASTRONOMICAL TIMEKEEPING

Another category of Islamic astronomical literature dealt with astronomical timekeeping. As stated above, the times of prayer in Islam are astronomically defined and the direction of prayer is towards Mecca. In addition, the Muslim calendar is defined in terms of the first visibility of the

[5] See Kennedy and Ghanem, *Life and Work of Ibn al-Shāṭir*.

lunar crescent. The science of astronomical timekeeping, called *ᶜilm al-mīqāt*, deals with these three problems from a mathematical point of view, not in terms of the primitive techniques of folk astronomy. Most of the literature dealing specifically with these subjects dates from the seventh/thirteenth century onwards; before that time the subjects were treated in more general works, such as *zīj*s.

The definitions of the times of prayer are such that the times vary from day to day and are dependent on geographical latitude. Already in the third/ninth century simple tables were compiled in Baghdad displaying the solar altitudes at the times of the daytime prayers throughout the year. In the early fourth/tenth century Ibn Amājūr compiled a table displaying the time as a function of solar or stellar altitude for the latitude of Baghdad, and another table displaying the time approximately for all latitudes. In later centuries corpuses of tables containing several thousand, if not tens of thousands, of entries were compiled for various centres of astronomical activity, including tables for reckoning time by the sun and stars and tables for regulating the times of prayer. In the seventh/thirteenth century an Egyptian astronomer compiled a table for finding the time of day or night by the sun or any star which would work for all latitudes; this table contains over a quarter of a million entries. Muslim astronomers also compiled auxiliary tables for solving all problems of spherical astronomy for all latitudes. The first such set was devised by Aḥmad b. ᶜAbdullāh Ḥabash al-Ḥāsib al-Marwazī in early third/ninth-century Baghdad, and the culmination of this tradition was reached by Shams al-Dīn Muḥammad b. Muḥammad al-Khalīlī in eighth/fourteenth-century Damascus. With very few exceptions these several hundred tables were first studied only in the 1970s. Indeed for the most part they were earlier not even known to exist, in spite of the fact that the main corpuses of tables for Cairo, Damascus and Istanbul, the main centres of *ᶜilm al-mīqāt*, survive in dozens of manuscripts.

Already in the third/ninth century Muslim scholars had solved the complicated problem of the determination of the direction of Mecca from a given locality. In the same century a Baghdad astronomer prepared a table displaying the *qiblah* as a function of terrestrial latitude and longitude, but based on an approximate formula. In the following centuries other such tables were prepared, but they are all overshadowed by a table compiled by al-Khalīlī in the eighth/fourteenth century which displays the *qiblah* as an angle in degree and minutes for all latitudes and longitudes, and which is based on an accurate formula and extremely carefully computed. Most *zīj*s contain lists of latitudes and longitudes of localities, and in some *zīj*s the *qiblah* values are also given. Again most *zīj*s present a method for finding the *qiblah* by calculation or geometrical construction. Such methods are also generally discussed in Islamic treatises on instruments.

ASTRONOMICAL INSTRUMENTS

A large category of Islamic astronomical literature deals with instruments for timekeeping and for solving other problems of spherical astronomy. Already in the second/eighth and third/ninth centuries Muslim astronomers were preparing treatises on the armillary sphere, the planispheric astrolabe and the sundial, all instruments of Greek origin. One of the most interesting features of some of these early Islamic treatises is the tables that they contain for marking the curves on astrolabes and sundials for different latitudes. The treatise of al-Farghānī (*fl. c.* 210/825) on the astrolabe contains tables for marking the almucantar and azimuth circles on the plates of astrolabes for each degree of terrestrial latitude. The treatise of Abū Jaᶜfar Muḥammad b. Mūsā al-Khwārazmī on sundials contains tables for drawing the hour-lines on sundials for a range of latitudes. Such tables, which are of considerable mathematical sophistication, represent a purely Islamic contribution, whose development can be traced through the centuries from ᶜAbbasid Iraq to the late Ottoman empire.

Islamic treatises on the astrolabe may deal with the construction or the use of the instrument. The treatise of Abū Saᶜīd Aḥmad b. Muḥammad al-Sijzī (*fl. c.* 360/970) deals with the different kinds of astrolabe retes with which the author was familiar. (The better-known treatise by al-Bīrūnī is based on this.[6]) The treatise of ᶜAlī b. Khalaf (*fl.* Toledo, *c.* 475/1082), known only in a translation in Old Spanish, deals with a universal astrolabe which does not need any plates for different latitudes. A series of treatises also originating in fifth/eleventh century Toledo deals with a simplification of this instrument consisting of a single plate known as the *shakkāziyyah*, and of the same plate with markings for the co-ordinate systems of both the celestial equator and the ecliptic, known as the *zarqāliyyah*, after the astronomer al-Zarqālī (d. 494/1100).

Islamic treatises on different kinds of computing devices in the form of a quadrant, notably the sinical quadrant with a trigonometric grid, and the horary quadrant with fixed or movable cursor for reckoning the time of day from solar altitude, date back to third/ninth-century Baghdad. A wide variety of types of quadrants is described by Abū ᶜAlī al-Marrākushī

[6] See below, ch. 24, 413.

(see below) who worked in Cairo in the seventh/thirteenth century, but not any kind of almucantar quadrant. In the early eighth/fourteenth century there appeared in Syria a series of treatises on the almucantar quadrant and modifications thereon, but in the earliest known Arabic treatises on the simple almucantar quadrant, the authors make no claim to have invented the instrument. The origin of the almucantar quadrant in Islam has thus yet to be explained; in Christian Europe it was introduced by Profatius in the thirteenth century.

As with literature on the quadrant, so Islamic literature on sundial theory and construction received new impetus in the seventh/thirteenth, eighth/fourteenth, and ninth/fifteenth centuries, notably in Mamlūk Egypt and Syria. In a seventh/thirteenth-century Egyptian treatise by al-Maqsī we find tables for the construction of horizontal sundials for different latitudes, and of vertical sundials for the latitude of Cairo for each degree of inclination to the meridian, as well as for sundials skew to both the meridian and the horizon. The number of treatises on sundials from this period is by no means matched by the number of extant sundials. With some notable exceptions most surviving Islamic sundials date from the late Ottoman period.

The most important Islamic treatise on instruments has yet to be studied properly. This is the *Jāmiᶜ al-mabādiᵓ wa-ᵓl-ghāyāt* of Abū ᶜAlī al-Marrākushī. It is a compendium dealing with spherical astronomy and instruments, based on earlier treatises most of which are no longer extant. The first half of this treatise dealing with spherical astronomy and sundials was translated by J. J. Sédillot in 1834. The other half dealing with instruments was studied in a rather haphazard fashion by L. A. Sédillot in 1844. Al-Marrākushī discusses a variety of analogue computer devices, an analysis of which, together with an investigation of his sources, would add much to our knowledge of Islamic instrumentation.

Islamic treatises on observational instruments are restricted to descriptions of individual instruments such as meridian quadrants for measuring altitudes in the meridian, until the appearance of the treatise on the instruments used at the observatory at Marāghah in the seventh/thirteenth century, written by one of the astronomers there, Muᵓayyad al-Dīn al-ᶜUrḍī. This treatise, and the later one by Taqī ᵓl-Dīn, discussing the instruments used at the observatory which he directed in Istanbul in the tenth/sixteenth century, have been published and investigated to establish the relationship of the instruments described and the instruments used in the earliest European observatories of the sixteenth century. No other treatises of consequence survive on the activities of the various Islamic observatories. One *Kitāb ᶜAmal al-raṣad* on the activities of the Afḍal-Baṭāᵓiḥī observatory in sixth/twelfth-century Cairo is no longer extant, though it was available to the Egyptian historian al-Maqrīzī in the ninth/fifteenth century. A. Sayili's valuable study, *The Observatory in Islam*, published in 1960, is based on all available material on observational instruments, and the introductions to a substantial number of *zīj*s, as well as extracts from medieval historians and geographers relating to observatories or observations.

AL-BĪRŪNĪ

The works of a scholar of the calibre and prolificity of al-Bīrūnī inevitably defy simple classification. This is already obvious from his *al-Āthār al-bāqiyah* on chronology, his *zīj* called *al-Qānūn al-Masʿūdī*, and his astrological work *al-Tafhīm*. Among his works on astronomy we may mention in particular the recently rediscovered *Kitāb Maqālīd al-hayʾah*, on the rules of spherical trigonometry and their application to spherical astronomy, extant in a unique manuscript in Tehran. In this work al-Bīrūnī presents not only the rules and their application, but also a historical discussion of the work of earlier Muslim astronomers in this field.

CONCLUSION

Any brief survey of the categories of Islamic astronomical literature will not do justice to the scope of a corpus of literature compiled during a period of time exceeding a millennium, in a society which considered astronomy one of the most important branches of scientific knowledge. Anyone who leafs through the pages of Fuat Sezgin's volume of his *Geschichte des arabischen Schrifttums* dealing with astronomy (vol. VI) will see the amount of scientific material available from the first four centuries of Islam. The amount of material available from later centuries is considerably greater. Three out of about 200 Islamic *zīj*s have been published. We have no published edition of the Arabic versions of the *Almagest*, or of any Arabic recensions or commentaries. The majority of published Arabic scientific texts were prepared in Hyderabad, most with no critical apparatus. There is an obvious need for reproductions in printed form of manuscripts of particular importance, since the historian of Islamic astronomy has to rely mainly on microfilms of manuscripts, which some libraries are unable or unwilling to supply.

In 1845 L. A. Sédillot, whose privilege it was to have access to the rich collection of Arabic and Persian scientific manuscripts in the Bibliothèque Nationale in Paris, wrote: "Each day brings some new discovery and illustrates the extreme importance of a thorough study of the manuscripts of the East." Given the vast amount of available material preserved in the libraries of the world, and the small number of scholars who are working in this field, Sédillot's statement is no less true now than it was over 140 years ago.

CHAPTER 16

ASTROLOGY

Astrology has had a deep and pervasive influence on the thought and culture of the Arabs and Persians; and it has also had effects on Arabic literature in that many metaphors and other tropes are based on the ideas and technical terminology of astrology. In another respect too it has been influential. Starting from the initial, now discredited, premise that astronomical events have a reflection in sublunary events, the astrologers sought to develop principles for the practical application of this premise by methods which include the matching of observed astronomical events with actual human events. This methodology, of relying on observation as a criterion for establishing general principles, is a strictly scientific one, and was a fruitful forerunner of the observational technique characteristic of true science and especially noteworthy in, for example, the clinical approach to medicine of Abū Bakr Muḥammad b. Zakariyyāʾ al-Rāzī. At the same time, it must not be supposed that astrology had a total dominance over Arab thought. At all periods there were individuals who, for either religious or purely intellectual reasons, rejected the initial premise of astrology and consequently the whole of the art.

THE SOURCES OF ARABIC ASTROLOGY

Methods of predicting the future on the assumption that the motions of the heavenly spheres are the efficient causes of changes in the sublunar world of the four Empedoclean elements were developed in Hellenistic Egypt, and became the "science" or "mathesis" of the Roman empire; thence it spread to India and to Iran. From Greek, Sanskrit, Pahlavi and Syriac, astrological texts were translated into Arabic, especially in the late second/eighth century; and then the main branches of Arabic astrology were established: genethlialogy (including anniversary themes), dealing with individuals; astrological history, dealing with peoples, rulers and religions; catarchic astrology, dealing with the forecasting of undertakings and the proper times for initiating actions; and interrogations, dealing with responses to queries. Most of our extant astrological literature was composed in the third/ninth century on the basis of these earlier translations; the outstanding astrologer of that period was Abū Maᶜshar, who wrote the "classic" texts on genethlialogy and astrological history, and formulated the philosophical rationale for astrology that satisfied later generations of believers. A few interesting introductions to astrology were written in the fourth/tenth and fifth/eleventh centuries, but thereafter (so far as is yet apparent) the only works of significance were compendia of the views of earlier authorities.

The period during which Arabic astrological literature was created, then, was very brief, but its extent is vast. Unfortunately, few texts have been studied in modern times, and even fewer edited. The following survey can, therefore, do little more than indicate the authors and the relations of their works to each other and to the tradition in general. It is not possible, though this is a history of literature, to discuss the literary merits of astrological texts. The Arabic is generally clear and straightforward, and only the technicalities of the subject at times plunge the uninitiated reader into incomprehension.

THE EARLIEST ASTROLOGICAL WORKS IN ARABIC

The earliest Arabic text relating to astrology that we know of happens to deal with celestial omens ultimately descended from the Old Babylonian texts included in *Enūma Anu Enlil*. This text, the *Apocalypse* of Daniel, is preserved for us only in a Greek translation made by one Alexius of Byzantium in AD 1245, who reports that the Arabic text that he translates was turned into that language from a manuscript discovered by Muᶜāwiyah (reigned 41–60/661–80) in the course of his campaign in the environs of Constantinople during the reign of Constans II (reigned AD 641–68).[1] The omens interpreted by the text include solar and lunar eclipses, haloes around the two luminaries, the new moon, comets, falling stars, rainbows, flashes, the reddening of the sky, thunder, lightning, rain, hail, earthquakes, etc. Other versions of the *Apocalypse* survive in Greek and in Syriac;[2] and there exist in Arabic three versions of a *Milḥah* or *Malḥamah* of Daniel,[3] of which

[1] *GAS*, VII, 312–17.

[2] G. Furlani, "Di una raccolta di trattati astrologici", *Rivista degli studi orientali*, VII, 1916–18, 885–9; and "Astrologisches aus syrischen Handschriften", *Zeitschrift der Deutschen Morgenländischen Gesellschaft*, LXXV, 1921, 122–8, esp. 122–5.

[3] G. Furlani, "Eine Sammlung astrologischer Abhandlungen in arabischer Sprache", *Zeitschrift der Assyriologie*, XXXIII, 1921, 157–68; Fahd, *La Divination Arabe*, 408–12; Ullmann, *Natur- und Geheimwissenschaften*, 293.

the longest is stated to have been translated from Syriac and to be based on Dhū ʾl-Qarnayn (Alexander), Balaʿam, Andronicus,[4] Ptolemy, Hermes and ʿUzayr (Ezra) or ʿAzīz the Scribe.[5] Such celestial omens are also described in some detail in the second book of Ptolemy's *Apotelesmatika*, and thence entered the Arabic tradition of astrology. Other texts in Arabic dealing with celestial omens are attributed to Hermes, who is the alleged author of numerous astrological treatises as well;[6] much of this Hermetic literature probably originated in Ḥarrān. Also belonging to the literature on celestial omens are the treatises dealing with predictions based on the twenty-eight lunar mansions[7] and the hemerologies.[8] Similar celestial omens were preserved among non-Muslim Syrians[9] and Mandaeans[10] under Arab domination.

The oldest treatise on genethlialogy that survives in Arabic is a *Kitāb al-Mawālid wa-aḥkāmihā* ("Book of Nativities and their Judgements") of Zarādusht.[11] This allegedly was first written in the language of the Dīn dabīrih (Avestan script), but was translated into Pahlavi and commented upon by Māhānkard b. Mihrziyār for Māhūya b. Māhānāhīdh the Marzubān in the year in which Ctesiphon fell to the Arabs (16/637). The Pahlavi version was turned into Arabic by Saʿīd b. Khurāsānkhurrah for the Ispahbad Sunbād, who served under Abū Muslim (132–7/750–5). This work deals with various technical details of interpreting the themes of natives (diagrams illustrating horoscopes) assuming that the reader has a fairly thorough knowledge of astrology already. The topics discussed include the effects of the sun in the several astrological places, the *haylāj* (prorogator) and the *kadhkhudāh* (lord of the significant luminary's term), the dodecatopos (the twelve astrological places), anniversary themes and the influence on natives of selected fixed stars. The whole is illustrated by examples datable to the Sasanid period. In part Zarādusht (or Māhānkard) has followed the Pahlavi

4 Cf. A. Mingana, "Some early Judaeo-Christian documents in the John Rylands library", *Bulletin of the John Rylands Library*, IV, 1917–18, 59–118. 5 Furlani, "Astrologisches", 125–8.

6 L. Massignon, "Inventaire de la littérature hermétique arabe" in A. J. Festugière, *La Révélation d'Hermès Trismégiste*, I, 2, Paris, 1950, 384–400; Ullmann, *Natur- und Geheimwissenschaften*, 289–93; *GAS*, VII, 50–8.

7 C. Pellat, *Abū Muḥammad ʿAbdallāh ibn Muslim ibn Qutayba al-Dīnawarī, Kitāb al-anwāʾ*, Hyderabad-Deccan, 1956; Fahd, *La Divination Arabe*, 412–17.

8 Fahd, *La Divination Arabe*, 483–88; R. G. Khoury, "Un fragment astrologique inédit attribué à Wahb b. Munabbih", *Arabica*, XIX, 1972, 139–44; M. J. L. Young, "An Arabic almanac of favourable and unfavourable days", *Journal of Semitic Studies*, XXVII, 1982, 261–79.

9 E. A. Wallis Budge, *Syrian Anatomy, Pathology and Therapeutics*, Oxford, 1913, I, 441–3, 546–53; II, 520–2, 648–55.

10 E. S. Drower, *The Book of the Zodiac*, London, 1949, 119–20, 127–54, 158–9, 164–83, 188–93; *GAS*, VII, 81–6.

11 D. Pingree, "Māshāʾallāh: some Sasanian and Syriac sources" in *Essays on Islamic Philosophy and Science*, Albany, 1975, 5–14; "Classical and Byzantine astrology in Sassanian Persia", *Dumbarton Oaks Papers*, XLIII, 1989, 227–39.

translation of Dorotheus of Sidon, which was turned into Arabic in about 184/800.

THE PERSIAN INFLUENCE

The existence of a strong astrological tradition in the Sasanid empire helps to explain the preponderance of Iranian astrologers among those who created an Arabic astrological literature in the early ʿAbbasid period. The Pahlavi texts with which they worked were primarily the translations made from Greek and Sanskrit in the third Christian century, [12] representing a conflation of Hellenistic astrology with elements derived from its Indian offshoot.[13] These Iranian astrologers include Nawbakht, Māshāʾallāh b. Atharī al-Baṣrī and Abū Ḥafṣ ʿUmar b. al-Farrukhān al-Ṭabarī; these three were joined by Muḥammad b. Ibrāhīm b. Ḥabīb al-Fazārī, who was descended from an old Arab family of Kufa, in casting the catarchic theme for the foundation of Baghdad on 3 Jumādā I 145/30 July 762 for al-Manṣūr.[14]

Nawbakht and his son Abū Sahl al-Faḍl (d. after 193/809),[15] who claimed descent from the Kayanian hero Gēv, the son of Gōdharz, but who converted from Zoroastrianism to Islam at al-Manṣūr's court, were the leading astrological advisers to that caliph (reigned 136–58/754–75). Nawbakht's sole known work is the brief *Risālah fī Sarāʾir aḥkām al-nujūm* ("Epistle on the Secrets of Judicial Astrology"), but Abū Sahl was more active as an author. He is said to have versified al-Ahwāzī's Arabic translation of *Kalīlah wa-Dimnah* for Yaḥyā b. Khālid al-Barmakī (d. 190/805) between 160/776 and 187/803, and to have translated Pahlavi books into Arabic in the Khizānat al-Ḥikmah under Hārūn al-Rashīd. Only fragments survive of his works, including an important passage from his *Kitāb al-Nahmaṭān fī ʾl-mawālid* on the transmission of science and its preservation in Iran[16]. Other books of his are known to have dealt with nativities, anniversary themes and interrogations. The descendants of Abū Sahl continued to practise astrology at the ʿAbbasid court during the first half of the third/ninth century;[17] al-Ḥasan b. Sahl is the one most frequently quoted by later astrologers.

12 D. Pingree, *The Thousands of Abū Maʿshar*, London, 1968, 7–10.

13 Pingree, "Māshāʾallāh", 5–8; "The Indian and pseudo-Indian passages in Greek and Latin astronomical and astrological texts", *Viator*, VII, 1976, 141–95.

14 D. Pingree, "The fragments of the works of al-Fazārī", *Journal of Near Eastern Studies*, XXIX, 1970, 103–23.

15 Ullmann, *Natur- und Geheimwissenschaften*, 303; D. Pingree, *Encyclopaedia Iranica*, I, London, 1985, 369; *GAS*, VII, 100–1, 114.

16 Pingree, *Thousands*, 9–12.

17 Ullmann, *Natur- und Geheimwissenschaften*, 308; A. Labarta, *Mūsā ibn Nawbajt: al-Kitāb al-Kāmil*, Madrid, 1982.

Māshāʾallāh[18] was a (Persian?) Jew from Basra who worked as an astrologer in Iraq from at least 145/762 until about 200/815.[19] The first to introduce elements of Aristotelian physics into Arabic, presumably from a Ḥarranian source, in his *De scientia motus orbis*, he relied for his astrological doctrines on Pahlavi (Dorotheus, Valens and the Indians[20]), Greek (Rhetorius) and Syriac (Ptolemy and Hermes probably) texts. Of his numerous works few survive in Arabic, though more are extant in Latin, Hebrew and Persian, and there are many fragments in these four languages as well as in Byzantine Greek. On genethlialogy his *Kitāb al-Mawālid al-kabīr* survives in a Latin translation made by Hugo of Sanctalla between AD 1141 and AD 1151, while his *Kitāb al-Mawālid*, based on Dorotheus and a Byzantine treatise of the sixth Christian century, not only survives in Latin,[21] but was plagiarized by Māshāʾallāh's pupil, Abū ʿAlī Yaḥyā b. Ghālib al-Khayyāṭ (d. first quarter of third/ninth century). Among his many other works the most noteworthy are those devoted to astrological history, a science perfected in Sasanid Iran.[22]

Fī ʾl-Qirānāt wa-ʾl-adyān wa-ʾl-milal ("On Conjunctions and Religions and Sects"), which Māshāʾallāh wrote shortly before 197/813, combines Zoroastrian millennianism with the theory of the revolutions of the conjunctions of Saturn and Jupiter through the four triplicities (i.e. the four groupings of three signs 120° and 240° distant from each other; thus Aries–Leo–Sagittarius; Taurus–Virgo–Capricorn, etc.). In its original form it predicted the downfall of the ʿAbbasid dynasty and the restoration of Iranian rule in 200/815; this was changed by the redactor who has preserved the text for us, Ibn Hibintā, who substitutes the triumph of Aḥmad b. Buwayh in 334/945.[23]

Fī Qiyām al-khulafāʾ wa-maʿrifat qiyām kull malik ("On the Rise of Caliphs and the Knowledge of the Rise of every King"), written shortly after 193/809, contains themes of the vernal equinoxes of the years in which the reign of each caliph down to Hārūn al-Rashīd began.[24] Such astrological histories were very popular in Islam.[25] For the proper interpretation of historical themes Māshāʾallāh wrote a number of theoretical works, some of which survive in Latin.

[18] Ullmann, *Natur- und Geheimwissenschaften* 303–6; Pingree, *Dictionary of Scientific Biography*, IX, 159–62; *GAS*, VII, 102–8, 324. [19] Pingree, "Māshāʾallāh", 9–12.

[20] Pingree, "Indian and pseudo-Indian passages", 149–51, 181–2; "Classical and Byzantine astrology".

[21] Kennedy and Pingree, *Astrological History of Māshāʾallāh*, 145–74.

[22] D. Pingree, "Historical horoscopes", *Journal of the American Oriental Society*, LXXXII, 1962, 487–502.

[23] Kennedy and Pingree, *Astrological History of Māshāʾallāh*, 1–125. [24] Ibid., 129–43.

[25] E. S. Kennedy, "Ramifications of the world-year concept in Islamic astrology", *Actes du Dixième Congrès International d'Histoire des Sciences*, Paris, 1964, I 23–43.

Māshāʾallāh's colleague, ʿUmar b. al-Farrukhān al-Ṭabarī,[26] was associated not only with al-Manṣūr, but, like Abū Sahl b. Nawbakht, also with Yaḥyā b. Khālid al-Barmakī. Also like Abū Sahl, he translated Pahlavi books into Arabic; due to him are Arabic versions of Dorotheus of Sidon[27] and a commentary on Ptolemy's *Apotelesmatika* (*Kitāb al-Arbaʿah*) which Abū Yaḥyā b. al-Baṭrīq translated for him. His major independent works are the *Kitāb al-Masāʾil*, on astrological interrogations, in 138 chapters, and the *Kitāb fī ʾl-Mawālid*, on genethlialogy, in three books; of both there exist Latin translations. In the latter of these two works he not surprisingly relies on Dorotheus, Ptolemy and Māshāʾallāh. There also survives in a Latin translation by John of Seville a fourth/tenth century or fifth/eleventh century reworking of his *Liber universus* on astrological history, based on the doctrine of Kanaka the Indian,[28] who is known to have been an astrologer in the court of Hārūn al-Rashīd and whose astrological history of the caliphs ends in the reign of al-Maʾmūn.[29]

A somewhat older contemporary of these early ʿAbbasid astrologers was Thawfīl b. Tūmā or Theophilus of Edessa, a Syrian Christian who was adviser to al-Mahdī and who died – allegedly at the age of ninety – on the 2 or 3 Muḥarram 169/15 or 16 July 785.[30] He wrote extensive works on military astrology, genethlialogy and catarchic astrology with interrogations; his sources were mainly Greek, but he had some knowledge of Indian astrology as well, presumably derived from Sasanid Iran. These works, though often quoted by Arabic writers, survive as complete entities only in Byzantine Greek versions that are probably due to Theophilus himself.

ASTROLOGY IN THE THIRD/NINTH CENTURY

Arabic astrology continued to be impressively influential during the reign of al-Maʾmūn, though the initial surge of translation activity diminished considerably; the third/ninth-century translators worked far more industriously in the field of astronomy than in that of astrology. The two most important authors of this period were al-Khayyāṭ,[31] and Abū ʿUthmān Sahl b. Bishr al-Isrāʾīlī[32] who served Ṭāhir b. al-Ḥusayn at Marw in Khurāsān

26 Ullmann, *Natur- und Geheimwissenschaften*, 306–7; Pingree, *Dictionary of Scientific Biography*, XIII, 538–9; *GAS*, VII, 111–13, 324–5.
27 D. Pingree, *Dorothei Sidonii Carmen astrologicum*, Leipzig, 1976.
28 D. Pingree, "The Liber Universus of ʿUmar ibn al-Farrukhān al-Ṭabarī", *Journal for the History of Arab Science*, I, 1977, 8–12.
29 Pingree, *Dictionary of Scientific Biography*, VII, 222–4; *GAS*, VII, 95–6.
30 Ullmann, *Natur- und Geheimwissenschaften*, 302; Pingree, "Indian and pseudo-Indian passages", 148–9; *GAS*, VII, 49–50.
31 Ullmann, *Natur- und Geheimwissenschaften*, 312–13; *GAS*, VII, 120–1.
32 Ullmann, *Natur- und Geheimwissenschaften*, 125–8, 309–12, 325.

(205–7/821–2) and the vizier al-Ḥasan b. Sahl b. Nawbakht in Baghdad. Al-Khayyāṭ wrote on genethlialogy a *Kitāb Aḥkām al-mawālid*, of which a large part, as we have noted before, was plagiarized from Māshāʾallāh, though Ptolemy and Dorotheus also appear to be among his sources; this work was twice translated into Latin – in AD 1136 by Plato of Tivoli and in AD 1153 by John of Seville. His treatise on interrogations, entitled *Kitāb al-Masāʾil*, has not been investigated. Sahl's works include a *Kitāb al-Aḥkām ʿalā ʾl-niṣbah al-falakiyyah* on interrogations, also largely dependent on Dorotheus;[33] there exist both Latin and Byzantine Greek translations. On catarchic astrology Sahl wrote a *Kitāb al-Ikhtiyārāt ʿalā ʾl-buyūt al-ithnay ʿashar* ("Book of Elections according to the Twelve Houses"), in structure at least imitating Theophilus' work on the same subject. The last book of some significance that we know to have been penned by Sahl is his *Kitāb Taḥāwīl sinī ʾl-ʿālam* ("Book of Revolutions of the Years of the World"), of which a summary is extant; in this summary, and therefore probably in Sahl's original, al-Khayyāṭ and Yaʿqūb b. Isḥāq al-Kindī[34] are cited.

A somewhat younger contemporary of al-Khayyāṭ and Sahl was Abū Bakr al-Ḥasan b. al-Khaṣīb (third/ninth century)[35] from Kufa. His *Kitāb al-Mawālid* is one of the most elaborate books extant on genethlialogy; it deals with all the implications for the native's life of each of the twelve astrological places. Concerning anniversary themes he composed a *Kitāb Taḥāwīl sinī ʾl-mawālid*. For his theories in both these works he is indebted to Dorotheus, Ptolemy, Hermes, Andarzghar, ʿUmar b. al-Farrukhān al-Ṭabarī and al-Ḥasan b. Sahl. Both treatises were translated into Latin, the former by Salio of Padua in the seventh/thirteenth century, the latter by Plato of Tivoli in the sixth/twelfth.

An acquaintance of Ibn al-Khaṣīb was Abū ʾl-ʿAnbas Muḥammad b. Isḥāq al-Ṣaymarī (213–75/828–88).[36] His *Kitāb Aṣl al-uṣūl* ("Book of the Basis of Bases") begins with a discussion of general astrological doctrines; a second section (if it is really part of this work) consists of valuable compendium on catarchic astrology and interrogations arranged in the order of the astrological places and derived from such sources as Zeno, Antiochus, Dorotheus, Valens, Zarādusht, Buzurgmihr, Jina the Indian and Māshāʾallāh.

33 V. Stegemann, *Dorotheos von Sidon und das sogenannte Introductorium des Sahl ibn Bišr*, Prague, 1942.

34 O. Loth, "Al-Kindi als Astrolog", *Morgenländische Forschungen*, Leipzig, 1875, 261–309; Ullmann, *Natur- und Geheimwissenschaften*, 313–14; F. Klein-Franke, "Die Ursachen der Krisen bei akuten Krankheiten", *Israel Oriental Studies*, v, 1975, 161–88; *GAS*, vii, 130–4, 326–7.

35 Ullmann, *Natur- und Geheimwissenschaften*, 308–9; *GAS*, vii, 122–4.

36 Ullmann, *Natur- und Geheimwissenschaften*, 325–6; *GAS*, vii, 152–3; Pingree, *Encyclopaedia Iranica*, i, 259.

A much larger compendium was composed by Abū Yūsuf Yaᶜqūb b. ᶜAlī al-Qaṣrānī,[37] who was in the retinue of the ᶜAlids of Ṭabaristān from at least 250/864 until 270/884.[38] His enormous *Jāmiᶜ al-kitāb* or *Kitāb al-Masāʾil*, on interrogations, comprises excerpts from the same authorities as had contributed to the second section of the *Kitāb Aṣl al-uṣūl* (though in far greater profusion) as well as from such additional authorities as Theophilus of Edessa and Stephanus Byzantinus.

ABŪ MAᶜSHAR JAᶜFAR AL-BALKHĪ

The most impressive astrologer writing in Arabic in the third/ninth century, however, was Abū Maᶜshar Jaᶜfar b. Muḥammad al-Balkhī (171–272/787–886).[39] He formulated the standard expression of Islamic astrological doctrine in its major fields of genethlialogy and astrological history, creating a synthesis of the Indian,[40] Iranian, Greek and Ḥarranian theories current in his day. Of particular importance were his philosophical justification of astrology in terms of a late neo-Platonic interpretation of Aristotelian physics,[41] a justification that he apparently borrowed from Ḥarrān, and his theory of the derivation of astrological knowledge of all civilized nations from an antediluvian revelation.[42] The major works in which his views were expressed are the *Kitāb al-Madkhal al-kabīr*, two works entitled *Kitāb Aḥkām al-mawālid*, and the *Kitāb Taḥāwīl sinī ʾl-mawālid* on genethlialogy and anniversary themes, and the *Kitāb al-qirānāt* and *Kitāb al-Nukat* on astrological history; of the first of these, which was translated into Latin by John of Seville in AD 1133 and by Hermann of Carinthia in AD 1140, Abū Maᶜshar wrote an epitome, the *Kitāb al-Madkhal al-ṣaghīr*, which was translated into Latin by Adelard of Bath in the early sixth/twelfth century and is probably the basis of the third book of the Byzantine *Mysteria* of Apomasar. The first five of the nine books of the *Kitāb Taḥāwīl sinī ʾl-mawālid* were also translated into Greek in about AD 1000,[43] and from

37 Ullmann, *Natur- und Geheimwissenschaften*, 314–5; D. Pingree, "Political horoscopes from the reign of Zeno", *Dumbarton Oaks Papers*, XXX, 1977, 135–50; *GAS*, VII, 138–9.

38 D. Pingree and W. Madelung, "Political horoscopes relating to late ninth century ᶜAlids", *Journal of Near Eastern Studies*, XXXVI, 1977, 247–75.

39 Pingree, *Dictionary of Scientific Biography*, I, 32–9; Ullmann, *Natur- und Geheimwissenschaften*, 316–24; *GAS*, VII, 139–51, 328–9; Pingree, *Encyclopaedia Iranica*, I, 337–40.

40 Pingree, "Indian and pseudo-Indian passages", 170–4.

41 R. Lemay, *Abū Maᶜshar and Latin Aristotelianism in the Twelfth Century*, Beirut, 1962; J. C. Vadet, "Une défense de l'astrologie dans le madḫal d'Abū Maᶜšar al-Balḫi", *Annales Islamologiques*, V, 1963, 131–80. 42 Pingree, *Thousands*.

43 D. Pingree, *Albumasaris De revolutionibus nativitatum*, Leipzig, 1968.

Greek into Latin in the seventh/thirteenth century. The *Kitāb al-Qirānāt* and the *Kitāb al-Nukat* were both turned into Latin by John of Seville. Abū Maᶜshar wrote many other influential works on interrogations and catarchic astrology and on special topics in genethlialogy, but of greater interest for the historian of astrology is the collection of his sayings, *Mudhākarāt*,[44] made by his pupil, Abū Saᶜīd Shādhān b. Baḥr, which contains a wealth of information about astrologers and astrological practice in Baghdad in the ᶜAbbasid period.[45] The author of the Byzantine version of the *Kitāb Taḥāwīl sinī ʾl-mawālid* wrote a Greek epitome of this work, which was translated into Latin in the seventh/thirteenth century.[46]

Of the well-known Ḥarranian scholars contemporary with Abū Maᶜshar the only ones that need here be mentioned are those who were involved in the explication of Ptolemy's *Apotelesmatika* in the translation of Ibrāhīm b. al-Ṣalt as revised by Ḥunayn b. Isḥāq. Thābit b. Qurrah (221–88/836–901)[47] commented on the first book, while Muḥammad b. Jābir b. Sinān al-Battānī (d. 317/929)[48] explained all four. Other commentaries were written by al-Faḍl b. Ḥātim al-Nayrīzī (d. *c.* 310/922),[49] probably at Baghdad, and by ᶜAlī b. Riḍwān (377–460/988–1068)[50] in Cairo. The last was translated into Latin by Aegidius de Thebaldis in the seventh/thirteenth century.

Falsely attributed to Ptolemy is the extremely popular *Kitāb al-Thamarah*, on which a commentary was written by Abū Jaᶜfar Aḥmad b. Yūsuf b. al-Dāyah[51] under the Ṭulunids in Egypt in about 287/900; R. Lemay is probably right in asserting that Aḥmad himself forged this *Centiloquium*. The work is a collection of sayings relevant to many aspects of astrology. There exist a Byzantine version[52] and Latin translations from the Arabic by Hugo of Sanctalla and John of Seville in the sixth/twelfth century, and by William of Aragon in the seventh/thirteenth; the Greek was turned into Latin by Giovanni Gioviano Pontano and George of Trebizond in the ninth/fifteenth century. The *Kitāb al-Thamarah* was also commented on by Naṣīr al-Dīn al-Ṭūsī.[53]

44 D. M. Dunlop, "The *Mudhākarāt fī ᶜIlm an-Nujūm* (Dialogues on Astrology) attributed to Abū Maᶜshar al-Balkhī (Albumasar)", *Iran and Islam*, Edinburgh, 1971, 229–46.

45 E.g. F. Rosenthal, "From Arabic books and manuscripts x: a list of astrological works from the 'Discussions' of Abū Maᶜshar and Shādhān", *Journal of the American Oriental Society*, LXXXIII, 1963, 454–6.

46 L. Thorndike, "Albumasar in Sadan", *Isis*, XLV, 1954, 22–32.

47 B.A. Rosenfeld and A.T. Grigorian, *Dictionary of Scientific Biography*, XIII, 288–95; *GAS*, VII, 151–2, 329.

48 W. Hartner, *Dictionary of Scientific Biography*, I, 507–16; Ullmann, *Natur- und Geheimwissenschaften*, 328–9; *GAS*, VII, 158–60.

49 A. I. Sabra, *Dictionary of Scientific Biography*, X, 5–7; Ullmann, *Natur- und Geheimwissenschaften*, 328; *GAS*, VII, 156.

50 R. Arnaldez, *Dictionary of Scientific Biography*, XI, 444–5; *GAS*, VII, 44.

51 Ullmann, *Natur- und Geheimwissenschaften*, 327–8; *GAS*, VII, 157.

52 E. Boer, *Claudii Ptolemaei Opera*, Leipzig, 1952, III, 2, pt.2.

53 Ullmann, *Natur- und Geheimwissenschaften*, 341–2; S. H. Nasr, *Dictionary of Scientific Biography*, XIII, 508–14.

LATER ARABIC ASTROLOGY

After the third/ninth century few astrological treatises were composed, and these were primarily handbooks for beginners or compilations of expert opinions for the adept. In Syria the only authority of note in the fourth/tenth century was Abū ʾl-Ṣaqr ʿAbd al-ʿAzīz b. ʿUthmān al-Qabīṣī[54] who dedicated his *Kitāb al-Madkhal ilā ṣināʿat aḥkām al-nujūm* ("Book of the Introduction to the Art of Judicial Astrology") to Sayf al-Dawlah, the Hamdanid ruler of Aleppo from 333/945 until 356/967. This elementary textbook is chiefly valuable now for its quotations from Hermes, Ptolemy, Dorotheus, Andarzghar, Māshāʾallāh and Yaʿqūb b. Isḥāq al-Kindī. It was translated into Latin by John of Seville in AD 1144, and became the most frequently published astrological text of the Renaissance period.

In Persia the well-known mathematician Abū Saʿīd Aḥmad b. Muḥammad al-Sijzī[55] in the late fourth/tenth century compiled a lengthy *Kitāb al-Jāmiʿ al-shāhī*, in which he summarizes various works and opinions of Abū Maʿshar, Zarādusht, Hermes, Ptolemy and Dorotheus.[56] Al-Sijzī also wrote a *Kitāb al-Qirānāt wa-taḥāwīl sinī ʾl-ʿalām* ("Book of the Conjunctions and the Revolutions of the Years of the World") on astrological history.[57]

Al-Sijzī's younger contemporary, Abū ʾl-Rayḥān al-Bīrūnī,[58] wrote many treatises dealing with particular points in astrology. His major surviving work in the field is the *Kitāb al-Tafhīm li-awāʾil ṣināʿat al-tanjīm* ("Book of Instruction in the Elements of the Art of Astrology").[59] Actually, the first two-thirds of this introduction to astrology deal with the elements of the other sciences – geometry, arithmetic and astronomy – that an astrologer should know; the last third is a useful collection of definitions of astrological terms and summaries of procedures in genethlialogy, catarchic astrology and interrogations. In others of his books, and particularly in his *Kitāb fī Taḥqīq mā li-ʾl-Hind*,[60] al-Bīrūnī informs his Arab readers in some detail about Indian astrology.

The most complete summary of Arabic astrology is the *Kitāb al-Bāriʿ*, compiled by al-Bīrūnī's contemporary, Abū al-Ḥasan ʿAlī b. abī ʾl-Rijāl,[61] astrologer to al-Muʿizz b. Bādīs, the Zirid ruler of north Africa from 406/1016 until 454/1062; Ibn abī ʾl-Rijāl apparently lived until at least the late 430s/1040s. The *Kitāb al-Bāriʿ* deals in eight books with interrogations,

[54] Ullmann, *Natur- und Geheimwissenschaften*, 332–3; Pingree, *Dictionary of Scientific Biography*, XI, 226; *GAS*, VII, 170–1.

[55] Ullmann, *Natur- und Geheimwissenschaften*, 333–4; Y. Dold-Samplonius, *Dictionary of Scientific Biography*, XII, 431–32; *GAS*, VII, 177–82, 333–4.

[56] Pingree, *Thousands*, 21–4.

[57] Ibid., 70–127.

[58] E. S. Kennedy, *Dictionary of Scientific Biography*, II, 147–58; Ullmann, *Natur- und Geheimwissenschaften*, 335; *GAS*, VII, 188–92.

[59] See below, ch. 24, 413–16.

[60] Ibid., 416–17.

[61] *EI*², "Ibn Abī ʾl-Ridjāl"; Ullmann, *Natur- und Geheimwissenschaften*, 335–7; *GAS*, VII, 186–8.

nativities, catarchic astrology, astrological history and astrological meteorology; its sources include a vast array of authorities,[62] the citations from which make it one of an historian's most valuable possessions. It was translated into Latin from the Old Castilian version made by Yehūdāh b. Mōsheh in AD 1254[63] by Aegidius de Thebaldis and Petrus de Regio in AD 1256. Ibn abī ᵓl-Rijāl also wrote one of the few poems on astrology in Arabic, the *Urjūzah fī ᵓl-aḥkām* ("Poem in the Metre *rajaz* on Judicial Astrology").

After the fifth/eleventh century a number of other vast compendia were written in Arabic, the usefulness of which varies with the obscurity of the works which they pillaged. Worthy of mention are the *Kitāb Majmūᶜ aqāwīl al-ḥukamāᵓ* written by Abū Saᶜīd Manṣūr b. ᶜAlī al-Dāmaghānī[64] in the early sixth/twelfth century; the *Kitāb Safīnat al-aḥkām* ascribed to an otherwise unknown al-Nuṣayrī;[65] the compilation composed by Ibrāhīm al-Nāṣirī[66] in 759/1358; and the *Kitāb al-Bulhān* of ᶜAbd al-Ḥasan b. Aḥmad b. ᶜAlī al-Iṣfahānī.[67]

There remain unmentioned in this chapter numerous treatises, anonymous or not, preserved in libraries throughout the world. The scholarly investigation of this vast literature has barely begun; it will take generations to arrive at the point where a technical history of Arabic astrology, treating in detail its sources and its influences as well as its internal development, can be written. The author of the present chapter only hopes to have correctly delineated the several stages of that internal development and to have identified the principal texts upon which future studies must be based.

[62] E.g. V. Stegemann, *Der griechische Astrologe Dorotheos von Sidon und der arabische Astrologe Abū ᵓl-Ḥasan ᶜAlī ibn abī ᵓr-Riğāl, genannt Albohazen*, Heidelberg, 1935.

[63] G. Hilty, *El Libro Conplido en los Iudizios de las Estrellas*, Madrid, 1954.

[64] Ullmann, *Natur- und Geheimwissenschaften*, 337–8.

[65] Ibid., 338–9; *GAS*, VII, 22–4, which ascribes this work to Naṣīr al-Dīn al-Ṭūsī.

[66] Ullmann, *Natur- und Geheimwissenschaften*, 343; Pingree, *Thousands*, 25–6; *GAS*, VII, 25.

[67] Ullmann, *Natur- und Geheimwissenschaften*, 344; *GAS*, VII, 24–5.

CHAPTER 17

GEOGRAPHICAL AND NAVIGATIONAL LITERATURE

The earliest surviving piece of Arabic literature which may fairly be described as an original geographical work is *al-Masālik wa-ʾl-mamālik* of Ibn Khurradādhbih, who was writing during the reign of the caliph al-Muʿtamid (reigned 256–79/870–92). By this time half a century had elapsed since the death of the magnificent al-Maʾmūn who is generally credited with the generous encouragement of the arts and sciences, and more than two centuries since the Arabs had first had their eyes opened to the dazzling novelties of the world outside their arid and barren peninsula. Ibn Khurradādhbih's work describes a vast, well-organized and well-known empire and clearly it must have had some antecedents. Our knowledge of these, however, is extremely fragmentary.

As the Muslim empire grew and became increasingly difficult to administer, its leaders began to feel the need for recorded information about their territories, if only for fiscal and military purposes. It may be surmised that a great deal more information of this kind was written down than we have any knowledge of. There are a few scattered and uninformative hints as to this kind of activity, such as the caliph ʿUmar b. ʿAbd al-ʿAzīz's ordering his newly appointed governor of Spain, in 100/718, to send him a description of "al-Andalus and its rivers", for he had it in mind to evacuate the Muslims from that remote and dangerous territory. For all the Umayyad period information is just as vague, but the first close contact with the Hellenistic world is indicated by Ibn al-Nadīm's account of the doings of Khālid b. Yazīd (d. 85/704), who ordered a company of Egyptian Greeks who were well acquainted with Arabic to translate books on the Art (i.e. of astronomy/astrology) from Greek into Arabic.[1] The names of some of these translators are known and it is certain that from very early in Umayyad times there existed a corps of translators ready to attempt to render the products of a millennium of Greek writing into a language which, less than a century before, had no written literature.

[1] *Fihrist*, trans. Dodge, 581.

It is not until the ᶜAbbasid period that we find ourselves on more solid ground and begin to perceive the emergence of a genuine geographical literature. It is perhaps owing to Greek influence that the earliest works have an astronomical bias. This coincided with the interests of the ᶜAbbasid government, one of whose first preoccupations was a desire to know the length on the earth's surface corresponding to a degree of the celestial sphere as a necessary preliminary to establishing a map of the empire. The tradition of this cosmographical bias was maintained permanently in the more or less lengthy sections on geodesy and astronomy which later became a conventional introduction to books on geography.

Despite this early contact with Greek, the impetus for the systematic approach to cosmography came from India. The first Arabic translation from Sanskrit known was the lost *Zīj al-Arkand* composed about 120/738. Seemingly it was derived from the *Khaṇḍakhādyaka* of Brahmagupta (b. AD 598). However, more solid information about this very obscure period is chiefly associated with Muḥammad b. Ibrāhīm b. Ḥabīb al-Fazārī (d. 191/806) and his *Sindhind*.

THE *SINDHIND*

The *Sindhind*, as such, is lost, and unfortunately there were two al-Fazārīs, father and son, who are confused in the sources, and there are other discordant and obscure features in the accounts. The clearest appears in its oldest form in the *Ṭabaqāt al-umam* of the Spaniard Abū ʾl-Qāsim Ṣāᶜid b. Aḥmad b. Ṣāᶜid al-Qurṭubī (d. 462/1070). The gist of Ṣāᶜid's account is that in 156/772 there arrived at the court of the caliph al-Manṣūr an Indian astronomer bringing with him astronomical tables computed in a manner hitherto unknown to the Arabs (these tables were apparently based on the sine rather than the chord). Al-Manṣūr ordered these tables to be put into Arabic and Muḥammad b. Ibrāhīm al-Fazārī undertook the task, making from them a book which astronomers called "the great *Sindhind*".[2] H. T. Colebrooke[3] was the first to recognize the equivalence of *sindhind* and the Sanskrit word *siddhānta* applied to a number of treatises on astronomy, and identified the work concerned as the *Brāhma(sphuṭa)siddhānta* composed in AD 628 by Brahmagupta. Al-Masᶜūdī too has something to say about this early Indian contact.[4] His account is characteristically muddled but has the merit of indicating the knowledge of the existence, if no more, of a book he calls *Arjabhaz*, which reflects the name of the famous earlier Indian astronomer Āryabhaṭa or his book *Āryabhaṭīya*. Thus the Arabs' first

[2] See al-Qifṭī, *Ikhbār al-ᶜulamāʾ bi-akhbār al-ḥukamāʾ*, 270. [3] *Algebra*, lxv.
[4] *Murūj*, I, 150; *Tanbīh*, 220.

contact with scientific geography was with that of India. The actual books which were the result of this contact are lost, but it is to be supposed that a great deal of the material survived in later works which are extant. It is difficult to distinguish the fruits of this direct contact with India because the Indians in turn had borrowed heavily from the Greeks, and when, soon after, this Indian influence on the Arabs was supplanted entirely by Greek, the earlier Greek material taken by way of India was naturally absorbed in the mass without much trace.

PTOLEMY

The *Arkand* formed the basis for some tables compiled by Abū Jaᶜfar Muḥammad b. Mūsā al-Khwārazmī, which no longer exist in their original form, but for present purposes another work of al-Khwārazmī is more important. This is his *Ṣūrat al-arḍ* ("Depiction of the Earth"). It is closely related to Ptolemy's *Geographia* (*Geographike Hyphegesis*). Since it is the earliest genuine geographical work in Arabic, and since, moreover, for the Arabs the great Greek authority on geography, in comparison with whom all others fade into insignificance, is Ptolemy, the question as to how the Arabs came into possession of their Ptolemaic information is an important one. The problem, in brief, is that the Arabs give much information on the authority of Ptolemy which clearly does come fairly directly from Ptolemy's *Geographia* and yet there is not extant in Arabic any work which may be described as a translation of it. Moreover, the reports of such a translation ever having been made are not clear. It is difficult to believe that a work which was so well known and so often quoted should never have existed in the form of a straightforward translation into Arabic. This seems, however, to be the case. No such translation is extant and there is no clear record that it ever existed.

The Ptolemy in question is Claudius Ptolemy, called in Arabic Baṭlamayūs (or Ibṭulumayūs, etc.) al-Qalūdhī of Alexandria, who flourished during the second century AD. Of his many works only two have a direct bearing on Arab geography: the *Geographia* and the *Megale Syntaxis*. The latter, known to the Arabs as the *Majisṭī* and to medieval Europe as the *Almagest*, was early (*c.* 180/796) translated into Arabic. It is a work on astronomy and deals with geography only in that in his Book One Ptolemy describes the division of the inhabited world into "climes". Here Ptolemy mentions some of the places situated within each clime. The *Geography*, as its Greek title indicates, is rather the work of a cartographer than a geographer in the modern sense. Ptolemy's attention is directed exclusively to establishing the positions of places. His work is therefore basically a list of topographical features with their latitudes and longitudes. Three possible translators of the *Geographia* are mentioned in Arabic sources. Two of these occur in the short note devoted to it by Ibn al-Nadīm in the *Fihrist*: "A bad translation was made for al-Kindī, then Thābit b. Qurrah made a good translation into Arabic. It is also to be found in Syriac."[5] But the later writer al-Qifṭī, obviously copying from the *Fihrist* or its source, says that the *Geographia* was translated not *for* but *by* al-Kindī. There are no references to these translations in the lists of Thābit's and al-Kindī's works elsewhere in the *Fihrist*. The geographer Ibn Khurradādhbih, addressing his dedicatee, makes a brief and obscure statement which might be interpreted to mean that he translated Ptolemy into Arabic. A Syriac version does indeed exist, but it is too condensed to be the source of the detailed Ptolemaic knowledge. Abū ʾl-Fidāʾ refers to *Rasm al-rubʿ al-maʿmūr* ("Drawing of the Inhabited Quarter") as "a book attributed to Ptolemy and put into Arabic for Maʾmūn",[6] and Ḥājjī Khalīfah (d. 1067/1657) speaks of "*Jughrāfiyā*: they put it into Arabic in the time of al-Maʾmūn but the Arabic version is not now to be found"[7]. It seems probable that Abū ʾl-Fidāʾ is actually referring to al-Khwārazmī's book, mentioned below, and Ḥājjī Khalīfah's reference is possibly based on his reading of Abū ʾl-Fidāʾ. The *Kitāb al-Malḥamah* described as being by Ptolemy and quoted by Yāqūt is quite clearly not a translation of the *Geographia*. A telling argument that there never was a straightforward Arabic version of the *Geographia* in existence in the second half of the third/ninth century is the fact that al-Yaʿqūbī, who himself composed a work on geography and was very well acquainted with the *Almagest*, as he shows by giving a detailed and accurate description of its contents in his *Taʾrīkh*, does not include the *Geographia* in his list of Ptolemy's works, nor does he mention it in his own geography, though by then its contents were certainly well known.

ABŪ JAʿFAR MUḤAMMAD B. MŪSĀ AL-KHWĀRAZMĪ

Thus no direct translation of the *Geographia* into Arabic survives and perhaps never existed. The question now to be posed is: is there any work in Arabic which, while not being a direct translation, may be considered to be a version of it? For instance, an arrangement with or without contemporary additions, derived perhaps via a Syriac version or a Greek source such as Theon subsequent to Ptolemy? The answer seems to be that there are two which come close to being so, inasmuch as almost all their information is

5 Trans. Dodge, II, 640.
6 *Géographie d'Aboulféda*, trans. J. T. Reinaud and S. Guyard, Paris, 1840, 22, 74.
7 *Kashf al-ẓunūn*, ed. G. Fluegel, London and Leipzig, 1835–58, II, 603.

taken unchanged from the *Geographia*. These are *Kitāb Ṣūrat al-arḍ* by Muḥammad b. Mūsā al-Khwārazmī (d. *c*. 236/850) and *ᶜAjāᵓib al-aqālīm al-sabᶜah ilā nihāyat al-ᶜimārah* ("Marvels of the Seven Climes to the End of Habitation") by Suhrāb, who was writing some fifty years later. These two books resemble each other very closely indeed so that only one need be discussed here. The *Ṣūrat al-arḍ*, as it now survives (in a single manuscript), seems to be incomplete. Like the *Geographia* it is in tabular form, and many of the individual entries are identical with those in the *Geographia*. Al-Khwārazmī must have suspected that many of these Ptolemaic entries were either imaginary (as in the case of many African places) or no longer identifiable in his day. He retained them, nevertheless, no doubt out of caution and reverence for Ptolemy. There are many new entries to cover places which had come into prominence since the rise of Islam. The arrangement however is quite different from Ptolemy's. Al-Khwārazmī organizes his material according to the longest-day clime system, frequently used afterwards by the Arabs, and he has separate lists for towns, rivers, mountains, etc. where Ptolemy lists them all together. Al-Masᶜūdī's description of the *Geographia* as it appears in the *Murūj* seems to derive from a version where Ptolemy's material had already been arranged somewhat after the manner of al-Khwārazmī, but what he describes is not identical with al-Khwārazmī's work as now extant – but neither is it an exact description of the *Geographia*.

Of al-Khwārazmī nothing is known beyond what is vouchsafed by the two or three lines in the *Fihrist* and a bald reference by al-Muqaddasī. He was attached to the famous Bayt al-Ḥikmah ("House of Wisdom") in Baghdad and his tables (*zīj*) were standard works both before and after al-Maᵓmūn's celebrated *raṣd* (observation, survey) which is about to be described. The caliph al-Wāthiq (reigned 227–32/842–7) had sent him on an unspecified mission to the king of the Khazar (on the north-west shore of the Caspian). This would be in 227/841. Al-Khwārazmī's arrangement of his information according to climes set a pattern followed by numerous authors after him. The basis of this system was to divide the inhabited world as then known, from the Fortunate (i.e. Canary) Islands in the West to the far extremity of China in the East, into strips parallel with the Equator bounded by parallels of latitude corresponding with particular values for the length of the longest day. These strips are called *iqlīm* (clime) and are numbered from One to Seven from South to North. Thus al-Khwārazmī's First Clime extends from the Equator to 16° 20' N because it is at this latitude that the longest day is thirteen hours. His Second Clime extends as far north as 24° 00', his latitude for a longest day of $13\frac{1}{2}$ hours; and so on. These figures are derived from Ptolemy and so were out of date by al-

Khwārazmī's time because of the change in the value of the obliquity of the ecliptic. By negligence, conscious choice, or reverence for Ptolemy, al-Khwārazmī ignored this fact. The system allows for one sub-equatorial clime, but to the south of this and to the north of the Seventh Clime ordinary human life is assumed to be impossible; in any case this is unknown territory. Within the climes, towns and other geographical features are described in order of longitude proceeding from West to East. (It may be mentioned here that Arab maps are oriented with the South towards the top of the sheet.) There are variations on this scheme, but they all have in common the principle of distinguishing the climes by reference to the length of the longest day. By chance this clime system places Iraq and its capital Baghdad in the Fourth, that is the central, Clime. Iraq thus, being in the middle of everything, has the maximum of every virtue. In this way there is a happy link with the other regional systems which begin by placing Iraq at the centre of the inhabited world.

GEODESY

During al-Maʾmūn's lifetime and under his active patronage (symbolized by the establishment of the Bayt al-Ḥikmah), the intellectual outburst characteristic of the early ʿAbbasid age was well under way. By this time the Arabs had fully mastered the astronomy of Ptolemy. It would seem that intellectual curiosity was the mainspring of their activity, because the results of their researches could have had little immediate practical value. It is sometimes said that the astronomers were largely motivated by a desire to know the exact direction of the *qiblah* from any given place for the guidance of individual Muslims as well as for the accurate orientation of mosques, and to be able to fix the times of prayer. But the fact is that the orthodox methods of determining these matters are rules of thumb having nothing to do with exact celestial observation, and in point of fact these topics are not often stressed by astronomical or geographical writers as a justification for their studies.

The Arabs were aware of the results of the famous measurements by Eratosthenes and Posidonius to determine the length on the surface of the earth corresponding with a degree of the celestial meridian. This is a basic dimension from which the size of the earth is known and which is at the foundation of all map-making. Al-Maʾmūn decided that the value of a degree should be redetermined, chiefly because the Greek value for this unit was expressed in *stadia* and there was doubt as to the ratio between the *stadium* and the Arab *mīl*. By now the *mīl* had been standardized, on the basis of the width of a barleycorn, at very close to 2,000 metres. This redetermination was carried out at least twice in different localities chosen for being flat and extensive. One of the best accounts of this procedure is given by al-Bīrūnī in his *Taḥdīd*.[8] Two parties of observers, armed with the best instruments obtainable, proceeded in opposite directions from a point on the plain of Sinjār in northern Mesopotamia along an exact north-south line, which they staked out with poles as they proceeded. As they progressed each party measured the distance travelled and observed the sun's meridian altitude day by day. When they found that the altitude had changed by one degree they retraced their steps, repeating their observations. These observations, adjusted for the change in the sun's declination while they were being made, were enough to determine the result, which was fifty-six *mīl*. Al-Bīrūnī goes on to state that other versions reported the result as $56\frac{2}{3}$ *mīl*, so that there was an urgent need in his day for a repetition of the observation, and he laments that circumstances had never permitted him to undertake it, though he had suitable sites and other methods in mind. In his later *Tafhīm*,[9] he gives the value of $56\frac{2}{3}$ without comment, having no doubt concluded – rightly – that this was a more accurate value.

FROM GEODESY TO *ADAB*

The astronomical and mathematical approach to the depiction of the world as represented by al-Khwārazmī and Suhrāb soon ceased to be the main preoccupation of writers on geography, and their writings began to take on a more human aspect. Mathematics and astronomy became the preserve of a separate technical literature, while places and people became drawn towards the domain of *adab*, general culture. That is not to say that Ptolemy and his disciples were forgotten. On the contrary, their influence remained very strong and for centuries after, on a global as opposed to a regional scale, the Ptolemaic view reigned supreme, though less and less understood, so that most writers on geography considered a section on the Ptolemaic system to be an indispensable part of their introductory matter. By this time the Muslims had acquired a great deal of knowledge and sophistication; they had been exposed to the freely speculative atmosphere of Greek thought; the government of the empire was, for the time being, in the hands of a class headed by a caliph who did not accept the narrowness of the orthodox religious outlook and had established an intellectual ambience that was wide-ranging, free-thinking and intoxicating. The cultured citizens of Baghdad had the feeling that the scope for their intellectual

[8] Partially ed. A. Z. V. Togan, *Bīrūnī's Picture of the World*, Delhi, 1938; and see below, ch. 24, 410–12.
[9] See below, ch. 24, 413–16.

activity was unlimited. Among these people there arose the concept of *adab*. One who aspired to be a possessor of *adab* – an *adīb* – considered that he ought to know something about everything and that there was no topic that did not merit serious investigation. At the same time the Islamic empire was by now very large and complicated, and its administrators needed information if they were to carry out the business of government efficiently. The Iranians were beginning to play a dominant role in intellectual and administrative affairs and clearly the new outlook, seen at its apogee in the "Classical" school of geography to be considered later, was, at least in part the result of peculiarly Iranian preoccupations. These factors (and others) explain how a different kind of geographical material began to attract literary men and to be incorporated into works which are not works of geography exactly but something else – works of edification or recreation (i.e. *adab*-books) or manuals for civil servants, or both in varying proportions. A sort of human geography is born.

The first of these cultured Iranianized administrators to compose a book on geography was ʿUbaydullāh b. al-Qāsim b. Khurradādhbih (d. *c.* 272/885). He seems to have been a typical *kātib* of his time, a literary person who wrote on various subjects, though little of his work has survived except for his geography. Information about him is exceedingly sparse. Indeed, it is to be remarked that compilers of biographies generally have little to say about geographers, no doubt because geography, not being easily definable, was never quite recognized as an independent discipline. A geographer therefore got into a biographical dictionary because he wrote on some other "recognized" subject. Ibn Khurradādhbih, for example, finds a place in Ibn al-Nadīm's *Fihrist* because he wrote also on music, and so is included in Ibn al-Nadīm's section on singers, boon companions, wits, etc. To Ibn al-Nadīm we owe the information that sometime during his life Ibn Khurradādhbih held the office of Director of Posts and Intelligence (*ṣāḥib al-barīd wa-ʾl-khabar*) and it was this activity, presumably, which prompted him to compose his *Kitāb al-Masālik wa-ʾl-mamālik* ("Book of Routes and Realms"). From here it is a facile step to see Ibn Khurradādhbih as the conscientious civil servant composing a manual for the benefit of his fellow functionaries. But this is pure speculation having no real support in the biographical data (a mere four lines in Ibn al-Nadīm) nor the *Masālik* itself. It must always be borne in mind that the citizens of ʿAbbasid Baghdad do not necessarily fit well into the categories of the twentieth century.

Ibn Khurradādhbih divides the world into four regions which clearly represent a Persian tradition. He knows about the seven Greek climes and also about the other Greek division into four regions: Europe, Libya, Ethiopia and Scythia. But these he merely mentions in passing. To his four main regions he adds an additional one, now conceived of as a separate fifth region, namely the Sawād of Iraq, the central metropolitan area where all the others meet. He begins his enumeration with the Sawād not because it is where Baghdad, the capital of the Islamic empire, stands, but because "the kings of Persia used to call it *dil īrānshahr*, that is to say 'the heart of Iraq'".[10] Not only does he quote the phrase in Persian, but he translates *īrān* as *ᶜirāq*, thus betraying a belief, explicit in other writers, that *ᶜirāq* is derived from or is a corruption of *īrān*. The boundaries between his four regions radiate from the Sawād as though it were the centre of a wheel of which they are the spokes. After the Sawād he deals with the *mashriq*, which broadly corresponds to modern Persia and Afghanistan, losing itself in India, China and Central Asia. Next comes the *maghrib*, which consists of northern Iraq, Byzantine territory, Syria, Egypt and all to the west of those. For the northern division he uses the term *jarbī*. This includes Armenia, Ādharbāyjān, Gīlān, Ṭabaristān and everything beyond. Finally the south (*tayman*) corresponds practically with the Arabian peninsula.

Much of this is simply itineraries, lists of districts and tax assessments, but there is a great deal of other information which takes the work well outside the category of manuals for administrators. For instance, it seems as if Ibn Khurradādhbih, in his reading, had collected references in the poets to places, for very frequently he interrupts the dry sequence of place-names to insert a fragment of poetry where the name occurs. Very often he puts in an item of historical information or an anecdote. Having dealt more or less systematically with his four regions he finishes his book with a mass of miscellaneous material: the Rādhāniyyah merchants; the Rūs (i.e. Scandinavians); marvels such as the volcano in Sicily or a place where it never stops raining.

Ibn Khurradādhbih's younger contemporary Ibn Wāḍiḥ al-Yaᶜqūbī uses the same divisions with the same terminology. His *Kitāb al-Buldān* ("Book of the Lands"), as now extant, is incomplete, so that we lack the whole of the *jarbī* and the first part of the *maghrib*. As usual nothing much is known about al-Yaᶜqūbī himself. He must have died about 287/900. Unlike his contemporaries Ibn Khurradādhbih, Ibn al-Faqīh al-Hamadhānī and Ibn Rustih, he seems not to have had a Persian background, being by descent Egyptian though always based on Baghdad. He travelled a great deal and acknowledges that he lost no opportunity to collect information, especially of a historical nature. He is perhaps to be classified rather as a historian than a geographer, for his major work is a substantial history remarkable for its detailed treatment of the pre-Islamic era. The *Kitāb al-Buldān*, composed in

10 *Kitāb al-Masālik wa-ʾl-mamālik*, 5.

276/889, betrays this historical bias, for all the copious non-geographical information which it provides is historical in character. The tone is sober. The literary embellishments of Ibn Khurradādhbih and his taste for marvels are conspicuously lacking. There is not a single line of verse in the whole book. He too begins his description of the Islamic world with Baghdad. The Persian inspiration for this treatment is not as clear as in Ibn Khurradādhbih but it is revealed by his phraseology: "I begin," he says, "with Iraq, because it is the middle of the world and the navel of the earth and I mention Baghdad because it is the middle of Iraq (*wasṭ al-ʿirāq*)." This is an exact echo of *dil īrānshahr*. Notable also by comparison with Ibn Khurradādhbih is his complete neglect of the lands outside the domination of Islam. For him they seem not to exist.

The tendency for the distinction between cultural and technical to become blurred, or for the failure of modern ideas of literary categories to apply to Classical Arabic literature, is even better exemplified by two other writers, Persian also, who flourished at this time. Abū ʿAlī Aḥmad b. ʿUmar b. Rustih (fl. 290/903) was a native of Isfahan who seems not to have made any journeys except for the Pilgrimage. Of his *al-Aʿlāq al-nafīsah* ("The Precious Objects") only Part Seven survives and even that ends in mid-air. This Part Seven does not possess any clear organization and one may only speculate as to the overall scheme of the voluminous work of which it formed part. It is sheer guesswork to characterize Ibn Rustih's work as "a rich source of information about all kinds of subjects that interested the cultivated classes of society".[11] However, the contents of Part Seven are nearly all of a geographical kind. Ibn Rustih begins with extensive quotations from the Qurʾān which he prefixes to a long section on cosmology where he sets forth the Greek theories on the sphericity of the earth, etc. This is followed by another long section on Mecca and Medina. These two features – the insistence on the compatibility of Quranic revelation with pre-Islamic Greek theory and the primacy in treatment accorded to the Islamic Holy Places – along with other scattered indications, lead A. Miquel[12] to suggest that Ibn Rustih was a supporter of the Shuʿūbiyyah, that is the party (naturally composed for the most part of Persians and Turks) who held that the Arabs, despite the fact that the Prophet was one of them, were not necessarily pre-eminent among nations. Ibn Rustih, the Persian nationalist, wished to demonstrate clearly, but with prudence, the virtues of a non-Arab race and of the period before God had bestowed the boon of Islam on mankind (i.e. when the Persian empire was at its height), and yet at the same time to demonstrate his attachment to

[11] EI[1] (suppl.), "Djughrāfiyā".

[12] Miquel, *La Géographie humaine du monde musulman*, 201.

Islam. However, even his Islam is unorthodox, for he seems to be attracted both to the Shīʿah and the Muʿtazilah. His interest in the non-Arab and non-Muslim or doubtfully Muslim Khazar, Bulghār, Rūs, etc., to the exclusion of practically all the western regions of Islam, may point in the same direction. The last part of *al-Aʿlāq al-nafīsah*, in its present truncated form, has nothing to do with geography. The hiatus between this and the previous geographical material is so marked that one might suppose it to be the break between Parts Seven and Eight of the original, but there is no break in either of the two manuscripts extant.

The process by which the province of geography becomes absorbed into the domain of *adab* reaches its climax in another *Kitāb al-Buldān* – that of Ibn al-Faqīh al-Hamadhānī. Ibn al-Faqīh imparts his information not, so to speak, for its own sake but in order to help his reader to attain his ambition to be an *adīb*. What he says is not meant to have any practical use. The utilitarian spirit, clear in al-Yaʿqūbī but becoming fainter as one goes from him to Ibn Khurradādhbih to Ibn Rustih, is here hardly to be perceived at all, and even there it is merely coincidental. Practically nothing is known about the author, nor are we quite clear as to the status of the book ascribed to him. It seems to be well established that Ibn al-Faqīh was a Persian, a native of Hamadhān, who was writing about 290/903, and that the *Kitāb al-Buldān* which we possess is an abridgement by one al-Shayzarī of an original some four or five times the length. As an *adīb*, not a dry geographer, Ibn al-Faqīh is under no obligation to deal with his geographical material in a systematic way. His order of treatment does not seem to follow any plan. It begins with Mecca and Medina and continues with Baḥrayn, then the Yemen, then Egypt. The Maghrib comes next, then Syria. The Islamic world is then left for a time for an excursion into the lands of Byzantium. After that come Iraq and Persia. Another excursion outside Islam to Armenia follows, and the discourse ends with Khurāsān. His geographical information is copiously enlivened with legendary or traditional matter, such as the long account of the city of al-Baht or the embassy to the Rūm. He loves numbers, especially when occurring in apothegms: "ʿAbdullāh b. ʿAmr b. al-ʿĀṣ said: 'There are ten blessings. In Egypt there are nine, in the rest of the earth one. Evil is in ten portions. In Egypt there is one portion, and in all the rest of the earth nine portions.'"[13] In addition to these remotely "geographical" chapters representative of "la littérarisation de thèmes jusque là réservés aux spécialistes"[14] there is a substantial section which has no connection with geography whatever: "The Conversion of Humour to Solemnity and of Solemnity to Humour" as well as numerous

[13] *Mukhtaṣar Kitāb al-Buldān*, 57. [14] Miquel, *La Géographie humaine du monde musulman*, 66.

shorter "irrelevant" passages. Characteristic of the *adīb* is the interest in linguistic matters. Ibn al-Faqīh offers etymologies for many toponyms. At one place he takes the opportunity to parade almost a whole page of *nisbah*-adjectives derived from names of places or peoples: *ṣughdī* daggers, *ṣīnī* saddles, *fārisī* cuirasses, *turkī* bowstrings, etc.

AL-BALKHĪ – AL-IṢṬAKHRĪ – IBN ḤAWQAL – AL-MUQADDASĪ

What some call the "Classical" school of Arabic geographical literature is formed by four writers spanning the century ending in about 390/1000. They are Abū Zayd Aḥmad al-Balkhī (? d. 322/934), Ibrāhīm b. Muḥammad al-Iṣṭakhrī (d. *c.* 350/961), Abū ʾl-Qāsim b. Ḥawqal (d. *c.* 380/990) and Muḥammad b. Aḥmad al-Muqaddasī (d. after 378/988).

Al-Balkhī's book is lost, but M. J. de Goeje[15] long ago demonstrated that al-Iṣṭakhrī's is based on it, though al-Iṣṭakhrī does not say so. Ibn Ḥawqal in turn composed a revised edition of al-Iṣṭakhrī's book. Al-Muqaddasī shows more independence than his predecessors but he was clearly in the same tradition. Of the three he alone indicates unmistakably that he had had al-Balkhī's book in his hand. He was not certain (at least at first) that the book under his eyes was actually the original al-Balkhī or al-Iṣṭakhrī's revision of it. This was the beginning of a confusion about these writers and their works which still persists and has even increased. The only substantial information about Abū Zayd al-Balkhī is that contained in the *Irshād al-arīb* of Yāqūt, but this contains textual and chronological difficulties which make it seem as though the information does not fit the man. It is especially remarkable that Yāqūt, himself the author of a famous geographical dictionary where al-Balkhī's book is referred to, not once refers to this book in his biography of al-Balkhī in the *Irshād*.[16] The confusion is compounded by the fact that the three books extant exist in widely differing recensions and it so happens that al-Muqaddasī's short statement on al-Balkhī exists in two quite different forms. The first form was written when seemingly he had concluded that the book was by al-Iṣṭakhrī, not al-Balkhī, but by the time he was writing the second version he seems to have decided that after all al-Balkhī was the true author. It is difficult to decide what to make of this. All one may say with confidence is that al-Iṣṭakhrī based his work on one of uncertain form by al-Balkhī. With somewhat less confidence one may add that al-Balkhī's work was basically a set of twenty maps to which the text was subsidiary. This set, known through its successors, is referred to by some European writers as the "Atlas of Islam".

[15] "Die Istakhrī Balkhī Frage". [16] 1, 141.

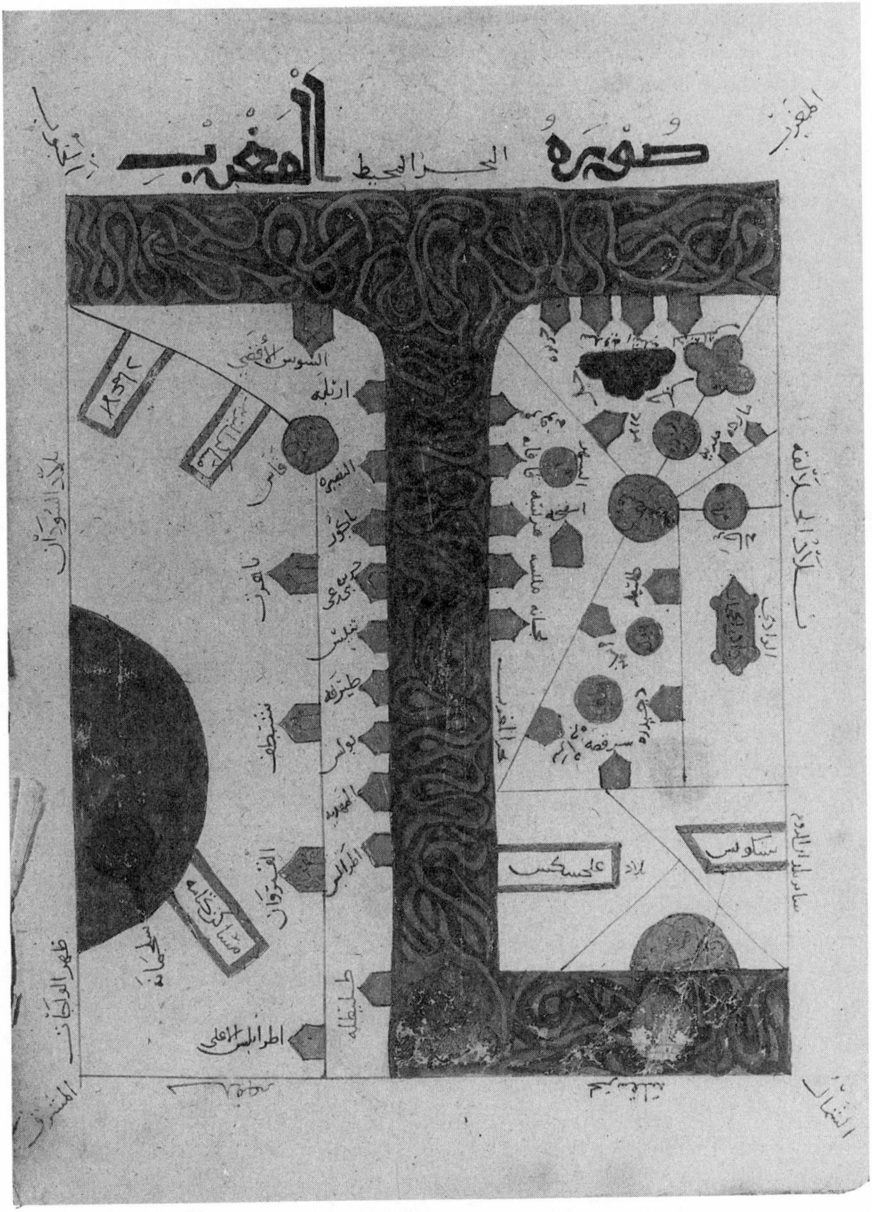

6 Map of north Africa (left) and Spain (right) from a manuscript (*c*. 596/1200) of the *Kitāb al-Masālik wa-ʾl-mamālik* of al-Iṣṭakhrī.

These maps and the underlying idea of how the world should be depicted are the important contribution of the Classical school. The methods used before them had been metaphysical or geometrical, reflecting ideas divorced from the practicalities of terrestrial life. Al-Iṣṭakhrī states his aim immediately in his opening paragraphs. He wants to list the regions of the earth *ᶜalā mamālik*, "according to kingdoms", by which it is clear that he means political regions, and so, by extension, regions defined by the character of the world's surface and its inhabitants rather than arbitrary lines. The maps are the important thing: "The aim of this book of mine is to give a depiction (*taṣwīr*) of these climes, which have not been mentioned by anyone that I know of."[17] Furthermore, although the principles apply to the whole world, the maps themselves and the accompanying text concern themselves with the Islamic world only. This is a deliberate restriction but is not explained. His series of twenty maps is preceded by a world-map, which represents the ancient idea of the world occupying the greater part of one hemisphere and being entirely surrounded by water. The separate regional maps are quite independent of one another; there is no question of any possibility of fitting the maps of adjoining regions together.

It does not seem that al-Iṣṭakhrī himself travelled very much, though the evidence is negative. His successor and continuator Ibn Ḥawqal, on the contrary, was addicted, as he says, to the reading of books on geography from early youth and later travelled extensively. Many of his journeys may be traced from references in his book. He hints several times at his partiality for the Faṭimids and it has been suggested that he was a secret agent for them. At one point he came face-to-face with al-Iṣṭakhrī, as a result of which encounter Ibn Ḥawqal decided to revise his predecessor's work. It appears that his intention at first was simply to rewrite it and improve its literary style but, in fact, and in the course of several recensions, he added much new material, largely as a result of his first-hand knowledge. In particular, his information on the Sahara is quite new. He breaks entirely new ground also in showing an interest in ordinary economic matters as opposed to marvels and curiosities. Despite a dependence on his predecessor which he does not acknowledge, his version is nevertheless a great improvement. On every page there are examples of some slight omission or addition or rearrangement by which he stamps his personality on his work and gives to it a liveliness which is lacking in al-Iṣṭakhrī's.

The Classical school culminates in a highly original author who may be said, in a very general way, to represent a nodal point where all the strands of geographical writing come together, only to part again as different

[17] *Kitāb al-Masālik wa-ʾl-mamālik*, 3.

strands. In Miquel's words: "S'il est permis de schématiser, on peut dire qu'avant elle la géographie est politique et mathématique, d'une part, littéraire et anecdotique de l'autre; après elle, elle évolue vers le dictionnaire, l'encyclopédie scientifique ou le récit de voyages."[18] Al-Muqaddasī seems to have led the life of a kind of cultured vagabond, for, in a remarkable autobiographical passage, he says that he has experienced all that may happen to a traveller except being a beggar or committing a serious crime. He goes on in a sustained passage of rhymed prose to name some of these experiences, from which, making due allowance for his boastful exuberance, one perceives an open-minded, ebullient, unconventional, inquisitive man who was ready to take the rough with the smooth and learn a lesson from every situation. His insistence on the value of seeing things for oneself and his evident pleasure in doing so are perhaps the chief attraction of *Aḥsan al-taqāsīm fī maᶜrifat al-aqālīm* ("The Best Classification, on the Knowledge of the Provinces" *c.* 380/990). He insists also on the methodical presentation of his information. Every region is described according to a fixed format. He has freed himself more or less completely from the al-Balkhī–al-Iṣṭakhrī–Ibn Ḥawqal framework, though restricting himself to the lands of Islam. His regions, still referred to as *iqlīm*, are now reduced from twenty to fourteen, of which he classifies six as Arab, the rest belonging to the non-Arabs (*aᶜājim*). He does not speak of "depicting" the regions of Islam, nor does he mention maps (although some of the manuscripts of *Aḥsan al-taqāsīm* are accompanied by versions of the Iṣṭakhrī maps).

AL-MASᶜŪDĪ

The celebrated Abū ʾl-Ḥasan ᶜAlī al-Masᶜūdī (d. *c.* 345/956) does not fit well into any school or tradition. In his exuberance and love of travel he resembles his junior contemporary al-Muqaddasī, while in his combining of different disciplines in one work he has something of the character of the earlier *adab*-writers, but also of the later encyclopaedists. He is generally thought of as a historian. The bulk of the contents of his two surviving works is historical in nature, but the introductions are chiefly geographical and there is much more geographical material embedded in the rest. Much has been written by Europeans about al-Masᶜūdī, perhaps because the *Murūj* was one of the first important Arabic works to circulate translated into a European language. Comment is often eulogistic in tone ("the Herodotus of the Arabs", "the Muslim Pliny"), following the example of

18 In al-Muqaddasī, *Aḥsan al-taqāsīm fī maᶜrifat al-aqālīm*, partially trans. A. Miquel, *La Meilleure Répartition pour la connaissance des provinces*, Damascus, 1963, xxiii.

Ibn Khaldūn, who calls him *imām li-ʾl-muʾarrikhīn*, "a leader for historians", though not exempting him from his general censure of historians for their uncritical approach to their sources. In common with his contemporaries and successors al-Masʿūdī saw his task as the transmitting of reports, not investigating them or commenting on their veracity or plausibility. His two surviving works are *Murūj al-dhahab* ("Meadows of Gold") and *al-Tanbīh wa-ʾl-ishrāf* ("Indication and Conspectus"), of which the first is much the better known. Al-Masʿūdī mentions or quotes thirty-six other books which he composed, but, as there is no surviving trace of the books themselves, nor any mention by any other writer that he ever had any of these works in his hand, it may be suspected that they never existed outside al-Masʿūdī's imagination. Little is known about the man himself. His education and background are obscure and there is no clue as to how he financed his travels. By his own account he was a great traveller and visited most of the lands of the Islamic empire except the Maghrib. He gives a great deal of original information of a geographical kind but his treatment is quite unsystematic. He moves erratically from one topic to another, mixing history, geography, law, religion, etc., leaving a trail of loose ends behind him. His chief virtue is perhaps his open-mindedness, which leads him to devote much space to the non-Islamic lands.

AL-BĪRŪNĪ

Al-Bīrūnī is not usually thought of as a geographer any more than al-Masʿūdī is. It is convenient to place these two together inasmuch as both men were universal spirits interested in everything and prepared to record their knowledge in books which cannot conveniently be categorized, but really there is little resemblance. Al-Bīrūnī's mind was that of a scientist in the modern sense. He is exact and lucid where al-Masʿūdī is blurred and obscure. His lifelong interests were mathematics and astronomy, and so his first great work *al-Āthār al-bāqiyah ʿan al-qurūn al-khāliyah* ("The Surviving Monuments of Past Centuries")[19] deals with calendars and problems, mainly mathematical, connected with them, but in the course of his exposition he has occasion to give much information about the various peoples whose chronology he is discussing.

Though really peripheral to geographical literature al-Bīrūnī deserves to be mentioned here, first, as one of the towering intellectual figures of medieval Islam, a universal genius capable of illuminating any topic he touched (for example, he realized that the soil of Lower Egypt is alluvium

[19] See below, ch. 24, 408–9.

brought down by the waters of the Nile from the mountains where they have their origin); and secondly, on a more mundane level, as one who added a detailed description of northern India to the stock of geographical knowledge lying ready to hand for the compilers and encyclopaedists to manipulate each according to his own ideas.

By the date of al-Bīrūnī's death al-Khwārazmī had been dead for two centuries. The astronomers, the *adab*-writers, the "Classical" school and all their adherents, known and unknown, had over these centuries amassed a huge stock of material about the Islamic lands and beyond, to which little new was destined to be added in the following centuries. The bricks had been made and were ready for conversion into buildings according to various plans.

"POST-CLASSICAL" GEOGRAPHERS: AL-BAKRĪ AND AL-IDRĪSĪ

The "Post-Classical" geographical writers, any more than their predecessors, are not readily classifiable. None of their works is purely geographical in any modern sense. Even those works of which the main concern is with topography and toponymy invariably contain a greater or lesser quantity of biographical, historical or other information. None of them pays attention to economic matters. On the other hand, works which are avowedly concerned with history or, to a lesser extent biography, will often contain geographical information which is deliberate and not merely incidental. Some writers continue the tradition of *al-Masālik wa-ʾl-mamālik* with little change in the method or in the material handled. Others reassemble the old material in a different form; for instance, by assigning it to regions defined in one way or another. Others put toponyms in alphabetical order as in a dictionary. Others again include a section on geography or cosmology as part of an encyclopaedia. It is difficult to perceive schools or trends or traditions so that any order of the treatment of these writers is artificial; one arrangement is as good as another. The two outstanding authors who carried on the "Classical" tradition are al-Bakrī (d. 487/1094) and al-Idrīsī (fl. 548/1154).

Abū ʿUbayd al-Bakrī was an Andalusian. The great difficulty in assessing his work is that the manuscripts of his work at present known cannot be made to yield a complete version of al-Bakrī's own original text. Some of them must be regarded as abridgements and some are possibly not even by al-Bakrī. The section on the Iberian peninsula, al-Bakrī's own homeland, is hardly longer than his account of the Sahara and the lands of the Blacks beyond it, and it differs from it in treatment. The fact that al-Bakrī's influence on his successors is apparently restricted to information on west

Africa suggests that his section on that region has circulated as a detached volume almost from the moment of its completion. It is on his account of west Africa that al-Bakrī's fame is founded. He must have had excellent sources for the *bilād al-sūdān* but it is not known what they were. He is a prime source for the history of that country and the spread of Islam there. His knowledge of the Slavonic peoples and of northern Europe too was more detailed than that of any of his predecessors.

Muḥammad b. Muḥammad al-Idrīsī is perhaps the best known to Europeans of all the Arab geographers, and that probably for the same reason as that which brought al-Masᶜūdī particularly to their notice. An abridgement of his work published at Rome in AD 1592 was one of the first Arabic books ever printed and a Latin translation was published in Paris twenty-seven years later. This early publication has generated a large literature on al-Idrīsī.

Not much is known about his life, possibly because he was ignored by his fellow Muslims as a renegade. He served the Norman king of Sicily, Roger II, and dedicated his book to him. His *Nuzhat al-mushtāq fī ᵓkhtirāq al-āfāq* ("The Pleasure of Him who Longs to Cross the Horizons"), alias *Kitāb Rujār* ("Roger's Book"), was finished in 548/1154. The manuscripts have always been accompanied by a set of maps in the Ptolemy–Khwārazmī tradition of which the antecedents are not known. The separate sheets of these maps are rectangles bounded by the requirements of the longest-day clime system. Their north-south dimension is determined by the length of the longest day and from East to West they measure sixteen degrees. The habitable part of the earth was thought to be contained within one hemisphere, i.e. 180 degrees, and a band ten degrees wide all round was occupied by the Surrounding Ocean. This left 160 degrees to be divided into ten sections. *Nuzhat al-mushtāq* was designed to accompany a large planisphere engraved on silver for Roger, which must have been a version of the first map of al-Idrīsī's set. This, unlike all the others, is circular and clearly is a descendant of the al-Iṣṭakhrī–Ibn Ḥawqal maps. Al-Idrīsī gives no indication that he knew anything of astronomical geography despite his division into astronomical climes, and it seems probable that he based his text on the maps, not the reverse. The introduction to the work is not very informative. The maps contain toponyms, most or all of Ptolemaic origin, which do not occur in the text, and there are signs that al-Idrīsī adapted his information to make it accord with the maps. This, and other suspicious features such as the too-frequent occurrence of conventional phrases, suggest that al-Idrīsī's work should be used with caution.

Some of al-Idrīsī's information is taken (without acknowledgement) from al-Bakrī, and al-Bakrī's hand may be perceived in a series of works whose writers plundered him for their chapters on Africa. The anonymous *Kitāb al-Istibṣār* ("Book of Reflection", completed 587/1191) is, as far as Africa is concerned, simply a revision in two layers, with a minimum of textual change, of al-Bakrī's text.

Almost a century and a half after al-Idrīsī, the Andalusian Abū ʾl-Ḥasan ʿAlī b. Mūsā b. Saʿīd composed a work of uncertain title which is based firmly on al-Idrīsī's work. The division into climes is the same as that of al-Idrīsī, but Ibn Saʿīd gives a plethora of actual latitudes and longitudes. Indeed, Ibn Saʿīd gives the impression even more than al-Idrīsī of having composed his work with a set of Ptolemy–Khwārazmī maps in front of him. His co-ordinates are not, of course, the result of astronomical or terrestrial observations; they are simply measured from the map. He provides a little fresh information on the authority of one Ibn Fāṭimah, of whom nothing is known. Later on the Syrian prince Abū ʾl-Fidāʾ (d. 732/1331) collated and arranged in scholarly fashion the work of many of his predecessors (whom he names) into a compendium, partly in tabular form, entitled *Taqwīm al-buldān* ("Survey of the Lands"). Abū ʾl-Fidāʾ's contemporary and fellow countryman Shams al-Dīn al-Dimashqī (d. 727/1327) incorporated very much the same material in *Nukhbat al-dahr fī ʿajāʾib al-barr wa-ʾl-baḥr* ("The Choice of the Age, on the Marvels of Land and Sea"). By this time the age of the compilers, arrangers and encyclopaedists had begun. To deal with these it is necessary to go back a century or so.

DICTIONARIES AND ENCYCLOPAEDIAS

In 656/1258 the Mongols occupied Baghdad and put a formal end to the ʿAbbasid caliphate. This catastrophe marked another stage in the political decline of the Islamic empire which had begun much earlier with the Buwayhids, the Saljūqs, etc., but it would be difficult to demonstrate that there was a parallel decline in literary activity. As far as geographical literature is concerned, the changes which may be discerned are largely inherent in the subject. The more information accumulates the greater the need for it to be presented in usable form. Hence the rise of a new kind of literature of which the aim is no longer primarily to gather but to shape. The interest of works composed under these circumstances may be as much in the manner of presentation as in the content.

The earliest of these classificatory works extant is apparently the *Muʿjam mā ʾstaʿjam* ("Dictionary of What is Found Incomprehensible") of al-Bakrī, the Andalusian writer previously mentioned. It is a repertory of only such place names as occur in the ancient literature, i.e. poetry and the Prophetic Tradition. The geographical information is of the scantiest, consisting for the most part of laconic statements, such as "a place in Najd" or "a watering-place in the territory of the Banū So-and-so". A great part of most entries is quotations of lines of verse where the name occurs, with some comment on its etymology. Al-Bakrī had no well-known followers in this genre and it was not until the beginning of the seventh/thirteenth century that the first genuine gazetteer saw the light. This was the *Muᶜjam al-buldān* ("Dictionary of Lands") of Yāqūt. Yāqūt b. ᶜAbdullāh al-Ḥamawī was a freed slave of Greek origin who worked tirelessly at his two great works of compilation until his death at Aleppo in 626/1229. His big biographical dictionary *Irshād al-arīb* has already been mentioned. *Muᶜjam al-buldān* is a vast compilation where place-names are listed in alphabetical order. There is an extensive introduction in which Yāqūt surveys the general field of geography and cosmology. It is in principle a world gazetteer. Yāqūt did not know very much about the more remote regions of the world, especially those outside the domain of Islam, and such information as he had about them he suspected of being unreliable. He dealt with it to the best of his ability. There is, for example, a very long chapter on Ṣīn, i.e. China, in which he says disarmingly: "Here is something about Furthest China, which I mention as I find it and do not guarantee its authenticity. If it is true, I will have achieved my aim; if it is not true you will know what people assert." He identifies his sources fairly scrupulously, which helps the reader to allow for anachronisms. One of these sources, much-quoted, is a lost *ᶜAzīzī* dedicated to the Faṭimid caliph al-ᶜAzīz by one Ḥasan al-Muhallabī. It may be deduced that this was an important work in the Classical tradition. Yāqūt's entries tend to follow a standard pattern. An entry begins by establishing the correct spelling and vocalization of the name and discussing its etymology. After this comes information of a more especially "geographical" kind, such as climate, water-supply, etc.; then it may deal with the history of the place, the customs of the inhabitants, and the like, usually terminating with brief biographies of celebrated people named after it. A great deal of verse is quoted. The *Muᶜjam al-buldān* remains to this day an indispensable tool for the Arabist. A useful abridgement of it was made a century later by Ṣafī ʾl-Dīn al-Baghdādī under the title *Marāṣid al-iṭṭilāᶜ* ("Observation Posts"). Yāqūt was the author of another book arranged alphabetically about places sharing the same name: *Kitāb al-Mushtarik waḍᶜan wa-ʾl-muftariq ṣuqᶜan* ("Book of Places which Share as to Spelling but Differ as to Situation").

It was through Yāqūt that most subsequent writers, few of whom show any originality or critical acumen or state any new facts, derived the information which they attribute to al-Bakrī, al-Muqaddasī, etc. This is true, for example, of Zakariyyāʾ al-Qazwīnī (d. 682/1283), who completed his two important books in 674/1275. The textual history of these books is complicated, but it is conventional to refer to one as the "Geography", with the putative title of *Āthār al-bilād* ("Monuments of the Lands") and to the other as the "Cosmography", with the probably correct title of *ʿAjāʾib al-makhlūqāt* ("Marvels of Created Things"). The first displays no originality except as to its arrangement. Basically al-Qazwīnī has simply redistributed a selection of Yāqūt's entries among the seven Ptolemy–Khwārazmī climes and put them in alphabetical order in each clime. This is not very inspired, but *ʿAjāʾib al-makhlūqāt* is a very different matter. It is the first Muslim cosmography. It is true that the long section on cosmography included in the *Rasāʾil* ("Epistles") of the Ikhwān al-Ṣafāʾ composed during the century centred on 300/912 seems to be the first attempt in Arabic to construct a coherent account of the natural world seen as a whole. However, this section is only part of a work which is in essence a statement of Ismāʿīlī doctrine and so is coloured by Ismāʿīlī propagandizing and esotericism. Al-Qazwīnī's "Cosmography" is the first attempt at a comprehensive exposition of the orthodox cosmographical ideas of the day. It contains nothing new, inasmuch as every item of information is to be found in earlier works. Its novelty lies in the fact of its methodical arrangement. It is divided into two parts, dealing respectively with supraterrestrial and terrestrial matters. The first part deals with the heavenly bodies and the spheres and the inhabitants of the outermost sphere, namely the angels, and ends with the problems of chronology. The second part deals with climatology, the climes, the seas and rivers, and the three natural kingdoms: mineral, vegetable and animal. Man is treated as part of the animal kingdom, as also are the *jinn* and the *ghūl*s considered by Muslim orthodoxy to occupy a position between mankind and the lower animals. *ʿAjāʾib al-makhlūqāt* has prompted many studies, not all favourable. A common accusation is that of lack of originality and specifically of plagiarism. This is justified from the modern European viewpoint, but to al-Qazwīnī and his contemporaries there was no such thing as the sin of plagiarism.

Of later compilatory works two may be mentioned: *Nihāyat al-arab* ("The Ultimate Goal") by Aḥmad al-Nuwayrī, and *Masālik al-abṣār fī mamālik al-amṣār* ("Pathways of Vision, on the Realms of the Regions") by Aḥmad b. Yaḥyā b. Faḍlullāh al-ʿUmarī (d. 749/1349). Only the first of these has been printed in its entirety. The framework of *Nihāyat al-arab* is cosmological. Four of its five sections deal respectively with heaven and earth; mankind; dumb animals; plants. In these al-Nuwayrī covers more or less the same ground as al-Qazwīnī but includes a large amount of literary matter. The fifth section deals with history, thereby showing that al-Nuwayrī followed his predecessors in not making a sharp distinction between geography, history and *adab*. Only a small proportion of al-ʿUmarī's encyclopaedia has been printed, although it seems that the scattered manuscripts could be assembled into the complete work. It is a voluminous compilation, apparently dealing with geography, history and biography on a geographical framework. It is especially valuable because, after a century and a half during which writers had been content to work over the old material, al-ʿUmarī produced a completely new and up-to-date description of west Africa collected partly from pilgrims passing through Cairo.

TRAVELLERS

Travel books, by which is meant accounts, direct or indirect, by travellers of their journeys, as opposed to more or less methodical presentations of geographical knowledge by persons who may or may not have made journeys, are an incidental but disproportionately valuable source of information. Not all are of much value. The medieval Muslim traveller travelled for trade or in search of learning, not to see the world. In either case the journey itself was a tiresome irrelevance. Traders were not in the habit of writing books, and the main interest of students was the scholars from whom they learnt, and who learnt from them as part of the network of oral transmission which authenticated Muslim learning.

The anonymous compilation known as *Akhbār al-Ṣīn wa-ʾl-Hind* ("News of China and India") was composed in 237/851 and therefore may be considered the earliest work in Arabic on human, as opposed to astronomical geography. The writer, mistakenly identified by earlier workers as "Sulaymān the Merchant", was probably a citizen of Sīrāf. He collected and recorded an unconnected series of short passages on the Far East which he had heard from eye-witnesses and written down in their own words. Despite the strictures of G. Ferrand,[20] who considered the language barbarous and the matter fabulous, J. Sauvaget argues convincingly that the deviations from linguistic propriety are, on the contrary, a guarantee of authenticity as being the actual words of the narrators, and that close scrutiny of the text and parallel texts leads to the conclusion that the information is in general veracious.

Aḥmad b. Faḍlān was sent by the caliph on an embassy to the king of the Bulghār in 309/921. His journey took him through Bukhārā, Khwārazm

[20] *Akhbār al-Ṣīn wa-ʾl-Hind*, trans. G. Ferrand, *Voyage du marchand arabe Sulaymân en Inde et en Chine*, Paris, 1922.

and the territories of various Turkic peoples to the capital of the Bulghār in the region of modern Kazan on the Volga. To Ibn Faḍlān's curiosity historians and, to a lesser extent geographers, owe an account of the Bulghār and their neighbours the Rūs and Khazar which is by far the most detailed for that time. Its original title is unknown.

Fabulous material easily finds its way into travellers' tales and, when such fictitious additions are obvious, they cast doubt on the rest which may be, on the face of it, true. This is the case with the Persian seaman and merchant Buzurg b. Shahriyār who wrote about 375/985 (in Arabic) a collection of stories misnamed *ʿAjāʾib al-Hind* ("Marvels of India") which sometimes strain credulity to breaking point and bring the work near to the frankly fictional stories exemplified in the Sindbad episodes of the *Thousand and One Nights*.

The tradition, especially among Andalusians, of combining the Pilgrimage with a study journey and then writing an account of it seems to have begun with Muḥammad b. Jubayr al-Kinānī, who left Granada on the first of his three journeys in 578/1183. Unlike most of his successors, however, for whom the journey was merely a vehicle for their literary or religious preoccupations, he became captivated by the spectacle of people and places and described them with a liveliness and vigour which his too-frequent attempts at a high-flown style do not spoil. His work, known simply as the *Riḥlah* ("Journey"), has been extensively plagiarized by later authors. In the same tradition, but on a far bigger scale, is the famous *Riḥlah* of another westerner, the Moroccan Muḥammad b. ʿAbdullāh b. Baṭṭūṭah.

Ibn Baṭṭūṭah set off from Tangier on his way to make the Pilgrimage in 725/1325. He duly performed his religious duty (as indeed he did several times subsequently), but his interest in travel for its own sake revealed itself from the beginning. It became, as he says, his ruling passion, so that he spent the next twenty-four years in almost continuous travelling, and did not set foot again in his native land until 750/1349. Even then he remained restless. After a visit to Granada he set off again and spent almost two years on a visit to the southern fringe of the Sahara, reaching Fez again in 754/1353. His *Riḥlah* was completed in 756/1357; then he disappeared from history. These journeys entitle him to be considered as one of the great travellers of history, comparable perhaps, in the scope of his travels and the copiousness of the information provided by his journal, with his near contemporary Marco Polo. His journeys took him through practically all the Muslim world of his day and outside it to India, Ceylon, the East Indies, East Africa, China and the territory of the Bulghār. He did not visit Europe except for Granada and an incidental call at Sardinia. His journeys were generally made on his own initiative, but he went to China as the envoy of the Sultan of Delhi and there are hints that he went to the Niger at the behest of the Sultan of Morocco. He was chief *qāḍī* of Delhi for several years.

The account of his travels, which is properly entitled *Tuḥfat al-nuẓẓār fī gharāʾib al-amṣār wa-ʿajāʾib al-asfār* ("The Gift of the Beholders, on the Peculiarities of the Regions and the Marvels of Journeys"), was put into literary form from Ibn Baṭṭūṭah's dictation by one Muḥammad b. Juzayy. It is a matter of debate whether certain problems evoked by the text are due to Ibn Baṭṭūṭah himself or to Ibn Juzayy's editorship. For example, it may be accepted that the "literary" embellishments are due to Ibn Juzayy, and probably the unacknowledged quotations from Ibn Jubayr are also by him. On the other hand, the insoluble contradictions in chronology and itinerary may be charitably attributed to Ibn Baṭṭūṭah's faulty memory after twenty-eight years of continual journeying during which he lost, as he says, many of such notes as he made. The account of the journey in China raises doubts because it seems to be too short and vague; the journey to the Bulghār is even more suspect. Despite these problems the *Riḥlah* has long been appreciated for its lively description of the known inhabited world at that time, particularly India, the lands of the Niger and Asia Minor at the beginning of Ottoman times. Ibn Baṭṭūṭah reveals himself as a rather conceited and callous person, but he was shrewd and practical, able to flourish in the most difficult circumstances and adept at obtaining the patronage and protection of powerful personalities.

NAVIGATIONAL LITERATURE

Arabic navigational literature, as known at present, forms a small corpus of highly specialized but extremely interesting writings on the fringe of the literary world. These writings are textbooks or manuals composed by practising seamen for their colleagues. Though the writers may have been persons of some education their readers were for the most part, it may be supposed, barely literate. These works have no artistic value despite the pretensions of at least one of the writers. To the errors due to the notorious carelessness of copyists are added those due to their total ignorance of the subject-matter, with the result that many passages are hardly intelligible. All the literature at present known is concerned with the Indian Ocean and its offshoots, the Red Sea and the Persian Gulf; there is no comparable literature extant concerning the Mediterranean.

Maritime trade between Arabia and India is well documented from remote antiquity, and it must be concluded that the pre-Islamic navigators in those seas were no less competent than the Muslims and that the Arabic literature carries on an ancient tradition. The manner of transmission is completely obscure. It was basically an oral tradition which did not often find its way into written form. Clearly it does not have its roots in traditional Muslim learning. It owes no demonstrable debt to the Arab geographers and astronomers. It reflects the closed world of seamen, different from the landsman's world and having its own independent customs and accumulated lore. There are striking instances of this aloofness. Ibn Mājid and Sulaymān al-Mahrī knew quite well that there was something wrong in the geometrical theory underlying some of their procedures, but apparently they never tried to rectify matters by seeing what the landsmen had to say. Similarly, they knew that the traditional lists of latitudes for various places differed as between the Arabs, the Gujaratis, the Cholas, etc., but they never seem to have tried to establish correct values by making observations on land, where very simple methods would have attained an accuracy far in excess of that obtainable with crude instruments on the heaving deck of a dhow driven by the monsoon (and that in the dark, for the Arabs' celestial navigation was based exclusively on the stars).

There are hints as to the existence of such a literature in Ibn Khurradādhbih and *Akhbār al-Ṣīn wa-ʾl-Hind* but the first writers whose names are actually given (by Ibn Mājid) flourished around 400/1009. A century or so later the "Three Lions", Muḥammad b. Shādhān, Sahl b. Abbān and Layth b. Kahlān, wrote navigational works of some kind which are no longer extant but of which Ibn Mājid apparently had copies. Ibn Mājid says that they were mere compilers, not navigators. After the Three Lions, apart from a few names, there is a blank until we arrive at Aḥmad b. Mājid.

Aḥmad b. Mājid was born about 840/1436 and died about 906/1500. All that is known about him (and his predecessors) is gleaned from his own works. As by his own account he spent fifty years at sea, it is not clear how or where he obtained his education, of which, nevertheless, he is very proud. Of his forty or so works the majority are in verse and deal with navigational questions. It is perhaps worthy of note that most of these verse productions are in conventional monorhyme, not couplets in the *rajaz* metre so commonly used for didactic poems. His most important works, however, the *Ḥāwiyat al-ikhtiṣār fī uṣūl ʿilm al-biḥār* ("Comprehensive Epitome on the Principles of Maritime Science"), and the *Fawāʾid* ("Useful Things"), are respectively in *rajaz* and prose. The contents of these works are technical. They purport to be composed according to a systematic plan but Ibn Mājid is very easily diverted from following his plan closely. The *Fawāʾid* is divided into twelve chapters called *fāʾidah* (of which word *fawāʾid* is the plural), as follows:

1 Introductory matter and some history of the subject
2 The qualities required in a pilot

3 The twenty-eight lunar mansions
4 Compass rhumbs
5 Miscellany
6 The types of route (i.e. coasting and ocean passages)
7 Latitude observations
8 *Ishārāt* (i.e. signs indicative of the ship's position, such as landmarks, seabirds, fish, changes of wind, etc.) and *siyāsāt* (policy and crew management etc.), followed by a detailed account of the west coast of India
9 An account of the coasts of the world as seen by a circumnavigator keeping the land to starboard
10 Important islands (without navigational detail)
11 Navigational seasons and monsoons
12 The Red Sea

It will be perceived that in practice this is anything but systematic. Chapters 9 and 10 are of no practical use to the navigator, while Chapter 12 and the second half of Chapter 8 are misplaced in a work on navigational theory. That is not to deny their undoubted value to the scholar.

Ibn Mājid has earned a certain notoriety in Europe because he is accused of being the man who piloted Vasco da Gama from Malindi to Calicut, so giving the Europeans access to India. This theory was propounded by Gabriel Ferrand[21] and is based on a passage in *al-Barq al-yamānī* by Muḥammad b. ʿAlāʾ al-Dīn al-Nahrawālī (d. 990/1582). Al-Nahrawālī mentions Ibn Mājid in a vague passage from which all one can deduce with certainty is that "early in the tenth century" (which began in AD 1494)... "a skilful navigator named Aḥmad b. Mājid" gave some advice to the "Frankish leader called *al-milandī*" (i.e. *almirante*, "admiral") as to how to get past an obstacle oddly defined as "a strait (*maḍīq*) with a mountain on one side and the Sea of Darkness on the other". This does not fit in with the Portuguese sources (which do not agree among themselves), nor with Ibn Mājid's own statements about the Portuguese, of whom he had heard but with whom, apparently, he had had no direct contact. G. R. Tibbetts and I. Khūrī,[22] the most recent commentators on this question, tend to the view that "our" Ibn Mājid was not the culprit. To exculpate him completely requires that al-Nahrawālī's use of the name be somehow explained away.

The advent of the Portuguese opened a new era in the Indian Ocean. The subject is not well documented but the traditional Arab navigators can

[21] In Ibn Mājid, *Kitāb al-Fawāʾid*, ed. G. Ferrand, Paris, 1921–8, ii.

[22] G. R. Tibbetts, *Arab Navigation in the Indian Ocean Before the Coming of the Portuguese, being a translation of Kitāb al-Fawāʾid ... of Aḥmad b. Mājid al-Najdī*, London, 1971, 9ff; Ibrāhīm Khūrī, "La *Ḥāwiya* de Aḥmad bin Māǧid", *Bulletin d'Etudes Orientales*, XXIV, 1971.

hardly have failed to appreciate the superior knowledge and methods of the Europeans and gradually to adopt them. Indeed, Ibn Mājid himself shows quite clearly in his *al-Sufāliyyah* his realization that the coming of the Portuguese would extend knowledge of the Indian Ocean to the southward. But Ibn Mājid's works, and even more his name, were remembered for several centuries more and may not quite be lost yet. His tradition was continued by one more known writer, namely Sulaymān al-Mahrī. He was a native of Shiḥr and wrote his *ᶜUmdah* ("Pillar") in 917/1511. That is all that is known about his life. Sulaymān knew about the *Ḥāwiyah* of Ibn Mājid and the *ᶜUmdah* follows the same plan, but, where Ibn Mājid is confused and wordy, Sulaymān is lucid and concise. To such a degree is this the case, according to Tibbetts,[23] that the works of Sulaymān are an indispensable key to the understanding of those of Ibn Mājid. Sulaymān is particularly good at illustrating his theory with practical examples. Later he revised the practical parts of the *ᶜUmdah* and reissued them separately as *Minhāj al-fākhir* ("The Way of the Proud") and then wrote a third work called *Tuḥfat al-fuḥūl* ("Present for the Masters") consisting of a revision of the theoretical parts of the *ᶜUmdah*. Finally, as his fourth work, Sulaymān wrote a commentary on the *Tuḥfah* which simply expands it to several times its length without adding anything either of substance or clarification.

[23] Tibbetts, *Arab Navigation*, 42.

CHAPTER 18

THE LITERATURE OF ARABIC ALCHEMY

THE NATURE AND AIMS OF ALCHEMY

Many thousands of pages have been written by modern scholars on the subject of alchemy, but it cannot be said that all the obscurities that render the subject so difficult have yet been satisfactorily elucidated. These obscurities include the actual definition of the term "alchemy", its origins in East and West, the authorship of many of the extant texts, the motives and beliefs of the alchemists, the methods they used and the identification of many of their materials. Only in the case of laboratory equipment and processes do we have any firm data, largely because most types of equipment used by the alchemists have survived into the present or recent past. Moreover, in several alchemical works, notably those of Abū Bakr Muḥammad b. Zakariyyā᾽ al-Rāzī, many pieces of equipment are clearly described and illustrated and can be understood by comparing them with their modern counterparts. Even so, although the basic purposes of the equipment can usually be determined, uncertainty as to the course of a given process may remain if we do not know the precise composition of the materials being processed.

Much of the obscurity of the subject is due to its esoteric nature and the consequent use made by its practitioners of analogy, allusion and cryptic utterances. A second difficulty lies in the tendency of many writers to attribute their own work to earlier, sometimes mythological, personages. A third problem, particularly for the student of Islamic alchemy, is the mass of manuscript material that has yet to be edited and studied. We shall have occasion to return to some of these problems a little later. Meanwhile it may be of service to set down the three broad categories into which proto-chemistry may be divided. (The terms for these categories are those used by Joseph Needham.[1])

Aurifiction

There are a number of artisanal crafts, predating the rise of alchemy, which demand varying degrees of empirical knowledge. These include the

[1] Needham, "The elixir concept".

manufacture of perfumes, glass, ceramics, inks, pigments and dyes. More relevant to our subject were the arts used by jewellers and smiths to imitate genuine substances such as gold, silver, gems and pearls. The term "aurifiction" applies to methods used for simulating gold. This could be achieved by "diluting" gold with other metals; by making gold-like alloys with copper, tin, zinc, nickel, etc.; by the surface-enrichment of such mixtures containing gold; by amalgamation gilding; or by the deposition of surface films of appropriate tints produced by exposure of the metal to the vapours of sulphur, mercury or arsenic or volatile compounds containing these elements. The deception of the client was not essential, for he might be quite content with an artifact of gold-like appearance. The artisan, however, would have been well aware that his product would not stand up to the ancient test of cupellation. In this test gold (or silver), with or without other metals, is heated with lead in a vessel made of bone-ash, a crucible or a shallow hearth, set in an oxidizing furnace with a reverbatory heat-flow. Lead monoxide (litharge) is formed, as well as the oxides of any base metals, and these separate with any other impurities, soaking into the porous ash and being blown off by the fumes, until a cake or globule of the precious metal remains. Cupellation does not separate gold and silver, but this could be achieved by the ancient method known as "dry parting" or "cementation". This process could also be used for the surface enrichment of a gold-containing alloy by the withdrawal of copper and silver from the external layers, so that an object thus treated would give a positive result to the touchstone, as the Hellenistic artisans certainly knew.

Aurifaction

Aurifaction, the attempt to produce gold (or silver) from base metals is commonly regarded as synonymous with alchemy. It is not possible here to discuss in any depth the ideas that led to the growth of alchemical thought. Some attempt must be made, however, to mention the most important concepts. Aristotle, though not an alchemist, formulated theories that are widely thought to be the basis of much alchemical thought. As is well known he taught that all substances are composed of four elements: fire, air, water and earth, which are distinguished from one another by their "qualities", these being the fluid (or moist), the dry, the hot and the cold. Each element possesses two of these, as follows:

Fire – hot and dry
Air – hot and fluid
Water – cold and fluid
Earth – cold and dry.

None of the four elements is unchangeable; they pass into one another through the medium of that quality which they possess in common; thus fire can become air through the medium of heat; air can become water through the medium of fluidity, and so on. Since each element can be transformed into any of the others, it follows that any kind of substance can be transformed into any other kind by so treating it that the proportions of its elements are changed to accord with the proportions of the elements in the other substance. The many hundreds of recipes given by the alchemists nearly all revert to this basic concept. One or more substances were subjected to chemical treatments such as roasting, amalgamation or calcination, and a substance known as the "philosopher's stone" or the "elixir" was applied to the resultant product. The preparation of this substance and its application to the materials to be transmuted could also involve elaborate chemical processing. Sometimes the operations were carried out under auspicious planetary influences. If everything had been carried out correctly, then pure gold would be produced.

Macrobiotics

The main ideas of macrobiotics include:

> (a) The conviction of the possibility of a chemically induced longevity . . ., (b) hope in a similar conservation of youth (c) speculation on what the achievement of a perfect balance of qualities might be able to accomplish, (d) the enlargement of the life-extension idea to life-donation or artificial generation systems, and (e) the uninhibited application of elixir chemicals in the medical treatment of diseases.[2]

Attempts to transmute base materials into gold, or to prolong life by chemical means, were, of course, bound to fail. Other early scientific work was also often based upon false premises. Valuable work was done in pneumatics, for example, before it was realized that aerostatic effects are caused by the weight of air. It is a little strange, therefore, that alchemists have been singled out for more than their fair share of ridicule, since many of them were serious seekers after truth, using the best theoretical assumptions that were known in their time. The ridicule may be partly explained by the fact that over the centuries many charlatans professed to be alchemists with the sole intention of deluding the unwary and so enriching themselves. Nevertheless, even serious alchemists must share part of the blame for the dubious status of their profession. They were either ignorant of, or chose to ignore, the assaying methods such as cupellation that were well known to the artisans. In other fields, for example machine technology, there was fruitful co-operation between scientists and craftsmen; if a

[2] Ibid., 258–9.

scientist ignored the advice of craftsmen then the machines he designed simply would not work. There is no simple answer to the failure of alchemists to seek practical advice.

Despite their refusal to put their results to well-tried testing procedures, the alchemists made an immense contribution to the development of modern chemistry and it is mainly this aspect of their work that has engaged the attention of historians of science. The esoteric side of alchemy, however, has an important place in the development of man's religious, philosophical and psychological thinking, and merits more serious attention than it has often received. According to T. Burckhardt,[3] the goal of alchemy "is the ripening, 'transmutation', or rebirth of the soul of the artist himself... In fact alchemy may be called the art of the transmutation of the soul". It is not necessary to believe, with Burckhardt, Ḥusayn Nasr[4] and others, that this essentially mystical side of the subject is the only "true" alchemy. It is clear that the subject cannot be properly investigated without taking this aspect of it into account. Unfortunately, the very nature of an occult system precludes any clear, rational presentation of its tenets. Alchemistic authors often imply that they preserve the secrets of alchemy by the use of allegory and simile in order to keep unqualified persons at a distance. Another technique was the dispersion of esoteric instruction among technical writings, so that only the initiated would grasp the meaning of the apparently irrelevant interpolated passages. Moreover, it was held that this true alchemy could only be passed on from a master to a pupil, not learned from books. It is hardly surprising, therefore, that a satisfactory definition of the term "alchemy", in all its aspects, has not yet been made.

ALCHEMICAL LITERATURE

Although the surviving literature is fragmentary and often of unknown authorship, it is clear that in the West alchemy came into being in Hellenistic Egypt. Artisanal practices, including the simulation of gold and other precious materials, were undoubtedly older than alchemy proper, and were one of the stimuli that led to the rise of alchemy. These practices are described in two surviving documents, usually identified as the Stockholm[5] and Leiden[6] manuscripts, dated to the third Christian century. About 200 BC Bolus of Mendes knew of certain techniques of colouring, and such

[3] *Alchemy–Science of the Cosmos*, 23. [4] *Islamic Science*, ch. 9.

[5] Now in Victoria Museum, Uppsala. Trans. with comm. O. Lagercrantz, *Papyrus Graecus Holmiensis*, Uppsala, 1913.

[6] Preserved in University Library, Leiden. Trans. and anal. M. Berthelot, *Collection des anciens alchimistes grecs*, Paris, 1887–8.

techniques, combined with neo-Platonic, Gnostic, Hermetic and Stoic ideas, with the underlying Aristotelian philosophy, helped alchemy to establish itself in Egypt. The writings of the Hellenistic alchemists themselves have survived only in a number of fragmentary manuscripts, many of which carry the names of legendary or celebrated figures such as Hermes, Isis, Moses, Ostanes (a legendary Persian sage) and Cleopatra. One or two others may not be pseudonyms: Mary the Jewess seems to have been a real person, and a great discoverer in practical science (the bain-marie is named after her). The oldest of these writings is probably the pseudo-Democritus, so called because it is attributed to the Greek philosopher Democritus, born about 470 BC. The pseudo-Democritus can be dated to the first century AD or to the last decades of the first century BC. The other writings were composed later – Comerius, the pseudo-Cleopatra and Mary the Jewess in the second century AD, others up to the end of the fourth century. An important figure was Zosimus of Panopolis who around AD 300 wrote an encyclopaedia of alchemy, parts of which have survived.

A considerable number of these Greek writings were translated into Arabic, but we have no exact information about the times and places of these translations. It seems, however, that the first were made towards the close of the second/eighth century, and that the greater part came to the Arabs in the third/ninth century. It is possible that in some cases there may have been intermediary translations into Syriac, but it is not clear whether Ḥunayn b. Isḥāq and his pupils took part in these translations. It is certain that the Arabs knew far more of the Greek pseudographic writers than have survived in Greek. Ibn al-Nadīm gives a long list of pseudographic authors,[7] and there are many mentions of them throughout the works of Arab alchemists. Only when many more of the Arabic alchemical writings have been edited and studied may it be possible to identify at least some of the Hellenistic sources. We must be careful, however, not to assume that the only sources of Arabic alchemy were Greek, simply because the written transmissions were from the Greek pseudographs. Needham has shown that Arabic alchemy contains elements that were absent from Greek alchemy but an essential feature of its Chinese counterpart. He points out that "the whole course of Hellenistic proto-chemistry was primarily metallurgical . . ., while Arabic joined with Chinese alchemy in the profoundly medical nature of its pre-occupations".[8] Macrobiotic ideas appear in the Jabirian writings and in the works of other Arab alchemical writers, and it seems almost certain that they were imported from China, where the characteristic form of Chinese alchemy had existed since the

[7] *Fibrist*, trans. Dodge, 849–50. [8] "The elixir concept", 259.

fourth century BC. No translations of Chinese works are known from the early centuries of Islam, but the two cultures had commercial relations from the second/eighth century onwards and non-literary transmissions could have occurred in alchemical matters as we know they did in other fields; for example, in paper-making and in techniques of siege-warfare.

For the beginnings of Arabic alchemy we have only reports of a legendary nature in the works of later alchemists. For example, the Umayyad prince Khālid b. Yazīd is said to have ordered Egyptian scholars to translate Greek and Coptic works on alchemy, medicine and astronomy into Arabic, and to have learned alchemy from a Byzantine monk by the name of Maryānos. While it is not improbable that Khālid took an interest in scientific subjects, there is no evidence to suggest that he was a founder of Arabic alchemy. Although there may have been other early Arab scholars who were interested in the subject, undoubtedly the most important name in early Arabic alchemy was that of Jābir b. Ḥayyān, long familiar to Western readers under the name of Geber, the medieval rendering of the Arabic word. Indeed, not only are the writings attributed to Jābir the earliest Arabic alchemical works to have survived, but they represent a peak of perfection that was never surpassed by later Arab scholars. As with other Arab scientists, Jābir was a polymath who concerned himself with all known branches of learning. He says that he wrote 300 books on philosophy, 1,300 books on mechanical devices and war-machines, etc. There were also hundreds of books on alchemy. A list of Jābir's works, together with the locations of surviving manuscripts, is given by P. Kraus[9] and, with additions, by F. Sezgin.[10] His writings are also listed by Ibn al-Nadīm.[11] According to the autobiographical statements to be found in Jābir's writings, his name was Abū Mūsā Jābir b. Ḥayyān and he is said to have lived from 103/721 until about 200/815. He studied under the imam Jaʿfar al-Ṣādiq and was also in favour with the Barmakids.

The attribution of these writings to a single personage, Jābir b. Ḥayyān, and even the existence of such a man, have been subjected to close scrutiny by scholars since the end of the thirteenth/nineteenth century. Indeed, even Ibn al-Nadīm[12] said that he spoke to a group of scholars who questioned Jābir's existence, although he himself accepted his historicity. A number of modern scholars, including M. Berthelot, E. O. von Lippmann, E. J. Holmyard, J. Ruska and others attempted to resolve the problem without coming to any definite conclusions.[13] In 1942–3 Paul Kraus published his monumental work on Jābir,[14] in which he set forth detailed arguments to

9 *Jābir b. Ḥayyān*, I, 3–166. 10 *GAS*, IV, 231–69. 11 *Fihrist*, trans. Dodge, 855–62.
12 *Ibid.*, 855. 13 For a discussion of these scholars' contribution to this debate, see *GAS*, IV, 175ff.
14 *Jābir b. Ḥayyān*, I, 1943; II, 1942.

show that Jābir was a legendary personage and that the Jabirian corpus was composed by a group of Ismāʿīlī scholars at the close of the third/ninth century and in the early decades of the fourth/tenth century. More recently Fuat Sezgin[15] has subjected the problem to close analysis and attempted a detailed refutation of Kraus's conclusions. He takes the view that the Jabirian writings are all attributable to Jābir b. Ḥayyān. An intermediate view is taken by Ḥusayn Naṣr,[16] who accepts the historicity of Jābir and his authorship of part of the corpus, to which followers of Ismāʿīliyyah doctrines added many treatises of their own. Clearly, there is no possibility here of discussing these widely differing opinions or offering any new conclusions. For those interested in investigating the matter further, there is no alternative to a close examination of the literature, particularly the writings of Kraus and Sezgin.[17] It must suffice to say that the present writer does not believe that Kraus's main conclusions have been undermined, but that Jābir b. Ḥayyān was a historical personage who may have initiated the study of alchemy in Islam. It is unlikely, however, that any of the Jabirian writings as they now stand were composed in the second/eighth century. Some of these writings are full-length books while others, though referred to as "books", are short treatises of only a few sheets. These writings are given individually or in groups by Ibn al-Nadīm and they have been tentatively given the following chronology: *Kitāb al-Raḥmah* ("Book of Mercy"), second half of the third/ninth century; the "112 books" and the "70 books", end of the third/ninth century; *Kutub al-Mawāzin* ("Books of the Balances"), beginning of the fourth/tenth century; the "500 books", around 432/1040. In the following discussion the name "Jābir" is used as a convenience for all the anonymous authors of these books.

The Jabirian corpus contains in its various parts virtually all that was known of alchemy at the time and indeed very little was added to this sum of knowledge later, except some practical advances in the way of new equipment and processes. All that can be mentioned here are some of the ideas that distinguish Jābir from his Hellenistic predecessors. The first of these is the quicksilver/sulphur theory. In quicksilver water and earth are present, sulphur contains fire and air and thus these substances together hold the four elements. When the particles of sulphur and quicksilver are mixed and enter into a close compound, the heat generates a process of maturation and cooking which results in the various kinds of metals. If the quicksilver is clean and the sulphur pure, if the quantities stand in ideal relation to one another and if the heat has the right degree, pure gold comes into being. If before maturation coldness enters, then silver is produced; if

[15] *GAS*, IV, 132–269. [16] *Islamic Science*, 199.

[17] Details of the various works will be found in Ullmann, *Natur- und Geheimwissenschaften*, 198–200.

dryness, then red copper. The more disturbing factors enter, the more low-grade the metals become. The alchemist, then, exerts himself to imitate nature. He tries to discover how much quicksilver and how much sulphur are contained in gold and how great the heat must be to bring about the maturation process. If he succeeds in establishing these conditions, he is able to synthesize gold. It should perhaps be added that "quicksilver" and "sulphur" did not necessarily mean for the alchemist the chemical elements Hg and S, but that by these terms he understood rather the basic principles of fluidity and inflammability.

Although the quicksilver/sulphur theory appears for the first time in the Jabirian corpus, it does not differ in essence from the methods used by the Hellenistic alchemists. Two other theories, however, do represent a radical departure from the principles and practices of earlier times. The theory of the balance was a highly speculative one, in which the alchemist attempted to assess the equilibrium of "natures" (heat, dryness, coldness and fluidity) in any given substance. An elaborate system of numerology was used in conjunction with the Arabic alphabet of twenty-eight letters to estimate the proportions of the natures in a substance. The "balance" was determined by giving numerical values to each letter of the alphabet and assigning these values to the letters in the name of the substance, whereupon the proportions of the natures in the substance could be calculated. These being known, according to the theory they could then be adjusted to produce another substance, usually gold, whose balance was known. This system, of which the foregoing is only an outline, undoubtedly had esoteric significance.

The idea of an elixir that could be used as a medicine or as a life-giving force appears for the first time in the West in the writings of Jābir. As mentioned earlier, the idea was probably diffused from China. The elixir, which could be prepared from animal, vegetable or mineral substances, could be used to prolong life or given as a medicine to desperately sick people. Even more startling is the so-called Science of Generation, concerned with the artificial asexual generation of plants, animals and even men, as well as the production of ores and minerals in Nature and in the laboratory, including the generation of the noble metals from the base. The transmutation of base metals into gold by means of an elixir is therefore but one specialized application of the theory.

The other great name of early Arabic alchemy is that of Abū Bakr Muḥammad b. Zakariyyāʾ al-Rāzī.[18] He is, of course, justly famous as a medical practitioner and teacher, but he also turned his attention to

[18] See below, ch. 21.

philosophy, logic, metaphysics, poetry, music and alchemy. Assuming that the dates of the composition of the Jabirian corpus are correct, he was a contemporary of the later Jabirian writers, but his views are very different from theirs. He wrote a number of alchemical works. He himself gives a list of twelve of his books, some of which have survived in manuscripts, although they have yet to be properly studied. His major work on the subject, not included in the twelve books, is *Kitāb al-Asrār* ("The Book of Secrets") to which he added a short supplementary book called *Kitāb Sirr al-asrār* ("The Book of the Secret of Secrets"). Ruska's annotated translation is given the latter title, but this is an error, since it is in fact the *Book of Secrets*.

From the *Book of Secrets* we receive the impression of a powerful mind much more interested in practical chemistry than in theoretical alchemy. Al-Rāzī did not accept Jābir's theory of the "balance", does not discuss the elixir of life and does not speculate about the esoteric meaning of alchemy. He believed, with the Hellenistic writers, that all substances are composed of the four "elements" and that therefore the transmutation of metals was possible. The object of alchemy was to effect this transmutation by means of elixirs, and also to "improve" valueless stones such as quartz and even glass with similar elixirs and so convert them into emeralds, rubies, sapphires, and the like. Al-Rāzī followed Jābir in assuming that the proximate constituents of metals were mercury and sulphur, but sometimes suggests a third constituent of a salty nature – an idea that occurs very frequently in later alchemical literature. Elixirs were of varying powers, ranging from those which could convert only 100 times their own weight of base metal into gold to those that were effective 20,000 times.

The *Secret of Secrets* foreshadows a laboratory manual and deals with substances, equipment and processes. Al-Rāzī in fact brought about a revolution in alchemy by reversing the relative importance of experiment and speculation. From the lists he gives of materials and apparatus it is evident that his own laboratory was very well equipped. It had vessels of all kinds, lamps and braziers, furnaces called athanors, smelting-furnaces, many kinds of tools, sand-baths, water-baths, filters of hair-cloth and linen, alembics, aludels, funnels, cucurbits and pestles and mortars. In addition, al-Rāzī gives details, often with illustrations, of the construction of more complicated pieces of equipment from these and other units.

His store-cupboard contained not only specimens of all metals then known, but pyrites, malachite, lapis lazuli, gypsum, haematite, turquoise, galena, stibnite, alum, green vitriol, natron, borax, common salt, potash, cinnabar, white lead, red lead, litharge, ferric oxide, cupric oxide, verdigris and vinegar. He drew up a scheme for the classification of all substances used in alchemy; here for the first time we meet with the now familiar division of substances into animal, vegetable and mineral.

The chemical processes described or mentioned by al-Rāzī include distillation, calcination, solution, evaporation, crystallization, sublimation, filtration, amalgamation and ceration, the last-named being a process for converting substances into pasty or fusible solids. Most of these operations were used in attempts at transmutation, which according to al-Rāzī were conducted as follows. First, the substances to be employed had to be purified by distillation, calcination, amalgamation or other appropriate treatment. Having freed the crude materials from their impurities, the next step was to reduce them to an easily fusible condition by means of ceration, which should result in a product that readily melted, without any emission of fumes, when dropped upon a heated metal plate. After ceration, the product was to be further disintegrated by the process of solution, which included dissolving in "sharp waters"; these were not generally acid liquids but alkaline and ammoniacal, though lemon juice and sour milk, which are weakly acidic, were sometimes employed. The solutions of the various substances, suitably chosen for the amount of "bodies", "spirits", etc., they were supposed to possess, were then brought together. The combined solutions were finally subjected to the process of coagulation or solidification, and if the experiment were successful the substance resulting would be an elixir.[19] In view of al-Rāzī's methodical approach and his insistence upon the necessity for practical work, he has been considered, rightly, as one of the main founders of modern chemistry.

An important alchemist of the first half of the fourth/tenth century, totally different in his attitudes from al-Rāzī, was Muḥammad b. Umayl al-Tamīmī. A number of his works have survived in manuscripts. Some of his writings are in the form of alchemical poetry. The *Risālat al-Shams ilā al-hilāl* ("Letter from the Sun to the Crescent Moon"), for example, consists of 448 verses, in which the "sun" represents the elixir and the "moon", mercury. An important work, extant in a number of manuscripts, is *Kitāb al-Māʾal-waraqī wa-ʾl-arḍ al-najmiyyah* ("The Silvery Water and the Starry Earth"). In the introduction to this work he tells us how he went with a friend to the temple of Būṣīr, which was known as "Joseph's Prison". Inside they found that the walls and ceiling were covered with inscriptions in hieroglyphics; these, which were a fund of alchemical wisdom, had been inscribed by Hermes. Ibn Umayl al-Tamīmī published these in his *Risālat al-Shams . . .*, and provided a commentary on those verses in *Kitāb al-Māʾal-waraqī . . .* The latter is an extremely important text, since it is a storehouse of

19 The foregoing outline of al-Rāzī's methods is a slightly condensed version of Holmyard's description in *Alchemy*, 86–8.

alchemical doctrines, particularly those of the ancient, pseudographic authors. Ibn Umayl subjects Jābir's work to occasional polemics and ignores al-Rāzī completely, as might be expected from a writer who obviously regarded the speculative, esoteric side of alchemy as its most important aspect.

Properly speaking, the great scientist, philosopher and physician Ibn Sīnā[20] cannot be considered as an alchemist at all, since in his *Kitāb al-Shifāʾ*, and elsewhere, he denied the main belief of the alchemists, namely the possibility of transmutation. Moreover, modern research has shown that most of the alchemical works that bear his name were not from his pen. One work that has survived exists only in a Latin translation with the title *Liber de anima*, which appears to date back to around the beginning of the sixth/twelfth century. Although this is probably a genuine work of Ibn Sīnā, it appears to have been subjected to alterations and revisions in the Latin version. The book is quite lengthy and deals with the nature, purposes and origins of alchemy and the processes needed for the preparation of the elixir. A number of earlier scholars and pseudographs are cited, including Pythagoras, Plato, Aristotle, Hermes, Maryānos, Jābir b. Ḥayyān, Dhū ʾl-Nūn al-Miṣrī, Abū Bakr Muḥammad b. Zakariyyāʾ al-Rāzī and Abū Naṣr Muḥammad b. Muḥammad al-Fārābī.

Another work attributed to Ibn Sīnā is the *Risālat al-Iksīr* ("Epistle on the Elixir"), which also exists in a Latin translation entitled *Avicennae ad Hasen regem epistola de re recta*. The work was in the form of a letter from Ibn Sīnā to Abūʾl-Ḥasan Sahl b. Muḥammad al-Sahlī and contains nine sections. In his introduction the writer says that he examined the works of the supporters and opponents of alchemy, but since he could not gain a true picture from these writings he formed his own opinions independently. The work includes descriptions of methods for colouring substances, synthesis and the preparation of the elixir. Careful and conscientious descriptions of various processes are given as well as of apparatus that seems to have been invented by the writer. The book in fact is a laboratory manual; Ibn Sīnā makes the point more than once that he always subjected his hypotheses to experimental tests.

Two important works were written in Spain in the latter part of the fourth/tenth century by Maslamah b. Aḥmad (d. 396/1005 or 398/1007). Although a native of Cordova he was known as al-Majrīṭī because of his long residence in Madrid. The works are *Kitāb Rutbat al-ḥakīm wa-mudkhal al-taʿlīm* ("The Sage's Step and the Entry into Learning"), and *Ghāyat al-ḥakīm* ("The Aim of the Wise"), an astrological work. Al-Majrīṭī was a

[20] See below, ch. 23.

noted astronomer and his leaning towards the natural sciences is reflected in *Rutbat al-ḥakīm*, which insists upon a good grounding in mathematics and science for the aspiring alchemist. This should include the study of mathematics in the pages of Euclid and Ptolemy, and of the natural sciences as taught by Aristotle or Apollonius of Tyana. Next the student should practise his hand in operation, his eye in examination, and his mind in reflection over chemical substances and reactions. The chemist should strive to follow Nature, whose servant he is, like the physician. The latter diagnoses the disease and administers a remedy, but it is Nature that acts.

The *Rutbat al-ḥakīm* contains very precise and intelligible instructions for the purification of gold and silver by cupellation and in other ways, serving to show that contemporary alchemy knew the discipline of the laboratory. Also, the author of the book describes an experiment, on the preparation of what is now called mercuric oxide, carried out on a quantitative basis. Very seldom in alchemical literature do we find even the slightest suggestion that pursuing the changes in weight that occur during a chemical reaction might lead to significant results; a procedure that, first methodically applied by Joseph Black in the middle of the twelfth/eighteenth century, has been for 200 years a guiding principle in the science of chemistry. It should be noted that the *Rutbat al-ḥakīm* was not written until 400/1009 or later, thus at least two years after the death of al-Majrīṭī. For this reason its author is sometimes called the pseudo-Majrīṭī, but it is possible that in this case, as in so many others, the work was edited and perhaps enlarged after the original author's death.

Although alchemical books continued to be written in the Arab world during the eighth/fourteenth and ninth/fifteenth centuries, there were fewer notable authors than in earlier times. Such books as were written were for the most part rearrangements or compendia of earlier works or commentaries on them. One of the last, and also one of the greatest of the medieval Arab alchemists, however, was ᶜIzz al-Dīn Aydamir al-Jildakī, an Egyptian, who died in 743/1342 or later. Almost nothing is known of his life, but he tells us that he spent seventeen years on extensive travels, which took him to Iraq, Asia Minor, the Maghrib, the Yemen, the Hijaz, Syria and Egypt, where he ultimately settled. Al-Jildakī represents the mystical and allegorical trend in Arabic alchemy, but there is evidence that he had real experience in practical operations and chemical substances. He wrote a large number of books, many of which have survived in manuscript, although in common with so many Arabic alchemical writings most of them await editing and study. His interests extended to *khawāṣṣ*, i.e. the magical properties of things, and to pharmacology, medicine and astrology, especially the attribution of metals and other substances to the seven planets. He often reflects on the parallels between natural and alchemical processes, and he attacks Ibn Sīnā who denied the possibility of artificial transmutation. He was not a writer of great originality and much of his work consists of commentaries upon the works of earlier writers. The value of his books lies in the great number of quotations that al-Jildakī saw fit to include in them, a value enhanced by the general accuracy with which the quotations are made. In many cases the original works from which the quotations were made are still in existence, and examination of them shows that al-Jildakī was a careful copyist; we may therefore with fair confidence accept as genuine other passages of which no earlier provenance is known.

One of his books, the *Nihāyat al-ṭalab* ("The End of the Search") is particularly rich in material as may be judged by the fact that he quotes from, or mentions, no fewer than forty-two works of Jābir and a large number of those of other authors, including Ibn Umayl al-Tamīmī, Ibn Sīnā, al-Majrīṭī, Khālid b. Yazīd and Abū Bakr Muḥammad b. Zakariyyāʾ al-Rāzī. Another book that would repay study is *Kitāb al-Burhān fī asrār ʿilm al-mīzān* ("The Book of the Proof in the Secrets of the Science of the Balance"). As its name implies, the book is concerned in part with the theory of the "balance" expounded by Jābir, but it also contains a wide range of valuable information. Al-Jildakī pays particular attention to the classification of animals, plants and minerals. For example, animals were categorized in seven groups: men, earthly demons, birds, wild animals, cattle, water animals and reptiles. Plants are also divided into seven groups, according to their connection with the seven planets, and their use in chemistry is discussed. Minerals are also catalogued, but in a less systematic manner. The *Burhān* is a very important work since it is virtually a summary of much of the knowledge accumulated in Islam up to the eighth/fourteenth century. It deals not only with alchemy but also with theology, philosophy, cosmology, physics, astrology and letter-magic. Arabic alchemy did not cease to be studied and practised after the time of al-Jildakī, but continued to have its serious adherents into the present century. We will conclude this brief survey, however, with a few words on the influence of Arabic alchemy on the development of its European counterpart.

While early medieval Europe was by no means lacking in skilful artisans such as dyers, painters, glass-makers, goldsmiths and others, there appears to have been no knowledge of alchemy in the West until it was introduced from Islam, a process beginning in the sixth/twelfth century. The greatest centre for the diffusion of Arabic knowledge into Europe was Spain – where the southern part of the peninsula was still under Muslim control. It was in Spain in AD 1144 that Robert of Ketton completed the first translation of an alchemical work from Arabic into Latin. It was in Toledo, however, that a school of translators rendered large numbers of Arabic scientific works into Latin. Prominent among these translators was Gerard of Cremona (*c.* 508–83/1114–87). Among alchemical works he translated a book of al-Rāzī and is also believed to have translated one of the works of Jābir. There were many other translations of alchemical works made at the same period; it is significant that many technical words had no equivalents in Latin and the translators were therefore obliged to supply these words by transliterating directly from Arabic. Such terms then became part of the scientific vocabularies of European languages. Examples in English are: alkali, alchemy, alcohol, athanor (a furnace), elixir, naphtha and many others. The same phenomenon occurs in other sciences and technologies.

Although one or two genuine works from the Jabirian corpus were translated into Latin, other works in Latin that carry the name of Geber are without known Arabic originals. It is of course possible that the study of as yet unedited works of the Jabirian writings may reveal a direct connection with the Latin Geber, but this seems to be unlikely. That the "Geber" treatises are based upon Arabic alchemical theory is not questioned, and it seems likely from various turns of phrase that their author knew Arabic. The general style, however, is quite different from that of any known writings of the Jabirian corpus, nor do they contain any typical Jabirian ideas such as the theory of the "balance" and the use of alpha-numerology. These works were probably written by a European scholar, but whatever their origin, they became the principal authorities in early Western alchemy and held that position for several centuries.

CHAPTER 19

ARABIC MEDICAL LITERATURE

None of the sciences received more patronage among the Arabs than that of medicine – a discipline which they acquired from the Greeks and in which they excelled most. The Arabic adage states: "al-ʿilm ʿilmān, ʿilm yarfaʿ wa-ʿilm yanfaʿ, fa-ʾl-rāfiʿ al-dīn wa-ʾl-nāfiʿ al-ṭibb" ("science is twofold, that which exalts and that which is useful – that which exalts is religion, and that which is useful is medicine"). Islam not only put medicine on a high level but also conferred the title of *ḥakīm* (wise) on medical practitioners, a term used by Muslims up to the present day in many areas. The association of medicine with religious learning is noteworthy, and is a pleasing feature of Muslim life; for according to a Tradition of the Prophet: "al-ʿilm ʿilmān, ʿilm al-fiqh li-ʾl-adyān wa-ʿilm al-ṭibb li-ʾl-abdān" ("science is twofold, theology and medicine").

Scientific medicine, from the death of Galen to the birth of William Harvey, was kept alive by the vigorous schools of the Byzantines and the Arabs. While among the neo-Latins in Europe, labouring under ignorance and superstition, it almost ceased to exist, and among the later Byzantines surviving in suspended animation rather than growth, under the rising crescent in the East we have to admire one of the most remarkable phases of the history of medicine, that which developed within the culture of Arabian civilization.

Prior to Islam there was very little medicine practised by the Arab tribes. There was no evidence of medicine men, shamans or any allusion to haruspices. Muḥammad himself claimed no miracles, and when he needed medical advice he sought the services of al-Ḥārith b. Kaladah – the first Arab physician who studied medicine at Jundīshāpūr; according to Tradition, however, Muḥammad gave certain advice concerning health and personal hygiene, which in its collected form was later known as *al-ṭibb al-nabawī*.[1]

With the advent of the conquests and the acquiring of lands far away from their original abodes, the Arabs could not fail to discover their lack of

[1] C. L. Elgood, "Ṭibb-ul-Nabī", *Osiris*, xiv, 1962, 38.

science, and in particular of medical science. They had no objection to receiving medical knowledge from the heathen Greeks, but though the main influence of Arab science was undoubtedly Greek, it was in the letter only, and not in the spirit. The Greek spirit never descended or could descend upon the true believers in Islam. No Muslim knew anything of Greek in the original; Greek writings had to be translated into Syriac and then into Arabic.

For effective purposes we may place the limits of Arabic medicine between the years 850–1250 (third to seventh centuries AH). These four centuries cover events of the highest importance for the history of the Arab intellect. Their medical knowledge was founded on philosophical and logical principles: on an induction proceeding by select experience, always observant, cautious and ascending slowly to the generalities of theory. This is abundantly illustrated, particularly in the works of Ibn Sīnā.

THE PERIOD OF TRANSLATION AND JUNDĪSHĀPŪR

The period of translation cannot be closely defined; it falls between roughly 132/750 and 236/850, but prior to that physicians in Jundīshāpūr were already translating some Greek material into Syriac and sometimes into Arabic. Such translations were sporadic. The earliest definitely alien influence that we can discern in the field of Arabic medicine, is in the nature of infiltration rather than direct translation. The earliest agents of this process appear to have been mostly Christians, and to a lesser extent Jews who had been under Sasanid rule and domiciled in Iraq and the south-western part of Persia. Such influence can be traced in the works of Ahrūn and Māsarjawayh who unquestionably drew on Greek sources, and who set forth fully the doctrines of the four elements (*iṣtaqissāt*), the four humours (*akhlāṭ*), and the four temperaments (*amzijah*).

According to Bar Hebraeus,[2] the medical Pandects (*Kunnāsh*) of Ahrūn were translated from Syriac by Māsarjawayh into Arabic. Others believe that they were translated by Sergius into Syriac from a Greek original. This statement fits in well with Ibn abī Uṣaybiᶜah's statement that Sergius, a monk from Raʾs al-ᶜAyn, was the first to translate both medical and philosophical works from the Greek language. On the other hand, Sezgin[3] states that Māsarjawayh not only translated Ahrūn's *Pandects* but also added two treatises of his own. Thus he is one of the first translators of medical works into Arabic, and also the earliest-known medical writer in that language. His other work *Kitāb fī abdāl al-adwiyah* ("Book on Substitutes

[2] Cited by Elgood, *Medical History of Persia*, 99. [3] *GAS*, III, 206–7.

for Drugs") is mentioned by C. L. Elgood, but M. Meyerhof rejects the authenticity of its authorship. Māsarjawayh's works must have been well received by early Muslim physicians, for Abū Bakr Muḥammad b. Zakariyyāʾ al-Rāzī repeatedly quotes him, using the introductory phrase, "wa-qāla al-Yahūdī".

Translation started in earnest in 215/830 when the caliph al-Maʾmūn established his famous institution the Bayt al-Ḥikmah ("House of Wisdom") in Baghdad. In this academy Nestorian scholars from Jundīshāpūr[4] began to translate from Greek manuscripts. The Arabic versions were put in their final forms by correction against their Greek originals. Added to this were translations from Persian and to a lesser extent Indian sources. Later, with the decline of Jundīshāpūr and the rise of the Bayt al-Ḥikmah, we witness the birth of Arabic medical literature in translation.

The best and most celebrated of all the translators was a gifted Christian Arab by the name of Ḥunayn b. Isḥāq al-ʿIbādī who was born in al-Ḥīrah in 192/808 and died in 260/873. He was the Erasmus of the Arabic Renaissance and was known later to the Latin West as Johannitius or Hunainus. The Introduction or Isagoge by Johannitius formed part of the anthology or collection of medical tracts, known as *Ars Medicinae Articella*, which later became the basis of the medical curriculum of the European universities.[5]

To evaluate briefly the importance of Ḥunayn's role as a transmitter of knowledge, it is important to know that Arabic scientific knowledge, until Ḥunayn's time, was not only meagre but also lacked the terminology which is so essential for the transmission of thought. Although the translation of Greek material into Syriac began in the first half of the sixth Christian century, most of such translations were of inferior quality. Many of the Syriac versions of Ḥunayn's works, of course, were ultimately done into Arabic, and so found their way into the Arabic corpus. Because of this early zeal for translation and the establishment of a tradition, the Arabs eventually came to possess (for example) translations of every one of Galen's works which were still studied in Greek centres of learning from the first/seventh to the third/ninth century. There can be no doubt that this great physician's medical works *in toto*, as well as his methods and results, were fully digested by all the later Arab physicians and became an integral part of their medical learning.

Ḥunayn's style was no mere pretty play with words but a search for Arabic vocabulary for the exact meaning equivalent to the Greek. He was the translator *par excellence* and faithful to the original Greek – a language which he mastered in his youth; thus he translates *chalazion* into *baradah*, and

[4] *EI*², "Gondēs͟hāpūr".

[5] Pearl Kibre, *Studies in Medieval Science*, I, London, 1984, 186; for the role of Ḥunayn in the translation movement as a whole, see below, ch. 28, 487–90.

pannus into *sabal* (*chalazion*: a small hailstone; a small hard swelling on the border of the upper eyelid; *pannus*: a piece of tattered cloth; a membrane-like vascularized tissue covering part or the whole of the cornea, a frequent complication of trachoma).

At a later date Ḥunayn's translations became not so much popular manuals as books of reference. For example, it was easier for a medical student to use ᶜAlī b. ᶜĪsā al-Kaḥḥāl's book on eye diseases *Tadhkirat al-kaḥḥālīn* ("Memorandum for the Oculists") than Ḥunayn's *ᶜAshr maqālāt* ("Ten Treatises on the Eye"). The *ᶜAshr maqālāt* has its faults, for there is a want of balance between the theoretical and the practical; and for a beginner, who is embarking on the study of eye diseases, this is rather difficult to follow. Ibn abī ᶜUṣaybiᶜah finds the arrangement of the treatise lacking in uniformity, and the contents abridged. He also states that he knew of an eleventh treatise which dealt with operative treatment. This observation is confirmed by Abū Bakr Muḥammad b. Zakariyyāᵓ al-Rāzī who refers to it in his *Kitāb al-Ḥāwī*. By composing a second book on ophthalmology for the use of his sons Dāwūd and Isḥāq, which he called *Kitāb al-Masāᵓil fī ᵓl-ᶜayn* ("Book of Questions on the Eye"), Ḥunayn introduced a new genre of Arabic medical literature – a kind of medical catechism which later became very popular among medical students (it may be noted that catechism series in English medical literature remained popular among medical students as late as the thirties and forties of this century).

THE PERIOD OF DEVELOPMENT AND ORIGINAL CONTRIBUTION

In less than a century, and after the accumulation of such medical material, Arab physicians displayed a conspicuous activity in the learning and teaching of medicine. One may say that this was the scholarly period following the period of translation. Study of what had been translated had trained them in careful observation and clear thinking. Although needing "aids to diagnosis", they were skilled enough to form their clinical methods, sometimes modified, but always along the same lines as their Greek predecessors.

The Arab physician, at first, was a generalist, not a specialist; he sought also to be an encyclopaedist and tried to elaborate a complete scheme of medical knowledge with an unreasoning reverence for *al-Awāᵓil* ("the Ancients"). This is well illustrated in the work *Firdaws al-ḥikmah* ("Paradise of Wisdom") of ᶜAlī b. Rabbān al-Ṭabarī who lived in the third/ninth century.[6] The *Firdaws* deals mainly with medicine proper, but also to some

[6] Date of birth not known, but Ṣiddīqī places it at about AD 785.

extent with philosophy, meteorology, zoology, psychology and astrology. This work is the first of its kind and one is justified in thinking that it was meant to be a textbook for medical students, for the author remarks: "But he who masters this book and fully fathoms and perpends it will find in it the greater part of what the young graduate needs of the science of medicine and the action of the natural forces in this microcosm and also of the macrocosm."[7]

In his introduction, ᶜAlī al-Ṭabarī addresses those intending to become physicians on how to approach their subject. He compares the medical profession with other skills, such as carpentry, sewing and other manual jobs, and goes on to say: "The skill of the medical profession cannot be acquired easily; it needs a period of apprenticeship and study, but those whose patience is short can still benefit from this book which, when compared with other books, is like a unique stone among other precious ones."[8]

Edward Granville Browne, in his *Arabian Medicine*, makes little attempt to describe the introduction of the *Firdaws*, but he enumerates the parts of the book, its chapters and discourses. Max Meyerhof gives a more detailed commentary, and enumerates 360 chapters. He describes briefly their contents and supplements his paper with a glossary of technical terms and a list of drugs and remedies. ᶜAlī al-Ṭabarī draws mainly on Greek sources and, apart from Hippocrates and Galen, he mentions Alexander of Aphrodisias, Stephanus of Alexandria and Pythagoras. There is also an evidence of some Indian elements, particularly in his section on materia medica. The only Arab authors quoted by him are Māsarjawayh, Yūḥannā b. Māsawayh and Ḥunayn b. Isḥāq.[9] Browne dismisses the book as "little more than a practitioner's *vade-mecum*".[10]

EDUCATION, PROFESSIONALISM AND SPECIALISM

In pre-Islamic and early Islamic times, the profession of medicine, as a general rule, passed from father to son, as in the case of the Bakhtīshūᶜ, the Māsawayh and the Qurrah families. The teaching of medicine followed Greek methods and was heavily tinged with an interest in rhetoric and debating. The ways in which the theoretical knowledge and practical skill needed for the exercise of the profession were acquired varied widely. We learn this from the biographies of physicians which have been handed down to us in many Arabic writings. Some students gained their knowledge and expertise by being apprenticed to a physician of repute for a certain period,

[7] Ṣiddīqī, *Firdaws al-ḥikmah*, 3. [8] Ibid. [9] Meyerhof, "Ṭabarī's Paradise of Wisdom", 6–54.
[10] *Arabian Medicine*, 44.

during which time they mastered their craft. Others were attached to a hospital where reading of public lectures to medical students seems to have been a common practice. The hospitals were well equipped with an adequate supply of books. Practical instruction was obtained by accompanying the physician on his rounds, and by observing and helping in the running of the clinics. Periods of hospital work were essential for young practitioners who were keen to improve their medical expertise and enhance their careers. It must have been rather difficult in some cases to attain such a goal; for, judging from certain letters found in the Cairo Genizah, it was important for the young aspirant to obtain letters of recommendation from a person of authority, such as a governor (*wālī*) or judge (*qāḍī*), and also a certificate of good character (*tazkiyah*) from the chief of police.[11]

There was a considerable diversity at all periods in the standard of medical education, as one would expect where there was no real and effective control of medical practice, either by licence or any other means. Throughout our period, to a small extent in the cities and almost exclusively in the country, the craft aspect of medicine remained dominant, and with it the traditional family education or apprenticeship became generally quite divorced from any scientific or theoretical basis. Nevertheless during the ᶜAbbasid and Faṭimid periods there was some gradual standardization of the medical curriculum. Some sort of qualifying examination was instituted at the time of the ᶜAbbasid caliph al-Muqtadir (reigned 295–320/908–32) when a case of malpractice came to his notice in 319/931. He thereupon, according to al-Qifṭī's *Ikhbār al-ᶜulamāᵓ bi-akhbār al-ḥukamāᵓ*[12], passed an edict that none should practise medicine in Baghdad unless he was able to satisfy Sinān b. Thābit (d. 331/943) of his competence in his profession. Such an edict represented an early, if not the first, attempt at the regulation of healing practices, and this could be considered one of the earliest examining and licensing boards.

During the fifth and sixth/tenth and eleventh centuries, when Arabic medicine reached its maturity, we notice a rise in the standards of medical tuition, professionalism and specialism. Special literature appeared to deal with most branches of medicine as well as subjects allied to medicine, or in some way or another related to the profession, such as pharmacy, dietetics, astrology, magic, medical etiquette and ethics. This literature was not necessarily written by specialists as we know them today. The generalists wrote their large volumes on all diseases in detail. Some included anatomy, materia medica and humoral pathology as well. Their works became more

[11] S. D. Goitein, *A Mediterranean Society*, II, Los Angeles, 1971, 250.

[12] Leipzig, 1903, 191.

encyclopaedias than textbooks. Al-Rāzī's *al-Ḥāwī*, al-Majūsī's *Kāmil al-ṣināʿah* and Ibn Sīnā's *Canon* are prominent examples. At a later date a new type of literature appeared on the scene: commentaries (*sharḥ*), concise works (*mūjiz*) and the more compact and tabulated works such as Ibn Jazlah's *Taqwīm al-abdān*. The idea behind the production of these books was to bring together much scattered material in one easily readable volume which the young practitioner and medical student could acquire cheaply. This type of literature was not necessarily an abridgement of the original work; for example the *Mūjiz al-Qānūn* of Abū ʾl-Ḥasan ʿAlī b. al-Nafīs (d. 687/1288) is not just a summary of the *Canon* as its title literally indicates, for,

> while in general the *Mūjiz* represents a condensation of the body of Arabian medical teachings as expounded in the *Qānūn*, it also contains many independent observations, judgements and illustrations which justify its being treated as a work illustrative of the Arabian system of medicine as taught in the thirteenth century, Ibn al-Nafīs having added his own observations to bring it into line with his own experience.[13]

Similarly it may be noted that in his commentary on the anatomical part of the *Canon*, the *Sharḥ tashrīḥ al-Qānūn*, Ibn al-Nafīs gives the first correct description in medical literature of the pulmonary circulation of the blood. Another category is the medical catechism, to which Ibn abī Uṣaybiʿah refers in the writings of many physicians, for example, the *Kitāb al-Iqtiḍāb ʿalā ṭarīq al-masʾalah wa-ʾl-jawāb* ("Abridged Book Using the Method of Question and Answer"), by Abū Naṣr Saʿīd al-Masīḥī (d. 589/1193).[14] Such a work would have been a valuable aid for any student, and it is the sort of book that could be consulted quickly by a young physician who was worried lest he had overlooked something obvious in his diagnosis. We should not neglect to note a fourth kind of literature, simply written, which was known as *ṭibb al-ʿāmmah* (popular medicine). This was to prove useful to the layman for self-medication, and to give brief advice about the best way of handling difficulties of health and disease. Such literature was written in the belief that, as far as possible, all knowledge should be available to anyone who seeks it. Evidence of such literature is found among the many medical fragments of the Cairo Genizah. It is usually written in simple colloquial language.

Another type of literature which is connected in one way or another with the medical profession includes books concerned with medical ethics, i.e. the doctor–patient relationship, doctor–doctor etiquette, wit and satire directed at physicians and hostile criticism of medicine. We learn from the

[13] M. J. L. Young, "The Arabian system of medicine in the thirteenth century" (unpublished Melbourne Ph.D. thesis, 1963), I, 90–1.

[14] Ghaliongi, *Questions on Medicine*.

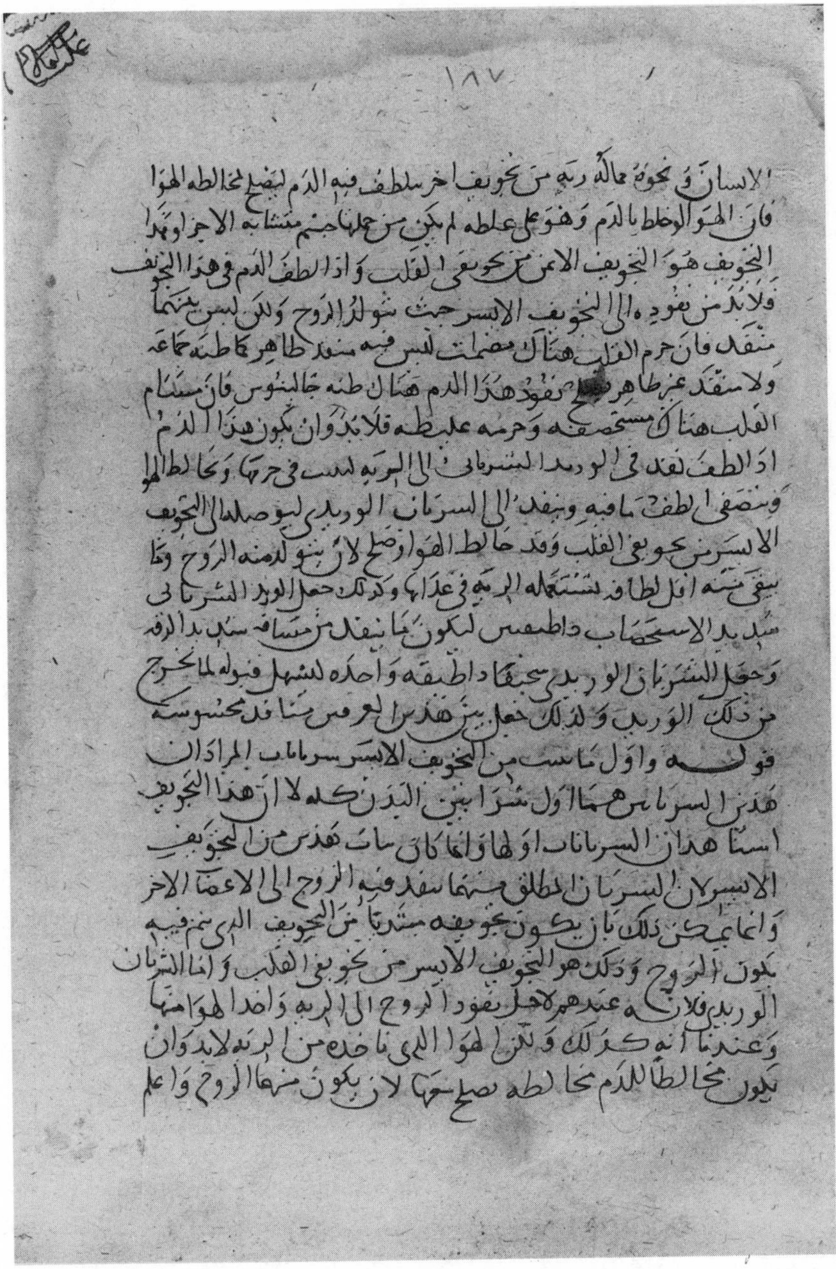

7 Page from a manuscript completed in 640/1242 of Ibn al-Nafīs' *Sharḥ tashrīḥ al-Qānūn*, showing the author's description (lines 2–10) of the pulmonary circulation of the blood.

introduction to the *Firdaws* the importance of the question of who should practise medicine, and what qualities he should acquire. According to ᶜAlī al-Ṭabarī a person intending to practise medicine should exhibit five virtues:

1 A continual concern to bring relief to all peoples alike
2 An earnest attempt to find out what is wrong with the patient
3 The realization that the physician is needed by both patricians and plebeians
4 An awareness of the physician's status among the public
5 The performance of professional duties only if God chooses (*bi-idhn Allāh*).

He goes on to say that a physician should be kind to his patients, content, and display compassion and decency (*ᶜiffah*). He should concern himself with deeds, not words; neither daring (*qadūm*) in his approach to treatment, nor talkative (*mikthār*), and claiming too much. ᶜAlī al-Ṭabarī hints also, in passing, at the doctor–doctor relationship: a physician should not seek to benefit from a colleague's faults, nor should he belittle another physician whose shortcomings he happens to come across.[15]

An anecdote has been preserved by Ibn abī Uṣaybiᶜah concerning the illness of the ᶜAbbasid caliph al-Nāṣir li-dīn Allāh (reigned 575–622/1180–1225) who complained of a stone in his bladder which caused retention of his urine. His personal physician, Abū ᵓl-Khayr al-Masīḥī, finding his case rather serious, consulted with another more skilled physician, Ibn ᶜUkāshah, who advised removal of the offending stone by surgery. The caliph declined such a hazardous operation. Thereupon a third physician, Abū Naṣr Saᶜīd al-Masīḥī, was called in, and he advised a conservative method of treatment with drugs which proved successful. The caliph became very angry and ordered that Ibn ᶜUkāshah should be executed. Then Abū Naṣr intervened and saved the life of his colleague.[16]

Aphoristic remarks are among the common features of medieval Arabic medical literature in their emphasis on medicine as a service to the community and on the physician's ethical behaviour. Medical aphorisms stressing ethical conduct were popular among medical men as well as among the public. Almost every renowned medical author, from Ḥunayn to Ibn Sīnā and Isḥāq al-Isrāᵓīlī (Isaac Judaeus) to Mūsā b. Maymūn (Maimonides), either composed his own aphorisms or wrote a commentary on those of Hippocrates or some other recognized classic of the genre. In

[15] Ṣiddīqī, *Firdaws al-ḥikmah*, 4.
[16] For further details and commentary on this episode, see al-Sāmarrāᵓī, *Mukhtaṣar taᵓrīkh al-ṭibb al-ᶜarabī*, I, 595–8.

this field a commentary not only pursued purely exegetical purposes but served also as a vehicle for the exposition of one's own cherished views. One of the best books on medical deontology is *Adab al-ṭabīb* written by Isḥāq b. ᶜAlī al-Ruhāwī (fourth/tenth century). He pointed out both the importance of the medical profession and the honour and the prestige attached to it. It is the duty of the physician to place the interest and welfare of his patient above all other considerations. The depreciation by one physician of another's professional skill may amount to serious professional misconduct. Al-Ruhāwī writes: "The philosophers can improve only the soul, but the virtuous physician can improve both body and soul. The physician deserves the assertion that he is imitating the acts of God, the exalted, as much as he can." He warns against those who: ". . . butter up the sultan with electuaries, select pretty women as good for one's health, give remedies for digestion, make one's hair beautiful, and incite sexual desire. In this way they attain access to people of wealth and authority."[17]

We are indebted to Shlomo Dov Goitein for exhaustive work on the Cairo Genizah, and for drawing our attention to the medical fragments it contains. Such fragments throw light on the qualitative aspect of medicine both as a science and profession as it was practised during the Faṭimid and the Ayyubid periods. In one Genizah fragment, for example, a physician writes to his wife describing how difficult it is for him to secure a living among fiercely competing physicians in the place where he is residing. In another we read how mercenary some physicians are, and how some of them attend the common people (*al-ᶜāmmah*) and others the upper class (*al-khāṣṣah*), i.e. plebeian and patrician – a timeless description of two-tier medicine.

Writing in the same vein, the Nestorian Abū ᵓl-Ḥasan al-Mukhtār b. ᶜAbdūn b. Buṭlān criticizes his colleagues. Ibn Buṭlān (d. after 455/1063) was one of the medical *literati*; for, while medicine was his vocation, he, like many of his colleagues in the lands of medieval Islam, saw that he should have some intellectual pastime which would serve to keep him in touch with the world outside his profession, and so in the evening of his life he ventured to travel. He left Baghdad, and during his sojourn in Mayyāfāriqīn he wrote his interesting book *Daᶜwat al-aṭibbāᵓ* ("The Physicians' Dinner Party"), in the style of a *maqāmah*. In this book Ibn Buṭlān set out to tackle every aspect of the medical profession of his day and those who practised it. He describes his encounter with his host, the old-established physician, and the new enthusiastic apprentice who was in attendance. He

17 M. Levey, "Medical ethics in medieval Islam", *Transactions of the American Philosophical Society*, III, 1967, 3.

8 Physicians' dinner party, showing the host with four guests and a lutenist, from a manuscript of *Daᶜwat al-aṭibbāʾ* by Ibn Buṭlān. This manuscript was completed in 672/1273.

lists, among other practitioners, pharmacists, oculists, phlebotomists and surgeons; and to each he allots a chapter.

There is reason to believe that most of the hostile criticism of the medical profession mentioned in this book, of which some proceeded from the public, may be attributed to genuine shortcomings in the various branches of the medical profession and the attitudes of the practitioners themselves and their relationship to each other. The author, in a witty and satirical style, brings out the connection between the medical profession as it stood and the events of the polities and societies in which the physicians found themselves. Ibn Buṭlān had an unhappy time during the three years he lived in Egypt, for ᶜAlī b. Riḍwān (d. 460/1068) conducted a hostile and protracted controversy with him which made him leave Cairo an embittered man. It may be that Ibn Buṭlān had hoped to secure for himself a position at the court of the caliph Maᶜadd al-Mustanṣir, who was well disposed to non-Muslim physicians, and it was this that immediately excited the wrath of his colleague Ibn Riḍwān.[18] The shifts and dishonesties that Ibn Buṭlañ describes in his book are said to have been imported by quacks and charlatans in a profession which should be wholly exempt from

[18] See Schacht and Meyerhof, *Controversy*.

them. He condemns the practice of those practitioners whose only aim is to get rich on the misery of their patients. He also attacks physicians of multiple interests, and those who demean themselves by trying to amass wealth by any and every means, such as having a share in a pharmacist's shop or by trading in shrouds. Here and there one comes across pearls of wisdom in the form of remarks, warnings, anecdotes or advice. For example, one must be careful in one's diet and one must eat to live and not live to eat. A physician should be careful in his approach to the treatment of his patients and not too drastic in his methods. He should be particularly on his guard in his relationships with his female patients, and should not take sides in family squabbles.

In his "Physicians' Dinner Party" Ibn Buṭlān writes from an intentionally subjective point of view and does not consider himself privileged, standing outside the orbit of humanity. He portrays an objectionable image of the physician of that age – an image that impugns the physician for specific reasons: his greed, incompetence and hubris. One must not overlook his timeless commentary on the state of medicine *vis à vis* the public: he warns against the cynics who deny medicine all positive meaning, and others who ridicule physicians, insisting that medicine is quite unable to cure diseases and that patients would be better if left to benevolent Nature. How aptly might one compare such critics to the therapeutic nihilists of the nineteenth century, on the one hand, and today's believers in faith healing and naturopathy, on the other.

The physician, although in general greatly revered and highly praised, is also not infrequently the target of wit and satire in Arabic literature – but this only applies to the unscrupulous, the ignorant, the pretentious and the quack. As a taunt at those who are proud of curing their patients, one may quote Abū ʾl-ʿAtāhiyah's disparaging verses following the death of Yūḥannā b. Māsawayh in 243/857:

Inna ʾl-ṭabība bi-ṭibbihi wa-dawāʾihi
Lā yastaṭīʿu difāʿa amrin qad atā
Mā li-ʾl-ṭabībi yamūtu bi-ʾl-dāʾi ʾlladhī
Kāna yubriʾu minhu fīmā qad maḍā?
Māta ʾl-mudāwī wa-ʾl-mudāwā wa-ʾlladhī
Jalaba ʾl-dawāʾa wa-bāʿahu wa-man ishtarā.

The physician, with his physic and drugs
Cannot avert a summons that hath come;
What ails the physician that he dies of the disease
Which he used to cure in time gone by?
There died alike he who administered the drug, and he who took the drug
And he who imported and sold the drug, and he who bought it.[19]

[19] Browne, *Arabian Medicine*, 8.

Two further verses, culled from his *Dīwān*, breathe the spirit of fatalism and scepticism:

Wa-qablaka dāwā ʾl-ṭabību ʾl-marīḍa
Fa-ʿāsha ʾl-marīḍu wa-māta ʾl-ṭabību.

And before you, a physician treated a patient
Then the patient survived and the physician died.[20]

Yā ṣāḥiba ʾl-saqami ʾl-ṭabība bi-dāʾihi
Ḥattā matā taḍnā wa-anta ṭabību?

O you who are afflicted, knowledgeable in his disease,
How long will you languish and you are a physician?[21]

In a similar vein are two more verses, from the popular romance of ʿAntarah b. Shaddād:

Yaqūlu laka ʾl-ṭabību dawāka ʿindī
Idhā mā jassa ẓandaka wa-ʾl-dhirāʿā
Wa-law ʿalima ʾl-ṭabību dawāʾa dāʾin
Yaruddu ʾl-mawta mā qāsā ʾl-niẓāʿā.

The physician says to thee, "I can cure thee",
When he feels thy wrist and thy arm;
But did the physician know a cure for disease
Which would ward off death, he would not suffer the agony of death.[22]

ENCYCLOPAEDIC MEDICAL WORKS

Examples of large encyclopaedic works are those of Abū Bakr Muḥammad b. Zakariyyāʾ al-Rāzī, ʿAlī b. al-ʿAbbās al-Majūsī and Ibn Sīnā. They differ both in style and presentation. Al-Rāzī's medical works are numerous. Some were translated into Latin, including his famous and original monograph on measles and smallpox, and his comprehensive manual *Kitāb al-Ḥāwī fīʾl-ṭibb* (*Liber continens* or "The Comprehensive Book").[23] The text of al-Rāzī's book *al-Kitāb al-Manṣūrī fīʾl-ṭibb*, which was dedicated to the governor of Rayy, al-Manṣūr b. Isḥāq (d. 302/914–5), was also translated into Latin as *Liber ad Almansorem* and was printed in AD 1481. It was studied by medical students, and medical men then knew it by heart. The commentators, especially at first, gave of the text only the beginnings of sentences after the pattern of Bible exegesis. These commentaries were written by members of the faculty of Pavia, and were used in the afternoon lectures on practical medicine as *ad lecturam Almansoris*. Much later, Sylvius and Vesalius still found it worthwhile to add to their wisdom that of al-Rāzī's *Almansorem*.

[20] Abū ʾl-ʿAtāhiyah, *Dīwān*, Beirut, 1964, 39. [21] Ibid., 42. [22] Browne, *Arabian Medicine*, 9.
[23] For the medical works of al-Rāzī see below, ch. 21, 373–7.

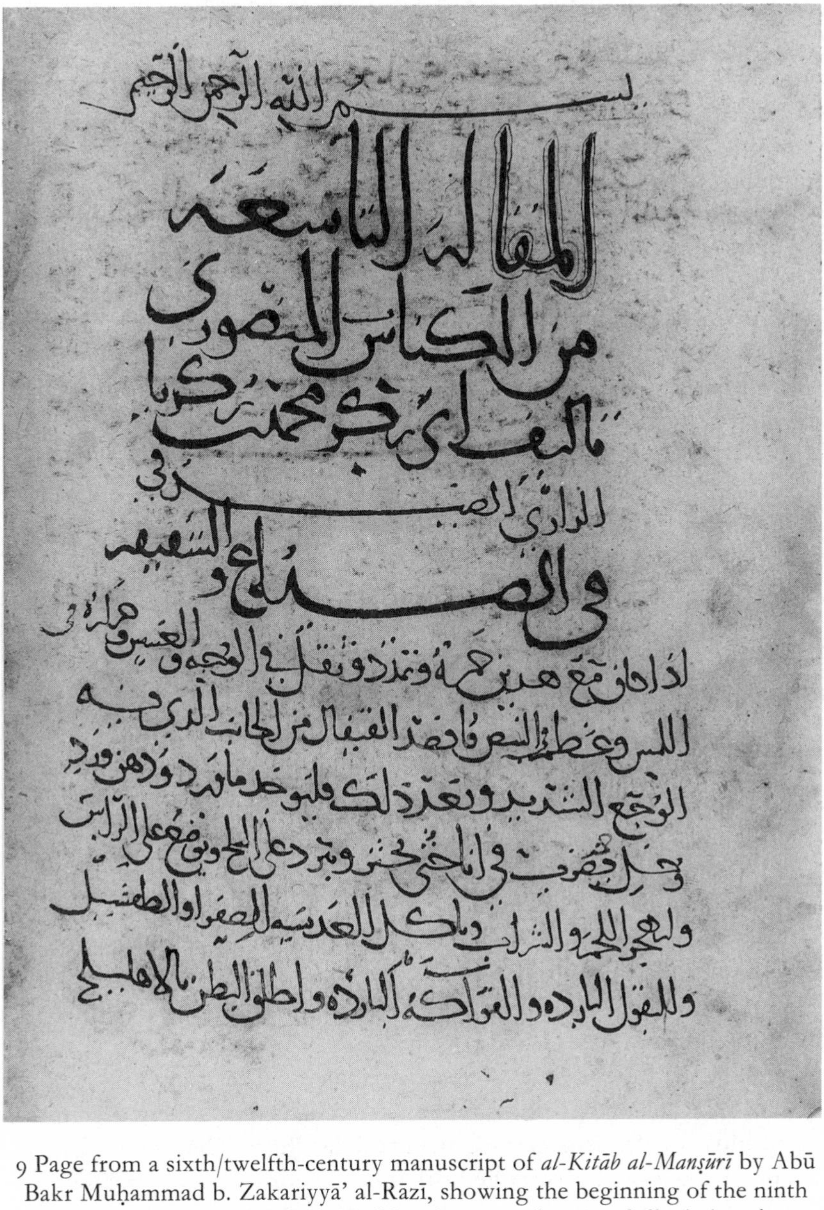

9 Page from a sixth/twelfth-century manuscript of *al-Kitāb al-Manṣūrī* by Abū Bakr Muḥammad b. Zakariyyā' al-Rāzī, showing the beginning of the ninth treatise, dealing with headache and hemicrany and ways of alleviating them.

Like all other physicians who lived in the first half of the ᶜAbbasid era ᶜAlī b. al-ᶜAbbās al-Majūsī (d. 384/994), known to Europeans as Haly Abbas, wrote his book *Kāmil al-ṣināᶜah* with the same kind of division into chapters as his predecessors. Accepting the theory of the four elements and the four humours he devised one more system of crases, dyscrases and crises, as of urine and the pulse. The book covers practice as well as theory; it is easy in style to follow, sententious and often aphoristic, and contains much original material including the first mention of anthrax. It superseded the work of al-Rāzī and became the authoritative work on anatomy. It is a much smaller work than the *Continens* of al-Rāzī, and more comprehensive than *ad Almansorem*. It is distinguished by its eminently practical character, and was first translated into Latin in AD 1127.

In the preface of his book *Kāmil al-ṣināᶜah*, al-Majūsī criticizes Muḥammad b. Zakariyyāʾ al-Rāzī for not referring to anatomy or surgery, which he, al-Majūsī, considered important, and because al-Rāzī made no mention at all of natural matters, such as the elements; on the other hand he goes on to say that al-Rāzī was very thorough, and "did not neglect the smallest thing required by the student of this art concerning the treatment of diseases". Elsewhere he remarks that al-Rāzī "treated his subject at too great length, and made his book too voluminous . . . this was the reason why most scholars were not able to order and purchase copies of the book".[24]

Of all the encyclopaedists Ibn Sīnā stands out as the most clear-thinking physician–philosopher; among the large number of books ascribed to him the most important from the medical point of view is *Kitāb al-Qānūn fī ʾl-ṭibb*, known to the Europeans as the *Canon*. In this work Ibn Sīnā presents us with the doctrine of Hippocrates and Galen modified by the system of Aristotle, together with illustrative material from later writers. It may be considered a *summa* of medical knowledge of the time. It contains a million words and is divided into five books with major and minor sections. The first book bears on generalities, offering an introduction to medicine, its definition and purpose. It covers anatomy, a discussion of the humours, temperaments, and the effect of the environment on health and disease. The second book deals with the simples (materia medica), their description, action and uses, their toxic properties and side-effects. Their side-effects, the author argues, can be ascertained either by experimentation (*tajribah*) or by analogy (*qiyās*). He supplements the theory of the four elements with the supposition that drugs act by their whole substance and not according to the elements they contain. The third book treats of special pathology and diseases of the various systems of the body. The fourth is concerned with general pathology of the body as a whole, such as fevers, crises (*buḥrān*),

24 Al-Majūsī, *Kāmil al-ṣināᶜah*, 5.

leprosy, surgery, dislocations and fractures. The fifth book is on compound drugs (pharmacopoeias and therapeutics).

Ibn Sīnā's clear thinking and keen observation are the two main pillars on which his medical works rest. He wrote minor treatises on special subjects, such as colic and the pulse, subdividing its varieties to an excessive degree.[25] He also wrote on conservation of health and on various compounds and their special uses. Humoral pathology was used by him as a device for selecting methods of possible treatment. Thus in the treatment of fevers, for example, he applies the humoral doctrine which implies that by controlling internal and external heats the imperceptible sustaining causal conditions of the disease can be altered in such a way that they can be removed by medicines, drug therapy or by other means. It thus narrows all major classes of medicines, be they simple or compounds, to warmers, coolers, purges or sudorifics; and it narrows the major non-medicinal treatment to the regulation of external heat by blood-letting, diet, baths, regimen (*ḥimyah*), exercise and massage (*ghamz*). This rational approach to treatment, he observes, influences for good not only the physical and vital pneumata but also the psychic.

Medicine and philosophy are linked in the works of Ibn Sīnā. He believed, like Aristotle before him, that where natural philosophy ends medicine begins. As a student, he had been well trained in philosophy, and in his later life he brought to this study the practical knowledge and experience of a competent physician. Thus he was able to point out the dependence of mental symptoms, such as anxiety and depression, upon bodily (physical) factors or vice versa. This embodies the modern theory of psychosomatic medicine, and this is well illustrated in the case of a lad who became ill because he was in love. When Ibn Sīnā was consulted he diagnosed the lad's complaint by feeling his pulse which became very rapid whenever the girl's town and place were mentioned.[26] A similar story is mentioned by ʿAlī al-Ṭabarī.[27]

In Book One of the *Canon*, Ibn Sīnā comments on the environment. He is well aware of the effects of the soil, water and winds on health. He opined that variations in the climate affect also the physical and mental conditions of the inhabitants, and may also to some degree account for the ups and downs of their activities. The parallel reference to environmental conditions by Ibn Khaldūn (732–808/1332–1406)[28], at a much later date, strongly supports Ibn Sīnā's statement in the *Canon*. Ibn Sīnā's remarks about the time of the year, the rising of constellations and changes of the seasons, winds and odour of the surroundings, show that prevalence of

[25] Browne, *Chahār Maqālah*, 140–1.
[26] Browne, *Arabian Medicine*, 85.
[27] Ṣiddīqī, *Firdaws al-ḥikmah*, 358.
[28] *Muqaddimah*, trans. Rosenthal, II, 376.

diseases was dependent on the climate, and throughout his chapter on the environment there are repeated references to seasonal diseases and their relationship to the equinox and solstice. He considers air as an essential element for the body and the spirit; for it acts as an adjuster in two activities: ventilation, which is helped by inhaling the fresh air, and purification by exhaling the foul air.

Ibn Sīnā may well have been indebted to his great predecessor Muḥammad b. Zakariyyāʾ al-Rāzī for some proportion of his clinical knowledge, though how much he owed to al-Rāzī who was born 115 years earlier is still not entirely clear; and if a provisional judgement is made on the capabilities of the two men, one might say that the originality of Ibn Sīnā probably lay in the theory of medicine, while that of al-Rāzī lay rather in its practice.

Ibn Sīnā was an indulgent physician, a keen observer and a perceptive diagnostician. His study of symptoms is brilliant, but his division of pain into fifteen varieties is more subtle than scientific. One cannot but admire his clinical findings and remarks concerning the association of diabetes with phthisis, the swelling of the groin with a septic leg, the clubbing of the fingers with the ulceration of lungs and finally malar flush with pneumonia. So far as we know he was the first to write a careful description of meningitis, and differentiate between meningitis proper and meningismus.

Ibn Sīnā's *Canon* prevailed in the medical world for six centuries and remained in use in Europe until the seventeenth century as the standard textbook in medical schools. The reason for this remarkable success lies in the fact that the medieval mind regarded medicine as a fixed body of unchanging truth, and the various scattered medical doctrines were collected by Ibn Sīnā into one vast corpus and set forth with great lucidity and logical cogency. He made any kind of new research unnecessary, and this particularly suited the temper of the Middle Ages. Science limited itself to possessing knowledge acquired by the Ancients, and the *Canon* contained nearly all that had been said up to that time by Greek and Arab physicians.[29] In speaking of the causation of disease, Ibn Sīnā discusses not only the conjoint causes of Galen but also the final and formal causes of Aristotle. This combination was very impressive to the medieval physician, who held that where Aristotle and Galen differed none could decide, and that where they agreed none could dissent.

SYNOPTIC MEDICAL LITERATURE

Abū ʿAlī Yaḥyā b. ʿĪsā b. Jazlah (d. *c.* 494/1100) was the first among the Arab physicians to produce a synoptic medical work. He wrote his book

[29] R. O. Moon, *The Relation of Medicine to Philosophy*, London, 1909, ch. 5.

Taqwīm al-abdān fī tadbīr al-insān ("Rectification of the Bodies in the Management of Man") after having studied medicine under Saᶜīd b. Hibatullāh at the famous ᶜAḍudī hospital in Baghdad. The book is the first of its kind which belongs to that synoptic genre of medical literature destined for the benefit of the literate lay reader and the medical student alike.[30] It is believed that Ibn Jazlah followed the example of Ibn Buṭlān, who wrote his *Taqwīm al-ṣiḥḥah* before him. A similar work is Ibn Jazlah's *Minhāj al-bayān fī mā yastaᶜmiluh al-insān* ("The Method of Demonstrating what Man Uses"). This was a popular work in which the name of the drug, its action and uses are well described in alphabetical order. ᶜAbdullāh Aḥmad b. al-Bayṭār (d. 646/1248) refers to the *Minhāj* in his work *al-Jāmiᶜ li-mufradāt al-adwiyah wa-ʾl-aghdhiyah* ("The Comprehensive Book on Simple Drugs and Foods"). Another writer of the same genre was Abū ʾl-Faraj b. al-Quff (631–85/1233–86). He wrote a synoptic commentary on Ibn Sīnā's *Canon*, a book on therapeutics, and his well-known work on surgery *Kitāb ᶜUmdat al-iṣlāḥ fī ᶜamal ṣināᶜat al-jarrāḥ* ("The Basis for the Betterment of the Surgeon's Work").

OPHTHALMOLOGY

Ophthalmology was one of the first medical specialties. The eye had received the attention of almost all physicians, and thus became included in all the encyclopaedic medical works. Eye diseases, and especially trachoma, known in Arabic as *ramad*, were endemic in western Asia and north Africa. Those who practised ophthalmology were called *kaḥḥālūn* (oculists) and those who were only cataract "couchers" were known as *qaddāḥūn*. The best-known works on eye diseases were Ḥunayn's *ᶜAshr maqālāt*, *Tadhkirat al-kaḥḥālīn* by ᶜAlī b. ᶜĪsā al-Kaḥḥāl and *al-Muntakhab fī ᶜilm al-ᶜayn* ("The Select Work on Eye Science") by ᶜAmmār b. ᶜAlī al-Mawṣilī (d. *c*. 400/1010).

The *Tadhkirat al-kaḥḥālīn* was completed by the end of the fourth/tenth century. It was written in a simple and easy style and was used extensively by oculists together with its many commentaries. It is one of the oldest books in Arabic on the anatomy of the eye and its diseases. It has been preserved in its entirety in the original Arabic. It was often consulted by the *muḥtasib* who was responsible for licensing oculists. Ibn abī Uṣaybiᶜah says of ᶜAmmār b. ᶜAlī al-Mawṣilī, the author of the *Muntakhab*, "he was a famous oculist and a practitioner of repute, with great experience in the treatment of eye diseases, and also a skilful eye surgeon." Max Meyerhof

[30] See A. B. Granville, *Catechism of Health*, London, 1932.

has translated that part of the *Muntakhab* which deals with cataract couching.[31]

Other Arab oculists[32] include Khalīfah b. ʿAlī al-Ḥalabī al-Kaḥḥāl (d. 654/1256) who wrote *al-Kāfī fī ʾl-kuḥl* ("The Sufficient in Eye Diseases"), Ṣalāḥ al-Dīn b. Yūsuf al-Ḥamawī, who lived in Ḥamāh in Syria (d. *c*. 696/1296) and wrote *Nūr al-ʿuyūn* ("The Light of the Eyes"), and lastly Abū ʿAlī Khalaf al-Ṭulūnī who started writing his book *Kitāb fī Tarkīb al-ʿaynayn wa-khilqatihimā wa-ʿilājihimā wa-adwiyatihimā* ("Book on the Composition of the Eyes, their Shape, Treatment and Medication") in 264/877 and finished it in 302/914. Ibn al-Nafīs's contribution to ophthalmology, his treatise on trachoma, should also be mentioned here.

PAEDIATRICS AND OBSTETRICS

The study of the production of sperm, the formation of the embryo and the nature of the baby was an enigma, and Arab physicians had to look back to Aristotle, Hippocrates and Galen for explanation and guidance in this difficult problem of procreation. Anatomically, the two sexes were presented as complementary, and both male and female were held to produce "sperma". Literature dealing with this subject is meagre, and the first work written in Arabic in this field is a translation of a Hippocratic work *Kitāb al-Ajinnah li-Buqrāṭ* ("Hippocrates on the Embryo"). This work is mentioned by Ibn al-Nadīm in his *Fihrist* as having been translated by Ibn Shahdā al-Karkhī, about whom he gives very little further information other than that "he translated badly from Syriac to Arabic".[33]

As far as paediatric literature is concerned, the first among the Arab physicians to write a separate treatise on this subject was Abū Jaʿfar Aḥmad b. Ibrāhīm b. al-Jazzār (282–369/895–979) who was the most celebrated pupil of Isḥāq al-Isrāʾīlī (d. between 295/907 and 343/955). The title of his treatise is *Siyāsat al-ṣibyān wa-tadbīruhum* (The Care of Children and their Management").[34] The treatise contains twenty-two chapters and the author deals with every aspect of prenatal, postnatal and neonatal care, and also the description and treatment of common children's diseases. He stresses the importance of breast-feeding and the choice of a healthy wet-nurse when mother's milk is insufficient.

Another treatise concerned with obstetrics and paediatrics is the as yet

31 *Las operaciones de cataracta*.
32 See J. Hirschberg, *History of Ophthalmology*, II, repr. Hildesheim, 1985.
33 See Lyons and Mattock, *Kitāb al-Ajinnah li-Buqrāṭ*.
34 M. H. al-Haylah, *Siyāsat al-ṣibyān wa-tadbīruhum*, Tunis, 1968.

unpublished work entitled *Maqālah fī Khalq al-insān* ("Treatise on the Creation of Man").[35] It is attributed to Abūʾl-Ḥasan Saʿīd b. Hibatullāh (437–95/1045–1101) who studied at Baghdad and became court physician to two ʿAbbasid caliphs, al-Muqtadī and his son al-Mustaẓhir. The author differs from his predecessor Ibn al-Jazzār in that he deals more with the basic medical sciences such as the anatomy of the male and female reproductive systems, sexual hygiene, menstruation, management of pregnancy and parturition. He draws chiefly on Greek sources, particularly Aristotle, Galen, Hippocrates and Soranus. The subject of growth and formation of the foetus receives more attention and there is a special chapter on miscarriage. Seven of its fifty chapters deal with children's diseases, child development and psychology related to pedagogy. There is also a chapter on birth control.[36]

On the subject of sex, Saʿīd b. Hibatullāh, like many other Arab physicians, discusses the harmful and beneficial effects of coition, frequency of indulgence in sexual relations and the indications and contra-indications of aphrodisiacs. Sexual activities, because of their excretory nature, were considered by Arab physicians as part of the "expulsive faculties" of the human body and therefore as leading to desiccation of the wholesome moistures; hence overindulgence was considered harmful. Attitudes to sexual matters in Islamic society should not be judged by standards that are totally alien to that society. In the early days of Islam the subject of sex was treated by the Prophet and his Companions in the most blunt and forthright terms, and during the formative period of Islamic law men of religion and unfeigned piety entered into the most detailed and serious discussions of sexual matters. This type of literature, dealing with subjects of a quasi-medical nature, is abundant, and many jurists, men of letters and physicians contributed to it.

MATERIA MEDICA AND MATERIA ALIMENTARIA

From the very early to comparatively late periods of the history of drug-lore, the preparation, action and uses of drugs were closely associated, often indeed identified, with witchcraft and divination. Islam tried to purge pharmacology of such practices; we find Arabic pharmaceutical tradition, on the whole, rational, clean and practical. The saying of the Prophet, "li-kulli dāʾin dawāʾ" ("for every disease there is a remedy"), is a religious explanation: it is left to the physician, through his knowledge and skill, to trace the right drug that God has created.

35 Cambridge University MS, Browne Collection.

36 Discussed by B. Musallam, *Sex and Society in Islam*, Cambridge, 1983.

The study of materia medica and other branches of natural history was carried out by the Arabs with no less vigour, and we owe to the ʿAbbasid epoch the discovery of plants and the inventions of many remedies which are still retained in many pharmacopoeias and used by many Muslims in the Indian subcontinent today. While trade was expanding between the Arabs and the rest of the world, many plants, drugs, minerals and other items useful to medicine came to the Arab practitioners. They took great interest in everything related to medicine. Sometimes they made long journeys for the purpose of securing certain plants or roots which they were unable to procure nearer home, or which they were anxious to obtain in a more perfect condition than was possible when they were purchased from the ordinary dealers.

One of the first to write a complete work on pharmacy was Abū Yūsūf Yaʿqūb b. Isḥāq al-Kindī. Since he lived in the era of translation, his medical formulary and his other works in this field bore the impression of Indian, Persian and Greek materials. Like Galen, Arab physicians considered Dioscorides' material the prime source and the foundation of their pharmacy. Dioscorides was first translated directly from Greek into Syriac by Ḥunayn while he was in the service of the caliph al-Mutawakkil. Then Stephanus son of Basilius translated the book from Greek into Arabic which was then revised by Ḥunayn in the same period. Other translations were made at later dates in Spain[37] and Diyār Bakr; the last translation was made in 547/1152 by Mihrān b. Manṣūr.[38]

ʿAbdullāh b. Aḥmad b. al-Bayṭār, second only to Dioscorides in the universality of his genius, but surpassing even that great man in his insatiable thirst for knowledge, had collected in his *al-Jāmiʿ li-mufradāt al-adwiyah wa-ʾl-aghdhiyah* all that the ancients knew of plants and herbs, 1,400 items of simples, animal, vegetable and mineral, based on his own observations and on over 150 authorities. Ibn al-Bayṭār, devoting himself to botany and materia medica, produced a work which served as a guide in these sciences until a very late period. His descriptions of some of the more valuable drugs, such as myrrh, asafoetida, squill and their different preparations are deserving of great praise. The efficacy of several remedies which he recommends has been admirably confirmed by later experience, such as the elm bark in skin diseases, male fern against worms and the use of infusion of the leaves of the willow tree to relieve pain in the joints. The compiler of the *Grete Herball* (printed by Peter Treveris at Southwark in 1526) noted that "the iuce of the leves of wilowe is good to delay the heate

[37] See below, 494–5.

[38] See M. M. Sadek, *The Arabic Materia Medica of Dioscorides*, Quebec, 1983, 17.

in fevers yf it be dronken"; if he could return now, and see the extent to which drugs based on salicin found in the willow leaves are used for this purpose and for the purpose of relief of pain he would feel that his statement had been confirmed to an extent of which he could scarcely have dreamed.[39]

Dispensing was not confined to pharmacists only; most physicians, such as al-Rāzī, Ibn Sīnā, Mūsā b. Maymūn and al-Zahrāwī wrote special treatises on the subject of drugs, their uses, and toxic effects and their antidotes. Jābir b. Ḥayyān is known to be the first to have written on poisons. Others like Yaḥyā b. al-Baṭrīq and ʿĪsā b. Māsah (third/ninth century) also wrote numerous and extensive accounts of the poisonous effects of drugs as well as their useful and therapeutic applications.

ASTROLOGY AND MEDICINE

The medieval physician interpreted the horoscope of his patient, and investigated the motions and conjunctions of the planets to help him in his diagnosis and prognosis; the modern practitioner consults the results of his blood-count, X-rays and electrocardiograms, etc. Almost every physician in ʿAbbasid times was something of an astrologer. This adherence to astrology or to the belief in the rule of the stars, i.e. the supposed influence of the heavenly bodies on human affairs, and especially upon the state of health and disease of the human body, was not a novel phenomenon of the later Middle Ages and early modern era. It was rather part and parcel of earlier medieval thought, as well as of antiquity. M. Ullmann lists a number of physicians who practised astrology, and one should not forget that there was always a conscious effort on the part of the proponents of medical astrology to lend respectability and plausibility to their belief by using the names of such physicians. Added to this there was also the keen rivalry between the astrologers and the physicians to earn favour with men of authority, such as caliphs and governors.[40] On the whole, however, astrology played only a small part in Arabic medicine. Charlatans and quacks, who mushroomed in the cities, were publicly ridiculed for their incompetent and foppish way of life. Nevertheless al-Rāzī, a great clinical observer who, with a critical mind, could describe the rhythm of the pulse so well as to distinguish between the regularly irregular and the irregularly irregular, included a short section in his book *al-Ḥāwī* on the influence of the stars on the crises of illnesses.

39 Agnes Arber, "From the medieval herbalism to the birth of modern botany" in E.A. Underwood (ed.), *Science Medicine and History*, 1, Oxford, 1953, 318.

40 Ullmann, *Islamic Medicine*, 111–14; Aḥmad al-Hāshimī, *Jawāhir al-adab fī inshāʾ lughat al-ʿArab*, Cairo, n.d., 271–5.

CHAPTER 20

AL-KINDĪ

Abū Yūsuf Yaʿqūb b. Isḥāq al-Kindī (*c.* 180–250/795–865) flourished in particular in the reign of al-Muʿtaṣim (reigned 218–27/833–42). It is said that he served as tutor to the caliph's son Aḥmad, to whom some of his writings are dedicated. Others are dedicated to the caliph himself. Most are short didactic pieces of strictly limited scope. A few dozen survive, some in Latin or Hebrew translation. Many more titles are recorded by the bibliographers, covering an enormous range of subjects. Al-Kindī wrote on questions of mathematics, logic, physics, psychology, metaphysics and ethics, but also on perfumes, drugs, foods, precious stones, musical instruments, swords, bees and pigeons. He wrote against the false claims of the alchemists, the atomism of the *mutakallimūn*, the dualism of the Manichaeans, and the trinitarian dogma of the Christians. He supported astrology, calculated the duration of the Arab empire, and speculated on the causes of natural phenomena such as comets, earthquakes, tides or the colour of the sky. He also took an interest in distant countries and ancient nations, collecting information on Socrates (whom he confused with Diogenes the Cynic), the Ḥarranians and the rites of India. A similar range of topics was later covered by al-Kindī's pupil Aḥmad b. al-Ṭayyib al-Sarakhsī, tutor and boon-companion of the caliph al-Muʿtaḍid (reigned 279–89/892–902). No doubt al-Kindī, too, had played the part of a cultured polymath who, wearing his learning lightly, strove to captivate, divert and instruct a courtly public. That aim explains the character also of his theoretical pieces. They are designed to afford the reader a glimpse of what "philosophy" (i.e. speculative science) can do, without unduly taxing his powers of attention.

At the same time al-Kindī makes it clear that philosophy is no easy matter. Philosophical knowledge, he says, consists in understanding why things are the way they are. Such understanding is not gained in a day. It requires protracted application to the contributions made by many men over many centuries. The aspiring philosopher must understand the mathematical sciences of the *quadrivium* (arithmetic, geometry, music and astronomy) before turning to the writings of Aristotle on logic, physics, metaphysics and ethics (for the philosopher seeks not only to know what is true but also to do what is right), in order then to move on to other sciences (such as astrology or medicine) building on those foundations.

The programme of philosophical study adopted by al-Kindī is that of sixth-century Alexandria. Much of his work is devoted to the restoration of the ancient curriculum. As the Graeco-Arabic translation movement was gathering momentum around him, al-Kindī was moved by the appearance in Arabic of Euclid, Ptolemy, and other mathematical classics to tackle the legacy of Aristotle. He took only a cursory interest in Aristotle's logic, summaries of which had been available for some time; and his moral writings scarcely rose above the level of popular wisdom literature. But he did break a lot of new ground in physics, metaphysics, and the theory of mind and soul that was supposed to bridge the gap between the two. We still have some of the versions of Aristotle he used: of the *De Caelo*, *Meteorology*, *Metaphysics* and perhaps the *De Anima*. Other parts of the *corpus Aristotelicum* may have been available to him in summaries. He was certainly familiar with the *Physics*, possibly through some version of the sixth-century commentary of John Philoponus of Alexandria. Some of those versions, if not all, seem to have been specially commissioned by al-Kindī from Christians capable of translating directly from Greek rather than, as was often done, from Syriac intermediaries.

There are, further, substantial remains of a large volume of subsidiary material assembled under the title of *Aristotle's Theology*, from the writings of the Aristotelian philosopher Alexander of Aphrodisias (*fl.* AD 200) and the neo-Platonists Plotinus (third century AD) and Proclus (fifth century AD). The title was later misunderstood. The *Theology of Aristotle* that has come down to us, as a book *by* Aristotle, is a chance collection of pages from the Kindī-circle Plotinus. The original *Theology* was a reader in the natural theology of Greek philosophy in the tradition of Aristotle – and, for that matter, Plato; for al-Kindī subscribed to the late Greek dogma of the ultimate unity of Plato and Aristotle, and in any case was more interested in the consensus of the Ancients than in their disagreements.

Unlike the translations of Aristotle, which closely follow the original Greek, the texts of the *Theology* are free adaptations. They share so many peculiarities with one another and al-Kindī's own writings that they must have been produced by a team collaborating, presumably under al-Kindī's direction. Another text bearing the hallmark of al-Kindī's workshop is an anonymous paraphrase of Aristotle's *De Anima*. It argues, among other things, that soul is a substance, that it is immortal, and that the celestial bodies have volition, sight and hearing – tenets shared by al-Kindī and the *Theology* but not by Aristotle's *De Anima*. Similarly, the *Theology* inserts into the philosophy of Alexander, Plotinus and Proclus a theory stated by al-Kindī as follows: "Strictly and primarily, action is the bringing into being (*taʾyīs*) of something from nothing (*al-aysāt min lays*). Action in that sense is clearly peculiar to God, the ultimate cause of everything. And in that special sense action is called origination (*ibdāʿ*)."[1] Accordingly, the God of the *Theology* is an originator (*mubdiʿ*), creating things from nothing. Neither Aristotle nor Alexander, Plotinus or Proclus had believed in creation from nothing. They had thought that there must always have been matter, motion, time – a view explicitly rejected by al-Kindī. The translator-adaptors of the Kindī circle evidently brought their ancient sources into accord, not only with one another, but also with their own beliefs. Since they changed what they disliked, they must have liked what they retained. The Kindī-circle *Theology* and *De Anima* give a much fuller picture than do al-Kindī's own writings of the kind of philosophy he was commending to his public. They are the first attempt in Arabic at gathering the best of pre-Islamic thought into a universal theory of God, mind, soul and nature. And they mark the beginning in the world of Islam of a tradition of "human science" (as opposed to the "divine science" of revelation) shared by intellectuals of different faiths.

The philosophy of al-Kindī and his circle is distinguished by certain idiosyncrasies of style and thought. Its most striking feature is a flamboyant and sometimes obscure vocabulary. Transliterated Greek terms (e.g. *hayūlā*, *fanṭāsiyā*,) are used more freely than in later Graeco-Arabic literature. Neologisms include nouns and verbs derived from Arabic particles (e.g. *huwiyyah*, *ayyasa*), and particles used as nouns (e.g. *al-ann*, *lays*, *ays*). Another characteristic is the use of certain set phrases to demarcate the stages of an argument (e.g. "To return to the matter in hand, we say that . . ."; "Thus it has now become clear that . . ."). It springs from a special concern with the structure of argument as evinced by some of al-Kindī's essays, where he takes great care to make his reasoning both clear and sound by proceeding in the manner of Euclid's geometry. For example, in arguing the finitude of the world, he painstakingly sets out a number of basic propositions which he endeavours to establish by showing that the opposite assumption in each case cannot be entertained because it leads to contradictions. No doubt it was Proclus' *Elements of Theology* (included, at least in part, in the Kindī-circle *Theology*) that inspired him to apply Euclid's procedure to questions of metaphysics. For that treatise comprises a whole system of metaphysics in a series of propositions argued *more geometrico*. Al-Kindī follows its lead also in other respects. For example, in arguing the createdness of the

[1] *Rasāʾil al-Kindī al-falsafiyyah*, ed. Abū Rīdah, I, Cairo, 1950, 182–3.

universe and the oneness of its creator, he heavily relies on the following propositions expounded by Proclus: that there can be no oneness without multiplicity; and that the oneness of all things possessed of multiplicity must be derivative.

Al-Kindī's insistence on creation from nothing sets him apart from the mainstream of later *falsafah*. (Another distinctive feature is his belief in astrology.) *Kalām* too was insisting on creation from nothing, and in some respects al-Kindī is closer to contemporary *kalām* than to later *falsafah*. Like the *mutakallimūn*, he believes in the supremacy of revelation, the need for rational explanation, and the efficacy of arguments *per impossibile* (if a proposition entails a contradiction, it cannot be true; and if one or the other of two propositions must be true, and one cannot be true, the other must be true). Such similarities are best explained by the fact that al-Kindī grew up at a time when smart society was under the sway of *kalām*. But the direction he took was frowned upon by the *mutakallimūn*. They rudely mocked his pretensions and, indeed, accused him of straying beyond the pale of Islam. In return we find al-Kindī muttering about opportunists trading in religious speculation for the sake of political influence and undeserved acclaim. Presumably he was referring to certain Muᶜtazilites who had the ear of the court at the time.

Some of al-Kindī's occasional remarks on reason and revelation hint at the source of his quarrel with the *mutakallimūn*. Truth, he holds, is the domain of reason. No truth of revelation can altogether be beyond the grasp of reason. But what, if that is so, is the point of having prophets? Should not the student of philosophy be able to dispense with revelation? Al-Kindī's answer is that scientific explanation moves but slowly. For all the knowledge accumulated by past philosophers, some of the truth eluded them. Prophets, by contrast, are spared the toil of theoretical enquiry (*naẓar*). The truth of what to us are the sweeping and sometimes cryptic pronouncements of scripture is revealed to them with full and instant clarity. To grasp that truth we must supply the arguments that will make it clear to our own, less inspired, minds. We cannot share the prophet's knowledge simply by repeating the pronouncements of scripture like mindless parrots. There is no knowledge without understanding, and no understanding without proper argument from first principles.

Al-Kindī's complaint is that the *mutakallimūn* argue *from*, not *to*, the truth of revelation; that they ignore the principles of mathematics and natural philosophy; and that they refuse to learn from the Greeks. The last point is the crucial one: the dispute is about the relevance to Muslim education of traditions of learning other than those developed in the first two centuries of Islam. (That attitude was not, of course, peculiar to the *mutakallimūn*, but al-Kindī's quarrel was with them in particular because they undertook, without reference to the Greeks, the kind of theoretical enquiry at which the Greeks had excelled.) Al-Kindī deplores the narrow Arabism of those disowning Greek science just because it had been ignored by earlier Muslims. His essay *Fī ʾl-Falsafah al-ūlā* ("On First Philosophy") opens with a memorable plea for alien wisdom: knowledge ennobles, whatever its source. On another occasion he is said to have claimed that Yūnān, the ancestor of the Greeks, had been a brother of Qaḥṭān, the ancestor of the southern Arabs (including his own tribe of Kindah), implying that Greek wisdom was not so alien after all. Clearly, the view that Muslim culture must be based squarely on the legacy (language, scripture, poetry and other institutions) of Arabia was already well entrenched. Al-Kindī's protest nicely illustrates that Arabic Hellenism (like, for the most part, the Shuʿūbiyyah movement) sprang from a preference for a more broadly based, more cosmopolitan culture. As an Arab nobleman, he was clearly not against the Arabs or the legacy of Arabia. There was no question of abandoning the Arabic language, or of replacing Arab lore with, say, Homeric mythology. Neither was one going to cultivate the legacy of the Greeks to the exclusion of anyone else's. One wanted to rejoice in the rich plurality of cultural traditions inherited by Islam. Greek science was too good a thing to pass over. The Arabic language was to be enriched by Greek words and concepts, but it was not to be Hellenized to anything like the extent that Syriac had been. Al-Kindī and his circle aimed for an idiom which for all the strange ideas it served to convey was soundly Arabic in structure. The language of the Kindī-circle *Theology* is prominently modelled on that of the Qurʾān.

Al-Kindī's campaign to expand the scope of Muslim education did not achieve its aim. *Falsafah* remained a foreign, un-Islamic science in most Muslim eyes. It must be rated as his greatest success that it remained at all, though his work had little influence on subsequent developments. His school, such as it was, came to an end with the execution of his pupil Aḥmad b. al-Ṭayyib al-Sarakhsī in Baghdad towards the end of the third/ninth century. For a while he had some following in the provinces. The philosopher–physician Isḥāq al-Isrāʾīlī of Ifrīqiyah (d. between 295/907 and 343/955) made extensive use of his writings and helped to spread his influence to the Jews of Andalusia and ultimately to the Latins. Abū Zayd Aḥmad al- Balkhī, whose philosophical writings are lost, professed himself to be a follower of al-Kindī. Other indications, too, suggest that al-Kindī was studied in greater Khurāsān. Ibn Sīnā may have known his work; he certainly knew some of the Kindī-circle *Theology*. So did the Ismāʿīlīs of early fourth/tenth-century Khurāsān, who revised their theology in the light of it. Perhaps al-Kindī's most abiding contribution to the history of *falsafah* lies in the textbooks he commissioned: the *De Caelo*, the *Metaphysics*, and above all the *Theology*. Yet though he is scarcely mentioned by al-Fārābī and other later philosophers (*falāsifah*), there may have been more of a continuity than they cared to admit. Some of al-Fārābī's most notable contributions – such as his fourfold division of reason (ʿ*aql*), his theory of prophecy in terms of the Aristotelian faculties of the soul, or his theory of moral action as the ultimate goal of philosophy – are foreshadowed in the writings of al-Kindī. The Alexandrian syllabus adopted by al-Kindī was never abandoned. And the close tie established by the Kindī circle between Aristotelian and neo-Platonic cosmology was never completely unpicked. Extensions and alterations notwithstanding, the edifice of classical *falsafah* continued to exhibit the original design of al-Kindī.

CHAPTER 21

AL-RĀZĪ

BIOGRAPHY AND RELIGIOUS VIEWS

Medieval authors have left confused and contradictory biographical accounts of Abū Bakr Muḥammad b. Zakariyyāʾ al-Rāzī (Rhazes), the most original physician–philosopher among the Arabic-speaking peoples.[1] He was born in Rayy (near modern Tehran) probably in 251/865. Physicians, he believed, should practise in great cities which abound in patients and skilful medical men;[2] hence his sojourn in Baghdad, where, in his youth, he studied and practised medicine at its hospital (*bīmāristān*).[3] Later he returned to Rayy, at the invitation of its governor, al-Manṣūr b. Isḥāq, to assume responsibility as director of its hospital. To this ruler al-Rāzī dedicated his *al-Kitāb al-Manṣūrī fīʾl-ṭibb* (*Liber ad Almansorem*)[4] and *al-Ṭibb al-rūḥānī* ("Spiritual Physic").[5] These two books were meant to be complementary: the former treats of diseases of the body, the latter, diseases of the soul.

Having achieved fame in Rayy, al-Rāzī returned to Baghdad to become head of its newly founded al-Muʿtaḍidī hospital, named after al-Muʿtaḍid (reigned 279–89/892–902). On account of political events, and in relation to high-ranking positions he had held, he resided on several occasions either in Baghdad or Rayy, but spent the last years of his life in Rayy suffering from glaucoma (*al-māʾ*), until he became blind and died in his birthplace around 313/925 or 320/932.

Al-Rāzī's self-restraint and modesty are best expressed in his own words, in *al-Sīrah al-falsafiyyah*:[6]

I have neither shown avarice nor extravagance; nor have I had any disputes or quarrels; nor have I ever acted unjustly against anyone. On the contrary, I have

[1] Ibn al-Nadīm, *Fihrist*, ed. G. Flügel, Leipzig, 1871–2, I, 299–301, 358; Kraus, *Epître de Bērūnī*; al-Qifṭī, *Ikhbār al-ʿulamāʾ*, 271–7; Ibn abī Uṣaybiʿah, *ʿUyūn al-anbāʾ* I, 309–21.

[2] Iskandar, "Ar-Rāzī on examining physicians", 495.

[3] A.Z. Iskandar, "L'âge d'ar-Rāzī au début de ses études de médecine", *al-Mashriq*, LIV, 1960, 168–77.

[4] Ibn al-Nadīm, *Fihrist*, I, 300; Kraus, *Epître de Bērūnī*, 6, no. 8; al-Qifṭī, *Ikhbār al-ʿulamāʾ*, 274; Ibn abī Uṣaybiʿah, *ʿUyūn al-anbāʾ*, I, 317.

[5] Kraus, *Epître de Bērūnī*, 19, no. 148; al-Qifṭī *Ikhbār al-ʿulamāʾ*, 273; Ibn abī Uṣaybiʿah, *ʿUyūn al-anbāʾ*, I, 315; for the Arabic text see Kraus, *Rasāʾil Falsafiyyah*, 1–96; A. J. Arberry, *The Spiritual Physick of Rhazes*, London, 1950.

[6] See above, ch. 11, 185.

been known to surrender my own rights. As regards food, drink, and amusement, my frequent guests know that I have never exceeded any reasonable limits. The same is also true of all the conditions of my life, as may be noted from my clothing and mount, and my servants and housemaids.[7]

In *al-Ṭibb al-rūḥānī*, in the first chapter "On the excellence and praise of reason", al-Rāzī asserts that reason (*ᶜaql*) is the ultimate authority which "should govern, and not be governed; should control, and not be controlled; should lead, and not be led".[8] He fought against absolute authority which, in religion, placed the prophets at the top of the list of mankind.[9] The system of the grading of men into classes was acceptable in the fifth-sixth/eleventh-twelfth century, as is clearly indicated in Sharaf al-Zamān Ṭāhir al-Marwazī's book on zoology.[10]

A lost book on religious criticism, *Fī Makhārīq al-anbiyāᵓ* ("On the Tricks of the Prophets"),[11] is attributed to al-Rāzī. According to him, religions breed enmity between people, and lead to wars and destruction. He claims that men do not need the authority of any of the prophets of the three monotheistic religions.[12] The fact that al-Rāzī was neither executed nor imprisoned on account of his heretical views reflects the tolerance of the fourth/tenth-century Muslim Iranian men of power. Rulers and princes, and al-Rāzī's numerous patients from all walks of life, held him in high esteem, and admired his much-needed medical skills. Nevertheless, al-Rāzī was censured; his *Fī Makhārīq al-anbiyāᵓ* was destroyed, and his views were refuted. One of his contemporaries, the Ismāᶜīlī Abū Ḥātim Aḥmad b. Ḥamdān al-Rāzī, wrote in *Aᶜlām al-nubuwwah* ("The Signs of Prophecy") that: "the heretic [al-Rāzī] claimed that by his wisdom he had understood what was unknown to his predecessors; he wrote a confused and foolish essay in which he said that he matched Hippocrates in the art of physic, and that in philosophy, he was an equal to Socrates."[13]

THE PHILOSOPHY OF AL-RĀZĪ

As a philosopher, al-Rāzī was a follower of Socrates; the difference between him and Socrates, he says, was in quantity (*kammiyyah*), not quality (*kayfiyyah*).[14] Al-Rāzī defends the philosophic conduct of Socrates, saying that people only mention the earlier period of his life, during which he had lived in seclusion and led an ascetic life; but he adds that, during these formative years, Socrates had devoted all his time to philosophy, a subject

7 *Rasāᵓil Falsafiyyah*, 110. 8 Ibid., 18. 9 Ibid., 293.
10 A. Z. Iskandar, "A doctor's book on Zoology: al-Marwazī's Ṭabāᵓiᶜ al-ḥayawān (Nature of Animals) re-assessed", *Oriens*, XXVII–XXVIII, 1981, 276. 11 See, for example, Ibn al-Nadīm, *Fihrist*, I, 301.
12 Kraus, *Rasāᵓil Falsafiyyah*, 292. 13 Kraus, "Raziana I", 303–4. 14 Kraus, *Rasāᵓil Falsafiyyah*, 100.

which he loved greatly. In his later life, Socrates led a normal life and participated in social activities.[15] Al-Rāzī disapproves of the monastic life of the Christians, and repudiates the idle life of Muslims who linger in mosques and refrain from earning a livelihood or doing any work.[16]

In *Kitāb al-ʿIlm al-ilāhī* ("The Divine Science"), another lost work from which fragments have survived in later sources, al-Rāzī explains his doctrine of the five pre-eternal principles (*al-qudamāʾ al-khamsah*):[17] Creator (*al-bāriʾ*), soul (*al-nafs*), matter (*al-hayūlā*), space (*al-makān*) and time (*al-zamān*). He writes: "I say that these five are pre-eternal, and that the world is created";[18] he rejected the Aristotelian tenet of the eternity of the world (*qidam al-ʿālam*).

The authority of books on medicine and philosophy was unacceptable to al-Rāzī. He devoted a large book, *Fī ʾl-Shukūk ʿalā Jālīnūs* ("Doubts about Galen"),[19] so far unpublished, to the criticism of precepts in twenty-eight of Galen's books, beginning with *al-Burhān* ("Demonstration"),[20] and ending with *al-Nabḍ al-kabīr* ("On the Pulse").[21] In his introduction to *al-Shukūk* al-Rāzī acknowledges with humility his debt to Galen, declaring that he himself is Galen's follower and disciple. Al-Rāzī adds that Galen was a leading master and a great teacher of both philosophy and medicine. Nevertheless, al-Rāzī argues that, since the art of healing is a philosophy, it can neither renounce criticism, nor can it tolerate submission to the authority of books. In *al-Shukūk*, al-Rāzī also writes that Galen censured his students and followers who accepted knowledge unsubstantiated by the demonstrative method.[22]

Al-Rāzī believed in the progress of scientific knowledge: he who studies the works of the ancients, gains the experience of their labour as if he himself had lived thousands of years spent on investigation.[23] In this precept, he repeats Galen's views in *Fī anna al-Ṭabīb al-fāḍil faylasūf* ("That the Excellent Physician is a Philosopher").[24]

[15] Ibid., 99–101. [16] Ibid., 105. [17] Ibid., 191–290.

[18] This statement appears in Abū Ḥātim Aḥmad b. Ḥamdān al-Rāzī's *Aʿlām al-nubuwwah*; see Kraus, *Rasāʾil Falsafiyyah*, 308; "Raziana II", 51.

[19] Ibn al-Nadīm, *Fihrist*, 1, 299; Kraus, *Epître de Bērūnī*, 13; al-Qifṭī, *Ikhbār al-ʿulamāʾ*, 273; Ibn abī Uṣaybiʿah, *ʿUyūn al-anbāʾ*, 1, 316; among the known MSS are: Bagdatli Vehbi, Istanbul, MS 1488/26, fols. 231b–248b; Majlis, Tehran, MS 3821, fols. 150b–185b; Millī Malik, Tehran, MS 4554/23, pp. 1–29. [20] Millī Malik, Tehran, MS 4554/23, p. 2, line 14.

[21] Ibid., p. 27, line 39.

[22] Ibid., p. 1, lines 20–36; see S. Pines, "Rāzī critique de Galien", *Actes du VIIᵉ Congrès International d'Histoire des Sciences, Jerusalem, 1953*, Paris, 480–7.

[23] Iskandar, "Ar-Rāzī on examining physicians", 496–7.

[24] *Galens Abhandlung darüber, dass der vorzügliche Arzt Philosoph sein muss* (arabisch und deutsch herausgegeben, *Nachrichten der Akademie der Wissenschaften zu Göttingen*. Phil.-hist. Kl., 1965, Abh. 1), ed. P. Bachmann, 18.

THE MEDICAL WRITINGS OF AL-RĀZĪ

Ibn al-Nadīm and al-Qifṭī mention that al-Rāzī compiled an index of his own works.[25] So far as is known all manuscripts of this index are now lost. He wrote about 200 works on medicine, philosophy, alchemy and other subjects; these vary in size from short treatises to voluminous textbooks and encyclopaedic works.

It is appropriate here to clarify uncertainties regarding two works: *al-Ḥāwī fī ʾl-ṭibb* ("The Comprehensive Book on Medicine")[26] and *al-Jāmiʿ al-kabīr* ("The Great Comprehensive Book"), which have always been wrongly considered identical, on account of the similarity between the meaning of the two Arabic words *al-Ḥāwī* and *al-Jāmiʿ*. The common roots *ḥawā* and *jamaʿa*, from which the titles are derived, both mean "collect" or "gather together".

Al-Ḥāwī fī ʾl-ṭibb

Evidence from manuscripts and printed sources of *al-Ḥāwī* (*Continens*) shows that it was merely a commonplace book, an *aide-mémoire*, and a private record of the author's comments and reflections on case-histories of his patients and on medical books written from the time of Hippocrates down to his own time. In the fourth/tenth century, *al-Ḥāwī* would probably have been considered the private library of a well-read physician.

The arrangement of the subject-matter in *al-Ḥāwī* gives the impression that the author probably had several study-files, each containing quires (*kurrāsāt*) for copying notes from reference books. He did not neglect to record even those opinions which seemed false to him, invariably adding his private comments and personal experiences and identifying them as his own with the possessive *lī* (mine). Sometimes he corrected statements which he quoted from reference books, and wrote remarks under such titles as, "mine, with amendments". Each of al-Rāzī's medical study-files was reserved for notes on a certain topic: one was specifically for diseases of the head, another for diseases of the chest, and so forth. These medical files might have been arranged in a certain systematic order, in accordance with the accepted method of writing medical books, beginning with the head and working downwards to the toes (*mina ʾl-qarn ilā ʾl-qadam*).[27] From these

25 Ibn al Nadīm, *Fihrist*, I, 299, 302; al-Qifṭī, *Ikhbār al-ʿulamāʾ*, 273.

26 *Kitāb al-Ḥāwī fīʾl-ṭibb (Continens of Rhazes), an Encyclopaedia of Medicine by Abū Bakr Muḥammad b. Zakariyyāʾ al-Rāzī (d.* A. H. *313*/AD *925)*, Hyderabad and Deccan, 1955–71.

27 See al-Rāzī's introductory sections to his books: *Ilā man lā yaḥḍuruh al-ṭabīb*, Wellcome Institute for the History of Medicine, WHS Or. 23, fol. 1b, lines 6–12; *al-Ṭibb al-mulūkī*, Bibliotheca Universitatis, Leiden, MS Or. 585/4, fol. 46a, lines 16–20.

private notes al-Rāzī selected subject-matter for his other written works, such as *al-Qūlanj* ("Colitis");[28] *al-Manṣūrī*;[29] *al-Jadarī wa-ᵓl-ḥaṣbah* ("Smallpox and Measles");[30] and *al-Adwiyah al-mufradah* ("Materia Medica").[31] Clinical observations concerning illnesses which affected al-Rāzī himself are recorded in *al-Ḥāwī*. In one remark, he writes on an effective treatment he used for inflammation of his uvula, by gargling with astringent and acid vinegar.[32] Again, learning by personal experience from a fever which attacked him, he writes a short private note: ". . . mine: During my sojourn in Baghdad, I was smitten by a fever accompanied by rigor. The pulse was increased and then I became feverish. No sweats came upon me. The fever then departed and did not recur. Accordingly, we should learn that when fever is accompanied by rigor it is not necessarily non-ephemeral; as the contrary is also true."[33] In another note, written strictly for private use, he writes on his swollen right testicle (a matter which did not worry him in the least because it was not painful) and adds that he used emetics continuously until his testicle became as it originally was.[34]

Al-Jāmiᶜ al-kabīr

It is understandable that al-Rāzī should have neglected to mention *al-Ḥāwī* by name in any of his other books, since authors do not cite the titles of their private notebooks. Ibn al-Nadīm and Ibn abī Uṣaybiᶜah mention *al-Jāmiᶜ al-kabīr* in al-Rāzī's bibliography, adding that it consists of twelve parts (*aqsām*). They disagree, however, on the titles of some of its parts, and confuse *al-Jāmiᶜ* with *al-Ḥāwī*.[35] Al-Rāzī refers several times to his book *al-Jāmiᶜ al-kabīr* and describes the lengthy years of hard work he had spent writing it. In his book *al-Sīrah al-falsafiyyah* he writes that he laboured hard for fifteen years, working night and day on the production of *al-Jāmiᶜ al-kabīr*, until his sight failed and the muscles of his hand were painfully strained (probably writer's cramp).[36] In another place in *al-Sīrah al-falsafiyyah* he mentions the titles of some of his medical writings as samples of his achievements, and concludes with the statement: "none of my

[28] Cf. subject-matter in *al-Ḥāwī* (VIII, 101–220) against the text of *al-Qūlanj*, Cambridge University Library, MS Add. 3516, fol. 48b, line 12–62b, line 11; Leiden Library, MS Or. 585/3, fols. 26a–45b.
[29] *Ḥāwī*, XIX, 241–404; *al-Manṣūrī*, Bodleian Library, MS Marsh 248, fols. 76, line 9–108, line 9.
[30] English trans. W. A. Greenhill, *A Treatise on the Small-Pox and Measles*, London, 1848. Greenhill (101–30) has shown that the text of *al-Jadarī wa-ᵓl-ḥaṣbah* is derived from *al-Ḥāwī*, Bodleian Library MS Marsh 156, fols. 282a, line 22–291b, line 19.
[31] *Ḥāwī*, XX, 1–617; *al-Adwiyah al-mufradah*, Wellcome Institute for the History of Medicine, WMS Or. 123, fols. 52b–86b. [32] *Ḥāwī*, III, 279.
[33] Ibid., XIV, 54; Bodleian Library, MS Marsh 156, fol. 82a, lines 4–6.
[34] Bodleian Library, MS Arab. b. 10, fol. 299a, lines 20–1.
[35] Ibn al-Nadīm, *Fihrist*, I, 300; Ibn abī Uṣaybiᶜah, *ᶜUyūn al-anbāᵓ*, I, 317–18.
[36] Kraus, *Rasāᵓil Falsafiyyah*, 110.

countrymen has ever produced any work to rival *Kitāb al-Jāmiʿ*, nor has my example been followed."[37]

Al-Rāzī also refers four times to *al-Jāmiʿ al-kabīr* in his book *al-Fuṣūl* ("Aphorisms"), which was written to serve as an introduction to medicine and to guide prospective physicians in choosing books from a reading list, and again he refers to *al-Jāmiʿ al-kabīr* in his *al-Aqrābādhīn al-mukhtaṣar* ("Abridged formulary") of which only one manuscript exists.[38] In his criticism of Galen's books, in *al-Shukūk*, al-Rāzī refers the readers several times to better accounts written in his book *al-Jāmiʿ al-kabīr*.[39]

In one section in *al-Ḥāwī*, on diseases of the eye, there is further evidence that al-Rāzī had intended to add a part on ophthalmology to the twelve parts of *al-Jāmiʿ al-kabīr*.[40] Besides, on the diagnosis of a composite attack of tertian and hectic fevers, he jots down a remark in *al-Ḥāwī* that he would make a thorough study of this subject and then would write down the results of his research in *al-Jāmiʿ al-kabīr*.[41]

Taken together the above-mentioned sources provide conclusive evidence that al-Rāzī wrote a medical encyclopaedia which he called *al-Jāmiʿ al-kabīr*, and that he had hoped to increase the number of its parts by two, one entitled *al-Jāmiʿ fī ʾl-ʿayn* and the second *al-Jāmiʿ fī ʾl-ḥummayāt*. Since he refers to *al-Jāmiʿ al-kabīr* in *al-Ḥāwī* these two works are evidently different.

In *Kitāb Ṣaydalat al-ṭibb* ("Pharmacology in Medicine"), which is merely a part of *al-Jāmiʿ al-kabīr*,[42] al-Rāzī states that pharmacology is a subsidiary branch of medicine. Nevertheless, studying this subject during leisure is a sign that a physician has great interest in his work. This subsidiary art should come second to a good grasp of the subjects on medicine proper or, at least, not before a good grounding in the minimum essentials in the basic subjects. Al-Rāzī was also aware that some gifted physicians are naturally equipped with the ability to study an art like pharmacy without any fear of being unable to master the theory and practice of medicine.

This book emphasizes an early date of specialization in Arabic pharmacology. A study of its text, together with a later text by al-Bīrūnī, *al-Ṣaydanah fī ʾl-ṭibb*,[43] should help to establish in a new dimension the history of Arabic pharmacy in relation to medicine. Galen distinguished between physicians and pharmacists. Al-Rāzī favoured this distinction and, according to him, books on pharmacy should contain, among other things, accounts of

[37] Ibid., 109. [38] Wellcome Institute for the History of Medicine, WMS Or. 9, fol. 24a, line 2.

[39] Millī Malik, Tehran, MS 4554/23, 19, lines 29–31, 40–1; fol. 20, lines 16–20, 23–5, 27–33.

[40] *Ḥāwī*, II, 26–7.

[41] Bodleian Library, MS Marsh 156, fol. 238a, lines 7–9 (al-Rāzī's private notes on *Kitāb al-Ḥummayāt* occupy fols. 2b, line 1–314b, line 4); see also *Ḥāwī*, XIV–XVI and XVII, 1–119.

[42] Ibn al-Nadīm, *Fihrist*, I, 300; Ibn abī Uṣaybiʿah, *ʿUyūn al-anbāʾ*, I, 318.

[43] See below ch. 24, 420–1.

origins and descriptions of pure and adulterated forms of drugs, good and bad specimens and virtues of drugs. These works are written for *ṣayādilah* (pharmacists), whom al-Rāzī considers to be specialists in a branch closely associated with medicine and contributing to it, but far from being physicians. Pharmacists should be mainly concerned with purchasing pure species of drugs, storing them safely, and ensuring non-adulteration of drugs.[44]

On the other hand, *aqrābādhīnāt* (formularies) are written by physicians for the use of practitioners. They contain recipes and instructions on the compounding of drugs, both for physicians who dispense their own drugs and for pharmacists who serve them. Al-Rāzī wrote an *aqrābādhīn*, called *al-Adwiyah al-murakkabah* ("Compound Drugs"),[45] which has been preserved in a few manuscripts.[46]

Medical education in the time of al-Rāzī was based mainly on reading Arabic translations of earlier books. Al-Rāzī thought that it would be useful to define the names of drugs, diseases and organs which, though transliterated, were not translated into Arabic. It was equally essential, in his opinion, to have a knowledge of foreign units of weight and measures for writing recipes, together with their equivalents in the Arab world, if foreign formularies were to be used at all by practising physicians.

Another part of *al-Jāmiᶜ al-kabīr* is entitled *Fī ᵓstinbāṭ al-asmāᵓ wa-ᵓl-awzān wa-ᵓl-makāyīl al-majhūlah al-wāqiᶜah fī kutub al-ṭibb* ("On Finding the Meaning of Unfamiliar Terms, Weights, and Measures Occurring in Books on Medicine").[47] *Fī ᵓstinbāṭ al-asmāᵓ* is a type of polyglot lexicon in which each unfamiliar term – whether Greek, Syriac, Persian, Indian or even Arabic – is placed in a column, followed by a definition or translation given in the opposite column. Although al-Rāzī wrote in his introduction to this part of *al-Jāmiᶜ al-kabīr* that he would mark the linguistic origin of each unfamiliar term, by writing next to it a certain letter of the alphabet, these key letters are very frequently missing from the text. Prospective editors of this particular book are likely to meet a wide range of etymological difficulties, in five different languages. A copyist, who probably knew very little about the text he was transcribing, says in a marginal remark: "these terms seem to be in different tongues; their obscure meanings are intelligible only to able linguists of sound judgement."[48] Al-Rāzī also writes, in

[44] Bodleian Library, MS Bod. Or. 561, fols. 1b, line 2–4a, line 13; Escorial MS 815, fols. 2b, line 2–4b, line 19.

[45] Ibn al-Nadīm, *Fihrist*, I, 300; Kraus, *Epître de Bērūnī*, 7, no. 13; al-Qifṭī, *Ikhbār al-ᶜulamāᵓ*, 274; Ibn abī Uṣaybiᶜah, *ᶜUyūn al-anbāᵓ*, I, 316.

[46] *GAL*, I, 269, no. 4; Bodleian Library, MS Marsh 537/3, fols. 158a–181a; Millī Malik, Tehran, MS 4573, pp. 1–14.

[47] Ibn al-Nadīm, *Fihrist*, I, 300; Ibn abī Uṣaybiᶜah, *ᶜUyūn al-anbāᵓ*, I, 318.

[48] Bodleian Library, MS Or. 561, fol. 55a. This part of *Kitāb al-Jāmiᶜ al-kabīr* was printed under the title of *al-Ḥāwī*, XXII, 61–412.

Fī ʾstinbāṭ al-asmāʾ, that he intentionally included exotic words with corrupt forms of Arabic spelling because these were frequently found written thus in the recipes in many medical books.

As a physician, al-Rāzī appreciated that men of noble birth were entitled to certain considerations in the prescription of medicines: unpleasant tastes of drugs should be hidden in sweet and palatable vehicles; hence his book *al-Ṭibb al-mulūkī* ("Royal Medicine"), in contrast with his work *Man lā yaḥḍuruh al-ṭabīb* ("He who has no Physician to Attend Him") also known as *Ṭibb al-fuqarāʾ* ("Medicine for the Poor").

Al-Rāzī's *Kitāb al-Khawāṣṣ* ("Properties of Things"),[49] so far unpublished, gives evidence of his opposition to scientific dogmas. In his introduction, he argues that properties attributed to things should be recorded in a book; nothing would be lost but the time of writing them down. These properties should neither be accepted nor denied unless experience (*tajribah*) proves them to be true or false:

> Since many wicked people tell lies with regard to such properties, and we do not possess decisive means to distinguish the truth of honest men from the false testimony of liars – save only actual experience – it will be useful not to leave these claims scattered but to collect and write them all . . . We shall not accept any property as authentic unless it has been examined and tried.[50]

Al-Rāzī was an experienced clinical observer. He read the case-histories of Hippocrates' *Epidemics* and decided that it would be useful for posterity to write his own case-histories, in which he recorded the patients' names and professions.[51] He gives an early example of an up-to-date clinical trial when he treats a group of patients suffering from meningitis (*sarsām*) with blood-letting and intentionally, as a control, leaves another group without blood-letting, so that he may form the right opinion.[52]

The medical works of al-Rāzī had a great influence on the teaching of medicine in the Latin West. He differentiated between smallpox and measles in his book *al-Jadarī wa-ʾl-ḥaṣbah*[53] in which he gives very interesting clinical details. This book was translated into many occidental languages; *al-Ḥāwī* and *al-Manṣūrī* were also translated into Latin, and remained for centuries among the textbooks used in European universities.

49 Ibn al-Nadīm *Fihrist*, I, 300; Ibn abī Uṣaybiʿah, *ʿUyūn al-anbāʾ*, I, 316, line 30.

50 Dār al-Kutub al-Miṣriyyah, Cairo, MS Ṭibb 141, fols. 120a, line 20–120b, line 4; A. Z. Iskandar, "Rhazes' clinical experience: new material", *al-Mashriq*, LVI, 1962, 237–8.

51 M. Meyerhof, "Thirty-three clinical observations by Rhazes (circa 900 AD)", *Isis*, XXIII, 1935, 321–56 (Arabic text 1–14).

52 Iskandar, *Catalogue of Arabic manuscripts*, 10–11 and no. 2; Iskandar, "Rhazes' clinical experience", 239; Bodleian Library, MS Marsh 156, fol. 167a, lines 7–12.

53 Ibn al-Nadīm *Fihrist*, I, 300; Ibn abī Uṣaybiʿah, *ʿUyūn al-anbāʾ*, I, 316; see above, n. 30.

CHAPTER 22

AL-FĀRĀBĪ

Unlike the changes which Muslim names frequently underwent in the Latin West, the last name of Abū Naṣr Muḥammad b. Muḥammad b. Tarkhān b. Awzalugh (or Uzlugh) al-Fārābī was barely altered, and it is as "Alfarabi" that it has been common to refer to him. Al-Fārābī's name, however, may be the only constant on which to seize at the moment, as contemporary scholarship challenges previous assessments of his work. Al-Fārābī appears increasingly as a disarmingly subtle thinker, an individualist with a civic conscience, a man who attempted to reconcile Plato and Aristotle, philosophy and theology, Athens and Mecca.[1] The syntheses attempted, however, are neither facile nor dogmatic, and proceed from a predominantly philosophical standpoint. The exact nature of al-Fārābī's philosophical credo, moreover, is still being questioned.

The question is complicated by the lack of a sure chronology for al-Fārābī's many compositions, and an equal ignorance of the particular circumstances which prompted each work in a given genre: the motivation, purpose and intended audience. With few sure criteria of a biographical or stylistic sort to assist them, scholars are forced to choose between differing statements and emphases in related texts, and even within the same text, to determine al-Fārābī's genuine convictions. Moreover, the work of Leo Strauss, Muhsin Mahdi and others has drawn attention to the likelihood that al-Fārābī deliberately shielded essential elements of his convictions from the eyes of the uncritical reader. Thus al-Fārābī has been a prime candidate for that approach to philosophy which emphasizes its esoteric nature, a nature at variance with the exoteric or apparent reading of a text.

Not much is known of al-Fārābī's private life. As his name indicates, he was born in Fārāb, a district and town adjacent to the Jaxartes river in Turkestan (Transoxania), in 256 or 257/870. His father was, it seems, a Turkish officer, with whom al-Fārābī presumably went to Damascus. It was there or in Khurāsān that he apparently began his philosophical studies, reportedly reading at night by lamplight, while working as a labourer in a

[1] See above, ch. 6, 78–87.

garden and vineyard during the day. The reduced circumstances this bespeaks inured al-Fārābī to the simple if not ascetic life. At no time then or later did he possess wealth or power, or seek them.

Rather, al-Fārābī sought out teachers of philosophy in Baghdad, where he advanced from the ranks of student to that of celebrated teacher. He commented on many of Aristotle's books, particularly his logical treatises, and his own summaries and more independent compositions show great familiarity with the Stagirite's thought in all its dimensions. Al-Fārābī's knowledge of Plato was more limited, though Plato's *Republic* and *Laws* play critical roles in his own political philosophy. Al-Fārābī's metaphysical doctrine, for its part, is an amalgam of neo-Platonic and Aristotelian thought.

Al-Fārābī's many writings and fame brought him, in his seventies, to the attention of the Shīʿī Ḥamdānī prince Sayf al-Dawlah (reigned 333–56/945–67), who in 330/942 invited him to join his court in Aleppo. There al-Fārābī received a modest subvention, and was left mostly to his own devices. He dressed as a Ṣūfī, but this was apparently more a statement of independence than of identification with the mystical fraternity.

Al-Fārābī's identification was first and foremost with philosophers, but unlike Socrates, for example, with whom he had much in common personally and philosophically, he did not antagonize the ruling class. Despite the general and not necessarily Islamic thrust of his writing, his philosophical views were not regarded as heretical, his political theory not seen as subversive. Indeed, in many ways he built bridges between the Muslim and Shīʿī (particularly Imāmī) state and the philosophical tradition. He was thus tolerated if not appreciated in Aleppo, where, apparently, he died in 339/950.

Al-Fārābī's fame continued to grow after his death, and he became widely known as "the Second Teacher", *al-muʿallim al-thānī* (after Aristotle, *the* teacher of philosophy in the Islamic world), the man who interpreted Aristotle, Plato and much of the later philosophical tradition to interested Muslims and Jews in the Arab world. The Latin West, receiving his translated works belatedly and partially, together with those of Ibn Sīnā and Ibn Rushd, did not appreciate him as much, though current interest in his thought may make up for medieval neglect.

Al-Fārābī's success is due in part to the ambience of Baghdad in his day. He studied there with Yūḥannā b. Ḥaylān, and held conversations with Abū Bishr Mattā b. Yūnus and others of that circle. These men were part of a continuous coterie of Christian Arab scholars who had kept the flame of philosophy and science from being extinguished in the generally constricted climate of Byzantium and early Islam. By the fourth/tenth century,

Baghdad had offered a haven to these philosophers, and allowed them to transmit their learning, translated into Arabic from Greek and Syriac texts. The curriculum taught was essentially that of Alexandria of the sixth century AD, itself a culmination of a long chain of commentaries on most of Aristotle's work, a good deal of pseudepigraphic neo-Platonic teachings and some, but not much, of Plato and other Greek writers.

Baghdad was a haven for this philosophical legacy of late antiquity, but it was also a challenge to it, as its proponents were forced to defend their teachings before a sceptical, and somewhat threatened traditionally minded Muslim intelligentsia. The teachings themselves bore the stigma of pagan origin and Christian transmission, and were thus doubly suspect to the Muslim faithful. More even than carrying the burden of guilt by association, however, philosophy was seen as adversarial to the traditional sciences of Islam by its very nature. It introduced as subjects necessary for the educated person's well-being and even eternal happiness areas of investigation remote from the Qurʾān, *tafsīr*, *Ḥadīth* and *fiqh*. Even the esteemed and more abstract studies of *kalām* and the Arabic language were thought to be challenged by the claims of the new sciences, particularly logic.

Al-Fārābī's task was to naturalize philosophy in Islam in a convincing manner, while at the same time not compromising philosophy itself. To do this he essentially disregarded the historical Christian association with the discipline, treating it in effect as a coincidental and peripheral fact; and considered the pagan dimension as a similarly negligible factor. Thus, for example, in commenting upon Aristotle's reference in *De Interpretatione* 23a 23 to many "first substances" (*prōtai ousiai*/*al-jawāhir al-uwal*) which are actual without having any potentiality, al-Fārābī says that this notion is "extremely obscure" (*aghmaḍ jiddan*), and that "the notion of 'the first substances' was almost taken for granted among Aristotle's contemporaries; for they used to believe in many gods. But what the people of his time and his country used to consider as gods people of our time consider as angels. Today, people believe them to be mortal, while Aristotle's contemporaries believed them to be eternal".[2]

In this manner, al-Fārābī subtly dissociates Aristotle from his polytheistic contemporaries, and relegates the philosophers' belief in many gods to the dustbin of history. "Angels" have taken the place of the fallen pagan gods in the cosmology of those (like himself) who follow Aristotelian teachings, he explains, adding that "today, people believe" angels to be mortal, i.e. non-eternal. Al-Fārābī does not say that he believes this, or that philosophers in general so believe, but that the general mass of people in his

[2] Zimmermann, *Al-Farabi's Commentary*, 185.

day (*ahl zamāninā*) do so. This is correct, as was al-Fārābī's observation that Aristotle's "gods" were considered as "angels" by Muslim (as well as Jewish and Christian) philosophers.

Whether gods or angels, however, the immortal status of these substances was not usually denied by the philosophers, who viewed them in non-theological terms as the "intelligences" (*al-ᶜuqūl*) of the spheres, their formal causes. Al-Fārābī sided with the philosophers on this issue, but as it is admittedly a complicated and "obscure" topic, far from the logical distinctions which are the main concern of his *De Interpretatione* Commentary, he was able to extricate himself from the discussion without further elaboration. That was fortunate, since elaborating upon his position would have undercut the general impression of sympathy with Muslim beliefs which he wished to make.

The *De Interpretatione* Commentary, which has now been extensively studied and commented upon, makes the point which al-Fārābī presents elsewhere as well, that logic is a universal tool for understanding the concepts which underlie all languages, and that it is not a grammar of any one specific language. Abū Bishr Mattā had already been subjected to public ridicule for claims similar to al-Fārābī's, the case against him made easier owing to his imperfect command of Arabic. Al-Fārābī could not be so easily faulted, and he is careful to translate the Syriac locutions of his predecessors, with their Christian associations, into Arabic. Yet al-Fārābī's technical terms and even syntactic constructions clearly bear the mark of their non-Arabic and ultimately Greek origins. He does not hesitate to use Greek linguistic forms as paradigms of his "universal" grammar. This may well have put off traditional grammarians and hurt al-Fārābī's own chances of being accepted by his contemporaries, yet it also speaks to a certain courage in his character. He was not prepared to present philosophy in any of its aspects as a parochial subject. Even as it was not inherently Greek or Christian, neither was it particularly Muslim. It had nothing to be ashamed of in its antecedents, and saw itself as their heir. Islamicization of the material could go only so far; philosophy was its own reality, not necessarily antagonistic to the traditional sciences of Islam, but not subservient to them either.

Al-Fārābī's teachings, even when cautious, bear signs of the incipient challenge philosophy presented to the orthodox guardians of the faith. For all his avoidance of theological issues in the *De Interpretatione* Commentary, for example, al-Fārābī is almost impaled on the horns of a dilemma in trying to reconcile God's foreknowledge and man's free will,[3] both seen as

[3] Ibid., cxvi, 83, 98.

required to assert divine justice as well as omniscience and omnipotence.

Al-Fārābī is brought into this problem by commenting upon Aristotle's (*De Interpretatione*, 9) belief, with which he concurs, that future events contingent upon external causes cannot be known definitely in advance of their occurrence. This, because future events as such do not exist as yet, and the possibility of their existing is just that, a possible and not a certain reality. It should not impugn God's omniscience, therefore, to have his knowledge "limited" to present and past realities. Moreover, al-Fārābī recounts the deleterious effects upon human beings of believing that all their actions are necessary and thus predestined, determined by God's foreknowledge.

However, despite the compelling logical and social reasons for accepting the non-definite and thus unknowable nature of future possibilities, and despite surely having known that similar claims had been made by the more liberal (but vanquished) Muᶜtazilah theologians, al-Fārābī claims that "all religions" affirm divine foreknowledge, and that it is therefore necessary to find a solution compatible with religious beliefs as much as with actual reality and popular opinions. Al-Fārābī's own solution is a variant of one suggested by Islamic theologians before him, namely, that both necessity and possibility, foreknowledge and freedom (of a sort) can coexist, that the intrinsic possibility of a thing is not altered by external causes which in effect determine its future, and which always have done so. In this view, a person retains the ability or "power" (*qadar*) to act; it is *his* ability, though the actual operation of the power is determined by God. This formulation, however, is not particularly satisfactory from a philosophical standpoint, and al-Fārābī appears to concede as much before terminating the discussion. His final observation on the *kalām*-type resolution he has adopted, however ambivalently, is that "this opinion is more helpful for religions" (*anfaᶜ fī ᵓl-milal*) than that of its opponents.

As this example indicates, al-Fārābī is prepared to come to terms with the religious tenets held by most Muslims of his day. As he intimates, however, ideally he would hope to find solutions that conform both to religious dogma, popular beliefs *and* actual reality (*al-amr al-mawjūd*). It is this latter criterion which effectively distinguishes him and all philosophers from the theologians of Islam, the *mutakallimūn*. For the dominant forms of *kalām* occasionalism and atomism, even in diluted form, tended to deny the autonomy of nature and of the subject viewing nature, while aggrandizing God's presence in the world. Al-Fārābī's conviction of the relative independence of man and nature from God, and of the reliability of man's senses and judgement, is his point of departure as a philosopher, that which he shares with Aristotle.

Al-Fārābī is particularly critical of *kalām* methodology. As he describes it in his *Iḥṣāʾ al-ʿulūm* ("Enumeration of the Sciences") and elsewhere, it is essentially apologetic and polemical, defending religious beliefs in a variety of ways, including the use of logical fallacies. Even where their reasoning is internally valid, however, the conclusions of *kalām* arguments are conjectural at best, since they are of a type of argument which does not lead to certain truth. This is dialectical reasoning, which, as he says in a number of places, uses premises which are commonly assumed ("famously" so, *al-mashhūrāt*) to be true, but which may well not be. These premises do not contain the incontrovertible and logically unassailable evident truths of the first principles or intelligibles (*al-ʿuqūl al-awāʾil*), and thus, unlike them, do not yield conclusions which are necessarily true. Thus *kalām* reasoning, even where well constructed, leads only to possibly true conclusions, propositions which cannot (or should not) justify full confidence or certainty in those who assert them.

There is, though, as al-Fārābī concedes, a degree of certainty and thus a measure of truth to dialectical arguments, since there is a possibility that they may be true. Likewise, rhetorical arguments may be true, though they are less likely to be, since their premises are more suspect, being patently conjectural (*maẓnūn*) and not widely known or accepted. Even poetry has its degree of truth, however remote initially, its erstwhile singular statements convertible to general syllogisms. Religion is said to make use of poetic discourse, even as its theologians use all the other forms of arguments as well, including sophistical reasoning where necessary.

There are thus five kinds of reasoning for al-Fārābī: demonstrative, dialectical, sophistical, rhetorical and poetic. In his various introductions and commentaries to Aristotle's works on the *Organon*, which al-Fārābī expands to include rhetoric and poetry, he deals with the syllogisms appropriate to each, conveying to the reader the merits and limitations of each form of discourse in relation to certain knowledge. Such knowledge is the goal of philosophical investigation, and for al-Fārābī it is clear that it is attained only by the demonstrative syllogism, as described by Aristotle in the *Prior* and *Posterior Analytics* (*Kitāb al-Qiyās* and *al-Burhān* respectively).

As he makes clear in his commentaries on these works and elsewhere, al-Fārābī's penchant is for formally structured, deductive reasoning, using premises which are known to be true essentially on non-empirical grounds. Following Aristotle, he believes this is how philosophy should operate in all its theoretical endeavours, in mathematics, physics and metaphysics, as well as in logic itself. At the same time, al-Fārābī realizes, with Aristotle, that most areas of life, those investigated by both the natural and social sciences, depend upon empirical evidence offered to the senses and upon non-necessary, inductively derived premises; and that most people base their beliefs upon accepted and conventional wisdom, relying on the teachings of both secular and religious authorities. All these sources of knowledge are trustworthy in principle, however limited their claim to certain truth must be. Still, a great deal of significant and vital knowledge may be had by pursuing investigations in these areas of practical philosophy. Accordingly, al-Fārābī has treatises on astronomy, the vacuum, medicine and alchemy, in addition to many compositions in the traditional subjects of physics and metaphysics; and he complements his commentaries on rhetoric and poetry with a work on music theory. In all these studies, al-Fārābī's preferred models are taken from Greek sources, an approach which is more successful in the sciences than in the arts, for which knowledge of Greek language and culture is more necessary.

Al-Fārābī's confidence in his ability to assimilate and interpret Greek culture to his Muslim audience stems from his conviction in the universality of the human condition, a condition both physical and spiritual. Man's rationality and sociability are viewed as part of a universe which is eminently and naturally ordered and benign. It is in this perspective that one should read al-Fārābī's analysis of the growth of language, and of the various rational and cultural skills which develop in each nation in the wake of this growth. As presented in the *Kitāb al-Ḥurūf* ("Book of Letters"), particularly, nations are seen to progress from the lesser forms of reasoning – rhetoric, dialectic and sophistry – to the greater, namely, demonstrative reasoning. Those citizens familiar with all these skills will appreciate the capabilities and applicable spheres of demonstrative syllogisms, but also know their limitations. Political science, for example, will be recognized at best as a mixture of dialectic and demonstrative reasoning, the dialectic coming as close as it can to certainty. It remains, however, essentially a dialectical art, dealing with probable assumptions only.

Discussing human society in general as he is – although the classical Greek experience is his ostensible model – al-Fārābī then claims that philosophers implement their beliefs by establishing a religion comprised both of theoretical ideas and of practical laws which reflect these ideas. As, however, most people cannot understand ideas in their abstract and syllogistically demonstrable manner, the religion is given a symbolic formulation, with figurative representations and imitations of the ideas. There can be an appropriate philosophical religion of this sort, al-Fārābī allows, a religion which correctly articulates the ideas of its founders or founder. Such a religion will be attuned to the language, mores and history of the people to which it is addressed, and express national traditions and aspirations. Yet al-Fārābī also points out the many corruptions which may befall religion, owing to human failings and the vicissitudes of history. Besides the popular tendency of people to treat familiar religious symbols as ultimate realities, foreign conquest can introduce a new religion the symbols of which are widely misunderstood from the start, not following from prior philosophical conceptualization. In instances such as these, the philosopher who appreciates the universality of truth and the relativity of religious symbolization is likely to be pitted against the popular defenders of the faith, its legislators and theologians. Religion can thus play a constructive role in society as well as a destructive one, depending on its relation to philosophy.

The secular and political interpretation of religion which al-Fārābī here offers is striking, but it is not his only interpretation of this phenomenon. In a number of similar compositions, and particularly in his major treatises, "The Political Regime" (*Kitāb al-Siyāsah al-madaniyyah*) and the "Principles of the Views of the Citizens of the Best State", as its latest learned editor and translator has called the *Kitāb Mabādiʾ ārāʾ ahl al-madīnah al-fāḍilah*, we find a view of the relation of philosophy and religion which is couched in more traditional terms, philosophically and conceptually. Admittedly, it is again the philosopher, the man who knows truth demonstratively, who is portrayed as the lawgiver and founder of the religion, and again religion is described in terms of figurative representation and imitation of abstract truth. In the best or ideal state, the philosopher is king, legislating practices as well as beliefs. Now, however, the philosopher-plus seems to be only a conduit for revelation from on high. His inspiration (*waḥy*) is said to come from the "Active Intellect" (*al-ʿaql al-faʿʿāl*), the heavenly substance which is responsible (in the Hellenistic scheme accepted by al-Fārābī and all other *falāsifah*) for imparting knowledge to man. The Active Intellect in turn is dependent ultimately on God for its action, if not for its being, so that it is Allāh – called so by name – who is really responsible for the religion revealed to his prophet and imam, introducing traditional terms as synonyms for the philosopher king.

Seen in this light, the true religion, the religion of the best city or state, can yet be subservient to philosophy and be its popular expression, but it would appear nevertheless to be authentically God-given, its resemblance to other religions of superficial significance. Accordingly, this approach affords a more conventional and religiously conciliatory impression than otherwise discernible in al-Fārābī's writing on this topic.

This impression is challenged, however, by the realization that al-Fārābī's doctrine of the Active Intellect is philosophically problematic and inconsistent. On the one hand, the Active Intellect, for all its religious identification – it is called "the Holy" as well as "the Faithful Spirit" (*al-rūḥ al-qudsī, al-rūḥ al-amīn*) – relates to all men equally. The emanation of ideas flows from it necessarily, in al-Fārābī's scheme, even as the First Cause, God, endows the Active Intellect (together with the rest of the world) with existence in a necessary way. Al-Fārābī has no general theory of divine will to account for particular acts of revelation; a fact which has led scholars to assume al-Fārābī regards revelation essentially as a function of its recipient, the person endowed with a superior intelligence. A prophet in this view is distinguished from a philosopher by his developed imagination only, but this faculty, as his intelligence, comes to him "naturally".

On the other hand, al-Fārābī describes the relation of the Active Intellect to the prophet in such a way that the former appears to act as a true "angel", intentionally delivering a message, which may involve future events, to a selected individual. The message, moreover, is said to be given in particular, even "sensible" (i.e. representational) terms, not as intelligibles or universals only, which the prophet then particularizes and stylistically adapts. This would, however, be quite an extraordinary feat for the Active Intellect, since as intellect it supposedly has no more an imaginative or sensory faculty than it has volition.

Another problem is presented by al-Fārābī's claim that the souls of the righteous philosophers survive death and consciously enjoy the next world.[4] Similarly though conversely, the wise but wicked souls are said to suffer eternal pain, while ignorant souls are doomed to complete annihilation. As is clear, the sole criterion for immortality is intellectual achievement, though the entire soul, with its physical faculties of pleasure and pain, is said to receive eternal being. This, despite the fact that al-Fārābī believes that the virtuous person is one who distances himself from physical pleasures. The soul, which nowhere in al-Fārābī is said to be eternal *a parte ante*, thus receives a status for which he has no real explanation.

Similarly lacking a satisfactory conceptual formulation are al-Fārābī's assertions regarding the possibility of an individual person's intellect achieving immortality. Al-Fārābī discusses this issue in a number of compositions including one called simply the *Risālah fī ʾl-ʿAql* ("Treatise on the Intellect"). Though his writings vary here and there, he is quite explicit and consistent on the developmental stages of a person's intellect, and on the nature of its final state of actualization, that in which it achieves immortality and perfection. It is then an "acquired intellect" (*ʿaql mustafād*), i.e. it has acquired its "own" substantive reality, the sum total of its intellections of essential being, and it is this individual immaterial intelligence which he claims survives man's physical demise. For al-Fārābī, this is accomplished without permanent conjunction or unification with the Active Intellect. The individual intellect has a partial relation with this universal source of intellection and intelligible or formal reality, but the ontological gap between the two is too great, apparently, ever to be

[4] Cf. *al-Madīnah al-fāḍilah*, ch. 16.

completely bridged. With the assistance of the universal intellect, and in a relation said to approximate union, the individual intellect for al-Fārābī takes its place in eternity as a discrete essence, the eternal intellect or realized form of a given person.

The difficulty with accepting al-Fārābī's stated position on its face value is based on a number of factors. For one, al-Fārābī emphasizes the individual and "natural" origins of the human intellect, originally created as part of man's nature, an innate "disposition" (*istiᶜdād*) of his imaginative faculty to abstract intelligible forms from objects of sensation or/and imagination. Al-Fārābī never explains how this generated intellect can become immortal, however perfected it is. Secondly, the lack in al-Fārābī's conceptualization of a permanent if only partial conjunction with the Active Intellect leaves the individual intellect suspended in air, without a substantive support in eternal being. It is for this reason that Ibn Rushd was led later to posit an essential identification of universal and individual intellects; while Ibn Sīnā, for his part, saw the Active Intellect as emanating all actual forms directly upon the individual intellect, thus ensuring its immortality. For Ibn Sīnā, the proliferation of immortal intellects – and souls – is part of the emanative process characteristic of the cosmic chain of being; a position al-Fārābī, with his greater concern for the autonomy of nature and human intellection, cannot so easily endorse.

The attainment of happiness is a major concern of al-Fārābī's writing, and it is the title of one of his treatises, *Taḥṣīl al-saᶜādah*. Yet "true happiness" (*al-saᶜādah bi-ˀl-ḥaqīqah*), would seem to be beyond al-Fārābī's grasp, if it is to be found only in an after-world to which one has to earn entrance primarily as a successful philosopher. This is al-Fārābī's main condition for achieving immortality, though it would appear that it is not his main view of true happiness, or at least of that sort of happiness with which he was comfortable philosophically. Real happiness for al-Fārābī is to be found with and for people, in designing and implementing the ideal society, or one close to the ideal. It is thus political philosophy, not metaphysics, which holds the key to distinguishing between true and false forms of happiness. Accordingly, al-Fārābī's political treatises go into great detail to delineate the various types of states or cities, and the natures of the leaders of each. Working with Plato's *Republic* as his model, al-Fārābī offers examples of political leadership suitable for Muslim as well as non-Muslim societies. Elsewhere, Plato is singled out for mention in teaching the respect which the philosopher–statesman must accord the conventions and religion of his society.

It would be misleading, however, to pretend al-Fārābī's politically oriented treatises are just that. There is a great deal of attention paid in them to metaphysical teachings, it being apparent that for al-Fārābī true happiness is to be had in the mastery of both theoretical and political philosophy. Yet we have said that at the critical juncture between the heavens and earth, in the relation between the Active Intellect and man, al-Fārābī's metaphysics breaks down. We can say further that al-Fārābī presents the main body of his cosmological doctrine in a mostly dogmatic way, not demonstrating its truth so much as assuming it. The most elaborate arguments he presents for the existence of God lead to a necessary being presiding over an eternal universe, a view which he could not very well press unduly on his fellow Muslims. Moreover, if al-Fārābī really believed there was an unbridgeable gap between the Active Intellect and an individual intellect, it would never be possible to know the ultimate truths, those beyond the Active Intellect itself, those concerning God himself.

It would seem that the neo-Platonic legacy was the metaphysical view which most appealed to al-Fārābī, though he may well have realized that it was not a demonstrably necessary position to hold. In his treatises describing the philosophy of Plato and Aristotle, he essentially ignores the metaphysical doctrines of both, probably indicating thereby that neither was convincing to him. In view of all this, it may not be far-fetched to believe that al-Fārābī presented a metaphysical scheme in which he had less than full confidence, one for which at least certain key aspects were described disingenuously. He was reported to have disavowed his belief in immortality in a now lost commentary on the *Nicomachean Ethics*, calling such a belief an old women's tale and claiming that there is no happiness other than political happiness.[5] If so, though, it is political happiness resting on a foundation more natural and empirical than it is metaphysical and analytical, with arguments of a dialectical rather than demonstrative nature. As such, al-Fārābī's ideal city is founded only on probable truths, and man's happiness depends on political views which could be wrong.

Al-Fārābī may well have known that there was little certainty to most of his political or metaphysical teachings. Like Socrates, al-Fārābī may have been aware of his ignorance, understanding that true happiness lies in the quest, and not in the attainment, of happiness. Outwardly, though, al-Fārābī prefers to follow Plato in appearing more confident and conformist; while allowing the sophisticated reader to realize the dilemma in which the philosopher finds himself. In the most radical but debateable formulation of this position, al-Fārābī's metaphysical scheme can be seen as the philosopher's religion, an abstract yet symbolic expression of ideas rooted in political necessity.

[5] Cf. S. Pines, "The limitation of human knowledge according to al-Farabi, Ibn Bajja and Maimonides" in I. Twersky (ed.), *Studies in Medieval Jewish History and Literature*, Cambridge, Mass., 1979.

CHAPTER 23

IBN SĪNĀ

Ibn Sīnā is outstanding among Arabic authors for the unusually warm reception which he has been given in Europe. The secret of his success is to be found in the way that his writings synthesize all the most original features of Muslim philosophy.

It is often claimed in histories of philosophy that Arabic philosophy's only merit is its transmission of Greek, mainly neo-Platonic, thought. This oversimplifies the subject in a misleading way, for, by dispensing with the need to analyse Arabic philosophy in its own right, it relieves the student of all the technical obstacles to an understanding of the subject. A strange language, a different religion, an altogether foreign cultural milieu: these and numerous other considerations are dismissed at once.

Ibn Sīnā's acceptance in the West is indicative of the affinity which exists between his outlook and European systems of thought, an affinity that is less strongly felt in the cases of other Arabic philosophers, although, like Ibn Sīnā, nearly all of them lived in times of crisis. The crises experienced in Ibn Sīnā's lifetime were not only of a political nature but arose mainly from antinomies between Muslim religious principles, and those of the cultures which were being assimilated by an expanding Islamic empire. The resulting conflicts were what in Western terms would be called antagonisms between faith and reason. Ibn Sīnā's solution to this aporia captured the minds of the medieval Christian world, not only as a solution in its own right, but also on account of the influence which it exercised on later Arabic philosophers: on Ibn Rushd, for example, who was to play such an important part in the renaissance of medieval Christian thought. Despite the disputes between them over many other matters, Ibn Rushd took his lead from Ibn Sīnā on the issue of the relationship between revelation and faith.

The purpose of the present exposition is to emphasize those aspects of Ibn Sīnā's thought which best illustrate the originality of its departure from, and superseding of, Greek philosophy.

BIOGRAPHICAL SKETCH

Ibn Sīnā was born in 370/980 and died some fifty years later in 428/1037. His full name was Abū ʿAlī al-Ḥusayn b. ʿAbdullāh b. al-Ḥasan b. ʿAlī b. Sīnā. Avicenna, the name by which he is known in the West, is of Andalusian origin. He was born in Turkestan, in Afshana, near Bukhārā, and is buried in Hamadhān, where he died. His Persian origins preclude speaking of his philosophy purely in terms of Greek features because, fluent both in Arabic and in Persian, his access to Iranian sources was direct and unmediated by Greek writers.

Ibn Sīnā can only be described as a very gifted child prodigy. Through failing to adapt to their environment, child prodigies all too often lose their way: Ibn Sīnā, though, was rescued by a feeling of dissatisfaction with his teachers, as a result of which, and thanks to the flexibility of Muslim education, he became self-taught. While still a child, he was initiated in religious studies by a private tutor; by the age of ten, he had memorized the Qurʾān. Indeed, it can be said that religious learning underlaid his formation in science. Besides the deep understanding of Islamic jurisprudence which he gained, instruction in the natural sciences complemented his religious education. It is known for certain that he had read the scientific encyclopaedia of the Ikhwān al-Ṣafāʾ at a very early age. Of all the sciences, however, excluding the sciences of religion, the one in which he was initiated in perhaps the shortest time was medicine, to which a Christian physician, ʿĪsā b. Yaḥyā, introduced him. He was renowed for his medical skills at the age of sixteen, to all intents and purposes instructing the students himself. The extraordinary cures that he performed on monarchs and princes won him the favour of sovereigns and, by the time he was twenty, the most celebrated rulers and physicians in the East were consulting him. At seventeen, he had cured the Samanid sultan Nūḥ b. Manṣūr (reigned 365–87/976–97); later, the amir Shams al-Dawlah recovered miraculously from a life-or-death struggle during which Ibn Sīnā spent over forty days at his bedside.

It is not unusual to hear of eastern intellectuals combining scientific and political activities. Ibn Sīnā was one such intellectual, alternating politics by day with nocturnal vigils of study and research. In his own words;

> At night I would return home, set out a lamp before me, and devote myself to reading and writing. Whenever sleep overcame me or I became conscious of weakening, I would turn aside to drink a cup of wine, so that my strength would return to me. Then I would return to reading. And whenever sleep seized me I would see those very problems in my dream; and many questions became clear to me in my sleep.

[1] W. E. Gohlman, *The Life of Ibn Sina*, Albany, 1974, 29–31.

It has to be admitted, nevertheless, that he was less successful in politics than in medicine or philosophy. He returned defeated, for example, from a military expedition with Shams al-Dawlah. Indeed, the political losses which he suffered (and for which he had none but himself to blame) led the military to sentence him to death. He was on the point of being executed but his life was spared because the amir, again ill in health, was forced to call once more on Ibn Sīnā's medical services. His salvation for political failure, in other words, lay in the dependence of monarchs on his powers of healing.

The work in which Ibn Sīnā's medical knowledge was cast is his *al-Qānūn fī ʾl-ṭibb*.[2] Not only is this a work which formed successive generations of eminent physicians until the late Middle Ages, but, as late as the end of the eleventh/seventeenth century, in the Universities of Montpellier and Louvain in France and Belgium, it was still being used as a textbook. This work is characterized by clarity and precision. Consider, for example, its description of pleuritic symptoms:

> The signs of pleurisy are unmistakable; first, continuous fever; secondly, violent and unremitting pain under the ribs, brought on particularly by heavy breathing; thirdly, short breaths, taken with difficulty; fourthly, a fast, faint pulse and, lastly, a dry cough. If the patient begins to cough up sputa, it is a sign that the lungs are diseased also.

Today, there are more exact methods for diagnosing pleurisy but modern science, nevertheless, cannot dispute the accuracy of Ibn Sīnā's observations. His great encyclopaedic works, and his writings on metaphysics, have medical titles: namely *al-Najāh* ("Salvation") and *al-Shifāʾ* ("Healing").

When Ismāʿīlī missionaries from Egypt arrived in Bukhārā, Ibn Sīnā's father and one of his brothers were among the many whom they converted. His own rejection of their attempts to convert him demonstrates his force of personality. Critical of the need for new ritual systems, he assimilated only those aspects of Ismāʿīlī philosophy which he deemed to be valid: notably, an interest in the natural sciences and, at the same time, a mystical inclination – the fusion of Egyptian gnosticism with Iranian occult sciences – which would manifest itself in his final metaphysical intuition.

In reality, he became a student of all the humanities, including Greek philosophy, although this was not to the exclusion of other subjects such as Euclidean geometry, with which he acquainted himself; he learned the "Indian numerals"[3] from a grocer; and also mathematics, physics and astronomy. The lack of teachers qualified to satisfy his intellectual curiosity in any subject forced him to become self-taught in all of them. When the

[2] See above ch. 19, 356–8. [3] See above ch. 14, 255.

philosopher al-Nātalī went to Bukhāra, for example, he stayed as the guest of Ibn Sīnā's father. Ibn Sīnā learned some logic with him but remained unconvinced at heart by the instruction that he was given and was led once again, therefore, to teach himself.

Metaphysics was the only subject in which the autodidactic method proved unsuccessful and, as Ibn Sīnā himself admitted, he found the subject quite inscrutable despite reading and rereading Aristotle's *Metaphysics* until he virtually knew the work by heart. Then, one day, he met someone by chance in a bookshop who recommended a work by al-Fārābī, probably his *Kitāb al-Ḥurūf* ("Book of Letters"). It was a revelation; it was the key to Aristotelian metaphysics. The incident is significant because it discloses the originality of the sources of Avicennian philosophy. It is generally argued, for example, that his neo-Platonism is no different from the Greek: yet, in adapting it to the Islamic world (as al-Fārābī had done before him), he modified and enriched it profoundly. Even more importantly, now that Greek neo-Platonism is known to have been inspired by Iranian science, the knowledge of Persian, which was his by birth, led Ibn Sīnā to draw directly on this inspiration at its source.

The apparent cause of Ibn Sīnā's death was dysentery, a disease to which he was prone, as he was to epilepsy also. Both are said to have brought him close to death on several occasions. In addition, according to his pupil and biographer, Abū ᶜUbayd al-Jūzajānī, he gave himself reckless treatment. He finally fell ill on a journey with his patron ᶜAlāʾ al-Dawlah; knowing (with the intuition on which he frequently acted in life) that he was about to die and that treatment was in vain, he is alleged to have remarked: "The governor who used to govern my body is now incapable of governing, and so treatment is no longer of any use."[4] There is a legend that his epitaph read: "His philosophy taught him no manners, and his medicine no cures."

Like most Arabic philosophers, Ibn Sīnā was both a prolific and a versatile writer during his relatively short lifetime. The bibliography compiled by G. C. Anawati contains 276 entries, including eight encyclopaedias and numerous treatises on logic, metaphysics, theology, mysticism and asceticism, physics, astronomy, music, medicine, mathematics, grammar, rhetoric and poetry.

ORIGINAL FEATURES OF IBN SĪNĀ'S WORKS

In his classification of the sciences Ibn Sīnā largely followed Aristotle. Taking the degree of abstraction of their subject-matter as his classificatory

[4] Gohlman, *Ibn Sina*, 89.

criterion, he distinguished three scientific classes, namely, the physical, the mathematical, and the metaphysical sciences.

Within the Hellenic metaphysical tradition, Ibn Sīnā was the first writer I know to have considered theology and ontology separately. His ontology is quite different in outline from the science of divinity: the subject of metaphysics, he boldly asserts, is not the Deity but "being as such". In order for something to be the subject of a science it is first necessary to prove its existence. The Deity, therefore, cannot be the subject of metaphysics since it is the aim of metaphysics to prove the existence of the Deity. This conception of the problem of the onto-theological bearing of metaphysics amounted to a genuine revolution in the subject. The formulations of St Thomas in the Prologue to his *Summa Theologica* virtually translate statements made by Ibn Sīnā.

In order to discover the originality of Ibn Sīnā's thought, it is important to bear its evolution in mind: superimposed on his Muslim faith, the tenets of which formed the basis of all his thinking, there is a fusion of Greek philosophy and Iranian neo-Platonism alongside Greek and Christian gnosticism. It is this synthesis of religion and philosophy, so characteristic of Arabic philosophy in general, and of Ibn Sīnā's in particular, which has been the primary cause of his influence in the West. For here was to be found, in a unique manner, the human framework which is needed to support religion.

Ibn Sīnā was an untiring metaphysician, deeply preoccupied with religious concerns and constantly restless in intellectual curiosity. Questions multiplied as his understanding of para-Islamic sciences advanced: where does the truth lie? In Islam or in Christianity? In Greece or Persia? India or Egypt? Or is it in all of them? Let us see how his mystical synthesis was accomplished, step by metaphysical step.

Like the neo-Platonists, Ibn Sīnā conceived the way to the Deity as a dual process of ascent and descent. The Deity is indivisible oneness. Since oneness can have knowledge neither of itself nor of others – because knowledge presupposes disunity, a dichotomy between the knowing subject and the object of knowledge – knowledge of the Deity must be extrapolated externally. This occasions the first consciousness, which, in itself and by its own nature, is nothing but pure possibility emanating necessarily from oneness. Ibn Sīnā described it as "possible by itself, necessary for Other". Having the form of possibility and the existence of a shadow, it stands in opposition to oneness, a nonentity on its own.

By contemplating itself as shadow, consciousness creates the essence of the supraelemental body of the first heaven. This ethereal body stands in need then of the spiritual motive power of a soul. All emanations are a consequence of knowledge, the products of intelligence. There are three main acts of intelligence, each of which creates a discrete entity: these entities are first, consciousness, which arises from contemplation of the Deity; secondly, the motivating soul of the first heaven, which derives from consciousness contemplating itself as possibility; thirdly, the celestial body, which is constituted by consciousness's third act of intelligence, namely, its contemplation of its own existence as possibility. Following Ptolemy's astronomical system composed of ten spheres, Ibn Sīnā proceeded down to a tenth consciousness. Each stage of the descent is based on a ternary process in which body, spiritual force (the soul) and intelligent consciousness are involved.

Distinguishing two functions of the soul as, on the one hand, the form of a body and, on the other, physically independent consciousness, was to depart from Aristotelianism in a vital way. The ten consciousnesses are called *karūbiyyūn*, cherubic intelligences or intellectual angels. It was Ibn Sīnā's doctrine on these heavenly angels, the motivating souls of the ten celestial spheres, which was to scandalize Ibn Rushd: namely, the doctrine that, lacking the faculties of the senses, they have no feelings but only pure insentient imagination. As a result, radical change was introduced into Islam, as the Quranic angels and archangels of revelation were transformed into superior consciousnesses. Indeed, it is those very archangels which we are to understand by the "active principle of understanding" such as occurs in Ibn Sīnā's epistemology. It is worth emphasizing the importance of the imagination in inferior souls.

In the hierarchy of intellectual emanations, the tenth, lacking the force with which to produce another unique consciousness and another unique soul, explodes and produces the multitude of human souls. From the emanation's shadow aspect issues sublunar matter in all its multiplicity. Ibn Sīnā spoke of the active principle of understanding, the last of the intellectual angels, as the form-giver. Our souls are created from it and, in reuniting with it, receive enlightenment (*ishrāq*), the means by which ideas, the forms of knowledge, are projected onto our souls. It follows, then, that knowledge is not an abstraction from sense perceptions, but the fruit of a similar process to that described by Muḥammad b. Muḥammad al-Fārābī in his enumeration of the various forms of human understanding. Human consciousness is empowered to know the intelligibility of sensory data: by uniting with the active principle of understanding, it is illuminated by an impression of the form of everything that is intelligible. Thus, its potential for understanding is realized. At the same time, knowledge of the intelligibility of sensory data, which the soul acquires by enlightenment, enables it to know itself as a purely intelligible entity. This makes understanding a habitual faculty of consciousness, which, in turn, facilitates knowledge of the source of enlightenment, the active principle of understanding, and so on to knowing the Deity. Consciousness, at this stage, comes to be known as acquired, or holy, understanding. It should be noted that this holy understanding can be experienced, in different ways, by the philosopher as well as by the prophet, as shown below.

It is manifestly apparent from this doctrine that Ibn Sīnā synthesized Aristotelianism, neo-Platonism, Iranian gnosticism, Islam and religious concepts. What, then, specifically, is most original about the philosophy? Ibn Rushd objected to it on the ground that, in the interplay between Aristotelianism and neo-Platonism, the latter prevailed. It is plain to see from our exposition that it hardly separated logic, and with it a theory of knowledge, from metaphysics, psychology and anthropology; nor, I would venture to add, did it distinguish between reason and revelation. Everything blends harmoniously in a continuous process of flux in which oneness produces multiplicity, and multiplicity reduces to oneness.

THEORY OF KNOWLEDGE

Ibn Sīnā's fusion of Islam with Graeco-Persian neo-Platonism was nowhere more apparent than in his general theory of human knowledge, which, in line with al-Fārābī, was based on a transference of the Quranic scheme of revelation. There, the Deity addresses one man, the Prophet, through the archangel Gabriel; in Ibn Sīnā's neo-Platonic scheme, the divine word is transmitted by the cherubic agent of understanding to any man who can hear it. The angel of revelation has been transformed, in other words, into a modified version of Aristotle's active principle of understanding. Aristotle was never explicit about whether this principle is intrinsic or extrinsic to man: according to Ibn Sīnā, for whom it is the last of the ten consciousnesses, it is definitely extrinsic, as al-Fārābī had said (albeit in such a way as to make of it, ultimately, a genuinely internal human principle). All knowledge is inspired by the Deity through the agency of enlightened understanding. We shall see below the degree to which Ibn Sīnā's true religious sentiments were influenced by this theory.

EMANATION OR CREATION?

Ibn Sīnā's metaphysical system was founded on the concept of emanation. What is not made explicit, however, is whether Ibn Sīnā was using this concept to denote a process within Divinity, operative at the instance of knowledge (which would permanently confine us, by nature, to Divinity), or whether he subscribed to the Christian tradition of creation. It is this uncertainty which has led many traditionalist Muslims to place Ibn Sīnā, and all philosophers in general, on the fringes of orthodoxy, some even regarding them as heterodox.

A distinction perhaps ought to be made at this point between the form and content of the concept of emanation: the anti-creationist terms in which it is formulated are, none the less, authentically creationist in content. While it is true that everything proceeds from and through knowledge, the effect of this knowledge is to create extrapolations which are external to Divinity. The essence of the first consciousness and, thus, of all beings in their multiplicity is sheer potentiality: that which is nothing by itself but necessary in terms of Other. On its own it is nothing; the necessity which it contracts in relation to Other cannot be referred to its essence, for this neither is, nor can be, necessary. Necessity is exclusively a function of existence. Since Divinity necessarily produces the existence of the world everything in it is eternal. These apparently simple assertions revealed a discrepancy between Ibn Sīnā's position and the Islamic affirmation that man and the world are temporal creations: we shall see, though, the explanation which he gave in order to preserve the integrity of his Quranic faith.

Ibn Sīnā's views also constituted a real revolution in metaphysics inasmuch as they introduced change into the conception of human nature. Man is not only form and substance: as a being whose reality is essential potentiality and existential Other-wise necessity, he simply combines essence and existence. This is however, not the place to embark on a study of the repercussions which these ideas had on the renaissance of Christian philosophy. It also goes without saying that their widespread interpretation as substantiating a distinction which corresponds to one that Arabs make in practice is of purely anecdotal interest, and without textual foundation. This has been proved sufficiently by the works of Manuel Alonso, Miguel Cruz Hernández, and the present writer. The distinction in question is nothing more than an intellectual construct, similar in this respect to the distinction which Ibn Sīnā established when he wrote that oneness is a contingent property of essence.

Of perhaps even greater transcendence in metaphysics, however, was the theory of analogy which derived from this conception of man. The broadening of Aristotle's binary opposition between form and substance in order to include an opposition introduced by Arabic philosophers, namely, that between existence and essence, presupposes an essential transformation of the concept of analogy. Intellectual development consists of the use of progressively more general concepts: from a knowledge of many men, for example, comes the universal concept of "man"; by comparing men with other beings we acquire more general concepts, such as "animal", "vegetable", "substance", etc. Finally, we arrive at the most general concept of all, that of "being". As long as we remain within the sphere of finite beings and intelligibility, we do not meet with any special obstacles to this broadening of our conceptual horizons. There are, however, areas of experience which elude us: can human categories comprehend infinity? This is the great dilemma of metaphysics.

Some philosophers believe that infinity can be described by a single, unequivocal term. Others, on the contrary, regard it as a far more complex and transcendent concept, for which reason they have developed a special, so-called analogous, term. What did Ibn Sīnā think? Can the Deity and other transcendent notions be subsumed by a single category? Here, we believe, is where Ibn Sīnā superseded Greek philosophy. L. Gardet tends towards the view that he was an exponent of the unambiguous character of the concept, whereas E. Gilson recognizes that he admitted the use of analogy of some sort.

Ibn Sīnā refers to *tashkīk* (ambiguity) and *kashf* (unveiling), and for the latter term he offers two synonyms, namely, *mushāhadah* and *ḥads*. The first has the meaning of sense perception ("testimony of the senses"); the second is conjecture ("intellectual intuition"). Both terms may be used equally to refer either to the senses or to the inner faculties. In metaphysics, they connote the final intuition in which metaphysical speculation culminates, the intuition of the soul in contemplation of absolute truth and beauty, in the act of which it is united with them, "receiving the impression of their form, becoming one with them in substance, willing to go their way". This is what led Gardet to opt for the unequivocally pantheistical character of the ontological identity of the Deity.

Naṣīr al-Dīn al-Ṭūsī prefers to give the term *mushāhadah* an epistemological rather than an ontological significance, a kind of *idrāk*, as much intellectual conception as sensory perception. It is this very intuitive character, the intuition, or perception, of transcendent contact, which differentiates Avicennian *ishrāqī* philosophy from Greek philosophy. When we reach the final stage of metaphysical intuition, even while awake, we can experience the invisible just as we experience it in dreams. *Ahl al-mushāhadah* was Ibn Sīnā's name for those who look for intellectual intuition, those, that is, who make a practice of intuitive, intellectual ascertainment of reality: "They are the people," he wrote, "who are steady in wisdom." The superiority of his philosophy in relation to the Peripatetic school is due to its synthesis of intuitive verification and verification by observation and reason. Peripatetic wisdom, Naṣīr al-Dīn al-Ṭūsī remarks, was purely discursive, whereas Avicennian wisdom, although it is founded on discourse and observation (*maʿa al-baḥth wa-ʾl-naẓar*), culminates in intuition (*bi-ʾl-kashf*). It is by intuition that "the ideas of 'being', 'thing', and 'necessary' are first engraved on the soul." Intuitive hints or inspirations such as these are what lead A. M. Goichon to see a connection between Ibn Sīnā and Kant: we shall see below the importance of *a priori* reasoning in Ibn Sīnā's psychology.

Returning to Ibn Sīnā's conception of analogy, two points can be made which, although fundamental, appear to have gone unnoticed until now. The ultimate intuition of being is arrived at through an insight, or conjecture, which, not unlike a vector, points towards the origin, or source, of being without ever succeeding in fully comprehending it. This was how Ibn Sīnā conceived the ascent towards unity. Where the path, as it might be called, descends, he resorted to the Iranian theory of participation; he was as familiar with the original source of this theory as Plato and Plotinus had been, from whom, therefore, it should not be thought to have been a loan. There is no doubt any longer about this Iranian influence. Ibn Sīnā remarks in his *Manṭiq al-mashriqiyyīn* ("Logic of the Easterners"): "The sciences very nearly reached us without passing via the Greeks."

In Zoroastrianism, a quadruple dualism may be discerned, beyond which is Ahura Mazda, the supreme, transcendent Deity. There is, first, the duality of the material world of the senses and the immaterial world of the intellect. This opposition produces the dichotomy between the opposed principles of good (Spenta Mainyu) and evil (Angra Mainyu) which preside over the immaterial and material worlds, respectively. Yet another dualism is established on the basis of these two worlds, the dualism of the twin process of ascent and descent. From Ahura Mazda, unique first cause, there is descent towards abstract or inferior divinities and towards both the intelligible and the sensible worlds. The reverse process, from the material world to the immaterial world, and to their corresponding first causes, is also possible. It is a process governed by the following laws:

1 That between the principles of good and evil (Spenta Mainyu and Angra Mainyu) there is no possibility of participation, neither on grounds of resemblance, nor of composition, nor of causation.
2 That between the principle of good and the principle of evil as it obtains in the good sensible world there can be no participation, because no relation of resemblance or of causation exists between them.
3 That between the principle of evil and the good sensible world there can be no participation, for the same reason.
4 That between the principle of good and the good sensible world

> participation is possible on the basis of the formal resemblance which exists between the first cause and its concomitant (as in the constant relation between cause and effect). The same applies to the relation of participation between the principle of evil and the evil sensible world. That participation between good and bad effects is possible in the material world: that is to say, both participate in the same being on the basis of composition, at least, if not of resemblance. (Zoroastrians deny that there is any resemblance between good and evil, meaning that there can be a mixture, or composition, of the two elements in the same being, without their being related in any other way than as constituent principles of the same being.)

There is a notable parallel between Zoroastrian metaphysics and Ibn Sīnā's. As is evinced quite clearly by its premises, his metaphysical system advocated true analogy, not uniformity. There are two factors which preclude compatibility between his concept of being and uniformity: first, the concept's unattainable, transcendent quality, owing to which the finite categories of human intelligence are only able to comprehend it referentially, in the form of a vector pointing towards infinity; secondly, the dual process required to give reality to the notion, a reality which first must be sought at the source of being before the notion can partake of that form of being which is possible in itself and necessary because of Other.

It was stated above that Ibn Sīnā shared certain points in common with Kant. In fact, there are, above all, two *a priori* aspects of thought that are developed in human understanding: one is the ontological argument proving the existence of the Deity; the other is the allegory of the flying man. Ibn Sīnā's ontological argument springs from the idea of necessary being, deducing the necessity of extra-mental existence from *a priori* mental activity. His theory on the theme of the flying man is regarded by one virtually uniform tradition of thought as a precedent for Cartesian subjectivism. The theory serves as a useful vantage-point from which to see how Ibn Sīnā attempted to reconcile his doctrine with the teachings of the Qurʾān.

The principal text in which Ibn Sīnā formulated his theory is a passage in his *al-Shifāʾ*:

> We say, then, that it would serve our purpose to imagine someone created in one stroke. The person thus created is perfectly normal in all but two respects: first, he lacks the faculty of sight for the contemplation of external objects; secondly, he is created in a void, soaring in mid-air, unaffected by the obligatory sensation of atmospheric pressure. Imagine, also, that his limbs were detached in such a way that they did not come into contact with one another. Would this person then affirm his own existence? Well, there can be no doubt that he would affirm the

existence of his essence, over and above which, however, he would not affirm the existence of his limbs or his internal organs, including his heart and brain, nor would he affirm the existence of any external object. Whether or not, in this state, he could even imagine a hand or any other limb, it would not be as a part or condition of his essence. All that he would affirm is his own essence, though he would not do so in terms of its length, breadth, or depth. As you know, something close is not the same as something distant; analogously, things which are affirmed differ from things which are not. Obviously, this person's body and limbs, which are not affirmed as existing, form a different being which belongs to his essence, the existence of which is affirmed. By the same token, therefore, the person affirming this can also affirm the existence of his soul as something which not only is not his body but is not body at all.[5]

This text has been understood by general consensus to be the self-expression of the soul, evidentially similar in many respects to the fruit of Cartesian doubt. That it is not a matter of absolute equivalence between the two, however, is underlined by E. Galindo's objection that there is no Cartesian doubt in Ibn Sīnā. Yet different starting-points do not in themselves alter the fact that the text can be read as a solution, in many ways, to Cartesian doubt (contrary to Galindo's view that they have nothing in common). Let us see where these solutions lie.

Ibn Sīnā was attempting to direct his interlocutor's soul, by an effort of imagination, to a self-internalized state of being. By abstracting sensory perception, he arrived at a subjectivism through which a fuller concentration on the essence of the soul could be achieved. The evidential results of the soul's self-replication are not subject to any sense of uncertainty, there being no point at which methodical Cartesian doubt is entertained: anything that is not evident in itself is separated out, for the simple reason that its existence does not belong to one's own essence. That is to say, in perceiving itself other than through the medium of extraneous images, the soul has an unquestionably certain sense of its own existence.

Within this system of thought, Ibn Sīnā could dispense with theories of pre-existent harmony, or of the infallibility of the Deity, in order to know his corporeal essence as an inalienable part of himself. This was so because the body is not of man's essence. The essence of being is the soul. Even a knowledge of matter is perhaps unnecessary, since it is unknowable, according to Aristotle and his Greek commentators. From which Ibn Sīnā concluded that there is nothing necessary about the resurrection of the body at the end of time. This at once brings us up against a fundamental problem: that of the relation between philosophy and revealed Islamic faith. Muslims believe in the resurrection of the body (even descriptions of other-worldly felicity are made predominantly in terms of the senses), so

[5] Bk. 1, sect. 1, para. 6.

what possibility is there of reconciling this contradiction between Ibn Sīnā's philosophy and Quranic revelation?

Nowadays, a secularized society is one of the modern ideals of much of the world: it is interesting, therefore, to see what the attitudes of the great thinkers of Islam were on the subject, since they achieved something very close to secularization, namely, the fusion of religion, or theology, and philosophy. Both these fields of learning embrace the whole of human nature: while philosophy concerns itself with the knowledge that humanity can have of the Deity, theology regulates human conduct, including the use of reason, in order to provide men with their means of salvation. It is by no means an easy task to co-ordinate both activities: in order to simplify things, pure philosophy disregards the religious domain, while religious fanaticism would enslave reason, even prohibiting sound criticism of the practical and theoretical deviations perpetrated by some religious leaders in their interpretations of the revelation. Might there not be some possibility of reducing the aporia concerning the relationship between these two activities in order to make them mutually compatible? Muslim thinkers and, particularly, philosophers are noted for their efforts in this direction. Let us briefly consider Ibn Sīnā's Islamic viewpoint.

Although already in Ibn Sīnā's time philosophy had been granted citizenship in the Muslim community, friction was still felt in matters over which there was no obvious possibility of agreement between the two parties. The subject of the creation is just one example of antagonism: in the Qurʾān, it is temporal; according to Ibn Sīnā, eternal. Conceived neo-Platonically, in the mode of an emanation, there is the danger that creation itself conflates the nature of Divinity and the nature of humanity, instead of presenting us as issuing from nothingness.

The problem of knowledge of the Deity is another theme fraught with antagonism. Ibn Sīnā took a neo-Platonic line, arguing that knowledge presupposes multiplicity because it divides the knowing subject from the object of knowledge. Furthermore, if the Deity were to know individuals singly, this would amount to their reduplication because, for Deity, to know is to create. Ibn Sīnā's solution was to argue that the Deity apprehends individuals in their universality but does not know them severally. Since there is no other cause of Divinity than Divinity itself, divine self-knowledge necessarily implies universal knowledge of cause and effect; the Qurʾān states categorically, however, that the Deity knows things in their specific uniqueness, down to the finest points of detail.

In regard to the aporia between Ibn Sīnā and the Qurʾān on the subject of the resurrection of the body, his position was that death liberates the soul and that, therefore, resuscitating the corpse would mean the soul's reincarceration in matter. Some writers have sought to dissociate him from this doctrine, preferring to see it as a defamatory attempt by al-Ghazālī to discredit him with certain consequences of his neo-Platonic premises, consequences which he never proclaimed but which are imputed to him nonetheless. Today, it has to be recognized that al-Ghazālī did not misinterpret him: although, in his most popular works, he professed acceptance of the Quranic creed on this doctrine, it is clear that he denied the resurrection of the body from his *Risālat al-Aḍḥawiyyah fī ᶜumr al-maᶜād.*

Ibn Sīnā does not appear to have been disturbed by this seeming antinomy between philosophy and revealed faith because for him it was not a case of two truths, one theological, the other philosophical, but of two methods of expressing the same truth. The Qurᵓān teaches with words that are accessible to ordinary people; if it spoke only of the purely spiritual pleasures of the afterlife, most believers, immersed as they are in the sensual pleasures of mundane living, would understand nothing and they would lose faith as a result, in terror. That is why the Qurᵓān describes the future life in sensory colour. The anthropomorphic language which it uses, though, is metaphorical, and its true interpretation must be left to philosophers, those who know how to discover the real spiritual meaning underlying its sensuous expressions. To present the people with the subtleties of theology would be to disfigure any image which they may have formed of the Deity. It is not that the metaphors as such are false, but that they need to be interpreted by those who know how to understand them.

Ibn Sīnā's text is itself quite explicit:

> Theologians effectively spend their days and nights, and every minute of their lives, exercising their spirits, sharpening their wits, and attuning their souls, the more readily to be able to penetrate these obscure concepts. Accordingly, they could well do with more light and an explanation of those expressions. Upon my word, that would be the day for unlettered Jews and Arab nomads! Had the Deity imposed on the Prophet the duty of professing subtle dogma in minute detail to the people at large, who are weak by nature and confined in their imaginations to a purely sensory reality; or had the Prophet been given, in addition to the responsibility of exacting from the people an immediate response to his own faith, the obligation to undertake their intellectual formation in preparation for the study of these concepts, then the burden would have been insupportable, far in excess of human capabilities. The people would need to be gifted with divine privileges of celestial inspiration and superior powers, in which case prophetic mediation in transmitting the word would be pointless.

Curiously, at this stage, Ibn Sīnā offers an interpretation of the Hebrew and Christian scriptures which implies a deep understanding on his part of the grounds for dialogue between their two religions. The falsity of certain Jews and Christians lies not in their having falsified the scriptures by selective editing or by capricious alterations of the texts, but in his own words:

What, then, will these objectors [his adversaries] have to say about the Hebrew scriptures, which are pure anthropomorphism from beginning to end? It is not that they have been falsified, for how could it be possible to falsify an entire body of scriptures shared by countless peoples from lands that are as far apart, and with aspirations that are as different, as those of the Jews and the Christians? Peoples, who are after all, hostile to one another.

Ibn Sīnā's benevolent attitude towards the Christian and Hebrew scriptures is striking. Benevolence of this kind, though, is not unusual among Muslim writers, of whom there always have been, from the Traditionist ʿAbdullāh al-Dārimī, in the third/ninth century, to Muḥammad ʿAbduh, in the thirteenth/nineteenth century, with Abū Ḥāmid al-Ghazālī and Ibn Khaldūn between them, those for whom the integrity of the text was never in doubt, only the ever-changing ways of interpreting its metaphorical meaning: in some cases the interpretation is correct; in others, erroneous.

Nevertheless, it should not be supposed that Ibn Sīnā was a sceptical rationalist. Everyone is agreed that he was a sincere believer, even though his actions may not have concurred always with his beliefs. Some say that his premature death was due to the excesses of his private life. His philosophy is, none the less, profoundly religious: that prophetic inspiration permeated his natural theology may be deduced from his epistemology, and mystical intuition is diffused throughout even the final phases of his metaphysics. He can be said to have made every effort to adapt neo-Platonism to Islam, even to the point of distortion where his theory of the immortality of the soul was concerned, a theory which he maintained for the sake of concordance with the Quranic doctrine of forfeits and favours in the afterlife.

Revealed faith influenced Ibn Sīnā in two ways. On the one hand, it gave rise to many of the philosophical difficulties which he confronted, bringing him to submit to the outward-directed practices of prayer and community life in Islamic society. At the same time, on the other hand, it induced him to modify his own philosophical standpoint in order to adapt to what he saw as the self-evident dogmas of the Qurʾān.

In conflicts between religion and philosophy, Ibn Sīnā inclined toward the latter, not because he dismissed the Qurʾān as false, but because accurate interpretation of the content of its metaphorical language depends on skilled human reasoning. The truth remains the same, but it is expressed differently in order to meet the particular requirements of its two separate audiences and, thereby, equip each for its own journey in life. He took the boldest of positions: the truth of revelation in any given case was to be judged by its use of metaphor and figurative language. Anthropomorphism was proof of veracity. Were revealed knowledge to be expressed openly in the form of explicit truths, or in terms of unfamiliar and unprecedented symbolism, then that more than anything would attest its falseness and lack of celestial authority.

All of this presupposes that the philosopher can attain the same heights as the prophet, which comes as no surprise after al-Fārābī's teachings on the subject. Both receive enlightenment from above, but the prophet surpasses the philosopher inasmuch as he receives enlightenment naturally, whereas the philosopher acquires its equivalent through spiritual, mystico-philosophical asceticism. Yet, while the prophet is worthier of popular faith because his words are adapted to the people, the philosopher, owing to intellectual capacity and constant application to the study of religious truth, is better able than the simple believer to understand the Qurʾān's true spiritual meaning.

Two clear and precise conclusions, I believe, emerge finally. There can be no denying that Ibn Sīnā's unparalleled attempt to synthesize philosophy and religion was valid in its own right, whether or not his doctrines are acceptable either from a Muslim or from a Christian point of view. Mere external authority will not bring a man to betray himself by acting against his own better judgement if, guided by the inner light of his own powers of reason, he sincerely accepts only what at each moment of his life he sees to be true. It is this synthesis of the philosophical and the religious which was the most original feature of Ibn Sīnā's thinking, and the key factor in explaining his influence on the renaissance of Christian philosophy in the Middle Ages. Today, this influence, already encountered above, is not in doubt. It derived from the fact that his philosophy came closer, than did almost any other, to Christian systems of thought, at the same time offering Christian theology a better footing on which to gain credibility in rationalist intellectual traditions.

The originality of Ibn Sīnā's philosophy has, it is hoped, been demonstrated sufficiently, both as regards a synthesis of previous philosophies, and also in respect of the fusion of revealed faith and philosophy which it accomplished. There was novelty too in several other aspects of his philosophical system, above all in its *rapprochement* of metaphysics and mysticism. Even today, his attempt to reconcile faith with the demands of human nature is still applicable. There can be no confusing him with others: his philosophy was unmistakably original.

CHAPTER 24

AL-BĪRŪNĪ AND THE SCIENCES OF HIS TIME

BIOGRAPHICAL BACKGROUND

Abū ʾl-Rayḥān Muḥammad b. Aḥmad al-Bīrūnī al-Khwārazmī, the most distinguished encyclopaedist of the Muslim scientists, was born in Khwārazm, apparently on the 3 Dhū ʾl-Ḥijjah, 362/4 September 973.[1] There is no firm etymology for his name "al-Bīrūnī", but according to Yāqūt it is a local dialect word applied to people who lived in a suburb.[2]

The date of al-Bīrūnī's birth is not well established. The only evidence for it is a note appended to a manuscript giving the above-mentioned date, and a statement by al-Bīrūnī himself giving his age in lunar years, which seems to corroborate that date.[3] The usual biographical sources do not devote much space to him, and none of them give any information on his early life. All we can assert about that period is that he had studied with someone close to the Khwārazm-Shah's court,[4] who also probably introduced him to this court. Later on he served Qābūs b. Wushmagīr (reigned 366–71/977–81 and 388–403/988–1012–13), the master of Jurjān, and to him he dedicated his first major work, *al-Āthār al-bāqiyah* (see below), in the year 1311 of Alexander (= AD 1000).[5] After some considerable turmoil in the political life of Khwārazm, al-Bīrūnī was apparently taken prisoner by the central Asian monarch Maḥmūd of Ghaznah (reigned 388–421/998–1030) about the year 407/1016, and it appears that al-Bīrūnī's knowledge of astrology saved him from certain death.[6] In another account, al-Bīrūnī was supposed to have been an invited guest at Maḥmūd's court,[7] in order "to attain the honour of attendance" at this new court. Niẓāmī, in his *Chahār Maqālah*, insinuates that al-Bīrūnī was "eager to go, having heard accounts of the king's [i.e. Maḥmūd's] munificent gifts and presents".[8] As an astrologer at Maḥmūd's court, al-Bīrūnī accompanied the monarch on his campaigns to India during 408–21/1017–30.[9] During these campaigns, al-

1 Bīrūnī, *al-Āthār*, in Sachau, *Chronologie*, xvi.
2 Yāqūt, *Irshād*, ed. A. Rifāʿī, Cairo, 1936–8, XVII, 180.
3 *Al-Āthār*, in Sachau, *Chronologie*, xxxxvi–xxxxviii.
4 Ibid., 184. 5 Ibid., xxiv–xxv, 194. 6 Ibn al-Athīr, *Kāmil*, IX, 264–5; Yāqūt, *Irshād*, 186.
7 *Niẓāmī ʿArūḍī Samarqandī*, ed. E. G. Browne, Cambridge, 1921, XI, 2, 119. 8 Ibid.
9 Yāqūt, *Irshād*, XVII, 186.

Bīrūnī must have found enough time to study some Sanskrit,[10] in order to translate Indian astronomical texts with the help of a *mutarjim* or a *mufassir*.

After the death of Maḥmūd of Ghaznah,[11] al-Bīrūnī's fortunes fluctuated considerably. He successively served the two sons of Maḥmūd, Masᶜūd, for whom he wrote *al-Qānūn al-Masᶜūdī*, till 432/1040, and Mawdūd, for whom he wrote his book on gems, apparently until 441/1049. In his later years, it would appear that he was not patronized by anybody, for he did not dedicate his book on pharmacology to anyone, as was his wont in other cases.[12]

To conclude this biographical sketch, it is important to note that the information collected from the available sources does not so far answer the most elementary questions about al-Bīrūnī. We do not know, for example, anything about his immediate family circumstances. And if we were to believe his own account as preserved in a line of sarcastic poetry,[13] he did not seem to have known much about it himself. In spite of the vague references to the relationship with Abū Naṣr Manṣūr b. ᶜAlī b. ᶜIrāq, we still do not know much about al-Bīrūnī's early education. Nor do we get any more information from al-Bīrūnī's own autobiographical poem preserved by Yāqūt,[14] which raises more questions than it answers, for he refers to his patrons in a chronological order, up to and including the patronage of the three Ghaznavid monarchs, without mentioning Masᶜūd among them, although he dedicated his major astronomical work *al-Qānūn al-Masᶜūdī* to him. On the other hand, he mentions, in the same poem, the Samanid ruler Manṣūr II b. Nūḥ (reigned 387–9/997–9), to whom he did not dedicate any work as far as we know.

AL-BĪRŪNĪ'S WORKS

According to al-Bīrūnī's *Fihrist*, composed in 427/1035–6,[15] his own works were grouped as follows:

1 Some eighteen works, of varying lengths, do not have a general title, but could be classified as astronomical in nature. Amounting to at least 3,985 folios, they were mainly written as commentaries on earlier works.

2 The next category, composed of some fifteen books, of at least 635 folios, is that of "longitudes and latitudes of cities and their direction

[10] D. Pingree, "Al-Bīrūnī's knowledge of Sanskrit astronomical texts" in P. Chelkowski (ed.), *The Scholar and the Saint*, New York, 1975, 72. [11] Ibn al-Athīr, *Kāmil*, IX, 398.
[12] Bīrūnī, *al-Ṣaydanah*, 15. [13] Yāqūt, *Irshād*, XVII, 189. [14] Ibid., 187.
[15] P. Kraus, *Epître de Bērūnī contenant le répertoire des ouvrages de Muḥammad b. Zakariyyāᵓ al-Rāzī*, Paris, 1936.

from one another".[16] One of these books, the *Taḥdīd nihāyāt al-amākin li-taṣḥīḥ masāfāt al-masākin*, ("The Determination of the Co-ordinates of Cities") which is still extant (see below), is given as being 100 folios long. In the published version it covers some 300 average-size printed pages.

3 Eight works, amounting to 230 folios, are classified as being "Arithmetical" (*ḥisāb*), and four are classified as related to mathematical astrology, rays (*shuʿāʿāt*) and transits (*mamarr*), with a total of 140 folios.

4 The category of "Instruments and their uses" included five works amounting to another 140 folios.

5 Works dealing with chronology, and not including his previously mentioned major work dedicated to Qābūs b. Wushmagīr, amounted to some five treatises totalling 245 folios.

6 Five treatises, of at least 180 folios, were devoted to comets, and were followed by a list of twelve works (of at least 845 folios) which could be loosely grouped as mathematical and meteorological in the sense of Aristotelian meteorology.

7 On astrology proper, al-Bīrūnī wrote seven works; the most important of them, being some 330 folios, is still extant. The other six amount to at least sixty-two folios. Four of them are still extant either in whole or in part.[17]

8 Without giving any indication as to their specific subjects or length, al-Bīrūnī claims to have translated, mainly from Persian, some thirteen treatises.

9 On doctrinal ideas (*ʿaqāʾid*), al-Bīrūnī wrote six treatises amounting to more than 725 folios. His book on India, which is still extant, covers 700 folios, and is included under this category.

10 Finally, al-Bīrūnī states that he had lost the original drafts of several works: he only recalled the titles of four of them. One, *al-Tanbīh ʿalā ṣināʿat al-tamwīh* ("Warning against the Craft of Deceit"), was devoted to an attack on astrology.

Works in progress included about ten books; some in a second edition, while others were only in first draft. These unfinished works included his

[16] Ibid., 32. [17] *GAS*, VII, 189f.

astronomical *magnum opus*, *al-Qānūn al-Masᶜūdī*, that is now published in three volumes of 1,500 printed pages (see below).

Taking a very conservative estimate, based only on the number of folios that were reported by al-Bīrūnī himself, and compared to those that are still extant and printed, al-Bīrūnī seems to have written more than what would now cover 20,000 average printed pages by the year 427/1035–6. This estimate does not include two of his major books, the *Jamāhir fī maᶜrifat al-jawāhir* ("Multitudes Regarding the Knowledge of Gems") and *al-Ṣaydanah* ("Pharmacology"), which were produced after that date. In sum then al-Bīrūnī's total output amounted to some 146 titles: ninety-six devoted to mathematical astronomy or related subjects, while the others ranged from chronology to mechanics, and included pharmacology, mineralogy, history, literature, religion and philosophy.

The following is a short assessment of some of the major works of al-Bīrūnī:

Al-Āthār al-bāqiyah ᶜan al-qurūn al-khāliyah ("The Surviving Monuments of Past Centuries"). This text is unique in the Middle Ages: it combines the technical astronomical information about the various religious sects and nations then known, in regard to their timekeeping and calendar schemes, with the literary and historical traditions of these sects and nations. After defining the basic units of time, the day, the month and the year, in Chapters 1 and 2 al-Bīrūnī discusses the various eras known to him in Chapters 3 and 4, listing in tabular form, from the beginning of time until his own day, the chronological reigns of the Assyrian kings, the Babylonians, the Macedonians, the Romans, the Christians – i.e. the Romans and Byzantines after Diocletian, the Persians before Alexander, the Ashkanians – the Persians after Alexander, the Sasanids and the Muslim caliphs. This section then concludes with a comparative table of ten eras, arranged in a triangular shape, beginning with the era of the Flood and ending with that of al-Muᶜtaḍid (reigned 279–89/892–902). Under each era, al-Bīrūnī gives the nature of the month and the year used in that calendar, and then gives the number of days that separates it from all the others.[18] With these tabular listings, al-Bīrūnī includes other information of a social and political nature.

The rest of the book is then devoted to a discussion of religious celebrations, starting with astronomical cycles, on which most of the religious feasts depended in the first place, and ending with a description of the lunar mansions that are pertinent to the Muslim lunar calendar. The religious groups whose feasts and customs are detailed in these chapters (9–

[18] *Al-Āthār*, in Sachau, *Chronologie*, 137.

20), include the Persians, the Soghdians, the Khwarazmians, the Jews, the Melkite Christians, the Monophysite Christians, the Nestorians, the Ḥarranians, the pre-Islamic Arabs, and the Muslims – all treated as nations. With each feast mentioned, al-Bīrūnī gives all the information that he had gathered about its customs, origins, and the various traditions connected with it. On the ninth of the Arabic month Dhū ʾl-Ḥijjah, for example, the Muslims celebrate the day of ʿArafāt, which is "the day of the great pilgrimage on ʿArafāt. It is so called because on that day people recognize (*taʿārafa*) each other at the time when they assemble for the performance of the rites of the pilgrimage, or, because Adam and Eve recognized each other after they had been driven out of Paradise in the place where people assembled, i.e. in ʿArafāt".[19] The popular etymology applied to geographical names, which is transparently used here, is a well-attested phenomenon, and al-Bīrūnī simply acts as a transmitter of these folk-tales and customs. On the other hand, he was much more critical in his treatment of the Jewish calendar (Chs. 7, 14) and ended up by producing the most authoritative account on the subject, not to be surpassed by any other medieval source, including the Hebrew sources themselves.[20]

In short, Bīrūnī's *al-Āthār al-bāqiyah* was an attempt to record all that was known of the various customs of ancient and medieval nations, with special attention to those rites and rituals that were based on astronomical notions and cycles.

Al-Asʾilah wa-ʾl-ajwibah ("Questions and Answers").[21] This text started as a correspondence between al-Bīrūnī and Ibn Sīnā, apparently initiated by al-Bīrūnī himself when he sent ten questions to Ibn Sīnā relating to Aristotle's *De Caelo*, and eight others dealing mainly with natural philosophy. In response, Ibn Sīnā cites the original questions and gives his own responses to each of them. Apparently, al-Bīrūnī was not satisfied with these answers and sent back to Ibn Sīnā a set of objections to his responses. Ibn Sīnā was apparently offended by al-Bīrūnī's rough language and did not pursue the matter any further. Instead, he gave al-Bīrūnī's objections to one of his students by the name of al-Maʿṣūmī,[22] who read them in a sarcastic spirit and wrote back his own rather harsh response.

All of this correspondence, which must have been carried out at some

[19] Ibid., 332–3. For an alternative etymological account, where the angel Gabriel is supposed to have taught Abraham the name of ʿArafāt, see Yaʿqūbī, *Taʾrīkh*, Beirut, 1960, I, 27.

[20] J. Obermann, *Maimonides' Sanctification of the New Moon*, New Haven, 1956, xliii f.

[21] Nasr, S. H., and Mohaghegh, M. (eds.), *Al-Bīrūnī and Ibn Sīnā: al-Asʾilah wa-ʾl-ajwibah*, Tehran, 1974.

[22] Ẓahīr al-Dīn abū ʾl-Ḥasan ʿAlī al-Bayhaqī, *Taʾrīkh ḥukamāʾ al-Islām*, ed. M. Kurd ʿAlī, Damascus, 1946, 102–3. It should be noted that *Taʾrīkh ḥukamāʾ al-Islām* is an alternative title for *Tatimmat ṣiwān al-ḥikmah*; see below, n. 24.

early point in al-Bīrūnī's life,[23] has survived and has been printed together in one booklet. But, although this correspondence is the least important in terms of its contents and contribution to al-Bīrūnī's intellectual character, it nevertheless revealed even to medieval biographers, and probably to al-Bīrūnī's own contemporaries, al-Bīrūnī's lack of ability in philosophical argumentation. Ẓahīr al-Dīn abū ᵓl-Ḥasan ᶜAlī al-Bayhaqī, for example, says in his biography of al-Bīrūnī: "He also engaged in disputations with Abū ᶜAlī [Ibn Sīnā], although he was not especially gifted in philosophical matters (*al-maᶜqūlāt*). And each can excel only in that for which he was created."[24] The same judgement is also repeated verbatim by al-Shahrazūrī.[25]

But even if it were true that al-Bīrūnī was not especially gifted in philosophical matters, he made up for this by being distinguished in the mathematical disciplines. It was on this ground that he finally revenged himself on Ibn Sīnā when he referred to him in the *Taḥdīd* in the following terms: "I have seen a treatise on the correction of the longitude of Jurjān . . . by Abū ᶜAlī . . . Ibn Sīnā."[26] After demolishing the contents of this treatise, he concludes: "Though Abū ᶜAlī is renowned for his intelligence and sound intuition, he is unreliable in a matter which requires practical experience."[27] Further on, in the same text, al-Bīrūnī goes on to say:

> However, Abū ᶜAlī is not reliable, and at least he should not have been confused by the figures of the altitudes of the stars in his very complicated method for the determination of the longitude, or he would have adopted for his determination a method which does not depend on the observation of the fixed stars by earlier observers. I suppose, if objections were raised against his method, he would put the blame for it on others.[28]

More than ten years later, when al-Bīrūnī wrote his *al-Qānūn al-Masᶜūdī*, he was still taunting Ibn Sīnā: "Abū ᶜAlī b. Sīnā said that he had verified the longitude of Jurjān as a result of his work there, and considered Ḥabash's [Aḥmad b. ᶜAbdullāh Ḥabash al-Ḥāsib al-Marwazī] determination of the longitude of Baghdad as replacing one of them [i.e. the two required eclipse observations]. This method, although correct in theory, is unattainable in reality."[29]

Taḥdīd nihāyāt al-amākin li-taṣḥīḥ masāfāt al-masākin. The edition of this text was based on a manuscript that was completed on 23 Rajab, 416/19 September 1025, and thus the book itself must have been composed

[23] It must have been written before the year 390/1000, the date of composition of the *Chronology*, for it is mentioned in it; see *al-Āthār*, in Sachau, *Chronologie*, 257.

[24] *Tatimmat ṣiwān al-ḥikmah*, Lahore, 1935, 62–3. [25] *Taᵓrīkh*, II, Hyderabad, 1976, 86.

[26] *The Determination of the Coordinates of Cities*, trans. J. Ali, Beirut, 1967, 166.

[27] Ibid., 167–8. [28] Ibid., 209. [29] 508–9.

sometime between 408/1017, the year al-Bīrūnī came to Ghaznah, and 416/1025, when the completed manuscript was copied. But since the text reports several observations taken at Ghaznah, some of them dated in 410/1019, we can assume that the composition was closer to 416/1025. Al-Bīrūnī described his reasons for writing the book:

My particular purpose, however, is to determine these data [i.e. co-ordinates] for the city of Ghaznah, the capital of the kingdom of the East, because, as a newcomer, I would like to consider it, by human reckoning, my homeland; though all true reckoning, in reality, is made by God only. In Ghaznah, as long as I am able to do so, I shall persevere in carrying on the observations and the scientific research on that which is constantly on my mind, namely, the determination of the true direction of the *qiblah*.[30]

The determination of the *qiblah* for Ghaznah, a somewhat difficult mathematical problem in itself, and involving the use of advanced spherical trigonometry,[31] gave al-Bīrūnī the chance to argue for the utility of mathematics and mathematical astronomy. Without mathematical geography, the determination of the *qiblah*, a religious injunction by itself, would be made impossible. Although this argument sounds like an apology for the mathematical sciences, it is nevertheless of crucial interest to the status of the "foreign sciences", including mathematics and astronomy, in contrast to the native or "religious sciences". Al-Bīrūnī pleads with his reader not to be an "extreme fanatic" who would "call everyone whose name ends with the letter 's' (*sīn*) a rejector of Islam and an atheist" (a reference to such famous non-Arab figures as Jālīnūs = Galen, Baṭlamiyūs = Ptolemy, Aristūtālīs = Aristotle),[32] despite the fact that some of Aristotle's "theories and beliefs run contrary to the beliefs of Islam".[33] But that should not lead to a rejection of logic, for "generally speaking, it is like grammar".[34]

Of course, accepting logic as a tool like grammar, and mathematics and astronomy as useful sciences, allows one then to respond to "the great need for ascertaining the direction of the *qiblah* in order to hold the prayer which is the pillar of Islam and also its pole".[35] And "if the investigation of distances between towns, and the mapping of the habitable world, so that the relative positions of towns become known [the subject-matter of the book], serve none of our needs except the need for correcting the direction of the *qiblah*, we should find it our duty to pay all our attention and energy to that investigation."[36]

The rest of the introduction is devoted to questions of natural philosophy related to the creation and formation of the habitable world. And it is in the discussion of these questions that one gains an understanding of the

[30] *Taḥdīd*, 32. [31] *EI*², "Ḳibla". [32] *Taḥdīd*, 6. [33] Ibid. [34] Ibid. [35] Ibid., 12. [36] Ibid., 13.

status of such research in al-Bīrūnī's time. Current geological theories, for example, were reviewed to explain the presence of fossils in parts of the habitable world that appear never to have been close to the sea. Other lost works on similar geological subjects, such as the work of Ibn al-ᶜAmīd (d. 360/970)[37] on the construction of cities, *Fī Bināᵓ al-mudun*, would have remained unknown if it were not for this research of al-Bīrūnī.

Besides the several methods for the determination of the *qiblah* discussed in this book, al-Bīrūnī also devotes extensive sections to other related problems of a practical nature, such as the determination of the local meridian, the distances between cities, methods of observation, etc.

Ifrād al-maqāl fī amr al-ẓilāl ("Treatise Devoted to the Question of Shadows"). As in the *Taḥdīd*, here too, al-Bīrūnī tries to elaborate on the distinction between the mathematical disciplines and philosophy. He argues that the world could hardly be understood without recourse to arithmetic and geometry. And anyone who denies that is not only indistinguishable from the common masses, but is also ignorant "of what impugns religion so that he might [properly] support it".[38]

In a long introductory section, al-Bīrūnī examines the uses of the word *ẓill* (shadow) from every perspective, with the astronomical relations always in mind, then concludes by defining two shadow functions, namely, the tangent and the cotangent (Chs. 9–10). The ensuing relationships between these functions and the other trigonometric functions are then discussed at great length (Chs. 11–12), and are followed by the practical methods for ascertaining the shadow functions (Chs. 13–17). The direct application of this research to religious matters is vigorously pursued by first determining the relationship of shadow measurements to the determination of the local meridian, and then the telling of the time which itself leads (Chs. 25–6) to a consideration of times of prayer and their indications by curves on astronomical instruments. These curves are the equivalent of our modern use of a graph for representing mathematical functions. Chapter 27 is devoted to a study of the advantages of using trigonometric functions over the Menelaus Theorem, and Chapters 28–30 conclude the discussion by bringing together all the miscellaneous material related to shadows.

Although al-Bīrūnī's purpose was apparently to define, in mathematical terms, the religious times of prayer, hence putting mathematics in the service of religion, the treatise could still be seen as an independent text on trigonometry. This should not be surprising, for, historically speaking,

[37] Ibn Khallikān, *Wafayāt*, v, 103f. [38] *Ifrād*, 6.

trigonometric functions were drawn directly from the study of shadow instruments and time-telling devices. The Arabic word for "tangent" is still *ẓill* which also means "shadow".

Istīʿāb al-wujūh al-mumkinah fī ṣināʿat al-asṭurlāb ("The Comprehension of the Possible Methods in the Art of the Astrolabe"). Although this text exists in several manuscript copies, and in several libraries around the world, it has not yet been studied by modern scholars despite its importance for the history of astronomy in general, and the study of instruments in particular. It not only surveys all the types of astrolabes known to al-Bīrūnī, a veritable anthology of the technical developments introduced into this originally Greek instrument up to the fifth/eleventh century, but also includes long discussions of the novelties for which various astrolabes became famous, as well as the theoretical foundations upon which they were based. While discussing the *zawraqī* astrolabe of Abū Saʿīd Aḥmad b. Muḥammad al-Sijzī, for example, al-Bīrūnī says:

> I have seen a simple astrolabe – it did not contain a northern or southern section – made by Abū Saʿīd al-Sijzī and called *al-zawraqī*. I liked it very much, for he had invented it by employing an independent theory, held by some people, stating that the apparent universal motion is due to the earth and not to the heavens. I earnestly believe that [such motion] is difficult to ascertain and analyse, and it should not concern those who depend on geometric lines, i.e. the engineers and the astronomers, for it does not invalidate their craft in any way. The natural philosophers, however, are the ones charged with the analysis of such problems and doctrines.[39]

The fact that some people, including al-Sijzī, did indeed believe that the earth was moving on its own axis, contrary to appearances and the doctrines of Ptolemy, is further confirmed by another reference from the seventh/thirteenth century which states: "According to the geometers [or engineers] (*muhandisīn*), the earth is in constant circular motion, and what appears to be the motion of the heavens is actually due to the motion of the earth and not the stars."[40]

Al-Tafhīm li-awāʾil ṣināʿat al-tanjīm ("Instruction in the Elements of the Art of Astrology"). This text, written about 420/1029, is the most comprehensive encyclopaedia on astrology that has survived from medieval times. Written in the form of question and answer for a woman by the name of Rayḥānah bint al-Ḥasan, who is otherwise unknown, it begins with long sections on geometry, arithmetic, astronomy, the astrolabe and its uses as

39 British Library, MS Or. 5593, fols. 40v–41r.
40 Aḥmad b. Ḥamdān al-Ḥarrānī, *Kitāb Jāmiʿ al-funūn*, British Library, MS Or. 6299, fol. 64v.

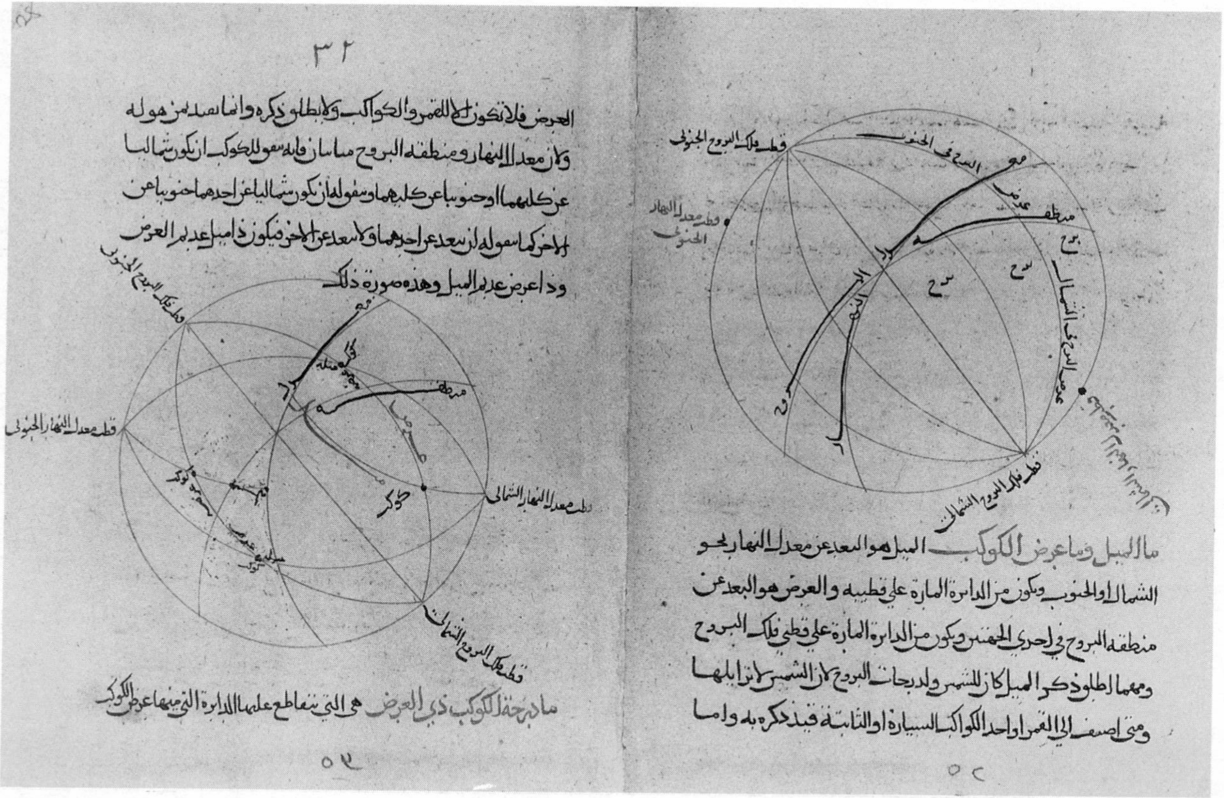

10 Diagrams from a sixth/twelfth-century manuscript of *al-Tafhīm li-awāʾil ṣināʿat al-tanjīm* by al-Bīrūnī, giving the author's answers to the questions "What is declination?" and "What is the latitude of a heavenly body?"

an observational instrument, and only then the last third of the book is reserved for astrology proper.

Because of this encyclopaedia, and because of al-Bīrūnī's employment as an astrologer, the question of his belief in astrology has been raised several times. According to Eduard Sachau, the editor and translator of al-Bīrūnī's *al-Āthar al-bāqiyah* and *Taḥqīq mā li-ʾl-Hind* for example, "it would hardly be intelligible why he [i.e. al-Bīrūnī] should have spent so much time and labour on the study of Greek and Indian astrology if he had not believed in the truth of the thing". Sachau claims that al-Bīrūnī remained "entangled in the notions of Greek astrology".[41] But the editor and commentator on the Persian version of al-Bīrūnī's *Tafhīm*, J. Humāʾī,[42] believes that al-Bīrūnī did not give much credence to the works of the astrologers.

The reason why these opinions regarding al-Bīrūnī's beliefs seem so contradictory is that although al-Bīrūnī himself must have worked as a professional astrologer,[43] he nevertheless wrote works in which he specifically attacked astrology. The title of one such work is mentioned by al-Bīrūnī himself in his *Fihrist* and in *al-Āthār al-bāqiyah*, but the book is unfortunately lost. Moreover one can gather enough of al-Bīrūnī's opinions that are scattered throughout his works to support the assertion that he was "studying the subject... to be able to warn the reasonable man away from it".[44] The same sentiment is put slightly differently by al-Bīrūnī himself when he says: "I mention this to protect the reader from the delusions [of astrology]."[45] And later on, in the same work he says: "We did not work in this art [of astrology] except to guide those who are asked about it to the right path."[46]

At this stage when Islamic astrology has still not been comprehensively surveyed, it is hard to say whether al-Bīrūnī was attacking mathematical astrology, a subject he indeed treated at great length in several books, or the folk-astrology which was little more than doctrinal statements with no mathematical interest. When al-Bīrūnī studied the problem of "the projection of rays", or "the equalization of houses", or "the transits of a planet", and developed the mathematical definitions and solutions of these problems in the most advanced spherical trigonometric terminology, did he believe in the influence of the "houses" or the "rays" or the "transits"? His absolute silence in regard to his own belief in these matters, and his constant references to other astrologers when introducing these problems by saying "according to them", lead the present author to suspect that al-Bīrūnī probably believed, like everyone else in medieval times who had

[41] *Taḥqīq*, xxvi. [42] Tehran, 1940. [43] Samarqandī, *Chahār Maqālah*.
[44] E. S. Kennedy, "The world-year concept in Islamic astrology", *Journal of the American Oriental Society*, LXXXIII, 1963, 23–43; E. S. Kennedy *et al.*, *Studies in the Islamic Exact Sciences*, Beirut, 1983, 351–71.
[45] *Al-Qānūn al-Masʿūdī*, 1469. [46] Ibid., 1479.

read Aristotle and Ptolemy carefully, that the planets do indeed have an influence on the physical make-up of the human being on this earth, but he himself dealt with the subject mainly because it lent itself to an advanced mathematical treatment, which in itself seems to have fascinated al-Bīrūnī. The tone in which he treated astrology in general as "the art of the decrees of the stars",[47] may give the reader the flavour of his way of thinking:

> The time has come that we mention the statements (*muwāḍaᶜāt*) expressed in the craft of the decrees of the stars (*ṣināᶜat aḥkām al-nujūm*), for most of those who ask are really seeking it with their questions, and because, according to the majority of people, it is the fruit of the mathematical sciences, in spite of the fact that our belief in this fruit and craft is comparable to that of the least of them.[48]

Tamhīd al-mustaqarr li-taḥqīq maᶜnā al-mamarr ("The Preparation of the Abode for the Determination of the Significance of the Transit"). This text is a good example of the method with which al-Bīrūnī treats astrological subjects. He takes one concept, in this case that of the *mamarr* (transit), states what the astrologers thought of it in "their craft",[49] gives a detailed survey of the general use of the terms, and then defines *mamarr* in mathematical terminology, always relating it to other astrological concepts which have been previously defined. After exhausting all the particular information that he had gathered about the specific concept, he gives several methods of his own to solve the problem or to sharpen the definitions. In each case he gives an anthology of all the methods he knew of from his predecessors who treated the same problem, but mainly to criticize those methods and validate his own. In such a historical survey, al-Bīrūnī manages to preserve for us in one form or another at least some of the contents of earlier works that are now presumed lost.

Taḥqīq mā li-ʾl-Hind min maqūlah maqbūlah fī ʾl-ᶜaql aw mardhūlah ("Ascertaining of Statements to be Accorded Intellectual Acceptance or to be Rejected Regarding India"). While in the company of Maḥmūd of Ghaznah, during the latter's forays into India, from 408/1017 to 421/1030, al-Bīrūnī seems to have gone beyond his role as the monarch's astrologer. He obviously had the time to learn at least some Sanskrit, gather a group of translators, and investigate several features of Indian life around that time. We also know that he arranged to have several Sanskrit books translated into Arabic. But during those years he must have kept copious notes about India, which were useful when, after the death of his original patron Maḥmūd, he decided to put them together into book form. The result is a manuscript of 700 folios, as described in his own *Fihrist*, and in English translation it fills a densely printed two-volume book.

47 *Tafhīm*, 210. 48 Ibid. 49 *Tamhīd*, 1.

"This book," al-Bīrūnī says, "is not a *polemical* one. I shall not produce the arguments of our antagonists in order to refute such of them as I believe to be wrong. My book is nothing but a *simple historic record of facts*";[50] facts about the Hindus in general: their beliefs, their social customs, their laws, their religion, their literature and grammar, their astrology and astronomy, and in short every aspect of Indian life as he had observed it. Of course, the subjects that interested al-Bīrūnī personally received a much greater attention, whether astronomical, chronological, meteorological or geographical.

Lest his account of India should be reduced to tales and stories, al-Bīrūnī planned it from the very beginning with a general educated Muslim reader in mind. Indian accounts are compared, whenever al-Bīrūnī felt they could be, with Greek, Ṣūfī and Christian doctrines, "in order to show the relationship existing between them".[51] In short, al-Bīrūnī managed to write a comparative anthropological account of Indian life around 421/1030, that "remains one of the most penetrating accounts we have of Indian society".[52]

Like others of his writings, this one too is a mine of information of al-Bīrūnī's views of his own society as it related to India. His critique of the early Arabic translations of Sanskrit sources, and the difficulties one usually faces while studying another culture, is more of a mirror that reflects al-Bīrūnī's own society rather than that of India. To get to the bottom of al-Bīrūnī's assessment of either civilization one has to weave through, and in between the lines of the whole book, being constantly alert to the innocently scattered remarks that look as if they were mentioned simply by free association. Such a detailed assessment is beyond the scope of the present survey.

Ghurrat al-zījāt ("The Finest Astronomical Tables"). This is only one of several Sanskrit books that al-Bīrūnī seems to have arranged to have translated into Arabic. On the basis of this text, which was apparently translated around 417/1026, both the original editor of the translation and David Pingree, who has studied it more recently, became convinced that al-Bīrūnī did not have an expert, direct knowledge of the Sanskrit astronomical sources. In fact, it has become doubtful whether he himself translated any of these sources. Pingree even suggests "that Bīrūnī's role in the production of the *Ghurrat al-zījāt* was confined to that of a sponsor, editor, and explicator of some pandit's incompetent effort".[53]

50 Sachau, *Alberuni's India*, 7. 51 Ibid.
52 *Taḥqīq mā li-ʾl-Hind*, ed. A. Embree, New York, 1971, v.
53 Pingree, "Al-Bīrūnī's knowledge of Sanskrit", 69.

Al-Qānūn al-Masᶜūdī. This is al-Bīrūnī's extensive astronomical work. In it he brings astronomical knowledge up to the early part of the fifth/eleventh century, and adds some of his own. The text is written in eleven treatises paralleling, more or less, the contents of a usual Islamic *zīj* (astronomical handbook), but containing additional discussions of a theoretical nature that are of the type encountered in Ptolemy's *Almagest*. It is in this book, for example, that one finds al-Bīrūnī incorporating his own observations with those of his predecessors to determine new parameters for planetary tables.[54] It is here too that new theoretical grounds were covered for the first time as in the case, for example, of determining the motion of the solar apogee, and concluding that the results reached were first, contrary to Ptolemy's hypothesis, and secondly, that the motion was distinct from the motion of precession as the later Muslim astronomers had thought.[55]

This text also contains new mathematical concepts and computational techniques. In it, for example, al-Bīrūnī analyses instantaneous motion and acceleration in such terminology that can best be understood if we assume that he had "mathematical functions" in mind.[56] Similarly, tables of planetary equations are adjusted in such a way as to facilitate their use by eliminating, whenever possible, the negative values of these tables, thereby reducing the computations to simple additions.[57]

It is unfortunate that this book has not yet received the attention that it deserves from modern historians of science, for it not only promises to be of great value for historians of Islamic astronomy, but may further increase our knowledge of the history of trigonometry, and change our accepted ideas about the general history of mathematics as well.[58]

Al-Jamāhir fī maᶜrifat al-jawāhir ("Multitudes on the Knowledge of Gems"). This text is divided into a long introduction and two treatises (*maqālah*): the first deals with precious stones and minerals, and the second deals with metals. In the introduction al-Bīrūnī discusses precious stones and metals in general and their social, economic and political roles, thereby producing a theory of government and ethics. In his statement of the purpose of his book he says that such studies should help rulers to distinguish, among other things, the genuine from the fake, for:

> There is no genuine thing in the hands of a just man without a fake in the hands of a corrupt one, trying to pass the fake as genuine. From such a person, and people like

54 E. S. Kennedy, "Al-Bīrūnī's *Masᶜūdic Canon*", *Al-Abḥāth*, XXIV, 1971, 77.

55 W. Hartner and M. Schramm, "Al-Bīrūnī and the theory of the solar apogee: an example of originality in Arabic science" in A.C. Crombie (ed.), *Scientific Change*, London, 1963, 206–18, esp. 216.

56 Ibid., 215.

57 Kennedy, "Al-Bīrūnī's *Masᶜūdic Canon*", 69, 70, 74.

58 For al-Bīrūnī's astronomical work *Maqālīd al-hayᵓah*, see above, ch. 15, 288.

him, arises the need for those in command to abide by the rules of government in order that they be worthy of the name of caliphs to God's creation, and the name of His shadow on this earth. They should be ready to equate, with the help of the Almighty, those of His creatures who are high in rank, and those who are low; the noble in birth, and the weak, and God will reward only those who succeed in doing so.[59]

As for money itself, whether gold or silver, al-Bīrūnī asserts that its value is in reality an arbitrary convention among people, for it has nothing in its essence to distinguish it for praise or blame: "And anything that does not contribute to man's sustenance and the preservation of his species, or to his dress and his defence against other men, or to his protection from heat and cold, or to his support in dispelling evil, that thing is not praiseworthy by itself, but is rather conventionally so."[60]

The treatise on precious stones begins with the generalized category *yāqūt*, discussing the various stones known in that category, their social and economic values, the semi-precious gems, anecdotes related to them and their use by various rulers, their colours, their physical properties, the time and place of their collection (as in the case of pearls), the names and descriptions given to them by lexicographers and jewellers, their values in various times and places, and ends with a discussion of glass and its by-products. In this discussion al-Bīrūnī also gives descriptions of the methods of preparation, if the stone is an artificial one like glass, its medical properties, if it has any, and the legends told about them to which he himself does not give much credence – as in the case of the talismanic stories concerning precious stones by ʿUṭārid b. Muḥammad al-Ḥāsib (third/ninth century).[61]

The second treatise begins with a discussion of metals in general, and the theory behind their formation. Mercury is discussed first, only because "the physicists (*ṭabīʿiyyūn*) have stated that sulphur was the father of fusible bodies, while mercury was their mother, and with the action of fire they all return to a quivering mercury".[62] But the metal of social and economic value was obviously gold, and that is taken up next. Having discussed gold in its linguistic context, al-Bīrūnī then gives all the anecdotes that he knows about it, discusses its economic value, its preparation and its mining, and concludes by taking gold as the reference metal for the specific weights of all other metals that he himself had determined. He takes the standard measure of gold to be 100 units, as he had taken the standard measure for the precious stones to be 100 units of emerald. Then he determined the specific weight of copper, for example, to be $45+\frac{1}{2}+\frac{1}{6}=45.66$ units of the standard weight of gold, which is 100 units. This gives a specific weight for

59 *Al-Jamāhir*, 8. 60 Ibid., 8–9. 61 Ibid., 217. 62 Ibid., 229.

copper of 0.46, which is the modern value. He repeats the same treatment for the other metals, always giving their specific weight with respect to gold. A comparison of these weights with the modern values confirms, even by modern standards, al-Bīrūnī's scientific methodology.[63]

Al-Ṣaydanah fī ʾl-ṭibb ("Pharmacology in Medicine"). This pharmacological encyclopaedia, containing more than 1,000 entries, was culled from earlier sources such as the *Materia Medica* of Dioscorides, containing some 827 entries, and the works of prominent physicians such as Abū Bakr Muḥammad b. Zakariyyāʾ al-Rāzī. In the process, al-Bīrūnī managed to consult the works of some 125 authorities, either for linguistic identification of the drugs discussed or for the medical information about each of the entries that he included in the collection.

The encyclopaedia itself, unlike the *Materia Medica* of Dioscorides which is arranged by subject-matter, is listed in a strictly alphabetic order, irrespective of the origin of the drugs, whether from plants, minerals, metals or animals. For each drug, as far as possible, al-Bīrūnī attempts to list the names of the drug (in Arabic, Syriac, Greek, Sanskrit, Hebrew, Persian, Soghdian and other languages), and follows this with a linguistic commentary to ascertain its exact identification and the way the Arabic name should be pronounced. This information is then followed by a physical description of the drug, the literary sources that mention it, its provenance, its medical uses, and finally its varieties that are found in nature.

Because of the several languages quoted by al-Bīrūnī in this work, it has been assumed that he was proficient in these languages. In light of more thorough research, however, it seems that, at best, al-Bīrūnī may have been able to use some of the dictionaries of these languages, and, with the exception of Arabic and Persian, he was by no means proficient in them. In the introduction to this book, al-Bīrūnī himself states that he learned both Arabic and Persian, and that neither of them was his mother tongue. But he goes on to say that "he preferred to be satirized in Arabic rather than be praised in Persian".[64] In modern times, and because of modern politics, this remark of al-Bīrūnī has created some controversy. Owing to the directions of al-Bīrūnī's travels, he has been acclaimed as a national scientist in the USSR, because he was born in the city now named after him near modern Khorezmskaya in Uzbekistan; in Iran because he spoke Khwarazmian, a dialect akin to Persian; in Pakistan and Afghanistan because he spent a good

[63] For a fuller table of specific weights, as determined by al-Bīrūnī and others, see A. Mieli, *La Science Arabe*, Leiden, 1939, 101.

[64] M. Meyerhof, "Das Vorwort zur Drogenkunde des Bīrūnī", *Quellen und Studien der Naturwissenschaften und der Medizin*, Berlin, 1932, III, 157–208, text 13.

part of his life in the Sind district and in Ghaznah, near modern Kabul; and in the Arab countries because he wrote in Arabic. His own inclination, however, if the introduction of this book is read properly, was to be identified first and foremost as a Muslim, who preferred to read and write scientific works in Arabic – the language of science at that time – and to leave Persian for works of entertainment.

CONCLUSION

The above survey of al-Bīrūnī's works covers only the most important ones which have survived and which are, with the exception of the *Astrolabe*, available in print. Other, minor works, such as his treatise on *Tasṭīḥ al-ṣuwar wa-tabṭīḥ al-kuwar* ("Planispheric projection"), and his treatise *Fī ʾstikhrāj al-awtār fīʾl-dāʾirah* ("The Extraction of Chords in a Circle")[65] have also survived and would have been included if this assessment had been intended to be exhaustive.

After this selective treatment of al-Bīrūnī's works, it may be of interest to consider some general questions that have not been touched on in the discussion of the individual works. Why, for instance, were none of his works translated into Latin during the intensive translation activity of the sixth/twelfth and seventh/thirteenth centuries? The subject-matter of those works could not have been the reason (as with the case of poetry, or Quranic commentaries), for he wrote on many subjects that were specifically sought after by the Latin translators, such as his work on astrology which would have been a much better text to translate than all the astrological texts that were in fact translated during that period. This obscurity of al-Bīrūnī in the Latin West may be partially related to the similar neglect which he received at the hands of the standard biographers in the Muslim East. We noted above that only Ibn abī Uṣaybiʿah managed to devote a few lines to al-Bīrūnī, and none were accorded him by al-Qifṭī or Ibn Khallikān. In the light of this, and in spite of his prolific production, we are forced to conclude that he was not considered by his contemporaries and immediate successors as a major figure.

Another reason for this relative obscurity may be sought in al-Bīrūnī's intellectual temperament itself. For although he was a student of the "foreign sciences" and natural philosophy, as his contemporaries would have seen him, still his discomfiture at the hands of Ibn Sīnā mentioned above exposed him as less than brilliant in that domain. Even the language that he used in the questions he sent to Ibn Sīnā, and in the objections that he

[65] First treatise in *Rasāʾil al-Bīrūnī*.

raised to the answers, barely hides the disdain with which he treated philosophical issues. Note also how quickly he dismissed the possibility of the motion of the earth as a philosophical issue that he was not prepared to entertain. This shortcoming of al-Bīrūnī was noted very clearly by the few biographers who devoted any space to him, such as Yāqūt and Ẓahīr al-Dīn al-Bayhaqī (quoted above), both saying that "he was not especially gifted in philosophical matters". In this connection one may also ask why al-Bīrūnī did not produce, as far as we know, any work in the same vein as that of his contemporaries Ibn al-Haytham[66] and Abū ᶜUbayd al-Jūzajānī,[67] or his successors such as Muʾayyad al-Dīn al-ᶜUrḍī, Naṣīr al-Dīn al-Ṭūsī, Quṭb al-Dīn al-Shīrāzī, and ᶜAlāʾ al-Dīn Aḥmad b. Ibrāhīm b. Muḥammad b. al-Shāṭir (d. 777/1375). All of these astronomers wrote objections to Ptolemaic astronomy; and some of them even proposed alternative models of their own, so that, when taken together, they represent a trend in Islamic astronomy that was distinguished by its rigorous attack against what was perceived to be a set of imperfections in Ptolemaic astronomy. This trend continued throughout the seventh/thirteenth and eighth/fourteenth centuries and culminated in the works of Copernicus, that were motivated by the same considerations and, in many aspects, adopted identical mathematical solutions to respond to these imperfections. Evidence has however recently come to light of a lost work by al-Bīrūnī, entitled *Ibṭāl al-buhtān bi-īrād al-burhān*, in which he argued against the Ptolemaic latitude theory. This finding changes our assessment of al-Bīrūnī's engagement with the new astronomy of his time.

In view of this temperament which kept his feet on the ground, so to speak, it becomes understandable why after solving the mathematical problem of the *qiblah* more than once in the *Taḥdīd*, al-Bīrūnī devoted a special section for the benefit of engineers that was introduced with the following words: "These methods [of mathematically determining the *qiblah*] are sufficient for those who wish to use elaborate methods, but as architects and artisans cannot work out the precise amounts which we have derived, they must proceed as follows."[68] In the same spirit, he also devised new techniques for artisans who had to construct projection lines on astrolabes and who were not especially knowledgeable in the geometric proofs of these projections, but skilled enough to seek higher precision. In his short treatise on planispheric projection, he says:

66 *Al-Shukūk ᶜalā Baṭlamiyūs*, eds. N. Shehaby and A. Sabra, Cairo, 1971.

67 G. Saliba, "Ibn Sīnā and Abū ᶜUbayd al-Jūzjānī: the problem of the Ptolemaic equant", *Journal for the History of Arabic Science*, IV, 1980, 376–403.

68 255.

There are those artisans who prefer arithmetical [methods] over the practical ones (*al-ṭuruq al-ṣināʿiyyah*) that are followed by all makers of astrolabes and other instruments that we know. For that reason, we repeat all that we have described so far in arithmetical terms, and account for the values of the diameters of the circles and the distances of their centres from the centre of the given circle, as well as the intersections of the lines with the circumference.[69]

In short, it seems that he himself was aware of his limitations and that he was content to confine himself to particular problems, and to leave the more general philosophical issues on one side, for he says: "We must limit ourselves to the works of the ancients, and devote our energy to correct, whenever possible, each and every mistake as we encounter it. For the one who attempts encompassing [all things] will lose the whole."[70]

[69] *Tasṭīḥ*, 18. [70] Ibid., 22.

CHAPTER 25

AL-GHAZĀLĪ

One of the greatest thinkers of the classical Islamic age and the man who influenced Islamic thought after the sixth/twelfth century more than any other was Abū Ḥāmid al-Ghazālī. Led by Muʿtazilites and philosophers such as Muḥammad b. Muḥammad al-Fārābī and Ibn Sīnā, Islamic thought had maintained certain modes of rationalism for 300 years; al-Ghazālī redirected it towards mysticism.

Today there are signs of al-Ghazālī's influence in the works of his successors including those of the great shaykh, Muḥyī ʾl-Dīn b. al-ʿArabī (560–638/1165–1240) who seems, at first glance, to have little in common with al-Ghazālī's conservatism. Al-Ghazālī's book *Iḥyāʾ ʿulūm al-dīn* ("The Revival of the Religious Sciences"), exceptional for its exalted tone of moral instruction, is still widely read in religious and learned circles and is occasionally reprinted in Cairo and Beirut. Of particular interest also is a shorter work called *al-Munqidh min al-ḍalāl* ("The Deliverer from Error"), which was written towards the end of his life and in which he describes certain periods of his life and summarizes his ideas on philosophy, mysticism and Ismaʿilism. In both these works, and in others also written in the last years of his life such as *Ayyuhā ʾl-walad* and *al-Qisṭās al-mustaqīm* ("The Correct Balance"), al-Ghazālī blends mysticism with jurisprudence and theology with philosophy.

PUPIL AND TEACHER

Poor but well-educated, the young al-Ghazālī visited the great cities of his time: Jurjān, Naysābūr, Baghdad and Damascus, in order to gain more knowledge which he could share with others. However, at the age of thirty-eight, while he was teaching in Baghdad, he underwent an acute spiritual crisis. For the six months during which this crisis lasted, he was quite unable to think as usual, and the experience changed his life radically and left a deep imprint on his later works.

Abū Ḥāmid Muḥammad b. Muḥammad b. Aḥmad al-Ghazālī was born in 450/1058 in the village of Ghazālah near the city of Ṭūs. Destroyed by the

Mongols in 617/1220, Ṭūs re-emerged later as Mashhad, and today houses the tombs of such famous figures as Hārūn al-Rashīd, the Imam ʿAlī al-Riḍā and the great Persian poet al-Firdawsī. Al-Ghazālī himself was buried near al-Firdawsī in 505/1111.

His father was a poor and illiterate man whose great pleasure in life was sitting with preachers and ulema. He dreamed of one of his sons becoming a brilliant scholar, and in fact his dream was realized in both his sons, Aḥmad and Muḥammad. Muḥammad studied the religious and linguistic sciences in Ṭūs and Jurjān and then went on to the Naysābūr Niẓāmiyyah College with some other students from Ṭūs. Here he studied the more advanced sciences of *fiqh* and theology under the celebrated teacher, the Imām al-Ḥaramayn, ʿAbd al-Malik b. ʿAbdullāh al-Juwaynī. At the college he also began studying logic and philosophy. Then, in 478/1085, the same year in which al-Juwaynī died, he met Niẓām al-Mulk, the Saljūq vizier, who was then staying in the camp in the eastern part of Naysābūr. Al-Ghazālī was invited to take part in a debate with some ulema which was attended by the vizier. His prowess caught the vizier's attention and in 484/1091 he was appointed to a professorship in the Niẓāmiyyah college in Baghdad. The following year Niẓām al-Mulk was assassinated by a young Ismāʿīlī. His son, Fakhr al-Mulk ʿAlī, who later became vizier to the Saljūq ruler Sanjar, suffered a similar fate.

In 483/1090, one year before al-Ghazālī moved to Baghdad, the Ismāʿīlī leader, al-Ḥasan b. al-Ṣabbāḥ had returned to Persia from Egypt and occupied the fortress of Alamūt. Here he instructed his followers in his own interpretation of Islam and the imamate. The numerous assassinations performed by this extremist group were among the reasons for the attack al-Ghazālī launched on Ismāʿīlī beliefs. In this connection he wrote *Faḍāʾiḥ al-Bāṭiniyyah* ("The Infamies of the Baṭinites"), which is sometimes called *al-Mustaẓhirī*, and *al-Qisṭās al-mustaqīm* in the form of an imaginary dialogue between himself and an Ismāʿīlī figure.

Al-Ghazālī wrote: "It has always been my practice, as a youth and as a man, to thirst for knowledge of the true nature of things . . . so that I can be freed from the bond of imitation (*taqlīd*)".[1] Judging from the great range and variety of his works, his claim would seem to be perfectly true. Once he had gained a thorough grasp of Shafiʿite jurisprudence, he wrote an exposition of it in five works, in addition to seven other books on *uṣūl al-fiqh*. The most famous of these, which vary in length and style, is *al-Mustaṣfā* ("The Choicest Portion"). His books on logic, such as *Miʿyār al-ʿilm* ("The Yardstick of Knowledge") and *Miḥakk al-naẓar fī ʾl-manṭiq* ("The Touch-

[1] *Munqidh*, 13.

stone of the Study of Logic") show him to have been an outstanding scholar in this field as well. He was able to summarize also the philosophy of al-Fārābī and Ibn Sīnā with originality and perception, discovering in them the system of Greek philosophy in its Arab clothing. His book *Maqāṣid al-falāsifah* ("The Aims of the Philosophers"), translated into Latin in the sixth/twelfth century, became an influential book among scholastic Christian theologians.[2] Al-Ghazālī's purpose in writing it was, in fact, to prepare the ground for his next work, *Tahāfut al-falāsifah*. This critical work won him a great deal of fame despite the technicality of its arguments.

SPIRITUAL CONVERSION

There are indications that when al-Ghazālī was teaching in Baghdad he began to enjoy his position as an *ᶜālim* and the privileges it accorded him. State officials consulted him in various matters of importance and pupils came from everywhere to study under him. However, in 488/1095 he began to have serious doubts about two things: first, the value of what he believed and taught, and secondly, the extent of his own certainty of belief. Like many pious Muslim thinkers of the time, al-Ghazālī believed that personal knowledge should spur one on to good deeds which please God and lead to salvation. A conflicting view was the Aristotelian one held by some philosophers that the purpose of knowledge was the achievement of mental satisfaction and enjoyment. However, being of the former opinion al-Ghazālī was inclined to criticize his own behaviour and aims. He thought that he had used his learning merely to gain prestige and acclaim. In order to put an end to this self-indulgence, he turned to Ṣufism, hoping also to find in the Ṣūfī experience an answer to his question about certainty. In his analysis of his spiritual sufferings, al-Ghazālī admits that for some time he was torn between his desire for the world which urged him to hold on to his position and prestige, and the call of his spirit which urged him to abandon his professorship to search for peace and certainty: "For almost six months, starting in Rajab, 488, I wavered between obeying the call of this world and its passions and obeying the call of the next world."[3]

During the first two months of this crisis period he suffered from a speech impediment and stopped lecturing. He doubted that mental conviction could exist and clung to a certain sort of sophistry which sees no certainty in anything. His mental illness was cured by divine light reaching his heart, touching him and restoring his faith in the exigencies of reason as

[2] See Manuel Alonso, "Influencia de Algazel en el mundo latino", *al-Andalus*, XXIII, pt. 2, 1958, 371–80; Badawī, *Muʾallafāt al-Ghazālī*, 56–8. [3] *Munqidh*, 16–17.

facts revealed by God and known intuitively rather than as proven by the discursive mind. Once he had reached this conclusion there grew in him a spiritual desire, which was perhaps mixed with a fear of death, to leave his work and go far away where he could live alone to contemplate and worship God. After four months of hesitation he decided to leave his academic post to his brother Aḥmad, a scholar with a reputation in his own right. Abū Ḥāmid divided most of his wealth among the poor of Baghdad, left enough for his family to live on, and left for Damascus, telling only a few of his friends of his destination.

After a short stay in Damascus, he went on to Jerusalem where he stayed for a while before returning to Damascus to live in the western minaret of the Umayyad mosque. In 489/1096 he went on pilgrimage to Mecca and then returned to Damascus to complete his famous work *Iḥyāʾ ʿulūm al-dīn* which he had begun in Jerusalem. The following year he returned to his family in Baghdad and took them to Khurāsān. When they reached Ṭūs he taught for a short time before resuming his ascetic life.

In 498/1104 a son of Niẓām al-Mulk, Fakhr al-Dīn ʿAlī, became vizier to Sanjar b. Malik-Shāh (490–552/1097–1157) in Naysābūr and persuaded al-Ghazālī to return to the Niẓāmiyyah college there. It is not known for certain how long he remained in this teaching post, but Fakhr al-Dīn was killed by an Ismāʿīlī on 10 Muḥarram 500/1106, and al-Ghazālī probably stopped teaching officially then. Some sources say that he went back to his home in Ṭūs and built a house for students and a *khānāqāh* for Ṣūfīs. He divided his time between his visitors and consolidating his knowledge of *Ḥadīth* in which he considered himself weak.

AL-GHAZĀLĪ'S STYLE

So far only those books which were definitely written by al-Ghazālī have been mentioned, but there are many other books and manuscripts which have also been attributed to him. Scholars such as W. Montgomery Watt, G. Hourani, L. Massignon and M. Bouyges have attempted to put his writings in chronological order. In a recent investigation, ʿAbd al-Raḥmān Badawī concluded that seventy-two of the works attributed to al-Ghazālī, which range from short treatises to whole volumes, are authentic. This total includes fifteen works which are not known to be extant, as well as a further twelve small treatises which are in fact either summaries of other works of his or chapters extracted from them or *fatāwā* of small size and importance. He points out also that al-Ghazālī used to revise his own books some considerable time after he had written them. He added to them, and sometimes referred to books he had written in the intervening years, so that his references cannot be relied upon to date a work, for they may refer to something he wrote later rather than earlier.[4]

Al-Ghazālī's style is not difficult in comparison with the styles of other Muslim thinkers. It has a certain eloquence and shows his desire to communicate with ordinary people and teach them. The multiplicity of the subjects dealt with by al-Ghazālī has attracted Arab scholars of every discipline to his work. Orientalists such as D. B. Macdonald, Margaret Smith, Carra de Vaux, Asín Palacios, J. Obermann, A. J. Wensinck and I. Goldziher have devoted attention to his work, although it may be pointed out that Carra de Vaux and Asín Palacios overemphasized the Christian influence in his works. Contrary to his tendency to conservatism, Abū Ḥāmid did in fact quote many sayings attributed to Jesus and used them both in the *Iḥyāʾ* and in other books he wrote as a mystic. He states clearly in the treatise *Ayyuhā ʾl-walad*[5] that he had studied "the gospel of Jesus", and his quotations show that he thought Islam and Christianity differed in belief but shared the same code of morality.

This irenic attitude of moderation and toleration is characteristic of al-Ghazālī and is responsible, to some extent, for his inconsistencies, especially those apparent in his attitude towards philosophers and theologians. These he criticized, while at the same time agreeing with some of their ideas and making use of their methods of argument. It has also been proved that many of the Prophetic Traditions quoted in the *Iḥyāʾ*, and which the Ṣūfīs believed to be genuine, were in fact spurious. Al-Ghazālī can perhaps be excused for this as he himself was not an authority on *Ḥadīth*, and in any case held the belief that a "weak" Tradition can be used to influence someone to act morally. However, a critical study of the Traditions (usually published in the margin of the *Iḥyāʾ*) by Abū ʾl-Faḍl ʿAbd al-Raḥman b. al-Ḥusayn Zayn al-Dīn al-ʿIrāqī (d. 806/1404) shows al-Ghazālī to have erred considerably in this respect.

As yet unmentioned are two important works of al-Ghazālī: *Mishkāt al-anwār* ("The Niche of Lights") and *al-Maqṣid al-asnā fī sharḥ maʿānī asmāʾ Allāh al-ḥusnā* ("The Most Exalted Aim in Explaining the Meanings of the Most Beautiful Names of God"). Written towards the end of his life, they both show that the philosophy he had once studied and attacked had left a deep impression on him and had drawn him to a modified version of Platonism. Another important work is *al-Iqtiṣād fī ʾl-iʿtiqād* ("The Golden Mean in Belief"). This study of major theological issues does not differ very much from other works of the Ashʿarite writers on the subject.

[4] Cf. Badawī, *Muʾallafāt al-Ghazālī*, 64, 70.

[5] 19.

THE PHILOSOPHY OF AL-GHAZĀLĪ

Al-Ghazālī directed much of his effort towards the examination of the abilities of rational man, and towards the investigation of the possibility of using them to gain knowledge unflawed by doubt. His investigations led him into criticism of the philosophical and the theological trends of his day because they each claimed to have reached certain truth. On the strength of his own experience, Abū Ḥāmid believed that such claims had to be confronted with doubt, because it is doubt which drives man to test accepted ideas with logic. He sees that doubt means more than "confusion of thought" or suspension of judgement. It is rather a sort of intellectual unrest which makes man question himself and search for answers. While doubt attacks the mind, it also opens the door for the insights of the heart which are not devoid of import.

Imitation and certainty

Something which al-Ghazālī felt to be a hindrance to the understanding of how to gain certain knowledge was the practice of fanatically adopting the ideas current among thinkers, or a bias towards a particular political group. Learned people followed celebrated thinkers, believing them to be perfect and infallible, and al-Ghazālī saw the danger of this sort of practice spreading into every sphere of thought. He saw that Muslim philosophers and their followers had been so dazzled by Greek philosophy and its mathematical proofs that they accepted without question Greek physics and metaphysics, making no effort to investigate for themselves the truth of these teachings. He wrote: "He who follows something blindly does not know he is doing so but believes himself to be in the right. He is so absolutely certain that he feels no need to criticize his belief that he is right and his opponent is wrong."[6] Here he is speaking of the uneducated masses whom he excused as being unauthorized to study what was beyond them. The effect of dogmatic faith on religious people was to make them unable to think for themselves or to criticize anything. Beliefs implanted into the young child become deeply rooted:

> Therefore the sons of Christians, of Rafiḍites, of Zoroastrians and of Muslims follow the beliefs of their fathers. Their beliefs are so unshakeable that they would not renounce them even if they were torn limb from limb. Yet they have never heard a single thing to prove the truth of their religion, neither an actual nor a formal proof.[7]

[6] *Iljām al-ʿawāmm*, 57. [7] Ibid., 56.

Although the Muᶜtazilites and Ashᶜarites claimed to have explored and examined the field of human knowledge, al-Ghazālī noticed that they dismissed all their opponents as unbelievers, even though the points of disagreement may have been minor. They followed the teachings of their school more rigidly than the ordinary people and "had shackled themselves by their beliefs, becoming the blindest of the blind".[8] Like the partisans of Greek philosophy they claimed that their teachings were infallible, thus excluding any other interpretations. Bigotry such as this drives truth away and makes it "something dependent upon men", whereas, in reality, "men are known through truth", that is, the truth imposes itself regardless of who utters it or who agrees with it. A proof might be accepted by a member of a theological school who might then discover that it had been put forward by a follower of another school; he would then reject it. People would accuse each other of being unbelievers, even though each theological doctrine is, by definition, an exercise of discretion (*ijtihād*), and there is room in religion for more than one judgement on any issue. Such blind faith lacks the support of spiritual insight and so is open to error and doubt.[9] It remains on the "lower level" of the accepted, never rising to the "higher level of perception". For such faith to have any certainty it must make use of intuitive understanding, which is something quite different from theological reasoning that rests mainly on assumptions, and also from philosophical innovations which for the most part contradict the basic principles of religion. This understanding is the resorting to the spiritual side of man for inspiration, to the heart which "understands and knows the reality of things".[10]

Al-Ghazālī was obviously not a pure philosopher who relied on purely logical arguments that are divorced from the facts of faith. Nor was he purely a mystic who relied on illumined visions of revelation (*kashf*) and attached no importance to the intellect. He aimed rather to blend intellect with spiritual inspiration, but was not always successful in fulfilling his aim. This explains why his critics have sometimes found a certain confusion in his writings. The heart of the matter, for him, was the difficulty of ever gaining "certain knowledge". This is because "the heart", by which he meant "the inspired mind", can only be fully effective when it has reached such a degree of perfection in *maᶜrifah* (knowledge) that it no longer needs to make use of rational proofs. "True knowledge" is making a decision about some issue with confidence in the rightness of one's decision. Certainty, from this point of view, is a belief which eliminates doubt and which regards the possibilities of negligence and error as unlikely.[11]

[8] *Fayṣal al-tafriqah*, 131. [9] Cf. *Iḥyāʾ*, III, 13. [10] Ibid., 5.

[11] Cf. *Mustaṣfā*, I, 43; *Munqidh*, 13–14.

Reason and faith

In the *Munqidh*, al-Ghazālī removes what he calls "certain knowledge" from the realms of theoretical reasoning, and places it instead in those of revelation and insight, where logical proof is unnecessary. In the *Iḥyāʾ* he virtually ignores the role of logic as something which shows us the validity of proof and legitimacy of conclusion. This is all in keeping with the general Ṣūfī view; but other works, such as *Miḥakk al-naẓar* and *Miʿyār al-ʿilm*, clearly attribute to logic great importance in the settling of disputes, and its universality as a tool of thought. In *al-Qisṭās al-mustaqīm*, he says plainly that it is logic which is the basis of God's message to man as mediated by the prophets. Spiritual inspiration lacks logic's universality; it is a gnostic gift for prophets and saints only, whereas logic, based as it is on the self-evident principles of reason, is used by rational man everywhere.

As the facts of revelation are a discourse to mankind they must be interpreted in the light of those things common to all men: reason and its tools of logic. Al-Ghazālī believed that if reason was untainted by prejudice and false ideas, it could then acquire "certain knowledge" of some issues at least. The facts of faith require rational understanding: "Reason is like the power of sound vision which sees well, and the Qurʾān is like the sun irradiating light everywhere . . . Hence reason *with* revelation is light with light."[12] Abū Ḥāmid rejects the idea that reason and faith are incompatible. According to him "whoever lacks a penetrating inner vision has only the superficialities of religion".[13] Reason brings us close to the deepest secrets of religion, and the light of faith can strengthen reason in its moral task.

The debate over the roles of reason and revelation had been in progress long before al-Ghazālī contributed to it. Was reason something with which the fundamentals of religion could be understood and logically proved, as the theologians in general claimed? Or was it, as the Ḥanbalites argued, something with which the data of religion could be accepted without attempting to prove or interpret anything? In search of a compromise, al-Ghazālī tried to combine the two views. Reason conceptualizes the discourse of revelation in order to accept it. However, reason, which does not make excessive use of technical terminology and argumentation, is the ideal way of restoring confidence in the facts and aims of revelation.

Although his belief in Ṣufism deepened a great deal after his spiritual crisis, Abū Ḥāmid did not abandon his belief that sound reason was both efficacious and essential for knowledge and morals as well. In the *Iḥyāʾ*[14] he describes four different aspects of reason, each of which has different

[12] *Iqtiṣād*, 3; cf. *Iḥyāʾ*, III, 17. [13] *Iḥyāʾ*, I, 87. [14] I, 85–9.

functions, which can all be incorporated into a wider concept of "the heart of man". There is, first of all, reason as a faculty which "distinguishes man from other beasts". With it he is able to expand his knowledge and conceive what he cannot see. Secondly, reason includes *ḍarūriyyāt*, i.e. self-evident principles of thought, such as the impossibility of something being in two places at the same time. Thirdly, reason can be applied to man's experience, as when he becomes skilled and prudent in dealing with new situations. Finally, reason is the faculty of reflection on "the consequences of different things and on the restraint of the desire for temporal pleasure". It is in this respect that it achieves "its final fruit", and in this capacity it can be seen as a moral imperative or conscience. The first two aspects of reason are innate, whereas the third and fourth are achieved through learning and practice. While knowledge of the *ḍarūriyyāt* is shared equally by all humanity, individuals vary in the extent to which they understand ideas and gain experience in life. Furthermore, the part which reason plays as a moral imperative differs not only from person to person, but also from stage to stage in the same person's life.

Reason, with its powers of criticism and appraisal, can correct the data of the senses and imagination. With reason it can be proved that a star is far bigger than it seems to the naked eye, and if imagination fails to provide us with a reliable evaluation of something, reason can.[15] This comparison between the inadequacy of the senses and the capability of reason is something al-Ghazālī stresses more than once. In *Mishkāt al-anwār*,[16] he concludes from such comparison that reason, in contrast to perception, can be aware of the infinity of number, and is also capable of self-awareness and self-criticism. It "penetrates to the very heart of things, it understands their real meaning and uncovers their purpose and cause". "Reason's domain consists of all being . . . it moves in it freely, judging it with soundness." Here he seems to be saying that reason is more than the faculty which determines one's conscience and more than the power of argumentation. What he means is inspired reason, or the heart, which follows the data of faith and interprets them in the light of divine illumination. The duty of ordinary reason is to keep inspiration from falling into inconsistency.

Reason and philosophy

A number of scholars have noticed a contradiction in al-Ghazālī's evaluation of rational knowledge: sometimes he testifies to its importance and lofty role, while at other times he denies these very things in order to

[15] *Miʿyār al-ʿilm*, 62–5. [16] 42–9.

establish religion's decrees as impregnable to rational examination. The *Tahāfut* could be viewed as an attack on rationalism as it denies the principle of causality and disproves the major rational arguments held by Muslim thinkers. Although he occasionally resorts to sophistry, his criticism does have some good points to make against the philosophers. His view seems to be that reason is not always incapable of achieving true knowledge or of removing its own ambiguities, but that it is incapable of exercising any authority in matters of faith which are directly based on revelation.

Al-Ghazālī aimed to show that philosophical beliefs, which are claimed to have been proved true, are not void of contradictions,[17] nor do they properly follow the rules of syllogism and inference. He openly admits the truth of the philosophers' advances in the fields of mathematics, because they have been rigorously proved and cannot be refuted by the precepts of the *sharīʿah*. He aimed to expose the inconsistency of those philosophers who were influenced by the neo-Platonic and Aristotelian schools of thought, such as al-Fārābī and Ibn Sīnā, in the realm of *ilāhiyyāt* (metaphysics, spiritual concerns). "Most of their beliefs are contrary to the truth,"[18] he claims. The twenty philosophical questions tackled in this work are interlinked and could be classified under the traditional headings of metaphysics (the first thirteen chapters) and physics (the final seven chapters).

The first and second questions deal with the refutation of the assertion that the world had no beginning and will have no end. The tacit preference shown by Muslim philosophers for the doctrine that "the world was as old as God" was a result of the neo-Platonic theory of emanation (*fayḍ*), which held that the world had emerged involuntarily from God, like light from the sun. This denies the involvement of divine will in creation and was criticized by theologians such as al-Bāqillānī (d. 403/1013) and Ibn Ḥazm for contradicting the basic principles of Islam. The theologians believed in the theory of "occurrence" which held that God had willed the creation of the world and had created it *ex nihilo*. Al-Ghazālī's refutation was more coherent and precise than those of his predecessors, although he did apparently benefit from Yaḥyā al-Naḥwī's (John Philoponus, d. AD 568) refutations of the writings of Proclus on this subject. According to Ibn al-Nadīm and al-Bīrūnī this work of al-Naḥwī was translated into Arabic and widely read.

Al-Ghazālī first presented the philosophical proofs regarding the world's eternity. He divided them into four categories and disproved each of them in turn. For example, the philosophers thought it was impossible for the

[17] Cf. *Tahāfut*, 43–5. [18] Preface to *Maqāṣid al-falāsifah*, 32.

mortal world to have emerged from the immortal God, and for there to have been a time when this world did not exist. The world, its motion, and the time engendered by them both were as eternal as God himself. On the basis of these judgements, the philosophers tended towards the belief that God's priority over the world is due to his own position or rank and is not connected to time. Al-Ghazālī said that the view that "the world came into being through an eternal divine will which demanded the world's existence at the time it began to exist"[19] was not a contradiction as the philosophers maintained.

He sees God's priority over the world as absolute when related to time, for time itself is something caused by the motion of the world and did not exist before the world was created. This means that God has always existed and had existed without the world. When he did create the world, it existed separately from him. The philosophers' assumption that time existed before the creation of the world is a fruit of the mind's inability to imagine the beginning of something which has not been preceded by something else. However, this is not difficult for the mind illumined by faith. The philosophers took it for granted that events happen in this world at particular times and that these are linked to previous events which also occurred at particular times, and so on. As this chain of events must eventually go back to the beginning they must originate in God the creator. If this is so, thought al-Ghazālī, then philosophers must accept that the world as a whole is something created by God at the particular time decided upon by his will.

A postulate which the philosophers believed to be indisputable was that of the inseparability of cause and effect. Al-Ghazālī aimed to disprove this doctrine so that a place would be left for religious miracles which are, by definition, a violation of the normal rules of nature. He also intended to prove the attributes of God, his omnipotence and ability to act in nature with absolute volition, which means that he can lead nature away from the established order. Abū Ḥāmid argues that what philosophers claim as the necessary relationship between what they call "cause", A, and "effect", B, is not based on an accurate view of phenomena. The objective view suggests that B occurs *with* or *after* A. If we take for an example the combustion of wood when wood comes into contact with fire, al-Ghazālī thought that "observing a phenomenon [the combustion, B] is proof that it happened with it [the fire, A] but not through it. Nor is fire the sole cause [of combustion]".[20] Causality is a relationship of coincidence (*maᶜiyyah*) between two phenomena and its result can have several different causes.

[19] *Tahāfut*, 50. [20] Ibid., 196.

Al-Ghazālī thought that "the cause" should be a "willing doer" instead. Wood and fire, etc., are not what philosophers claim to be causes, and if actions can be attributed to natural substances it is only in a metaphorical sense. The special properties of things do not act for themselves but are for the use of God who is the true deliberate doer. The link of causality, concludes al-Ghazālī, is one that was invented by man on the strength of the succession of events he is accustomed to seeing among natural phenomena. David Hume (d. 1190/1776) made a similar analysis, arguing that causality is founded only on that to which man is mentally accustomed. In al-Ghazālī's view fire is not the cause of combustion of substances, nor is drinking water the reason for the quenching of thirst. Burning and quenching occur by way of their coincidence with fire and drinking. God may remove this connection and so the properties of things may change: fire, for example, could lose its heat, as it did when Abraham was thrown into it. This is how miracles can be explained.

God and the world

Al-Ghazālī admits that in the *Tahāfut* he confined himself to trying to disprove the philosophers' arguments, and did not try to put forward any constructive ideas of his own on the same subjects. He wrote: "I speak to them only as someone refuting them, not as someone proving something else."[21] He promised to put forward his views on various questions of divinity in *Qawāʿid al-ʿaqāʾid* ("The Bases of Beliefs"). We find a long chapter of the same title in the *Iḥyāʾ*,[22] which does not deviate significantly from Ashʿarite teaching. There are, however, contained in the *Tahāfut* his implicit views on the issue of God and the world which are of a philosophical nature themselves. One of his pupils, Abū Bakr Muḥammad b. ʿAbdullāh b. al-ʿArabī, remarked that: "Our master Abū Ḥāmid entered the world of the philosophers but when he wanted to leave it he could not."[23]

An argument which emerges clearly is that philosophers cannot maintain those attributes of God mentioned in the revelation. According to the Qurʾān God is omniscient, living, almighty and has a purpose, and in these attributes lies the explanation for his creation of the world. The world did not emanate from him as an inevitable consequence of his nature, but emerged as the result of his knowledge, will and power. Putting his finger on the weak spot of the theory of emanation, al-Ghazālī asks how is it that there emanated from the one God only one mind? In the *Iḥyāʾ*[24] and other

21 Ibid., 83. 22 I, 89–125. 23 Quoted by Ibn Taymiyyah in *Naqd al-manṭiq*, Cairo, 1951, 56.
24 I, 106.

works he accepts as valid the proof commonly used by theologians to show that the world was created by God out of nothing. The premises of this proof are that every occurrent (*ḥādith*) must have a cause, and that the world itself is occurrent because it has within it both movement and rest which occur in time. Something which contains occurrents is an event itself and, as all events must have a cause, we can only conclude that God is the cause of the creation of the world. This sort of proof is termed "cosmological". Another version of it which was common among philosophers was based on the concepts of the contingent and the necessary and stemmed also from Aristotelian metaphysics.

On the subject of divine knowledge, Ibn Sīnā believed that God knows particular entities and events "in universal terms unsubsumable by time". God knows the events and their causes because they originate through him. He does not know them as things subject to their "becoming" in time and place. This seems to be al-Ghazālī's version of Ibn Sīnā's view which states: "God knows every particular thing from a universal view."[25] Ibn Sīnā did not say that "God knows all particulars", because this would mean that God's knowledge would be always changing owing to the multiplicity of events and things. Thus God's knowledge of something, mankind for example, is of a universal type and not a knowledge of individual men, their actions or the events in their lives. Al-Ghazālī saw that this philosophy would jeopardize the very foundation of the *sharīʿah* because it means that God does not know if a man obeys him or not, and so there can be no basis for reward and punishment. His conclusion was that "God's knowledge of creatures is a single, eternal and unchanging entity", and that no analogy could be made between divine and human knowledge.[26]

Divine omniscience had an important consequence because it led on to the belief in predestination, which rules out all possibility of free will for man. "The will of God", in al-Ghazālī's view, encompasses everything that happens "on heaven and on earth . . ., good and evil". It is the reason for every event which is known by God before it takes place. If so, then everything, including man's actions, has been predetermined by God. Al-Ghazālī openly admits this when he says that all man's suffering and joy form "perfect justice . . . everything happens because it should and it happens in the way and to the degree that it should".[27] Therefore this world, with everything that exists and occurs in it, is the best possible world because it was created by the omnipotence and all-embracing justice of God. If we suppose that God can do only good, to the exclusion of evil, then we subtract from his absolute perfection by attributing a sort of

[25] *Najāh*, Cairo, 1938, 247. [26] Cf. *Tahāfut* 165–6; *Iḥyāʾ*, I, 90. [27] *Iḥyāʾ*, IV, 258.

inability and penury to him. These cannot be divine attributes, and we must therefore consider this world to be the best possible one. This point was later quoted with commendation by Muḥyī ʾl-Dīn b. al-ʿArabī, and a similar argument can be found in the works of Gottfried Wilhelm Leibniz (d. 1128/1716).

Al-Ghazālī calls this world, in which many things fall within man's experience, the "visible world" (*ʿālam al-shahādah*) or the "world of domination" (*ʿālam al-mulk*), referring to the domination of God. This view of the world is complemented by a belief in another world which exists beyond ours, and is called "the invisible world" (*ʿālam al-ghayb*). This includes those entities which are named symbolically the Divine Pen, the Tablet, the Way, etc.[28] Al-Ghazālī uses these terms, "visible world" and "invisible world", which are derived from Quranic terminology, to build up an ontological schema similar to that of Plato. We read in *Mishkāt al-anwār* that "this visible world is a trace of that invisible one and the former follows the latter like a shadow". This means that everything around us is made in the image of an ideal form in heaven.[29] He comes close to Platonism once again when he says that man grows in knowledge from perceiving things in the world to rational knowledge about intermediate causes, such as the sun and angels, then to gnostic insights leading him to the invisible world. Naturally this requires a spirituality which only prophets and saints (*awliyāʾ*) possess.

THE ṢŪFĪ ANTHROPOLOGY

Man, al-Ghazālī thought, is a creature who bears a message and exists for some purpose. His purpose is to know the phenomena of this world, to make use of them in performing what is required from him. Hence through faith and good action he progresses to the stage of the original nature of Adam. Man's distinguishing characteristic, however, is that he is the epitome of this world.[30] This Greek view of microcosmos had found its way into different areas of Islamic thought through the writings of Yaʿqūb b. Isḥāq al-Kindī and the Ikhwān al-Ṣafāʾ ("the Brethren of Purity"), and we see once again that al-Ghazālī did not in the end reject philosophy but made those ideas of it which did not contradict Islam more widely known.

In the *Iḥyāʾ* he says that what distinguishes individual man is his spirit. God breathed the first spirit into Adam, from whom it has spread throughout mankind. So the spirit has descended from "the creative imperative" and is an obscure mystery as the mind cannot discern its

[28] Ibid., 250. [29] *Mishkāt al-anwār*, 51, 66, 67. [30] Ibid., 17.

essence. It has what he calls "the religious motive", which makes it long for its divine source and brings it into conflict with passion and carnal desires.[31] Man feels he is an exile in this world, but he must contemplate both the world and what is hidden in himself so that he can know where he has come from, and where he will return at the end of his wandering. His presence on earth has been planned by God to test his faith and his ability to raise himself up to the spiritual levels which are within his own reach: "Man cannot reach God, may he be praised, unless he lives in this world: he must break away from the lower level in order to reach the higher one."[32]

MORALITY AND EDUCATION

Al-Ghazālī was led by his reflection on the various aspects of man's spiritual ascent to investigate the bases of practice (*muᶜāmalah*), i.e. the interaction between faith in the heart of the believer and action in his daily life. This investigation is the cornerstone of morality in Ṣufism, and is the subject of most of the third and fourth volumes of the *Iḥyāᵓ* and the entire treatise *Ayyuhā ᵓl-walad*. His advice and exhortations to the reader who is following the spiritual path are clear, and he adds to the persuasiveness of his argument by using sayings and stories from earlier mystics. At first glance he seems to be merely re-presenting topics for which other works were renowned, such as the *Risālah* of Abū ᵓl-Qāsim al-Qushayrī, *Qūt al-qulūb* by Abū Ṭālib al-Makkī and other earlier Ṣūfī works. What he does, in fact, is to criticize these works for not rising to the level of a theory of moral behaviour, but merely presenting "some of the results of good morals."[33] We should, therefore, look more closely at his attempt to close the gap between the theory of morality and Ṣūfī directives on behaviour.

He defines morals as "the image and interior form of the spirit" and moves away from the view that would limit morals to being either an objective or subjective characteristic of human action. He does not exclude from morality a person who, for example, tends to be generous but does not reveal this inclination owing to external obstacles. On the other hand, there are people who are mean by nature but who pretend to be generous, and in the light of this we must regard a good deed as being one which is combined with the right intention. From another standpoint, morals are the result of the interaction of forces such as perception, anger and desire, and the balance of "equality among these forces" is therefore essential. Without it man's behaviour cannot be directed by good morals which are praise-

[31] Cf. *Iḥyāᵓ*, IV, 63. [32] Ibid., III, 5; cf. IV, 215. [33] Ibid., III, 52, 53.

worthy. Here al-Ghazālī is obviously combining in his own way Platonic and Aristotelian elements of ethics.

Man is able to correct himself if he consciously applies himself to doing so. This is proved by the counsel and exhortations repeated by spiritual teachers, which would not have been passed down from one generation to the next if they had not been significant. They are a constant invitation to us to change what we can of our natures, and they can "lead us to salvation and to God most High".[34] Al-Ghazālī explains that the aim behind the strife against the carnal soul is not to repress anger and desire completely, for this is impossible. Instead it aims to return them to a level of disciplined moderation which is "the medium between two extremes". Judged by this rule, anger becomes "a good form of zeal when it is free from rashness and cowardice".[35] Generally speaking, morals exist to make man powerful within the limits dictated by reason.

Most people have to strive for moral perfection first through the education they receive when young, and then through self-discipline, and striving (*mujāhadah*) when adult. An example of such exercise is to do something one is unaccustomed to doing and to persevere with it so that it gradually becomes an acquired habit in which one takes pleasure. If a proud man perseveres in performing acts of humility he can, in time, become humble. If the miserly man makes himself perform acts of liberality he can become generous.[36] Al-Ghazālī understood the mutual influence of the willing heart and the performing body: the heart orients itself to acquiring good morals while the body does what is known as good. Hence "every characteristic of the heart influences the body so that it moves in accordance with that characteristic, and every action of the body may have an influence on the heart."[37]

The third volume of the *Iḥyāʾ* consists mainly of descriptions of moral weaknesses or vices which al-Ghazālī calls "things which destroy", such as avarice, hypocrisy and indulgence in desires. By contrast most of the fourth volume is concerned with what he calls "things which bring salvation", such as repentance, gratitude, trust in God and love. These had been discussed by earlier Ṣūfīs such as al-Muḥāsibī, al-Kalābādhī and al-Sarrāj al-Ṭūsī (d. 378/988), and were called "stations" (*maqāmāt*), because the Ṣūfī advances spiritually by rising to them one by one in hierarchical steps. In works which followed the *Iḥyāʾ*, al-Ghazālī went further and concentrated on the maxims of moral behaviour. The first of these is for man to act towards God like an obedient slave, and the second is to feel obliged to

[34] Ibid., 55–6. [35] Ibid., 57. [36] *Mīzān al-ʿamal*, 48. [37] *Iḥyāʾ*, III, 59.

behave towards others as he himself likes them to behave to him in the same situation. This is the basis for the mutual respect so frequently found in modern ethics, the principles of which include the categorical imperative, but Abū Ḥāmid bases his view on the *ḥadīth* which says: "The believer loves for his brother what he loves for himself." The third principle is that knowledge should be used to purify the heart, and the fourth that man should not keep for himself any of the benefits of the world other than enough food for one year.[38]

Al-Ghazālī firmly believed that, unlike human physical features, human nature is not immutable, but can be moulded by moral instruction. This belief led him to form ideas on the ideal way to bring up and educate the young. He believed that natural inclinations and instincts should not be suppressed entirely because they are needed for essential tasks in life. "Desire was created for some benefit and is an essential part of nature" and its vital aim is obvious, if one thinks, for example, of the desire for food and sexual gratification.[39] A child's soul "has been created imperfect but capable of being made perfect through moral instruction and nourishment with knowledge".[40] The instruction he recommended included evoking in the child's mind a love of ascetism in both food and dress, forbidding him to associate with bad friends, instilling in him good table manners and the rudiments of worship. He should be made accustomed to activity and not be allowed to sleep during the day. He should be brought up to be polite and generous to his companions, and to listen carefully to those older than himself.[41]

These, and similar recommendations, aim at keeping the child away from anything which might cause depravity and at developing his sense of moral standards. Al-Ghazālī warns against anything which could have a bad influence on children's morals, even though such things may sometimes be thought to have a positive side. For example, he thought that children should not hear "poems in which love and things related to love are mentioned".[42] On the question of reward and punishment, al-Ghazālī believed that children need to be given encouragement in front of others when they do something good, so that they act in this way habitually. If a child does something wrong, he should be ignored the first time, especially if he is ashamed. If he does it again, he should be admonished privately and the gravity of his offence should be explained without scolding him too much. This is so that the child "does not become indifferent to rebuke or to doing wrong" and so that "these words may not lose their effect on his heart".[43]

[38] Cf. *Ayyuhā ʾl-walad*, 59–63. [39] Cf. *Iḥyāʾ*, III, 56–7. [40] *Mīzān al-ʿamal*, 52.
[41] *Iḥyāʾ*, III, 72–4. [42] Ibid., 73. [43] Ibid.

He believed also that play had special significance in developing a young person's intelligence; because it is a diversion from study, it can make the child ready and eager to learn: "Preventing a child from playing and burdening him with constant study only deadens his heart, numbs his intelligence and spoils his life so much that he plays tricks to escape studying."[44] In another context, however, al-Ghazālī held that children should receive spiritual teaching, be taught to be ascetic, and be forbidden to study theology (*kalām*) and disputation.[45]

FREEDOM AND POLITICS

The general outlines of al-Ghazālī's concept of freedom are not very different from those of the Ashᶜarite doctrine. Man, he believed, is "predestined in choice". In the action of a fire, for example, there is no element of choice because the properties of fire and combustible materials, and the conditions necessary for combustion exist without any awareness or choice on their part. At the other extreme the actions of God are by absolute choice, unmixed with hesitation, because they flow from his omniscience. Between these two extremes lies the action of man, which is what al-Ghazālī means by "predestined in choice".

It is true that sometimes man's choice of action seems to suggest an inner freedom, but al-Ghazālī thought this choice an expression of "a personal will suggested by the mind".[46] The human will is not absolutely free since it is subject to the deliberation of the mind. Man's ability to act is also subject to his will, and the action itself, such as movement in a place, is subject to ability (*qudrah*). To al-Ghazālī these three elements of will, ability and action seem to have been predestined from eternity as part of an inescapable determinism. This theory is not inconsistent with his theological view that "It is Almighty God who is the original doer of everything".[47] Man exists as a doer in a different way: he has been created with his ability related to his will and also with knowledge. Action is attributed to man metaphorically, in the same way that a criminal's execution can be attributed to the man who actually wields the axe, or to the judge who sentenced him, or to the ruler who set up the court.

Man's will is based on his ability to distinguish between good and evil, and this distinction is one kind of rational understanding. The action which the will carries out seems to be subject to the judgement of reason. Human actions are predestined in that in each man there are preordained possibilities which have not been chosen by him. In every man there is a particular

[44] Ibid.; cf. *Mīzān al-ᶜamal*, 110. [45] *Iḥyāʾ*, I, 94. [46] Ibid., IV, 254. [47] Cf. ibid., 255–6.

will and reason which guide him in his practice; but, from an ontological perspective, actions in this world seem to be the result of the divine volition which creates in the heart of man a will, deliberation and motives. Every event in this world is, in the final analysis, a completion of the volition of God.[48] After al-Ghazālī's death this sort of fatalism became a fundamental belief of the various Ṣūfīs, and some, such as Tāj al-Dīn b. ʿAṭāʾallāh ʿAbbās al-Sakandarī, went much further and believed that the will of man should be abandoned to the extent that he is no more than a faint shadow on the divine will which governs every situation and event.

The mission for which man was created is that of knowledge and worship and for this he needs a safe society in which to live. Social and political conditions are formed partly by men and partly by the will of God: "Man can only sometimes protect his spirit, body, property, home and food, but He cannot be truly religious unless these worries are taken care of" (by a potent state).[49] The function of the political system is, therefore, to protect individuals and to provide them with safety so that they can devote themselves to their personal affairs. Al-Ghazālī considered a country's security as a basis for government and essential for the collective welfare of its citizens. Government must be established on the principles of unity and sovereignty: "There can be no system of religion without a system in the secular world [i.e. the state] which can only exist through a leader who commands obedience."[50] One should remember that al-Ghazālī lived at a time of widespread political dissension, and so felt a need for an authority which would bring about political unity, demonstrate its sovereignty and regulate cultural and political life. With no such authority in existence people begin to behave in accordance with their own prejudices, which lead to dissent and destruction. In the treatise *al-Tibr al-masbūk fī naṣīḥat al-mulūk* ("Ingots of Gold for the Advice of Kings"; translated into Arabic from the original Persian in 595/1199), and generally attributed to al-Ghazālī, the state's rights of control and sovereignty are emphasized, and also the duties which must be assumed by the ruler. The ruler's duty is to care for his people and to commit himself to the ideals of fairness and justice, for justice is the value which upholds any government's legitimacy. One of the bases for justice was the striving of the ruler and his appointed governors to see that the law of the land was applied equally strictly to all citizens. For this he gave the following rule to all those in positions of responsibility: "In everything that comes before you, believe that you are one of a group of citizens and that the citizen is your equal. So do not accept

[48] Cf. *Iqtiṣād*, 12. [49] Ibid., 105–6. [50] Ibid., 105.

for any Muslim what you do not accept for yourself; if you do otherwise you betray and mislead the people under your rule."[51]

In the *Iḥyāʾ*,[52] however, al-Ghazālī makes no mention of justice in government but concentrates on what he saw as the main functions of the state: the preservation of order and the facilitation of what is in the public interest. This requires a strong ruler, even if he is unjust and autocratic. Such ideas on rule and leadership were formed while al-Ghazālī was living under the protection of the ʿAbbasid caliph al-Mustaẓhir (reigned 487–512/1094–1118). As the caliph and his officials were al-Ghazālī's patrons, it is not surprising to find him defending the legitimacy of the ʿAbbasid caliphate and attacking its enemies, such as the Ismāʿīlīs. The belief in *shūrā* (consultation), or, in other words, appointing a leader after an election, was disregarded by the ʿAbbasids in favour of the system of hereditary rule introduced by the Umayyads. Al-Ghazālī recommended the principle of *al-shawkah*, or "might", in the holding of leadership. According to this principle a man becomes the legitimate caliph merely by gaining the agreement of those who hold power in the Muslim community. The position of caliph, founded on such *shawkah*, is assumed to be strengthened by the mass support of followers and adherents and the obedience of other people.[53] The acknowledged leader should have mature understanding, soundness of sight and hearing, be free, not a slave, male, not female, and a member of the Prophet's tribe of Quraysh. The necessity of this last condition was doubted by al-Juwaynī.[54]

DIVINE LOVE AND BEAUTY

The object of all cognitive endeavour made by godly men is, according to al-Ghazālī, divine love. It is also the last spiritual station, the end of the Ṣūfī path to God. The other stations, such as trust in God, patience and asceticism, are preparatory stages through which the traveller on this path must pass before he can reach his goal of divine love. This sort of love cannot be reached unless man fights against his earthly desires and distractions and turns with his entire will to God. The link between love and knowledge is based on the belief that "love can only be attained after knowledge . . . If one finds in his awareness of an object delight and comfort, then this object is loved by the cognizant".[55] Divine love is more

[51] *Al-Tibr al-masbūk*, 23; for the second part of this work, see above, ch. 10, 166–7.
[52] II, 140–1. [53] Cf. *Faḍāʾiḥ al-Bāṭiniyyah*, 177–8.
[54] Cf. Abū ʾl-Maʿālī ʿAbd al-Mālik al-Juwaynī, *Kitāb al-Irshād*, ed. M. Y. Mūsā and ʿA. ʿA. ʿAbd al-Ḥamīd, Cairo, 1951, 426–7. [55] *Iḥyāʾ*, IV, 296.

than a state of excitement; it is something deep which gives spiritual impetus, and in which knowledge and action towards others are fused so that the person who follows this path is both pleasing to God and happy in himself. What characterizes a man who loves God is his lack of interest in mundane pleasures and the way he rids himself of any concern for them.

At the root of what we call "love" in man is a kind of egoism or self-love. Man loves both himself and his own existence and will instinctively try to preserve it. We know that man hates death and avoids places which endanger his life. He loves the things around in direct proportion to their ability to prolong his life:

> Man loves these things, not for what they are, but for the link between them and the continuance and completion of his own life. He may love his son even though he receives nothing from him and bears hardships for his sake simply because his son will live on after him. In the survival of his offspring he sees a way that he can survive . . . as though he will form part of his successor when he no longer lives himself.[56]

Love stems from the group of functions vital for the continuation of one's life and is a kind of inbuilt defence system for an existence which is permanently fragile. This is the reason why people tend to love those who treat them well, for, if one person acts kindly to another, he strengthens the latter's power to exist, and man loves those who sustain this power and his dignity as well. Man can, however, also love something for its sensuous beauty or for its own sake, regardless of any utilitarian value it might have: "This is love which is true and strong, which is sure of its own permanence. It is caused by beauty *ipso facto*, for all beauty is loved by the one who is cognizant of it and who loves it for its own sake."[57] Beauty cannot be reduced to one type; it lies in the object's own perfection which can be enjoyed by someone who is aware of it. Nor is beauty confined to the perfection of things perceived by the senses, but includes everything described as "good". The meaning of beauty (*ḥusn, jamāl*) can be extended to include goodness and virtue. This sort of beauty is perceived by inner vision, not by the physical sense of sight.[58]

If we look next at the motives for love we find that they all lead to God. Man loves what will preserve his existence, and it is God who gives and sustains life by creating the means for its continuance: "If the gnostic loves himself, . . . then he must love that which benefits and perpetuates his own existence. If he does not, he knows neither himself nor his Lord. Love is the fruit of knowledge."[59] If a man loves those who do good to him he will be led to his true benefactor, God, and human beings are good to one another because of God's goodness and compassion towards them. Divine grace

[56] Ibid., 297. [57] Ibid., 298. [58] Ibid., 299. [59] Ibid., 301.

comes from the absolute wisdom which is not motivated by any desire or demand for gain. The beauty manifested in visible objects and the inward beauty of character are loved equally by man, and reason which is enlightened by faith shows that God is the eternal source of all beauty beheld in this world. If man can gain such mystical intuitions about the reasons for love and the attraction of beauty, he can find pleasure in knowing God and his ways of directing the course of the world, and he may reach the station of divine love.

Among Sunnīs al-Ghazālī enjoys the designation *Ḥujjat al-Islām*, ("the Authority of Islam"). This recognizes the fact that he defended the bases of Islamic belief, and Islamic thought looked for guidance after his day to both philosophy and Ṣūfī concepts in an attempt to interpret religious teachings with attention to their deepest significance. But al-Ghazālī emphasized that intellectual thought must be limited by the data of faith, that it must serve them and that it must bring them closer to the common people. This conservative attitude had a negative effect on the philosophic movement; after his death it lost its brilliance and independence as the philosophical works of thinkers like Ibn Rushd were exposed to much open hostility.

As for Ṣufism, which he had expected to provide the solution to the question of doubt and certainty, it was, 200 years after his death, unable to maintain its predominance over Islamic thought. The sixth/twelfth and seventh/thirteenth centuries saw the high point of its growth; thereafter it began to decline as concern with the organization of the various Ṣūfī orders grew and special rituals were invented and miracle-mongering prevailed. It became, in short, a breeding ground for all kinds of irrationalism. The work of al-Ghazālī has, however, retained its influence up to the present day; his book *Iḥyāʾ ʿulūm al-dīn* being generally recognized as his greatest contribution to religious literature.

CHAPTER 26

CHRISTIAN ARABIC LITERATURE IN THE ᶜABBASID PERIOD

Christian Arabic literature in its widest sense comprises all the writings of Christians whose tongue is Arabic, but here we shall be concerned principally with the religious literature of Arabic-speaking Christians. The Arabization of Christian populations in north Africa and western Asia under the empire of Islam took place over some three centuries, proceeding most rapidly in Syria and Palestine, and being substantially complete in north Africa by the fourth/tenth century.

In spite of Georg Graf's five-volume study, *Geschichte der christlichen arabischen Literatur*, Christian Arabic literature is still relatively unknown, and the various relevant publications are scattered. Some forty volumes have been published in the *Patrologia Orientalis* series (Paris) and in the *Corpus Scriptorum Christianorum Orientalium* (Louvain) together with translations into European languages. More recently, a further ten or so volumes have been brought out in the *Patrimoine Arabe Chrétien* (Jounieh and Rome). The *Bulletin d'Arabe Chrétien* (1976–83) attempted to provide an annual bibliography, and from 1987 this task has been assumed by the review *Parole de l'Orient* (Kaslik, Lebanon).

Rather than follow Graf and classify the various authors in terms of their respective communities a thematic classification has been chosen here. However, given limitations of space, this may run the risk of providing little more than an inventory. The reader will find it easy enough to fill out what is said here by recourse to Graf's *Geschichte* (or to Nasrallah's *Histoire du mouvement littéraire dans l'église melchite* in the case of Melkite authors). In some places, particularly in the theological section, the writer's own research has made a synthesis possible. In more general terms, the writer has managed to examine personally about 80 per cent of the works mentioned.

BIBLICAL EXEGESIS

I shall not be concerned here with translations of the Bible, which are fairly common. They are interesting in regard to the attempts that were made to improve upon them, in terms both of accuracy and elegance. Especially noteworthy are the translations of the four Gospels into rhymed prose, and that of the Psalms into *rajaz* verse. Nor shall I be concerned with commentaries upon difficult passages in the Bible, which tend to be written in order to vindicate a particular theological position. This is the case with the commentaries of Sāwīrus b. al-Muqaffaᶜ, Bishop of al-Ashmūnayn, of Abū Zakariyyāᵓ Yaḥyā b. ᶜAdī, or of Abū ᶜAlī ᶜĪsā b. Isḥāq b. Zurᶜah, in the fourth/tenth century; with those of ᶜAbdullāh b. al-Ṭayyib or of Elijah of Nisibin in the fifth/eleventh century; with those of Ibrāhīm b. ᶜAwn in the sixth/twelfth century; with those of Ibn al-Rāhib, of Buṭrus al-Sadamantī and, above all, with those of Abū ᵓl-Faḍāᵓil Ṣafī ᵓl-Dawlah b. al-ᶜAssāl, in the seventh/thirteenth century. These texts belong more to theology or to philosophy than to exegesis. I shall therefore restrict myself to the study of Biblical commentaries in the strict sense, that is, those where the author comments upon a particular book in the Bible, just as in a *tafsīr* a scholar will comment upon a particular *sūrah* in the Qurᵓān.

There is only one complete commentary on the Old Testament in Arabic, written by the famous doctor and philosopher Abū ᵓl-Faraj ᶜAbdullāh b. al-Ṭayyib (d. 435/1043). He is the author of a complete commentary on the whole of the Bible, and he took his inspiration from authors writing in Syriac, for example Īshūᶜdād of Marw on Genesis. His commentary is philosophical, theological and spiritual in nature.

At the end of the sixth/twelfth century, Abū ᵓl-Fakhr Marqus b. Qanbar, a Coptic priest from Damietta who became a Melkite, wrote a commentary upon the whole of the Pentateuch which was symbolic, allegorical and Christological in outlook. It is a very spiritual commentary, in which everything stands as a symbol for Christian realities: the Church and the sacraments, in particular baptism, penance and the eucharist. It was this commentary which helped to bring about the formation of a small group of the faithful which was opposed to the Coptic patriarch, especially on account of the emphasis it placed upon the need for confession. Four versions of this *tafsīr* are known, a long one, a medium length one, a short one and an abridged one.

The Psalms have always played an important part in all Christian communities. It is therefore no surprise to find four commentaries on them, deriving from the four great eastern Christian communities of the period: a Nestorian one, by Abū ᵓl-Faraj ᶜAbdullāh b. al-Ṭayyib, a Melkite one, by ᶜAbdullāh b. al-Faḍl al-Anṭākī (fifth/eleventh century), a Jacobite one, by Dionysius b. al-Ṣalībī (sixth/twelfth century), and a Coptic one by Simᶜān b. Kalīl b. Maqārah (sixth/twelfth century).

Finally, we have a commentary on the Book of Daniel, with an introduction (which, unlike the commentary itself, has been published) in which the author reviews the story of Daniel, refutes those Jews who maintain that Daniel was not a prophet, and tries to explain why it was that Daniel was so much honoured in Babylon and not in Jerusalem. This commentary was the work of Abū ʾl-Sirrī Bishr b. al-Sirrī, a Melkite priest from Damascus who flourished about 246/860, and who was known above all as a translator and commentator on the New Testament and as an author of liturgical homilies.

In the third/ninth century, Ibn al-Sirrī translated and commented on the Gospels, a work which is lost, though it is mentioned by al-Asʿad Abū ʾl-Faraj b. al-ʿAssāl (d. 648/1250). In about 226/840 in Mesopotamia, Nonnus, Bishop of Nisibin, wrote a commentary on the Gospel of John, but only the Armenian translation has survived. In the fourth/tenth century, Sāwīrus, Bishop of al-Ashmūnayn (d. during patriarchate of Philotheus, AD 979–1003) composed a commentary on the Gospels which is no longer extant. In the following century, Abū ʾl-Faraj ʿAbdullāh b. al-Ṭayyib left a vast commentary on the four Gospels, in large part inspired by that of Theodore of Mopsuestia (al-Maṣṣīṣah), but also by Church Fathers such as John Chrysostom, and even by two Latin authors, Ambrose of Milan and Augustine; this commentary is preceded by a masterly general introduction on the need for exegesis. From Egypt we have a commentary upon Matthew's Gospel by Simʿān b. Kalīl (sixth/twelfth century), which makes extensive use of the Church Fathers (Eusebius, Athanasius, Chrysostom, Basil, Gregory of Nyssa, Ephraim, Cyril of Jerusalem and Sāwīrus of Antioch). Finally, in the seventh/thirteenth century, Buṭrus al-Sadamantī isolated the principles governing the interpretation of the Scriptures in his famous treatise on hermeneutics, *al-Qawl al-ṣaḥīḥ fī ālām al-Sayyid al-Masīḥ*.

As far as the Acts of the Apostles and the Catholic epistles are concerned, we only have the translation and commentary of Ibn al-Sirrī, preserved in an autograph Kufic manuscript dated AH 253 (=AD 867) (Sinai Arab. 151). This same author added a number of glosses to his translation of the works of St Paul.

Al-Muʾtaman b. al-ʿAssāl (d. after 664/1265) composed a general introduction to the Epistles of St Paul, consisting of a life of the saint, and a summary of the purpose and context of each epistle, together with a listing of doctrinal and ethical themes. Al-Muʾtaman b. al-ʿAssāl's collaborator, al-Wajīh Yūḥannā al-Qalyūbī, left an extensive commentary on St Paul's Epistle to the Romans and, it would appear, on the two Epistles to the Corinthians.

Finally, the Apocalypse of St John the Divine was the object of two different commentaries in the course of the seventh/thirteenth century, by Būlus al-Būshī, Bishop of Cairo, and Abū Isḥāq ᶜAlam al-Riʾāsah Ibrāhīm b. Kātib Qayṣar (d. second half of seventh/thirteenth century). The latter devotes himself to linguistic researches, comparing the various manuscripts one with the other (Greek, Syriac, Coptic and Arabic) in order to discover the true meaning of the text.

CANON LAW

From the second/eighth century, the Christian communities began to translate a number of canon law collections from Greek, Coptic or Syriac into Arabic. The Melkites of Syria seem to have been the first to set this process in motion. Once translated, the texts circulated rapidly from one country to another, with each community upon occasion adding its own improvements. The collections that appeared in the third/ninth century were ordered chronologically, and it was only in the fifth/eleventh century that the first systematic compilations, known as nomocanons, were tentatively assembled, attaining their most perfect form in the seventh/thirteenth century, particularly with the nomocanon (*majmūᶜ*) of Abū ʾl-Faḍāʾil Ṣafī ʾl-Dawlah b. al-ᶜAssāl. In the following only the systematic compilations are cited:

1. The first compilation, assembled at some point prior to AD 1028, is that of Abū Ṣāliḥ Yuʾannis (rather than Yūnus) b. ᶜAbdullāh, who is supposed to have been a Copt (though he is more likely to have been an Iraqi). It is a small, fairly rudimentary compilation, classified in terms of forty-eight summaries (*jumlah*). The introduction is of particular interest, being cast in the form of answers to five doubtful points: Why is there canon law, when no such thing exists in the Gospels? Why is the law of talion not applied? Why are there no laws respecting worldly goods (succession and so on)? Why has there been legislation regarding marriage? Why is divorce prohibited? Basically, each of these points can be seen as a response to one major question, namely, why does Christianity not have a *sharīᶜah*, as Islam does?

2. In the same period, Abū ʾl-Faraj ᶜAbdullāh b. al-Ṭayyib drafted his *Fiqh al-Naṣrāniyyah*, a compilation which is both chronological and systematic. The systematic part consists of three sections: civil law (marriage, divorce, inheritance, wills, bailment, sale and purchase, slavery, testimony, oath, taxation), ecclesiastical law (liturgical prescriptions and

canon law for clerics) and social law (hospitals, schools, monasteries). This compilation had considerable influence on Ibn al-ᶜAssāl (see below).

3 The Coptic patriarchs promulgated various statutes: Christodoulos (AD 1047–77), on liturgical questions; Cyril II (AD 1078–92), on pastoral and administrative questions; Gabriel II Ibn Turayk (AD 1131–45), on similar matters, but on inheritances also. The latter left a nomocanon in seventy-four well-structured chapters, dealing with civil and religious law.

4 In 584/1188, Mīkhāʾīl, Bishop of Damietta, composed a large nomocanon which was mainly concerned with religious and liturgical questions, but also dealt with the care of the sick and the poor, with relations with Muslims and heretics, with magic, marriage, slavery and with the rules of succession.

5 In the wake of the crisis which shook the Coptic Church at the beginning of the seventh/thirteenth century, and which ended with the patriarchal seat remaining empty from AD 1216 to AD 1235, the synod of bishops entrusted Abū ʾl-Faḍāʾil Ṣafī ʾl-Dawlah b. al-ᶜAssāl with the task of drafting a canonic compilation which would serve as a norm in the case of any dispute. He completed it in 635/1238. This work, which was fifty-two chapters long, enjoyed considerable success: in the following century it was translated into Geᶜez (and from this language into Italian and English), and served as a model for the other oriental Christian communities, and for the Maronites in particular. It still serves, even today, as a basis for the codification prevailing in these Churches. This work is of an unrivalled scientific quality; it also represents an attempt to adapt to Muslim law in matters concerning the civil code.

6 More or less at the same period in Egypt, Mīkhāʾīl, Bishop of Athrīb and Malīj, also composed a large canonic compilation which, in spite of its intrinsic worth was eclipsed by that of Ṣafī ʾl-Dawlah b. al-ᶜAssāl.

CHRISTIAN THEOLOGY

Theological writings are the main genre within Arab Christian thought, and serve best to express its essential nature. They are dealt with in detail in the second volume of Graf's study and, as regards the Melkites, in the work of Nasrallah. I shall here merely try to draw out a few of the major themes. A number of the dogmatic works are exclusively addressed to Christians: these are generally Christological controversies. The remainder are directed at Muslims, even when they are ostensibly addressed to Christians. Indeed, Arab Christian theology is always, in some way, apologetic, since it is obliged to defend itself against continual Muslim attack.

The oriental communities were divided over Christology. All of them affirmed that Christ was truly God and truly man, but each gave a different account of the relation between these two aspects of Christ. This gave rise to three different schools (*madhāhib*): the Monophysites (Copts, western Syrians or Suryān and Armenians); the Nestorians; and the Melkites (Byzantines and Maronites).

It is fair to say that every self-respecting theologian wrote at least one treatise in defence of his own *madhhab* and in criticism of the others. The most important ones were, in chronological order:[1]

Timothy I (N), Theodore abū Qurrah (M), Abū Rā'iṭah al-Takrītī (S), ʿAlī b. Dāwūd al-Arfādī (S), Saʿīd b. Baṭrīq (M), Abū Zakariyyā' Yaḥyā b. ʿAdī (S), Sāwīrus b. al-Muqaffaʿ (C), Abū ʿAlī Naẓīf b. Yumn (M), Abū ʿAlī ʿĪsā b. Isḥāq b. Zurʿah (S), Abū 'l-Faraj ʿAbdullāh b. al-Ṭayyib (N), Elijah of Nisibin (N), ʿAbdullāh b. al-Faḍl al-Anṭākī (M), Abū Naṣr Yaḥyā b. Jarīr al-Takrītī (S), Dionysius b. al-Ṣalībī (S), ʿAfīf b. al-Makīn b. Mu'ammil (M), Būlus al-Anṭākī (M), Ignatius II (S), Īshūʿyāb b. Malkūn (N), Buṭrus Sāwīrus al-Jamīl, Bishop of Malīj (C), Abū 'l-Faḍā'il Ṣafī 'l-Dawlah b. al-ʿAssāl (C) and his brother al-Mu'taman b. al-ʿAssāl (C), Mīkhā'īl, Bishop of Athrīb and Malīj (C).

However, many of these theologians, having expounded the differences between the Christological schools, go on to emphasize the deeper agreement uniting them over fundamental issues. This is the case, in particular, with Timothy I, Abū Rā'iṭah, Abū 'l-Faraj ʿAbdullāh b. al-Ṭayyib, Yaḥyā b. Jarīr al-Takrītī, Abū 'l-Faḍā'il Ṣafī 'l-Dawlah b. al-ʿAssāl and al-Mu'taman b. al-ʿAssāl. Some of these theologians go still further, and devote separate chapters or even entire treatises to demonstrating how Christians are unanimous in their faith. In the treatise by ʿAlī b. Dāwūd al-Arfādī (beginning of the fourth/tenth century), entitled *Kitāb Ijtimāʿ al-imānah wa-mukhtaṣar al-diyānah* ("The Agreement of Belief and Epitome of Religion"), the author emphasizes that divisions between Christians have four causes, namely, ignorance, passion, fanaticism and a desire for power (*jahl*, *hawā*, *ʿaṣabiyyah*, *riyāsah*). Sāwīrus b. al-Muqaffaʿ deals with differences in custom (fasting, circumcision and the preparation of the eucharist) and judges that all the variations are legitimate, because they do not affect what is essential. Abū ʿAlī Naẓīf b. Yumn (d. 380/990), a Melkite philosopher and physician

[1] C = Coptic; M = Melkite; N = Nestorian; S = west Syrian.

of Baghdad, first of all explains that the three schools agree over content (*maᶜnā*), although they may differ in the expressions (*ᶜibārah*) that they use. Then he tries to justify philosophically the position of each of the three schools! Abū ᵓl-Faḍāᵓil Ṣafī ᵓl-Dawlah b. al-ᶜAssāl, in the eighth chapter of his *Fuṣūl mukhtaṣarah fī tathlīth al-ittiḥād* ("Brief Chapters on the Triplication of Unity"; written in 639/1242), demonstrates that the disagreement turns upon a handful of philosophical terms. Once he has explained and justified the opinions of the three schools, he says why it is that he prefers that of the Jacobites. Mīkhāᵓīl, Bishop of Athrīb and Malīj, in Lower Egypt, composed around 643/1245 a treatise in two parts, the first part of which shows that Christians are unanimous over the essential articles of dogma, namely, the Trinity and unity of God and the divinity and humanity of Christ. The second part of the treatise is concerned with the differences, which were caused by Satan: Mīkhāᵓīl expounds the opinion of the Nestorians, the Melkites, the Franks and the Armenians, refutes what seems to him to be erroneous and sets out the difference between Nestorius and the Nestorians of his own time. He concludes by saying that one should not rebaptize a Christian, but only one who has totally renounced his faith (for instance, a Christian who has become a Muslim and wishes to return to the faith, or a non-Christian).

The majority of Muslims think that Christians are not monotheists. This dogma has therefore to be firmly established. Arab theologians attempt to establish Christian monotheism through two different approaches, namely, tradition and reason (*naql* and *ᶜaql*). The argument from tradition follows three different paths: (a) the invocation of Holy Scripture: this is the way adopted by, for example, Abū Rāᵓiṭah al-Takrītī (third/ninth century), Sāwīrus b. al-Muqaffaᶜ of al-Ashmūnayn, Elijah of Nisibin (d. after 440–1/1049), the anonymous author of the Sbath Manuscript 1129 and by al-Muᵓtaman b. al-ᶜAssāl; (b) an appeal to the Qurᵓān itself: two texts in particular are crucial here, the third interview of Elijah of Nisibin with the vizier al-Maghribī, and the anonymous Sbath Manuscript 1129; (c) an appeal to Muslim tradition: thus Elijah of Nisibin bases his case upon the commentators (in particular Abū Jaᶜfar Muḥammad b. Jarīr al-Ṭabarī) and upon the theologians (in particular al-Bāqillānī), while the anonymous author of the Sbath Manuscript relies on the jurists and Traditionists.

The argument from reason follows a number of different philosophical paths. Thus Abū Rāᵓiṭah al-Takrītī explains that Christian monotheism is the height of perfection: by contrast with every created being, God is one as regards substance (because he is simple) and triune as to number; thus "nothing resembles him" (Qurᵓān, xlii.11). ᶜAbd al-Masīḥ al-Kindī (third/ninth century) formulates a response to the objection, based on the Qurᵓān, that God has neither companion nor son. However it was Abū Zakariyyāʾ Yaḥyā b. ʿAdī, the master of Aristotelianism in Baghdad after the deaths of Abū Bishr Mattā b. Yūnus and Abū Naṣr Muḥammad b. Muḥammad al-Fārābī, who, refuting Abū Yūsuf Yaʿqūb b. Isḥāq al-Kindī, shows that there are for Aristotle not three kinds of One but six, and that God is one in his quiddity and multiple in his attributes; he is a unity which includes otherness (*ghayriyyah*).

A number of theologians, notably an anonymous author of the second/eighth century and, above all, Elijah of Nisibin, conclude their exposition with a declaration of monotheistic faith which is in the purest Islamic style.

Theologians expound the doctrine of the Trinity in three different ways:

1 They may appeal to Scripture. This approach entails showing that the Trinity was foreshadowed in the Old Testament and made manifest in the New Testament. One author in every two (beginning with Abū Rāʾiṭah al-Takrītī) adopts this method.

2 They may employ analogies, as with many of the Church Fathers. The idea is a simple one, namely, if we consider the created world, we find in it many examples of one and the same reality being expressed in three different forms. One uses both natural analogies (springs, trees, apples and, above all, the sun) and corporeal analogies (soul, mind and body; soul, intelligence and speech; soul, speech and life; the finger composed of three joints).

3 They may undertake an analysis of the divine attributes. In this case, one sets out from philosophical triads, in particular from the neo-Platonic triad (the good, the wise and the powerful) or from the Aristotelian triad (the intellect, the intelligent and the intellected: *ʿaql ʿāqil nafsih wa-maʿqūl li-nafsih*) "discovered" by Yaḥyā b. ʿAdī, or from other triads which accord with the philosophical system of the authors of the treatises. If asked why it is that they restrict themselves to three attributes, they answer that they are concerned with the attributes of essence (*ṣifāt*), such as being, life and wisdom, which are distinguished from relative attributes (*ṣifāt al-iḍāfah* or *nisbiyyah*) and from attributes of action (*ṣifāt al-fiʿl*).

In order to establish the divinity of Christ, most of the theologians set out from the Quranic assertion that Christ is the "word of God" (*kalimat Allāh*). Since the word of God is inseparable from him and coeternal with him, Christ is coeternal with God and inseparable from him. Elijah of Nisibin pioneered another method. Comparing Christ to the prophets, he showed that he was superior to each of them considered individually

(Adam, who was conceived without human seed, John the Baptist, who was a virgin, Moses the thaumaturge, Enoch, who was raised up into the sky), and to all of them considered as a category (owing to his being exempt from sin, and owing to the fact that he was the word of God and not merely created by the word of God).

There were three different ways of establishing the incarnation (*tajassud*, *ittiḥād* or even *ittiṣāl*):

1 Many theologians searched through the Old Testament for prophetic announcements of this dogma.

2 Yaḥyā b. ʿAdī followed a more philosophical path. Taking as his starting-point the nature of God as gift-giver *par excellence* (*jawwād*), who cannot help but give the best that he has, that is, himself, Yaḥyā b. ʿAdī establishes the necessity (*wujūb*) of the incarnation. Only a lack of generosity (*bukhl*) or powerlessness (*ʿajz*) on God's side could prevent him from giving such a gift, and these two faults are incompatible with God's nature; and on man's side only, an incompatibility between God and man could prevent this gift; and this would be opposed to the fact that God created man, and in his own image. Once one has established the possibility and the necessity of the union between God and man, one has to conclude that it necessarily took place. If the creation is an act of generosity (*jūd*) by God for man, God, through the incarnation, completes his love for man.

3 Abū ʾl-Faḍāʾil Ṣafī ʾl-Dawlah b. al-ʿAssāl rehearses the above arguments and adds a third, which is also a traditional one, namely, that man, in order to perfect his nature, has need of God.

The basic exposition of the truth of Christianity is to be found in a work by Abū Rāʾiṭah al-Takrītī, in response to a question by the Muʿtazilite Abū Maʿn Thumāmah al-Baṣrī (d. *c.* 213/828). His account was then repeated, with a number of different variants, by dozens of theologians, including Ḥunayn b. Isḥāq al-ʿIbādī.[2] The gist of the argument is that Christianity has been accepted by both scholars and the ignorant, even though its dogmas are opposed to reason and its morality is opposed to sensual pleasures. Scholars, however, only accept what is contrary to reason, and the ignorant what is contrary to sensual pleasure, if they are constrained to do so. Now there are two kinds of constraint (*qahr*), namely, miracles and the sword, and no one has been forced to become a Christian at swordpoint. People

[2] Kh. Samir, "Liberté religieuse", 93–121.

must therefore have been constrained by miracles, which necessarily come from God. The allusion to Islam is clear here. Ḥunayn goes on to add further refinements to the argument, making a distinction as regards conversion between good and bad criteria.

HISTORY

History is a genre to which Arab Christian authors have given considerable attention. Here we will first consider a number of minor works and histories of medicine and science, and will then discuss a number of major works at greater length. There are some twenty or so minor works that deserve to be mentioned, either on account of their intrinsic merit, or on account of their author. They are here given in chronological order, concluding with the fifth/eleventh century.

From the third/ninth century there are seven works: the *Kitāb al-Mushāhadāt wa-ʾl-akhbār* of the vizier Abū ʾl-ʿAbbās al-Faḍl b. Marwān b. Māsarjīs al-Naṣrānī (156–250/773–864); the two books of Yūsuf b. Ibrāhīm b. al-Dāyah, foster-brother of the caliph al-Muʿtaṣim, born in 180/796 and died in 265/878, who was an important historian of culture and wrote an *Akhbār Abī Nuwās* and a *Kitāb fī Anwāʿ al-akhbār*; the general history of Ḥunayn b. Isḥāq; the *Kitāb Akhbār al-ḥawārī* of Ibrāhīm b. ʿĪsā (third/ninth century); the abridged history of the monk Hārūn b. ʿAzzūr, which extends from Adam until the end of the third/ninth century, and which was later used by Abū Saʿīd ʿUbaydullāh b. Jibrīl (d. 450/1058) and by Ibn abī Uṣaybiʿah; and the general history of Qays al-Mārūnī (beginning of fourth/tenth century), which extends from the creation of the world until the reign of al-Muktafī (reigned 289–95/902–8), which al-Masʿūdī valued highly.

A further seven works belong to the following century: the *Kitāb al-Firdaws fī ʾl-taʾrīkh* of Qusṭā b. Lūqā, who died at the beginning of the fourth/tenth century; the history of the kings and dynasties from Adam to Constantine, composed by the Egyptian Melkite monk Athanasius, and commended by al-Masʿūdī; the lost history of Yaʿqūb b. Zakariyyāʾ al-Kaskarī, which surpassed the work of other Christians, according to al-Masʿūdī; the history of the Greek and Byzantine kings and philosophers written by the philosopher Abū Zakariyyāʾ Danḥā (fourth/tenth century) around 313/925; an anonymous chronicle preserved in the church of al-Qusyān in Antioch but now lost, mentioned by al-Masʿūdī; the shortened version of the history of Abū Jaʿfar Muḥammad b. Jarīr al-Ṭabarī, which ʿArīb b. Saʿd al-Qurṭubī (fourth/tenth century) abridged and completed in regard to the Maghrib and Andalusia, together with his *Ṣilat taʾrīkh al-*

Ṭabarī, which covers the years 291–320/904–32. (The last two works are still extant.)

In the fifth/eleventh century numerous works appeared, including *The History of the Nestorian Patriarchs*, by Yūḥannā b. al-Ṭabarī; the history of the monk Theophilus, *Taʾrīkh Thawfīl al-rāhib al-muʾarrikh*, which extends from Adam to the fifth/eleventh century; the world history of the Nestorian monk Abā, which dates from the fifth/eleventh century; the *Zīj al-Tawārīkh* of Yaḥyā b. Jarīr al-Takrītī, which extends from Adam to 473/1080; and the work of Mīkhāʾīl b. Badīr, who translated in 481/1088 a section from the Coptic history of the patriarchs of Alexandria into Arabic. (This last work is still extant.)

The important role which Christians played in Arab medicine and science is well known. A number of Christian writers composed histories of medicine, and there is good reason to suppose that they invented this genre, which was to culminate in the work of Ibn abī Uṣaybiʿah. Of these it is essential to mention the following: in the third/ninth century, among numerous other works, the *Nawādir al-falāsifah wa-ʾl-ḥukamāʾ* ("Anecdotes of the Philosophers and Sages") of Ḥunayn b. Isḥāq, together with his *Ādāb al-muʿallimīn al-qudamāʾ* ("Mores of the Ancient Teachers"); the *Akhbār al-aṭibbāʾ* ("Accounts of Physicians") and the *Akhbār al-munajjimīn* ("Accounts of Astrologers") of Yūsuf b. Ibrāhīm b. al-Dāyah; the *Taʾrīkh al-aṭibbāʾ* ("History of Physicians") and the *Adab al-ṭabīb* ("Etiquette of the Physician")[3] of Isḥāq b. ʿAlī al-Ruhāwī; the *Akhbār al-aṭibbāʾ* of Fathyūn b. Ayyūb al-Turjumān (middle of third/ninth century), quoted more than thirty times by Ibn abī Uṣaybiʿah; and the *Taʾrīkh al-aṭibbāʾ* of Isḥāq b. Ḥunayn (d. 289/910–11).

In the following centuries among works of this kind were the *Kitāb Sharḥ madhāhib al-Yūnāniyyīn* ("Commentary on the Doctrines of the Greeks") of Qusṭā b. Lūqā; the *Manāqib al-aṭibbāʾ* ("Feats of the Physicians") of ʿUbaydullāh b. Jibrīl, the last of the Bakhtīshūʿ family; the *Daʿwat al-aṭibbāʾ*[4] of Abū ʾl-Ḥasan al-Mukhtār b. ʿAbdūn b. Buṭlān, which was completed in Constantinople in 445/1053; and the *Bustān al-aṭibbāʾ wa-rawḍat al-alibbāʾ* ("Garden of the Physicians and Meadow of the Intelligent") of Ibn al-Muṭrān, the personal physician of Ṣalāḥ al-Dīn, who embraced Islam two years before his death in 587/1191.

The great surviving historical works began to appear in the course of the fourth/tenth century. They tend to be ecclesiastical histories, but with an admixture of secular history. They often provide information which was

[3] See above, ch. 19, 351. [4] See above, ch. 19, 351–3.

unknown to Muslim historians, being based upon Greek, Syriac or Coptic documents to which the latter had no access. Furthermore, in several cases, eyewitnesses are involved. In all of them a novel point of view, that of the minorities, is presented, and they display an unusual concern for detail. We know of three other important works from this period. *Naẓm al-jawhar* of Saᶜīd b. Baṭrīq, the Melkite patriarch of Alexandria from AD 933 to AD 940, is concerned with secular and ecclesiastical history from the earliest times up until 326/983. Another Melkite, Maḥbūb Qusṭanṭīn (fourth/tenth century), Bishop of Manbij, drafted a universal history, *Kitāb al-ᶜUnwān*, which extends from the creation to 330/942; unfortunately the only known manuscript stops short at 150/767, but it is worth noting that for this latter section he employed an eyewitness account, as contained in the universal history of the Maronite astronomer Theophilus of Edessa, who died in 169/785. Once again in Egypt, in the latter half of the same century, Sāwīrus b. al-Muqaffaᶜ compiled, on the basis of arduous researches in the Coptic monasteries, a history of the Church entitled *Kitāb Siyar al-biᶜah al-muqaddasah* ("Biographies of the Holy Church") commonly known as the "History of the Patriarchs of Alexandria". There is, however, good reason to suppose that the definitive version of the work should be attributed to Abū ᵓl-Barakāt Mawhūb b. Manṣūr, who was deacon of Alexandria at the end of the fifth/eleventh century. Mawhūb b. Manṣūr also composed a *Kitāb al-Majāmiᶜ* ("History of the Ecumenical Councils"), which is both historical and theological in content and is intended to be a response to the history of Saᶜīd b. Baṭrīq. It was translated into Geᶜez in the ninth/fifteenth century.

Four major works have come down to us from the fifth/eleventh century. The chronicle of Elijah, Nestorian Bishop of Nisibin, is written in parallel columns in Syriac and Arabic. The first part covers the years from 25/645 to 409/1018, while the second part is a computational treatise (*zīj*), with concordance tables between the different eras; the entire work was composed prior to 417/1026. The Melkite Yaḥyā b. Saᶜīd al-Anṭākī wrote a *Kitāb al-Dhayl* ("Supplement") to the history of Saᶜīd b. Baṭrīq, which extends from 326/938 to 425/1034. This work is an important source for the Faṭimid epoch in Egypt and in Syria, and also for relations with Byzantium. Saᶜīd b. Baṭrīq lived in Alexandria, where he wrote his history around 396/1006, redrafting it several years later. Finally, in 405/1014, he went to Antioch and, on the basis of new documents, composed his final version. So objective was this work that it was used, from the sixth/twelfth century, by Muslim historians such as ᶜAbd al-Raḥmān b. al-Munqidh (d. 588/1192). The *Chronicle of Siirt* (named after a small town in Kurdistan, where the manuscript was found), was written by a Nestorian author around 429/1036, who was particularly concerned with ecclesiastical history, and who drew upon dozens of Syriac and Arabic sources. In the manuscript as we now have it the chronicle stops at the year 30/650. The deacon and Coptic notable Abū ᵓl-Barakāt Mawhūb b. Manṣūr b. Mufarrij al-Iskandarānī (*c.* 416–97/1025–1103) collated the entire history of the Patriarchs of Alexandria, originally undertaken by Sāwīrus b. al-Muqaffaᶜ, and composed the lives of the twelve Patriarchs who ruled from 266–485/880–1092; this task occupied him for six years, from 481–7/1088–94. He died having completed the biography of Mīkhāᵓīl IV (485–95/1092–1102), but his text has not survived. In the sixth/twelfth century, if one excepts the historians of the Coptic patriarchs (Yūḥannā b. Saᶜīd b. Yaḥyā b. Mīnā, known as Ibn al-Qulzumī (wrote about 517/1123), and the Coptic Patriarch Marqus III Ibn Zurᶜah, 1166–89), there are only two histories worthy of mention. About 545/1150 the Nestorian Mārī b. Sulaymān (sixth/twelfth century) composed a huge religious encyclopaedia entitled *al-Majdal li-ᵓl-istibṣār wa-ᵓl-jadal* ("The Tower for Insight and Dispute"). In the fifth chapter of the fifth part, he inserted a lengthy ecclesiastical history, in which he enters on the scene in person after the catholicos Makkīkhā I (485–504/1092–1110).[5]

In AD 1209, the Coptic shaykh Abūᵓl-Makārim Saᶜdullāh b. Jūrjīs b. Masᶜūd composed a history of churches and monasteries. The sole surviving manuscript (Munich Arab. 2570) is incomplete and disarranged. In its present form it covers the churches and monasteries of Egypt (Cairo and the Delta), Sinai, Jerusalem and Palestine, Syria, Iraq, Turkey and even Rome. This work is replete with precise historical information on the churches, their construction and destruction, their architecture and decoration, etc.

There are, therefore, two histories written by Copts which are worthy of attention in the first half of the seventh/thirteenth century (up to 656/1258), if one excludes the universal history written by al-Makīn Jūrjīs, surnamed Ibn al-ᶜAmīd, after 660/1262. Between 605/1208 and 612/1215 Abū Ṣāliḥ the Armenian wrote a history of churches and monasteries, of the same type as the preceding. Starting at Cairo, he works up the Nile Valley, describing in detail Upper Egypt and Nubia, with an appendix on Ethiopia, the Maghrib and Andalusia. It has been claimed that this history is merely the second part of the above-mentioned history by Abū ᵓl-Makārim, but an examination of the two histories shows that we are dealing with two different

[5] Mārī b. Sulaymān, *al-Majdal*, ed. H. Gismondi, Rome, 1899, 156.

authors. Al-Nushūʾ abū Shākir b. al-Rāhib Sanāʾ al-Dawlah abī ʾl-Makārim Buṭrus b. al-Muhadhdhab (seventh/thirteenth century) composed a *Kitāb al-Tawārīkh*, which extends from Adam to the year 655/1257, and consists of three parts: a treatise on astronomy and chronology (Chs. 1–47); a universal chronicle, Islamic and ecclesiastical in nature, which amounts to almost two-thirds of the work (Chs. 48–50); and a compendium of the history of the first seven ecumenical councils (Ch. 51). The work enjoyed great success among Christians while the author was still alive, and was used by al-Muʾtaman b. al-ʿAssāl and al-Makīn Jūrjīs; it is frequently quoted by al-Maqrīzī and Ibn Khaldūn, and was translated into Geʿez by ʿEnbaqom about 920/1514, in which form it became a classic. The famous *Chronicum Orientale*, translated for the first time into Latin in 1651 by Abraham Ecchellensis (Ibrāhīm al-Ḥāqilānī), is merely a mediocre compendium of Chapters 48–50, done by an anonymous author of the seventh/thirteenth century.

RELIGIOUS ENCYCLOPAEDIAS

It was four centuries before the need was felt to assemble religious knowledge into encyclopaedias. This genre was to develop mainly in the sixth–seventh/twelfth–thirteenth centuries. During the epoch with which we are concerned there are four works which are worthy of note. *Al-Murshid* ("The Guide") was composed by Abū Naṣr Yaḥyā b. Jarīr al-Takrītī, a Syro-Orthodox author by whose hand we have six works concerned with astrology, medicine, mathematics, history and theology. His encyclopaedia consists of fifty-four chapters and is concerned with theology, liturgy, spirituality and law. He is quoted by Yāqūt in his *Muʿjam al-buldān*, by Ibn abī Uṣaybiʿah, and by the Coptic encyclopaedists.

In Mārī b. Sulaymān's encyclopaedia *al-Majdal* all the religious themes are touched upon: philosophy, theology, liturgy, sacraments, spirituality, morality and history. He quotes many earlier texts but rarely gives his sources. Biblical quotations abound. He normally employs rhymed prose. Shams al-Riyāsah abū ʾl-Barakāt b. Kabar (d. 724/1324) calls him ʿAmr b. Mattā al-Ṭīrhānī!

About 662/1263 the Coptic al-Muʾtaman b. al-ʿAssāl finished drafting his *summa theologica*, entitled *Majmūʿ uṣūl al-dīn wa-masmūʿ maḥṣūl al-yaqīn*, a remarkable philosophico-theological encyclopaedia in seventy chapters. In this he tried to gather together the whole of the Arab Christian heritage and to organize it in a systematic manner.

In 669/1270 al-Nushūʾ Abū Shākir b. al-Rāhib composed his *Kitāb al-Burhān*, a religious *summa* consisting of fifty questions concerned with philosophy, theology, morality and spirituality. His theodicy (Chs. 28–40) is based upon the *Kitāb al-Arbaʿīn* of Fakhr al-Dīn al-Rāzī.

CHAPTER 27

JUDAEO-ARABIC LITERATURE

The medieval period witnessed a vigorous and variegated output of Arabic literature written by Jews, which in virtue of both its intellectual and linguistic enrichment of Jewish and Arabic culture deserves to be included in any historical survey of Arabic letters.

Judaeo-Arabic literature arose at a time when the majority of Jews lived beneath the dominion of Islam, when the latter itself was at the height of its cultural achievements. A decline began to set in at the end of the ʿAbbasid period, when the employment of Hebrew for literary purposes started to gain ground. There were two factors, one external, the other internal, that caused the decline of Judaeo-Arabic letters. First cultural introversion and a subsequent inadequacy in Classical Arabic, and secondly the fostering of an elaborate Hebrew culture in the wake of the Hispanic schools of translation, which was then propagated throughout the Mediterranean after the expulsions from Spain in 1391 and 1492. However a distinctly vernacular brand of Arabic continued to be written, albeit among the culturally less favoured classes, right down to modern times, when in the wake of the European enlightenment the Jews experienced a cultural renaissance (*nahḍah*) and the revival of a certain form of literary Arabic. In north Africa a "classicized vernacular" was employed to express the new themes inspired by the European Haskalah, whereas in the East the Arabic employed, sometimes in Arabic characters, was nearer the standard language.

Hitherto the term "Judaeo-Arabic" has been applied generally to all writings of the Arabic language copied into Hebrew characters for the use of Jewish readers, irrespective of whether these writings had any specifically Jewish traits. Such an indiscriminate characterization has sometimes proved misleading and even provoked some disapproving and often unwarranted protest.

While it is true that the bulk of what is called Judaeo-Arabic literature does possess a distinctive character and a specific literary tradition peculiar to a clearly defined religio-ethnic society which differentiates it from general Arabic letters, there is an unfortunate tendency to classify as

Judaeo-Arabic Arabic texts which are Judaic only in transmission but not in content. If Judaeo-Arabic literature is defined as: "the writings composed in Arabic by Jewish authors concerned with topics of predominantly Jewish interest, generally – but not exclusively – employing the Hebrew script and often presupposing some degree of familiarity with Hebrew", then such a definition would satisfactorily accommodate Jewish writings composed in the Arabic script, though primarily intended for internal Jewish circulation. Several Bible translations and commentaries in Arabic script believed to have been copied for the use of Qaraites have been preserved, mainly in the Cairo Genizah. It is not clear whether this resort to Arabic letters was due to their alienation from the Hebrew script, as contended by Joshua Blau,[1] or whether it was to avoid the eventual profanation of the Hebrew script written on paper. It is thought that early authors such as Saᶜadyah and Isḥāq b. Sulaymān al-Isrāʾīlī may well have written some of their works intended for external circulation in Arabic characters. An Arabic manuscript of Maimonides' *Guide for the Perplexed*, presumably for the use of Muslims, has been published by H. Atay.[2] The above definition would however exclude Arabic writings of a general character transliterated into Hebrew letters, despite the fact that the latter may confer upon them a specific orthographical form, irrespective of whether their authors were of the Jewish faith. The latter, which include *inter alia* scientific, medical and philosophical works, are to be qualified simply as Arabic compositions in Hebrew transliteration. The copying of works of Muslim authors into Hebrew characters can hardly transform them into Judaeo-Arabic, for it is merely a convenient expedient comparable to the transliteration of Arabic into Syriac letters (*karshūnī*) for the use of the Christians of the Orient, or equally the copying of Judaeo-Arabic texts into Arabic characters for the use of Arabists! Thus a Qurʾān copied into Hebrew characters (as found in the Genizah T–S Ar. 51.62 and in other manuscripts) is no more a Judaeo-Arabic work than certain early European prints which represented Arabic in Hebrew transcription, simply because their readers were unfamiliar with the Arabic script, or because no Arabic fount was available at the time. For example, the Arabic notes to the first Latin printing (Basel, 1543) of the Qurʾān by Th. Bibliander (Buchmann), are in Hebrew characters! Attention may also be drawn to J. H. Hottinger's *Historia Orientalis*. In the first edition (Zürich, 1651) all the Arabic texts are printed in Hebrew characters, following a system which differs slightly

[1] *Emergence and Linguistic Background of Judaeo-Arabic*, Jerusalem[2] 1981, 43.

[2] Ankara, 1974. Fragments of an Arabic text with Hebrew script quotations, presumably for the use of Jews, has however been preserved in the Genizah (T–S Ar. 18(1) 141, NS 306. Ar. 42.42, AS 178.222, Misc. 24.85, AS 178.228, T–S Misc, 24.85, AS 178.228 and New York, JTS ENA 3916.19 and ENA 3920.5).

from that employed in Judaeo-Arabic texts; in the subsequent edition of 1666, the selfsame texts appear in Arabic script, presumably after an Arabic fount had become available.

Without going as far as to postulate that Judaeo-Arabic is a separate language, it is nonetheless undeniable that it does exhibit linguistic features which are truly distinctive and characteristic. Besides the degree of Hebraic elements, which are determined by the subject-matter and usually demonstrate a remarkable conformity with Arabic morphology and syntax, the written language also contains a higher percentage of neo-Arabic features than Muslim literary Arabic. This is probably due to the fact that the Jews were less inhibited by the stylistic ideals of Classical Arabic. This curious mixture of neo-Classical and Classical elements is best described as a Middle Arabic Standard and affords an enlightening insight into the analytic structure of Middle Arabic, betraying at the same time many instances of hypercorrection motivated by a desire to maintain a Classical resonance. Instances of Judaeo-Arabic texts provided with Hebrew vocalization, which is more discriminative than Arabic, furnish a faithful reflection of the contemporary Arabic pronunciation and the process of modification and elimination of certain vowels and consonants, mirrored by parallel phenomena in modern Arabic dialects. Furthermore, in contrast to the classical idiom, Judaeo-Arabic tends to be loose and imprecise.

ORIGINS

Although the Jews inhabited places in the Arabian peninsula several centuries prior to the rise of Islam, there is no evidence that they had a distinct written Arabic tradition, despite the dubious report that they corresponded with Muḥammad in Arabic written in Hebrew letters.[3]

In the wake of the Islamic conquests and the diffusion of Arabic as a cultural medium, the conquered Jewish populations, who had previously spoken Aramaic in the East and Berber or Romance in the West, gradually adopted the Arabic language for most, though not all, of their literary needs. It was claimed both by the Judaeo-Arabic authors themselves and later by orientalists, that this adoption was necessitated by the inadequacy of Hebrew or Aramaic to express the new concepts that were being forged. This justification ignores the fact that Arabic too had to contend with the same difficulties, although by the time it was employed in the first Judaeo-Arabic works of any significance it had already acquired considerable sophistication. Secondly, in the legal domain, where Arabic was later to

[3] Cf. Aḥmad b. Yaḥyā al-Balādhurī, *Futūḥ*, Cairo, 1932, 460.

express some of the most sacred concepts of Judaism, there already existed a richly developed technical idiom, predominantly Aramaic. However as knowledge of the latter declined, since it had no sacred character, it was gradually and unregretfully superseded by Arabic, particularly as the new forms of legal literature had been inspired by Arabic models. Thirdly, in the domain of poetry, where language was required to be at its richest, paradoxically Jews continued to compose in Hebrew. This option had serious consequences for the subsequent development of Judaeo-Arabic literature and deserves to be briefly dwelt upon in more detail. It would seem that the sacred language persisted in this domain where there already existed a tradition of Hebrew composition, i.e. the synagogal liturgy. Furthermore, the academic institutions, such as the mosque and the *madrasah*, which would have provided the Jews with the proficiency necessary in composing Arabic poetry, were inaccessible to them. There may also have been ideological motives, inspired by the spirit of the Shuᶜūbiyyah which prompted Jews to demonstrate the Hebrew language's ability to vie, linguistically, with Arabic. A more recent suggestion has been that the choice of language was determined by a level of register. Where in the dominant culture a prestige register was employed, such as in the case of Classical Arabic poetry, then Hebrew would replace it. On the other hand, where a Middle Arabic register was used, such as in scientific writings, then Judaeo-Arabic was correspondingly employed.[4]

In addition to these considerations, two further factors suggest a certain reticence on the part of the Jews towards the dominant culture. While it is true that Arabic eventually permeated all areas of Jewish literary expression, penetrating into the most sacred of sectors, this process of acculturation was relatively slow, for it was not until the third/ninth century that the first Judaeo-Arabic writings of any significance emerged. This may be due to the fact that the principal centres of Jewish learning, such as the great academy of Sura in southern Iraq and the lesser academy of Pumpeditha (Anbār), were situated in the Aramaic-speaking countryside where Arabization made slow progress. It was only at the beginning of the fourth/tenth century that both these institutions were transferred to Baghdad. Secondly, prior to its assimilation by Jews, Arabic culture underwent a Hebraization. Despite the existence of Arabic works in Arabic characters, the overwhelming proportion of Arabic works in Hebrew transliteration that have been found in the Cairo Genizah suggest that the majority of Jews were not proficient in the reading and writing of Arabic script. Even the greatest Jewish sage of the Middle Ages, Mūsā b. Maymūn (Moses

[4] Cf. C. Rabin, "Hebrew and Arabic in medieval Jewish philosophy", *A. Altmann Festschrift*, Alabama, 1979, 235–45.

Maimonides), chose to compose his Arabic medical writings, intended for non-Jewish circulation, in Hebrew characters (as found in the Genizah manuscripts T–S Ar. 21.112 and Misc. 34.24). This may not necessarily have been the result of an internal reluctance, but the outcome of the prohibition imposed upon *dhimmīs* by the Muslim environment against the utilization of the Arabic script. Ibn Qayyim al-Jawziyyah (d. 751/1350) states "they must be prevented from learning to write Arabic even for the purpose of engraving their signets".[5] According to some authorities it was forbidden to teach *dhimmīs* Arabic or even to sell them religious or scientific books written in the Arabic script. Even as late as 1044/1634 the bibliophile Jacob Roman, writing to J. Buxtorf of his project to establish an Arabic printing press in Constantinople, states: "But the Arabic cannot be in Arabic characters but Hebrew ones, since we cannot print in Arabic letters in this city, for the Muslims will not hear of it."[6] Indeed it would seem from the episode of Abū Munajjā[7] that the writing of a Qurʾān in Arabic script by a *dhimmī* was punishable by death.[8]

SCOPE

The great bulk of the literary production of the Jews in the Arabic language is religious in character and largely indifferent to aesthetic considerations. Consequently it is difficult to speak of *belles-lettres* in the stricter sense of the term, although works of significant artistic value are not lacking. Likewise, the long literary tradition of the Jews of the Orient had mainly been confined to religious themes of a legislative and homiletical character; contact, however, with the ramified and diversified culture of the new Muslim civilization not only infused such traditional disciplines as theology and religion with a novel spirit of rationalism and systematization, but also created entirely new areas of study, such as philosophy, philology, exegesis, history and science. Although the compositions of Jews in the fields of medicine and astronomy were of considerable significance, their non-confessional character excludes them from the present survey, which will mainly take into account works of Jewish philosophy and theology. For the sake of convenience Judaeo-Arabic works have been classified under the following headings: Theology and philosophy; Philology and exegesis; Legal literature; *Belles-lettres*. The main centres of Jewish learning of this period, Baghdad, al-Qayrawān, Andalusia and later Cairo, proved perhaps

5 *Sharḥ al-shurūṭ al-ʿumariyyah*, ed. S. Ṣāliḥ, Damascus, 1961, 111.

6 Cf. M. Kayserling, "Richelieu, Buxtorf et Jacob Roman", *Revue des Etudes Juives*, VIII, 1884, 93.

7 Ibn Duqmāq, *Description de l'Egypte*, Cairo, 1893, V, 46–7.

8 Knowledge of Arabic or Persian Script could be grounds for forced conversion to Islam. See J. Wolff, *Researches and Missionary Labours*, London, 1835, 177.

to have been the most fruitful, and their contribution to the Jewish heritage has been the most lasting.

THEOLOGY AND PHILOSOPHY

The first outstanding thinker of the Judaeo-Arabic period was Saᶜadyah Gaᵓōn b. Yūsuf al-Fayyūmī (269–331/882–942), who was a significant grammarian, lexicographer, exegete and translator of the Hebrew Bible. Born in Egypt, he journeyed to Baghdad at a mature age, where he became *gaᵓōn* or head of the Academy of Sura. In his theological treatise *Kitāb al-Amānāt* ("Book of Opinions"), he presents the tenets of the Jewish faith in the light of the Muᶜtazilite *kalām*. Although Saᶜadyah is usually considered to be the first Jewish philosopher, it would seem that Jews had already engaged in philosophical activities prior to his time.[9] Among other theologians who made use of *kalām* was his younger contemporary, Dāwūd b. Marwān b. Muqammiṣ (*fl. c.* 300/900), whose philosophical treatise, *ᶜIshrūn maqālāt* ("Twenty Discourses"), dealing with problems of *tawḥīd* and *ᶜadl*, has only partially been preserved.[10] Believed to have returned to Judaism from Christianity, he also wrote a refutation of the Christian faith, *al-Radd ᶜalā ᵓl-Naṣārā*, parts of which have recently been discovered in the Cairo Genizah.

The heterodox sect of Jews known as the Qaraites, against whom Saᶜadyah directed some of his writings, were also deeply influenced by *kalām*. Yaᶜqūb b. Isḥāq al-Qirqisānī (d. *c.* 318/930) wrote a voluminous treatise on legal and theological matters, *Kitāb al-Anwār wa-ᵓl-marāqib*, ("Book of Lights and Look-outs"), which has been published from manuscripts in Arabic characters. Of comparable importance is the Qaraite theologian and polyglot, Abū Yaᶜqūb Yūsuf b. Ibrāhīm al-Baṣīr (fifth/eleventh century) who endeavoured in his treatise *al-Muḥtawī* ("Compendium") to harmonize the dogmas of Qaraism with the principles of *kalām*.[11]

The school of al-Qayrawān is dominated by the figures of Isḥāq b. Sulaymān al-Isrāᵓīlī, physician of ᶜUbaydullāh, founder of the Faṭimid dynasty, and his disciple Dūnash b. Tamīm (second half of fourth/tenth century), and draws its inspiration from neo-Platonic sources such as the pseudo-*Theology of Aristotle*. Unfortunately the Arabic originals of their writings have for the most part been lost, although Isḥāq's works, in the

[9] Cf. F. Rosenthal, "A Jewish philosopher of the tenth century", *Hebrew Union College Annual*, XXI, 1948, 155–73; S. Pines, "A tenth-century philosophical correspondence", *Proceedings of the American Academy for Jewish Research*, XXIV, 1955, 103–36.

[10] Cf. G. Vajda, "La finalité de la création de l'homme selon un théologien juif du IXᵉ siècle", *Oriens*, XV, 1962, 61–85.

[11] Cf. G. Vajda, "La démonstration de l'unité divine d'après Yūsuf al-Baṣīr", *G. Scholem Festschrift*, Jerusalem, 1967, 285–315.

Latin translation of Gerard of Cremona, were very popular, and they were one of the first books of Judaeo-Arabic origin to be printed (at Lyons in AD 1515).[12] A similar destiny was granted to the greatest Judaeo-Arabic neo-Platonist, Sulaymān b. Gabirol (d. *c.* 442/1050), the original of whose *Yanbūᶜ al-ḥayāh*, known to the Latin schoolmen as *Fons vitae*, has survived only in fragments. On the other hand the spiritual and ethical manual of another Andalusian, Baḥya b. Paquda (d. *c.* 463/1070) *al-Hidāyah ilā farāᵓiḍ al-qulūb* ("Guide to Duties of Hearts") has been preserved and published in the Arabic original. While professing an admixture of neo-Platonic and Muᶜtazilite doctrines, the work is profoundly indebted to Ṣūfī pietism. To the Andalusian neo-Platonic school also belongs Abū Hārūn Mūsā b. ᶜEzra (*c.* 447–530/1055–1135), whose philosophical anthology, *Maqālat al-Ḥadīqah* ("Essay of the Garden") has preserved several earlier texts of paramount importance.[13]

Although neo-Platonic themes continue to pervade the system of thought of Ibn ᶜEzra's friend, the foremost Hebrew poet, Abū ᵓl-Ḥasan Yehūdāh ha-Lēvī (d. *c.* 535/1140), the latter is perhaps the most original and independent philosopher writing in Judaeo-Arabic. His book, popularly known as the *Kuzari*, the full title of which is *al-Ḥujjah wa-ᵓl-dalīl fī naṣr al-dīn al-dhalīl* ("Arguments and Proofs on Behalf of the Disparaged Religion"), is an eloquent defence of the Jewish faith presented as a fictitious dialogue between a rabbi and the King of the Khazars. Utilizing the premises and conclusions of philosophy, ha-Lēvī tries to demonstrate the inadequacy of rational speculation.

The theological and philosophical productivity of the Arabic-speaking Jews reached its culmination in the works of Mūsā b. ᶜUbaydullāh b. Maymūn (Maimonides, d. 601/1204 Cairo), who is also the greatest Jewish figure of the medieval period. His *Dalālat al-ḥāᵓirīn* ("Guide for the Perplexed"), based on the tenets of Arabic Aristotelianism, especially as interpreted by al-Fārābī, became a classic and was translated into Hebrew in the author's lifetime by Shĕmūᵓel b. Tibbon. Although the *Guide* became a subject of emulation and commentary for generations to come, Maimonides' own descendants, in contrast to their forbear's rationalistic bent, espoused a decidedly more mystical form of thought, deeply influenced by Ṣufism. Maimonides' own son Abū ᵓl-Munā Abraham b. Mūsā al-Maymūnī (d. 635/1237) composed a voluminous theological and devotional manual

12 Cf. A. Altmann and S. M. Stern, *Isaac Israeli*, Oxford, 1958; G. Vajda, "Nouveaux fragments arabes du commentaire de Dunash b. Tamim sur le 'Livre de la Creation'", *Revue des Etudes Juives*, 1954, 37–61; P. B. Fenton, "Gleanings from Mōšeh ibn 'Ezra's Maqâlat al-Hadîqa", *Sefarad*, XXXVI, 1976, 285–98.

13 Cf. P. B. Fenton, *La Maqāla al-Ḥadīqa de Moise Ibn ᶜEzra, Etudes sur le Judaïsme médiéval*, XII, to appear Leiden, 1992.

entitled *Kifāyat al-ᶜābidīn*, in which he extols the virtues of Ṣūfīs. His son ᶜUbaydullāh also penned a mystical opuscule called *al-Maqālah al-ḥawḍiyyah* ("Treatise of the Pool"), in which he develops the typically Ṣūfī idea that the heart must be cleansed like a pool before it can receive the pure water of gnosis. The last dignitary of the Maimonidean dynasty to hold office, David II b. Joshua (*c.* 736/1335–813/1410) continued this tradition in his *al-Murshid ilā al-Tafarrud* ("The Guide to Detachment"), which bears the stamp of the *ishrāqī* Ṣūfī school of Shihāb al-Dīn Yaḥyā al-Suhrawardī (d. 587/1191). Together with his *Maqālat tajrīd al-ḥaqāᵓiq al-naẓariyyah*, in which he combines Jewish and Islamic mysticism, this was probably the last important work of Judaeo-Arabic philosophy, with the exception of Yūsuf b. Waqār of Toledo (*fl.* first half eight/fourteenth century), who, in his *al-Maqālah al-jamīᶜah* ("The Treatise of Conciliation"), makes a similar but more systematic attempt to reconcile Jewish mysticism (*qabbālāh*) and philosophy.[14]

The as yet little explored philosophical compositions of the Yemeni Jews, who continued to write in Middle Arabic until modern times, also produced some noteworthy contributions, the most outstanding of which is perhaps the *Bustān al-ᶜuqūl* ("Garden of Intellects") by Něthanᵓel b. al-Fayyūmī (d. *c.* 545/1150), which betrays the influence of Ismāᶜīlī thought and quotes freely from the Qurᵓān in support of the author's theories.

PHILOLOGY AND EXEGESIS

In addition to his precursory pursuit of philosophy, Saᶜadyah was also among the founders of a new kind of Biblical exegesis involving the systematic study of grammar and lexicography. His works in this field, often composed as a sequel to the Qaraites' intensive investigation of scripture, were later overshadowed by the Hispanic school, and have been only incompletely preserved. Fragments from the Genizah were published as early as 1868 in Odessa by A. Firkowitsch.[15] His successor, Shěmūᵓel b. Ḥōfnī (d. 426/1034) of Baghdad, was also the author of an Arabic translation and commentary on the Pentateuch.[16] The purpose of Ibn Ḥōfnī's work too, was partly to counteract the Qaraites who made important contributions in this field. Of particular importance are Sulaymān b. Ruḥaym (fourth/tenth century) who composed several Biblical

[14] Cf. G. Vajda, *Recherches sur la philosophie et la Kabbale dans la Pensée Juive du Moyen Age*, Paris, 1962, 116–297.

[15] The most important publication is the *ᵓEgrōn, Kitāb Uṣūl al-shiᶜr al-ᶜibrānī*, ed. N. Allony, Jerusalem, 1969, where further bibliography is given.

[16] First published in Arabic characters by I. Israelsohn, St Petersburg, 1886; 2nd edn in Hebrew characters, A. Greenbaum, Jerusalem, 1980.

commentaries, of which the original Arabic has been preserved, and his prolific contemporary, Abū ᶜAlī Ḥasan b. ᶜAlī al-Baṣrī, known in Hebrew as Yefet b. ᶜAlī, who translated the entire twenty-four books of scripture into Arabic and commented on them.[17] The Jerusalem school of Qaraites likewise produced a number of significant grammarians and lexicographers, the most outstanding of whom was Abū Sulaymān Dāwūd b. Ibrāhīm al-Fāsī (fourth/tenth century), author of the Biblical dictionary *Jāmiᶜ al-alfāẓ*. Among the early works of this discipline composed in the West was the *Risālah* of Yehūdāh b. Quraysh of Tāhart, in which he urges the Jews of Fez to study Aramaic as well as Arabic in order to gain a deeper understanding of scripture.

Surprisingly, it was not until the end of the fourth/tenth century that the true nature of the triliteral Hebrew root was recognized, thus inaugurating a new era in the history of Hebrew philology. The tardiness with which this realization came about was perhaps due to the grammarians' intimacy with the Hebrew language, which consequently obscured their perspective, or it may alternatively have been due to their conviction that Hebrew had a specific genius distinct from Arabic, their main model of emulation.

Among the distinguished series of Hispanic grammarians, two names are particularly prominent, those of Abū Zakariyyāʾ Yaḥyā b. Dāwūd b. Ḥayyūj (d. beginning of fourth/eleventh century) who elaborated on the triliteral theory, and his disciple Abū ʾl-Walīd Marwān Yōnah b. Janāḥ, who wrote an Arabic grammar and lexicon of Biblical Hebrew. Mention may also be made of Abū Ibrāhīm Isḥāq b. Barūn (d. 495/1100) who wrote a dissertation on comparative Arabic and Hebrew philology.[18]

The quantity of the equally brilliant exegetical achievements of the Hispanic school that has survived is less conspicuous. Isḥāq b. Yehūdāh b. Ghiyāth's (d. 482/1089) commentary on Ecclesiastes betrays a marked neo-Platonic leaning, whereas the surviving works of both Mōsheh b. Gikatilla and Abū Zakariyyāʾ Yaḥyā Yehūdāh b. Balᶜam (fifth/eleventh century) show a predilection for grammatical analysis.

In the East, Abū ʾl-Munā Abraham, already referred to, also composed a lengthy commentary on Genesis and Exodus wherein he interprets certain aspects of the Biblical narrative in terms of Ṣūfī ethics. One of the last great exegetes of the Orient and, curiously, one of the first to be resuscitated by modern scholarship, was Tanḥūm b. Yōsēf Yerūshalmī (d. *c.* 650/1250), who composed lexicographical and exegetical observations on several Biblical texts as well as compiling a dictionary of Maimonides' *Mishneh Tōrāh*.[19]

[17] Some of his works were edited in the nineteenth century by J. J. L. Bargès in Paris.

[18] Cf. P. Wechter, *Ibn Barūn's Arabic Works on Hebrew Grammar and Lexicography*, Philadelphia, 1964.

[19] Partially published by B. Toledano: *al-Murshid al-Kāfī*, Tel Aviv, 1961.

LEGAL LITERATURE

One of the oldest disciplines of Jewish literature, legal writings, through their contact with Islamic culture, developed a tendency towards codification. Notwithstanding their purely Jewish concern, numerous works dealing with various aspects of Jewish ritual, such as legal manuals, liturgical treatises, *responsa* and Talmudical commentaries, were composed in Arabic. Here too Saᶜadyah laid the foundations amongst other writings with his recension of the Jewish prayer book annotated with Arabic rubrics. Ḥefeṣ b. Yaṣliaḥ (d. sixth/twelfth century), native it seems of al-Qayrawān, wrote a detailed disquisition on the 613 precepts of the Jewish law entitled *Kitāb al-Sharāʾiᶜ* ("Book of Laws").[20] Also from al-Qayrawān was Nissīm b. Yaᶜaqōb b. Shāhīn (*c.* 380–450/990–1060), portions of whose Arabic commentary on the Talmud have come down to us.[21] The most authoritative commentary on the Mishnah is that of Maimonides, originally written in Arabic, as were his numerous *responsa*, of which several autographs have been discovered in the Cairo Genizah.[22]

The output of legal writings in Qaraite circles was quite considerable. Worthy of note are al-Qirqisānī's *Kitāb al-Anwār*, referred to above, and Yūsuf al-Baṣīr's ritual code, *Kitāb al-Istibṣār* ("Book of Clarification"), finished in 428/1036, which has not yet been studied or published.

BELLES-LETTRES

Historical and geographical works are virtually unknown in Judaeo-Arabic, and since poetry, narrative and poetical prose were almost exclusively written in Hebrew, few Judaeo-Arabic writings can be qualified as artistic compositions in the strict sense of the term. Even those that come close to this description, such as Ibn Shāhīn's collection of edifying tales, *Kitāb al-Faraj baᶜda al-shiddah*,[23] had theological overtones. Indeed the purpose of this latter work was to discourage Jews from reading Muslim works of a similar vein, by providing them with a Jewish alternative that encouraged at the same time faith in a divine justice.

A unique representative of the *adab* genre, the *Kitāb al-Muḥāḍarah wa-ʾl-mudhākarah*, was penned by the foremost Hebrew poet of Spain, Mōsheh b. ᶜEzra. The author discusses the history and art of Hebrew poetry, displaying an uncommon appreciation of the literary and stylistic beauty of

[20] Partially published by B. Halper: *Book of Precepts*, Philadelphia, 1915.

[21] Cf. S. Abramson, R. *Nissim Gaon Libelli Quinque*, Jerusalem, 1965.

[22] *Commentary on the Mishnah*, ed. with a Hebrew trans. by Y. Qāfiḥ, Jerusalem, 1963–8; *Responsa*, ed. A. Freimann and J. Blau, Jerusalem, 1957–86.

[23] Ed. J. Obermann, *The Arabic Original of Ibn Shahin's Book of Comfort*, New Haven, 1933; published in Arabic characters and reviewed by D. H. Baneth in *Kirjath Sefer*, XI, 350–7.

the Bible. Although more philosophical in nature, the sequel to this work, the *Maqālat al-Ḥadīqah fī maᶜānī ᵓl-majāz wa-ᵓl-ḥaqīqah* ("Garden of Metaphorical and Literal Meaning"), as its title suggests, is also devoted to the question of rhetoric. When viewed in the light of the Shuᶜūbiyyah trends in Andalusia, the literary appraisal of scripture, developed in these two works, besides their didactic content, represents a Jewish reaction to the doctrine of the inimitable literary supremacy of the Qurᵓān as upheld by Muslim theology.

ARABIC IN HEBREW CHARACTERS

Although beyond the scope of Judaeo-Arabic as defined above, the vast volume of Arabic literature copied into Hebrew characters warrants at least a brief description. The extent of this literature, which has not been fully evaluated,[24] is of considerable significance not only as a register of the Arabic cultural influence on Judaism, but also because the copies of Arabic texts in Hebrew letters, when they do not represent the only surviving copies of primary works, often preserve superior readings owing to the fact that the Hebrew character is less prone to consonantal ambiguity than unpointed Arabic.

These include a number of Arabic translations of classical works, unknown in Arabic transmission, such as the longer version of the pseudo-*Theology of Aristotle*, preserved in several Genizah manuscripts,[25] as well as philosophical and scientific texts of the Muslim period which have otherwise been lost.[26] As the practice of medicine was widespread amongst the Jews, this science is particularly well represented in Hebrew-letter versions. Among those not recorded by M. Steinschneider, which have not been preserved in Arabic characters, are Muẓaffar al-Dīn al-Baᶜlabakkī's (*fl.* 630/1232) *Mufarriḥ al-nafs* (Genizah MS, Cambridge Or. 1035) and Hibatullāh b. Jumayᶜ's (d. 594/1198) history of medicine *al-Risālah al-Ṣalāḥiyyah* (MS Fenton, JA5). Curiously too there exists a Muslim commentary on Maimonides' Hebrew code, the *Mishneh Tōrāh*, composed by a Muslim, ᶜAlāᵓ al-Dīn al-Muwaqqit, preserved in Hebrew characters.[27] An interesting

24 A considerable amount of material, especially in the Genizah, has come to light since M. Steinschneider's "Manoscritti arabici in caratteri ebraici", *Bollettino Italiano degli Studi Orientali*, NS, 1877, 65–79, 82–7, 128–34, 333–8, and "Schriften der Araber in hebräischen Handschriften", *Zeitschrift der Deutschen Morgenländischen Gesellschaft*, XLVII, 1893, 335–84.

25 P. B. Fenton, "The Arabic and Hebrew versions of the *Theology of Aristotle*" in J. Kraye, W. Ryan and C. Schmitt (eds.), *Pseudo-Aristotle in the Middle Ages*, London, 1986, 241–64.

26 The well-known *Calendar of Cordova*, ed. R. Dozy, 1873, was also based on a MS in Hebrew characters.

27 British Library, Add. 27.294, described by G. Margoliouth in "A Muhammadan commentary on Maimonides' Mishneh Torah", *Jewish Quarterly Review*, XIII, 1901, 488–507, and E. Strauss, *The Jews in Egypt and Syria*, Jerusalem, 1944, I, 353–6 (in Hebrew).

parallel to this phenomenon is afforded by the existence of an Arabic translation of a Hebrew chronicle, the *Sefer ha-yūḥasīn*[28] by Abraham Zacuto (d. Damascus? *c.* 921/1515).

As a bibliographical corollary to this field of study, mention may be made of the several Hebrew translations of Arabic works of which the originals are at present lost. Until this century, certain works of the foremost Muslim philosophers, such as al-Fārābī, al-Ghazālī, Ibn Bājjah and al-Baṭalyawsī, were only known, at least in published form, by their Hebrew versions. An important neo-Platonic source, of which a Hebrew version only has been preserved, is the pseudo-Empedocles, *Book of Five Substances*.[29] Indeed, as the Jews were prominently involved in the translation of Arabic works into Hebrew and Latin, it could be advantageous to speculate in the interest of textual criticism whether these translations were made from copies of Arabic works made in Hebrew characters.[30] Many of the foremost classics of Judaeo-Arabic literature were translated into Hebrew and some have exercised a lasting influence right down to modern times. This process was already initiated in the fifth/eleventh century with the school of Tobias b. Mōsheh, who translated important Qaraite texts for the benefit of the non-Arabic reading sectarians of Byzantium. Likewise the Ibn Tibbon dynasty (southern France, sixth-seventh/twelfth-thirteenth centuries) made translations of Judaeo-Arabic works for the benefit of French Jews. Later translations were primarily the consequence of a decline in the command of classical Judaeo-Arabic and also a cultural shift towards an increased use of Hebrew, mainly propagated by the Spanish exiles. Finally, there are even instances of Judaeo-Arabic works being "translated" into vernacular Arabic, sometimes curiously enough from Hebrew versions, for example, the "translation" of Saᶜadyah's version of the Pentateuch into vernacular Arabic by Issakhar b. Sūsan in the tenth/sixteenth century,[31] and the translation into "Berber" (i.e. vulgar Arabic) of Baḥya b. Paquda's *Hidāyah ilā farāʾiḍ al-qulūb* by Issakhar Sitruk.[32] We may also note *Tolĕdōt Yaᶜaqōb Yōsēf* (Jerba, 1954), a rendition into vulgar Arabic of Ibn Tibbon's translation of Maimonides' *Thamānī fuṣūl*, by the last of the Judaeo-Arabic Mohicans, Yūsuf Renassia (d. 1964), Rabbi of Constantine.[33]

28 MS Leiden, cod. Ar. 1499 (2).

29 Ed. D. Kaufmann, *Studien über Salomon Ibn Gabirol*, Budapest, 1899, 1–63.

30 E.g. Nicolaus Praepositus' *Antidotarium*; cf. Steinschneider, "An introduction to the Arabic literature of the Jews", *Jewish Quarterly Review*, XII, 1900, 500–1.

31 Cf. MS Sassoon 159, *Catalogue*, I, 63.

32 Jerba, 1919.

33 Yosef Renassia de Constantine, *Commentaire du Perek de Maimonide avec les 8 chapitres . . . traduits en Judaeo-Arabe*, Jerba, 1954.

THE STUDY OF JUDAEO-ARABIC LITERATURE

Though it is true that the scientific study of Judaeo-Arabic literature was founded by the indefatigable efforts of Moritz Steinschneider (1816–1907) who, in 1845, at the time of the great works entitled *bibliothecae*, conceived of a *Bibliotheca Arabico-Judaica* (finally published in 1902), the great bibliographer did have some noteworthy predecessors. To be sure, knowledge of and interest in Arabic works had never ceased among oriental Jewry, who were still copying and composing Judaeo-Arabic works at the end of the ninth/fifteenth century. One of the last prolific copyists and authors of the East was Saʿadyah b. Dāwūd al-ʿAdanī (active 850–90/1446–85). Symptomatically his *Madkhal al-tashwīq li-ʾl-ghāfilīn* was translated into Hebrew in the nineteenth century by Menasheh Sithōn (d. 1876) of Aleppo. The first Judaeo-Arabic printed work, Saʿadyah Gaʾon's Arabic version of the Pentateuch, appeared in Hebrew characters in the Polyglot Pentateuch of Constantinople in 953/1546. Bibliographers have failed to recognize that this was in fact the first Arabic work to have been printed in the East. This version was subsequently transcribed into Arabic characters and used in the Paris Polyglot (1645) by Gabriel Sionita (1577–1648), and later by Edward Pococke (1604–91) in the Walton Polyglot (London, 1657). Pococke's interest in the Arabic writings of the Jews had no doubt been aroused by William Bedwell (1561–1632) of Tottenham, a pioneer of Arabic studies in modern England, and later, while serving as Anglican chaplain to the English merchants in Aleppo, Pococke made a special effort to acquire the Judaeo-Arabic manuscripts which now form part of the extensive holdings of the Bodleian Library, Oxford. Furthermore the same scholar was also responsible for the first printing of a Judaeo-Arabic work in the West, an annotated selection from a manuscript acquired in Aleppo, and now known to be an autograph of Maimonides' Arabic commentary on the *Mishnah*, entitled *Porta Mosis* (Oxford, 1655). This was incidentally also the first work printed in Hebrew characters at Oxford, if earlier transcriptions of Arabic into Hebrew characters are discounted. Pococke's publications of Arabic may have been inspired by the scholarly collector Jacob Roman, whom he had befriended during his stay in the East (1637–41),[34] and who had conceived a similar project in 1634 to print the works of Maimonides in Judaeo-Arabic and Latin in Constantinople.[35] Pococke's collection generated much interest, and Oxford henceforth became an important centre for a host of subsequent scholars whose interests, favoured by post-Reformation trends, were primarily in the grammatical and exegetical works composed by the Jews in

[34] L. Twells, *Life of Dr E. Pococke*, London, 1816, 46.

[35] See above, 465.

the Arabic tongue. The French orientalist Jean Gagnier (1670–1740), later to become professor of Arabic at Oxford, prepared an edition of Ibn Ḥayyūj's treatise on punctuation.[36] German scholars, too, made the pilgrimage to Oxford, such as H. Paulus (1761–1851), who published Saᶜadyah's version of Isaiah in Arabic characters from an Oxford manuscript (Jena, 1790). The following year, Christian Friedrich Schnurrer (1724–1822), author of the famous *Bibliotheca arabica auctam nunc atque integram*,[37] published part of Tanḥūm Yerūshalmī's commentary on Judges at Tübingen, which renewed the interest in this late exegete initiated by Pococke, and was later pursued by Th. Haarbrücker (commentary on Samuel, Halle, 1842), W. Cureton (commentary on Lamentations, London, 1843) and S. Munk (commentary on Habakkuk, Paris, 1843). It must not be forgotten that the oriental manuscript collections of Europe were still very modest and that interest in Tanḥūm was prompted less by his intrinsic value as a late eclectic writer, than by the fact that he was one of the rare Judaeo-Arabic authors whose works were available at that time in the West.

Solomon Munk (1803–67), a French orientalist of Prussian origin, must be considered together with Steinschneider as among the foremost promoters of Judaeo-Arabic studies. His contributions on Judaeo-Arabic lexicographers and philologists,[38] as well as his monumental edition of the Arabic original of Maimonides' *Guide for the Perplexed* (Paris, 1856–66, 400 years after the first printing of Ibn Tibbon's Hebrew version in Rome), completed when Munk was already totally blind, are significant milestones. His work was continued by Joseph Derenbourg (1811–95) who undertook the edition of Saᶜadyah's exegetical works as well as the grammatical writings of Ibn Janāḥ,[39] complementing the dictionary by the same author edited earlier by the Oxford orientalist and noted Judaeo-Arabist A. Neubauer (1837–1901).

Noteworthy amongst those who also worked in Oxford was the Polish scholar B. Goldberg (1800–84), who collaborated with J. J. L. Bargès (well known for his publication of some works of Yefet b. ᶜAlī the Qaraite) on the edition of Ibn Quraysh's *Risālah* (Paris, 1857).

The second generation of the "Science of Judaism" included Ignaz Goldziher (1850–1921), who ever since his doctoral dissertation devoted to Tanḥūm Yerūshalmī made important contributions to Judaeo-Arabic literature. The historical school founded by H. Graetz (1817–91) produced

36 See *Biographie Universelle*, Paris, xv, 1856, 361–2. In 1727 Gagnier published a specimen of Saᶜadyah's *Kitāb al-Amānāt* in Arabic with a Latin translation.

37 Halle, 1811.

38 "Notice sur Joseph ben Jehouda", *Journal Asiatique*, xiv, 1842, 1–70; "Notice sur Abou ʾl-Walid Merwan ibn Djana'h", *Journal Asiatique*, xvi, 1850, 1–427.

39 *Oeuvres complètes de* R. *Saadia ben Iosef al-Fayyoumi*, Paris, 1893–1900; *Opuscules et traités d' Abou ʾl-Walid Merwan Ibn Djanah*, Paris, 1880.

a number of outstanding Judaeo-Arabic scholars, among them being W. Bacher (1850–1913), who worked mainly on grammatical texts, A. Harkavy (1835–1919) and S. Poznanski (1864–1921), who dealt with Geonic and exegetical material. Among the pupils of the great orientalist Theodor Nöldeke of the University of Strassburg, three at least devoted their efforts to the furtherance of Judaeo-Arabic studies: I. Friedländer (1876–1920), A. S. Yahuda (1877–1951), a Jew of Baghdadi origin, and H. Hirschfeld (1854–1934). The latter was to pioneer the investigation of the Judaeo-Arabic literary texts in the Cairo Genizah, brought to Cambridge by Solomon Schechter in 1896.

Research into the Genizah collections of England, Russia and later, America, was to open up a new era in Judaeo-Arabic studies. While P. Kokowzow (1861–1942) and A. Borisov (1903–42) collated the grammatical and philosophical writings of the Leningrad Genizah, collected by the Qaraite scholar A. Firkowitsch and now virtually inaccessible to western scholars, J. Mann (1888–1940) worked on the documentary material, mainly in Cambridge, paving the way for the modern school of S. D. Goitein.

In his research on Judaeo-Arabic philology, S. Skoss (1884–1953) also exploited the grammatical writings preserved in the Genizah. His work has been carried on by present-day scholars such as S. Abramson, N. Allony and M. Zucker. Bordering on the field of Genizah research L. Nemoy and A. S. Halkin have been prominent in the editing of major Judaeo-Arabic texts, whereas the Jerusalem school established by D. H. Baneth (1893–1973) and his pupil J. Blau has laid the scientific basis for the philological study of these texts. The industrious Yemeni scholar, Y. Qāfiḥ, is continuing to edit or re-edit and translate into modern Hebrew several classical Judaeo-Arabic texts, while his compatriot Y. Raṣābī has made important contributions to the bibliography of Yemeni Judaeo-Arabic literature. Of late the foremost master of Judaeo-Arabic philosophical literature has been the French scholar G. Vajda (1908–81).

CONCLUSION

Despite the broadening interest in Judaeo-Arabic studies in recent decades, especially in the wake of the dissolution of a Jewish presence in Arab lands, much primary research remains to be done, mainly in the editing and exploiting of hitherto unpublished yet prominent texts. The possibilities of research afforded by the mass of Arabic writings harboured by the Cairo Genizah appear unlimited. There remain many uncatalogued collections of material, and the harvest of Arabic Bible translations and exegetical texts promises to be particularly abundant. Progress in this respect is hindered by the refusal of the Soviet authorities to make available the considerable treasures of Judaeo-Arabic literature to be found in the Leningrad collections. On the other hand, little progress has been made in research into the sizeable literary output of Yemeni Jewry, much of which still remains in manuscript.[40] Indeed even some of the important works mentioned by Skoss over twenty-five years ago in his proposed programme of further studies in Judaeo-Arabic literature have neither been published nor adequately investigated.[41] It is only when this task has been achieved that a proper appraisal can be attempted of the important status Judaeo-Arabic literature deserves, both as a reflection and a repository of the wider sphere of Arabic letters.

[40] Some philosophical texts have been published by Y. Qāfiḥ in *Sefunot*, XVI, 1980; others have been pointed out by F. Rosenthal in "From Arabic books and manuscripts V; a one-volume library of Arabic philosophical and scientific texts in Istanbul", *Journal of the American Oriental Society*, LXXV, 1955. The Yemeni Jews also composed some poetry in Arabic: cf. W. Bacher, *Die Hebräische und Arabische Poesie der Juden Jemens*, Budapest, 1910.

[41] S. Skoss, "Suggestions for further studies in Judaeo-Arabic literature" in S. Löwinger, J. Somogyi and A. Scheiber (eds.), *I. Goldziher Memorial*, II, Jerusalem, 1958, 42–9.

CHAPTER 28

THE TRANSLATION OF GREEK MATERIALS INTO ARABIC

The Arabic translation movement begins among non-Arabs, non-Muslims, neo-Muslims or heretical Muslims, as one phase of a much larger process at the interface between cultures. The Greek to Syriac translating which preceded and accompanied the translation of Greek works into Arabic is another phase of the same larger process.[1] A salient aspect of this great meeting of eastern and western civilizations is the Hellenization of Islam. For all the centres of intellectual activity in western Asia during the formative period of Islamic civilization – the surviving Christian centres of medical, logical, historical and Biblical learning at Edessa, Nisibin, and Qinnasrīn, the Talmudic academies of Sura and Pumpeditha, the medical centre of Jundīshāpūr, the pagan astronomical and astrological centre at Ḥarrān, the fire temples of Magian Persia, the Buddhist centres of Balkh, and the Indian observatories of Ujjain[2] – exhibit traditions of learning centuries old and deeply imbued with the spirit of Hellenism and with detailed knowledge of the Greek sciences and arts, often studied in the original texts, or (for us even more important) in translation or adaptation.

The new Islamic civilization which presided over the dissolution of the Sasanid Persian empire and effectively sealed the "lower tier" of former Byzantine provinces against Byzantine political control, which absorbed large numbers of Jewish, Christian, pagan and Magian converts and imposed the terms for coexistence with the unconverted, was not and by the very nature of its success could not be so radically creative or destructive as to exclude all that it found in the new-won lands. The religion at the core of that civilization was consciously akin to Judaism and Christianity in their Hellenized phases and from the beginning had assimilated what was amenable to it and rejected only what it could not absorb. Correspondingly, with translation from the Greek we find tremendous openness in the early centuries of Islam, only later followed by a gradual closing of the floodgates of Greek influence. This openness is neither passive nor undirected but is

[1] See *CHALUP*, ch. 22.

[2] See De Lacy O'Leary, *How Greek Science Passed to the Arabs*, London, 1948, 105, 150.

motivated from the start by an active and witting search for solutions to pragmatic problems.

Beyond the Greek arts and sciences, in poetry, history, fiction and drama, the Greek materials enter more haphazardly. The influences become more complex and subtle than in technical and scientific fields. Not that the Arabic writers were incapable, but because the works, even if translated, were of indirect application to the concrete problems Arabic writers confronted. As the content of Islam gradually defined itself, there was reaction as well as selection. But by the time it was possible clearly to discern the underlying premises of Greek thought and contrast them with a coherent body of Islamic ideas, the movement was completed and the mark had been made: what had been sought in the Greek canon had been made over into Arabic, and what was assimilable – not without struggle, but all the more decisively for that – had become constitutive in the new Islamic identity.

The cosmopolitan character of the movements that fostered knowledge of Greek sciences is pronounced under the early ʿAbbasids, who regarded the achievement of a certain form of cultural integration under their Islamic banner as a central mission of the dynasty. The increasingly systematic sponsorship of translation from the Greek during these reigns reflects the policy of the monarchs and their viziers to adopt what they saw as the most useful elements of the pre-Muslim substrate cultures as a matter of expediency or even urgency.

When al-Manṣūr (reigned 136–58/754–75) laid the foundations of Baghdad in 146/762, he was attended by two astrologers, Nawbakht (d. *c.* 160/776–7) and Māshāʾallāh (d. *c.* 200/815), a Persian (former Zoroastrian) and a Jew from Balkh. Nawbakht, a translator from Pahlavi, wrote works on astrology and related subjects. Māshāʾallāh (Albumasar) wrote on astral "sympathies". Their task was to plan the city to optimize such influences. Great care was taken in selecting the hour for the deposition of the foundation stone. Al-Manṣūr felt no qualms in using sciences of non-Arab origin and pagan premises. His vizier, Khālid b. Barmak, came from a line of Buddhist abbots of Balkh who became Zoroastrians not long before the Muslim conquest. As Muslims, the Barmakids were ministers, commanders, governors – virtual creators of the ʿAbbasid vizierate. Their power reached its acme in the reign of Hārūn al-Rashīd before their great purge in 187/803. The influence was a Hellenizing one; for the family had extensive knowledge of what Greek civilization had to offer. In Umayyad times the translating and adapting of Greek works had been sporadic and of no great quality or intellectual penetration. Under the early ʿAbbasids translation became a regular state activity. Manuscripts were sought out.

Free adaptation gave way to commentary. Objective standards and philological methods came to govern the translation procedure. Within a single lifetime evolving canons of accuracy and clarity rendered obsolete the work of several generations of earlier translators. A vast amount of new matter was translated, no longer for purely *ad hoc* needs, but sometimes in a conscious effort to complete an author's canon, or support the growth of a science – not for praxis, but for comprehension, as a prelude to original work.

One tradition has it that the *Siddhānta* (an astronomical treatise and tables) of the Hindu mathematician Brahmagupta (b. AD 598) was first translated in the reign of al-Manṣūr, but finding the work too difficult for its intended recipients (who had hoped, no doubt, to apply it to astrological and other "practical" calculations), Jaᶜfar al-Barmakī advised Hārūn al-Rashīd to prepare the ground by sponsoring translations of Euclid's *Elements* and Ptolemy's *Megale Syntaxis*, the *Almagest*. The story is dubious, but it gives a sense of the exploratory nature of the first Arabic enquiries into the Greek sciences: the impelling interest in solutions to practical problems, the discovery of unsuspected complexities and the resort to the more comprehensive, logically elementary and conceptually radical founts of Greek science. With Ptolemy came not merely data (which the Arabs – once oriented – could observe for themselves), but the Ptolemaic cosmos, with its *Weltanschauung*, and the conception that science offers models of explanation rather than pictures of the universe. With Euclid came not merely the theses of geometry, which might be rediscovered empirically, but the imperious and compelling ideals of mathematical rigour and system and of science as a pure, theoretical enterprise.[3]

The Greeks themselves were not always universal in their outlook, but (like Egypt to the Greeks) their thought represented a vast widening of horizons for Islam. Greek thought was often most challenging where it was parochial, and so strikingly alien to the notions a Muslim had been raised to take for granted. Al-Ghazālī dated the birth of his critical awareness from his recognition of other cultures.[4] But Greek literature offered more than the exotic: its disciplines promised to replace naive with critical thinking; its ideals might undercut the dogmas of the disciplines themselves. As al-Ghazālī observed, once the glass of unquestioning faith is broken, it cannot be repaired unless melted down and formed anew.

Greek writings were seen initially, in the phrase Richard Walzer was fond of citing, as a treasure house of truth – a body of data to be drawn

3 See B. Spinoza, *Ethica* I, app., ed. C. Gebhardt, II, 79, ll.29ff. As al-Ghazālī urges (see below, n. 45), it is not the content of mathematics but its pretensions to rigour that challenge faith. For models of explanation, see Maimonides, *Guide*, II, 9, 24; cf. II.

4 *Al-Munqidh min al-ḍalāl*, ed. F. Jabre, Beirut, 1959, 10–11; trans. 61.

upon. The official translating institution at Baghdad was called Bayt al-Ḥikmah ("House of Wisdom"); the library from which it grew, Khizānat al-Ḥikmah ("Storehouse of Wisdom").[5] The ideal of learning as an ongoing dialectic pursued for its own sake was at the start just another of the notions which lay in the library amongst the books.

The medical capabilities of Jundīshāpūr, not far distant from Baghdad, were of more immediate interest. Founded by Nestorians fleeing Byzantine persecution in the sixth century AD, the school/hospital, under Sasanid imperial protection, laid the basis for the Islamic *bīmāristān*. The ancient linkage of Greek medicine with the cult of Asclepius had long been cut, and the physicians followed a cosmopolitan tradition joining Greek, Syrian, Persian, Hindu and Jewish scholars in the common enterprise. The Greek texts and Syriac summaries used were prototypes for the work of the Arabic translators. In 148/765 al-Manṣūr invited the director of the complex, Jūrjīs b. Jibrīl b. Bakhtīshūʿ (d. 154/771) to heal his stomach. The treatment was successful and the physician was kept at court for several years, leaving the hospital under his son Bakhtīshūʿ (d. 185/801). The latter in turn served al-Hādī, brother and predecessor of Hārūn al-Rashīd. Even the intrigues which caused his dismissal could not prevent his recall in an emergency in 171/787 and ultimate selection as chief court physician. He, his son Jibrīl (d. 212/828) and grandson Bakhtīshūʿ (d. 256/870) continued in the service of Hārūn, al-Amīn, al-Maʾmūn, al-Muʿtaṣim, al-Wāthiq and al-Mutawakkil. A descendant, Jibrīl b. ʿUbaydullāh b. Bakhtīshūʿ (d. 396/1006) served under the Buwayhids and Marwanids and was wooed bootlessly by the Faṭimids. The powerful Christian house of Bakhtīshūʿ (Pahlavi for "Saved of Jesus") served the ʿAbbasids far longer than the Barmakids and nearly as stormily. Jūrjīs is credited with the authorship of a pandect. Jibrīl, his grandson, was a patron of translators. Abū Saʿīd ʿUbaydullāh b. Jibrīl (d. 450/1058) wrote a medical/philosophical dictionary and a treatise on love. Neither genre existed in Arabic before the penetration of Greek medical thinking.[6] At the earliest stage there was little thought of the effects which delving into the sciences behind the Greek arts might have, but there was curiosity.

THE BEGINNINGS OF THE TRANSLATION MOVEMENT

Muḥammad b. ʿAbdullāh b. al-Muqaffaʿ is listed among the first translators of Greek logical and medical works into Arabic in the time of al-Manṣūr.[7]

[5] See *EI*², "Bayt al-ḥikma", and above, ch. 19.

[6] See *EI*², "Bukhtīshūʿ"; Sarton, *Introduction*, I, 522, 537, 573; Ibn al-Nadīm, *Fibrist*, trans. B. Dodge, 697.

[7] *EI*², "Ibn al-Muḳaffaʿ"; Peters, *Aristotle and the Arabs*, 59.

The more celebrated father, ᶜAbdullāh b. al-Muqaffaᶜ, was a wealthy member of the secretarial class. His well-known translations of Persian works, adaptation from the Pahlavi of the Indian favourite *Kalīlah wa-Dimnah*, and the surviving original works bearing his name reflect his Iranian and Zoroastrian background, and his rationalist bent. The same discontent with narrowness that shines through in the father's translation/adaptations may have impelled the son to look into the logic of Aristotle and the findings of Greek medical science. According to the tradition,[8] his forays into the *Organon* carried him as far as the *Posterior Analytics*. Known to the Arabs as the "Book of Demonstration", this work had reputedly seemed forbidding to the Bishops of Ḥarrān and Edessa. They may not have banned it, but their commentaries and translations do huddle around the earlier parts of the *Organon*. In time the Arabic *Posterior Analytics* would represent the demands of proof, against which all arguments of *kalām* and the sciences must be tested. Repression in the first years of the translation movement might have halted the natural progress to the *Posterior Analytics*, but, in fact, the pressure was in the opposite direction, and the development was irreversible: one cannot unlearn the claims of rigour.

In Umayyad times, Māsarjawayh, a Jewish physician, had translated the *Pandects* of Ahrūn of Alexandria, a Monophysite, probably from Syriac, during the reign of Marwān I (reigned 64–5/683–85). Now Abū Yaḥyā b. al-Baṭrīq (i.e. Patricius, d. *c.* 182–90/798–806) translated Hippocrates and Galen, the *Tetrabiblos* of Ptolemy and other writings at the behest of al-Manṣūr. Hārūn's interest in astronomy again was practical: the rise of the ᶜAbbasids was seen as an epoch signalled in the stars, and the rulers were eager to know their share in history. Māshāʾallāh's *Kitāb al-Duwal wa-ʾl-niḥal* is not the "Book of States and Creeds", but, takes *dawlah* (pl. *duwal*) in its astrologically freighted sense, i.e. "The Book of Epochs and Heritages".[9] Astrology however rests on astronomy. Ibn al-Baṭrīq's translation for al-Manṣūr of Ptolemy on judicial astrology was commented upon by ᶜUmar b. al-Farrukhān al-Ṭabarī and complemented by Muḥammad b. Ibrāhīm b. Ḥabīb al-Fazārī's translation from the Sanskrit of the *Siddhānta* (*Sindhind*).[10] Muḥammad (d. 191/806) was apparently continuing work begun by his father, Ibrāhīm al-Fazārī (d. 161/777), an expert on astronomy and the calendar, and the first Muslim to construct an astrolabe. He is said to have started work on the *Siddhānta* in the middle of the second/eighth century.

8 See Fakhry, *Islamic Philosophy*, 6; Madkour, *L'Organon d'Aristote*, 31–2. Al-Fārābī's claims to primacy in penetrating the *Posterior Analytics* are known to be tendentious – partly from his own testimony. See F. W. Zimmermann, *Al-Fārābī's Commentary on Aristotle's De Interpretatione*, Oxford, 1981, cv–cxii.

9 Cf. *Rasāʾil Ikhwān al-Ṣafāʾ* in Goodman, *The Case of the Animals vs. Man*, 5–7, 30, 72–5, 160.

10 Cf. above, ch. 17, 302.

Māshāʾallāh had already written a book on the technique of astrolabe construction. But not until the late third/ninth century, when Isḥāq b. Ḥunayn and Thābit b. Qurrah had published revised versions of the *Almagest* and *Tetrabiblos*, and Yaḥyā b. Manṣūr and Aḥmad b. ʿAbdullāh Ḥabash al-Ḥāsib al-Marwazī had corrected the astronomical tables, was Arabic astronomy soundly grounded. Observations were still being refined in the ninth/fifteenth century under Ulugh Beg.

Hārūn al-Rashīd routinized and enlarged translation activity. The caliph's education under Barmakid influence doubtless contributed to this. Rich manuscript collections were in the booty he won at Amorium and Ankara, and al-Manṣūr acquired Euclid and Greek books on the physical sciences by a diplomatic request to the Byzantine emperor. The library gathered at Baghdad was a reference tool for physicians and astronomers, and large enough to need a librarian. Hārūn appointed a translator of Persian works, al-Faḍl, son of the Nawbakht who had served his grandfather in the founding of Baghdad.[11]

As the recurrent lineages show, the interest in Greek arts and sciences was sufficiently sustained to support a class of specialists; and the materials these experts produced held and enlarged their initial interest and that of their patrons. Thus the movement grew. Yaḥyā b. al-Baṭrīq, whose father had translated for al-Manṣūr, went far beyond his father, working in a team under al-Ḥasan b. Sahl al-Sarakhsī, who had a concerted interest in astrology. Besides such medical works as Hippocrates' *On the Signs of Death* and Galen's *De Theriaca ad Pisonem*, Yaḥyā translated into Arabic Aristotle's *De Caelo et Mundo*, *De Anima*, *Meteorologia*, the nineteen zoological books and a version of Plato's *Timaeus*.[12] Although the last may have been Galen's compendium, and the *De Anima* was probably from Themistius' version, these accessions of major works of Greek speculative philosophy mark a turning-point. The *Timaeus* is the *locus classicus* of Greek cosmological enquiry. Its key thematic sentences, which solve the Greek problem of change (and, in principle, the monotheistic problem of creation) by the bold expedient of distinguishing the intellectual from the sensible realm, are strikingly placed at the beginning of the Arabic translation of Galen's version[13] – more prominently than in the original dialogue, which requires pages of preliminaries before setting forth the famous argument, which Galen highlights like a student text. *De Caelo* bears Aristotle's vigorous

11 O'Leary, *Greek Science*, 151–3. For Hārūn's raids, see Hitti, *History*, 310. For al-Manṣūr and al-Maʾmūn's gathering Euclid and other MSS, see Ibn Khaldūn, *Muqaddimah*, trans. Rosenthal, 115–6.

12 Sarton, *Introduction*, 536; Fakhry, *Islamic Philosophy*, 8–9.

13 *Galeni Compendium Timaei Platonis* in P. Kraus and R. Walzer (eds.), *Corpus Platonicum Medii Aevi. Plato Arabus*, London, 1951, I, 3–4; trans. 36ff.

refutation of the view that the world has a beginning. *De Anima* argues for the view that neither body nor soul, but only the intelligence is immortal. These works presented considerable challenges to the dogmatically inclined. Controversy, for that very reason, rendered access to them imperative.

Yaḥyā b. al-Baṭrīq's Syriac translations apparently included Aristotle's *Historia Animalium* and *Politica*.[14] That he worked with the *Politics* is a tantalizing fact, for it is the only work of Aristotle to the best of our knowledge not translated into Arabic during the great age of translations from the Greek. While searching for the *Politics* for the caliph, Yaḥyā is said to have found the apocryphal *Secretum secretorum* (*Sirr al-asrār*), a medley of folk wisdom and superstitions about diet, physiognomy and many other subjects, which circulated widely throughout the Middle Ages under the false banner of its ascription to Aristotle. The Arabic introduction represents Yaḥyā as the translator of this *mélange* from a Greek original unknown to us, perhaps in fact a Syriac collation from Greek sources.[15] The translators were interested in every sort of useful knowledge; the very distinction between critical and popular thought was among the flotsam brought in with the widening eddy of their interest. Such distinctions were certainly not among the original objects of their enquiry.

What was sought was what was useful, but the concept of the useful was itself becoming enlarged. From one point of view Plato's theory of ideas might prove useful; so could rigorous logic and theoretic knowledge, or Aristotle's speculations on justice and statecraft. Translations were undertaken initially to learn the therapy for a given disease, to solve a practical problem of geometry or engineering, to make available methods by which future events could be predicted or human fortunes made secure, to acquire tools for refuting a theological adversary. But the Greek works bear with them their own context, assumptions, cross references – above all, their own problematic. One work leads on to another. Insensibly but inexorably, pragmatic interest breeds academic expertise, the drive to completeness, of scholarship or system. Whole sciences become the empires to annex – mathematics, logic, medicine, physics, astronomy, metaphysics.

By the end of the second/eighth century support for translating had widened. Physicians, gentleman-scholars and courtiers sponsored translations, and the translators took on disciples, scribes and amanuenses. Bookbinding and paper-making had become important crafts, and the work of the translators met the small but eager market for the preconcerted knowledge that booksellers could dispense. The churches too were active.

[14] Sarton, *Introduction*, 556. [15] Fakhry, *Islamic Philosophy*, 8–9.

Theodore abū Qurrah (*c.* 122–205/740–820),[16] the first Christian author of important works in Arabic, championed the thought of John of Damascus (d. *c.* 131/748) among the pagans, Manichaeans, Jews, Muslims and Ṣabians. As the Arabic translator of Damascene's work and as a polemicist in his own right, he played a yet larger role: his work invites, in fact demands, a Muslim and a Jewish Arabic *kalām*, in much the way that exposure to Aristotle would tempt the speculatively inclined to try their hands at *falsafah*, and as, in fact, two centuries before, exposure to Jewish and Christian scriptures had provoked Muḥammad first to conceive an Arabic *qurʾān*. By the third/ninth century al-Jāḥiẓ could write that every Muslim deems himself a *mutakallim*.

AL-MAʾMŪN AND THE TRANSLATION OF GREEK WORKS

Al-Maʾmūn went far beyond his father in establishing routine support for the translation of Greek works. His famous Bayt al-Ḥikmah, formally instituted at Baghdad in 215/830, sponsored translation as its main activity and employed a regular staff of scholars including the learned Christian Yūḥannā b. Māsawayh (d. 243/857), whose father had served at Jundīshāpūr, and who had been physician to Hārūn and director of the Baghdad *bīmāristān*; al-Ḥajjāj b. Maṭar, translator of Ptolemy and Euclid; Yaḥyā b. al-Baṭrīq; Sahl b. Hārūn and Saʿīd b. Hārūn; the "curator", Salmān of Ḥarrān; a supporting staff of copyists, binders and other skilled workers; and the celebrated brothers known as the Banū Mūsā b. Shākir, whose learning and wealth made them scientists and patrons of translation in their own right.

Compared with the Khizānat al-Ḥikmah or library of Hārūn, al-Maʾmūn's Bayt al-Ḥikmah was a far more ambitious institutional undertaking, patterned more on the example of Jundīshāpūr. The shift in conception is significant: learning is not seen as quite so static and complete as in the previous generation; scholarship is an activity, and the academy is its aegis. The library remains the nucleus, with the Greek texts at its scientific core. But the library is a planned collection. Salmān, a translator of Aristotle and conversant with Pahlavi, was sent with a delegation of scholars to Constantinople for manuscripts. Al-Maʾmūn sought repeatedly but failed to lure away the Byzantine mathematician Leo, head of the imperial university at Constantinople. Investigators from the Bayt al-Ḥikmah set up observatories at Baghdad and near Palmyra. They correctly measured the inclination of the ecliptic at 23° 33′ and accurately calculated the circumference of the earth.

[16] *EI*², "Abū Ḳurra"; Peters, *Allah's Commonwealth*, 118–19.

Besides sponsoring the Bayt al-Ḥikmah, al-Maʾmūn was a patron of philosophers, philologists, Traditionists, jurists, mathematicians, physicians, alchemists and astrologers. Yet we must not confuse the caliph's liberality with liberalism. G. Sarton[17] is surprised that al-Maʾmūn "combined in a remarkable way free thought and intolerance", by supporting Muʿtazilite rationalism and at the same time persecuting anti-Muʿtazilites, but the association of rationalism with liberalism is modern. Al-Maʾmūn's Muʿtazilism had more in common with the school's Kharijite antecedents than with "free thought". What is rationalistic in Muʿtazilism is the belief that human reason is adequate to determine whom it is appropriate for God to condemn. The translation policy was not a purely intellectual programme and would not have been undertaken solely on the basis of such justifications. Al-Maʾmūn's power rested on a complex balance of ethnic, credal, personal and political dynamics. His publishing four treatises on behalf of the Muʿtazilite thesis of the created Qurʾān played a part in the maintenance of that balance.[18] So did his abortive attempt to reunite the Shīʿah and the Sunnīs by declaring the Shīʿī pretender ʿAlī al-Riḍā (d. 203/818) his heir, on the Sunnī grounds that he was the man most fit to be caliph. Al-Maʾmūn appears to have inaugurated his notorious *miḥnah* or "inquisition" in an attempt to restrain traditionalism. The same, it seems, can be said of the programme of translating Greek works. The patronage was pragmatic in motive. Ultimately its political odour harmed the very growth the caliph sought to foster. As F. E. Peters remarks: "The 'foreign sciences' supported and encouraged so assiduously by al-Maʾmūn may have suffered in the end by their association with the Caliph's Shiʿite and Muʿtazilite sympathies."[19]

THĀBIT B. QURRAH

Yet the scope of the heightened translation activity and the fuller articulation of thought it fostered far outran any initial aim of the original sponsors. The Banū Mūsā b. Shākir became rivals to al-Maʾmūn in the quest for manuscripts, sending their own agents to Byzantium. They are said to have spent some 500 gold dinars a month on translation, and used the work to write pioneering Arabic treatises on machines, mathematics, astronomy and theologically freighted topics like the atom and the eternity of the world.[20] Among the translators they patronized were the Ṣabian mathema-

17 *Introduction*, 557–8.

18 See W. M. Watt, *The Formative Period of Islamic Thought*, Edinburgh, 1973, 179.

19 *Allah's Commonwealth*, 169.

20 Sarton, *Introduction*, 560; Ibn al-Nadīm, *Fihrist*, trans. Dodge, 585; Fakhry, *Islamic Philosophy*, 10. For the writings of the Banū Mūsā b. Shākir, see above, ch. 14, 264–6.

tician Thābit b. Qurrah (221–88/836–901) and the great translator/physician Ḥunayn b. Isḥāq.

The Ṣabians, pagan star-worshippers of Ḥarrān, by a genial fiction were identified (in al-Maʾmūn's time) with the Quranic monotheists known as "al-Ṣābiʾah". They were thus deemed "Scripturaries" (*ahl al-kitāb*), subject like Jews and Christians to differential taxation, but not to compulsory Islamization. The Ḥarranian tradition was in fact a surviving vestige of the astral religiosity widely popular in late antiquity. It preserved systematic knowledge of Greek astrology, neo-Pythagoreanism and philosophy. With the Ṣabians of Ḥarrān, as with the Nestorians and Monophysites, philosophy of a certain sort was vital to communal survival. So Thābit did not work in isolation. He founded a school of mathematicians and astrologers continued by his son, two grandsons and a great-grandson. Among other works, they translated Archimedes and Appolonius of Perga, valuable texts for engineering but also for physical theory and geometry. The neo-Pythagorean ontology/number theory developed by the neo-Platonist Nicomachus of Gerasa was well known to Thābit, who produced an Arabic version of his (second century AD) "Introduction to Arithmetic", the *Kitāb al-Madkhal ilā ʿilm al-ʿadad*.[21] Thābit moved on from his post with the Banū Mūsā to serve as astrologer to the caliph al-Muʿtaḍid. His translations from Greek and Syriac included a compendium of medical writings and improved versions of Ptolemy's *Almagest* and Euclid's *Elements*. He commented on Aristotle's *Physics* – the prime source for the analyses of time, motion, causality and matter by which philosophers defended the eternity of the cosmos – and wrote a *Kitāb fī Ṭabāʾiʿ al-kawākib wa-taʾthīrātihā* ("On the Natures and Influences of the Stars"), to give the conceptual backgrounds of the astrological art, whose results were widely sought by monotheists, but whose pagan underpinnings were not fully acknowledged by them.[22] Besides Thābit's numerous works on mathematics and astrology, he wrote a work on ethics, an "Elucidation of the Allegories of Plato's Republic", a work on music, and paraphrases of Aristotelian logical works.[23] All the work is of a piece: for initiates of neo-Pythagorean neo-Platonism mathematicals were the intermediary reality between Platonic forms and particulars. The stars were the linkage between embodied and disembodied being. Ethics and politics were the importation into life of mathematically harmonious relations discovered by logic, exampled in the heavens, and echoed in musical harmonies.

[21] Ed. W. Kutsch, Beirut, 1959; for Thābit's translations, see Hitti, *History*, 314.
[22] See S. M. Stern, "New information about the authors of the 'Epistles of the Sincere Brethren'," *Islamic Studies*, III, 1964, 407, 412–13; cf. Maimonides, *Guide*, III, 29–30.
[23] Fakhry, *Islamic Philosophy*, 17; 168, n. 18.

ḤUNAYN B. ISḤĀQ

Ḥunayn b. Isḥāq al-ʿIbādī[24] is the most significant individual translator and noted by Ibn Khallikān as the most industrious. Son of a Nestorian Arab pharmacist of al-Ḥīrah, Ḥunayn was bilingual in Syriac and Arabic. He studied medicine at Baghdad under Yuḥannā b. Māsawayh of the Bayt al-Ḥikmah, himself a pupil of Jibrīl b. Bakhtīshūʿ and translator of items from the booty manuscripts of Ankara and Amorium. Unable to cope with Ḥunayn's enquiries, Yuḥannā dismissed him. Ḥunayn may have travelled to Byzantium or Alexandria. When he reappeared in Baghdad after more than two years' absence he had mastered Greek. Ibn Māsawayh put him to work as a translator; but he soon left, preferring to work for independent patrons, such as the Banū Mūsā. He became chief physician to the caliph al-Mutawakkil, who is said to have supported a translation institute under Ḥunayn. Exposed to the usual court intrigues, Ḥunayn was imprisoned for some months; his property and library were sequestered, but he regained favour and held his medical post until his death. According to tradition, the cause of the caliph's displeasure was the physician's refusal on religious and Hippocratic grounds to procure a poison. The story itself is the stuff of palace legends. But poisons were among the earliest subjects of interest in the translation repertoire, and a work by Galen on antidotes was among the first Ḥunayn attempted to translate as a youth.

Ḥunayn translated works on medicine, philosophy, astronomy, mathematics and magic. He translated the Septuagint and oversaw translations by his son Isḥāq (d. 289/911), nephew Ḥubaysh b. al-Ḥasan, and disciples ʿĪsā b. Yaḥyā, Yaḥyā b. Hārūn, Stephanus son of Basilius and Mūsā b. Khālid. Since none of these collaborators had Ḥunayn's mastery of Greek, he usually did a primary translation into Syriac or sometimes Arabic. Isḥāq and Ḥubaysh gave their work from the Greek to Ḥunayn for checking. Even before Ibn al-Nadīm works of his disciples were fathered upon Ḥunayn because his son's name is simply the reverse of his own, while Ḥubaysh is orthographically nearly identical to his in Arabic script.

Ḥunayn exercised critical control throughout his career over the output of his disciples, but their work should not be underrated. Ḥubaysh was an important medical translator, and it was Isḥāq, Ḥubaysh and ʿĪsā who took primary responsibility for translating philosophic and mathematical materials, including nearly all of Aristotle. Isḥāq rendered the *Categories*, *Hermeneutics*, *De Generatione et Corruptione*, *Nicomachean Ethics* with Por-

24 Sarton, *Introduction*, 611, 613; Hitti, *History*, 312–3; Fakhry, *Islamic Philosophy*, 13–4; see also above, ch. 19, 344–5.

phyry's commentary, the spurious *De Plantis*, and parts of the *Metaphysics* as well as Plato's *Sophist* and *Timaeus.* He also translated Alexander of Aphrodisias, Porphyry, Themistius, Nemesius of Edessa, Proclus, Euclid, Archimedes, Ptolemy and other Greek thinkers, and wrote on pharmacology and the history of medical ideas.

In Ḥunayn's *Risālah* on his translations of Galen, some 129 Galenic works are listed, of which he names about 100 that he translated personally into Syriac or Arabic. For some he states doubts as to authenticity, based on the ancient sources; some, he confesses, are known to him only by title: he has searched for a work but failed to find it. A few of the works he saw in Greek Ḥunayn found himself without opportunity to translate. From the bibliography of Abū Bakr Muḥammad b. Zakariyyāʾ al-Rāzī,[25] we know that some of Galen's works escaped Ḥunayn's list, perhaps in part because he wrote the *Risālah* while deprived of access to his library, as he complains several times in the course of it.[26] While all of his translations presumably had some patron, Ḥunayn was clearly directing his efforts and those of his collaborators in the immense task of translating Galen systematically. Plainly held useful by its architect, the project was far from *ad hoc*. The works of Galen address whole families of problems, but must be allowed to proceed in their own way, thematically and systematically. Ḥunayn's efforts ensured that Greek answers did not enter Arabic literature without Greek questions. The impact was heightened by the critical standards Ḥunayn set.

As a young man Ḥunayn could impress others by reciting Homer in Greek. But he later saw that his first attempts at translating technical works were faulty; he returned, more experienced, to rework these. Recognizing that earlier translations into Syriac by Sergius of Raʾs al-ʿAyn and Ayyūb of Edessa were flawed, sometimes unintelligible, he redid these as well. As al-Ṣafadī long after pointed out,[27] the old translators tended to proceed word by word. This inevitably led to inaccuracies, as there were not always exact equivalences between Greek and Arabic terms. Often the early workers would simply set down transliterations; their attempts to mimic dead metaphors and preserve Greek syntax made their translations opaque. Ḥunayn recognized the sentence as the unit of meaning and translated *ad sensum*. Yet he overcame the penchant of some early translators for loose

[25] "Fī ʾstidrāk mā baqiya min kutub Jālīnūs mimmā lam yadhkuruh Ḥunayn wa-lā Jālīnūs fī Fihristih" ("On completing the listing of the remaining books of Galen which are not mentioned by Ḥunayn, nor by Galen in his Index"); see Ibn al-Nadīm, *Fibrist* trans. Dodge; *EI*[2], "Djālīnūs", "Ḥunayn".

[26] G. Bergsträsser, *Ḥunayn b. Isḥāq über die syrischen und arabischen Galen-Übersetzungen*, Leipzig, 1925; "Neue Materialen zu Hunain Ibn Ishaq's Galen-Bibliographie", *Abhandlungen für die Kunde des Morgenlandes*, XVII, 2, 1932; M. Meyerhof, "New light on Hunain ibn Ishaq and his period", *Isis*, VIII, 1926.

[27] Quoted by F. Rosenthal in "Galen: *On Medical Experience*", *Isis*, XXXVI, 1945/6, 253; cf. Peters, *Allah's Commonwealth*, 64.

paraphrase and summary. He struggled to create an Arabic and Syriac technical vocabulary. Recognizing the need for good texts, he worked with his colleagues on the collation of a critical text, taking account of variant readings, before beginning to translate, and emending his translations where important variants later turned up. Such methods set the standard for subsequent translators. Except in mathematics, which Ḥunayn never perfectly mastered, his translations are generally the first that did not require alteration for use by later readers.

Besides his work on Galen from his youth until just before his death,[28] Ḥunayn translated Hippocrates and assisted with the *Materia Medica* of Dioscorides, the standard Arabic pharmacopoeia: none of his disciples had his command of the Greek names of herbs and drugs. His decision to specialize in Galen was by no means casual. Galen may not have been the greatest Greek physician, but he was comprehensive, and his clarity had made his works standard texts in Alexandria. Galen's teleological thinking had won him favour among monotheists long before the birth of Islam, and his balance of theory and empiricism made him attractive to medieval physicians who valued originality and openness to clinical experience, but also hankered for a firm conceptual and methodological framework. Galen's eclectic work in philosophy, moreover, aided in integrating medical learning in a broader framework of scientific culture.

The corpus led naturally to philosophic studies: Galen's treatise *On Demonstration*, his work on *Hypothetical Syllogisms*, his *Ethics*, and his paraphrases of Plato's *Sophist*, *Parmenides*, *Cratylus*, *Euthydemus*, *Timaeus*, *Statesman*, *Republic* and *Laws*, his Peripatetic treatise on the unmoved mover, *Introduction to Logic* and work on the *Number of the Syllogisms* were all translated by Ḥunayn, ᶜĪsā or Isḥāq into Syriac or Arabic or both, often for Muḥammad b. Mūsā b. Shākir. Ḥunayn and ᶜĪsā translated a work of Galen's entitled *That the Best Physician should also be a Philosopher*. It was natural to move on to works by Plato, Aristotle and their successors. To Ḥunayn and Isḥāq are ascribed translations, paraphrases, elucidations and abridgements of Plato's *Republic*, Aristotle's *Categories*, *De Interpretatione*, *Analytica*, *Topica*, *Sophistica*, *Rhetorica*, *Physica*, *De Anima*, *Metaphysica*, *De Caelo* and *Magna Moralia*; and from the same school came numerous other translations of Aristotelian and neo-Platonic works.

In his own right, Ḥunayn wrote summaries and outlines, introductions, anthologies, even medical catechisms in the manner of the Syriac Church.

[28] Ḥunayn reports translating a Galenic work poorly from a bad MS into Syriac as a youth. At about forty, with a pupil, he made a critical text, which he retranslated using his new method. Still later he made a new translation for Abū Jaᶜfar Muḥammad b. Mūsā b. Shākir (d. 259/873). His Arabic *De Partibus Artis Medicae*, begun some two months before his death from his own Syriac version, was completed by his son.

There were also works on ophthalmology, and reportedly, a world history. Extant are a treatise on the essential non-physicality of light, a neo-Platonic *topos*,[29] and, in abridged form, a moderate apologetic work directed in part against Islam. Useful to translators was Ḥunayn's *Greek Grammar*, but there is a speculative as well as a practical thrust in a treatise on the tides or on alchemy; and, in writing on the salinity of sea water, or on the rainbow, Ḥunayn exhibits interests in which the speculative side is dominant. All of his works[30] illustrate an acculturation of Greek thought within Arabic literature which goes far beyond praxis. His anthology of philosophical anecdotes bears much of the Hellenistic spirit. The dialogue between Christianity and Islam is conducted via Greek dialectic; and, when a monotheist ophthalmologist seeks the nature of light, he knows that this is a theologically freighted issue and turns to Aristotle and the neo-Platonists, much as his contemporaries sought in Galen and Hippocrates a scientific understanding of the human body and its management and care.

A beneficiary of the first phase of translating activity was the Arab prince Abū Yūsuf Yaᶜqūb b. Isḥāq al-Kindī,[31] called the philosopher of the Arabs. He employed two Christian translators, Astat (Eustathius), who translated for him most of Aristotle's *Metaphysics*, and Ibn Nāᶜimah al-Ḥimṣī, who rendered the enormously influential pseudo-Aristotelian *Theology of Aristotle*.[32] The first original philosophic thinker in Islam, al-Kindī was not radically creative. He had independence of mind. But he knew that Greek materials held a rich experience which a physician or philosopher could little afford to ignore – materials structured into sciences with unexampled authority.

Al-Kindī was asked, or so he says (for the mention of such an enquiry gave occasion for an intimate discourse, dedicatory note and clear statement of a problem, as the *Risālah* evolved from letter to essay) to outline thoughts useful in combating depression. His patron, plainly, thought of metaphysic as a higher physic and hoped for a sort of verbal amulet to "keep constantly before his eyes" and so defeat anxiety and sorrow. The recipient got more than he bargained for. Al-Kindī offered a fair dose of anecdotes and wise sayings, as expected in a consolation, but added a vivid line of argument. Analysis of anxiety and sorrow leads to a rectification of the concept of happiness: anxiety is fear of loss; sorrow is the pain of loss. To free ourselves of these we must disengage from all that can be lost and yearn only for what we can hold without the fear of loss. But all things external can be lost. Only ideas are gained and held without dependence on externals.

[29] *Fī ʾl-Ḍawʾ wa-ḥaqīqatih*, ed. and trans. L. Cheikho, *Mashriq*, II, 1899.
[30] See Fakhry, *Islamic Philosophy*, 12–15. [31] See above, ch. 20.
[32] Fakhry, *Islamic Philosophy*, 17–19.

Like all the materials in the *Risālah fī ʾl-Ḥīlah li-dafʿ al-aḥzān* ("On How to Banish Sorrow") this argument is abstracted from late Greek philosophy.[33] Still the cure is not acquired cheaply. We must look upon our loved ones as already lost if we are not to suffer sharply when we lose them. But further we must adopt an epistemology and ontology like Plato's – positions of consequence for our way of life, but also for our idea of God. Al-Kindī defends his catholicity, adapting Aristotle's acknowledgment of his predecessors and echoing Philo Judaeus (*fl.* AD 39) by applying the sentiment to the insights of pagan philosophers: we should gratefully accept truth, even partial, where we find it – but not passively, for, as Aristotle also said, we must follow where argument leads.[34] The precept is close to al-Kindī's heart. His arguments are painstaking, often overcautious, striving to state each premise and turn. But, as he picks his way through a complex deduction, al-Kindī shows convincingly that it is argument, not authority, that he follows. And he does not follow blindly: almost all the best philosophers held that the divine ideas eternally imply the existence of particulars – thus that the world must be eternal. But al-Kindī adds creation to Aristotle's four kinds of change.

TRANSLATION AFTER ḤUNAYN

The post-Ḥunayn phase in the translation of Greek works begins with Thābit's contemporaries active in the late third/ninth early fourth/tenth centuries, Abū ʿUthmān al-Dimashqī and Qusṭā b. Lūqā. Al-Dimashqī was a Muslim disciple of Ḥunayn's, attached long after his teacher's death to ʿAlī b. ʿĪsā, "the Good Vizier," and assigned by him to the superintendence of the hospitals of Baghdad, Mecca and Medina. Besides medical works he translated Aristotle's *Topics*, *Nicomachean Ethics*, *Physics* IV (time, place, the void), *De Generatione et Corruptione*, Euclid, Porphyry's *Isagoge*, and treatises by Alexander of Aphrodisias on colours, disembodied substances and growth.[35] The *Ethics* now reveals philosophy in full autonomy, seeking the good life and presenting the *summum bonum* as the divine life of the philosopher who directs all personal and public affairs, practical and speculative, by the rule of reason. The ethos is not obviously that of the Bible or the Qurʾān: Aristotle holds that one theft does not make a thief, or one affair an adulterer, but there was a public interested in what philosophy as such had to say about ethics and was prepared to defer questions of whether and how the views of the philosophers squared with scripture.

33 In M. A. Abū Rīdah (ed.), *Rasāʾil al-Kindī al-falsafiyyah*, Cairo, 1950; H. Ritter and R. Walzer, *Studi su al-Kindi*, II, Rome, 1938.

34 See A. L. Ivry, trans., *Al-Kindī's Metaphysics*, New York, 1974, 57ff.

35 See M. Meyerhof, "New Light on Ḥunain Ibn Isḥâq and his period", *Isis*, VIII, 1926, 710; Fakhry, *Islamic Philosophy*, 17–18.

Qusṭā was a Christian, perhaps Greek by birth, as his name (Constans?) suggests. Born in Baalbek (Heliopolis), he earned his bread as a physician and made his name as a medical translator. He excelled in philosophy, astronomy and mathematics. Aristotle, Plutarch, Diophantus, Theodosius, Autolycus, Hypsicles, Aristarchus of Samos and Hero were among the authors he translated freshly or in revision, at which he was a specialist. As a physician and thinker Ibn al-Nadīm rates him in some ways above Ḥunayn. A fine stylist in Greek, Syriac and Arabic, Qusṭā travelled in Byzantine lands, securing works for translation. He wrote on poisons and antidotes, psychology, the atom, politics, logic, history and Greek thought.[36]

Abū Bishr Mattā b. Yūnus, the great Christian logician, founded the last major line of translators. A Greek from Syria, he was a student of al-Quwayrī, a logician–commentator; of al-Marwazī, a Syriac-speaking physician; of one Theophilus; of the Muslim secretary, theologian and physical theorist, Ibn Karnīb; and of a certain Benjamin, perhaps Benjamin al-Nihāwandī, the second founder of Qaraism. Abū Bishr was the teacher of Muḥammad b. Muḥammad al-Fārābī, whom Arabic tradition styles (after Aristotle) "the Second Teacher". Among Abū Bishr's many translations were the commentaries of Alexander of Aphrodisias on Aristotle's *De Caelo*, *De Generatione et Corruptione* and the theologically crucial book *Lambda* of the *Metaphysics* with Alexander of Aphrodisias' commentary. Such works barred later philosophers from making as free as al-Kindī had with the ideas of change and generation. Abū Bishr commented on the *Organon*, including the *Posterior Analytics*,[37] and wrote on the conditional syllogism, the bastion of propositional logic.

The ancient rivalry of propositional and class logic was crucial to the intellectual revolution in which philosophy was to claim dominance over theology, and al-Fārābī would affirm the world's eternity and avow neo-Platonic emanation as the truth behind the scriptural myth of creation. For in the hypothetical syllogistic of the *kalām* any proposition could be entertained. There was no *a priori* basis to exclude anything imaginable. But in the predicate logic of Aristotle certain events (including *ex nihilo* creation) could be ruled out *a priori*, as argued in *Physics* IV, *De Caelo*, and other now classic *loci*.[38]

Abū Zakariyyā᾿ Yaḥyā b. ᶜAdī, a disciple of Mattā, was a Jacobite, west Syrian, Christian. Like his master he was known as a logician; he openly polemicized against the method and theses of the *kalām*, refuting the atomism of the *mutakallimūn*, refining on their doctrine of the unity of God,

36 Fakhry, *Islamic Philosophy*, 15; Sarton, *Introduction*, 602; Ibn al-Nadīm, *Fihrist*, trans. Dodge, 611, 584, 588, 602, 604, 694, 743.

37 Ibn al-Nadīm, *Fihrist*, trans. Dodge, 631, 628, 629; Fakhry, *Islamic Philosophy*, 16.

38 See L. E. Goodman, *RAMBAM*, New York, 1976, 170–4.

clarifying the ideas of infinity and modality, and rejecting *kalām* attempts to reconcile free will with predestination through the (ultimately Stoic) doctrine of moral appropriation (*iktisāb*). Besides the texts on logic long studied in Jacobite circles and the texts relevant to eternalism – *De Generatione et Corruptione*, *Physics* VIII and perhaps the *Metaphysics* – Yaḥyā translated the *Topics*, *Sophistica*, *Laws* and *Poetics*, commenting on the *Topics*, *Physics* VIII and the *Metaphysics* selectively, and *De Generatione et Corruptione* in full.[39]

It is a commonplace that Arabic writers did not understand Aristotle's *Poetics*. If this means they did not derive from it an Aristotelian theory of literature, nothing could be more true. But readers of Arabic in the fourth/tenth century were not seeking a theory of literature. They were seeking a theory of religion. If scripture was not literal truth about creation, revelation and salvation, how should it be understood? The *Topics*, dealing with the varied contexts and intentions of statements, was a natural starting-point for this enquiry; the *Sophistica* was a natural continuation. But the *Poetics* climaxes the search, addressing discourse that is true, not literally, but on a higher plane, symbolically or morally. Seen as a work on logic of a sort, an extension of the *Rhetorica*, which deals with persuasive arguments, the *Poetics* was understood to explicate claims which appeal indirectly, via symbols, to the emotions, and thus do the work of arguments without conceptual articulation. In its own way poetry does more than many arguments can do: it can purge the ethos and instil intentions, when successful, whereas few arguments evoke more than intellectual assent.

Aristotle had sought to fathom how a Sophocles could convey truths emotively. Al-Fārābī saw that a prophet too was a poet who clothed philosophic concepts in images and language. Plato's *Laws* showed how philosophic insights, brought by symbol to the imagination, might be instituted in a society without all men first becoming philosophers. One could suddenly comprehend what Muḥammad and the rest had been about. The best Abū Bakr Muḥammad b. Zakariyyāʾ al-Rāzī had managed with the prophets was to make them out as frauds. Now a moral and spiritual truth was visible philosophically behind all the rhetorical and dialectical arguments, reliance on vivid pictures and threats.

Abū ʿAlī ʿĪsā b. Isḥāq b. Zurʿah (331–99/942–1008) and al-Ḥasan b. Suwar, known as Ibn al-Khammār (330–408/942–1017) were Jacobite members of the school of Yaḥyā b. ʿAdī. Ibn Zurʿah, probably a physician but known as a merchant persecuted for alleged intrigues with Byzantium, rendered from the Syriac Aristotle's *De Generatione Animalium*, *Historia Animalium*, *Metaphysics* (*Lambda*), *Sophistica* and Nicholas of Damascus'

39 See also above, ch. 26.

(first century BC) Five Books on Aristotle's philosophy. He is rated "accurate" by Ibn al-Nadīm and wrote several works marshalling the ideas found in the Greek disciplines.[40] Like Thābit b. Qurrah, Ibn Zurʿah translated some Proclus. But what was for the Ḥarranian an act of piety left unfinished at his death was in the Christian an expression of confidence. The vigorous eternalism and militant polytheism of Proclus were challenges to be met with philosophic candour, not heresies to be feared.

Ibn al-Khammār too translated mainly from the Syriac: the standard first portion of the *Organon* (*Isagoge*, *Categories*, *Hermeneutics*, *Prior Analytics*) in the middle-Platonist recension of Albinus, a work on ethics, and less central works like Aristotle's *Meteorologica* and the *Problems* of Theophrastus. He commented twice on the *Isagoge* and wrote on diabetes, pregnancy and other medical topics, essays on images caused by water vapour (mists, the rainbow, the halo of the moon), treatises on friendship, matter, and the life of the philosopher. He was something of an authority on ancient philosophy, having read Porphyry on the subject in Syriac. He reconciled Christian views with those of the philosophers, and, like al-Fārābī, applied philosophy in interpreting the idea of prophetic revelation and scriptural law.

The last major translator was the Nestorian Abū ʾl-Faraj ʿAbdullāh b. al-Ṭayyib (d. 435/1043), secretary to the Catholicos Elias I and a physician–philosopher under the ʿAḍudids of Baghdad. His works were largely paraphrases and commentaries on the medical, physiological, logical and philosophical works of Hippocrates, Aristotle, Galen and other Greeks. One work addressed the Aristotelian distinction between mind and soul.[41] Three known physicians were his students.

THE END OF THE TRANSLATION MOVEMENT

By the mid-fifth/eleventh century the great translation movement was largely over, although some activity continued for two centuries more. The main phase lasted some 300 years. Even in the West, which generally lagged behind Baghdad,[42] the main interest came in the fourth/tenth century. A new translation of Dioscorides' *Materia Medica* was made in Cordova in 339–40/951 under the Byzantine monk Nicholas, sent to the court of the Umayyad caliph ʿAbd al-Raḥmān III (reigned 300–50/912–61) by Constantine VII – rendering usable the emperor's prior gift of a brilliantly illustrated manuscript of the work. On a much reduced scale and highly dependent on what was done in the eastern Muslim empire, the western

40 Fakhry, *Islamic Philosophy*, 17–18; Ibn al-Nadīm, *Fihrist*, trans. Dodge, 632.

41 *GAL*, I, 635; see also above, ch. 26.

42 See Goodman, *Ibn Tufayl's Hayy Ibn Yaqẓān*, 12–14.

translation activity too was fostered among non-Muslims and non-Arabs. The Jewish vizier, scholar, linguist, physician, diplomat, patron of scholarship and letters and community leader, Ḥasday b. Shaprūṭ (294–365/905–75) over-saw the work on Dioscorides and other such efforts. In the West, the great stream of translations was over by the beginning of the fifth/eleventh century.[43] ʿAbd al-Raḥmān's son, al-Ḥakam II (reigned 350–66/961–76) is said to have gathered a library of some 400,000 volumes, acquired by agents throughout the eastern lands, and he founded twenty-seven schools in Cordova, with scholarships for the indigent. But by now the bulk of the scholarly repertoire was accessible in Arabic.

If we ask why translation ended when it did, we must begin with the fact that there was a reaction within Islam against the rationalism of the Muʿtazilah, particularly against their presumption to know the determinants of God's will. The anti-Muʿtazilite turn of thought and heart gained the upper hand politically during the reign of al-Mutawakkil (reigned 232–47/847–61). Many of the forces that had encouraged translation now militated against it. But while some writers may speak darkly of the forces of reaction, the anti-Muʿtazilite swing – although it did spill over to antipathies against all things Greek – did not by itself halt the translation movement. No mere official policy could be perfectly effective. Al-Maʾmūn's enforced Muʿtazilism certainly had not been. Al-Mutawakkil himself sponsored translations; and in his reign a new school of philosophy and medicine, bearing traditions of Antioch and Alexandria, flourished in Ḥarrān,[44] the school of Thābit b. Qurrah and his disciples, in which Apollonius of Perga and Archimedes were translated and Ḥunayn's rendering of Euclid was improved. Thābit himself was enthusiastically supported by the caliph al-Muʿtaḍid; and his work was carried on, as we have seen, down to the generation of his great-grandson. The most celebrated of Thābit's disciples, the astronomer al-Battānī, was a convert to Islam, but his surnames, al-Ḥarrānī and al-Ṣābiʾ, preserve the memory of his pagan heritage. Important translating continued in the East in respectable volume for nearly 200 years after the accession of al-Mutawakkil.

The notion that translation was halted by religious reaction, moreover, is simplistic, suggesting that there was a pristine, self-conscious, quintessential Islam latent throughout the translation period, knowing itself as the antithesis to Muʿtazilism and to all rationalism, scientific enquiry, practical technology, and even Greek mysticism, Greek ethics, Greek magic and astrology. There was no such religion and cannot have been. For such a trend of thought would require its possessors in their supposed naivety to

[43] See G. F. Hourani, "The early growth of the secular sciences in Andalusia", *Studia Islamica*, XXXII, 2, 1970, 143–56. [44] See Hitti, *History*, 314.

know Greek science and art in detail and to anticipate the impact of its interaction with Islam. The "reaction" was in fact but one aspect of the increasingly complex manifestations of that very interaction. Once the theories of Greek sciences and arguments of Greek philosophers began to be stated and understood in the Islamic world, there were naturally those like Abū Bakr Muḥammad b. Zakariyyāʾ al-Rāzī who grew critical of Islam, others who grew suspicious of the new methods, even to the point of rejecting mathematics, as Abū Ḥāmid al-Ghazālī records,[45] and still others, the vast majority of those who could pretend to learning, who set about reconciling and balancing in diverse ways. Al-Ghazālī himself, often seen as a leader of the anti-Hellenic reaction, was one of those Islamic thinkers whose work, in matter and form, is a product of creative/critical interaction with the materials of Greek literature. He writes, for example, in the introduction to his celebrated *Iḥyāʾ ʿulūm al-dīn* that a precedent for his mode of organizing that work is the tabular format used by Abū ʾl-Ḥasan al-Mukhtār b. ʿAbdūn b. Buṭlān in his highly original *Taqwīm al-Ṣiḥḥah* ("Maintenance of Hygiene"). Ibn Buṭlān[46] helped plan the Mirdasid hospital of Aleppo, sought to regulate Christian worship there, engaged in a famous controversy about Greek medical contributions with the Egyptian Ibn Riḍwān, wrote in Constantinople about the eucharist, planned the hospital of Antioch, and sought (before retiring as a monk) to reform medical treatment throughout Iraq and the environs, preferring "cool" to "hot" therapies. As for al-Ghazālī, neither his philosophic critique of "the philosophers" nor his neo-Platonic construction of Ṣufism would have been possible without mastery of the matter and method of Greek philosophy.[47]

A more informative and less circular answer than the mere label of reaction to our question about the ending of the translation movement might be found in the suggestion that the translators had completed their work. Several strands of evidence converge to confirm this hypothesis: we observe less primary work in the later phases of the movement, much revision and retranslation. Commentaries and supercommentaries continually revert to the same expanding but clearly unified family of issues. A definite corpus of works is uncovered and explored. Greek dramas are not among them. Ḥunayn, who could recite from Homer as a youth, found time to render some 100 works of Galen, many in more than one version; and he

[45] *Munqidh*, ed. Jabre, 20–1; trans. 74–5. [46] See above, ch. 19. 351–3.

[47] See A. J. Wensinck, *La Pensée de Ghazzālī*, Paris, 1940; L. E. Goodman, "Ghazālī's argument from creation", *International Journal of Middle Eastern Studies*, II, 1971, 67–85, 168–88; "Did Ghazālī deny causality?", *Studia Islamica*, XLVII, 1978, 83–120.

translated numerous other authors, but never Homer.[48] We can understand an interest in Themistius, Theophrastus or Proclus, but when Thābit b. Qurrah must translate Epaphroditus' *Commentary on Aristotle's Account of the Halo of the Moon*, while no reader of Greek seeks to open to his contemporaries the poetry of Sappho or Archilochus or the *History* of Thucydides, written, as its author states, for all the ages, we must observe a definite focus in what Arabic literature would acquire from the Greek. Once this interest was met, translation naturally would slow. In Arabic letters from the time of Ibn Sīnā we do not find a thirst for new materials but an endeavour to assimilate, synthesize, and – not only in al-Ghazālī but in Ibn Sīnā himself – to overcome the influence of the Greeks.

For this reason, a full account of the translation movement would properly be complemented by a more extended discussion of the growth and change of Greek ideas after the closing of the Greek book, when Greek themes, problems and methods had taken a life of their own within Arabic literature. The Arabic writers schematized the impact somewhat as follows: first there were the Greek arts and sciences, taken over more or less entire, preserving their form, content, assumptions and techniques – now practised, investigated and advanced in Arabic. Among the Greek arts were medicine, mechanics, alchemy, judicial astrology and magic. Among the Greek sciences were mathematics, logic, epistemology, physics, psychology, metaphysics, ethics, politics and aesthetics, each with its own sub-branches and characteristic Greek style and focus. Second come the effects of Greek translation literature and its ideas, formal and material, upon the Muslim disciplines: *kalām*, *tafsīr* and its hermeneutic principles; *fiqh* and *uṣūl al-fiqh*; *Ḥadīth*; and *taṣawwuf* (Ṣufism). Thirdly, one should explore the thematic and formal impact of Greek translation on Arabic narrative and imaginative writing – poetry, fiction, *adab* or polite letters, history, geography and fantasy, to discover where and how the Arabic writers take up, put down, tie off or twist the Greek thread. Rationalism, mysticism and empiricism are amongst the persistent themes, spiced by a curious blend of traditions which define an interest in secular love (as an alternative to erotic mysticism), held for centuries in a distinctive symbiosis with legal and theological positivism.

48 Theophilus of Edessa did translate some parts of the *Iliad*, but the translation made no impression on Arabic literature and was not preserved. See Hitti, *History*, 311.

CHAPTER 29

DIDACTIC VERSE

Arabic didactic verse (*shiᶜr taᶜlīmī*) aims solely at teaching a particular genre of knowledge. Many Arab critics do not regard it as true poetry, since it is devoid of emotion and imagination, both of which are essential constituents of poetry, besides metre and rhyme. In other words, they consider it as versified prose.

Didactic verse is instructive, adding to one's knowledge and aiming at improving one's morals. It pleases the ear and aids the memory. It is known to go as far back as the dawn of Greek history. In all probability, the Greeks borrowed the idea from the Sumerians, as so much of Greek civilization is traceable to ancient Mesopotamia. But the Arabs were influenced in this, as in so many other cultural aspects, by the Greeks and the Indians, rather than by Mesopotamia. Arabic didactic verse may be categorized under the following headings:

1 Epigrammatic and gnomic verses (i.e. pertaining to maxims or aphorisms) that date back to the time of the Jāhiliyyah, for which Zuhayr b. abī Sulmā, al-Nābighah al-Dhubyānī (d. AD 604) and Labīd b. Rabīᶜah were well known.
2 Fables, parables, songs, riddles, maxims, proverbs, monologues and dialogues, particularly of the ᶜAbbasid era. An example of this kind of literature is the *Dīwān* of Umayyah b. abī ᵓl-Ṣalt (d. *c.* 9/630), whose didactic verses were turned into prose by al-Jāḥiẓ.
3 Theological, medical and grammatical treatises which cover a wide range, for example, the *Alfiyyah* of Jamāl al-Dīn Muḥammad b. Mālik, 1,000 verses in *rajaz* metre to help students to learn by heart the intricacies of Arabic grammar.
4 Verses that are not primarily didactic, but are none the less instructive. Much Arabic verse falls within this category, such as Abū ᵓl-Ṭayyib Aḥmad al-Mutanabbī's odes descriptive of the campaigns of Sayf al-Dawlah.

An outstanding example of didactic poetry is the versification of *Kalīlah wa-Dimnah*, originally translated into Arabic by ᶜAbdullāh b. al-Muqaffaᶜ. It was turned into verse by a number of poets. There is no doubt that the first to do so was Abān b. ʿAbd al-Ḥamīd al-Lāḥiqī (132–200/750–815), who rendered it into 14,000 verses which he presented to Yaḥyā b. Khālid al-Barmakī. It is regrettable that the version is lost save for seventy-six verses preserved by Abū Bakr Muḥammad b. Yaḥyā al-Ṣūlī in his *Kitāb al-Awrāq*. The following lines are typical of this interesting work:

Hādhā kitābu kadhibin wa-miḥnah
Wa-hwa ʾlladhī yudʿā "Kalīlah wa-Dimnah"
Fīhi dalālatun wa-fīhi rushdu
Wa-hwa kitābun waḍaʿat-hu ʾl-Hindu
Fa-waṣafū ādāba kulli ʿālimi
Ḥikāyatan ʿan alsuni ʾl-bahāʾimi
Fa-ʾl-ḥukamāʾu yaʿrifūna faḍlah
Wa-ʾl-sukhafāʾu yashtahūna hazlah
Wa-hwa ʿalā dhāka yasīru ʾl-ḥifẓi
Ladhdhun ʿalā ʾl-lisāni ʿinda ʾl-lafẓi.[1]

This is a book of fiction and tribulations
Known as *Kalīlah and Dimnah*.
In it there is guidance and wisdom.
It is a book written by the Indians,
Wherein they described the manners of scholars
As related by the tongues of wild beasts.
Philosophers uphold its merit,
Light-minded people enjoy its humour.
Meanwhile, it is easy to memorize,
Sweet on the tongue to recite.

It goes on:

Wa-inna man kāna daniyya ʾl-nafsi
Yarḍā mina ʾl-arfaʿi bi-ʾl-akhassi
Ka-mathali ʾl-kalbi ʾl-shaqiyyi ʾl-bāʾisi
Yafraḥu bi-ʾl-ʿaẓmi ʾl-ʿatīqi ʾl-yābisi
Wa-inna ahla ʾl-faḍli lā yurḍī-him
Shayʾun idhā mā kāna lā yuʿnī-him.[2]

And he who is low and mean
Consents to exchange the lofty for the base;
Not unlike the poor wretched dog
Who rejoices at the sight of an old dry bone.
Indeed, people of high merit will not be satisfied
With anything that is not acquired by means strenuous and hard.

Al-Lāḥiqī composed another important didactic poem, the "Poem of fasting and alms-tax". Even its title is versified:

Qaṣīdatu ʾl-ṣiyāmi wa-ʾl-zakāti
Naqalaha Abānu min fami ʾl-ruwāti.

[1] Ṣūlī, *Awrāq*, 1–52. [2] Ibid., 48.

The poem of fasting and alms-tax
Related by Abān from the narrators' mouths.

It opens thus:

Hādhā kitābu ʾl-ṣawmi wa-hwa jāmiʿu
Li-kulli mā qāmat bihi ʾl-sharāʾiʿu
Min dhālika ʾl-munzalu fī ʾl-Qurʾāni
Faḍlan ʿalā man kāna dhā bayāni.[3]

This is the Book of Fasting comprising
All that has been ordained by divine laws,
Including what has been revealed in the Qurʾān,
As well as what is related by eloquent authoritative people.

Apparently the Lāḥiqīs were a family of poets who had a special flair for didactic verse, for Abān al-Lāḥiqī had a son, Ḥamdān by name, who composed an elegant poem (over 100 lines in length) on the art of love, which opens with a reproach to poets and scholars for neglecting such an art:

Mā bālu ahli ʾl-adabi
Minnā wa-ahli ʾl-kutubi?
Qad waḍaʿū ʾl-ādāba
Wa-atbaʿū ʾl-kitāba
Li-kulli fannin daftaru
Munaqqaṭun muḥabbaru
Siwā ʾl-muḥibbīna fa-lam
Yarʿaw lahum ḥaqqa ʾl-dhimam
Fī ʿilmi mā qad jahilū
Wa-mā bihi qadi ʾbtulū![4]

What is the matter with the writers
And authors among us?
They write on literature
And produce books.
For each art there is a [special] volume
Carefully written with all the dots put in,
Except that [of love and] lovers
For they (the writers) have had no care to preserve their (the lovers') rights
In the matter of [a branch of] learning of which they were ignorant
And by which they have not been afflicted!

Ḥamdān proceeds to enumerate fifteen varieties of lovers, but with no prescription for treatment or cure.

All these lines, like the bulk of didactic verse, are in *rajaz*, a kind of iambic metre, with the foot *mustafʿilun* (- - *v* -) repeated two or three times in each half-verse. This has a jingling sound that imprints itself on the memory

[3] Ibid., 51. [4] Ibid., 57.

better than any other metre. Other metres, such as *ṭawīl* (long), *basīṭ* (simple), *kāmil* (perfect), and *ramal* (trilling), may be used in didactic verse, but to a lesser extent. Jamāl al-Dīn Muḥammad b. Mālik handled all these metres with considerable dexterity. Apart from his *Alfiyyah*, in *rajaz*, he composed *Lāmiyyat al-afʿāl* or *Kitāb al-Miftāḥ* ("The L-Rhyming Ode on Verbs" or "Book of the Key") consisting of 114 lines in *basīṭ* metre.[5] He composed also *Tuḥfat al-mawdūd fī ʾl-maqṣūr wa-ʾl-mamdūd* ("Gift to the Beloved regarding Nouns with Final Short or Long 'a'") consisting of 162 lines rhyming in "a",[6] the *Kitāb al-Iʿlām bi-muthallathāt al-kalām* ("The Book of Information concerning Triliteral Words") in *muzdawij* form (i.e. *rajaz* with rhyming half-verses) on triliteral verbs, consisting of a forty-nine-line poem in *kāmil* metre, dealing with verbs in which the middle radical of the imperfect may be pointed with more than one vowel, and *Kitāb al-Iʿtidād fī ʾl-farq bayna ʾl-ẓāʾ wa-ʾl-ḍād* ("The Reliable Book for Distinguishing between *Ẓāʾ* and *Ḍād*").[7]

Didactic verse found its way into the exposition of theology, logic and medicine. Many examples are still in manuscript form. A whole *rajaz*-poem has been composed discussing, from a religious point of view, the use of toothpicks! It opens thus:

Ayā sāʾilan nafʿa ʾl-siwāki wa-ḥukmahu
Wa-mā fīhi min aḥkāmi fiqhin wa-ḥikmati, . .

O you who ask about the benefit
Of using toothpicks and how to employ them,
And about the rules of law and wisdom
Concerning them . . .

The concluding line, typical of many didactic poems, reads:

Wa-akhtimu naẓmī bi-ʾl-ṣalāti musalliman
ʿAlā ʾl-Muṣṭafā ʾl-Mukhtāri Hādī ʾl-Bariyyati.[8]

I close my verses with blessing and greetings
To the Chosen, Selected one (i.e. the Prophet Muḥammad),
The True Guide of God's creation.

Another poem, *Manẓūmah fī ʾl-fiqh* ("Didactic Poem on Jurisprudence"), deals with the precepts of the Ḥanafite school. It begins with the "Book of Prayers" and ends with a "Chapter on the prohibitions concerning the preparations for pilgrimage". It goes back to the seventh/thirteenth century. The first part is missing, but the extant verses open thus:

Furiḍat ʿalā mukallafin qad aslama
Wa-ʿan maḥīḍin wa-nifāsin salima.[9]

[5] Ziriklī, *Aʿlām*, VII, 111. [6] *GAL*, I, 363. [7] Ibid. [8] Raʾūf, *al-Āthār*, II, 277, 399.
[9] Ibid., 399.

[Pilgrimage] is incumbent on every adult
Who has embraced Islam, except for women
In their menstrual or post-natal periods.

As already stated, much of Arabic didactic verse is still in manuscript and unpublished, because it has long fallen out of fashion and is today frowned upon rather than encouraged. There is, however, hardly a classical poet who did not write some didactic poetry. These poets may be tabulated as follows:[10]

A *The pre-Islamic period*

Zuhayr b. abī Sulmā (AD 530–627)
Ṭarafah b. al-ᶜAbd (d. *c.* AD 569)
ᶜAdī b. Zayd al-ᶜIbādī (d. AD 604)
Labīd b. Rabīᶜah (AD 560–661)

B *The earlier and later ᶜAbbasid periods*

Abū ʾl-ᶜAtāhiyah (130–211/748–826)
Abū Tammām (192–231/807–46)
Ibn Durayd (d. 321/933)
Abū ʾl-Ṭayyib Aḥmad b. al-Ḥusayn al-Mutanabbī (303–54/915–65)
Abū ʾl-Fatḥ al-Bustī (d. 401/1010 or 401/1011)
Abū ʾl-ᶜAlāʾ al-Maᶜarrī (d. 449/1057)
Zayn al-Dīn b. al-Wardī (d. 749/1349)

C *Modern period*

Nāṣīf al-Yāzijī (1214–87/1800–71)
Maḥmūd Sāmī ʾl-Bārūdī (1255–1322/1839–1904)
Aḥmad Shawqī (1285–1351/1868–1932)
Muṭrān Khalīl Muṭrān (1289–1369/1872–1949)
Maᶜrūf al-Ruṣāfī (1292–1365/1875–1945)
Jibrān Khalīl Jibrān (1301–50/1883–1931)

Although rudiments of didactic verse are found in pagan times as maxims and gnomic verses,[11] it was not established as a distinct genre of Arabic poetry until the advent of the Hesiod of the Arabs, Abān b. ᶜAbd al-Ḥamīd al-Lāḥiqī, who is the true father of didactic Arabic verse.[12] It was he who made it an established genre of poetry, although, prior to him, Ṣafwān al-Anṣārī (*fl.* second/eighth century)[13] had categorized in verses the merits

[10] See Ḥannā al-Fākhūrī, *al-Ḥikam wa-ʾl-amthāl*, Cairo, n.d., 89.
[11] Cf. *CHALUP*, 90f, 116–17.
[12] Ṭāhā Ḥusayn, *Ḥadīth al-arbiᶜāʾ*, II, Cairo, 1962, 220.
[13] Abū ᶜUthmān ᶜAmr b. Baḥr al-Jāḥiẓ, *al-Bayān wa-ʾl-tabyīn*, ed. ᶜAbd al-Salām Muḥammad Hārūn, I, Cairo, 1968, 27f.

of the earth and the minerals and precious stones contained therein. Abān, however, devoted practically the whole of his poetry to this genre. He versified historical, theological and fictitious themes. In history, he versified the biography of Ardashīr and Khusraw Anūshirvān. He also wrote in verse on the origin of creation, including some verses on logic.[14] It was he who inspired Abū ʾl-ʿAtāhiyah to compose his long ode *Dhāt al-amthāl*, the poem of 4,000 proverbs.[15] Muḥammad b. Ibrāhīm al-Fazārī also followed in Abān's footsteps, composing a long *muzdawijah*, a double-rhymed *rajaz*-poem which, according to Yāqūt,[16] runs into ten volumes, in three-hemistich lines. It begins thus:

Al-ḥamdu li-ʾllāhi ʾl-ʿAliyyi ʾl-Aʿẓami
Dhī ʾl-faḍli wa-ʾl-majdi ʾl-Kabīri ʾl-Akrami
Al-Wāḥidi ʾl-Fardi ʾl-Jawādi ʾl-Munʿimi.

Praise be to God, the High, the Great,
Lord of grace, Glorious, Munificent,
Unique, Generous, All Bestowing.

Historians in their turn were unable to stay outside the sphere of didactic verse, for soon ʿAbd al-Malik al-Aṣmaʿī composed an ode on past kings, mighty rulers and extinct nations.[17] Other poems along similar lines are:

1 Nashwān b. Saʿīd's *Qaṣīdah Ḥimyariyyah*.
2 Yaḥyā b. Ḥakam al-Ghazāl's (*fl.* first half of third/ninth century) *rajaz*-poem on the conquest of Spain.
3 Ibn al-Muʿtazz's 419 *rajaz*-lines on the biography of al-Muʿtaḍid.
4 ʿAlī b. al-Jahm's (d. 249/863) *rajaz*-poem on world history down to his time.
5 Ibn ʿAbd Rabbihi's long *rajaz*-ode on the reign of ʿAbd al-Raḥmān III in Spain.
6 Tammām b. ʿĀmir b. ʿAlqamah's poem on the history of Spain.
7 The fifth/eleventh-century historical *rajaz*-ode by ʿAbd al-Jabbār al-Mutanabbī (*fl. c.* 537/1142) from Alcira.
8 Lisān al-Dīn b. al-Khaṭīb's *Raqm al-ḥulal fī naẓm al-duwal*, most of which is on the western dynasties.[18]

Some, like Ibn Dāniyāl, claimed that they resorted to versification of history for the sake of brevity, while others employed events as a kind of satire (*hijāʾ*).[19] This may be observed in such verses as:

Unbiʾtu anna fatātan kuntu akhṭubuhā
ʿUrqūbuhā mithlu shahri ʾl-ṣawmi fī ʾl-ṭūli[20]

14 Shawqī Ḍayf, *al-ʿAṣr al-ʿAbbāsī al-awwal*, Cairo, 1966, 190–1.
15 *Aghānī*, IV, Cairo, 1931, 36–7; Ḥijāb, *Maʿālim al-shiʿr*, 102.
16 *Irshād*, XVII, Cairo, 1926–7, 118.
17 Jāḥiẓ, *Ḥayawān*, VI, 149.
18 Rosenthal, *Muslim Historiography*, 184ff.
19 Ibid., 181.
20 Ṭāhā Ḥusayn, *Min Taʾrīkh al-adab al-ʿArabī*, II, Cairo, 1971, 249.

I was told of a girl to whom I was about to be betrothed
That she had a hock as long as the month of fasting.

Similar verses with a touch of cynicism occur in Abū ʾl-ʿAtāhiyah's *Dīwān*. From this time onwards didactic poetry tends toward a cynical, pessimistic philosophy. Says Abū ʾl-ʿAtāhiyah:

Lidū li-ʾl-mawti wa-ʾbnū li-ʾl-kharābi
Fa-kullukumu yaṣīru ilā tabābi.[21]

Give birth to children destined to die and build up for destruction.
Surely everyone of you is doomed to annihilation.

To soften these harsh thoughts, he couched them in the most musical metres – to take a case in point:

Hammu ʾl-qāḍī baytun yuṭrib
Qāla ʾl-qāḍī lammā ʿūtib
Mā fī ʾl-dunyā illā mudhnib
Hādhā ʿudhru ʾl-qāḍī wa-ʾqlib![22]

The *qāḍī*'s sole care is an affecting verse.
When he was reproached he said:
"None is there in this world who sins not."
This is the *qāḍī*'s excuse, so change the last word round!

He means that the dot on the Arabic letter *dhāl* in the word *ʿudhr* (excuse), is to be transferred to the first letter, *ʿayn* (ʿ), converting it into *ghayn*, the resulting word, *ghadr*, meaning "perfidy". This school of satirical didacticism was developed further by Abū ʾl-Ṭayyib Aḥmad al-Mutanabbī who caricatured his contemporaries and produced a burlesque versified history of the first half of the fourth/tenth century. Most of his satires on Kāfūr (reigned 355–7/966–8), the Ikhshidid ruler of Egypt, fall into this category.

The art reaches its climax, however, with the advent of the blind poet–philosopher, al-Maʿarrī, more especially in his *Luzūmiyyāt* ("Fettered Poems") wherein the poet employs more than one rhyme letter. He made philosophy the main theme of his didactic verse. Al-Maʿarrī was a strong believer in predestination, as may be perceived in the following lines:

Mā bi-ʾkhtiyāriya mīlādī wa-lā haramī
Wa-lā ḥayātī, fa-hal lī baʿdu takhyīru?
Wa-lā iqāmata illā ʿan yaday qadarin
Wa-lā masīra idhā lam yuqḍa taysīru![23]

I had no option about my birth, old age
Or my life. How can I then claim to have free will?
I cannot rest [in one place] save through the hands of Fate
Nor can there be journeying, if fate does not ordain it!

[21] Ḥannā al-Fākhūrī, *Taʾrīkh al-adab al-ʿArabī* Beirut, n.d., 426.
[22] Abū ʾl-ʿAtāhiyah, *Dīwān*, Cairo, 1947, 301. [23] *Luzūmiyyāt*, 1, Cairo, 1891, 322.

Two other poets who put aphorisms (*ḥikam*) into didactic verse are Abū ʾl-Fatḥ ʿAlī al-Bustī who became well known for his *nūniyyah* (n-rhyming) poem of sixty lines, the opening lines of which are:

Ziyādatu ʾl-marʾi fī dunyāhu nuqṣānu
Wa-ribḥuhu ghayra maḥḍi ʾl-khayri khusrānu.[24]

The longer a man lives the shorter his life is.
His gain other than simple goodness is but loss.

Zayn al-Dīn b. al-Wardī was celebrated for his *lāmiyyah* (l-rhyming) poem of seventy-seven verses. For him all ground he trod was home and any group who reciprocated his love and affection was his family. Unlike Abū ʾl-ʿAtāhiyah, Abū ʾl-Ṭayyib Aḥmad al-Mutanabbī and al-Maʿarrī, Ibn al-Wardī was optimistic, cheerful and realistic with a religious tendency. A selection of verses culled from his *lāmiyyah* will suffice to give an idea of his outlook:

Iʿtazil dhikra ʾl-aghānī wa-ʾl-ghazal
Wa-quli ʾl-faṣla wa-jānib man hazal
Wa-daʿi ʾl-dhikra li-ayyāmi ʾl-ṣibā
Fa-li-ʾayyāmi ʾl-ṣibā najmun afal
Wa-ʾhjuri ʾl-khamrata lā taḥfil bihā
Kayfa yasʿā li-junūnin man ʿaqal?

Ay bunayya ʾsmaʿ waṣāyā jamaʿat
Ḥikaman khuṣṣat bihā khayru ʾl-milal
Uṭlubi ʾl-ʿilma wa-lā taksal fa-mā
Abʿada ʾl-khayra ʿalā ahli ʾl-kasal!

Wa-ʾtruki ʾl-dunyā fa-min ʿādātihā
Takhfīḍu ʾl-ʿālī wa-tuʿlī man safal.

Lā taqul aṣlī wa-faṣlī abadan
Innamā aṣlu ʾl-fatā mā qad ḥaṣal.
Qad yasūdu ʾl-marʾu min ghayri abin
Wa-bi-ḥusni ʾl-sabki qad yunfaʿ zaghal
Wa-kadhā ʾl-wardu mina ʾl-shawki wa-hal
Yanbutu ʾl-narjisu illā min baṣal?

Ḥubbu-ka ʾl-awṭāna ʿajzun ẓāhirun
Fa-ʾghtarib talqa ʿani ʾl-ahli badal
Fa-bi-mukthi ʾl-māʾi yabqā āsinan
Wa-surā ʾl-badri bihi ʾl-badru ʾktamal![25]

Shun all mention of songs and flirtation
Say the decisive word [of truth], avoid the jester.
Abandon talk about the days of youth,
For the star of those youthful days has set.
Avoid wine-drinking – have naught to do with it!

[24] Fākhūrī, *Taʾrīkh al-adab*, 711; Shawqī Ḍayf, *Taʾrīkh al-adab al-ʿArabī: ʿaṣr al-duwal wa-ʾl-imārāt*, Cairo, 1980, 634. See also pp. 416–23, 627–35.

[25] Fākhūrī, *al-Ḥikam wa-ʾl-amthāl*, 70–1.

How can one endowed with intelligence aspire to folly?
My son, hearken to testaments [handed down] replete with
Aphorisms with which the best of creeds has been endowed.
Seek out knowledge! Be not indolent!
Far indeed is prosperity from idle folk.
Abandon worldliness, for the wont
Of the world is to humble the mighty and raise the lowly.
At no time speak of "my honour and my noble birth".
A lad's nobility lies in what he himself achieves, no more!
A man can come to rule as lord, without a [noble] father.
Through skilled smelting, debased metal can be made usable;
So also the rose springs from a thorn.
And does not the narcissus grow but from a bulb?
Your love of your home country is plain weakness.
Travel in foreign parts, and you will find those who will take your family's place.
Through remaining stagnant water turns brackish;
And the new moon, travelling by night, becomes a full moon.

Another example of didactic satire is to be found in the *maqāmāt* (assemblies) of Badīᶜ al-Zamān al-Hamadhānī and al-Ḥarīrī, both of whom deplore the circumstances of their time, when begging became the norm amongst a group of scholars, resulting in the rise of the literature of mendicancy (*adab al-kudyah*). In it the poet instructs others how to obtain their living by dubious means and trickery, employing a range of obscure expressions and diction to enable the learner to extend his vocabulary. A grotesque picture is painted by al-Ḥarīrī in a cleverly composed poem of this genre.[26]

Polemicists, likewise, kept pace with sages, grammarians and historians in employing didactic verse. Maᶜdan al-Aᶜmā al-Shīᶜī al-Shumayṭī (*fl.* second/eighth century), Imāmī Shīᶜī polemicist, wrote a lengthy poem on Shīᶜī sects and the tenets of other sects, upholding the extreme Shumayṭī sect above them all. Bishr b. al-Muᶜtamir (d. 210/825), the Muᶜtazilite, employed verse to convey his sectarian arguments. Two poems that he wrote on these lines were more akin to natural history than polemics, for he mentions in them insects and various other kinds of animals. In the same category are al-Ḥakam b. ᶜAmr al-Baḥrānī's (*fl.* second/eighth century) ode on strange creatures, and that of Hārūn, the client of the Azd, in his description of the elephant.[27]

Al-Sayyid al-Ḥimyarī (d. *c.* 173–8/789–94), the ᶜAbbasid poet of the Shīᶜah, made his contribution to didactic verse by versifying (and taking a sectarian viewpoint of) all the tales relating to the Prophet Muḥammad and

[26] See Ṣafāʾ Khulūṣī, *Taʾrīkh al-adab al-ᶜAbbāsī*, Baghdad, 1966, 120–2.
[27] Jāḥiẓ, *Ḥayawān*, II, 286; *Bayān*, I, 23; III, 75, 356; VI, 80; VII, 76.

his cousin ʿAlī.[28] It is said that he composed no less than 2,300 poems on their house, the Banū Hāshim.[29] He is also quoted as an authority on geographical didactic verse (see below) by Abū Muḥammad al-Ḥasan b. Aḥmad al-Hamdānī,[30] when he refers to Tabin in the Yemen. Al-Ḥimyarī says:

Hallā waqafta ʿalā ʾl-aṭlāli min Tabini
Wa-mā wuqūfu kabīri ʾl-sinni bi-ʾl-dimani?

Why did you not halt at the traces of the deserted encampment at Tabin?
But what point is there in an old man lingering over ruins?

The theme is conventional. The ruins evoke memories of the poet's beloved and his youth.[31]

Al-Ḥimyarī apart, other poets have also rendered the biography of the Prophet into verse, prominent among them being:

Al-Fatḥ b. Mismār (d. 663/1264–5)
ʿIzz al-Dīn al-Dīrīnī (d. 697/1297)
Fatḥ al-Dīn b. al-Shahīd (d. 793/1391)
Abū ʾl-Faḍl ʿAbd al-Raḥmān b. al-Ḥusayn Zayn al-Dīn al-ʿIrāqī (d. 806/1404), who composed an *Alfiyyah* on this theme[32]
Shihāb al-Dīn b. ʿImād al-Dīn al-Aqfahsī (d. 808/1405)
Ibrāhīm b. ʿUmar al-Biqāʿī (d. 885/1480)

The greatest length of any versified biography of the Prophet, however, was reached by Ibn al-Shahīd in his 25,000 line *rajaz*-epic entitled *al-Fatḥ al-qarīb fī sīrat al-Ḥabīb*.[33]

It is interesting to note that didactic verse covered a wide and varied range of literary curiosities. Among others we may remark on a poem on the manners and etiquette of sexual intercourse, entitled *Qurrat al-ʿuyūn bi-sharḥ naẓm Ibn Yāmūn fī ʾl-nikāḥ al-sharʿī wa-adabih* ("The Delight of the Eyes concerning the Commentary on Ibn Yāmūn's Poem on Legal Intercourse and its Etiquette") by Abū Muḥammad Mawlānā al-Tihāmī Kannūn al-Idrīsī al-Ḥasanī (*fl.* tenth/sixteenth century).[34] It consists of 101 *rajaz*-lines, the two half-verses rhyming internally, interspersed with a commentary that constantly refers to the Prophet's practice (*sunnah*) and sayings (*Ḥadīth*), along with quotations from other similar didactic poems. The subject is approached from both psychological and hygienic aspects. A man, for instance, is not supposed to touch his newly wed wife before performing his ablutions with her. Both must perform the sunset (*maghrib*) and late-

[28] Ḥijāb, *Maʿālim al-shiʿr*, 101. [29] Aḥmad ʿAṭiyyatullāh, *al-Qāmūs al-Islāmī*, III, Cairo, 1970, 588.
[30] *Ṣifat Jazīrat al-ʿArab*, ed. D. H. Müller, Leiden, 1884–91, 174. [31] See *CHALUP*, 46ff.
[32] Rosenthal, *Muslim Historiography*, 398. [33] Arberry, "The Sira in verse", 65.
[34] 2nd edn, Cairo, 1367/1948.

evening (*ʿishāʾ*) prayers. Then she should stand behind him and perform two *rakʿah*s saying "Amen!" after his supplication and prayers for their well-being and the success of their marriage.

The tradition of didactic verse has continued up to modern times. Its outstanding modern exponent has been the poet laureate Aḥmad Shawqī, who excelled all others. He devoted to it half of the fourth volume of *al-Shawqiyyāt* under the heading *al-Ḥikāyāt* ("Tales"), followed by *Dīwān al-aṭfāl*, ("Children's Anthology"), which differs little from the previous section, as it contains mostly animal fables with a line or two appended to conclude them with a moral. A fair example of Shawqī's technique in didactic verse is illustrated in the lines:

> *Saqaṭa ʾl-ḥimāru mina ʾl-safīnati fī ʾl-dujā*
> *Fa-bakā ʾl-rifāqu li-faqdihi wa-taraḥḥamū.*
> *Ḥattā idhā ṭalaʿa ʾl-nahāru atat bihi*
> *Naḥwa ʾl-safīnati mawjatun tataqaddamu.*
> *Qālat: khudhūhu kamā atānī sāliman,*
> *Lam abtaliʿhu li-annahu lā yuhḍamu!*[35]

> At night the ass fell from the ship.
> His comrades mourned his loss,
> And prayed God to be merciful to him.
> But lo and behold, when the dawn broke,
> A wave advanced towards the ship,
> Brought him alongside and said:
> "Take him back safe and sound.
> I have not swallowed him,
> Because he is indigestible!"

Besides his original fables, Shawqī versified a number of fables by Aesop, Phaedrus and La Fontaine.

With regard to geography, Yāqūt's *Muʿjam al-buldān* is full of didactic verse. Particular attention in this genre should also be drawn to Abū Muḥammad al-Ḥasan b. Aḥmad al-Hamdānī's *Ṣifat Jazīrat al-ʿArab*, the description of the Arabian peninsula which abounds in geographical didactic lines. Especially notable in this respect is *Urjūzat al-Ḥajj* (a *rajaz*-poem on the Pilgrimage route in the Yemen) by Aḥmad b. ʿĪsā al-Radāʿī (d. 420/1030), which consists of 127 five-lined stanzas, making 635 lines altogether.[36] This is a practical type of didactic verse useful to travellers, merchants and of course the pilgrims themselves, and forms a distinct genre on its own. Pilot-books in mnemonic verses are best exemplified in the works of Ibn Mājid[37] of the late ninth/fifteenth century, but they doubtless have an ancestry going back to ʿAbbasid times.

[35] Fākhūrī, *Taʾrīkh al-adab*, 995. [36] Hamdānī, *Ṣifat*, 235–79. [37] See above, ch. 17, 325–7.

In modern times, ᶜAbd al-Majīd Luṭfī (b. 1904) composed a long ode on the rivers, mountains and small villages of Iraq, the names of which otherwise are very difficult to remember. Both ᶜAbbās al-Khalīlī and his younger brother Jaᶜfar al-Khalīlī[38] have enriched modern Arabic didactic verse by translations from Persian into Arabic.

[38] J. T. Hamill, "Jaᶜfar al-Khalīlī and the modern short story in Iraq" (Michigan doctoral diss., 1972); Arabic trans. Wadīᶜ Filasṭīn and Ṣafāʾ Khulūṣī, Baghdad, 1976.

GLOSSARY

The majority of Arabic terms used in this volume are included here, but those terms which occur in one place only, and are there provided with a definition, are generally excluded.

abjad Alphabet; system of numerical expression in which the twenty-eight letters of the Arabic alphabet represent the units, tens and hundreds up to 1,000.
adab *Belles-lettres*; refinement, culture.
adab al-kudyah Literature of mendicancy.
adab al-qāḍī Duties of a judge.
ʿādah Custom; customary law.
ʿadhāb al-qabr Punishment of the grave.
adīb Writer of *adab*; man of letters.
ʿadl Of good character; just, equitable, fair. Justice, fairness.
afʿāl al-muqārabah Verbs of appropinquation.
Ahl al-Bayt The Family of the Prophet.
ʿajam (pl. ***aʿājim***) Non-Arabs, Persians.
ʿajz Powerlessness, impotence.
akhbār Reports, anecdotes, history, annals.
akhlāṭ The (four) humours.
ʿālam al-ghayb The invisible world; a world beyond the present one.
ʿālam al-mulk World of dominion; the present world.
ʿālam al-shahādah The visible world.
alfiyyah Poem of 1,000 verses.
ʿālim (pl. ***ʿulamāʾ***) Scholar, savant, scientist; the term "ulema" (***ʿulamāʾ***) is used to describe the class of men of religious learning who constitute the nearest thing in Islam to a clergy.
ʿamal Work, action; judicial practice; grammatical operation.
ʿāmil Word governing another in syntactical regimen, regent, "operator".
ʿāmil al-sūq Market inspector; the original term for the ***muḥtasib***.
al-ʿāmmah The common people.
amr Command; divine power of mandate.
amṣār (sing. ***miṣr***) Fortress cities established or maintained by the Arabs in the early days of their empire.
amzijah (sing. ***mizāj***) The (four) temperaments in humoral theory.
anwāʾ Meteorological and celestial phenomena.
ʿaqāʾid (sing. ***ʿaqīdah***) Doctrines, beliefs.
ʿaqd Contract, agreement, legal transaction; document, deed.
ʿaqīdah (pl. ***ʿaqīdāt***) Compendium of dogma.

ᶜaql Intellect, discernment; rationality, mind.
ᶜaql faᶜᶜāl Active intellect.
aqrābādhīn (pl. **aqrābādhīnāt**) Formulary; composite medicament.
ᶜArafāt Hill outside Mecca where part of the ceremonies of the annual Muslim **ḥajj** or pilgrimage are held.
asbāb al-nuzūl The occasions and circumstances of the Quranic revelations.
Ashᶜarites Followers of Abū ʾl-Ḥasan ᶜAlī al-Ashᶜarī (260–324/873-4–935), who was the founder of orthodox Islamic scholasticism (**kalām**).
askudār Scroll on which are recorded details of in- and out-letters.
atābak Turkish title, meaning lit. "father-prince", given to guardians of Saljūq and other Turkish princes; in time **atābaks** became governors and founders of dynasties.
āthār Traditions.
al-awāʾil Forbears; the ancients (authors, religious authorities, etc.).
ayyām al-ᶜArab "Days" of the Arabs; pre-Islamic tribal battles.
ᶜazzābah Members making up the levels of the Ibāḍī "circle" (**ḥalqah**).

bāb Sub-chapter, esp. in **Ḥadīth** literature; (in Ismāᶜīlī usage) chief **dāᶜī** under the imam (also known as **dāᶜī al-duᶜāt**).
badāʾ Doctrine of the Shīᶜah which envisages the possibility of God changing his mind.
barāʾah (In Ibāḍī usage) dissociation from other Muslims.
baradah Chalazion; a small swelling on the upper eyelid.
barakah Blessing; holiness, virtue as inherent spiritual power.
al-Bāriʾ The Creator.
barīd Post, mail.
barrānī Exterior.
basīṭ A metre employed in Arabic poetry.
basmalah The invocation, "In the name of God, the Compassionate, the Merciful".
bāṭin Interior, hidden (knowledge); esoteric.
bīmāristān Hospital for the sick.
Bohras Shīᶜī sect concentrated mainly in Gujarat and Bombay.
buḥrān Crisis (of an illness).
bukhl Meanness, parsimony.

dāᶜī Religio-political missionary; propagandist for a **daᶜwah**.
ḍaᶜīf (In Ibāḍī usage) "weak" imam; political appointment of a man not normally fully qualified for the position.
Dār al-Hijrah (In Shīᶜī usage) place of refuge; new (Faṭimid) state.
Dār al-ᶜIlm Cairo institute of higher learning founded in the reign of the Faṭimid al-Ḥākim.
ḍarūriyyāt Self-evident principles of thought.
daᶜwah Mission; religio-political organization headed by the chief **dāᶜī**; religious summons, especially among the Ismāᶜīlīs and similar groups.
dawlah (pl. **duwal**) Cycle, rotation; change of time, epoch; dynasty; state, country.
dhāʾiᶜ Widespread; popular.
dhawq Taste, inkling.

dhimmī Non-Muslim protected by the Islamic state; Christian or Jew.
difāʿī (In Ibāḍī usage) a temporary imam charged with some specific task, normally the defence of the state.
dīwān Register; a department of the Islamic bureaucracy; collection of poetry by a single author or from a single tribe.
dīwān al-muṣādarāt Diwan or department of confiscations.
dīwān al-zimām wa-ʾl-istīfāʾ Diwan or department of financial control and accounting.
duʿāʾ Private prayer, as opposed to ritual prayer (***ṣalāh***).
durrāʿah Sleeved coat; the distinctive garb of the ***kuttāb*** or state secretaries.

faḍāʾil (sing. ***faḍīlah***) Virtues, merits.
fāʾidah (pl. ***fawāʾid***) Advantage; chapter, section, heading; information conveyed (in a word or sentence).
falsafah Philosophy.
faqīh (pl. ***fuqahāʾ***) One learned in Islamic jurisprudence.
al-faraj baʿd al-shiddah "Relief after misfortune": designation of certain types of literary anecdote.
faṣl (pl. ***fuṣūl***) Section, chapter.
fatḥ (pl. ***futūḥ***) Conquest, victory.
fatwā (pl. ***fatāwā***) Legal response given by a ***muftī*** to a question of law addressed to him; Islamic equivalent of Roman *responsa prudentium*.
fayḍ (Neo-Platonic) theory of emanation.
fiʿl Action, verb.
fihrist Index, catalogue, list.
fiqh Islamic jurisprudence.
firqah (pl. ***firaq***) Sect.
fitnah Dissension, civil war; particularly after the murder of ʿUthmān.
furūʿ al-fiqh "Branches of law"; positive law as opposed to ***uṣūl***.
furūq Legal distinctions.
futuwwah Chivalrous qualities of a young man; ideal of chivalry. Term applied to certain chivalrous organizations. In Ṣufism an ethical ideal of altruism.

ghamz Massage.
ghayb What is hidden; the world of mystery.
ghaybah Occultation or temporary disappearance of the imam in Shīʿī doctrine.
ghayriyyah Otherness; altruism.
ghāzī Originally one who took part in a ***ghazwah*** (raid); later used to designate those who pursued the Holy War against non-Muslims.
ghubār Dust; the name given to the western form of the numerals used by the Arabs, which were the immediate precursors of modern European numerals.
ghūl Ghoul, desert demon appearing in different guises to men; goblin, ogre.

ḥadd (pl. ***ḥudūd***) Limit; divine ordinance; legal punishment; (logical) definition; (grammatical) rule; rank in the hierarchy of the ***daʿwah*** in Ismāʿīlī terminology.
ḥadd and ***muṭṭalaʿ*** Regulation and intuition of the true import of a Quranic verse.
ḥadīth (With a capital) the corpus of Traditions of the sayings and doings of the Prophet; (with small initial) such a Tradition.

ḥādith Occurrent, happening; appearing for the first time, having had a beginning.
ḥads Conjecture; intuition.
ḥajj The annual pilgrimage to Mecca in the month of Dhū ʾl-Ḥijjah.
ḥakīm Wise; medical practitioner.
ḥāl (pl. ***aḥwāl***) State; a spiritual state of enlightenment or rapture on the Ṣūfī path; circumstantial qualifier in Arabic grammar.
ḥamalat al-ʿilm Ibāḍī missionaries.
handasah Geometry, engineering.
ḥaqāʾiq Truths, facts; term used of philosophical works of Ismāʿīlī literature.
ḥarf Letter, particle.
ḥasan Category of ***ḥadīth*** situated between "sound" (***ṣaḥīḥ***) and "weak" (***ḍaʿīf***); fair, good; structurally correct in grammar.
Haskalah (Hebrew) Enlightenment. The European Enlightenment of the eighteenth century strongly influenced the cultural development of the Jews. The leaders of the Jewish Enlightenment wanted to introduce the Jews to wider horizons, hoping thereby to free them from their cultural ghetto and enable them to participate in the developments of European civilization.
hayʾah, ***ʿilm al-hayʾah*** Astronomy.
haylāj Prorogator in astrology.
hayūlā Matter.
hijāʾ Satire, versified lampoon.
Hijrah Muḥammad's migration from Mecca to Medina in AD 622.
ḥikmah (pl. ***ḥikam***) Wisdom; aphorism; rationale, reason.
ḥīlah (pl. ***ḥiyal***) Legal device, stratagem, for the purpose of *in fraudem legis agere*; mechanical device, machine.
ḥimyah Diet, regimen.
ḥisāb Arithmetic, reckoning, computation.
ḥisāb al-yad Hand arithmetic, finger mathematics, using the fingers as an aid to calculation.
ḥisbah The duties of the ***muḥtasib***.
ḥizb (pl. ***aḥzāb***) Litany, incantation.
ḥujjah (pl. ***ḥujaj***) Proof; a term applied to the prophets as proofs of God to the world; the highest ranking ***dāʿī*** in any particular sector of the ***daʿwah***, subordinate only to the chief ***dāʿī***.
ḥusn Beauty.
huwiyyah Essence, nature, identity.

Ibāḍīs Surviving sect of the Khawārij or Kharijites.
ʿIbādī Nestorian Christian.
ʿibārah Expression
ibdāʿ Creating things from nothing; originating.
iḍāfah Grammatical annexation.
idrāk Attainment, accomplishment; realization, perception; consciousness; understanding.
ʿiffah Virtue, chastity; probity, honesty.
ighlāq Abstruseness.
iʿjām (lit. "making foreign") Adding dots to letters of similar shape in order to distinguish between them.

iʿjāz Inimitability of the Qurʾān.
ijāzah Licence given by a scholar to his pupil, authorizing the latter to transmit and teach a text.
ijmāʿ Consensus; the consensus of the Islamic community.
ijtihād Exertion; right and duty of forming one's own opinion on how the rules of law are to be interpreted.
ikhāʾ Brotherhood; friendship.
ikhtilāf Disagreement; difference of opinion between different schools of law.
Ikhwān al-Ṣafāʾ "Brethren of Sincerity" (or "Purity"). They composed their *Rasāʾil* between AH 350 and 375; these *Rasāʾil* attempt to fuse the teachings of neo-Platonism with the ideas of Ismaʿilism.
iktisāb Doctrine of moral appropriation.
ilāhiyyāt Metaphysics; spiritual concerns.
ilhām Illumination; inspiration through divine revelation.
ʿillah (pl. ***ʿilal***) Cause; defect, especially gap in chain of authentic transmission of a ***ḥadīth***.
ʿilm Knowledge; science; mere book-learning as opposed to ***maʿrifah***.
ʿilm al-ʿadad The science of number.
ʿilm al-ḥisāb The science of reckoning, including both algebra and arithmetic.
ʿilm al-lughah Lexicography; the science of language.
ʿilm al-mīqāt Science of astronomical timekeeping.
ʿilm al-rijāl Science of trustworthy authorities in ***Ḥadīth***.
ʿilm al-ṭuruq Science of roads, knowledge of itineraries.
imām Leader, especially religious leader; the head of the Islamic community according to the Shīʿah; paragon; leader in communal prayer (***ṣalāh***).
Imāmī Twelver Shīʿī.
imām muḥtasib A leader of the Ibāḍīs when the state is not properly constituted; the title ***imam*** here is a *politesse*, and in fact rationalizes the position of certain individuals in history.
īmān Faith, being a believer.
inshāʾ Art of drawing up official documents.
iqlīm Clime; one of the seven zones parallel with the equator into which geographers divided the inhabited world.
iqṭāʿ Administrative grant, whereby the state granted its fiscal rights over lands that remained juridically the property of their previous owners. Such a grant was held in lieu of payment from the public treasury for service.
iqtiṣād Moderation, circumspection; economy.
iʿrāb The inflectional terminations of nouns and verbs.
irādah The aspiration of the ***murīd*** to undertake the journey of the soul to God.
ishārāt Indications, hints; type of Ṣūfī exegesis of the Qurʾān which seeks to avoid the presumption of binding the divine will; signs indicative of a ship's position (navigation).
ishrāq Illumination, enlightenment; illuminative philosophy. The name given to illuminative wisdom advocated by Shihāb al-Dīn al-Suhrawardī (d. 587/1191), who drew upon a revival of Zoroastrian angelology, neo-Platonic cosmology and in particular the metaphysical works of Ibn Sīnā. From these sources and his own spiritual experience al-Suhrawardī created the ***ishrāqī*** philosophy, or the philosophy of illumination, a description of ecstatic and mystical experience in the framework of philosophical ideas.

ishrāqī Illuminative; pertaining to illuminative philosophy.
ism Given name; noun.
ismiyyah Nominality.
isnād Chain of authorities, in particular in ***Ḥadīth*** and historical writings.
isrāʾīliyyāt Jewish traditions used to amplify Quranic allusions.
isṭaqissāt The (four) elements according to Greek and Islamic physical theory.
istiḥsān "Approval"; a discretionary opinion in breach of strict analogy in Islamic law; method for the determination of decisions when conflicting principles compete for consideration.
istiṣḥāb al-ḥāl Presumption that a fact is valid failing proof to the contrary.
istiṣlāḥ Juridical procedure whereby the public interest is taken into account.
istiṭāʿah The "ability" to act, or freedom of will.
Ithnā ʿAshariyyah "Twelvers", Imāmīs; the most important sect of the Shīʿah, and the official form of Islam in Persia.
ittiḥād Union; (in Christian usage) incarnation.
ittiṣāl Unitedness, union; contact, communication.

jabr Compulsion; doctrine of predestination.
al-jabr wa-ʾl-muqābalah The two basic operations of Arabic algebra.
Jabrites Believers in predestination.
Jāhiliyyah The term used by Muslim writers to denote the period before Muḥammad's mission.
jāʾiz Permissible.
jamāl Beauty.
jarbī In Ibn Khurradādhbih a geographical area including Armenia, Ādharbāyjān, Gīlān, Ṭabaristān and countries beyond.
jawāb (pl. ***ajwibah***) An answer, reply.
jawhariyyah (Divine) substance in Islamic theology.
jawwād Giver of gifts.
jidhr Unknown root in algebra.
jinn Invisible beings that may be harmful or helpful to human beings; demons.
jizyah Poll-tax; capitation tax.
jūd Generosity; act of divine love.
jumlah Sentence (in grammar); summary.

kabīrah (pl. ***kabāʾir***) Great sin, grave offense, atrocious crime.
kadhkhudāh Lord of the significant luminary's term in astrology.
kāfir Unbeliever.
kaḥḥāl Oculist.
kāhin Pre-Islamic soothsayer.
kalām Speech; scholastic theology.
kāmil Metre employed in Arabic poetry.
kammiyyah Quantity.
karāmah (pl. ***karāmāt***) Grace, thaumaturgic and charismatic gifts.
karshūnī Arabic written in Syriac letters.
karūbiyyūn Cherubim, cherubic intelligences, intellectual angels.
kasb, ***iktisāb*** Acquisition; personal initiative.
kashf Uncovering; exposure, unveiling; revelation, illumination.
kashf, ***ẓuhūr*** The period of open rule of the imams (Ismāʿīlī usage).

kātib (pl. ***kuttāb***) Secretary; clerk in government service.
kātib al-amwāl Secretary for finance.
kātib al-inshāʾ Secretary for correspondence.
kayfiyyah Quality.
Kaysāniyyah A Shīʿī subsect which supported al-Mukhtār b. abī ʿUbayd.
khabar Political or military intelligence; grammatical predicate.
khabbāz Baker; public baker of the market.
kharāj At first taxes or tribute generally, then specialized to mean land tax as opposed to poll tax.
khārij External.
al-khāṣṣah The elite; upper class.
khawāṣṣ Magical properties of things.
khawf Fear, dread.
Khojas A closed caste of Indian Ismāʿīlī Muslims, most of whom are followers of the Agha Khan.
kitāb (pl. ***kutub***) Writing; scripture; book; in ***Ḥadīth*** a division approximating to a chapter.
kitābah Writing; the art of the secretary.
kurrāsah (pl. ***kurrāsāt***) Quire; gathering of a book.

lāmiyyah Poem rhyming in 'l'.
laqab (pl. ***alqāb***) (Earlier) name alluding to a personal characteristic; (later) honorific title.
lughz (pl. ***alghāz***) Riddle.
luṭf Divine favour; grace.

maʿānī al-Qurʾān Minutiae of the meanings of the Qurʾān.
maʿārīḍ al-kalām Vagaries of speech, linguistic ambiguities.
madhhab (pl. ***madhāhib***) Procedure; opinion, belief; creed, doctrine; movement, school; orthodox rite of jurisprudence.
maʾdhūn Assistant to a ***dāʿī.***
maḍīq Strait.
maḍnūn bihā Esoteric.
madrasah (pl. ***madāris***) School, college; institution of higher learning, frequently attached to a mosque.
maghāzī Early Muslim military expeditions in which the Prophet took part.
Maghrib The Islamic West; north-west Africa; in Ibn Khurradādhbih it means northern Iraq, Byzantium, Syria, Egypt and the lands to the west of these.
maḥabbah Love.
mahdī "Rightly guided one": a messianic figure who will remove injustice from the world and bring about an era of justice for the oppressed.
maʿiyyah Relationship of coincidence between two phenomena.
majāz al-Qurʾān Lexical and syntactical usage of the Qurʾān.
majlis (pl. ***majālis***) Meeting, session; scholarly discussion, salon; (in pl.) written record of such discussions.
majmūʿ Collected; totality, sum; nomocanon.
makān Space, place.
makfirah (In Ibāḍī usage) a major sin requiring formal repentance (***tawbah***).
mamarr Transit.
maʿmūl fīh "Operated upon"; grammatical term applied to that part of an

utterance which is the object, in contradistinction to its ʿ***āmil***, or "operator".

maʿnā Meaning, content.

manāqib Virtues, great deeds, feats, exploits; laudatory biography.

manzilah Status (in grammar).

al-manzilah bayna ʾl-manzilatayn Intermediate position; the position adopted by the Muʿtazilites in Islam with regard to a major sinner: he was neither a true believer nor an unbeliever; he was in between and would be punished by God.

maqāmah (pl. ***maqāmāt***) Assembly, session, meeting; a genre of Arabic literature written in rhymed prose presenting a short dramatic scene; stage of spiritual development; station of the mystic path.

maʿqūlāt Philosophical matters; things that are intelligible or rational; categories.

maʿrifah Knowledge; immediate knowledge of the divine; gnosis.

masʾalah (pl. ***masāʾil***) Problems; *quaestiones*.

mashīkhah Written document enumerating the teachers or ***shaykhs*** under whom a scholar has studied.

Mashriq The Islamic East; lands to the east of Egypt; in Ibn Khurradādhbih it means Persia and Afghanistan, extending into India, China and Central Asia.

mashriqī Illuministic; pertaining to "Oriental" wisdom or philosophy, and closely related to ***ishrāq***.

massāḥ (pl. ***mussāḥ***) Land surveyor.

mathnawī Type of poetry in couplets.

matn (pl. ***mutūn***) Text (lit. "backbone").

mawḍiʿ Syntactical function of a word which determines its vocalization.

mawlā (pl. ***mawālī***) Client, non-Arab Muslim.

maẓālim Complaints (concerning miscarriages or denials of justice).

miḥnah Inquisition; ordeal, tribulation, misfortune.

mikthār Talkative, garrulous.

mīl Unit of measurement in Arabic, standardized at close to 2,000 metres.

al-milal wa-ʾl-niḥal literature. Literature devoted to comparative religion.

millah Religious community; denomination; creed.

mīqāt (pl. ***mawāqīt***) Prayer times.

miqyās (pl. ***maqāyīs***) Analogical pattern in grammar.

miʿrāj Ascent; the Prophet's midnight journey to the seven heavens, made on the 27th Rajab from Jerusalem.

mithāl Example.

mīzān Balance; balance of divine justice.

muʿāmalah Practice; the interaction between faith in the heart of the believer and action in his daily life.

mubdiʿ Creating things from nothing; originator.

mubtadaʾ Grammatical subject.

mufassir One who explains a text; exegete.

muftī An authoritative specialist in Islamic law, competent to issue a ***fatwā***.

muḥaddith Ḥadīth scholar, collecting and studying the ***Ḥadīth***.

muḥāl Wrong, perverted; intrinsically meaningless in grammatical usage.

muhandis Engineer; geometer.

muḥdath Caused: used in regard to the doctrine that the Qurʾān is caused.

muhmal Neglected; combinations of radicals not used in Arabic words.

muḥtasib Inspector of the market; Islamic official whose role can be traced back to the Byzantine *agoranomos* or market inspector.

mujāhadah (Moral) striving.

muʿjam Alphabet; dictionary.
mūjiz Concise; abstract, epitome.
muʿjizah Miracle, wonder.
mukabbir (pl. ***mukabbirūn***) Pronouncing the formula "***Allāh akbar***" ("God is very great"); one who chants this.
mukāsir Assistant to a ***dāʿī***, next in rank after ***maʾdhūn***.
muʾmin Believer.
munāsabah Appropriateness of the literary sequence of the verses and ***sūrahs*** of the Qurʾān.
Murjiʾites A sect which arose in the Umayyad period which suspended judgement against believers who had committed sins.
musajjaʿ Composed in rhymed prose.
musannāt Dams with sluices.
mushāhadah Seeing, vision; contemplation.
musnad Work of ***Ḥadīth*** in which individual ***ḥadīth*** can be attributed to the Prophet himself.
mustafʿilun A foot of poetry consisting of two long, one short and one long syllable.
mustajīb Candidate seeking admission to the Ismāʿīlī ***daʿwah***.
mustaʿmal In use; combinations of radicals actually used in words.
mustaqīm Straight, right; making sense grammatically.
mutʿah Marriage contracted on a temporary basis.
mutakallim (pl. ***mutakallimūn***) Scholastic theologian; speaker (in grammar), as opposed to person addressed (***mukhāṭab***).
mutarjim Translator.
Muʿtazilah Theological school which created the speculative dogmatics of Islam.
muzdawij Double; a type of double-rhymed poem.

nafs Soul
nafy Grammatical negation.
nahḍah Renaissance.
nāḥin (pl. ***nuḥāh***) Grammarian.
naḥw grammar; syntax.
naḥwī (pl. ***naḥwiyyūn***) Grammarian.
nāʾib ʿan al-fāʿil Agent of the passive verb.
naql Conveying, transmission; translation; copy; tradition.
naskh "Book-hand" style of Arabic script (contrasted with *kufic*); abrogation, cancellation, repeal.
naṣṣ Content, purport, text; constituting a proof.
naṣṣ jalī Public designation of a successor.
naṣṣ khafī Private designation of a successor.
naʿt (pl. ***nuʿūt***) Description; title descriptive of rank.
nāṭiq A prophet who has revealed a new law, such as Muḥammad, or an expected lawgiver.
nāʿūrah Water-wheel, noria.
naẓar Theoretical enquiry.
nisbah Kinship, relationship, affinity; derivative form (ending in *-ī*) of a name or other noun; see *CHALUP*, 19.
nūniyyah Poem rhyming in "n".

qabīḥ Ugly, bad; structurally incorrect in grammar.
qadar Divine foreordaining, predestination; fate, destiny.
Qadarites The earliest school of philosophy in Islam, which believed in human free will.
qaddāḥ Coucher for cataract.
qāḍī Judge of a ***sharīʿah*** court.
qaḍiyyah Lawsuit; (legal) case, cause, question, affair.
qadūm Bold, audacious.
qahr Constraint.
qāʾid Leader, especially a military leader; tribal chief.
qalam daqīq Fine style of handwriting.
qalam jalīl Thick style of handwriting.
qanāh (pl. ***qunī***) Subterranean irrigation channel or conduit; stream, waterway.
Qarāmiṭah Qarmaṭians, an extremist Ismāʿīlī movement. It founded a state in eastern Arabia in 281/894 which lasted until the end of the fifth/eleventh century.

qaṣaṣ Stories (coll.); didactic narratives used by Ṣūfīs; fables.
qiblah Direction to which Muslims turn in praying (towards the Kaʿbah in Mecca).
qidam al-ʿālam Eternity of the world.
qirāʾah (pl. ***qirāʾāt***) Recitation of the Qurʾān; variant reading of the Qurʾān.
qiyās Analogy; the process of arriving at a legal decision by analogy.
al-qudamāʾ al-khamsah The five pre-eternal principles: Creator, soul, matter, space, time.
qudrah Power, ability.
quṭb (pl. ***aqṭāb***) Axis, pivot, pole; head of the hierarchy of ***awliyāʾ***, or saints.
quwwah Power, faculty.

Rādhāniyyah A group of Jewish merchants who traded between Europe and the lands of Islam (mentioned by Ibn Khurradādhbih).
Rafiḍites A division of the Shīʿīs who forsook Zayd b. ʿAlī b. al-Ḥusayn b. ʿAlī b. abī Ṭālib; used by Sunnīs for any sect of the Shīʿīs.
rajʿah "Return" of the imam from death or occultation in the doctrine of the Shīʿah.
rajaz A metre employed in Arabic poetry, though considered inferior to the other classical metres.
rakʿah The words and actions involved in Islamic ritual prayer, involving a bending of the torso from an upright position, followed by two prostrations.
ramad Ophthalmia; eye disease.
ramal Name of a poetical metre.
ramz (pl. ***rumūz***) Symbol, sign.
raṣd Astronomical observation.
raʾy Opinion; individual reasoning; exercising opinion in arriving at a legal decision.
ribā Excess, interest, usury.
risālah (pl. ***rasāʾil***) Epistle; literary genre in the form of a letter.
rizq Livelihood, means of living; subsistence, sustenance; boon.
ruʾyah Vision or visibility of God.

sabab Cause; the motivating cause for doing an act (a constituent of ***istiṭāʿah***, or ability to act).

sabal Pannus; tissue covering whole or part of the cornea of the eye.

Ṣābiʾah Name of two different sects: (1) the Mandaeans, a Judaeo-Christian gnostic sect in Iraq; (2) the Ṣabians of Ḥarrān, a pagan sect in existence as late as the fifth/eleventh century.

safīr Envoy, ambassador; (in Shīʿī usage) designation of the leaders through whom the twelfth imam communicated with his followers.

ṣaghīrah (pl. ***ṣaghāʾir***) Venial sin; minor mistake.

Ṣaḥābah The group of the Companions of the Prophet.

ṣāḥib al-barīd wa-ʾl-khabar Director of posts and intelligence.

sajʿ Balanced and rhyming prose; utterance originating with pre-Islamic soothsayers, of primitive style, short and with a single, invariable monorhyme at the end of each member.

Salafiyyah A "return to sources" school in Islam (end of nineteenth century).

ṣalāh Canonical prayer.

ṣāmit Imam who does not reveal a new law, but who is the chief exponent and interpreter of the existing law.

sāqiyah Irrigation device using chains of pots for raising water, driven by animal power.

ṣarf Morphology.

sarsām Meningitis.

satr Concealment; period of concealment, i.e. the first stage of Faṭimid history.

ṣawm Fasting.

ṣaydalī (pl. ***ṣayādilah***) Pharmacist.

shahādah Testimony; the bearing witness that there is no deity but God and that Muḥammad is his messenger; the Muslim creed.

shakk Doubt, misgiving.

shakkāẓiyyah Astrolabe having a single plate.

sharḥ Systematic commentary.

shārī (In Ibāḍī usage) a full, plenipotentiary imam in a period of the expanding state (***ẓuhūr***).

sharīʿah The corpus of Islamic law.

sharṭ (pl. ***shurūṭ***) Stipulation; legal document; (in Ibāḍī usage) condition of limiting legal authority (e.g. the phrase "***lā sharṭ ʿalā ʾl-imām***").

shawkah Might, power of political leadership.

al-shayʾ Lit. "the thing": "x", the unknown quantity in algebra.

shaykh Elder, chief, head (of a tribe); teacher, master.

Shīʿah (adj. ***Shīʿī***) Sect who hold that headship of the Islamic community belongs only to descendants of ʿAlī and Fāṭimah.

shiʿr taʿlīmī Didactic verse.

shuʿāʿāt Rays; beams; spokes.

shūrā Consultative council; the council of electors appointed by the caliph ʿUmar to choose his successor.

Shuʿūbiyyah Anti-Arab political and literary movement, especially strong in Iranian circles.

shuyūkh al-ḥirfah (lit. "***shaykhs*** of the craft") Designation often used of masters of the Ṣūfī way, though properly referring to the guilds of ***futuwwah***.

ṣifāt al-dhāt Essential attributes of God.

ṣifāt al-fiʿl Attributes of action, with reference to God.

ṣifāt al-iḍāfah or ***nisbiyyah*** Relative attributes.

ṣifāt sharʿiyyah Legal epithets.
sijill Record, writing; ***qāḍī***'s judgement.
ṣināʿat al-iʿrāb The art of inflection; morphology.
sīrah (pl. ***siyar***) Way of acting, conduct; life, biography, especially of the Prophet; story; theological epistle sent between different Ibāḍī communities; (in the pl.) biographies, heroic deeds, campaigns; branch of the ***sharīʿah*** dealing with the conduct of military expeditions and the rights to be accorded enemies; laws of war.
al-ṣirāṭ The bridge of judgement which spans hell.
sīrat al-ḥalqah The book of the organization of the "circle" of ulema and neophytes directing the north African Ibāḍī communities.
siyāsah (pl. ***siyāsāt***) Statecraft, administration; (in navigation) crew management.
sunnah Way, path; customary practice, usage sanctioned by tradition; the sayings and doings of the Prophet which have been established as legally binding.
Sunnī Muslim who believes that the ***sunnah*** cannot be overridden by any human authority (for practical purposes antithetical to Shīʿī).
sūrah A chapter of the Qurʾān.

ṭabaqah (pl. ***ṭabaqāt***) Layer; generation, class; (in the pl.) collective biography.
taʾbīd Perpetual negation (in grammar).
tābiʿūn (sing. ***tābiʿ***) Successors, the generation after the Prophet's Companions (***Ṣaḥābah***).
tadbīr al-mulk Kingship, statecraft.
tadwīn Committing to writing.
tafsīr Quranic exegesis.
taḥmīd Eulogy.
tajassud Becoming corporeal; materialization; incarnation.
tajribah Experience; experimentation.
takhliyat al-shuʾūn Freedom of circumstances (a constituent of ***istiṭāʿah***, or ability to act).
ṭalab al-riʾāsah Pursuit of leadership; rivalry.
taʾlīf Literary composition.
talqīn Rote learning.
taʿmiyah Obscurity in expression.
tamyīz Specifying element in grammar.
taqdīr Interpolation of an elucidatory phrase in exegesis; (in grammar) paraphrasing of unexpressed forms or meanings.
taʿqīd Complexity.
taqiyyah Dissimulation of one's real beliefs when in fear of one's life.
taqlīd Imitation; clinging to tradition; reference to the Companions of the Prophet; reliance on the teaching of a master; adopting the doctrine of a school of law for a particular transaction.
taqsīm Dichotomous classification (grammar).
taqwā Godliness, piety.
taqwīm Ephemerides.
taʾrīkh Dating; history, annals.
ṭarīqah Way; term for the Ṣūfī path; mystical method, system or school for following such a path.
tarjamah (pl. ***tarājim***) Translation; biography.

taṣawwuf Mysticism.
tashbīh Anthropomorphism; regarding God as resembling corporeal things.
tashkīk Ambiguity.
taṣʿīb Making difficult; being intentionally obscure.
taṣwīr Depiction.
taʿṭīl Annulment; denying God all attributes (as opposed to ***tashbīh***).
tawḥīd The doctrine of the unity of God.
ṭawīl A meter employed in Arabic poetry.
taʾwīl Esoteric or allegorical interpretation of the Qurʾān or law; the process of extracting the ***bāṭin*** from the ***ẓāhir***.
tawṣiyah Enjoining of good counsels.
taʾyīd Reinforcement (grammar).
taʿyīn al-mubham Naming the unnamed; term of Quranic exegesis denoting the effort to make everything known.
tayman The south; in Ibn Khurradādhbih virtually identical with the Arabian peninsula.
taʿziyah Consolation on bereavement.
tazkiyah Pronouncement of a person's integrity; attestation of upright character.
ṭibb al-ʿāmmah Popular medicine.
al-ṭibb al-nabawī "Prophetical medicine"; medical recommendations and teachings attributed to the Prophet Muḥammad.

ummah Folk; the Islamic community.
ʿurf Customary law.
ʿushr Tithe.
uṣūl al-fiqh The "roots" or theoretical bases of Islamic law.

waʿd Promises.
Wahhābiyyūn Followers of Muḥammad b. ʿAbd al-Wahhāb (1115–1201/1703–87), who aimed at the restoration of pure Islam by doing away with all innovations (***bidaʿ***).
waḥy Divine inspiration of a prophet.
waʿīd Admonitions.
walī (pl. ***awliyāʾ***) Saint.
wālī (pl. ***wulāh***) Ruler, governor.
waqf Form of mortmain under which property is rendered inalienable and the income devoted to charitable purposes.
wāqifah A sect whose line of imams has ended and is expecting a ***Mahdī*** or ***qāʾim***, such as the Qarmaṭians or the Twelver Shīʿīs, unlike those who believe in a continuing imamate, such as the Faṭimids or the Nizārī Ismāʿīlīs today.
waṣāyā Testaments, or admonitions, designed to instruct by moralizing. A form of literature characteristic of Ṣufism.
waṣī; ***asās*** Executor of a prophet's will or the head of a series of imams, such as ʿAlī b. abī Ṭālib after Muḥammad, or Aaron after Moses.
wilāyah (In Ibāḍī usage) association with other Muslims.
wird (pl. ***awrād***) Litanies compounded of ***adhkār*** or remembrance formulae.
wizārah Office of vizier or minister.
wujūb Necessity.

wuqūf (In Ibāḍī usage) suspended judgement concerning the status of a member of the community; an intermediate position between association (***wilāyah***) and dissociation (***barāʾah***).

yajūz*, *lā yajūz "It is allowed"; "it is not allowed" (prescriptive terms in grammar).
yaqīn Certainty, conviction.
yāqūt Precious stone, gem.

zāhid Ascetic.
ẓāhir Exterior; external sense, literal meaning; exoteric.
Ẓāhirī School of law relying on the literal (***ẓāhir***) meaning of the Qurʾān.
zakāh Alms-tax of prescribed amount.
zamān Time.
zarqalliyyah Astrolabe having one plate with markings for the coordinate systems of both the celestial equator and the ecliptic.
zīj (pl. ***zījāt***) Astronomical table.
ẓill (pl. ***ẓilāl***) Shadow, tangent.
ziyārah Visitation (to holy place or shrine).
ẓuhūr The full realization of an Ibāḍī state.

BIBLIOGRAPHY

GENERAL BIBLIOGRAPHY

Blachère, R. *Histoire de la littérature arabe*, Paris, 1952–64.

Brockelmann, C. *Geschichte der arabischen Litteratur* and Suppls. I–III, Leiden, 1943–9.

The Cambridge History of Arabic Literature: Arabic Literature to the End of the Umayyad Period, ed. A. F. L. Beeston, T. M. Johnstone, R. B. Serjeant and G. R. Smith, Cambridge, 1983.

The Cambridge History of Arabic Literature: ʿAbbasid Belles Lettres, ed. Julia Ashtiany *et al.*, Cambridge, 1990.

Dictionary of Scientific Biography, New York, 1970–80.

The Encyclopaedia of Islam, 1st edn, Leiden, 1913–42; 2nd edn, Leiden and London, 1960– .

The Encyclopaedia Judaica, Jerusalem, 1972.

Graf, G. *Geschichte der christlichen arabischen Literatur* (Studi e Testi 118, 133, 146, 147, 172), Vatican, 1944–51.

Huart, C. *La Littérature Arabe*, Paris, 1902; trans. as *A History of Arabic Literature*, London, 1903.

Ibn Khaldūn, ʿAbd al-Raḥmān b. Muḥammad *al-Muqaddimah*, ed. E. Quatremère, Paris, 1858–68; trans. F. Rosenthal, 3 vols., London, 1958.

Ibn Khallikān, Shams al-Dīn Aḥmad b. Muḥammad *Wafayāt al-aʿyān wa-anbāʾ abnāʾ al-zamān*, ed. Iḥsān ʿAbbās, Beirut, 1968– ; Eng. trans. MacGuckin de Slane, Paris, I, 1842; II, 1843.

Ibn al-Nadīm, Muḥammad b. Isḥāq *Kitāb al-Fihrist*, ed. G. Flügel, Leipzig, 1871–2; Cairo, 1929; trans. Bayard Dodge, *The Fihrist of al-Nadim*, New York, 1970.

Ibn abī Uṣaybiʿah, Muwaffaq al-Dīn abū ʾl-ʿAbbās Aḥmad *ʿUyūn al-anbāʾ fī ṭabaqāt al-aṭibbāʾ*, ed. A. Müller, Königsberg, 1884.

Ikhwān al-Ṣafāʾ *Rasāʾil*, ed. F. Dieterici (*Die Abhandlungen der Ikhwān al-Ṣafāʾ in Auswahl*), Leipzig, 1886.

al-Jāḥiẓ *Kitāb al-Ḥayawān*, ed. ʿAbd al-Salām Hārūn, Cairo, 1938–45.

Kātib Čelebi, Ḥajjī Khalīfah Muṣṭafā b. ʿAbdullāh *Kashf al-ẓunūn ʿan al-asāmī wa-ʾl-funūn*, ed. and trans. G. Flügel, Leipzig and London, 1835–58.

Lewis, B., and Holt, P. M. (eds.) *Historians of the Middle East*, London, 1962.

Nallino, C. A. *Raccolta di Scritti editi e inediti*, V, Astrologia–Astronomia–Geografia, Rome, 1944.

Nasr, S. H. *An Annotated Bibliography of Islamic Science*, Tehran, 1975– .

Nicholson, R. A. *A Literary History of the Arabs*, Cambridge, 1907.

al-Nuwayrī, Aḥmad *Nihāyat al-arab fī funūn al-adab*, Cairo, AH 1342–48.

Pearson, J. D. *Index Islamicus*, Cambridge, 1958– .
al-Qifṭī, Jamāl al-Dīn abū ʾl-Ḥasan ʿAlī b. Yūsuf *Ikhbār al-ʿulamāʾ bi-akhbār al-ḥukamāʾ*, ed. J. Lippert, Leipzig, 1903.
Rosenthal, F. *A History of Muslim Historiography*, Leiden, 1952, 1968.
Sarton, G. *Introduction to the History of Science*, Baltimore, 1927.
Sezgin, F. *Geschichte des arabischen Schrifttums*, Leiden, 1967– .
Shorter Encyclopaedia of Islam, Leiden, 1974.
Storey, C. A. *Persian Literature: a Bio-Bibliographical Survey*, II, London, 1958.
Suter, H. "Die Mathematiker und Astronomen der Araber und ihre Werke", *Abhandlungen zur Geschichte der Mathematischen Wissenschaften*, X, 1900 and XIV, 1902; additions by H. J. P. Renaud, *Isis*, XVIII, 1932.
Ullmann, M. *Die Medizin im Islam* (Handbuch der Orientalistik, I Abt., Ergänzungsband VI, i), Leiden and Cologne, 1970.
Die Natur- und Geheimwissenschaften im Islam (Handbuch der Orientalistik, I Abt., Ergänzungsband VI, ii), Leiden and Cologne, 1972.
Walzer, R. *Greek into Arabic*, Oxford, 1962.
Yāqūt al-Ḥamawī *Irshād al-arīb ilā maʿrifat al-adīb*, ed. D. S. Margoliouth, London, 1923–31; A. Rifāʿī, Cairo, 1936–8.
Muʿjam al-buldān, ed. F. Wüstenfeld, Leipzig, 1869.
al-Ziriklī, Khayr al-Dīn *al-Aʿlām*, Cairo, 1954–9.

1 SUNNĪ THEOLOGY

ʿĀdil al-ʿAwwāʾ *al-Kalām wa-ʾl-falsafah*, Damascus, 1964.
Allard, M. *Le Problème des attributs divins dans la doctrine d'al-Ašʿarī*, Beirut, 1965.
Alonso, M. *Teología de Averroes: estudios y documentos*, Madrid, 1967.
al-Āmidī, Sayf al-Dīn *Ghāyat al-marām fī ʿilm al-kalām*, ed. Ḥasan Maḥmūd ʿAbd al-Laṭīf, Cairo, 1971.
Anawati, G. C. "Culture humaine et science religieuse. La place du Kalām (théologie musulmane) dans l'organisation du savoir", *IBLA*, VII, Tunis, 1944.
Arberry, A. J. *Revelation and Reason in Islam*, London, 1957.
Asín Palacios, M. *Abenházam de Córdoba y su historia crítica de las ideas religiosas*, Madrid, 1927–32.
al-Baghdādī, ʿAbd al-Qāhir *Kitāb Uṣūl al-dīn*, Istanbul, AH 1346.
Ess, J. van "The logical structure of Islamic theology" in G. E. von Grunebaum (ed.), *Logic in Classical Islamic Culture*, Wiesbaden, 1970.
Gardet, L. and Anawati, G. C. *Introduction à la théologie musulmane*, Paris, 1948.
Grunebaum, G. E. von *Theology and Law in Islam*, Wiesbaden, 1971.
Horowitz, S. *Über den Einfluss der griechischen Philosophie auf die Entwicklung des Kalam*, Breslau, 1909.
Horten, M. *Muhammedanische Glaubenslehre. Die Catechismen des Faḍālī und des Sanūsī übersetzt und erläutert*, Bonn, 1916.
Macdonald, D. B. *Development of Muslim Theology, Jurisprudence and Constitutional Theory*, London, 1972.
McCarthy, R. *The Theology of al-Ašʿarī*, Beirut, 1953.
Nader, A. "Bibliographie concernant le kalam", *Bulletin de Philosophie Médiévale*, XV, 1973.

Niewohner, F. "Bibliographie d'ouvrages en langues européennes concernant le kalam", *Bulletin de Philosophie Médiévale*, XVI–XVII, 1974–5.

Pareja, F. M. "Historia de la espiritualidad musulmana" in Juan Flors (ed.), *Historia de la Espiritualidad*, Barcelona, n.d.

al-Shahrastānī *Asch-Schahrastâni's Religionspartheien und Philosophen-Schulen*, trans. T. Haarbrücker, Halle, 1850–1.

Stieglecker, H. *Die Glaubenslehren des Islam*, Munich, 1959.

Sweetman, W. J. *Islam and Christian Theology*, London, 1967.

Wensinck, A. J. *The Muslim Creed: its Genesis and Historical Development*, Cambridge, 1932.

Les Preuves de l'existence de Dieu dans la théologie musulmane, Amsterdam, 1936.

al-Ẓawāhirī, M. al-Ḥusaynī *al-Taḥqīq al-tāmm fī ᶜilm al-kalām*, Cairo, 1939.

Zbinden, E. *Die Djinn des Islam*, Bern, 1953.

2 SHĪᶜĪ THEOLOGICAL LITERATURE

al-Ashᶜarī, Abū ᵓl-Ḥasan ᶜAlī b. Ismāᶜīl *Kitāb Maqālāt al-Islāmiyyīn*, ed. H. Ritter, Wiesbaden, 1963.

al-Ashᶜarī, Saᶜd b. ᶜAbdullāh al-Qummī *Kitāb al-Maqālāt wa-ᵓl-firaq*, ed. Muḥammad Jawād Mashkūr, Tehran, 1963.

al-Faḍl b. Shādhān al-Naysābūrī *al-Īḍāḥ*, ed. Jalāl al-Dīn al-Ḥusaynī al-Urmawī, Tehran, 1972.

al-Ḥillī, al-ᶜAllāmah al-Ḥasan b. Yūsuf b. al-Muṭahhar *al-Bāb al-ḥādī ᶜashar*, Tehran, AH 1370; trans. W. Miller, *A Treatise on the Principles of the Shīᶜite Theology*, London, 1958.

Kashf al-murād fī sharḥ tajrīd al-iᶜtiqād, being a commentary on Naṣīr al-Dīn al-Ṭūsī's *Tajrīd al-iᶜtiqād*, Qumm, AH 1377.

Ibn Bābawayhi

Risālat al-Iᶜtiqādāt in al-Ḥillī, *al-Bāb al-ḥādī ᶜashar*, Tehran, AH 1370; trans. A. A. A. Fyzee, *A Shīᶜite Creed*, Oxford, 1942.

Kamāl al-dīn wa-tamām al-niᶜmah, ed. ᶜAlī Akbar al-Ghaffārī, Tehran, AH 1395.

Kitāb al-Tawḥīd, ed. Hāshim al-Ḥusaynī, Tehran, AH 1387.

al-Kashshī, Abū ᶜAmr Muḥammad b. ᶜUmar *Rijāl al-Kashshī*, in the recension of Muḥammad b. Ḥasan al-Ṭūsī, *Ikhtiyār maᶜrifat al-rijāl*, ed. Ḥasan al-Muṣṭafā, Mashhad, AH 1348.

al-Kulaynī, Abū Jaᶜfar Muḥammad b. Yaᶜqūb *al-Uṣūl min al-kāfī*, ed. ᶜAlī Akbar al-Ghaffārī, Tehran, AH 1388.

al-Mufīd, Abū ᶜAbdullāh Muḥammad b. Muḥammad

Awāᵓil al-maqālāt fī ᵓl-madhāhib al-mukhtārāt, ed. ᶜAbbāsqulī S. Wajdī, Tabrīz, AH 1371.

al-Fuṣūl al-ᶜasharah fī ᵓl-ghaybah, Najaf, 1951.

Kitāb al-Irshād fī maᶜrifat ḥujaj Allāh ᶜalā ᵓl-ᶜibād, ed. Kāẓim al-Mūsawī al-Miyāmiwī, Tehran, AH 1377; trans. I. K. A. Howard, *The Book of Guidance into the Lives of the Twelve Imams*, London, 1981.

Kitāb Sharḥ ᶜaqāᵓid al-Ṣadūq, or *Taṣḥīḥ al-iᶜtiqād*, ed. ᶜAbbāsqulī S. Wajdī (printed in same volume as *Awāᵓil al-maqālāt*), Tehran, AH 1371.

al-Murtaḍā, al-Sharīf Abū ᵓl-Qāsim ᶜAlī b. al-Ḥusayn

Jumal al-ᶜilm wa-ᵓl-ᶜamal, Najaf, AH 1387.

Kitāb al-Shāfī fī ʾl-imāmah, Tehran, AH 1301.
al-Uṣūl al-iʿtiqādiyyah in *Nafāʾis al-makhṭūṭāt*, II, ed. Muḥammad Ḥasan Āl-Yāsīn, Baghdad, 1954.
al-Najāshī, Aḥmad b. ʿAlī *Kitāb al-Rijāl*, Tehran, n.d.
al-Nawbakhtī, Abū ʾl-Muḥammad al-Ḥasan b. Mūsā *Firaq al-Shīʿah*, ed. H. Ritter, Istanbul, 1931.
al-Qummī, Abū ʾl-Ḥasan ʿAlī b. Ibrāhīm *Tafsīr al-Qummī*, ed. Ṭayyib al-Mūsawī al-Jazāʾirī, Najaf, AH 1386.
al-Ṭūsī, Abū Jaʿfar Muḥammad b. al-Ḥasan *Fihrist kutub al-Shīʿah*, ed. A. Sprenger and Mawlāwī ʿAbd al-Ḥaqq, Calcutta, 1835.
Kitāb al-Ghaybah, Tabrīz, AH 1322.
Talkhīs al-Shāfī, ed. al-Ḥasan al-Mūsawī al-Kharsān, Najaf, 1963.
al-Ṭūsī, Naṣīr al-Dīn *Sharḥ al-Muḥaṣṣal* in Fakhr al-Dīn Muḥammad b. ʿUmar al-Rāzī, *Kitāb al-Muḥaṣṣal*, Cairo, AH 1322.
Tajrīd al-iʿtiqād in al-Ḥillī, *Kashf al-murād*, Qumm, AH 1377.

3 IBĀḌĪ THEOLOGICAL LITERATURE

Cook, M. *Early Muslim Dogma*, Cambridge, 1981.
Cuperly, P. "L'Ibadisme au XIIème siècle. La Aqida de Abu Sahl Yahya", *IBLA*, CXLIII, CXLIV, 1979.
"Muḥammad Atfayyaš et sa Risâla šâfiya fi baʿḍ tawâriḫ ahl wâdi Mizâb," *IBLA*, CXXX, 1972.
Ennami, A. K. "A description of new Ibāḍī manuscripts from North Africa", *Journal of Semitic Studies*, XV, 1970.
Ess, J. van "Untersuchungen einiger ibāḍitischen Handschriften", *Zeitschrift der Deutschen Morgenländischen Gesellschaft*, CXXVI, 1976.
Lewicki, T. "Les historiens, biographes et traditionnistes Ibāḍites – wahbites de l'Afrique du Nord du VIIIe au XVIe siècle", *Folia Orientalia*, III, 1961.
"La répartition géographique des groupements Ibāḍites dans l'Afrique du Nord au moyen-Age", *Rocznik Orientalistyczny*, XXI, 1957.
Moreno, M. M. "Note de teologica Ibāḍita", *Annali dell'Istituto Orientale di Napoli*, NS III, 1949.
Motylinski, A. de C. "Bibliographie du Mzab", *Bulletin de Correspondence Africaine*, III, 1885.
Rubinacci, R. "La Purità Rituale secondo gli Ibāḍiti", *Annali dell'Istituto Orientale di Napoli*, NS VI, 1957.
Schacht, J. "Bibliothèques et manuscrits abadites", *Revue Africaine*, C, 1956.
Schwartz, W. *Die Anfänge der Ibāḍiten in Nordafrika* (Studien zum Minderheiten-problem im Islam, VIII,), Wiesbaden, 1983.
Ǧihād unter Muslimen (Studien zum Minderheitenproblem im Islam, VI, part 2), Wiesbaden, 1980.
Smith, G. R. and Wilkinson, J. C. "The Omani manuscript collection at Muscat", *Arabian Studies*, IV, 1978.
Wilkinson, J. C. "Bio-bibliographical background to the crisis period in the Ibāḍī Imāmate of Oman", *Arabian Studies*, III, 1976.
"Ibāḍi *Ḥadīth*: an essay on normalization", *Der Islam*, LXII, 1985.
The Imamate Tradition of Oman, Cambridge, 1987.

4 QURANIC EXEGESIS

Abbott, N. *Studies in Arabic Literary Papyri*, II, *Qurʾānic Commentary and Tradition*, Chicago, Oriental Institute Publications, LXXVI, 1967.

Abū ʿUbaydah, Maʿmar b. al-Muthannā *Majāz al-Qurʾān*, ed. F. Sezgin, Cairo, 1954–62.

al-Bayḍāwī, ʿAbdullāh b. ʿUmar, *Anwār al-tanzīl wa-asrār al-taʾwīl*, Cairo, 1887.

Birkeland, H. *Old Muslim Opposition against Interpretation of the Koran*, Oslo, 1955.

al-Bukhārī, Muḥammad b. Ismāʿīl *al-Ṣaḥīḥ*, Cairo, 1896.

Burton, J. *The Collection of the Qurʾān*, Cambridge, 1977.

"The origin of the Islamic penalty for adultery", *Transactions of the Glasgow University Oriental Society*, XXVI, 1978.

al-Dānī, Abū ʿAmr ʿUthmān b. Saʿīd *Kitāb al-Muqniʿ*, ed. O. Pretzl, Istanbul, 1932.

al-Dhahabī, Muḥammad H. *al-Tafsīr wa-ʾl-mufassirūn*, Cairo, 1976.

al-Farrāʾ, Abū Zakariyyāʾ Yaḥyā b. Ziyād *Maʿāni al-Qurʾān*, Beirut, 1955, 1980.

Gätje, H. *Koran und Koranexegese*, Zürich, 1971.

Goldziher, I. *Die Richtungen der Islamischen Koranauslegungen*, Leiden, 1921, 1952.

Horst, H. "Zur Überlieferung im Korankommentar aṭ-Ṭabarīs," *Zeitschrift der Deutschen Morgenländischen Gesellschaft*, CIII, 1953.

Ibn al-ʿArabī, Abū Bakr Muḥammad b. ʿAbdullāh *Aḥkām al-Qurʾān*, Cairo, 1957.

Ibn al-ʿArabī, Muḥyī ʾl-Dīn abū ʿAbdullāh Muḥammad b. ʿAlī *The Bezels of Wisdom [Fuṣūṣ al-Ḥikam]*, trans. R. W. J. Austin, London, 1980.

Tafsīr al-shaykh, Cairo, 1866.

Ibn ʿAṭiyyah, Abū Muḥammad ʿAbd al-Ḥaqq, *Kitāb al-Jāmiʿ al-muḥarrar al-ṣaḥīḥ al-wajīz fī tafsīr al-Qurʾān al-ʿazīz* (introduction only); see A. Jeffery, below.

Ibn Ḥayyān, Muḥammad b. Yūsuf, *al-Baḥr al-Muḥīṭ*, Riyāḍ, 1969.

Ibn Qutaybah, ʿAbdullāh b. Muslim *Kitāb Taʾwīl mukhtalif al-ḥadīth*, Cairo, 1966.

al-Jaṣṣāṣ, Abū Bakr Aḥmad b. ʿAlī *Aḥkām al-Qurʾān*, Cairo, 1928.

Jeffery, A. *Kitāb al-Maṣāḥif* [Abū Bakr b. abī Dāʾūd], Cairo, 1936.

Materials for the History of the Text of the Qurʾān, Leiden, 1937.

Two Muqqadimahs on the Qurʾān Sciences, Cairo, 1954, 1972.

Mālik b. Anas *al-Muwaṭṭaʾ*, Cairo, 1929.

Muqātil b. Sulaymān *Tafsīr al-khams miʾat āyah min al-Qurʾān*, ed. Isaiah Goldberg, Shfaram, 1980.

Muslim b. al-Ḥajjāj *Ṣaḥīḥ*, Cairo, 1911.

al-Naysābūrī, Niẓām al-Dīn al-Ḥasan b. Muḥammad *Gharāʾib al-Qurʾān wa-raghāʾib al-furqān* (marg. Ṭabarī, *Tafsīr*), Būlāq, 1910.

Nöldeke, T. *Geschichte des Qorans*, Leipzig 1909–19, I and II ed. Fr. Schwally; III, ed. G. Bergsträsser and O. Pretzl, Hildesheim, 1961.

al-Qummī, ʿAlī b. Ibrāhīm *Tafsīr al-Qummī*, Beirut, 1968.

al-Qurṭubī, Muḥammad b. Aḥmad *al-Jāmiʿ li-aḥkām al-Qurʾān*, Cairo, 1952.

al-Rāzī, Fakhr al-Dīn Muḥammad b. ʿUmar *Mafātīḥ al-ghayb*, Tehran, n.d.

Rippin, A. "Ibn ʿAbbās's al-Lughāt fīʾl-Qurʾān", *Bulletin of the School of Oriental and African Studies*, XLIV, 1, 1981.

Stauth, G. *Die Überlieferung des Korankommentars Muǧāhid b. Ǧabrs*, Giessen, 1969.

al-Suyūṭī, Jalāl al-Dīn *al-Durr al-Manthūr fī tafsīr al-Maʾthūr*, Cairo, 1896.

al-Itqān fī ʿulūm al-Qurʾān, Cairo, 1935.

Tafsīr al-Jalālayn, Cairo, 1924.

al-Ṭabarī, Abū Jaʿfar Muḥammad b. Jarīr *Jāmiʿ al-Bayān ʿan taʾwīl āy al-Qurʾān*, Būlāq, 1905; ed. M. Shakir, 1955.
al-Ṭabarsī, al-Faḍl b. al-Ḥasan, *Majmaʿ al-bayān fī tafsīr al-Qurʾān*, Qumm, 1914.
al-Thaʿālibī, ʿAbd al-Raḥmān, *al-Jawāhir al-ḥisān fī tafsīr al-Qurʾān*, Algiers, 1905.
al-Ṭūsī, Muḥammad b. al-Ḥasan, *al-Tibyān fī tafsīr al-Qurʾān*, Beirut, 1957.
Wansbrough, J. *Qurʾanic Studies*, Oxford, 1977.
al-Zamakhsharī, Maḥmūd b. ʿUmar *al-Kashshāf ʿan ḥaqāʾiq al-tanzīl*, Cairo, 1948.
al-Zarkashī, Badr al-Dīn Muḥammad b. ʿAbdullāh *Kitāb al-Burhān fī ʿulūm al-Qurʾān*, Cairo, 1957.
Zayd, M. *al-Naskh fī ʾl-Qurʾān al-Karīm*, Cairo, 1963.

5 THE PROSE LITERATURE OF ṢUFISM

ʿAbdullāh al-Anṣārī al-Harawī *Manāzil al-sāʾirīn*, ed. L. de Beaurecueil, Cairo, 1954.
Munājāt wa-naṣāʾiḥ, Berlin, 1924.
ʿAfīfī, Abū al-ʿAlāʾ *al-Malāmatiyyah wa-ʾl-ṣūfiyyah wa-ahl al-futuwwah*, Cairo, 1364/1945.
Arberry, A. J. *Sufism: An Account of the Mystics of Islam*, New York, 1950.
ʿAṭṭār, Farīd al-Dīn *Tadhkirat al-awliyāʾ*, ed. R. A. Nicholson, Leiden, 1905; trans. A. J. Arberry, *Muslim Saints and Mystics: Episodes from the Tadkhirat al-Awliyāʾ*, London, 1966.
al-Ḥallāj, Manṣūr *Akhbār* . . ., ed. L. Massignon and Paul Kraus, Paris, 1936.
Ḥamīrī, Muḥammad b. abī ʾl-Qāsim *Durrat al-asrār*, Tunis, AH 1304.
al-Ḥujwīrī, ʿAlī *Kashf al-maḥjūb*, trans. R. A. Nicholson, London, 1959.
Ibn ʿAṭāʾallāh al-Sakandarī *al-Ḥikam al-ʿAṭāʾiyyah wa-ʾl-Munājāt al-ilāhiyyah*, Damascus, n.d.; trans. V. Danner, Leiden, 1973.
Laṭāʾif al-minan, Tunis, AH 1304.
Tāj al-ʿarūs wa-qamʿ al-nufūs, Cairo, AH 1304.
al-Tanwīr fī isqāṭ al-tadbīr, Cairo, 1390/1970.
al-Iṣfahānī, Abū Nuʿaym Aḥmad *Ḥilyat al-awliyāʾ*, Cairo, 1351–7/1932–7.
al-Jīlī, ʿAbd al-Karīm *al-Insān al-kāmil fī maʿrifat al-awāʾil wa-ʾl-awākhir*, Cairo, 1292/1875.
al-Kalābādhī, Abū Bakr M. *al-Taʿarruf li-madhhab ahl al-taṣawwuf*, ed. A. J. Arberry, Cairo, 1352/1933; ed. Maḥmūd al-Nawawī, Cairo, 1388/1969.
al-Makkī, Abū Ṭālib *Qūt al-qulūb fī muʿāmalat al-Maḥbūb*, Cairo, 1310/1933.
Massignon, Louis *Essai sur les origines du lexique technique de la mystique musulmane*, Paris, 1959.
al-Nabhānī, Ismāʿīl *Jāmiʿ Karāmāt al-awliyāʾ*, Cairo, 1929.
Nicholson, R. A. *Studies in Islamic Mysticism*, London, 1914 and Cambridge, 1967.
al-Qushayrī, ʿAbd al-Karīm *al-Risālah al-Qushayriyyah*, Cairo, AH 1284; ed. ʿAbd al-Ḥalīm Maḥmūd, Cairo, n.d.
al-Sarrāj, ʿAbdullāh *Kitāb al-Lumaʿ fī ʾl-taṣawwuf*, Leiden, 1914; ed. ʿAbd al-Ḥalīm Maḥmūd and Ṭāhā ʿAbd al-Bāqī Surūr, Cairo, 1380/1960.
al-Shaʿrānī, ʿAbd al-Wahhāb *al-Ṭabaqāt al-kubrā*, Cairo, AH 1305.
Smith, Margaret *Readings from the Mystics of Islam*, London, 1972.
al-Tirmidhī, Muḥammad b. ʿAlī al-Ḥakīm, *Kitāb Khatm al-wilāyah*, ed. H. I. Yaḥyā, Beirut, 1965.
Trimingham, J. Spencer *The Sufi Orders in Islam*, Oxford, 1971.

6 PHILOSOPHICAL LITERATURE

Anon. *Qiṣṣat Salāmān wa-Absāl*, condensed by Naṣīr al-Dīn b. al-Ḥusayn al-Ṭūsī in *Sharḥay al-Ishārāt*, Cairo, 1325/1907, II; trans. H. Corbin in *Avicenna and the Visionary Recital*, New York, 1960, part I, section 21.

Badawī, ʿAbd al-Raḥmān *Histoire de la Philosophie en Islam*, Paris, 1972.

Charlton, W. "Is philosophy a form of literature?", *British Journal of Aesthetics*, XIV, 1974.

"Moral beauty and overniceness", *British Journal of Aesthetics*, XX, 1980.

Hourani, George F. "Ibn Sīnā's 'Essay on the Secret of Destiny'", *Bulletin of the School of Oriental and African Studies*, XXIX, 1966.

Ḥunayn b. Isḥāq al-ʿIbādī *Qiṣṣat Salāmān wa-Absāl* (trans. from the Greek), in *Tisʿ rasāʾil*, Istanbul, 1298/1881; trans. H. Corbin in *Avicenna and the Visionary Recital*, New York, 1960, part I, section 20.

Ibn Bājjah, Abū Bakr Muḥammad b. al-Ṣāʾigh *Fī ʾttiṣāl al-ʿaql bi-ʾl-insān* in Majid Fakhry (ed.), *Rasāʾil Ibn Bājjah al-Ilāhiyyah*, Beirut, 1968; ed. and trans. Miguel Asín Palacios, *Al-Andalus*, VII, 1942.

Ibn al-Nafīs, ʿAlāʾ al-Dīn ʿAlī b. abī ʾl-Ḥazm *al-Risālat al-Kāmiliyyah fī ʾl-Sīrah al-Nabawiyyah*, ed. and partially trans. M. Meyerhof and J. Schacht, Oxford, 1968.

Ibn Ṭufayl, Abū Bakr Muḥammad b. ʿAbd al-Malik *Ḥayy ibn Yaqẓān*, ed. and trans. L. Gauthier, Beirut, 1936; trans. S. Ockley, London, 1708, repr. 1711; trans. L. E. Goodman, New York, 1972.

Leamon, O. "Does the interpretation of Islamic philosophy rest on a mistake?", *International Journal of Middle Eastern Studies*, XII, 1980.

Lerner, R., and Mahdi, M., eds. *Medieval Political Philosophy: A Sourcebook*, Ithaca, New York, 1971, part I.

Mahdi, M. "Averroës on Divine Law and Human Wisdom" in J. Cropsey (ed.), *Ancients and Moderns*, New York, 1964.

Ibn Khaldun's Philosophy of History, Chicago, 1964.

"Islamic theology and philosophy", *Encyclopaedia Britannica*, 15th edn, 1974.

"Remarks on the *Theologus Autodidactus* of Ibn al-Nafīs", *Studia Islamica*, XXXI, 1970.

Natanson, M., and Johnstone, H. W., eds. *Philosophy, Rhetoric and Argumentation*, Pennsylvania, 1965.

Pines, S. (translator's introduction) "The philosophic sources of the Guide of the Perplexed" in Moses Maimonides, *The Guide of the Perplexed*, trans. S. Pines, introductory essay by Leo Strauss, Chicago, 1963.

Sharif, M. M., ed. *A History of Muslim Philosophy*, Wiesbaden, 1963–6.

Strauss, Leo "How Fārābī read Plato's *Laws*" in *What is Political Philosophy? and Other Studies*, Glencoe, Ill., 1959, section 5.

"On a forgotten kind of writing" in *What is Political Philosophy? and Other Studies*, Glencoe, Ill., 1959, section 2.

Persecution and the Art of Writing, Glencoe, Ill., 1952.

al-Suhrawardī, Shihāb al-Dīn Yaḥyā b. Ḥabash *Qiṣṣat al-ghurbah al-gharbiyyah*, ed. H. Corbin, *Oeuvres philosophiques et mystiques de . . . Sohrawardi* (*Opera Metaphysica et Mystica*, II, i), Tehran, 1952; trans. W. M. Thackston, *The Mystical and Visionary Treatises of . . . Suhrawardi*, London, 1982.

7 ARABIC LEXICOGRAPHY

al-Azharī, Muḥammad b. Aḥmad *Tahdhīb al-lughah*, ed. A. S. M. Hārūn *et al.*, Cairo, 1964–7.

Blachère, R. "Al-Ǧawharî et sa place dans l'évolution de la lexicographie arabe" in E. Paret (ed.), *Analecta*, Damascus, 1975.

Diem, W. *Das Kitâb al-Ǧîm des Abû ʿAmr aš-Šaibânî. Ein Beitrag zur arabischen Lexikographie*, Munich, 1968.

al-Fīrūzābādī, Muḥammad b. Yaʿqūb *al-Qāmūs al-muḥīt wa-ʾl-qābūs al-wasīṭ al-jāmiʿ li-mā maḍā min lughat al-ʿArab shamāṭīṭ*, Cairo, 1952.

Gätje, H. "Arabische Lexikographie: ein historischer Überblick", *Historiographia Linguistica*, XII, 1985.

Ghaly, M. M. S. "Arabic dictionaries, an annotated, comprehensive bibliography", *Mélanges de l'Institut dominicaine d'études orientales du Caire*, X, 1970; XII, 1974.

Haywood, J. A. *Arabic Lexicography: its History and its Place in the General History of Lexicography*, Leiden, 1965.

Ibn Durayd, Abū Bakr Muḥammad b. al-Ḥasan *al-Jamharah fī ʾl-lughah*, Hyderabad, AH 1345–52; repr. Beirut, n.d; ed. Ramzi Baalbaki, Beirut, 1987–8.

Ibn Fāris, Aḥmad b. Zakariyyāʾ *Muʿjam maqāyīs al-lughah*, ed. A. S. M. Hārūn, Cairo, AH 1366–71.

Ibn Manẓūr, Muḥammad b. Mukarram *Lisān al-ʿArab*, Būlāq, AH 1300–8; another edn, Beirut, 1955–6.

Ibn Sīdah, Abū ʾl-Ḥasan ʿAlī b. Ismāʿīl *al-Muḥkam wa-ʾl-muḥīṭ al-aʿẓam*, ed. M. al-Saqqāʾ and Ḥusayn Naṣṣār, Cairo, 1958–73.

al-Mukhaṣṣaṣ fī ʾl-lughah, Cairo, AH 1316–21; repr. with index of quotations (*shawāhid*) by A. S. M. Hārūn, Beirut, AH 1386.

al-Jawharī, Abū Naṣr Ismāʿīl b. Ḥammād *Tāj al-lughah wa-ṣiḥāḥ al-ʿarabiyyah*, ed. A. A. G. ʿAṭṭār, Cairo, 1956.

al-Khalīl b. Aḥmad *Kitāb al-ʿAyn*, I, ed. A. Darwīsh, Baghdad, 1967; II, ed. M. al-Makhzūmī, Baghdad, 1981.

Kraemer, J. "Studien zur altarabischen Lexikographie nach Istanbuler und Berliner Handschriften", *Oriens*, VI, 1953.

Krenkow, F. "The beginnings of Arabic lexicography till the time of al-Jauharī, with special reference to the work of Ibn Duraid", *Journal of the Royal Asiatic Society* (centenary suppl.), 1924.

Lane, E. W. *An Arabic-English Lexicon Derived from the Best and Most Copious Eastern Sources*, London, 1863–77; repr. New York, 1955–6; Beirut, 1968; Tehran, n.d.; London, 1984.

Marçais, W. "La lexicographie arabe", *Articles et Conferences*, Paris, 1961.

Rundgren, F. "La lexicographie arabe" in P. Fronzaroli (ed.), *Studies in Semitic Lexicography*, Florence, 1973.

Vix, H. "Survey of useful Arabic reference materials", *al-ʿArabiyyah*, XII, 1979.

Wild, S. *Das Kitāb al-ʿain und die arabische Lexikographie*, Wiesbaden, 1965.

al-Zabīdī, Abū ʾl-Fayḍ Muḥammad Murtaḍā *Tāj al-ʿarūs min jawāhir al-qāmūs*, Cairo, AH 1306–7; Kuwait, 1965– .

al-Zamakhsharī, Abū ʾl-Qāsim Maḥmūd b. ʿUmar *Asās al-balāghah*, Cairo, 1960.

8 ARABIC GRAMMAR

al-Astarābādhī, Raḍī ʾl-Dīn Muḥammad *Sharḥ Kāfiyat Ibn al-Ḥājib*, Istanbul, 1275/1857–8.

Bakalla, M. H. *Arabic Linguistics: an Introduction and Bibliography*, London, 1983.

Bobzin, H., and Versteegh, C. H. M. (Kees) (eds.) "Studies in the history of Arabic grammar", *Zeitschrift für Arabische Linguistik*, xv, 1985.

Bohas, G., and Guillaume, J.-P. *Etudes des théories des grammairiens arabes*, I, *Morphologie et phonologie*, Damascus, 1984.

Carter, M. G. "An Arab grammarian of the eighth century A.D.", *Journal of the American Oriental Society*, XCIII, 1973.

Arab Linguistics, an Introductory Classical Text with Translation and Notes (Ibn Ājurrūm), Amsterdam, 1981.

"Les origines de la grammaire arabe", *Revue des Etudes Islamiques*, XL, 1972.

"When did the Arabic word *naḥw* first come to denote grammar?", *Language and Communication*, v, 1985.

Diem, W. "Bibliographie: Sekundärliteratur zur einheimischen arabischen Grammatikschreibung", *Historiographia Linguistica*, VIII, 1981.

Elamrani-Jamal, A. *Logique aristotélicienne et grammaire arabe, étude et documents*, Paris, 1983.

al-Fārisī, Abū ʿAlī *Kitāb al-Īḍāḥ*, ed. H. S. Farhoud, Cairo, 1969.

Haarmann, U. "Religiöses Recht und Grammatik im klassischen Islam" in W. Voigt (ed.), *XVIII Deutscher Orientalistentag*, Wiesbaden, 1974.

Howell, M.S. *Grammar of the Classical Arabic Language*, Hyderabad, 1886–1911.

Ibn al-Anbārī, Abū ʾl-Barakāt ʿAbd al-Raḥmān b. Muḥammad *al-Inṣāf fī masāʾil al-khilāf. Die grammatischen Streitfragen der Basrer und Kufer*, ed. G. Weil, Leiden, 1913.

Lumaʿ al-adillah fī uṣūl al-naḥw, ed. A. Amer, Stockholm, 1963.

Ibn Bābashādh, Ṭāhir b. Aḥmad *al-Muqaddimah al-muḥsibah*, ed. A. ʿAbd al-Karīm, Kuwait, 1977.

Ibn Fāris, Abū ʾl-Ḥusayn Aḥmad *Kitāb al-Ṣāḥibī fī fiqh al-lughah*, ed. M. Chouémi, Beirut, 1963.

Ibn Hishām, Jamāl al-Dīn ʿAbdullāh b. Yūsuf *Qaṭr al-nadā wa-ball al-ṣadā. La Pluie de rosée, étanchement de soif*, trans. A. Goguyer, Leiden, 1887.

Ibn Jinnī, Abū ʾl-Fatḥ ʿUthmān *Khaṣāʾiṣ al-ʿarabiyyah*, ed. M. A. al-Najjār, Cairo, 1952–6.

Ibn Maḍāʾ al-Qurṭubī *al-Radd ʿalā ʾl-nuḥāh*, ed. S. Ḍayf, Cairo, 1968.

Ibn Mālik, Jamāl al-Dīn Muḥammad b. ʿAbdullāh *Tashīl al-fawāʾid*, ed. M. K. Barakāt, Cairo, 1968.

La ʾAlfiyyah d'Ibn Mālik, suivi du Lāmiyyah du même auteur, ed. and trans. A. Goguyer, Beirut, 1888.

Ibn al-Sarrāj, Muḥammad b. al-Sarī *al-Mūjaz fī ʾl-naḥw*, ed. M. Chouémi, and B. Damerji, Beirut, 1965.

al-Uṣūl fī ʾl-naḥw, ed. A. H. al-Fatlī, Najaf, 1973.

Ibn Yaʿīsh, Abū ʾl-Baqāʾ Yaʿīsh b. ʿAlī *Sharḥ al-Mufaṣṣal*, ed. G. Jahn, Leipzig, 1882–6.

al-Iṣfahānī, Lughdah *al-Mukhtaṣar fī ʾl-naḥw*, ed. ʿA. al-Fatlī in *Mawrid*, III, 1974.

al-Mubarrad, Abū ʾl-ʿAbbās Muḥammad b. Yazīd *Kitāb al-Muqtaḍab*, ed. M. A. K. ʿUḍaymah, Cairo, 1963–8.
Sībawayhi, Abū Bishr ʿAmr b. ʿUthmān *Le Livre de Sībawaih, traité de grammaire arabe*, ed. H. Derenbourg, Paris, 1881–9, repr. Hildesheim, 1970.
Sibawaihi's Buch über die Grammatik, trans. G. Jahn, Berlin, 1895–1900; repr. Hildesheim, 1969.
Kitāb Sībawayhi, Būlāq, 1898–1900; repr. Baghdad, 1965.
Troupeau, G. *Lexique-Index du Kitāb de Sībawayhi*, Paris, 1976.
Versteegh, C. H. M. *Greek Elements in Arabic Linguistic Thinking*, Leiden, 1977.
"Current bibliography on the history of Arabic grammar", *Zeitschrift für Arabische Linguistik*, XII, 1984.
al-Zajjājī, Abū ʾl-Qāsim *al-Īḍāḥ fī ʿilal al-naḥw*, ed. M. al-Mubārak, Cairo, 1959.
al-Jumal, ed. M. Ben Cheneb, Paris, 1957.
al-Zamakhsharī, Abū ʾl-Qāsim Maḥmūd b. ʿUmar *al-Mufaṣṣal*, ed. J. P. Broch, Christiania, 1879.

9 ISLAMIC LEGAL LITERATURE

Aghnides, N. P. *Mohamedan Theories of Finance*, New York, 1916.
Coulson, N. J. *A History of Islamic Law*, Edinburgh, 1964.
Fyzee, A. A. A. *Outlines of Muhammadan Law*, ed. D. Pearl, Oxford, 1983.
Liebesny, H. J. *The Law of the Near and Middle East*, Albany, 1975.
Pearl, D. *A Textbook on Muslim Law*, London, 1979.
Schacht, J. *Introduction to Islamic Law*, Oxford, 1964.
The Origins of Muhammadan Jurisprudence, Oxford, 1950.

10 ADMINISTRATIVE LITERATURE

Ben Shemesh, A. *Taxation in Islam*, Leiden, 1958–69.
Björkman, W. *Beiträge zur Geschichte der Staatskanzlei im islamischen Ägypten*, Hamburg, 1928.
Bosworth, C. E. "Abū ʿAbdallāh al-Khwārazmī on the technical terms of the secretary's art: a contribution to the administrative history of mediaeval Islam", *Journal of the Economic and Social History of the Orient*, XIII, 1969, 113–64.
"An early Arabic Mirror for Princes: Ṭāhir Dhū ʾl-Yamīnain's epistle to his son ʿAbdallāh (206/821)", *Journal of Near Eastern Studies*, XXIX, 1970, 25–41.
Løkkegaard, F. *Islamic Taxation in the Classic Period, with Special Reference to Circumstances in Iraq*, Copenhagen, 1950.
Mez, A. *The Renaissance of Islam*, Eng. trans. S. Khuda Bakhsh, Patna, 1937.
Richter, G. *Studien zur Geschichte der älteren arabischen Fürstenspiegel*, Leipzig, 1932.
Rosenthal, E. I. J. *Political Thought in Medieval Islam: an Introductory Outline*, Cambridge, 1968.
Sourdel, D. *Le Vizirat ʿabbāside de 749 à 936 (132 à 324 de l'Hégire)*, Damascus, 1959–60.

11 ARABIC BIOGRAPHICAL WRITING

Auchterlonie, P. *Arabic Biographical Dictionaries: a summary guide and bibliography*, Durham, 1987.
Bulliet, R. W. *The Patricians of Nishapur*, Cambridge, Mass., 1972.
"A quantitative approach to medieval Muslim biographical dictionaries", *Journal of the Economic and Social History of the Orient*, XIII, 1970.
Grunebaum, G. E. von *Medieval Islam: A Study in Cultural Orientation*, Chicago, 1946.
Hafsi, Ibrahim "Recherches sur le genre 'Ṭabaqāt' dans la littérature arabe", *Arabica*, XXIII, 1976; XXIV, 1977.
Ḥasan, Muḥammad ʿAbd al-Ghanī *al-Tarājim wa-ʾl-siyar*, Cairo, 1955.
Holt, P. M. "Three biographies of al-Ẓāhir Baybars", *Medieval Historical Writing in the Christian and Islamic Worlds*, ed. D. O. Morgan, London, 1982.
Morray, D. W. *The Genius of Usāmah ibn Munqidh: aspects of Kitāb al-Iʿtibār by Usāmah ibn Munqidh*, Durham, 1987.
Pellat, C. "Peut-on connaître le taux de natalité au temps du Prophète? A la recherche d'une méthode", *Journal of the Economic and Social History of the Orient* XIV, 1971.
Petry, C. F. *The Civilian Elite of Cairo in the Later Middle Ages*, Princeton, 1981.
Rosenthal, F. "Die arabische Autobiographie", *Studia Arabica*, I, Rome, 1937.
ʿUṭbah, ʿAbd al-Raḥmān *Maʿa ʾl-maktabah al-ʿArabiyyah*, Beirut, 1984.

12 HISTORY AND HISTORIANS

Abbott, N. *Studies in Arabic Literary Papyri*, I, Historical Texts, Chicago, 1957.
Baumstark, A. *Geschichte der syrischen Literatur*, Bonn, 1922.
Cahen, C. *La Syrie du Nord à l'époque des Croisades*, Paris, 1940.
Canard, M. *Histoire de la dynastie des Hamdanides*, Algiers, 1951.
Daniel, E. I. "The anonymous history of the Abbasid family and its place in Islamic historiography", *International Journal of Middle Eastern Studies*, XIV, 1982.
al-Dūrī, ʿAbd al-ʿAzīz *Baḥth fī nashʾat ʿilm al-taʾrīkh ʿinda ʾl-ʿArab*, Beirut, 1960.
Hunger, H. *Geschichte der byzantinischen Literatur*, Münster, 1978.
Ibn al-Ṣayrafī *al-Ishārah ilā man nāla al-wizārah*, ed. A. Mukhlis, *Bulletin de l'Institut Français d'Archéologie Orientale du Caire*, XXV, 1924.
Idris, H. R., *La Berbérie orientale sous les Zirides*, Paris, 1962.
Madelung, W. "Abū Isḥāq al-Ṣābī on the Alids of Tabaristan and Gīlān" *Journal of Near Eastern Studies*, XXVI, 1967.
"The identity of two Yemenite MSS", *Journal of Near Eastern Studies*, XXXII, 1973.
Margoliouth, D. *Lectures on Arabic Historians*, Calcutta, 1930.
Morgan, D. O. (ed.) *Medieval Historical Writing in the Christian and Islamic Worlds*, London, 1982.
al-Munajjid, Ṣalāḥ al-Dīn *al-Muʾarrikhūn al-Dimashqiyyūn*, Cairo, 1956.
al-Muṭahhar al-Maqdisī *Kitāb al-Badʾ wa-ʾl-taʾrīkh*, ed. C. Huart, Paris, 1899–1919.
Rotter, G. "Abu Zurʿa al-Dimashqi und das Problem der frühen arabischen Geschichtsschreibung in Syrien", *Die Welt des Orients*, VI, 1971.
"Zur Überlieferung einiger historischen Werke Madāʾinīs in Tabaris Annales", *Oriens*, XXIII–XXIV, 1974.

Sezgin, F. *Abū Miḥnaf: ein Beitrag zur Historiographie der Omayadenzeit*, Leiden, 1971.
Talbi, M. *L'Emirat Aghlabide*, Paris, 1966.
Wüstenfeld, F., *Die Chroniken der Stadt Mekka*, Leipzig, 1858–1861.

13 FAṬIMID HISTORY AND HISTORIANS

Becker, C. H. *Beiträge zur Geschichte Aegyptens*, Strassburg, 1903.
Bryer, D. R. W. "The origins of the Druze religion", *Der Islam*, LII, 1975; LIII, 1976.
Cahen, Claude "Quelques chroniques anciennes rélatives aux derniers Fatimides," *Bulletin de l'Institut Français d'Archéologie Orientale du Caire*, XXXVI, 1937.
Casanova, P., "Les derniers Fatimides", *Mémoires publiés par les membres de l'Institut Français d'Archéologie Orientale du Caire*, VI, 1897.
Gacek, A. *Catalogue of Arabic Manuscripts in the Library of the Institute of Ismaili Studies*, London, 1984–5.
Goeje, M. J. de *Mémoire sur les Carmathes du Baḥrain et les Fatimides*, Leiden, 1886.
Goriawala, Muᶜizz *A Descriptive Catalogue of the Fyzee Collection of Ismāᶜīlī Manuscripts*, Bombay, 1965.
Guyard, S. *Fragments rélatifs à la doctrine des Ismaélis*, Paris, 1874.
Hamdani, Abbas *The Beginnings of the Ismāᶜīlī Daᶜwa in Northern India*, Cairo, 1956.
Hamdānī, Ḥusayn *al-Ṣulayḥiyyūn*, Cairo, 1955.
"The history of the Ismāᶜīlī Daᶜwat and its literature during the last phase of the Fatimid empire," *Journal of the Royal Asiatic Society*, 1932.
"Some unknown Ismāᶜīlī authors and their works", *Journal of the Royal Asiatic Society*, 1933.
Hammer-Purgstall, J. von *The History of the Assassins*, trans. O. C. Wood, 1968, from German original of 1835.
Ḥasan Ibrāhīm Ḥasan and Ṭāhā Sharaf
al-Muᶜizz li-dīn Allāh, Cairo, 1947.
ᶜUbaydullāh al-Mahdī, Cairo, 1947.
Ḥasan b. Yaᶜqūb al-Hamdānī *Ṣifat Jazīrat al-ᶜArab*, ed. Muḥammad b. ᶜAlī al-Akwaᶜ al-Ḥiwālī, Beirut, 1983; Riyāḍ, 1984.
Hodgson, M. G. S. *The Order of the Assassins*, The Hague, 1955.
Hollister, J. N. *The Shīᶜa of India*, London, 1953.
Ḥusayn, Muḥammad Kāmil *Ṭāʾifat al-Ismāᶜīliyyah*, Cairo, 1959.
Ivanow, Wladimir *A Guide to Ismāᶜīlī Literature*, London, 1933.
Ismāᶜīlī Literature: A Bibliographical Survey, Tehran, 1963.
Kāmil Ḥusayn, M. *Fī Adab Miṣr al-Fāṭimiyyah*, Cairo, 1963.
Kraus, Paul "La bibliographie Ismaélienne de W. Ivanow", *Revue des Etudes Islamiques*, VI, 1932.
Lane-Poole, Stanley *History of Egypt in the Middle Ages*, London, 1901.
Lewis, B. *The Assassins*, London, 1967.
Löfgren, O., and Traini, R. *Catalogue of the Arabic Manuscripts in the Biblioteca Ambrosiana*, Vicenza, 1975–81.
Madelung, W. "Das Imāmat in der frühen ismailitischen Lehre", *Der Islam*, XXXVII, 1961.
Mājid, ᶜAbd al-Munᶜim *Nuẓum al-Fāṭimiyyīn wa-rusūmuhum*, Cairo, 1955.
Ẓuhūr khilāfat al-Fāṭimiyyīn wa-suqūṭuhā, Cairo, 1977.

Massignon, L. "Esquisse d'une bibliographie Carmathe", *E. G. Browne Festschrift*, London, 1922.
O'Leary, De Lacy *A Short History of the Fatimid Khalifate*, London, 1923.
Poonawala, I. K. *Biobibliography of Ismāʿīlī Literature*, Malibu, California, 1977.
Quatremère, E. "Mémoires historiques sur la dynastie des Khalifes Fatimides", *Journal Asiatique*, II, 1836; III, 1837.
Sacy, Silvestre de *Exposé de la religion des Druzes*, Paris, 1838.
Sayyid, Ayman Fuʾād *Maṣādir taʾrīkh al-Yaman fī ʾl-ʿaṣr al-Islāmī*, Cairo, 1974.
"Lumières nouvelles sur quelques sources de l'histoire Fatimide en Egypte", *Annales Islamologiques*, XIII, 1977.
al-Shayyāl, Jamāl al-Dīn *Majmūʿat al-wathāʾiq al-Fāṭimiyyah*, Cairo, 1958.
Stern, S. M. *Fatimid Decrees*, London, 1964.
Tajdin, Nagib *A Bibliography of Ismāʿīlism*, Delmar, New York, 1985.
Wüstenfeld, F. *Geschichte der Fatimiden-Chalifen*, Göttingen, 1881.
Zāhid, ʿAlī *Taʾrīkh-i-Fāṭimiyyīn-i-Miṣr* (in Urdu), Hyderabad, 1948.

14 MATHEMATICS AND APPLIED SCIENCE

al-Hassan, Ahmad Y., and Hill, Donald R. *Islamic Technology: An Illustrated History*, Paris and Cambridge, 1986.
Hill, Donald R. *Arabic Water-Clocks*, Institute for the History of Arabic Science, Aleppo, 1981.
A History of Engineering in Classical and Medieval Times, London, 1984.
Mieli, A. *La Science Arabe*, Leiden, 1966.
Nasr, S. H. *Science and Civilization in Islam*, Cambridge, Mass., 1968.
Wiedemann, E. *Aufsätze zur Arabischen Wissenschaftsgeschichte*, Hildesheim and New York, 1970.

15 ASTRONOMY

Caussin de Perceval "Le livre de la grande table Hakémite, observée par le Sheikh . . . ebn Iounis . . .", *Notices et Extraits des Manuscrits de la Bibliothèque Nationale* (Paris), VII, 1804.
Debarnot, M. T. *Al-Bīrūnī, Kitāb Maqālīd ʿilm al-hayʾa – La Trigonométrie Sphérique chez les Arabes de l'Est à la fin du Xᵉ siècle*, Damascus, 1985.
Goldstein, B. R. *Al-Biṭrūjī: On the Principles of Astronomy*, New Haven and London, 1971.
Theory and Observation in Ancient and Medieval Astronomy, London, 1985.
Hartner, W. "The Islamic astronomical background to Nicholas Copernicus", *Studia Copernicana*, XIII, 1975.
Heinen, A. M. *Islamic Cosmology: A Study of as-Suyūṭī's al-Hayʾa al-saniya*, Wiesbaden, 1982.
Kennedy, E. S. "The exact sciences in Iran under the Seljuqs and Mongols" in *Cambridge History of Iran*, V, Cambridge, 1968.
"The digital computer and the history of the exact sciences", *Centaurus*, XII, 1967.
"A survey of Islamic astronomical tables", *Transactions of the American Philosophical Society* (Philadelphia), XLVI, 1956.

Kennedy, E. S., and Ghanem, I. *The Life and Work of Ibn al-Shāṭir: An Arab Astronomer of the Fourteenth Century*, Aleppo, 1976.
Kennedy, E. S., and Haddad, F. I. "Geographical tables of medieval Islam", *al-Abḥāth*, XXIV, 1971.
Kennedy, E. S., and King, D. A. "Astronomy in the medieval Maghrib", *Journal for the History of Arabic Science*, VI, 1982.
King, D. A. *Islamic Astronomical Instruments*, London, 1987.
Islamic Mathematical Astronomy, London, 1986.
Mathematical Astronomy in Medieval Yemen, Malibu, California, 1982.
A Survey of the Scientific MSS in the Egyptian National Library, Indiana, 1986.
"Astronomical alignments in medieval Islamic religious architecture", *Annals of the New York Academy of Sciences*, 1982.
"On the astronomical tables of the Islamic Middle Ages", *Studia Copernicana*, XIII, 1975.
"Astronomical timekeeping (ʿ*ilm al-mīqāt*) in medieval Islam", *Actes du XXIX*ᵉ *Congrès International des Orientalistes*, Paris, 1973.
"The astronomy of the Mamluks", *Muqarnas*, 1982.
King, D. A., and Saliba G. (eds.) *From Deferment to Equant: Studies in the History of Science in the Ancient and Medieval Near East in Honor of E. S. Kennedy*, New York, 1987.
Kunitzsch, P. *Untersuchungen zur Sternnomenklatur der Araber*, Wiesbaden, 1961.
Livingston, J. "Naṣīr al-Dīn al-Ṭūsī's al-Tadhkira: a category of Islamic astronomical literature", *Centaurus*, XVII, 1972–3.
Mayer, L. A., *Islamic Astrolabists and their Works*, Geneva, 1956.
Nallino, C. A. *al-Battani sive Albatenii Opus Astronomicum* (Pubblicazioni del Reale Osservatorio di Brera in Milano, XL), Milan and Rome, 1899–1907; repr. Frankfurt, 1969.
Neugebauer, O. "The astronomical tables of al-Khwārizmī", *Kgl. Danske Vidensk. hist.-fil. Skrifter*, 4:2, 1962.
Pingree, D. "The fragments of the works of al-Fazārī", *Journal of Near Eastern Studies*, XXIX, 1970.
"The fragments of the works of Yaʿqūb ibn Ṭāriq", *Journal of Near Eastern Studies*, XXVI, 1968.
"The Greek influence on Early Islamic mathematical astronomy", *Journal of the American Oriental Society*, XCIII, 1973.
"Indian influence on Sassanian and Early Islamic astronomy and astrology", *Journal of Oriental Research, Madras*, XXXIV–V, 1964–6.
Savage-Smith, E. *Islamicate Celestial Globes*, Washington, 1985.
Sayili, A. *The Observatory in Islam*, Ankara, 1960.
Schmalzl, P. *Zur Geschichte des Quadranten bei den Arabern*, Munich, 1929.
Schoy, C. "Gnomonik der Araber" in E. von Bassermann-Jordan (ed.), *Die Geschichte der Zeitmessung und der Uhren*, Berlin and Leipzig, 1923.
Sédillot, J.-J. *Traité des instruments astronomiques des Arabes*, Paris, 1834–5.
Sédillot, L. A. "Mémoire sur les instruments astronomiques des arabes", *Mémoires présentés . . . à l'Académie Royale . . . de l'Institut de France*, I, 1844.
Prolégomenes des tables astronomiques d'Oloug-Beg, Paris, 1853.
al-Ṣūfī, ʿAbd al-Raḥmān b. ʿUmar *Kitāb Ṣuwar al-kāwakib al-thābitah*, Hyderabad, 1954.

Suter, H. "Die astronomischen Tafeln des Muḥammed ibn Mūsā al-Khwārizmī in der Bearbeitung des Maslama ibn Aḥmed al-Madjrīṭī und der latein. Übersetzung des Adelard von Bath", *Kgl. Danske Vidensk. Skrifter*, 7. R., Hist. og filos. Afd., 1914, III, part I.

Tekeli, S. "Nasirüddin, Takiyüddin ve Tycho Brahe'nin Rasat Aletlerinin Mukayesesi", *Ankara Universitesi Dil ve Tarih-Coğrafya Fakültesi Dergesi*, XVI, 1958.

Toomer, G. J. "A survey of the Toledan tables", *Osiris*, XV, 1968.

Vernet Ginés, J. *Contribución al Estudio de la Labor Astronómica de Ibn al-Bannāʾ*, Tetuan, 1952.

16 ASTROLOGY

Carmody, F. J. *Arabic Astronomical and Astrological Sciences in Latin Translation*, Berkeley-Los Angeles, 1956.

Catalogus Codicum Astrologorum Graecorum, Brussels, 1898–1954.

Fahd, T. *La Divination Arabe*, Leiden, 1966.

Kennedy, E. S., and Pingree D. *The Astrological History of Māshāʾallāh*, Cambridge, Mass., 1971.

Steinschneider, M. *Die Hebräischen Übersetzungen des Mittelalters und die Juden als Dolmetscher*, Berlin, 1893.

17 GEOGRAPHICAL AND NAVIGATIONAL LITERATURE

Abū ʾl-Fidāʾ, Ismāʿīl b. ʿAlī *Taqwīm al-buldān*, ed. J. T. Reinaud and M. de Slane, Paris, 1840.

al-Bakrī, Abū ʿUbayd ʿAbdullāh ʿAbd al-ʿAzīz *al-Masālik wa-ʾl-mamālik* (N.W. Africa), ed. M. de Slane, Algiers, 1911.

Muʿjam mā ʾstaʿjam, ed. M. al-Saqqāʾ, Cairo, 1945–9.

Buzurg b. Shahriyār *ʿAjāʾib al-Hind*, ed. P. A. Van der Lith and trans. M. Devic, Leiden, 1883.

Colebrooke, H. T. *Algebra with Arithmetic and Mensuration from the Sanskrit*, London, 1817.

al-Dimashqī, Shams al-Dīn *Nukhbat al-dahr fī ʿajāʾib al-barr wa-ʾl-baḥr*, ed. A. Mehren, St Petersburg, 1886.

de Goeje, M. J. "Die Istakhrī-Balkhī Frage", *Zeitschrift der Deutschen morgenländischen Gesellschaft*, XXV, 1871.

Honigmann, E. *Die Sieben Klimata*, Heidelberg, 1929.

Ibn Baṭṭūṭah, Muḥammad b. ʿAbdullāh *Tuḥfat al-nuẓẓār fī gharāʾib al-amṣār wa-ʿajāʾib al-asfār*, ed. and trans. C. Defrémery and B. R. Sanguinetti, Paris, 1853–8.

Ibn Faḍlān, Aḥmad b. Ḥammād *Risālah*, ed. Sāmī al-Dahhān, Damascus, 1959.

Ibn al-Faqīh, Abū Bakr Aḥmad b. Ibrāhīm al-Hamadhānī *Mukhtaṣar Kitāb al-Buldān*, ed. M. J. de Goeje, Leiden, 1885.

Ibn Ḥawqal, Abū ʾl-Qāsim *Ṣūrat al-arḍ*, ed. M. J. de Goeje, Leiden, 1873; ed. J. H. Kramers, Leiden, 1938.

Ibn Jubayr, Abū ʾl-Ḥusayn Muḥammad b. Aḥmad *Riḥlah*, ed. W. Wright, 1852; trans. R. J. C. Broadhurst, London, 1952.

Ibn Khurradādhbih, ʿUbaydullāh b. al-Qāsim *Kitāb al-Masālik wa-ʾl-mamālik*, ed. M. J. de Goeje, Leiden, 1889.

Ibn Mājid, Aḥmad *Ḥāwiyat al-ikhtiṣār fī uṣūl ʿilm al-biḥār*, ed. and analysis I. Khūrī, "La Ḥāwiya de Aḥmad bin Maǧid", *Bulletin d'études orientales*, XXIV, 1971.

Kitāb al-Fawāʾid, facsimile text in G. Ferrand, *Instructions nautiques et routiers arabes et portugais*, I, Paris, 1921; ed. Ibrāhīm Khūrī, Damascus, 1971.

Ibn Rustih, *Kitāb al-Aʿlāq al-nafīsah*, ed. M. J. de Goeje, Leiden, 1892.

Ibn Saʿīd, Abū ʾl-Ḥasan ʿAlī b. Mūsā *Basṭ al-arḍ fī ʾl-ṭūl wa-ʾl-ʿarḍ*, ed. J. Vernet Ginés, Tetuan, 1958.

al-Idrīsī, Muḥammad b. Muḥammad *Nuzhat al-mushtāq fī ʾkhtirāq al-āfāq*, ed. A. Bombaci, U. Rizzitano, R. Rubinacci and L. Veccia Vaglieri, Naples-Rome, 1970–(in progress).

al-Iṣṭakhrī, Ibrāhīm b. Muḥammad *al-Masālik wa-ʾl-mamālik*, ed. M. J. de Goeje, Leiden, 1870; ed. Muḥammad Jābir ʿAbd al-ʿĀl al-Ḥīnī, Cairo, 1961.

al-Khwārazmī, Muḥammad b. Mūsā *Kitāb Ṣūrat al-arḍ*, ed. H. von Mžik, Leipzig, 1926.

Krachkovsky, I. J. *Arabskaya geografičeskaya literatura*, Moscow-Leningrad, 1957; trans. Ṣalāḥ al-Dīn ʿUthmān Hāshim, *Taʾrīkh al-adab al-jughrāfī al-ʿarabī*, Cairo, 1963–5.

Kramers, J. H. "Geography and commerce" in Sir T. Arnold and A. Guillaume (eds.), *The Legacy of Islam*, Oxford, 1931.

al-Masʿūdī, Abū ʾl-Ḥasan ʿAlī *Murūj al-dhahab*, ed. and trans. A. C. Barbier de Maynard and Pavet de Courteille, Paris, 1861–77.

al-Tanbīh wa-ʾl-ishrāf, ed. M. J. de Goeje, Leiden, 1893–4.

Miquel, A. *La Géographie humaine du monde musulman jusqu'au milieu du 11ᵉ siècle*, Paris and The Hague, 1973, 1975, 1980.

al-Muqaddasī, Shams al-Dīn Abū ʿAbdullāh Muḥammad b. Aḥmad *Aḥsan al-taqāsīm fī maʿrifat al-aqālīm*, ed. M. J. de Goeje, Leiden, 1887, 1906.

Nallino, C. A. "Al-Ḫuwârizmî e il suo rifacimento della Geografia di Tolomeo", *Atti della* R. *Accademia dei Lincei*, CCXCI, 1894.

Ptolemy *Almagest*, trans. G. J. Toomer, London, 1984.

Claudii Ptolemei Geographia, ed. C. F. A. Nobbe, Leipzig, 1888–93.

al-Qazwīnī, Zakariyyāʾ b. Muḥammad *ʿAjāʾib al-makhlūqāt wa-āthār al-bilād*, ed. F. Wüstenfeld, Göttingen, 1848.

Ṣafī ʾl-Dīn, ʿAbd al-Muʾmin al-Baghdādī *Marāṣid al-iṭṭilāʿ*, ed. T. Juynboll (*Lexicon geographicum*), Leiden, 1852–64.

Ṣāʿid al-Andalusī *Ṭabaqāt al-umam*, ed. L. Cheikho, Beirut, 1912.

Suhrāb, Ibn Sarābiyūn *ʿAjāʾib al-aqālīm al-sabʿah ilā nihāyat al-ʿimārah*, ed. H. von Mžik, Leipzig, 1930.

Sulaymān al-Mahrī *ʿUmdah*, text in G. Ferrand, *Instructions nautiques et routiers arabes et portugais*, II, Paris, 1925.

al-ʿUmarī, Shihāb al-Dīn b. Faḍlullāh *Masālik al-abṣār fī mamālik al-amṣār*, partial ed. (N. Africa and Spain) H. H. ʿAbd al-Wahhāb, Tunis, n.d.; and (Mali) Ṣalāḥ al-Dīn al-Munajjid, Beirut, 1963.

al-Yaʿqūbī, Aḥmad b. abī Yaʿqūb *Kitāb al-Buldān*, ed. M. J. de Goeje, Leiden, 1892.

Yāqūt al-Ḥamawī *Kitāb al-Mushtarik waḍʿan wa-ʾl-muftariq ṣuqʿan*, ed. F. Wüstenfeld, Göttingen, 1846.

18 THE LITERATURE OF ARABIC ALCHEMY

Burckhardt, T. *Alchemy – Science of the Cosmos, Science of the Soul*, trans. W. Stoddart, Baltimore, 1971.

Geber, *The Works of Geber*, trans. R. Russell, London, 1678; new edn, E. J. Holmyard, London and Toronto, 1928.

Holmyard, E. J. *Alchemy*, Harmondsworth, 1957.

Kraus, P. *Jābir b. Ḥayyān*, I, Cairo, 1943; II, Cairo, 1942.

Naṣr, Ḥusayn *Islamic Science: An Illustrated Study*, London, 1976.

Needham, J. *Science and Civilization in China*, V, part 2, Cambridge, 1974.

"The elixir concept and chemical medicine in East and West", *Journal of the Chinese University of Hong Kong*, II, 1974.

al-Rāzī *Al-Rāzī's Buch Geheimnis der Geheimnisse*, trans. and annot. J. Ruska, Berlin, 1937.

Sherwood Taylor, F. *The Alchemists, Founders of Modern Chemistry*, New York, 1949; London, 1951.

19 ARABIC MEDICAL LITERATURE

al-Anṭākī, Dāwūd *al-Tadhkirah*, Cairo, AH 1325.

Browne, E. G. *Arabian Medicine*, Cambridge, 1921.

Chahār Maqālah, Cambridge, 1921.

Campbell, D. *Arabian Medicine*, London, 1926.

Elgood, C. L. *A Medical History of Persia and the Eastern Caliphate*, Cambridge, 1951.

Ghaliongi, P. *Questions on Medicine for Scholars*, Cairo, 1980.

al-Haylah, M. H. *Siyāsat al-ṣibyān wa-tadbīruhum*, Tunis, 1968.

Ḥunayn b. Isḥāq al-ʿIbādī *Kitāb al-Masāʾil fī ʾl-ʿayn: Livre des questions sur l'oeil de Honein b. Ishaq*, ed. P. Sbath and M. Meyerhof, Cairo, 1938.

ʿAshr maqālāt, Hyderabad, 1964.

Meyerhof, M. *Las operaciones de cataracta de ʿAmmār b. ʿAlī al-Mauṣilī*, Barcelona, 1937.

"Ṭabarī's Paradise of Wisdom", *Isis*, XVI, 1931.

al-Sāmarrāʾī, Kamāl *Mukhtaṣar Taʾrīkh al-ṭibb al-ʿarabī*, Baghdad, 1984– .

Schacht, J. and Meyerhof, M. *The Controversy between Ibn Buṭlān and Ibn Riḍwān*, Cairo, 1973.

Ṣiddīqī, M. Z. *Firdaws al-ḥikmah*, Berlin, 1929.

Ullmann, M. *Islamic Medicine*, Edinburgh, 1978.

20 AL-KINDĪ

Altmann, A., and Stern, S. M. *Isaac Israeli*, London, 1958.

Atiyeh, G. N. *Al-Kindi: The Philosopher of the Arabs*, Rawalpindi, 1966.

Endress, G. *Proclus Arabus*, Beirut and Wiesbaden, 1973.

Ivry, A. L. *Al-Kindi's Metaphysics*, Albany, 1974.

al-Kindī, Abū Yūsuf Yaʿqūb b. Isḥāq *Rasāʾil al-Kindī al-falsafiyyah*, ed. M. A. Abū Rīdah, Cairo, 1950–3.

Rescher, N. *Al-Kindi: An Annotated Bibliography*, Pittsburgh, 1964.

Rosenthal, F. "Al-Kindi and Ptolemy", *Studi Orientalistici in Onore di Giorgio Levi della Vida*, II, Rome, 1956.

Zimmermann, F. W. "The origins of the so-called *Theology of Aristotle*" in J. Kraye, W. F. Ryan and C. B. Schmitt (eds.), *Pseudo-Aristotle in the Middle Ages*, London, 1986.

21 AL-RĀZĪ

Channing, J. *Rhazes de variolis et morbilis, Arabice et Latine*, London, 1766.
Hau, F. R. "Taqrīr al-Rāzī ḥawla ʾl-zukām al-muzmin ʿinda tafattuḥ al-ward", *Journal for the History of Arabic Science*, I, 1977.
Heym, G. "Al-Rāzī and alchemy", *Ambix*, I, 1938.
Iskandar, A. Z. *A Catalogue of Arabic Manuscripts on Medicine and Science in the Wellcome Historical Medical Library*, London, 1967.
"Ar-Rāzī on examining physicians: *K. Miḥnat al-Ṭabīb*", *al-Mashriq*, LIV, 1960.
"Rhazes' K. al-Murshid aw al-fuṣūl (The Guide or Aphorisms), with texts selected from his medical writings", *Revue de l'Institut des Manuscrits Arabes*, VII, 1961.
'A study of ar-Rāzī's medical writings, with selected texts and English translations' (Oxford doctoral diss., 1959).
Koning, P. de *Traité sur le calcul dans les reins et dans la vessie par Abū Bakr Muḥammad ibn Zakarīyā al-Rāzī*, trans. and text, Leiden, 1896.
Trois Traités d'anatomie arabes, trans. and text, Leiden, 1903.
Kraus, P. *Epître de Bērūnī contenant la répertoire des ouvrages de Muḥammad b. Zakarīyā ar-Rāzī*, Paris, 1936.
"Raziana I", *Orientalia*, IV, 1935.
"Raziana II", *Orientalia*, V, 1936.
Rasāʾil Falsafiyyah li-Abī Bakr Muḥammad b. Zakariyyāʾ al-Rāzī, Cairo, 1939.
Leclerc, L. *Histoire de la médecine arabe*, Paris, 1876.
Mohaghegh, M. *Fīlsūf-i-Rayy Muhammad Ibn-i-Zakarīyā-i-Rāzī*, Tehran, 1970 (Persian; preface and introduction in English).
Nadjmabadi, M. *Bibliographie de Rhazes "Aboubakr Mohammad Ibn Zakarria Razi", celèbre médecin et philosophe iranien*, Tehran, 1960 (Persian).
Partington, J. R. "The chemistry of Rāzī", *Ambix*, I, 1938.
al-Rāzī, Abū Bakr Muḥammad b. Zakariyyāʾ *al-Kitāb al-Manṣūrī fī ʾl-ṭibb*, ed. G. Colin and H. P. J. Renaud, Rabat, 1941.

22 AL-FĀRĀBĪ

Arberry, A. J. "Farabi's canons of poetry", *Rivista degli Studi Orientali*, XVII, 1938.
Davidson, H. "Alfarabi and Avicenna on the active intellect", *Viator*, III, 1972.
Dunlop, D. M. "Al-Fārābī's *Eisagoge*", *Islamic Quarterly*, III, 1956.
"Al-Fārābī's introductory risālah on logic", *Islamic Quarterly*, III, 1956.
"Al-Fārābī's introductory sections on logic", *Islamic Quarterly*, II, 1955.
"Al-Fārābī's paraphrase of the *Categories* of Aristotle", *Islamic Quarterly*, V, 1959.
al-Fārābī, Abū Naṣr Muḥammad b. Muḥammad *Falsafat Aflāṭūn*, ed. and trans. F. Rosenthal and R. Walzer, London, 1943.
The Fuṣūl al-Madanī: Aphorisms of the Statesman, ed. and trans. D. M. Dunlop, Cambridge, 1961.

Iḥṣāʾ al-ʿulūm (Catalogo de las Ciencias), ed. and trans. A. González Palencia, Madrid, 1953.
al-Jamʿ bayna raʾyay al-ḥakīmayn Aflāṭūn al-ilāhī wa-Arisṭūṭālīs, ed. and trans. F. Dieterici, in *Alfārābī's Philosophische Abhandlungen*, Leiden, 1890 (text), 1892 (trans.).
Kitāb al-Alfāẓ al-mustaʿmalah fī ʾl-manṭiq, ed. Muhsin Mahdi, Beirut, 1968.
Kitāb al-Ḥurūf, ed. Muhsin Mahdi, Beirut, 1969.
Kitāb al-Millah wa-nuṣūṣ ukhrā, ed. Muhsin Mahdi, Beirut, 1968.
Kitāb al-Siyāsah al-madaniyyah, ed. Fawzī Najjār, Beirut, 1964.
al-Madīnah al-fāḍilah, ed. F. Dieterici, Leiden, 1895.
Risālah fī ʾl-ʿAql, ed. M. Bouyges, Beirut, 1938.
Taḥṣīl al-saʿādah, Hyderabad, 1345/1926.
Talkhīṣ Nawāmīs Aflāṭūn: Compendium Legis Platonis, ed. and trans. F. Gabrieli, London, 1952.
Galston, M. "A re-examination of "Al-Fārābī's neoplatonism", *Journal of the History of Philosophy*, XV, 1977.
Madkour, Ibrahim *La Place d'al-Fārābī dans l'école philosophique musulmane*, Paris, 1934.
Mahdi, Muhsin "Alfarabi against Philoponus", *Journal of Near Eastern Studies*, XXVI, 1967.
"Remarks on Alfarabi's Attainment of Happiness" in G. F. Hourani (ed.), *Essays on Islamic Philosophy and Science*, Albany, 1975.
Mahdi, Muhsin (trans.) *Alfarabi's Philosophy of Plato and Aristotle*, Glencoe, 1962.
Rescher, N. *Al-Fārābī: An Annotated Bibliography*, Pittsburgh, 1962.
Steinschneider, M. *Al-Farabi*, St Petersburg, 1869; repr. Amsterdam, 1966.
Strauss, Leo "Farabi's Plato" in S. Lieberman (ed.), *Louis Ginsberg Jubilee Volume*, New York, 1945.
Walzer, R. (ed. and trans.) *Al-Farabi on the Perfect State*, Oxford, 1985.
Zimmermann, F. W. (trans.) *Al-Farabi's Commentary and Short Treatise on Aristotle's De Interpretatione*, Oxford, 1981.

23 IBN SĪNĀ

Alonso, M. "La 'Al-anniyya' de Avicena y el problema de la esencia y existencia", *Pensamiento*, XIV, 1958.
Anawati, G. C. "Bibliographie de la philosophie médiévale en terre d'Islam pour les années 1959–1969", *Bulletin de Philosophie Médiévale*, X–XII, 1968–70.
Essai de Bibliographie Avicennienne, Cairo, 1950.
Cruz Hernández, M. *La Metafísica de Avicena*, Granada, 1949.
"Algunos aspectos de la existencia de Dios en la filosofía de Avicena", *Al-Andalus*, XII, 1947.
"El avicenismo de Duns Escoto", *De Doctrina Ioannis Duns Scoti: Acta Congressus Scotistici Internationalis* (Oxford-Edinburgh, 1966), I (Studia Scholastico-Scotistica, 1), Rome, 1968.
"La distinción aviceniana de la esencia y la existencia y su interpretación en la filosofía occidental", *Homenaje a Millas-Vallicrosa*, I, Barcelona, 1954.
"Sentido y naturaleze de la prueba aviceniana de la existencia de Dios", *Proceedings of the XIth International Congress of Philosophy* (Brussels, 1953), XIV, 1953.

Galindo, E. "'L'homme volant' d'Avicenne et le 'Cogito' de Descartes", *IBLA*, XXI, 1958.

Gardet, L. *La Pensée religieuse d'Avicenne (Ibn Sînâ)*, Paris, 1951.

"La connaissance suprême de Dieu (*maᶜrifat Allāh*) selon Avicenne", *IBLA*, XIV, 1951.

Gilson, E. "Avicenne et les origines de la notion de cause efficiente", *Proceedings of the XIIth International Congress of Philosophy* (Venice, 1950), IX, 1960.

"Les sources gréco-arabes de l'augustinisme avicennisant", *Archives d'Histoire Doctrinale et Littéraire du Moyen Age*, IV, 1929–30.

Goichon, A. M. *Lexique de la langue philosophique d'Ibn Sînâ*, Paris, 1938.

Gómez Nogales, S. *Horizonte de la Metafísica aristotélica*, Madrid, 1955.

"Constitutivos metafísicos del ser según Ibn Ḥazm", *Al-Andalus*, XXIX, 1964.

La filosofía musulmana y su influjo determinante en el pensamiento medieval de Occidente, Madrid, 1969.

"Situación actual de las investigaciones sobre filosofía musulmana en España", *Dialogo Ecumenico*, VIII, 1967.

Ibn Sīnā, Abū ᶜAlī al-Ḥusayn *Anthologie des textes poétiques attribués à Avicenne*, eds. and trans. H. Jahier and A. Noureddine, Algiers, 1960.

Asbāb ḥudūth al-ḥurūf, trans. K. I. Semaan, Lahore, 1963.

al-Ilāhiyyāt, Cairo, 1960.

al-Ishārāt ilā ᶜilm fasād aḥkām al-nujūm, summarized by A. F. M. Mehren in "Vues d'Avicenne sur l'astrologie" in *Homenaje a D. Francisco Codera*, Saragossa, 1904.

al-Ishārāt wa-ʾl-tanbīhāt, ed. S. Dunyā, Cairo, 1960.

Kitāb al-Nafs, ed. F. Raḥmān, London, 1959.

Manṭiq al-mashriqiyyīn, Cairo, 1910.

Maqālah fī ʾl-Nafs in S. Landauer (ed. and trans.), "Die Psychologie des Ibn Sīnā", *Zeitschrift der Deutschen Morgenländischen Gesellschaft*, XXIX, 1875.

al-Qānūn fī ʾl-ṭibb, Cairo, 1877.

Risālat al-Aḍḥawiyyah fī ᶜUmr al-maᶜād, ed. and trans. F. Lucchetta, Padua, 1969.

Risālat Ḥayy b. Yaqẓān, ed. and trans. A. M. Goichon, Paris, 1959.

Risālat al-ḥudūd, in A. M. Goichon (ed. and trans.), *Introduction à Avicenne: son Epître des définitions*, Paris, 1933.

Risālat al-Ṭayr, in A. F. M. Mehren (ed. and trans.), *Traités Mystiques . . . d'Avicenne*, Leiden, 1891.

al-Shifāʾ, ed. I. Madkour, Cairo, 1952–75.

al-Urjūzah fī ʾl-ṭibb, ed. and trans. H. Jahier and A. Noureddine, Paris, 1956.

ᶜUyūn al-ḥikmah, in A. Badawī (ed.), *Mémorial Avicenne, 5: Avicennae fontes sapientiae*, Cairo, 1954.

Mahdavi, Y. *Bibliographie d'Ibn Sina*, Tehran, 1954.

Marmura, M. E. "Avicenna's psychological proof of prophecy", *Journal of Near Eastern Studies*, XXII, 1963.

Teicher, J. "Gundissalino e l'Agostinismo avicennizzante", *Rivista di Filosofia Neo-scolastica*, XXVI, 1934.

Vajda, G. "Bibliographie d'Ibn Sina" (Abstracta Islamica), *Revue des Etudes Islamiques*, XXII, 1954.

Wickens, G. M. (ed.) *Avicenna: Scientist and Philosopher. A Millenary Symposium*, London, 1952.

24 AL-BĪRŪNĪ AND THE SCIENCES OF HIS TIME

al-Bīrūnī, Abū ʾl-Rayḥān Muḥammad b. Aḥmad *al-Āthār al-bāqiyah ʿan al-qurūn al-khāliyah*, Arabic text in *Chronologie Orientalischer Völker*, ed. E. Sachau, Leipzig, 1878; English trans. E. Sachau, London, 1879; Persian trans. by Akbar Danāseresht, Tehran, 1974, contains additional material not known to Sachau.

Ghurrat al-zījāt, ed. N. A. Baloch, Sind, 1973.

Ifrād al-maqāl fī amr al-ẓilāl, Hyderabad, 1948.

al-Jamāhir fī maʿrifat al-jawāhir, ed. F. Krenkow, Hyderabad, AH 1355.

Kitāb al-Ṣaydanah fī ʾl-ṭibb, ed. M. Said and R. Ilahi, Karachi, 1973.

Kitāb Tasṭīḥ al-ṣuwar wa-tabṭīḥ al-kuwar in A. Saidan (ed.), *Dirāsāt*, IV, 1977.

al-Qānūn al-Masʿūdī, Hyderabad, 1954–6.

Rasāʾil al-Bīrūnī, Hyderabad, 1948.

al-Tafhīm li-awāʾil ṣināʿat al-tanjīm, printed in facsimile and trans. R. Wright, *Elements of Astrology*, London 1934.

Taḥdīd nihāyat al-amākin li-taṣḥīḥ masāfāt al-masākin, ed. P. Bulghakov, *Majallat Maʿhad al-Makhṭūṭāt al-ʿArabiyyah*, 1962.

Taḥqīq mā li-ʾl-Hind..., ed. E. Sachau, London, 1888; trans. E. Sachau, *Alberuni's India*, London, 1914.

Tamhīd al-mustaqarr li-taḥqiq maʿnā al-mamarr, Hyderabad, 1948.

Boilot, D. J. "L'oeuvre d'al-Beruni. Essai bibliographique", *Mélanges de l'Institut Dominicain d'Etudes Orientales*, II, 1955; III, 1956.

Ibn al-Athīr *al-Kāmil fī ʾl-taʾrīkh*, Beirut, 1965–6.

Kennedy, E. S. "al-Bīrūnī's *Masudic Canon*", *Studies in the Islamic Exact Sciences*, Beirut, 1983.

A Commentary upon Bīrūnī's Kitāb Taḥdīd al-Amākin, Beirut, 1973.

"Late medieval planetary theory", *Isis*, LVII, 1966.

al-Munajjid, Ṣalāḥ al-Dīn "al-Bīrūnī wa-ʾl-lughah al-ʿArabiyyah", *Al-Bīrūnī Commemoration Volume*, Karachi, 1979.

Saliba, G. "Arabic astronomy and Copernicus", *Zeitschrift für Geschichte der Arabisch-Islamischen Wissenschaften*, I, 1984.

"al-Bīrūnī", *Dictionary of the Middle Ages*, II, New York, 1983.

"A Damascene astronomer proposes a non-Ptolemaic astronomy", *Journal for the History of Arabic Science*, IV, 1980.

"The development of astronomy in medieval Islamic society", *Arab Studies Quarterly*, IV, 1982.

"The first non-Ptolemaic astronomy at the Maraghah School", *Isis*, LXX, 1979.

"The original source of Quṭb al-Dīn al-Shīrāzī's Planetary Model", *Journal for the History of Arabic Science*, III, 1979.

Togan, A. Z. V. (ed.) *Bīrūnī's Picture of the World* (partial ed. of *Taḥdīd nihāyat al-amākin*), Delhi, 1938.

25 AL-GHAZĀLĪ

al-Aʿṣam, A. *al-Faylasūf al-Ghazālī*, Beirut, 1974.

Asín Palacios, M. *La Espiritualidad de Algazel y su Sentido cristiano*, Madrid, 1934–40.

Badawī, ᶜAbd al-Raḥmān *Muʾallafāt al-Ghazālī*, Kuwait, 1977.
Dunyā, S., *al-Ḥaqīqah fī naẓar al-Ghazālī*, Cairo, 1965.
al-Ghazālī, Abū Ḥāmid Muḥammad *Ayyuhā ʾl-walad*: Arabic text with French trans. by T. al-Ṣabbāgh, Beirut, 1951.
Faḍāʾiḥ al-Bāṭiniyyah, ed. ᶜA. Badawī, Cairo, 1964.
Fayṣal al-tafriqah bayn al-Islām wa-ʾl-Zandaqah, ed. S. Dunyā, Cairo, 1961.
Iḥyāʾ ᶜulūm al-dīn, 5 vols. Vol. v is supplementary containing al-Ghazālī's *al-Imlāʾ ᶜalā Ishkālāt al-Iḥyāʾ* with other works by other authors, Beirut, n.d.
Iljām al-ᶜawāmm ᶜan ᶜilm al-kalām, Cairo, AH 1351.
al-Iqtiṣād fī ʾl-iᶜtiqād, Cairo, AH 1320.
al-Maqāṣid al-asnā fī sharḥ maᶜānī asmāʾ Allāh al-ḥusnā, ed. F. A. Shehadi, Beirut, 1971.
Maqāṣid al-falāsifah, ed. S. Dunyā, Cairo, 1961.
Miḥakk al-naẓar fī ʾl-manṭiq, ed. M. B. al-Naᶜsānī, Beirut, 1966.
Mishkāt al-anwār, ed. A. ᶜAffīfī, Cairo, 1964; trans. W. H. T. Gairdner, *The Niche for Lights*, London, 1924.
Miᶜyār al-ᶜilm, ed. S. Dunyā, Cairo, 1961.
Mīzān al-ᶜamal, Beirut, 1979.
al-Munqidh min al-ḍalāl, ed. ᶜA. Maḥmūd, Cairo, 1964.
al-Mustaṣfā, Cairo, AH 1322.
al-Qisṭās al-mustaqīm, ed. V. S. al-Yasūᶜī, Beirut, 1959.
Tahāfut al-falāsifah, ed. M. Bouyges, Beirut, 1962; trans. S. A. Kamilī, *Incoherence of the Philosophers*, Lahore, 1958.
al-Tibr al-masbūk fī naṣīḥat al-mulūk, trans. into Arabic from the original Persian in 595/1199; ed. M. M. Abū al-ᶜUlā, Cairo, 1967; trans. F. R. C. Bagley, *Ghazālī's Book of Counsel for Kings*, London, 1964.
Jabre, F. *Essai sur le lexique de Ghazālī*, Beirut, 1970.
La Notion de la Maᶜrifa chez Ghazālī, Beirut, 1958.
Laoust, H. *La Politique de Ghazālī*, Paris, 1970.
Maḥmūd, Z. N. (ed.) *Abū Ḥāmid al-Ghazālī fī ʾl-dhikrā al-miʾawiyyah al-tāsiᶜah li-mīlādih*, Cairo, 1962.
Obermann, J. *Der Philosophische und Religiöse Subjektivismus Ghazalis*, Leipzig, 1921.
Othmān, A. I. *The Concept of Man . . . in the Writings of al-Ghazālī*, Cairo, 1960.
Smith, Margaret *al-Ghazālī the Mystic*, London, 1944.
al-ᶜUthmān, ᶜA. *Sīrat al-Ghazālī wa-aqwāl al-mutaqaddimīn fīh*, Damascus, 1961.
Watt, W. M. *The Faith and Practice of al-Ghazālī*, London, 1953.
Muslim Intellectual: A Study of al-Ghazālī, Edinburgh, 1963.
Wensinck, A. J. *La Pensée de Ghazālī*, Paris, 1940.

26 CHRISTIAN ARABIC LITERATURE IN THE ᶜABBASID PERIOD

Allard, M. "Les chrétiens à Bagdad", *Arabica*, IX, 1962.
Cheikho, L. *al-Makhṭūṭāt al-ᶜArabiyyah li-katabat al-naṣrāniyyah*, Beirut, 1924.
Les savants arabes chrétiens en Islam, 622–1300, ed. Camille Héchaimé, *Patrimoine Arabe Chrétien*, 5, Jounieh and Rome, 1983.
"al-Tawārīkh al-naṣrāniyyah fī ʾl-ᶜarabiyyah", *al-Mashriq*, XII, 1909.
Graf, G. "Exegetische Schriften zum Neuen Testament in arabischer Sprache bis zum 14. Jahrhundert", *Biblische Zeitschrift*, XXI, 1933.

Ḥaddād, Rashīd *La Trinité divine chez les théologiens arabes (750–1050)*, Paris, 1985.
"Al-Wajh al-naṣrānī li-ᵓl-thaqāfah al-ᶜarabiyyah", *al-Waḥdah*, XIV, Sidon, 1975.
Nasrallah, J. *Histoire du mouvement littéraire dans l'église melchite*, III (AD 969–1250), Louvain and Paris, 1983.
Samir, Kh. "Bibliographie du dialogue islamo-chrétien", part 1: Du 7ᵉ au 10ᵉ siècle; part 2: 11ᵉ au 12ᵉ siècle; part 3: Elie de Nisibe (975–1046); part 4: Addenda et corrigenda aux auteurs arabes chrétiens des 11ᵉ au 12ᵉ siècle; part 5: Girgi moine de Saint-Siméon en 1217, *Islamochristiana*, I, II, III, V, VII, 1975, 1976, 1977, 1979, 1981.
"Liberté religieuse et propagation de la foi chez les théologiens arabes chrétiens du IXᵉ siècle et en Islam", *Tantur Yearbook 1980–81*, Jerusalem, 1982.
"Madkhal ilā ᵓl-turāth al-ᶜarabī ᵓl-masīḥī", *al-Masarrah*, LXVII, 1981; reprinted in augmented form in *Theological Review*, V, 1982; *Ṣadīq al-Kāhin*, XXIII, 1983.
"Une théologie arabe pour l'Islam", *Tantur Yearbook 1979–1980*, Jerusalem, 1981.
"La tradition arabe chrétienne. Etat de la question, problèmes et besoins", *Actes du premier congrès international d'études arabes chrétiennes* (Goslar, septembre, 1980) in Khalil Samir (ed.), *Orientalia Christiana Analecta*, Rome, 1982.
"al-Turāth al-ᶜarabī ᵓl-masīḥī ᵓl-qadīm wa-tafāᶜuluh maᶜa ᵓl-fikr al-ᶜarabī ᵓl-islāmī", *Islamochristiana*, VIII, 1982.
"L'unicité absolue de Dieu. Regards sur la pensée chrétienne arabe", *Lumière et Vie*, CLXIII, 1983.
Samir, Kh. (ed.) *Actes du deuxième congrès international d'études arabes chrétiennes* (Oosterhesselen, septembre, 1984), *Orientalia Christiana Analecta*, Rome, 1986.
Troupeau, G. "La littérature arabe chrétienne du Xᵉ au XIIᵉ siècle", *Cahiers de Civilisation Médiévale*, XIV, 1971.

27 JUDAEO-ARABIC LITERATURE

Abraham b. Mūsā b. Maymūn *Commentary on Genesis and Exodus*, ed. with a Hebrew trans. by E. Wiesenberg, Letchworth, 1959.
Kifāyat al-ᶜābidīn; partial ed. S. Rosenblatt, *The Highways to Perfection of Abraham Maimonides*, New York, 1927; Baltimore, 1938; part 2, ed. N. Dana, Ramat Gan, 1989.
Abū ᵓl-Ḥasan Yehūdāh ha-Lēvī *al-Ḥujjah wa-ᵓl-dalīl fī naṣr al-dīn al-dhalīl*, ed. D. H. Baneth, Jerusalem, 1977.
Baḥya b. Paquda *al-Hidāyah ilā farāᵓiḍ al-qulūb*, ed. A. S. Yahuda, Leiden, 1912.
Blau, J. "Jüdische Literatur" in H. Gätje (ed.), *Grundriss der Arabischen Philologie*, II, Wiesbaden, 1987, 394–99.
Blau, J. (ed.) *Judaeo-Arabic Literature: Selected Texts*, Jerusalem, 1980.
Dāwūd b. Joshua Maimonides *Murshid ilā al-Tafarrud*, *Qōbeṣ ᶜal Yad*, XI, 1984.
al-Fāsī, Dāwūd b. Abraham *The Kitāb Jāmiᶜ al-Alfāẓ of David b. Abraham al-Fāsī*, ed. S. Skoss, New Haven, 1936–45.
Fenton, P. B. *Mōreh ha-pĕrīšūt*, Jerusalem, 1987.
Goldziher, I. "Mélanges Judéo-Arabes", *Revue des Etudes Juives*, XLIII–L, 1898–1905.
Halkin, A. S. "Judaeo-Arabic literature" in L. W. Schwartz (ed.), *Great Ages and*

Ideas of the Jewish People, New York, 1956.
"Judaeo-Arabic literature" in L. Finkelstein (ed.), *The Jews*, New York, 1960.
Hirschfeld, H. *Arabic Chrestomathy in Hebrew Characters*, London, 1892.
"The Arabic portion of the Cairo Genizah at Cambridge", *Jewish Quarterly Review*, xv–xx, 1903–8.
Hoerning, R. *Six Karaite Manuscripts of Portions of the Hebrew Bible in Arabic Characters*, London, 1889.
Ibn Ghiyāth, Isḥāq b. Yehūdāh *Commentary on Ecclesiastes*, *Ḥames Megillōt*, Jerusalem, 1962.
Ibn Ḥayyūj, Abū Zakariyyāʾ Yaḥyā b. Dāwūd *Le Livre des Parterres Fleuris*, ed. J. Derenbourg, Paris, 1886.
Ibn Janāḥ, Abū ʾl-Walīd Marwān Yōnah, *The Book of Hebrew Roots*, ed. A. Neubauer, Oxford, 1875.
Marx, A. "Some notes on the use of Hebrew type in non-Hebrew books" in *Biographical Essays: A Tribute to Wilberforce Eames*, New York, 1924, 381–408.
Mōsheh b. ʿEzra *Kitāb al-Muḥāḍarah wa-ʾl-mudhākarah*, ed. A. S. Halkin, Jerusalem, 1975.
Mūsā b. Maymūn *Dalālat al-ḥāʾirīn*, ed. with French trans. S. Munk, Paris, 1856–66; new edn with Hebrew trans. Y. Qāfiḥ, Jerusalem, 1972.
Nĕtanʾel b. al-Fayyūmī *Bustān al-ʿuqūl*, ed. Y. Qāfiḥ, Jerusalem, 1954.
al-Qirqisānī, Yaʿqūb b. Isḥāq *Kitāb al-Anwār wa-ʾl-marāqib*, ed. L. Nemoy, New York, 1939–43.
Saʿadyah Gaʾōn *Kitāb al-Amānāt*, ed. S. Landauer, Leiden, 1880.
Kitāb Jāmiʿ al-ṣalawāt wa-ʾl-tasābīḥ, ed. S. Assaf, I. Davidson and I. Joel, Jerusalem, 1941.
Steinschneider, M. *Die Arabische Literatur der Juden*, Frankfurt am Main, 1902; repr. Hildesheim, 1964.
ʿUbaydullāh b. Abraham b. Mūsā b. Maymūn *al-Maqālah al-Ḥawḍiyyah*, ed. P. B. Fenton as *Obadyah Maimonides' Treatise of the Pool*, London, 1981.
Vassel, E. *La Littérature populaire des Israélites tunisiens*, Paris, 1904–7.
Yehūdāh b. Quraysh *Jehuda ben Kureisch, Epistola de Studii Targum Utilitate*, ed. J. J. L. Bargès and D. B. Goldberg, Paris, 1857.

28 THE TRANSLATION OF GREEK MATERIALS INTO ARABIC

Badawi, Abdurrahman *La Transmission de la Philosophie Grecque au Monde Arabe*, Paris, 1968.
Dunlop, D. M. *Arab Civilization to A.D. 1500*, London, 1971.
Fakhry, Majid *A History of Islamic Philosophy*, New York, 1983.
Goodman, L. E. *The Case of the Animals vs. Man before the King of the Jinn*, New York, 1978.
Ibn Tufayl's Hayy Ibn Yaqzan, 2nd edn, Los Angeles, 1983.
Hitti, P. K. *History of the Arabs*, London, 1956.
Madkour, Ibrahim *L'Organon d'Aristote dans le monde Arabe*, Paris, 1969.
Maimonides, Moses *Guide for the Perplexed*, trans. M. Friedländer, London, 1925.
Peters, F. E. *Allah's Commonwealth*, New York, 1973.
Aristotle and the Arabs, New York, 1968.
The Harvest of Hellenism, New York, 1970.

Rosenthal, Franz *The Classical Heritage in Islam*, London, 1975.
Walzer, R. *Greek into Arabic*, Oxford 1962.

29 DIDACTIC VERSE

al-Aḥdab, Ibrāhīm *Farāʾiḍ al-laʾālī*, Beirut, AH 1312.

Arberry, A. J. "The Sira in verse" in George Makdisi (ed.), *Arabic and Islamic Studies in honour of Hamilton A. R. Gibb*, Leiden, 1965.

al-Fākhūrī, Ḥannā *Funūn al-adab al-ʿArabī: al-fann al-taʿlīmī; al-ḥikam wa-ʾl-amthāl*, Cairo, *c.* 1956.

Grunebaum, G. E. von "On the origin and development of Arabic *muzdawij* poetry", *Journal of Būlāq Near Eastern Studies*, III, 1944.

al-Hamdānī, al-Ḥasan *Ṣifat Jazīrat al-ʿArab*, ed. D. H. Müller, Leiden, 1884–91.

Ḥijāb, Muḥammad Nabīh *Maʿālim al-shiʿr wa-aʿlāmuh fī ʾl-ʿaṣr al-ʿAbbāsī al-awwal*, Cairo, 1973.

Ibn al-Athīr, Ḍiyāʾ al-Dīn *al-Mathal al-sāʾir*, Būlāq, AH 1282.

Ibn Mālik, Jamāl al-Dīn Muḥammad *Alfiyyah* (Sharḥ Ibn ʿAqīl), ed. Fr. Dieterici, Leipzig, 1851.

Ibn al-Muʿtazz, ʿAbdullāh "Urjūzah", *Zeitschrift der Deutschen Morgenländischen Gesellschaft*, XL, 1886; XLI, 1887.

Khulūṣī, Ṣafāʾ *Fann al-taqṭīʿ al-shiʿrī wa-ʾl-qāfiyah*, Beirut, 1977.

al-Maqqarī, Aḥmad b. Muḥammad *Nafḥ al-ṭīb*, ed. R. Dozy *et al.*, Leiden, 1855–61.

al-Maqrīzī, Aḥmad b. ʿAlī *al-Khiṭaṭ*, Būlāq, AH 1270.

al-Maydānī, Abū ʾl-Faḍl Aḥmad *Majmaʿ al-amthāl*, ed. Muḥammad Muḥyī ʾl-Dīn ʿAbd al-Ḥamīd, Cairo, 1955.

Raʾūf, ʿImād ʿAbd al-Salām *al-Athār al-khaṭṭiyyah fī ʾl-maktabah al-Qādiriyyah fī Jāmiʿ al-Shaykh ʿAbd al-Qādir al-Jīlānī*, Baghdad, n.d.

Shawqī, Aḥmad *al-Shawqiyyāt*, ed. M. S. al-ʿUryān, IV, Cairo, 1373/1956.

Somogyi, J. de "A qasida on the destruction of Baghdad by the Mongols", *Bulletin of the School of Oriental and African Studies*, VII, 1933–5.

al-Ṣūlī, Abū Bakr Muḥammad b. Yaḥyā *Kitāb al-Awrāq*, ed. J. Heyworth-Dunne, London, 1936.

Wahbah, Magdi *A Dictionary of Literary Terms* (*English-French-Arabic*), Beirut, 1974, s.v. "Didactic".

INDEX

Aba the Nestorian 456
Abān b. ʿAbd al Ḥamīd al-Ḷāḥiqī 499–500, 502, 503
al-ʿAbbād, Aḥmad 61
al-ʿAbbādī, Muḥammad b. Aḥmad 173
ʿAbbās b. Firnās 180
ʿAbbasids *see individual caliphs*
ʿAbd al-ʿAzīz b. Muhtadā 24
ʿAbd al-Azīz b. Shaddād 215, 227
ʿAbd al-ʿAzīz b. Yūsuf 163
ʿAbd al-Ghanī al-Nābulusī 75
ʿAbd al-Ḥamīd b. Yaḥyā 155, 161
ʿAbd al-Ḥaqq b. ʿAṭiyyah 48
ʿAbd al-Jabbār, Qaḍī 31
ʿAbd al-Laṭīf al-Baghdādī 184, 231
ʿAbd al-Malik (caliph) 190
ʿAbd al-Qādir al-Jīlānī 61, 62, 66, 68
ʿAbd al-Raḥmān III al-Nāṣir 495, 503
ʿAbd al-Raḥmān b. ʿAlī (al-Qāḍī al-Fāḍil) 223–4, 228
ʿAbd al-Raḥmān b. Muʿāwiyah (ʿAbd al-Raḥmān I al-Dākhil) 182
ʿAbd al-Raḥmān b. Rustam 33
ʿAbd al-Raḥmān b. ʿUmar al-Ṣūfī 280, *281*, 282
ʿAbd al-Wahhāb b. ʿAbd al-Raḥmān b. Rustam 34, 35
ʿAbduh, Muḥammad 403
ʿAbdullāh b. ʿAbbās 43, 44, 45–6
ʿAbdullāh b. ʿAbd al-ʿAzīz 35
ʿAbdullāh b. ʿAmr b. al-ʿĀṣ 311
ʿAbdullāh b. Buluggin b. Bādīs 214
ʿAbdullāh b. Jaʿfar 18, 236, 237
ʿAbdullāh b. Masʿūd 145
ʿAbdullāh b. Muḥammad al-Miyānajī *see* ʿAyn al-Quḍāt ʿAbdullāh al-Hamadhānī
ʿAbdullāh b. Ṭāhir 159, 166
ʿAbdullāh b. Yaḥyā al-Kindī (Ṭālib al-Ḥaqq) 33
ʿAbdullāh al-Anṣārī al-Harawī *see under* al-Anṣārī
abjad numerical system 254–5
ablutions 26, 42, 507–8
Abraham 13, 28, 51, 72, 435
Abraham Ecchellensis 459
Abramson, S. 475
abrogation (*naskh*) 18, 28, 30, 43, 46, 148
Absāl and Salāmān 105
abṣār ("outer eye") 54
Abū ʾl-ʿAbbās Aḥmad 36
Abū ʿAbdullāh Muḥammad b. abī Sufyān 34, 36
Abū ʿAbdullāh Muḥammad b. Bakr al-Nafūsī 36
Abū ʿAbdullāh al-Shīʿī 239
Abū ʿAlī al-Ḥasan b. ʿAlī al-Baṣrī (Yefet b. ʿAlī) 469, 474
Abū ʿAmr al-Shaybānī 112
Abū ʾl-ʿArab Muḥammad b. Aḥmad b. Tamīm 175, 215
Abū ʾl-Aswad al-Duʾalī 119
Abū ʾl-ʿAtāhiyah 353–4, 502, 503, 504, 505
Abū Bakr (caliph) 17
Abū Bakr b. ʿAbd al-Raḥmān 141
Abū Bakr b. ʿAbdullāh b. Aybak al-Dawādārī 216, 240
Abū Bakr Muḥammad b. ʿAbdullāh al-ʿArabī 49, 435
Abū ʾl-Barakāt Hibatullāh b. Malkā al-Baghdādī al-Baladī 242
Abū ʾl-Barakāt Mawhūb b. Manṣūr b. Mufarrij al-Iskandarānī 457, 458
Abū ʾl-Faraj ʿAbdullāh b. al-Ṭayyib *see* Ibn al-Ṭayyib
Abū ʾl-Faraj al-Iṣfahanī 58, 216
Abū ʾl-Fatḥ ʿAlī b. Muḥammad al-Bustī *see* al-Bustī
Abū ʾl-Fidāʾ, Ismāʿīl b. ʿAlī 226, 304, 319
Abū Ghānim Bashīr b. Ghānim al-Khurāsānī 35
Abū Ḥanīfah 142, 143, 144; anecdote 181; *ʿaqīdah* 14; *isnād*s 141; *Musnad* 142; school of 142, 152
Abū ʾl-Ḥasan Yehūdāh ha-Lēvī 467
Abū Hāshim 196
Abū Ḥātim al-Aṣamm 60
Abū Ḥātim Sahl b. Muḥammad al-Sijistānī 132
Abū ʾl-Ḥawārī Muḥammad b. al-Ḥawārī 36, 37
Abū ʾl-Ḥayyān al-Tawḥīdī 204
Abū Isḥāq Ibrāhīm b. Hilāl al-Ṣābiʾ *see* al-Ṣābiʾ
Abū Jābir Muḥammad b. Jaʿfar al-Izkawī 37
Abū Kāmil Shujāʿ 256
Abū ʾl-Khayr al-Masīḥī 348
Abū Layth Naṣr b. Muḥammad al-Samarqandī 153

Abū ᵓl-Maᶜālī Muḥammad b. ᶜUbaydullāh 238
Abū ᵓl-Maḥāsin Yūsuf b. Taghribirdī 175, 176, 222, 240
Abū ᵓl-Makārim Saᶜdullāh b. Jūrjīs b. Masᶜūd 458, 459
Abū Manṣūr ᶜAbd al-Qāhir b. Ṭāhir al-Baghdādī 238
Abū Maᶜshar Jaᶜfar b. Muḥammad al-Balkhī 291, 297–8, 299
Abū Mikhnaf 193
Abū ᵓl-Muᶜarrij 35
Abū Muḥammad ᶜAbd al-Raḥmān al-Rāzī 173
Abū Muḥammad al-Ḥasan b. Mūsā b. Nawbakht 27, 205–6, 238
Abū Muḥammad Mawlānā al-Tihāmī Kannūn al-Idrīsī al-Ḥasanī 507–8
Abū ᵓl-Munā Abraham b. Mūsā al-Maymūnī 467, 469
Abū Munajjā 465
Abū Nuᶜaym al-Iṣfahānī 63
Abū Rāᵓiṭah al-Takrītī 451, 452, 453, 454
Abū Sahl al-Faḍl b. Nawbakht 293, 295, 482
Abū Sahl Ismāᶜīl b. ᶜAlī b. Nawbakht 27
Abū Saᶜīd Aḥmad b. Muḥammad b. Ziyād 60, 69
Abū Saᶜīd al-Kudamī 37, 38
Abū Ṣāliḥ the Armenian 222, 241, 458
Abū Ṣalt 215
Abū Shāmah, Shihāb al-Dīn abū ᵓl-Qāsim ᶜAbd al-Raḥmān 185, 223, 226, 228
Abū Shujāᶜ Ẓāhir al-Dīn Muḥammad al-Rūdhrāwarī 204, 246
Abū Sufrah ᶜAbd al-Malik b. Sufrah 35
Abū Sufyān Maḥbūb b. al-Raḥīl 34, 34, 35
Abū Ṭālib al-Makkī 69, 72
Abū Tammām 502
Abū al-Ṭayyib al-Lughawī 107
Abū ᶜUbayd ᶜAbdullāh ᶜAbd al-ᶜAzīz al-Bakrī 215, 240, 317–18, 318–19, 319–20
Abū ᶜUbayd al-Jūzajānī 392, 422
Abū ᶜUbayd al-Qāsim b. Sallām 106
Abū ᶜUbaydah Maᶜmar b. al-Muthannā 46, 106
Abū ᶜUbaydah Muslim b. abī Karīmah 33, 34, 35
Abū ᵓl-Wafāᵓ al-Būzajānī 160, 253, 283
Abū Yaḥyā b. al-Baṭrīq (Patricius) 295, 481
Abū Yaᶜlā b. al-Farrāᵓ 150, 157
Abū Yaᶜqūb al-Sijistānī 240
Abū Yaᶜqūb Yūsuf b. Ibrāhīm al-Baṣīr 466, 470
Abū Yaᶜqūb Yūsuf b. Ibrāhīm al-Warjalānī 38
Abū Yazīd al-Bisṭāmī 60, 61, 67
Abū Yūsuf: on Abū Ḥanifah and Abū Laylā 142; and formation of Ḥanafite school 142; on *ikhtilāf al-madhāhib* 152; and *Kitāb al-Jāmiᶜ al-kabīr* 144; works 142; *Kitāb al-Kharāj* 142, 144, 157, 159, 192; *Kitāb al-Radd* 142, 143
Abū Zakariyyāᵓ Yaḥyā b. abī Bakr al-Warjalānī 232, 239
Abyssinia 173
Acts of the Apostles 448
adab al-kudyah (literature of mendicancy) 506
Adab al-sulūk (Ṣūfī work) 66–7
ᶜādah (customary law) 141
Adam 13, 72, 74, 184, 437, 454
ᶜAdan 243
Adelard of Bath xviii, 297
ᶜAdī b. Zayd al-ᶜIbādī 502
al-ᶜĀḍid (Faṭimid caliph) 243
ᶜadl (justice) 6, 140, 466
administration: dating system 197; Egypt 162, 242; law xvii, 142; *see also*: administrative literature; *dīwān*s; intelligence service; postal service; secretaries; taxation
administrative literature xvii, 155–67; anecdotes 163–4, 165; biography 163–4; Byzantine influence 158; chancery documents 163, 164, 201, 223–4; *ḥisbah*, manuals of 150, 160–1; as historical source 201; on irrigation system 158; on land management 159–60; "Mirrors for Princes" 165–7, 204, 232; Persian influence 158, 159; on postal and intelligence services 158, 164; practical manuals 156–61, 301, 108; on statecraft 165–7; on taxation 159–60; treatises for secretaries 157–8, 161–3
admonitions, Ṣūfī 60
ᶜAḍud al-Dawlah 203, 206
ᶜAḍudī hospital, Baghdad 359
adultery, penalty for 42–3
Aegidius de Thebaldis 298, 300
aerostatics 263, 330
Aesop 508
afᶜāl al-muqārabah (verbs of appropinquation) 125
al-Afḍal (Yemeni prince) 108, 222
al-Afḍal b. Badr al-Jamālī 244
afḍal (most excellent, of imam) 16, 17, 19
Afḍal-Baṭāᵓiḥī observatory, Cairo 288
Afghanistan 276
ᶜAfīf b. al-Makīn b. Muᵓammil 451
al-Aflaḥ b. ᶜAbd al-Wahhāb, Abū Saᶜīd 35
Africa, east 38
Africa, north: Christian populations 446; Faṭimid rule 236, 239–40; local law 143, 151; map *313*; *see also*: Berbers; Maghrib; Morocco; Sahara
Africa, west 317–18, 322, 342
afterlife 79, 98, 99–100, 101, 386–7, 388; rewards and punishments 100, 403, 440
Agakhān III 247
agrumiya ("grammar") 134
ahl al-ḥadīth 10, 143
ahl al-ḥadīth wa-ᵓl-naql 10
ahl al-kalām wa-ᵓl-ᶜaql 10
Aḥmad b. ᶜAbdullāh 37
Aḥmad b. ᶜAlī b. Maᵓmūn 184
Aḥmad b. Buwayh 294

Aḥmad b. Ḥanbāl 145
Aḥmad b. al-Muᶜtaṣim 364
Aḥmad al-Burnusī Zarrūk 69
Ahrūn of Alexandria 343, 481
al-Aḥwal, Muḥammad b. Nuᶜmān 20, 21
al-Ahwāzī 293
aḥzāb (litanies) 67
ᶜĀʾishah (wife of Prophet Muḥammad) 43
akhbār (type of historical writing) 189, 195, 196
Akhbār majmūᶜah (anon.) 219
Akhbār al-Ṣīn wa-ʾl-Hind 322
al-Akhfash al-Awsaṭ 124
akhlāṭ see humours
Akkadian technical terminology 159
al-Akwaᶜ, al-Qāḍī Ismāᶜīl 243
ᶜAlāʾ al-Dawlah 392
Alamūt 244–5, 246, 425
al-ᶜAlawī, ᶜAlī b. Muḥammad 213
al-ᶜAlawī, Yaḥyā b. Ḥamzah 238
Albinus 494
Albumasar *see* Māshāʾallāh
alchemy xv, xvii, 327–41; aurifaction 329–30, 335; aurifiction 328–9; balance, theory of 335, 336, 340; and chemistry xvii, 331, 336, 337, 339; Chinese 332–3, 335; compendia 339; Egyptian 331–2; elixirs 330, 335, 336, 337, 338; equipment 328, 336, 338; esoteric aspects 328, 331, 335, 338, 339–40; European 340–1; Hellenistic 331–2, 334, 335; Ibn Sīnā 338, 340; Jabirian corpus 332, 333–5, 336, 340, 341; al-Jildakī 339–40; macrobiotics 330, 332; manuals 336, 338; numerology 335; processes 328, 336, 337, 338; pseudographs 328, 332, 338; quicksilver/sulphur theory 334–5, 336; Abū Bakr Muḥammad b. Zakariyyāʾ al-Rāzī 328, 335–7, 338, 340, 341; Science of Generation 335; substances 336–7; translations 332, 333, 341; vocabulary 341
Aleppo 229, 230, 379, 496
Alexander of Aphrodisias 346, 365, 366, 488, 491, 492
Alexander III of Macedon ("the Great", Dhū ʾl-Qarnayn) 79, 81, 165–6, 292
Alexandria: education 365, 369, 380, 489; *History of Patriarchs of*, 456, 457, 458; traditions passed to Ḥarrān 495; water-clock 262
Alexius of Byzantium 291
Alfonso X of Castile 270
algebra 254, 255–6
"algorithm" 255
ᶜAlī, Zāhid 247
ᶜAlī b. al-ᶜAbbās al-Majūsī 348, 354, 356
ᶜAlī b. abī Ṭalḥah 44
ᶜAlī b. abī Ṭālib 3, 16, 60, 141, 189, 507
ᶜAlī b. Dāwūd al-Arfādī 451
ᶜAlī b. al-Ḥusayn b. ᶜAlī Zayn al-ᶜĀbidīn 16, 17, 67
ᶜAlī b. Ibrāhīm al-Qummī 24, 48
ᶜAlī b. ᶜĪsā b. Dāwūd ("the Good Vizier") 164, 491
ᶜAlī b. ᶜĪsā al-Kaḥḥāl 345, 359
ᶜAlī b. ᶜĪsā b. Māhān 157
ᶜAlī b. Jahm 503
ᶜAlī b. Khalaf 286
ᶜAlī b. Munqidh 220
ᶜAlī b. Riḍwān 298, 352, 496
ᶜAlī b. al-Ṣayrafī 222, 245
ᶜAlī al-Hādī 23
ᶜAlī al-Hamadhānī 60
ᶜAlī al-Riḍā: on creation of Qurʾān 28; imamate 20–1, 22; on *istiṭāᶜah* 25; al-Maʾmūn declares heir 21, 485; and Qummī Traditionists 24; tomb 425
allegory 73, 331, 399–400; Ṣūfī 56, 68, 70, 71
Allony, N. 475
Almohad empire 11, 213, 231–2
Almoravids 11, 213, 231
alms (*al-zakāh*) 10, 140, 142, 157, 499–500
Alonso, Manuel 396
alphabets 108–9
ᶜamal: grammatical operation 125; judicial practice 141, 148, 151
Amari, Michele 215
al-Aᶜmash, Ibn Mihrān 181
amber; magnetism 257
ambiguity 397; of Arabic script 115, 119, 178, 463, 471; in *ḥiyal* literature 130; of Qurʾān 41, 119
Ambrose of Milan 448
Āmid, Mesopotamia 257
al-Amīn (caliph) 480
al-Āmir (caliph) 243
ᶜAmmār b. ᶜAlī al-Mawṣilī 359–60
Amorium, booty from 482, 487
amr (divine power of mandate) 6, 9
ᶜAmr b. ᶜAbdullāh b. Layth al-Qabᶜah 182–3
ᶜAmr al-Makkī 69, 72
al-amr bi-ʾl-maᶜrūf (moral imperative) 7
ᶜAmrūs b. al-Fatḥ 37
amzijah (temperaments) 343, 356
analogy *see qiyās*
anatomy 347, 356
Anawati, G. C. 392
Anbār (Pumpeditha) 464
ancient world 166, 169, 212; *see also individual civilizations*
Andalusia *see* Spain
Andarzghar 296, 299
Andronicus 292
anecdotes 205, 309; in administrative literature 163–4, 165; animal 181–2; in biography 118, 180–3, 186, 350
angels 13, 14, 25, 321, 380–1; arch- 13, 394, 395
animal stories 181–2, 273, 508
Ankara, booty from 482, 487
annals 196–7

al-Anṣārī, Muḥammad b. ʿAbdullāh 138
al-Anṣārī, Ṣafwān 502–3
al-Anṣārī al-Harawī, ʿAbdullāh 63, 67, 74
al-Anṭākī, ʿAbdullāh b. al-Faḍl 447, 451
al-Anṭākī, Abū Bakr 241
al-Anṭākī, ʿĀṣim 56, 66
al-Anṭākī, Būlus 451
al-Anṭākī, Yaḥyā b. Saʿīd 219, 241, 457
ʿAntarah b. Shaddād 354
anthrax 356
anthropomorphism (*tashbīh*) 8, 11, 20, 21, 23, 27, 34
Antioch, Syria 455, 457, 495
Antiochus 296
Anūshirvān, Khusraw 165, 166, 183, 503
Anūshirwān b. Khālid, Sharaf al-Dīn Abū Naṣr 218
anwāʾ books 275
Aparvīz, Khusraw 165
aphorisms 350, 356, 505
aphrodisiacs 361
Apocalypse of St John the Divine 449
Apollonius of Perga 251, 252, 486, 495
Apollonius of Tyana 339
apologetic: Christian 451; Islamic 2; Judaeo-Arabic 467; Ṣūfī 64, 70–1
ʿaqāʾid (doctrinal ideas) 407
ʿaqd see contracts
al-Aqfahsī, Shihāb al-Dīn b. ʿImād al-Dīn 507
ʿaqīdāt (compendia of dogma) 14–15
ʿaql see reason
al-ʿaql al-faʿʿāl ("Active Intellect") 385–6, 388
aqrābādhīnāt (formularies) 376
al-Aʿrābī, Abū Saʿīd Aḥmad b. Muḥammad b. Ziyād 60, 69
Arabic language: Arabicization of Copts, Syriac and Greek speakers 212; colloquial and dialect xvi, 107, 219, 220, 461, 463, 472; foreign etymologies 116; Jews' adoption of 461, 463–4; lexical development 115, 116, 249, 344, 366, 368, 463–4, 489; loan-words in other languages 341; Middle 464, 468; philosophers' use 76; rhetoric 125; *see also:* *ʿarabiyyah*; translation; *and under* scripts
ʿarabiyyah (classical Arabic usage) xvi, 106–7, 112, 113, 114, 116, 117, 124, 130
ʿArafāt, day of 409
Aramaic language 116, 463, 464, 469
Archimedes: on hydraulics and dynamics 259; "Method" 252; translations 251, 486, 488, 495; water-clocks 263, 267, 268
architecture 249
archives 201–2, 208, 211, 227
Arḍ al-Hind 33
Ardashīr 503
al-Arfādī, ʿAlī b. Dāwūd 451
ʿArīb b. Saʿd al-Qurṭubī 201, 203, 214, 455
Aristarchus of Samos 492
Aristotle xvi: and Alexander the Great 79, 81, 165–6; and alchemy 332, 338, 339; al-Bīrūnī on 409–10, 411, 426, 421–2; on creation 366, 372, 436, 492; demonstrative syllogism 383; in education 339, 364–5, 380; on elements 329–30, 332; Ḥarranians and 294, 481; Ibn al-Haytham's commentary 257; Ibn Sīnā on 100, 395, 409–10, 421–2; Ibn Ṭufayl on 96, 100, 104; immortality, supposed 97; "just, lawful and fair" 122; on knowledge 395, 400, 426; literary style 77; on manual work 262; and medicine 356, 357, 358, 360, 361; metaphysics 388, 396, 433, 436 (Plato's harmonized with) 78–87, 365, 369, 378; neo-Platonism and 369; on parts of speech 128; physics 294, 297; sciences, classification of 392; translation 481, 482–3, 484, 489, 491; on unity of God 380, 453
WORKS: *De Anima* 482, 483; *De Caelo et Mundo* 409–10, 482–3; *De Interpretatione* 380–2; *Ethics* 79, 98, 100, 104, 487, 491–2; *Mechanical Problems* 272–3; *Organon* 481, 492, 494; *Physics* 486; *Poetics* 493; *Politics* 483; *Posterior Analytics* 383, 481, 492; *Prior Analytics* 81, 383
see also under al-Fārābī, Abū Naṣr Muḥammad
Aristotle, Theology of (pseudo-Aristotle) 365, 466, 471, 490
arithmetic 160, 254–5; al-Bīrūnī on 407, 411; numerals 254–5, 391; sexagesimal system 255, 278
Armenian church 232, 451, 452; in Egypt 222, 241, 244
Armenian language 108, 448
armillary sphere 286
Ars Medicinae Articella 344
arsenic 329
Arwā bint Aḥmad, Sayyidah 243
Āryabhaṭa 302
asbāb al-nuzūl (dating of Qurʾān) 44–5
asceticism 52, 54, 58; Plato's pious ascetic 83, 84–6
Asclepius 480
al-Ashʿarī, Abū ʾl-Ḥasan ʿAlī b. Ismāʿīl xvi, 7–9, 19, 22, 205, 238
al-Ashʿarī, Saʿd b. ʿAbdullāh al-Qummī 238
Ashʿarism 4, 7–9, 50; al-Ghazālī and 428, 430, 435; *see also* al-Ashʿarī, Abū ʾl-Ḥasan
al-Ashraf (Yemeni prince) 108
ʿĀṣim al-Anṭākī 56, 61n, 66
Asín Palacios, Miguel 428
al-ʿAskarī, Abū ʾl-Ḥasan ʿAlī 23
askudār (scroll) 158
al-Aṣmaʿī, Abū Saʿīd ʿAbd al-Malik b. Qurayb 106, 503
al-ʿAsqalānī *see* Ibn Ḥajar
Assassins 186, 224
assaying methods 329, 330
al-Astarābādhī, Raḍī ʾl-Dīn Muḥammad 135
Astat (Eustathius) 490

astrolabes 267, 280, 286; *abjad* system 255; al-Bīrūnī on 267, 286, 413, 422–3; early Islamic 481–2; makers 262, 481; *shakkāziyyah* 286; *zarqāliyyah* 286; *zawraqī* 413
astrology xv, xvii, 290–300; Babylonian 291; al-Bīrūnī and 288, 299, 405, 407, 413, *414*, 415–16, 421; Byzantine 295, 296; ephemerides and 280; and foundation of Baghdad 293, 478; Greek 290, 291–2, 293, 295, 297, 301, 415 (Ptolemy) 292, 294, 295, 296, 298, 299, 416, 481; Ḥarranian 292, 297, 298, 486; Indian 290, 293, 295, 297, 299, 415; Yaᶜqūb b. Isḥāq al-Kindī and 296, 299, 364, 367; Latin West and 294, 295, 296; mathematical 407, 415; medicine and 347, 363; origins 290–1; Persian 290, 292–3, 293–5, 297, 299; philosophy and 297, 367; Ṣūfī literature on 64; translations 290, 291–2, 294, 295, 296, 481, 482; *zīj*s on 277
astronomy xv, 274–89; Banū Mūsā and 249; al-Bīrūnī on 277, 279, 283, 288, 406, 408–9, 411, 413, 418; Byzantine 294, 296; Christian 248, 459; chronology 288; computer analysis, modern 283; crescent visibility 280, 284–5; development of Islamic xvii, 274–5, 307; earth's movement 413, 422; ephemerides 279–80; equatoria 267, 280; geography and 302, 318; Greek 276, 282, 301, 333; Indian 248, 274, 276, 280, 406; instruments 261, 262, 267, 286–8, 413 (*see also* astrolabes); Jewish contribution 465; Latin West 296; al-Maᵓmūn and 484; mathematical 253–4, 276–83, 411, 418; numerical notation 278; observatories 287–8, 484; Persian 251, 274, 276, 294; philosophy and 76, 291; planetary positions 277, 279; pre-Islamic folk 274, 275; Ptolemy and 274, 279, 394, 418, 479; tables *see zīj*s; theoretical 279, 283–4; time-keeping 284–6; translation 276, 294, 295, 296, 301, 333, 481–2; trigonometry and 254–4, 277, 278–9, 282–3; uranography 277, 280, *281*, 282; *see also*: eclipses; prayer (times); *qiblah; zīj*s
Atābaks 220, 227, 229
Atay, H. 462
Athanasius (Church Father) 448
Athanasius (Melkite) 455
āthār (Traditions) 139, 140, 141
"Atlas of Islam" 312–15
ᶜAṭṭār, Farīd al-Dīn 63, 68
Aubrey, John 175
Augustine, St 448
aurifaction 329–30, 335
aurifiction 328–9
authority, religious 3–4, 304, 371
autobiography: Ayyubid era 231; biographers quote 169, 183–7, 406; in didactic writings 185–6; emphasis on outer events 183; Greek 183; memoirs 218 (*see also* Usāmah); al-Muqaddasī 315; Nizārī works 244; spiritual 185 (*see also under* al-Ghazālī); in travel literature 186
Autolycus 492
automata 261, 262, 263, 266, 270, 272, 273
Avestan script 292
Avicenna *see* Ibn Sīnā
ᶜAwānah 193
awrād (Ṣūfī collects) 67–8
Awrangzīb ᶜĀlamgīr, Muḥyī ᵓl-Dīn 154
al-ᶜAwtabī, Salamah b. Muslim 37
al-Awzāᶜī 59, 142, 143, 145
Āyīn-nāmah 166
ᶜAyn al-Quḍāt ᶜAbdullāh al-Hamadhānī 70
al-ᶜAynī, Badr al-Dīn 217
ayyām al-ᶜArab (pre-Islamic tribal battles) 189
Ayyūb of Edessa 488
Ayyubid era 231, 235–30, 244; *see also under*: Faṭimids, historiography
Azd 33
al-Azdī, ᶜAbd al-Ghanī b. Saᶜīd 241
al-Azdī, Abū Zakariyyāᵓ Yazīd b. Muḥammad 206
al-Azdī, Ibn Ẓāfir 221, 224, 246
al-Āzharī, Muḥammad b. Aḥmad 111, 114, 116
al-ᶜAẓīmī, Muḥammad b. ᶜAlī 217, 220, 221
al-ᶜAzīz (Faṭimid caliph) 211, 241, 320
ᶜAzīz the Scribe 292
al-Azraqī 212
ᶜ*azzābah* councils 36

Babylon 159, 251, 291, 448
Bacher, W. 475
Bacon, Roger 258
badāᵓ (change in the Divine will) 16–17, 18, 25, 28, 30, 32
Badakhshānī school 242, 246, 247
Badawī, ᶜAbd al-Raḥmān 427–8
Badr al-Jamālī 241, 243, 244
Baghay, battle of 36
Baghdad: al-Basāsīrī's occupation 241, 242; as centre of world 310; Christian scholars 379–80; cultural centre 27, 126, 249, 310; foundation 293, 478; histories 174, 206, 218, 226; hospitals 359, 370, 484, 491; intellectual milieu 379–80; Jewish learning 464, 465–6; libraries 293, 480, 482, 484; Mongol occupation 231, 319; Niẓāmiyyah College 425; observatory 484; Saljūq dominance 31; water-clocks 262; *see also* Bayt al-Ḥikmah
al-Baghdādī, ᶜAbd al-Laṭīf 184, 231
al-Baghdādī, Abū Manṣūr ᶜAbd al-Qāhir b. Ṭāhir 238
al-Baghdādī, Ṣafī ᵓl-Dīn 320
al-Bahlawī, Abū Muḥammad ᶜAbdullāh b. Muḥammad b. Barakah 37, 38
Bahrām Chūbīn 165

al-Baḥrānī, al-Ḥakam b. ʿAmr 506
Baḥrayn 33, 238, 239, 242
al-Baht 311
Baḥya b. Paquda 467, 472
Bakhtīshūʿ (Abū Saʿīd ʿUbaydullāh b. Jibrīl) 455, 480; descendants 480, 487
Bakhtīshūʿ b. Jibrīl 480
Bakhtīshūʿ b. Jūrjīs 480
al-Bakrī, Abū ʿUbayd 215, 240, 317–18, 318–19, 319–20
Balaʿam 292
Baʿlabakkī, Muẓaffar al-Dīn 471
al-Balādhurī 193, 195, 199, 200
balances 260
balancing of wheels 270
al-Balawī, Abū Muḥammad ʿAbdullāh al-Madīnī 210
al-Balkhī, Abū Zayd Aḥmad 312, 315, 368
Baneth, D. H. 475
Banū Hāshim 507
Banū Mūsā: construction of machines 262; *Kitāb al-Ḥiyal* 249, 264, *265*, 266; as patrons 249, 487; and translation movement 264, 484, 485–6, 487, 489
al-Bāqillānī 433, 452
Bar Hebraeus 343
barakah (virtue) 64
Bargès, J. J. L. 474
barīd see postal service
Barmakids 155, 164, 293, 333, 482
al-Barrādī 35
al-Bārūdī, Maḥmūd Sāmī 502
baṣāʾir (inner eye) 54
al-Basāsīrī 241, 242
Bashīr b. abī ʿAbdullāh Muḥammad b. abī Sufyān Maḥbūb al-Raḥīlī 36
Basil 448
al-Baṣīr, Abū Yaʿqūb Yūsuf b. Ibrāhīm 466, 470
basīṭ metre 501
basmalah 64
Basra: historical documents 190; Ibāḍī *daʿwah* 33, 34; Kufan antagonism 124, 126–7, 134, 137; Muʿtazilism 31; Sībawayhi and 122, 124, 126; Ṣufism 59; Sufyān al-Thawrī's school of law 143; tidal mills 261; traditions 43
al-Baṣrī, Abū ʿAlī al-Ḥasan b. ʿAlī (Yefet b. ʿAlī) 469, 474
al-Baṣrī, Abū Maʿn Thumāmah 454
al-Baṭāʾiḥī, al-Maʾmūn 222, 245
al-Baṭalyawsī, Abū Muḥammad ʿAbdullāh b. Muḥammad 472
bāṭin (esoteric knowledge) 52, 54
Baṭlamayūs al-Qalūdhī *see* Ptolemy, Claudius
al-Battānī, Abū ʿAbdullāh Muḥammad b. Jābir b. Sinān 253, 277, 298, 495
Baydaq 232
al-Bayḍāwī, ʿAbdullāh b. ʿUmar 52
Bayhaq 219
al-Bayhaqī, Abū ʾl-Faḍl Muḥammad b. Ḥusayn 209–10
al-Bayhaqī, Ẓahīr al-Dīn abū ʾl-Ḥasan ʿAlī b. Zayd b. Funduq 184, 219, 410, 422
Bayt al-Ḥikmah 305, 306, 344, 480, 484
Bedwell, W. 473
Benjamin al-Nihāwandī 492
Berber language 108, 463, 472; translation of Qurʾān 11
Berbers 33, 240, 241
Bergsträsser, G. 142
Berthelot, M. 333
Bianquis, Thierry 211
Bible 193–4; and conception of Qurʾān 484; epistles as literary form 61; exegesis 446–9, 462, 465, 468–9, 471, 475; translations 446–7, 462, 473, 475, 487; *see also individual books*
Bibliander, Th. (Buchmann) 462
bidʿah (innovation) 12
Bidpay 165
bīmāristān see hospitals
biography xvii, 168–87; anecdotes 118, 180–3, 186, 350; of Assassins 224; chancery documents preserved in 164; characteristics 178–83; characterization 180; emphasis on outer events 170–1, 172, 180, 183; Faṭimid 239, 241; genealogy 170, 172–3, 179, 184; in geographical works 317, 322; of grammarians 118, 137; Greek 169; and *Ḥadīth* 153, 168–9, 172, 173, 194; identification of persons with similar names 178, 218; individual biographies 177–8; Maghribī 232; medical practice described in 174, 179–80, 346; memoirs *see* autobiography; of non-Muslims 169–70, 179; Persian 170, 232; prosopography 170, 187; sources 170; *ṭabaqāt* 153, 171, 189, 194–5; in technical dictionaries 107; on viziers and secretaries 163–4, 222; Zaydī 213; *see also*: autobiography; dictionaries, biographical; hagiography; *sīrah; and under*: historiography; Ibadism; law; Ṣufism
al-Biqāʿī al-Shāfiʿī, Ibrāhīm b. ʿUmar 507
Birjandī, Raʾīs al-Ḥasan b. Ṣalāḥ Munshī 245
birth control 361
al-Bīrūnī al-Khwārazmī, Abū ʾl-Rayḥān Muḥammad b. Aḥmad xviii, 405–23; assessment 422–3; autobiographical poem 406; biographers on 410, 421, 422; calendars 316–17, 408–9 (geared) 267; on coinage 419; on gems 406, 408, 418–20; geographical works 307, 316–17, 411; geometry 421; and Greek tradition 415; and Ibn Sīnā 409–10, 421–2; life 405–6, 411; on motion of earth 413, 422; observational method 259, 419–20, 422; patronage 405–6; and philosophy 422, 433;

on physics 257, 259; trigonometry 283, 288, 412–13
WORKS 406–21; *al-As'ilah wa-'l-ajwibah* 409–10, 421–2; *al-Āthār al-bāqiyah* 405, 408–9, 415; *Fī 'stikhrāj al-awtār fī 'l-dā'irah* 421; *Fihrist* 406–8, 415, 416; *Ghurrat al-zījāt* 417; *Ifrād al-maqāl fī amr al-ẓilāl* 412–13; *Istīʿāb al-wujūh al-mumkinah fī ṣināʿat al-asturlāb* 413; *al-Jamāhir fī maʿrifat al-jawāhir* 406, 408, 418–20; *al-Qānūn al-Masʿūdī* 406, 408, 410, 418; *al-Ṣaydanah fī 'l-ṭibb* 408, 420–1; *al-Tafhīm li-awā'il ṣināʿat al-tanjīm* 413, *414*, 415–16; *Taḥdīd* 407, 410–12, 422; *Taḥqīq mā li-'l-Hind* 416–17; *Tamhīd al-mustaqarr li-taḥqīq maʿnā al-mamarr* 416; *al-Tanbīh ʿalā ṣināʿat al-tamwīh* 407, 415; *Tasṭīḥ al-ṣuwar wa-tabṭīḥ al-kuwar* 421
see also under: Aristotle; astrolabes; astrology; astronomy; India; pharmacy; trigonometry
Bishr b. al-Muʿtamir 506
al-Bisyānī (Bisyāwī), Abū 'l-Ḥasan ʿAlī b. Muḥammad 38, 148
al-Biṭrūjī 284
Björkman, W. 161
Black, Joseph 339
Blau, J. 462, 475
Blois, F. de 237
blood, pulmonary circulation of 348, *349*
blood-letting 268, 352, 377
Bohra *dāʿīs* 235, 246, 247
Bolus of Mendes 331
Bombay; Bohra *dāʿī* 235, 246
book-binding xix, 483, 484
books: as booty 482, 487; certificates of reading 208; distribution xix, 198, 199, 200, 207–8, 229; Greek, acquired in Byzantium 482, 484, 485; Usāmah on loss of 186; *see also*: libraries; printing; textbooks
Borisov, A. 475
Boswell, James 175, 181
botany 198, 362
Bouyges, M. 427
Brahmagupta 302, 479
Brethren of Purity *see* Ikhwān al-Ṣafā'
Brockelmann, C. 274
Browne, E. G. 346
Buchmann, Th. 462
Bukhārā 206, 209
al-Bukhārī, Abū ʿAbdullāh Muḥammad b. Ismāʿīl 42, 43–4, 173, 197
Bulghārs 311, 322–3, 324
Bulliet, Richard W. 176
Būlus al-Anṭākī 451
Būlus al-Būshī, Bishop of Cairo 449
al-Bundārī 219
al-Būnī, Aḥmad 64
Burckhardt, T. 331
al-Burnusī Zarrūk, Aḥmad 69
Burzōē 183
Būṣīr; "Joseph's Prison" 337
al-Bustī, Abū 'l-Fatḥ ʿAlī b. Muḥammad 156, 502, 505
Buṭrus al-Sadamantī 447, 448
Buṭrus Sāwīrus al-Jamīl, Bishop of Malīj 451
Buwayhid era 156, 157, 203, 204, 480
Buxtorf, J. 465
al-Būzajānī, Abū 'l-Wafā' 160, 253, 283
Buzurg b. Shahriyar 323
Buzurgmihr 165, 297
Byzantium: and administrative literature 158; Arab relations with 163, 457, 482; astrology 295, 296; astronomy 294, 296; books for translation acquired from 482, 484, 485; Christian Arab scholars 379; Christology 451; and Faṭimids 241; historiography 232, 233; Judaeo-Arabic literature printed in 473–4; mathematics and science 248, 379; medicine 342; Qaraites 472; water-clocks 262; *see also* Constantinople

Cahen, Claude 160
Cairo: Afḍal-Baṭā'iḥī observatory 288; Dār al-ʿIlm (Ismāʿīlī library) 241, 243; Genizah 347, 348, 351, 464, 466, 470, 475; Jewish learning 465–6; Lamak b. Mālik's mission to 242, 243
calculus, integral 252
Calendar of Cordova 275
calendars: al-Bīrūnī on 267, 316–17, 408–9; al-Bīrūnī's geared 267; crescent visibility 280, 284–5; Faṭimid 240; folk astronomy recorded in 275
caliphs: al-Ghazālī defends 443; and law 142, 144; "Mirrors for Princes" 165–7; panegyrics 245; *see also individual caliphs and* imamate
calligraphy 65, 162
Cambridge Chronicle 215
Cambridge University 175, 475
camera obscura 258
canals (*qanāts*) 252, 258
capillarity 260
Carmathians 202, 237–8, 239, 242
Castile: language 108, 300; time-pieces 270, 272
cat, anecdote about 182
cataract couchers (*qaddāḥūn*) 359
catechisms: *ʿaqīdāt* as 15; Christian, imitation of 137, 489; medicine 345, 348, 489, *see also masā'il*
causality 46, 48, 434–5, 486
celibacy; Ṣufism on 74
cementation (metallurgy) 329
centres of learning, provincial 250; *see also individual places*
certificates of reading 208
chancery writings 155–6, 201, 223–4
charlatans 330, 363

chemistry, modern 331, 336, 337, 339
cherubim (*karūbiyyūn*) 394, 395
chess-players 205
China 320, 323–4; alchemy 332–3, 335; technology 257, 266, 333
Cholas 325
chords (trigonometry) 253, 302, 421
Christendom: Ibn Sīnā's influence 379, 389, 404; Muslim influence on learning in 272, 315, 368, 377, 379, 389, 404, 426; northern, al-Bakrī on 318; *see also individual countries*, Latin (translation), *and under* medicine
Christian Arabic literature xviii–xix, 446–60; analogy 453; apologetic 451; canon law 449–50, 459; encyclopaedias 458, 459–60; linguistic studies 449; publication 446; theology 2, 450–5; translation into Arabic 343, 344, 365, 380, 446–7, 493–4 (of Bible) 446–7, 462, 473, 475, 487 (canon law) 449, 450 (sponsorship of) 483–4; translation into Armenian 448; *see also* Bible (exegesis) *and under* historiography
Christianity xv; Arab scholars' contribution 379–80; Bakhtīshū[c] family 480; catechisms 137, 489; Christology 451, 452, 453–4; ecumenical councils 459; Georgian 233; al-Ghazālī and 403, 428, 429; gnosticism 393; Gospels 13, 448; historiography 193–4, 232, 241, 455–9, 459–60; Ibn Sīnā on 402–3; Incarnation 454; Jewish polemic against 466; Logos 8, 453; medicine xviii, 248, 450, 456, 496; miracles 454–5; missionaries 137; morality 459, 460; and Mu[c]tazilism 454; mysticism 1; in north Africa 446; philosophy 396, 460, 494; rebaptism 452; in Syria 446, 451, 489; Syriac literature 212, 447, 462; theology 2, 450–5, 459, 460; translators, *see under* Christian Arabic literature; Trinity 2, 5, 13, 364, 452–3; *see also individual churches and*: Christian Arabic literature; Jesus; monasticism
Christodoulos (Coptic patriarch) 450
chronicles, abridged 224–5, 227
Chronicum Orientale 459
chronology 277, 407, 459
churches, Christian; histories 459–60
Cleopatra (alchemist's pseudonym) 332
clepsydra, steelyard 260
climate and health 356, 357–8
climes (geographical regions) 303, 305–6, 308, 315, 318
clocks *see under* time-keeping
closed-loop systems 270, 273
codes, secret 163
coinage 193, 208, 419
Colebrooke, H.T. 302
Comerius 332
comets 291, 364, 407
commerce; origins of algebra in 256
community (*ummah*) 10, 189, 191; Ibāḍī concept 39
Companions of the Prophet: assemble Qur'ān 43; biographies of xvii, 168, 169, 171, 172; exegesis of Qur'ān 48; Traditions 43, 47, 48, 139, 140, 141, 168
compasses, magnetic 257, 326
compendia: astrology 299–300; dogma 14–15; geography 319; law 147–8; *see also*; dictionaries; encyclopaedias
computers: computing devices 286–7; modern electronic 283
conditional syllogism 492
consensus (*ijmā*[c]) 10, 12, 34, 37, 47; in *uṣūl al-fiqh* 141, 144, 148
Constantine VIII (Byzantine emperor) 495
Constantinople 287, 473–4, 484
constitutional law xvii, 157, 192–3
contracts, legal 130, 140, 144
control systems 263, 265–6, 270, 273
Copernicus, Nicolas 284
Coptic church: Biblical exegesis 447; canon law 449, 450; Christology 451; crisis, C7th/13th 450; historiography 456, 457, 458; patriarchate 447, 450, 456, 457, 458; religious encyclopaedias 459–60
Coptic language 212; translation (to Arabic) 333, 449, (to Ge[c]ez) 450
copyists 207–8, 324, 473, 484
Cordova: *Anonymous Work of*, 213; *Calendar of*, 275; al-Ghazālī's works burned 11; historiography 213–14; judges 173, 182; library xix; translation in 494–5; Umayyad caliphate 213, 481, 495; water-mills 262
corn 176, 261
correspondence: Aristotle's supposed 79, 81, 165–6; diplomatic 201, 239; Ṣūfī 59, 61–2, 65, 70–1; *see also* epistles
cosmography 302, 321
cosmology 310, 320, 482
cosmos, concept of 479
cotangent 411
court ceremonial 142
craftsmen 258, 262, 330–1, 422–3
cranks, mechanical 266, 270, *271*
creation, views on 14, 25, 30, 503; Aristotle 366, 372, 436, 492; al-Ghazālī 433–4, 435–6; Ibn Sīnā 100, 395–6, 401; Ya[c]qūb b. Isḥāq al-Kindī 367; al-Rāzī 372; Shi[c]ite 20, 21; *see also*: emanation; occurrence; *and under* Qur'ān
creed, Muslim (*shahādah*) 10
crescent visibility 280, 284–5
Crusaders 186, 223, 245
Ctesibius 263
cupellation 329, 330, 339
Cureton, William 474
customs and toll systems 160
Cyril II (Coptic patriarch) 450

Cyril of Jerusalem 448

daftar al-sanah (ephemerides) 279
al-Dāmaghānī, Abū Saʿīd Manṣūr b. ʿAlī 300
Damascus 59, 220, 427; historiography 174, 190, 209, 220–1, 226; water-clocks 262, 267–8
Damascus Chronicle 220–1
dams 261–2
Danḥā, Abū Zakariyyāʾ 455
al-Dānī, Abū ʿAmr ʿUthmān b. Saʿīd 184
al-Dānī, Aḥmad 72
Daniel (astrologer) 291–2
Daniel, Book of 447–8
Danishpazuh 244
Dār al-ʿIlm, Cairo 241, 243
dār al-hijrah (Faṭimid state) 236
al-Dārimī, ʿAbdullāh 403
al-Darjīnī, Abū ʾl-ʿAbbās Aḥmad b. Saʿīd 35, 232
ḍarūriyyāt (principles of thought) 432
al-Dasūqī, Ibrāhīm b. ʿAbd al-ʿAzīz 61
dating system 197, 201–2
David (prophet) 13
al-Dawādārī, Abū Bakr b. ʿAbdullāh b. Aybak 216, 240
daʿwah: *see*: Ḥāfizī; Nizārī; Ṭayyibī *daʿwah*s, *and under*: Faṭimids; Ibaḍism
al-daʿwah al-hādiyah (Ismāʿīlī movement) 236
Dāwūd b. Ḥunayn 345
Dāwūd b. Joshua Maimonides *see* Maimonides
Dāwūd b. Marwān al-Raqqī b. Muqammiṣ 466
Dāwūd II Joshua 468
Day of Judgement 14
al-Daylamī, ʿAlī b. Muḥammad 72
al-Daylamī, Muḥammad b. al-Ḥasan 238
Debarnot, M. T. 282
debates, public 124
decimal place-value system 254, 255
Deity *see* God
Delhi 324
Democritus, *pseudo-* 332
demography 176
demonstrative method *see* observational method
Derenbourg, J. 474
Descartes, René 252
descent *see* genealogy
determinism *see* freedom
al-Dhahabī, Muḥammad b. Aḥmad 53, 178, 207, 231, 246
*dhimmī*s (Christians and Jews) 465
Dhū ʾl-Nūn al-Miṣrī 52, 59, 338; epistles 61, 62, 66; *qaṣaṣ* 71, 72
Dhū ʾl-Yamīnayn, Ṭāhir 165, 166
diabetes 358
diacritical marks; origins 119
dialects *see under* Arabic language
dictionaries *see* lexicography *and under individual types below*
dictionaries, biographical 62–3, 168, 169–76, 187, 215, 232; Arabic creation 233; arrangement 171, 172; autobiographies included in 183–4; centennial 171, 176; general 171, 175–6; geographical information in 308; local 171, 172, 174–5, 206, 221, 229–30; on persons notable in particular field 171, 172–4; as registers of vital data 176–6; types 171–2
dictionaries, geographical 107, 312–15, 319–22; *see also* dictionaries, biographical (local)
dictionaries, medical 376–7, 480
dictionaries, polyglot 107–8, 376–7
dictionaries of synonyms 107
dictionary of Mishneh Tōrāh 469
didactic prose 56, 59, 185–6
didactic verse (*shiʿr taʿlīmī*) xix, 498–509; aphorisms 505; categorization 498; establishment of genre 502–3; fables 498, 508; Greek 498; metres 498, 500–1; modern 502, 508, 509; on Muḥammad's life 506–7; polemic 506; pre-Islamic 498, 502; satire 503–4, 506; Shiʿite 506–7; Ṣūfī 56, 59; *see also under individual disciplines*
dil īrānshahr (centre of world) 309, 310
al-Dimashqī, Abū ʿUthmān 491–2
al-Dimashqī, Shams al-Dīn 319
al-Dīnawārī, Abū Ḥanīfah Aḥmad 198, 199, 200
Diogenes the Cynic 364
Dionysius b. al-Ṣalībī 447, 451
Dionysius Thrax 119
Diophantus 251, 492
Dioscorides 420, 489, 494–5
diplomacy 163, 201, 239, 242, 322–3, 482
al-Dīrīnī, ʿIzz al-Dīn 59, 507
disciplines, academic; lack of demarcation 191, 199, 315
divination 64, 361
divorce, law on 449
*dīwān*s 115, 155, 163
Ḍiyāʾ al-Dīn b. al-Athīr 156, 227
Diyār Bakr 220, 221, 362
documents: administrative 163, 164, 201, 223–4; legal (*shurūṭ*) 152
dogma: scientific 377; theological 12–14, 14–15, 429
Dorotheus of Sidon 293, 295, 296, 297, 299
doubt: Cartesian 399–400; al-Ghazālī on 429, 479; *shakk* 34
dreams, interpretation of 174
dredging machine *265*
drugs *see* pharmacy
Druzes 240, 241
duʿāʾ (invocations) 67
al-Duʾalī, Abū al-Aswad 119
al-Dubaythī 218
Dujayl 184

Ḍumām b. Sā'ib 35
Dūnash b. Tamīm 466
al-Dūrī, ʿAbd al-ʿAzīz 196
durrāʿah (secretary's sleeved coat) 164
Dushanbe, library of 246
dust-board 255
dynamics 259

earth, motion of 413, 422
eclipses 258, 277, 280, 291
Edessa 248, 481
education 367–8, 439, 440–1; *see also*: grammar (pedagogy); *madrasah; and under*: Alexandria; medicine; philosophy; secretaries
Egypt: administration 162, 242; alchemy 331–2; archives 191; Armenians 222, 241, 244; astrology 290, 298; astronomy 285; Ayyubid period 225, 244, 245 (*see also under* historiography; *below*); biography 173, 222; Faṭimid period 18, 162, 234 (conquest) 239 (al-Ḥākim) 240–1 (Maʿadd al-Mustanṣir) 241–2, 244 (last phase) 225, 245–6 (*see also under* historiography *below*); gnosticism 391; Hellenistic 290, 331–2; historiography 197 (pre-Faṭimid) 193 (Faṭimid) 210, 211, 212, 213, 221–2, 225, 246, 457 (Ayyubid) 225, 226, 228–9, 230, 457 (Mamluk) 221, 228; Ibaḍism 33; Ikhshidid period 210, 211, 504; Mamlūk period 225, 230, 287; time-keeping 285, 287; treatises for secretaries 162; Ṭulunid period 210, 298; Usāmah in 221; viziers 222, 245; *see also*: Alexandria; Cairo
Ehrenkreutz, A. S. 160
elements 336, 329–30, 343, 356
elephant 506
Elgood, C. L. 344
Elias I (Catholicos) 494
Elijah of Nisibin: chronicle 457; theology 447, 451, 452, 453, 453–4
elixirs 330, 335, 336, 337, 338
emanation (*fayḍ*) 53, 395–6, 433, 435, 492
ʿEnbaqom 459
encampment, deserted (literary *topos*) 507
encyclopaedias: geographical 315, 319–22; Ibn Sīnā 391; medical 347–8, 354, *355*, 356–8, 420–1; religious, Christian 458, 459–60
Enoch 454
Enūma Anu Enlil 291
Epaphroditus 497
ephemerides 279–80
epigrammatic verse 498
epigraphy 208
epistles 61–2; Aristotle and Alexander's supposed 165–6; New Testament 61, 448; Ṣūfī 61–2, 65; *see also*: correspondence; Ikhwān al-Ṣafā'
epistolary style (*musajjaʿ*) 156
epitome (*mūjiz*) xix, 348
equatoria 267, 280
Eratosthenes 306
Escurial library 211, 226
esoteric works: alchemy 328, 331, 335, 338, 339–40; *bāṭin* 52, 54; al-Fārābī 378; al-Ghazālī 102–3, 104; Ismāʿīlī *ta'wīl* 234, 243; Muḥyī 'l-Dīn b. al-ʿArabī 74
ethics: Greek and Persian 165–6; al-Kindī on 365; medical 347, 348, 350–4; Ṣūfī 74; Thābit b. Qurrah on 486
etiquette literature: medical 347, 348, 350–1; Ṣūfī 66–7
Etna, Mount 309
etymology 70, 109, 116, 312, 409
Euclid: *Elements* 251, 254, 486; on geometry 252, 391; influence 251, 339, 365, 479; al-Khāzinī on 259; Yaʿqūb b. Isḥāq al-Kindī uses method 366; philosophical concepts 479; translations 482, 484, 486, 488, 491, 495
Euphrates, river 261
Eusebius 448
Eustathius (Astat) 490
evidence, law of 140, 152, 449
exchequer 155
exegesis *see under*: Bible; Qur'ān
experiment *see* observational method
eye: anatomy and functioning 258; *see also* ophthalmology

fables 498, 508; *see also Kalīlah wa-Dimnah*
faḍā'il literature 206
al-Faḍḍālī, Muḥammad 15
al-Faḍl b. Shādhān al-Naysābūrī 19, 23, 24
faith: and gnosis, Ṣūfī 57; and Islam 29, 30; and reason 8, 389, 431–2, 445; and revelation 389; Shīʿīs on 25–6, 29, 30
al-Fā'iz (Faṭimid caliph) 185, 243
Fakhr al-Mulk ʿAlī 425, 427
falsafah (philosophy) 1; neologism 115; *see also* philosophy
al-Fārābī, Abū Ibrāhīm Isḥāq b. Ibrāhīm 114
al-Fārābī, Abū Naṣr Muḥammad b. Muḥammad xviii, 77, 78–87, 378–88; on afterlife 79, 98, 99–100; on Aristotle 81–2, 83, 84, 98, 378, 379, 388, 467 (on *De Interpretatione*), 380–2 (on *Ethics*) 79, 98, 100; on creation 492; dissemination of works 102, 379, 472; esoteric writings 378; on freedom 381–2; on grammar 128–9, 381; and Greek philosophy 384, 426, 433; Ibn Sīnā and 392; Ibn Ṭufayl on 96, 98–100, 101, 104; *Liber de Anima* cites 338; life 378–9; on logic 128–9; metaphysics 379, 384, 387, 388, 392, 404, 433; on music 257; observational method 383, 384; on Plato 80–1, 82–6, 378, 379, 387, 388; political philosophy 379, 388; as polymath 384;

popular philosophy 86–7; on prophetic revelation 493, 494; on reasoning 382–3, 384, 394, 424; style 77; syntheses 378, 380, 426, 433; theory of knowledge 381–2, 395
WORKS: chronology 378: *Falsafat Aflāṭūn* 85; *Iḥṣāʾ al-ʿulūm* 383; *al-Jamʿ bayna raʾyay al-ḥakīmayn* 78–83, 84, 85; *Kitāb al-Ḥurūf* 384; *Kitāb Iḥṣāʾ al-ʿulūm* 250; *Kitāb Mabādiʾ ārāʾ ahl al-madīnah al-fāḍilah* 98, 385; *Kitāb al-Siyāsah al-madaniyyah* 98, 385; *Risālah fī ʾl-ʿaql* 386; *Talkhīṣ Nawāmīs Aflāṭūn* 83, 84–5
al-Farāhīdī, al-Rabīʿ b. Ḥabīb 34, 35, 38
al-Farghānī, Abū ʾl-ʿAbbās Aḥmad 286
al-Farghānī, Abū Muḥammad ʿAbdullāh b. Aḥmad b. Jaʿfar 203, 210–11, 229
al-Fārisī, Abū ʿAlī al-Ḥasan b. Aḥmad b. ʿAbd al-Ghaffār 129, 131
al-Farrāʾ, Abū ʾl-Ḥusayn Muḥammad b. abī Yaʿlā 153, 173
al-Farrāʾ, Abū Yaʿlā Muḥammad b. al-Ḥusayn b. 150, 157
al-Farrāʾ, Abū Zakariyyāʾ Yaḥyā b. Ziyād 46, 123, 124–5, 126, 129
al-Fāsī, ʿAbd al-Raḥmān b. ʿAbd al-Qādir 151
al-Fāsī, Abū Sulaymān Dāwūd b. Ibrāhīm 469
fasting 10, 140, 150, 499–500
fatāwā (legal responses) 34, 35, 36, 153–4
al-Fatḥ b. Mismār 507
Fatḥ al-Dīn b. al-Shahīd 507
Fathyūn b. Ayyūb al-Turjumān 456
Fāṭimah bint al-Ḥusayn b. al-Ḥasan b. ʿAlī b. abī Ṭālib 237
Fāṭimah bint Muḥammad 16, 172, 237
Faṭimids: Ḥāfiẓī *daʿwah* 243, 245; last phase 425–6; Nizārī *daʿwah* 242, 243, 244–5, 246, 247; north African period 236, 239–40; period of concealment (*satr*) 235, 236–8, 240; reign of al-Ḥākim 240–1; reign of al-Mustanṣir 241–3; Ṭayyibī *daʿwah* 242, 243–4, 246
and ʿAbbasids 236, 240, 241; Ayyubid conquest 221, 225, 244, 245; biography 239, 241; and Byzantium 241; calendar 240; *daʿwah* 234, 234–5, 238, 242 (*see also* Nizārī *and*; Ṭayyibī *below*); defeat Ibāḍīs at Baghay 36; Egypt, rule in *see under* Egypt; elite nature of movement 234; genealogy 235, 236–7, 239; historiography 210, 214, 216, 221–2, 225, 238, 239–40, 240–1, 242–6, 457; (*see also under* Egypt); Ibn Ḥawqal supports 314; imamate 210, 236–8; and Jibrīl b. Bakhtīshūʿ 480; libraries 235; *majālis* writings 242; and Muʿtazilism 242; Nizārī *daʿwah* 242, 243, 244–5, 246, 247; range of literature 235; secrecy of literature 235; and Syria 220–1, 234, 244–5, 457; Ṭayyibī *daʿwah* 242, 243–4, 246; and Yemen 222, 238, 239, 241–2, 242–3, 246; *see also under* Egypt
fayḍ see emanation
al-Fazārī, Ibrāhīm 481
al-Fazārī, Muḥammad b. Ibrāhīm b. Ḥabīb 293, 301-3, 481, 503
Ferrand, G. 322, 326
fevers 375
Fihrist al-Majdūʿ 247
fiqh see law
firaq literature (on sects) 238
al-Firdawsī 425
Firkowitsch, A. 468, 475
al-Fīrūzābādī, Muḥammad b. Yaʿqūb 74, 108, 114–15
fitnah (dissension) 34, 192
flight, early attempt at 180
Flood 13
footwear, cleansing of (*masḥ ʿalā ʾl-khuffayn*) 26, 42
formularies (*aqrabādhīnāt*) 376
fossils 412
fountains 261, 262, 264, 270
fractions, decimal 254, 255
Franks 220, 221, 223, 452; *see also* Crusades; Europe
freedom and determination 3, 4, 6, 14; al-Ashʿarī on 8–9; al-Fārābī on 381–2; al-Ghazālī on 436–7, 441–2; Muʿtazilites on 6, 27, 30; Shīʿīs on 20, 21, 25, 27, 29, 30
Friedländer, I. 475
fulling; water-powered machinery 261
funeral for pet animal 182
furūʿ al-fiqh 148, 149–50, 152
furūq (legal term) 150
Fyzee, A. A. A. 247

Gabriel, archangel 13, 395
Gabriel II Ibn Turayk 450
Gacek, A. 235
Gagnier, J. 473–4
Galen: Ibn al-Haytham and 183, 257; Ibn Sīnā's synthesis with Aristotle 356, 358; on pharmacy 362, 375, 487; philosophy 489; on procreation 360, 361; Abū Bakr Muḥammad b. Zakariyyāʾ al-Rāzī on 372; teleology 489; translation of 344, 481, 482, 487, 494 (Ḥunayn's), 183, 488, 489, 490, 497
Galindo, E. 400
Gardet, L. 397
gazetteers 158, 320–1
gears 258, 266–7
Geber *see*: Jābir b. Ḥayyān; Jabirian corpus
Geʿez language, translation into 450, 457, 459
gems 406, 408, 418–20, 503
genealogy: in biography 170, 172–3, 179, 184; Faṭimid 235, 236–7, 239; in historiography 194; in *maghāzī* 189; and pension rights 189; technical dictionaries 107; Umayyad nobility 195

genethlialogy 290, 291, 292, 294, 295, 296, 297
Genizah (Cairo); manuscripts 462, 464, 466, 468, 470, 471, 475
geodesy 302, 306–7, 484
geographical co-ordinates 277, 283, 406–7
geographical literature 301–24; as *adab* 307–12, 322; administrative manuals 158, 301, 308; *Akhbār al-Ṣīn wa-ʾl-Hind* 322; arrangement of works 320–1; astronomical contents 302, 318; biographical dictionaries as 308; al-Bīrūnī 307, 316–17, 411; "Classical school", C4th/10th 312–15; climes 303, 305–6, 308, 315, 318; compendia 319; dictionaries and encyclopaedias 107, 312–15, 319–22; didactic verse 507, 508–9; early literature 301–2; al-Fazārī; gazetteers 158, 320–1; geodesy 302, 306–7; Greek 301, 302, 303 (*see also under* Ptolemy); history intermingled with 205, 230, 240, 309–10, 315, 317, 322; human geography develops 308, 314, 322; Indian 302–3, 317, 323, 324, 326; on magnetic phenomena 257; maps 312, *313*, 314; mathematical 411; mechanical technical information in 261; Persian 308; poetry quoted in 309, 320; Post-Classical 317–19; regional divisions 314; for secretaries 308; *Sindhind* 302–3, 481; travellers' writings 322–4; Umayyad era 301; *see also* al-Khwārazmī *and other authors*
geology 412
geometry 252–3; al-Bīrūnī 411, 421; of chords 253, 302, 421; conic sections 252; Euclid on 252, 391; navigational literature 325; in philosophy 76
George of Trebizond 298
Georgian Christianity 233
Gerard of Cremona 255, 341, 467
Gēv son of Gōdharz 293
al-Ghāfiqī 108
Ghālib, Muṣṭafā 247
Ghars al-Niʿmah Muḥammad 203
ghaybah see occultation
ghayriyyah see unity of God
al-Ghazāl, Yaḥyā b. Ḥakam 503
al-Ghazālī, Abū Ḥāmid Muḥammad b. Muḥammad xvi, xviii, 424–5; and Ashʿarism 428, 430, 435; autobiography 62, 101–2, 185, 424, 426, 479; on beauty 444–5; on causality 434–5; on certainty 426, 430, 431; and Christianity 403, 428, 429; on creation 433–4, 435–6; critical awareness 479; on divine knowledge 436; on doubt 429, 479; on education 439, 440–1; esoteric works 102–3, 104; on freedom 436–7, 441–2; on God and world 435–7; and Greek ideas 426, 429, 433, 496; and *Ḥadīth* 427, 428; Hebrew translations 472; and Ibn Sīnā 100, 402, 426, 433; on imitation 429–30; on intuition 427; jurisprudence 425; life 106–7, 424–7, 431, 433, 445 (spiritual crisis), 424, 426–7, 431; on logic 425–6, 431; on love 443–5; metaphysics 429, 433–5, 437; microcosmos 437; morality 438–40; mysticism *see* Ṣufism *below*; on neo-Platonism 433, 496; Persian background 166–7; philosophy changed by xvi, 445; Platonism 428; physics 433; on politics 442–3; on reason 11, 62, 70, 424, 430, 431–5, 445; sources 64; style 427–8; successors 424, 445; Ṣufism xvi, 10–11, 54, 62, 70, 101–2, 424, 426, 431, 445, 496; toleration 428, 429, 435; tomb 425; on visionary experience 90, 91, 92, 95, 96, 98, 102–3
  WORKS 427–8; *ʿAjāʾib al-qalb* 62; *Ayyuhā ʾl-walad* 424, 428, 438; *Bidāyat al-hidāyah* 62; *Faḍāʾiḥ al-Bāṭiniyyah* 425; *Iḥyāʾ* 14, 64, 73, 424, 427, 428, 431–2, 435–6, 437–8, 439, 443, 445, 496; *al-Iqtiṣād fī ʾl-iʿtiqād* 428; *Jawāhir al-Qurʾān* 102; *Kīmiyāʾ al-saʿādah* 70; *Maqāṣid al-falāsifah* 426; *al-Maqṣad al-asnā* 102–3, 428; *Miḥakk al-naẓar* 425–6, 431; *Mishkāt al-anwār* 103, 428, 432, 437; *Miʿyār al-ʿilm* 425, 431; *Mīzān al-ʿamal* 101; *Mīzān al-iʿtidāl* 70; *al-Munqidh min al-ḍalāl* 62, 101–2, 185, 424, 431; *al-Mustaṣfā* 149, 425; *Naṣīḥat al-mulūk* 166–7; *Qaṣīdat al-ṭayr* 68; *Qawāʿid al-ʿaqāʾid* 435; *al-Qisṭās al-mustaqīm* 424, 425, 431; *Risālat al-Aḍḥawiyyah fī ʿumr al-maʿād* 402; *al-Tibr al-masbūk fī nasīḥat al-Mulūk* 442–3; *Tahāfut al-falāsifah* xvi, 101, 426, 433, 435
al-Ghazālī, Shihāb al-Dīn Aḥmad 68, 72, 425, 427
Ghazna, al-Bīrūnī at 405–6, 411
Ghaznavids; panegyric of 209–10; *see also* Maḥmūd of Ghazna
ghubār numerals 255
*ghūl*s 321
gilding, amalgamation 329
Gilson, E. 397
*ginān*s (Islamo-Hindu mystical poetry) 246
glaucoma (*al-māʾ*) 370
globe, celestial 258
gnomic verse 498, 502
gnosis 57, 69, 71, 72, 468
gnosticism 332, 391, 393, 395
God, attributes of: Christians on 453; Muʿtazilites on 5, 27, 30; power to act 6, 9, 382; Shīʿīs on 20, 21, 22, 23, 24–5, 27, 28, 30; Ṣūfīs on 64; visibility (*ruʾyah*) 5, 24, 28, 30; *see also*: anthropomorphism; knowledge (divine); word of God
Goeje, M. J. de 312
Goichon, A. M. 398
Goitein, S. D. 351, 475
gold 419–20; *see also*: aurifaction; aurifiction
Goldberg, B. 474

Goldstein, B. R. 284
Goldziher, I. 41, 428, 474
Graetz, H. 474
Graf, G. 446, 450
grain 161, 176, 261
grammar xvi–xvii, 118–38; abstraction 125–6, 137; C3rd/9th-C4th/10th 127–32; C5th/11th 132–3; C6th/12th 133–8; commentaries 132, 134; concise grammars 134–5, 137; early 120–1, 123; Greek influence 119, 126, 128, 131, 381; and *Ḥadīth* 130, 136; hierarchies 121, 130; Hispanic school 468, 469; Ḥunayn b. Isḥāq 490; and Islam 124, 132, 136; Judaeo-Arabic writings 465, 468–9, 475; jurisprudence; methods adopted from 120, 122, 123, 129–30; language as "speech acts" 25, 121, 122; law and 118, 122, 129–30 (procedures adopted from *fiqh*) 120, 122, 123, 129–30; logic and 125, 127–9, 130, 135, 380, 381; manuals for secretaries 161–2; Muʿtazilite influence 129; *naḥw* 118; origins 119–20; pedagogy 123–6, 127, 132–3, 136, 138 (simplified grammars), 131, 134–5, 137; philosophy and 118, 125–6, 127–9, 137; polemical literature 126, 133; primitive 120–1; Quranic 9–10, 45–9, 119; Sībawayhi 122–3; simplified grammars 131, 134–5, 137; substitutability 123; Ṣūfī literature 57; and *sunnah* 130; terminology 122–3, 125–6, 129, 136; and theology 128; "universal" 381; unmarked vs. marked distinction 121; verse treatises 498, 501; versified grammars 135–6; *see also individual grammarians and*: morphology; phonology; syntax
grammarians 18, 137
Granada 175, 214
gravity 260
gravity, specific 259, 419–20
Greek tradition 497; microcosmos concept 437; schools in Asia Minor 248; *see also individual authors and under individual disciplines and* Greek language (translation)
Greek language: decline in use 212; glossaries 108; grammar 119, 126, 128, 131; loan-words from 116
translation to Arabic xv, xix, 477–87; Bayt al-Ḥikmah 344, 480; Byzantium as source of manuscripts 482, 484, 485; canon law 449; Christian translators 344, 365, 380, 493–4; historiography 193–4; Ḥarranians 298, 495 (*see also* Thābit b. Qurrah); Hebrew character versions 472; Yaʿqūb b. Isḥāq al-Kindī's school 365, 366, 368, 490–1; pragmatic motivation 483, 485, 496–7; patronage 481, 482, 483, 484–5, 485–6, 487 (Banū Mūsā) 264, 484, 485–6, 487 (Hārūn al-Rashīd) 481, 482 (Khālid b. Yazīd), 301, 333 (al-Maʾmūn) 484–5; reasons for end of 495–7; in Spain 363, 461, 468, 469, 472, 495; Syriac intermediate translations 248, 343, 449, 487; systematic organization 483; (*see also under individual disciplines and Greek writers, and*: Ḥunayn b. Isḥāq; Thābit b. Qurrah)
translation to Byzantine Greek 296
Gregory of Nyssa 448
Griffini, E. 142
Gryaznevitch, P. A. 210
Gujarat, India 246, 325

Haarbrücker, Th. 474
Ḥabash al-Ḥāsib al-Marwazī, Aḥmad b. ʿAbdullāh 253, 276, 278, 285, 410, 482
ḥadd: Ismāʿīlī term 234; legal term 52, 140
al-Hādī 165, 480
al-Hādī ilā ʾl-Ḥaqq, Abū ʾl-Ḥusayn Yaḥyā b. al-Ḥusayn 213
Ḥadīth xv; *ahl al-ḥadīth* 10, 143; criteria for inclusion 43; on doing as you would be done by 440; and early historiography 189, 190; al-Ghazālī and 427, 428; Ibaḍism and 38; *ʿilm al-rijāl* (science of trustworthy authorities) 168–9, 172, 173, 194; and linguistic studies 107, 112, 130, 136; oral transmission 170; as root of law 139, 148–9; al-Ṭabarī's approach to 47; in al-Zamakhsharī 49; *see also* Traditions
Ḥaḍramawt 33, 34, 38, 243
ḥads (intuition) 397
al-Ḥāfiẓ (Faṭimid caliph) 243, 245
Ḥāfiẓī *daʿwah* 243, 245
hagiography 56, 60–1, 65, 68, 168, 177–8, 216
al-Ḥājib Jaʿfar b. ʿAlī 239
ḥajj see Pilgrimage
al-Ḥajjāj b. Maṭar 484
al-Ḥajjāj b. Yūsuf (governor of Iraq) 119
Ḥājjī Khalīfah (Kātib Celebi) 304
al-Ḥakam II xix, 495
al-Ḥakam b. ʿAmr al-Baḥrānī 506
al-Hakamī, ʿUmārah b. abī ʾl-Ḥasan 184–5, 222, 245
al-Ḥākim (caliph) 240–1
al-Ḥākim al-Naysābūrī 171
ḥāl (circumstantial qualifier) 121
Halkin, A. S. 475
al-Ḥallāj, Manṣūr 57, 60, 69, 73
Halm, H. 235, 247
Haly Abbas *see* al-Majūsī
al-Hamadhānī, ʿAlī 60
al-Hamadhānī, ʿAyn al-Quḍāt ʿAbdullāh 70
al-Hamadhānī, Badīʿ al-Zamān 59, 135, 506
al-Hamadhānī, Ibn al-Faqīh 309, 311–12
al-Hamadhānī, Muḥammad b. ʿAbd al-Malik 202, 203, 216–17
Ḥamāh, Syria 258, 226–7
ḥamalat al-ʿilm (Ibāḍī missionaries) 34, 38

al-Ḥamawī, Ṣalāḥ al-Dīn b. Yūsuf 360
Ḥamdān b. ʿAbd al-Raḥīm 220
Ḥamdān al-Lāḥiqī 500
Ḥamdān Qarmaṭ 237
al-Hamdānī, Abū Isḥāq Ibrāhīm b. Qays 37–8
al-Hamdānī, Abū Muḥammad al-Ḥasan b. Aḥmad 212, 507, 508
Hamdānī, Ḥusayn 237, 246–7
al-Hamdānī, Sulṭān al-Khaṭṭāb 243, 244
Hamdanids of Ṣanʿāʾ 243
al-Ḥāmidī, Ḥātim b. Ibrāhīm 242, 244
al-Ḥāmidī, Ibrāhīm b. al-Ḥusayn (*dāʿī muṭlaq*) 243, 244
Ḥammād b. abī Sulaymān 141
Ḥamzah b. ʿAlī b. Aḥmad 241
Ḥanafite school 141, 142; analytical work 146; *āthār* 141; code of law 49; compendium 147; didactic verse 501–2; *fatāwā* 153–4; foundation 142; and *ḥiyal* 151–2; on *ikhtilāf al-madhāhib* 152; on law of succession 149; on *shurūṭ* 152; on *uṣūl al-fiqh* 141, 148, 149; on *waqf* 149–50
Ḥanbalite school 141, 145; biography 173; foundation 145; historiography 217–18; and *ḥiyal* 151; on public law and administration 157; on reason 431; *ṭabaqāt* on early jurists 153; theologians and 8, 12, 14
handasah see geometry
ḥaqāʾiq (Ismāʿīlī literary term) 234, 243
al-Ḥāqilānī, Ibrāhīm (Abraham Ecchellensis) 459
al-Harawī 70
Ḥarāz region, Yemen 243
al-Ḥarīrī, Abū ʾl-Ḥasan al-Qāsim 59, 135, 506
al-Ḥārith b. Kaladah 342
al-Ḥārithī, Muḥammad b. Ṭāhir 243–4
Harkavy, A. 475
harmonic system 257
Ḥarrān: and Aristotle 294, 481; astrology 292, 297, 298; new school under al-Mutawakkil 248, 495; Ṣābiʾ family of historians 202–3, 2–4; Sabian sect 170, 202, 248, 364, 484, 486; time-keeping and calendar 409; translation 248, 495
Hārūn, client of the Azd 506
Hārūn b. ʿAzzūr 455
Hārūn b. al-Yamān 34
Hārūn al-Rashīd (caliph): administrative treatise for 142; and Barmakids 164, 478, 479; and Khizānāt al-Ḥikmah 293; tomb 425; and translation movement 293, 479, 481, 482, 484
ḥasan (structurally correct) 122, 125
Ḥasan, Muḥammad ʿAbd al-Ghanī 175, 178
al-Ḥasan b. Aḥmad 239
al-Ḥasan b. ʿAlī (caliph) 16, 17
al-Ḥasan b. al-Ḥusayn al-Khallāl 174
al-Ḥasan b. Nūḥ 244
al-Ḥasan b. Qāhir b. Muhtadī b. Hādī b. Nizār 245
al-Ḥasan b. al-Ṣabbāḥ 244, 425
al-Ḥasan b. Sahl b. Nawbakht 293, 296
al-Ḥasan b. Sahl al-Sarakhsī 482
al-Ḥasan b. Suwar, Ibn al-Khammār 493–4
al-Ḥasan al-ʿAskarī 23, 26
al-Ḥasan al-Baṣrī 4–5, 58, 59
al-Ḥasan al-Sīrāfī 127
al-Ḥasanī, Abū Muḥammad Mawlānā al-Tihāmī Kannūn al-Idrīsī 507–8
Ḥasdāy b. Shaprūṭ 495
Hāshim, Banū 507
Haskalah 461
Hava, J. G. 115
haylāj (prorogator) 292
al-Haytham b. ʿAdī 35
Ḥayy b. Yaqẓān, story of 87–8, 99, 104, 105
Hebrew: literary use 461, 472 (poetry) 464, 470; mathematics 251; translation (from Arabic) 364, 467, 472 (to vernacular Arabic) 472; trilateral root 469; *see also under*: scripts; translation
Ḥefeṣ b. Yaṣliaḥ 470
Hellenism *see* Greek tradition
Hellenistic world: alchemy 331–2, 334, 335; astrology 290, 293; astronomy 274; Egypt 290, 331–2; geographical literature 301; statecraft and ethics 165–6
hemerologies 292
Hermann of Carinthia 297
Hermes 292, 294, 296, 299, 332, 337, 338
Hermetism 332
Hernández, Miguel Cruz 396
Hero of Alexandria 259, 263–4, 265, 492
Hibatullāh b. Jumayʿ 471
hijāʾ (satire) 353–4, 503–4, 506
ḥikam (aphorisms) 350, 356, 505
ḥikmah (rationale of language) 128
Hilāl b. al-Muḥassin al-Ṣābiʾ 156, 203–4, 246
Hilalian invasion 241
al-Ḥillī, al-Ḥasan b. Yūsuf b. al-Muṭahhar 32
al-Ḥillī, Najm al-Dīn Jaʿfar 148
al-Ḥimyarī, al-Sayyid 506-7
Hinduism 417
Hippocrates: ʿAlī al-Ṭabarī uses 346; aphorisms 350; case-histories 377; Ibn Sīnā uses 356; on procreation 360, 361; translation 481, 482, 489, 490, 494
Hirschfeld, H. 475
ḥisāb al-yad (hand arithmetic) 255
ḥisbah, manuals of 150, 160–1
Hishām b. ʿAbd al-Malik 181, 249
Hishām b. al-Ḥakam 19, 20, 21, 22, 24, 25; school of 22–3
Hishām b. Sālim al-Jawālīqī 20, 21, 22
"Histories of the Ancients" 82, 85
historiography xv, xvii, 188–233; on ʿAbbasid revolution 196; abridged chronicle genre

224–5; aim to narrate, not comment 316; Almohad 231–2; on ancient world 194, 212, 457; annals 196–7; archives 201–2, 208, 211, 227; arrangement 195, 196–7, 232; Ayyubid era 225, 226, 228–9, 230, 231, 233; biography and 164, 176–7, 179–80; Buwayhid era 203, 204; Byzantine 232, 233; Christian Arabic xviii, 193–4, 232, 241, 455–9, 459–60; classical period 201–16; and community consciousness 191; Coptic 456, 457, 458; of Crusades 223; dating system 201–2; didactic verse 503; distribution 198, 199, 200, 229; dynastic 224; early, to time of al-Ṭabarī 189–201; *faḍāʾil* literature 206; genealogy in 194; geography intermingled with 205, 230, 240, 309–10, 315, 317, 322; Greek 194, 457; and *Ḥadīth* 189, 190, 195; Ḥamāh, historians from 226–7; Ḥanbalite school 217–18; Ḥunayn b. Isḥāq 490; Ibāḍī 232; identification of individuals with similar names 218; Ismāʿīlī 239; *isnād*s 200; Judaeo-Arabic 465; and jurisprudence 191–3; local histories 198, 206, 209, 225; Maghribi 193, 211, 215, 231–2, 455; Mamlūk 221, 228, 233; "Mirrors for Princes" as 166; north African 211, 213, 214–15; obituary notices 218, 228; objectivity 192, 200, 209, 220; oral tradition 189, 193–4, 195, 220; on Palestine 223; on pre-Islamic period 193–4, 309; regionalism 207, 209; on religious sects and schisms 205–6; Ṣābiʾ family 202–3, 204; Saljūq period 218–19, 226; secretaries and 198, 203; Shiʿite 198, 239; sources 190–1, 201–2, 207–9, 229; Spanish 193, 213–14, 215, 231–2, 455; Syriac language 212, 457; Syrian 217, 219–21, 223, 225–30, 457; Tradition and 195, 189, 190; translation 193–4; tribal influence 190; on vizierate 163, 205, 208; *see also individual authors*, panegyric, *and under*: Egypt; Faṭimids; Persia; Yemen
ḥiyal: legal 130, 144, 151–2, 160; mechanical technology 261
Holmyard, E. J. 333
Homer 488, 497
hospitals: Christian 450, 496; Muslim 347, 359, 370, 480, 484, 491, 496
Hottinger, J. H. 462–3
Hourani, G. 427
Howell, M. S. 134
Ḥubaysh b. al-Ḥasan 249, 487
Hūd b. Maḥkam al-Hawwārī 37
Hugo of Sanctalla 294, 298
al-Ḥujūrī, Abū Muḥammad Yūsuf 231
al-Ḥujwīrī, ʿAlī 65
Hūlāgū (Mongol leader) 245
Humāʾī, J. 415
Hume, David 435
humour 66, 71, 311
humours (*akhlāṭ*) 334–5; and medicine 343, 347, 356, 357, 361
Ḥunayn b. Isḥāq al-ʿIbādī 487–90; autobiography 183; Banū Mūsā patrons of 249; Christian theology 454–5, 489, 490; on medicine 183, 346, 350, 456 (ophthalmology) 345, 359, 490; translator 87, 249, 264, 298, 332, 344–5, 362, 487–9, 495 (of Galen) 183, 488, 489, 490, 497
hunting 186, 187
Ḥusām al-Dīn Sālār 283
Ḥusayn, M. Kāmil 247
al-Ḥusayn b. ʿAlī b. abī Ṭālib 16, 17, 192
Ḥusayn Naṣr 331, 334
al-Ḥusayn al-Wazzān 66
Hyderabad 288
hydraulics 258–9, 266
hydrostatics 258–9, 263
hygiene 26, 42, 507–8
Hypsicles 492

Ibaḍism xv, 33–9; biography 35, 215, 232; *daʿwah* 33, 34, 38; dissimulation 36; exegesis 34, 37, 38; Faṭimids defeat at Baghay 36; in Ḥaḍramawt 38; historiography 232; imamates 33–4, 36–7, 38; law xvii, 34, 35, 36, 37, 38, 141, 148; in Maghrib 33, 35, 36, 37, 38, 214; political community 39; *sīrah*s 36; in ʿUmān 36–7, 38; Wahbiyyah Ibaḍism 34; Yemeni campaigns 38; *ẓuhūr* (realization of Ibāḍī state) 33–4, 34–6
Ibn ʿAbbād, al-Ṣāḥib 110–11, 163
Ibn ʿAbbād al-Rundī 62
Ibn al-Abbār 215
Ibn ʿAbbās (ʿAbdullāh b. ʿAbbās) 43, 44, 45–6
Ibn ʿAbd al-Ḥakam 192, 193, 210, 213
Ibn ʿAbd Rabbihi 166, 214, 503
Ibn ʿAbd al-Raʾūf 160
Ibn ʿAbd al-Wahhāb 12
Ibn ʿAbd al-Ẓāhir 241
Ibn ʿAbdūs al-Jahshiyārī 164, 205
Ibn abī ʾl-Dam, Qāḍī 225, 226
Ibn abī Karīmah, Abū ʿUbaydah Muslim 33, 34, 35
Ibn abī Randaqah al-Ṭurṭūshī 167
Ibn abī ʾl-Rijāl, Abū ʾl-Ḥasan ʿAlī 299–300
Ibn abī Ṭāhir Ṭayfūr 206
Ibn abī Ṭayyiʾ 225–6, 228, 229, 230
Ibn abī Uṣaybiʿah, Muwaffaq al-Dīn abū ʾl-ʿAbbās Aḥmad 230, 231; anecdote from 350; biographies 169, 359, 374, 421 (information on practice of medicine) 179–80; history of medicine 456; on medical catechisms 348; sources 174, 183, 184, 455, 459; on translation from Greek 343, 345; *ʿUyūn al-anbāʾ* 174, 183, 184
Ibn abī Zayd al-Qayrawānī 147

Ibn al-ʿAdīm, Kamāl al-Dīn 217, 220, 221, 229–30, 246
Ibn Ājurrūm 134
Ibn akhī Muḥsin 216
Ibn ʿAlqamah 503
Ibn Amājūr 285
Ibn al-ʿAmīd, Abū ʾl-Faḍl Muḥammad b. al-Ḥusayn 163, 412
Ibn al-ʿAmīd, al-Makīn Jūrjīs 458, 459
Ibn al-Anbārī, Abū ʾl-Barakāt ʿAbd al-Raḥmān b. Muḥammad 137, 170, 173, 179, 180
Ibn al-ʿArabī, Abū Bakr Muḥammad b. ʿAbdullāh 49, 435
Ibn al-ʿArabī, Muḥyī ʾl-Dīn abū ʿAbdullāh Muḥammad b. ʿAlī: apologetic 70; esoteric writing 59, 74; exegesis 54–5, 59; al-Ghazālī's influence 424, 437; Logos principle 72, 73–4; on saints 61, 63; and *sharīʿah* 55, 74; sources 61, 74; style 57, 74; on unity of God 59, 69, 72
WORKS: *Fuṣūṣ* 73–4; *Futūḥāt* 73; *Iṣṭilāḥāt* 70; *Muḥāḍarāt al-abrār* 61
Ibn al-ʿArīf 181
Ibn ʿAsākir, Abū ʾl-Qāsim ʿAlī b. al-Ḥasan 58, 174, 209, 221
Ibn al-ʿAssāl, Abū ʾl-Faḍāʾil Ṣafī ʾl-Dawlah 447, 449, 450, 451, 452, 454
Ibn al-ʿAssāl, al-Asʿad Abū ʾl-Faraj 448
Ibn al-ʿAssāl, Muʾtaman 448, 451, 452, 459–60
Ibn ʿAṭāʾallāh al-Sakandrī 60, 62, 442
Ibn al-Athīr, Ḍiyāʾ al-Dīn 156, 227
Ibn al-Athīr, ʿIzz al-Dīn: Atābak history 229; on Ismaʿilism 246; *al-Kāmil fī ʾl-Taʾrīkh* 207; later historians use 228, 230; sources 215, 227; style 217; *Usd al-ghābah fī maʿrifat al-Ṣaḥābah* 169
Ibn al-Azraq al-Fāriqī 206, 220
Ibn Bābā al-Qāshī 224
Ibn Bābashādh, Abū ʾl-Ḥasan Ṭāhir b. Aḥmad 132–3, 182
Ibn Bābawayh al-Ṣadūq, Abū Jaʿfar Muḥammad b. ʿAlī 28–9, 30–1
Ibn Bājjah, Abū Bakr Muḥammad b. Yaḥyā b. al-Ṣāʾigh: Hebrew translations 472; Ibn Ṭufayl on 90–1, 92, 93, 95, 96–8, 101, 104; style 77; theoretical astronomy 284
Ibn Bannāʾ 277
Ibn Barakah al-Bahlawī, Abū Muḥammad ʿAbdullāh b. Muḥammad 37, 38
Ibn Barūn, Abū Ibrāhīm Isḥāq 469
Ibn Bashkuwāl 232
Ibn Bassām (d. prob. 542/1147) 232
Ibn Baṭṭūṭah, Muḥammad b. ʿAbdullāh 67, 186, 323–4
Ibn al-Bayṭār, ʿAbdullāh b. Aḥmad 359, 362–3
Ibn Buṭlān, Abū ʾl-Ḥasan al-Mukhtār b. ʿAbdūn 359, 456, 496; *Daʿwat al-aṭibbāʾ* 351, *352*, 353
Ibn Dāniyāl 503
Ibn al-Dāyah, Abū Jaʿfar Aḥmad b. Yūsuf 210, 298
Ibn al-Dāyah, Yūsuf b. Ibrāhīm 455, 456
Ibn Duqmāq 241
Ibn Durayd, Abū Bakr Muḥammad b. al-Ḥasan 111–12, 116, 502
Ibn ʿEzra, Abū Hārūn Mūsā 467, 470–1
Ibn Faḍlān, Aḥmad b. Ḥammād 322–3
Ibn al-Faqīh, Abū Bakr Aḥmad b. Ibrāhīm al-Hamadhānī 309, 311–12
Ibn al-Faraḍī 232
Ibn al-Fāriḍ, ʿUmar 57, 58
Ibn Fāris, Aḥmad 112–13, 130, 131
Ibn al-Farrāʾ, Abū Yaʿlā Muḥammad b. al-Ḥusayn 150, 157
Ibn Fāṭimah 319
Ibn al-Furāt, Abū ʾl-Fatḥ al-Faḍl b. Jaʿfar 127
Ibn al-Furāt, Muḥammad 215, 217, 222, 226
Ibn Ghiyāth, Isḥāq b. Yehūdāh 469
Ibn Gikatilla, Mōsheh 469
Ibn Ḥabīb al-Sulamī al-Qurṭubī, Abū Marwān ʿAbd al-Malik 213
Ibn al-Ḥaddād 217
Ibn Ḥajar al-ʿAsqalānī, Aḥmad b. ʿAlī 169, 176, 191, 200
Ibn al-Ḥājib 133, 134–5, 136, 137
Ibn Ḥamdūn 217
Ibn Ḥammād, Abū ʿAbdullāh Muḥammad b. ʿAlī 215, 239
Ibn Hāniʾ 239
Ibn Ḥawqal, Abū ʾl-Qāsim 240, 312, 314, 315
Ibn Ḥawshab 239, 242
Ibn al-Haytham, Abū ʿAlī al-Ḥasan: on astronomy 283, 284, 422; autobiography 183, 184; Galen's influence on 183; geometry 252; on optics 257–8
Ibn Ḥayyān, Abū Marwān Ḥayyān b. Khalaf 214
Ibn Ḥayyān, Muḥammad b. Yūsuf b. ʿAlī 48
Ibn Ḥayyūj, Abū Zakariyyāʾ Yaḥyā b. Dāwūd 469, 474
Ibn Ḥazm, ʿAlī 9–10, 11, 148, 214, 238, 433
Ibn Hibinta 294
Ibn Hishām, Jamāl al-Dīn ʿAbdullāh b. Yūsuf 133, 136
Ibn Hofnī, Shĕmūʾel 468
Ibn ʿIdharī al-Marrākushī 232, 239
Ibn al-ʿImrānī 217
Ibn ʿIrāq, Abū Naṣr Manṣūr b. ʿAlī 276, 283, 406
Ibn Isfandiyār 203
Ibn Isḥāq 193
Ibn Iyāḍ 74
Ibn Jaʿfar al-Izkawī, Abū Jābir Muḥammad 37
Ibn Janāḥ, Abū ʾl-Walīd Marwān Yonah 469, 474
Ibn al-Jawzī 70, 216, 217, 228, 246
Ibn Jazlah, Abū ʿAlī Yaḥyā b. ʿĪsā 348, 358–9
Ibn al-Jazzār, Abū Jaʿfar Aḥmad b. Ibrāhīm 179–80, 360

Ibn Jinnī, Abu ʾl-Fatḥ ʿUthmān 111, 113, 125, 130–1
Ibn Jubayr al-Kinānī, Abū ʾl-Ḥusayn Muḥammad b. Aḥmad 186, 323, 324
Ibn Juljul, Abū Dāwūd Sulaymān b. Ḥassān 174
Ibn Jumayʿ Hibatullāh al-Isrāʾīlī 471
Ibn Juzayy, Muḥammad 324
Ibn Kabar, Shams al-Riyāsah abū ʾl-Barakāt 459
Ibn Karnīb 492
Ibn Karrām, Muḥammad 57
Ibn Kaysān 126, 131
Ibn Khalaf, ʿAlī 286
Ibn Khaldun, Abū Zayd ʿAbd al-Raḥmān b. Muḥammad: arrangement of material 224; on Banū Mūsā 266; on Christian and Hebrew scriptures 403; on dream interpretation 174; on environmental conditions 357; on Ibn Raqīq 214; on *kalām* 1; *Kitāb al-ʿIbar* 239–40; life 231; on al-Masʿūdī 316; on philosophy 1–2; sources 185, 222, 459; on Ṣufism xvi
Ibn Khallikān, Shams al-Dīn abū ʾl-ʿAbbās Aḥmad b. Muḥammad: anecdotes 180–1, 182; al-Bīrūnī omitted 421; genealogical details 179; on Ḥunayn b. Isḥāq 487; on Ismaʿilism 246; sources 215; *Wafayāt al-aʿyān* 169, 175, 230
Ibn al-Khaṣīb, Abū Bakr al-Ḥasan 296
Ibn Khayyāṭ, Khalīfah 195, 197
Ibn Khurradādhbih, ʿUbaydullāh b. al-Qāsim: *Kitāb al-Masālik* 158, 301, 308–9, 325; life 308; style 310, 311; and translation of Ptolemy 304
Ibn Maḍāʾ al-Qurṭubī 137
Ibn Māhān 157
Ibn Mājid, Aḥmad 325–7, 508
Ibn Mālik, Jamāl al-Dīn Muḥammad b. ʿAbdullāh 133, 135–6, 498, 501
Ibn Mālik al-Ḥammādī 238
Ibn Manẓūr, Muḥammad b. Mukarram 114, 115
Ibn Māsarjis al-Naṣrānī, Abū ʾl-ʿAbbās al-Faḍl b. Marwān 455
Ibn Muʿādh 283
Ibn al-Mudabbir 161
Ibn Mughīth 152
Ibn al-Muhannā 108
Ibn al-Munqidh, ʿAbd al-Raḥmān 458
Ibn al-Muqaffaʿ, ʿAbdullāh 142, 166, 183, 194, 481, 498
Ibn al-Muqaffaʿ, Muḥammad b. ʿAbdullāh 480–1
Ibn Muqlah 162
Ibn al-Mutawwaj 241
Ibn al-Muʿtazz, ʿAbdullāh 90, 124, 503
Ibn al-Muṭrān 456
Ibn Muyassar, Tāj al-Dīn Muḥammad b. ʿAlī b. Yūsuf 211, 221, 230, 246
Ibn al-Nadīm, Muḥammad b. Isḥāq 200; on alchemical authors 332; on Archimedes 263; on Banū Mūsā 264; on early jurists 139, 153; on Jābir b. Ḥayyān 333, 334; on Abū Bakr Muḥammad b. Zakariyyāʾ al-Rāzī 373, 374; on translations 301, 304, 360, 487, 492; on various authors 20, 308, 433; on viziers and secretaries, 163–4
Ibn al-Nafīs 87, 348, *349*, 360
Ibn Nāʿimah al-Ḥimṣī 490
Ibn al-Najjār 218
Ibn Naṭṭāḥ 196, 210
Ibn al-Naẓar al-Samʾūlī 38
Ibn al-Naẓīf 225, 226–7
Ibn al-Qalānisī 209, 220, 226, 227, 246
Ibn al-Qāsim 145
Ibn Qayyim al-Jawziyyah, Shams al-Dīn abū ʿAbdullāh Muḥammad b. abī Bakr 74, 465
Ibn Qudāmah 148
Ibn al-Quff, Abū ʾl-Faraj 359
Ibn al-Qulzumī, Yūḥannā b. Saʿīd b. Yaḥyā b. Mīnā 458
Ibn Quraysh 474
Ibn Qutaybah: grammatical textbook falsely attributed to 137; historiography 198, 199; on Ṣūfīs 56
WORKS: *Adab al-kātib* 161; *Kitāb al-Anwāʾ* 275; *ʿUyūn al-akhbār* 59, 166
Ibn al-Qūṭiyyah 213–14
Ibn al-Rāhib 447
Ibn Rāhwayh 179
Ibn Raqīq of al-Qayrawān 214–15
Ibn al-Rāwandī 242
Ibn Rushd xvi; hostility to views 445; on *ikhtilāf al-madhāhib* 152; on intellects 387; importance in West 379, 389; on Ibn Sīnā 394, 395; style 77; theoretical astronomy 284
Ibn Rustam, ʿAbd al-Raḥmān 33
Ibn Rustih, Abū ʿAlī Aḥmad b. ʿUmar 309, 310–11
Ibn al-Ṣabbāgh, Muḥammad 61, 62
Ibn Saʿd, Muḥammad 171, 172–3, 179, 194–5
Ibn al-Ṣaghīr 214
Ibn Saḥnūn 124
Ibn al-Sāʿī, Tāj al-Dīn ʿAlī b. Anjab 231
Ibn Saʿīd, Abū ʾl-Ḥasan ʿAlī b. Mūsā 319
Ibn al-Sarrāj, Abū Bakr Muḥammad b. al-Sarī 128, 129, 131
Ibn al-Ṣayrafī, ʿAlī 162, 222, 245
Ibn Shaddād, ʿAbd al-ʿAzīz 215, 227
Ibn Shaddād, Bahāʾ al-Dīn Yūsuf b. Rāfiʿ 177
Ibn Shaddād, ʿIzz al-Dīn 178, 225, 228, 229, 230
Ibn Shādhān 19, 23, 24
Ibn Shahdā al-Karkhī 360
Ibn al-Shahīd 507
Ibn Sharaf 215
Ibn al-Shāṭir 278, 284, 422

Ibn Sīdah, Abū ʾl-Ḥasan ʿAlī b. Ismāʿīl: *al-Muḥkam* 107, 111, 114, 115; *al-Mukhaṣṣaṣ* 107, 111
Ibn Sīnā, Abū ʿAlī al-Ḥusayn xviii, 389–404; on "Active Intellect" 387; alchemy 338, 340; allegory 68, 399–400; on analogy 396–7, 398, 399; aphorisms 350; autobiographical material 184; al-Bīrūnī and 409–10, 421–2; on Christian and Hebrew scriptures 402–3; on consciousness 393–4, 395; on creation 100, 395–6, 401; al-Fārābī's influence 392; and Greek philosophy 100, 391, 392, 393, 397, 426, 433; Ḥayy b. Yaqẓān 105; Ibn Ṭufayl on 90, 98, 100–1, 102, 104; inductive method 343; influence on Christian West 379, 389, 404; intuition 391, 397–8; and Judaism 402–3; jurisprudence 390; on knowledge (divine), 401, 436 (as reward of love) 72 (theory of) 395; life 390–2, 403; mathematical approach 251; medicine 348, 354, 356–8, 390, 391, 392; metaphysics 391, 392, 393–5, 395–404, 433; on music 257; mysticism 72, 391, 404; neo-Platonism 395, 403; observational method 343, 356; on optics 257; and Oriental wisdom 88, 90, 91–2, 95, 96, 100–1; originality 392–5; Persian influences on 390, 391, 392, 395, 398–9; on pharmacy 363; on philosopher and city 87; philosophy and Islam reconciled in 390, 391, 395, 396, 399–403; politics 390–1; as polymath 391–2; rationalism 424; on resurrection of body 400–1, 401–3; sciences, classification of 250, 392–3; style 77; synthetical philosophy 389, 393, 395, 396, 399–400, 400–4; on theology 390, 393, on unity of God 69, 393
WORKS 392; *Canon* (*Kitāb al-Qānūn fī ʾl-ṭibb*) 348, 356–8, 359, 391; *Fī Aqsām al-ʿulūm al-ʿaqliyyah* 250; *Ḥayy b. Yaqẓān, Risālat al-Ṭayr* 87; *al-Ishārāt wa-ʾl-tanbīhāt* 69, 87, 91–2, 105; *al-Najāh* 391; *Qaṣīdat al-Ṭayr* 68; *Risālah fī ʾl-ʿIshq* 72; *al-Shifāʾ* 88, *89*, 100–1, 104, 257, 391, 399–400
Ibn al-Sirrī, Abū ʾl-Sirrī Bishr 447–8
Ibn Taghribirdī, Abū ʾl-Maḥāsin Yūsuf 175, 176, 222, 240
Ibn Ṭarāwah 137
Ibn Taymiyyah 11–12, 151
Ibn al-Ṭayyib, Abū ʾl-Faraj ʿAbdullāh 447, 448, 449–50, 451, 494
Ibn Tibbon, Shěmūʾel 467, 472, 474; descendants 472
Ibn Ṭufayl, Abū Bakr Muḥammad b. ʿAbd al-Malik 87–105; on Andalusian philosophic culture 95–8; on Aristotle 100, 104; cryptic disclosure 99, 88–98; on expression of visionary experience 88-98; on al-Fārābī 98–100, 101, 104; on al-Ghazālī 98, 101, 102–3; Ḥayy b. Yaqẓān story 87–98, 99, 104, 105; on Ibn Bājjah 90–1, 92, 93, 96–8, 101, 104; on Ibn Sīnā 98, 101, 102, 104; own path to truth 103–5; on philosopher and city 87–98, 99; on religion and philosophy 99; style 77
Ibn Tūmart 11
Ibn Ṭuwayr 221–2
Ibn ʿUkāshah 350
Ibn al-Ukhuwwah, Muḥammad 161
Ibn ʿUmar family 227
Ibn Umayl al-Tamīmī 337–8, 340
Ibn al-Wardī, Zayn al-Dīn 502, 505–6
Ibn Wāṣil 225, 226, 228–9
Ibn Yaʿīsh, Abū ʾl-Baqāʾ Yaʿīsh b. ʿAlī 134, 135
Ibn Yūnus, ʿAbd al-Raḥmān 210
Ibn Yūnus, ʿAlī 253–4, 277, 278, 280
Ibn Ẓafar, Muḥammad b. ʿAbdullāh 167
Ibn al-Zubayr, al-Rashīd 242
Ibn Zūlāq, Abū ʾl-Ḥusayn 241
Ibn Zūlāq, Abū Muḥammad al-Ḥasan b. Ibrāhīm b. al-Ḥusayn 210, 211, 241
Ibn Zūlāq, Ibn abī ʾl-Ḥusayn 241
Ibn Zurʿah, Abū ʿAlī ʿĪsā b. Isḥāq 447, 451, 493–4
Ibrāhīm b. ʿAwn 447
Ibrāhīm b. Hāshim 24
Ibrāhīm b. ʿĪsā 455
Ibrāhīm b. Muḥammad b. Mudabbir 161
Ibrāhīm b. al-Ṣalt 298
Ibrāhīm al-Ḥāqilānī (Abraham Ecchellensis) 459
Ibrāhīm al-Nakhaʿī of Kufa 141, 143
Ibrāhīm al-Nāṣirī 300
Idrīs (prophet) 72
al-Idrīsī, Muḥammad b. Muḥammad 240, 317, 318, 319
Ifrīqiyah 174–5, 211, 213, 214–15
Ignatius II (west Syrian patriarch) 451
iʿjām (orthographical device) 119
iʿjāz see Qurʾān (inimitability)
ijāzah (authorization for transmission of *isnād*) 200
ijmāʿ see consensus
ijtihād 12, 37, 430
Ikhshidids 210, 211, 504
ikhtilāf al-madhāhib (legal differences) 146, 152
Ikhwān al-Ṣafāʾ (Brethren of Purity) 179; on arithmetic 254; cosmography 321; date and authorship of *Rasāʾil* 238; Faṭimids and 243; Ibn Sīnā reads 390; on mathematics and logic 251; microcosmos 437; neo-Platonism 238, 240, 250; scholasticism 250; works introduced into Spain 179
iktisāb (moral appropriation) 9, 493
ʿillah (grammatical cause) 125
ʿilm al-ʿadad (science of number) 254
ʿilm al-farāʾiḍ (law of succession) 149
ʿilm al-ḥisāb (science of reckoning) 160, 254–5; *see also*: algebra: arithmetic
ʿilm al-lughah see lexicography

ᶜ*ilm al-mīqāt* (astronomical time-keeping) 284–6
ᶜ*ilm al-mukāshafah* (science of unveiling) 103
ᶜ*ilm al-rijāl* see under *ḥadīth*
ᶜImād al-Dīn al-Iṣfahānī *see under* al-Iṣfahānī
Imām al-Ḥaramayn *see* al-Juwaynī, Abū ʾl-Maᶜālī
imams: *ḍaᶜīf* 33, 37; *difāᶜī* 34, 37; Faṭimid; concealment 236–8; Ibāḍī 33–4, 36–7, 38; *shārī* 33, 37, 38; Shiᶜite 3, 16–20, 25, 26, 27, 29, 30–1; succession to Muḥammad 3, 141; *see also* occultation
īmān see faith
immortality: of individual intellect 386–7, 388; of soul 98, 99–100
India: al-Bīrūnī and 299, 317, 405–6, 407, 415, 416–17; didactic poetry 498; numerals 255, 391; phonetic theory 109; Portuguese in 326–7; statecraft and ethics 165; *see also* Sanskrit *and under* Ismaᶜilism *and individual disciplines*
inheritance, law on 449
inshāʾ (chancery style) 155–6
instruments, scientific *see under*: alchemy; astronomy
"Intellect, Active" (*al-ᶜaql al-faᶜᶜāl*) 385–7, 388
intellect, individual; immortality 386–7, 388
intellectual ambience, ᶜAbbasid 204, 307–8, 371, 379–80, 481
intelligence service (*khabar*) 158, 164, 201, 308
interest, monetary 140
intuition 391, 397–8, 427
iqlīm see climes
iqṭāᶜ 157, 204
iᶜrāb (grammatical inflection) 46, 48
irādah (acts of divine volition) 6
Iran *see* Persia
Iraq: as centre of world 157, 306, 309; etymology of name 309
al-ᶜIrāqī, Fakhr al-Dīn Ibrāhīm 73
al-ᶜIrāqī al-Kurdī, Abū ʾl-Faḍl ᶜAbd al-Raḥmān b. al-Ḥusayn Zayn al-Dīn 428, 507
irrigation 158, 159, 258
ᶜĪsā b. Aḥmad b. Muḥammad b. Bashīr al-Rāzī 214
ᶜĪsā b. Māsah 363
ᶜĪsā b. Yaḥyā 390, 487, 488, 489
Isaac 13, 28
Isaac Judaeus (Isḥāq b. Sulaymān al-Isrāʾīlī) 350, 360, 368, 462, 466–7
al-Iṣfahānī, ᶜAbd al-Ḥasan b. Aḥmad b. ᶜAlī b. al-Ḥasan 300
al-Iṣfahānī, Abū ᶜAbdullāh Ḥamzah b. al-Ḥasan 205
al-Iṣfahānī, Abū ʾl-Faraj 58, 216
al-Iṣfahānī, Abū Nuᶜaym Aḥmad 63
al-Iṣfahānī, Abū Shujāᶜ Aḥmad 147
al-Iṣfahānī, ᶜImād al-Dīn Muḥammad b. Muḥammad al-Kātib 207, 218–19, 222–3, 226, 228
al-Iṣfahānī, Lughdah 131
Isḥāq b. Ḥunayn b. Isḥāq 345, 456, 482, 487–8, 489
Isḥāq b. Rāhwayh 179
Isḥāq b. Sulaymān al-Isrāʾīlī (Isaac Judaeus) 350, 360, 368, 462, 466–7
Isḥāq b. Yehūdāh b. Ghiyāth 469
Ishmael 13, 28
ishrāqī see Oriental wisdom
Īshūᶜdād of Marw 447
Īshūᶜyāb b. Malkūn 451
Isis (alchemist's pseudonym) 332
Islam: and Arabic language 115, 116, 124, 130, 132; authority 3–4, 304, 371; calendar 409; Christian scholars in early 379; faith and 29, 30; al-Ghazālī defends 445; grammar and 124, 132, 136; Hellenic influence on 50; law and morality 140; and medicine 342, 350, 361; philosophy reconciled with 390, 391, 395, 396, 399–403; revelation, nature of 40, 395; *see also individual aspects*
Ismāᶜīl b. ᶜAbbād, al-Ṣāḥib 110–11, 163
Ismāᶜīl b. Jaᶜfar 18, 25, 28, 236, 237
Ismāᶜīl al-Tamīmī 241
Ismaᶜilism: Alamūt, al-Ḥasan b. al-Ṣabbāḥ in 425; *al-daᶜwah al-hādiyah* 236; doctrine of return of Muḥammad b. Ismāᶜīl 237–8; al-Ghazālī on 424, 443; historiography 239; history of movement 18, 234, 236, 239; Ibn Sīnā and 391; Ikhwān al-Ṣafāʾ on 250, 321; in India 235, 243, 244, 245, 246; Jabirian corpus on 334; Yaᶜqūb b. Isḥāq al-Kindī's influence 368–9; libraries 235, 241, 243, 246; Muḥyī ʾl-Dīn b. al-ᶜArabī and 74; and neo-Platonism 238, 240, 250, 321; philosophy 240; and Qarmaṭians 237–8; in Yemen 243, 468; *see also* Faṭimids
ismiyyah (nominality) 125
*isnād*s: in biography 170; in exegesis 44, 47, 48; in historiography 200; in jurisprudence 141, 143
isrāʾīliyyāt (Israelite stories) 45, 46, 194
Issakhar b. Sūsan 472
Iṣṭakhr (Persepolis) 249
al-Iṣṭakhrī, Ibrāhīm b. Muḥammad 312–14, 315
Istanbul observatory 287
istiḥsān (juridical procedure) 3, 130, 141, 145, 148
istiṣḥāb al-ḥāl (juridical procedure) 3
istiṣlāḥ (juridical procedure) 3, 148
istiṭāᶜah (ability to act) 20, 21, 25
Ithnā ᶜAshariyyah 236
Ivanow, W. 236–7, 242, 246–7
ᶜIzz al-Dīn b. al-Athīr *see* Ibn al-Athīr
ᶜIzz al-Dīn b. Shaddād *see under* Ibn Shaddād

Jabal Nafūsah 36
Jābir b. Aflaḥ 283, 284

Jābir b. Ḥayyān, Abū Mūsā (Geber): works attributed to 333–4, 341; *see also* Jabirian corpus
Jābir b. Zayd, Abū Shaᶜthāʾ 35
Jabirian corpus: alchemical theories 334–5; attribution 333–4; later writers on 336, 338, 340; Latin works 341; macrobiotics 332; on poisons 363
jabr see predestination
al-jabr (algebra) 254, 255–6
Jabrites 4
Jacobite church 447, 452, 493–4
al-Jaᶜdī, ᶜUmar b. ᶜAlī 171
Jaᶜfar b. Aḥmad, Abū ᶜAbdullāh 239
Jaᶜfar b. Manṣūr al-Yaman 239
Jaᶜfar b. Yaḥyā al-Barmakī 479
Jaᶜfar al-Ṣādiq (Shīᶜī imam) 17–18, 333; on attributes of God 24; on *badāʾ* 18, 25, 28; on free will 25; on occultation of imam 26; on Qurʾān 25, 29, 59; succession to 18, 20, 236, 237; transmission of exegeses 48
Jāhiliyyah *see* pre-Islamic period
al-Jāḥiẓ: biography 170; on grammar as science 131–2; on al-Ḥasan al-Baṣrī 58, 59; on *kalām* 484; al-Kirmānī on 240; on secretaries 164; and Umayyah b. abī ʾl-Ṣalt 498; works attributed to 166
al-Jahshiyārī, Ibn ᶜAbdūs 164, 205
Jalāl al-Dīn Mängübirti (Khwārazm-shāh) 219
Jalam b. Shaybān of Multan 239
al-Jannābī, Abū Ṭāhir 239
Jarbah Island 36
jarbī (region of world) 309
al-Jaṣṣāṣ, Abū Bakr Aḥmad b. ᶜAlī 49
al-Jawālīqī, Hishām b. Sālim 20, 21, 22
Jawdhar, al-Ustādh 214, 239
Jawhar al-Ṣiqillī 241
al-Jawharī, Abū Naṣr Ismāᶜīl b. Ḥammād 110, 113–14, 116, 180
jawhariyyah (substance of God) 22
al-Jawziyyah, Shams al-Dīn abū ᶜAbdullāh Muḥammad b. abī Bakr b. Qayyim 74, 465
al-Jazarī, Abū ʾl-ᶜIzz Ismāᶜīl b. al-Razzāz 262–3, 268–70
Jazīrah; historiography 225, 227
al-Jazūlī, Shaykh 64
al-Jazzār, Aḥmad b. Ibrāhīm b. 215
Jerusalem 221, 223, 427, 469, 475
Jesus: Islamic beliefs about 13, 14; Ṣūfī views on 72, 74
jewellers 329
Jews: academic opportunities 464; and Arabic language 461, 463–4; astronomy 465; Baghdad academies 464, 465–6; biographies of 170; in Cairo 465–6; calendar 409; and Christianity 466; on Daniel 448; epistolary form 61; Ibn Sīnā on 402–3; law 153, 463–4, 469, 470; of Maghrib 463; medicine xviii, 465, 471; mysticism (*qabbālāh*) 468; *nahḍah* (cultural renaissance) 461; poetry 464, 470; of al-Qayrawān 470; rationalism 465; sciences 465; scriptures 13, 402–3, 484; in Spain 461, 465–6, 467, 468, 469, 471; and Ṣufism 467–8, 469; Sura, academy of 464, 466; theology 2; translators 343, 472; *see also*: Judaeo-Arabic literature; Qaraites
Jibrān Khalīl Jibrān 502
Jibrīl b. Bakhtīshūᶜ 480, 487
Jibrīl b. ᶜUbaydullāh b. Bakhtīshūᶜ 480
jihād (Islamic neologism) 115
al-Jīlānī, ᶜAbd al-Qādir 61, 62, 66, 68
al-Jildakī, ᶜIzz al-Dīn Aydamir 339–40
al-Jīlī, ᶜAbd al-Karim 73
Jina the Indian 296
jinn 13, 321
jizyah (tax) 142, 156
Job 74
Johannitius *see* Ḥunayn b. Isḥāq al-ᶜIbādī
John the Baptist 454
John Chrysostom 448
John of Damascus 484
John the Divine, St 449
John Philoponus of Alexandria (Yaḥyā al-Naḥwī) 365, 433
John of Seville 295, 296, 297, 298, 299
Johnson, Samuel 106, 181
Jones, Sir William 175
"Joseph's Prison", Būṣīr 337
Judaeo-Arabic literature xviii–xix, 461–76; apologetic 467; *belles-lettres* 470–1; decline, post-ᶜAbbasid 461, 472; definition 461–2; exegesis 446–9, 468–9, 475; historiography 465; history of studies 473–5; legal writings 153, 469, 470; linguistic features 463; new disciplines resulting from Arab contact 465; origins 463–5; philology 463, 465, 468–9, 475; philosophy 465, 466–8, 469; polemic 185, 466; printing 467, 473–4; scope 465–6; in Spain 467, 469; theology 466–8; in Yemen 468, 475, 476; *see also*: Bible (translations); Genizah
Judaism *see* Jews
judges, biography of 172, 173, 182–3
al-Julandā b. Masᶜūd 33
jūmatria see geometry
jumlah (sentence) 122, 125
al-Junayd, Abū ʾl-Qāsim b. Muḥammad 61, 63, 66, 68, 69
al-Jundī, Khalīl b. Isḥāq 147
Jundishāpūr, school at 248, 342, 343, 344, 480, 484
jurisprudence (*fiqh*) *see* law
Jurjān 410, 425
al-Jurjānī, ᶜAbd al-Qāhir 133
Jūrjīs b. Jibrīl b. Bakhtīshūᶜ 480
justice, divine (*ᶜadl*) 6, 140, 446
Justinian 248

al-Juwaynī, Abū ʾl-Maʿālī ʿAbd al-Malik b. ʿAbdullāh b. Yūsuf (Imām al-Ḥaramayn) 149, 425, 443
al-Juwaynī, ʿAlāʾ al-Dīn ʿAṭāʾ-Malik b. Muḥammad 244, 246
al-Juwaynī, Saʿd al-Dīn 231
al-Juwwānī, al-Sharīf 241
al-Jūzajānī, Abū ʿUbayd 392, 422

Kaʿbah 13
kabāʾir (mortal sins) 6
kadhkhudāh (astrological term) 292
kāfir (unbeliever) 6–7, 12
Kāfūr 504
kaḥḥālūn (oculists) 352, 359
*kāhin*s (soothsayers) 156
al-Kalābādhī, ʿAbū Bakr Muḥammad 65, 70, 439
kalām see: speech; theology
al-Kalbī, Hishām 194
al-Kalbī, Muḥammad b. al-Sāʾib 46
Kalīlah wa-Dimnah 165, 183, 293, 481, 498–9
kalimat Allāh (word of God), Christ as 453
Kamāl al-Dīn b. al-ʿAdīm 217, 220, 221, 229–30, 246
kāmil metre 501
Kanaka the Indian 295
Kant, I. 398, 399
al-Karajī, Abū Bakr Muḥammad b. al-Ḥasan al-Ḥāsib 252
Karbalāʾ, battle of 16
al-Karkhī, Maʿrūf 60
karshūnī script 462
karūbiyyūn (cherubim) 394, 395
kasb 9
kashf (unveiling) 397
al-Kāshī, Ghiyāth al-Dīn Jamshīd 255
al-Kaskarī, Yaʿqūb b. Zakariyyāʾ 455
Kay Kāwūs b. Iskandar 167
Kaysāniyyah 16–17
Kennedy, E. S. 276, 284
Kepler, Johannes 258
khabar (intelligence service) 158, 164, 201, 308
khabar (predicate) 125
Khābūr, river 261
Khadduri, Majid 144
Khalaf al-Aḥmar 135
Khālid b. Barmak 478
Khālid b. Ṣafwān 59
Khālid b. Yazīd b. Muʿāwiyah 301, 333, 340
Khalīfah b. ʿAlī al-Ḥalabī al-Kaḥḥāl 360
Khalīfah b. Khayyāṭ 195, 197
al-Khalīl b. Aḥmad 106, 109, 116, 121, 135; *Kitāb al-ʿAyn* 110–11, 112
Khalīl b. Isḥāq al-Jundī 147
Khalīl Muṭrān 502
al-Khalīlī, ʿAbbās 509
al-Khalīlī, Jaʿfar 509
al-Khalīlī, Shams al-Dīn Muḥammad b. Muḥammad 285
al-Khallāl, al-Ḥasan b. al-Ḥusayn 174
kharāj (tax) 142, 156
al-Kharaqī 283
Khārijah b. Zayd b. Thābit 141
Kharijites xv, 3–4, 33, 214; *see also* Ibaḍism
al-Kharrāz 66, 70
al-Kharzanjī 111
al-Khaṣṣāf, Abū Bakr Aḥmad b. ʿUmar 150, 152
al-Khaṭīb al-Baghdādī (Abū Bakr Aḥmad ʿAlī) 174, 221
al-Khaṭṭāb 244
khawāṣṣ (properties of substances in magic) 339
al-Khayyām, Ghiyāth al-Dīn abū ʾl-Fatḥ ʿUmar b. Ibrāhīm 254, 256, 259
al-Khayyāṭ, Abū ʿAlī Yaḥyā b. Ghālib 294, 296
Khazars 305, 311, 323
al-Khāzinī, Abū ʾl-Fatḥ ʿAbd al-Raḥmān al-Manṣūr 259–60
al-Khiraqī, ʿUmar 148
Khizānat al-Ḥikmah 293, 480, 484
Khojas 246
Khudāy-nāmah (Pahlavi work on statecraft) 166
al-Khujandī, Abū Aḥmad 283
al-Khuldī 72
Khurāsān: administrative literature 157, 159; al-Ghazālī in 427; historiography 194, 210; Ibaḍism 33; Yaʿqūb b. Isḥāq al-Kindī's influence 368
Khūrī, I. 326
Khurshāh, Rukn al-Dīn 245
al-Khushanī, Muḥammad b. al-Ḥārith 173, 182
Khusraw Anūshirvān 165, 166, 183, 503
Khusraw Aparvīz 165
al-Khuzāʿī, Ḥāmid 59
Khwārazm 405, 409
al-Khwārazmī, Abū ʿAbdullāh Muḥammad b. Aḥmad 157–8, 159, 250, 255–6, 266
al-Khwārazmī, Abū Jaʿfar Muḥammad b. Mūsā: geography 303, 305–6, 307; on Indian numerals 255; on sundials 286; *Ṣūrat al-arḍ* 303, 305–6, 307; *zīj*s 253, 276, 277, 305
Khwarazmian glossaries 108
Kilwa, east Africa 38
al-Kindī, ʿAbdullāh b. Yaḥyā 33
al-Kindī, ʿAbd al-Masīḥ 452–3
al-Kindī, Abū Umayyah Shurayḥ b. al-Ḥārith 179
al-Kindī, Abū Yūsuf Yaʿqūb b. Isḥāq xviii, 364–9, on Aristotle 364–5, 453; and astrology 296, 299, 364, 367; on creation 367; and education 367–8; and Greek learning 304, 366, 367–8; life 364; linguistic innovation 366, 368; metaphysics 365, 366–7; microcosmos concept 437; mind and soul, theory of 365; and *mutakallimūn* 367–8; on pharmacy 362; on physics 365; as polymath 257, 364, 365; on prophecy 369; on reason 367–8, 369;

al-Kindī, Abū Yūsuf Yaʿqūb b. Isḥāq (*cont.*)
Risālah fī ʾl-Ḥīlah li-dafʿ al-aḥzān 490–1; school of 365–6, 368, 490–1, 491; style 77; translation 365, 366, 368, 490–1, 492
al-Kindī, Muḥammad b. Yūsuf 59, 173, 264
"Kings, Book of" (Persian) 194
Kirmān 33
al-Kirmānī, Awḥad al-Dīn Ḥāmid b. abī ʾl-Fakhr 73
al-Kirmānī, Ḥamīd al-Dīn Aḥmad b. ʿAbdullāh 240
al-Kirmānī al-Qurṭubī al-Andalusī, ʿUmar b. ʿAbd al-Raḥmān 179
al-Kisāʾī, Abū ʾl-Ḥasan ʿAlī b. Ḥamzah 123–4, 126
Kitāb al-Hāwī (anon.) 160
Kitāb al-Istibṣār (anon.) 319
Kitāb al-ʿUyūn wa-ʾl-ḥaqāʾiq (anon.) 211
kitābah (secretary, art of) 157–8, 161–2
kitmān (secrecy) 36
knowledge: Aristotle on purpose of 426; divine 51, 100, 381–2, 401, 436; Ibn Sīnā's theory of 395; as reward of love 443–5; *see also*: books; gnosis; oral tradition
Kokowzow, P. 475
Kraus, P. 247, 333–4
al-Kudamī, Abū Saʿīd 37, 38
Kufa: antagonism with Basra 124, 126–7, 134, 137; Faṭimid *dāʿī* 238; Ḥanafite school originates in 141; historical documents 190; Shīʿah and 16; Ṣufism 59; Traditions 43
al-Kūfī, Abū Jaʿfar 213
al-Kulayni, Abū Jaʿfar Muḥammad b. Yaʿqūb 24–7, 28, 29
Kunitzsch, P. 282
Kurdish apologetic literature 71
Kūshyār 283
kuttāb (sing. *kātib*) *see* secretaries
kutub al-anwāʾ (books on meteorological and celestial phenomena) 275
kutub al-hayʾah (type of astronomical literature) 283–4
al-Kutubī, Muḥammad b. Shākir b. Aḥmad 176

La Fontaine, Jean de 508
Labīd b. Rabīʿah 498, 502
al-Lāḥiqī, Abān b. ʿAbd al-Ḥamīd 499–500, 502, 503
al-Lāḥiqī, Ḥamdān 500
Lamak b. Mālik al-Ḥammādī 242–3
lamps, self-filling 264
lan, Zamakhsharian 134
land: grants of (*iqṭāʿ*) 157; management 159–60; measurement 252, 306; taxation 156–7
language: al-Fārābī on growth of 384; and law 107; as speech acts 25, 121, 122; *see also individual languages and*: grammar; lexicography; philology
Latham, J. D. 161
Latin: glossaries 108; translation from Arabic xviii, 472 (alchemy) 341 (astrology) 294, 295, 296, 298, 300 (astronomy) 296 (*Chronicum Orientale*) 459 (al-Ghazālī) 426, (Ibn Sīnā) 379, 389, 404 (Yaʿqūb b. Isḥāq al-Kindī) 364 (Qurʾān) 462 (Abū Bakr Muḥammad b. Zakariyyāʾ al-Rāzī) 354, 377
latitude observations 325, 326
law, canon 449–50, 459
law, Jewish 153, 463–4, 469, 470
law, pre-Islamic 139 law, Roman 153
law and legal literature, Islamic xv, xvii, 139–54; and administration 142; on adultery 423; biography of jurists 153, 172, 173, 182–3; on caliphate 142, 144; Christian adaptation 450; commercial 140, 144; compendia 147–8; constitutional 157, 192–3; of contracts 130, 140, 144; criminal 140; customary 141; documents (*shurūṭ*) 152; early jurists 47, 139, 140–6; evidence 140, 152; family 140, 423; al-Ghazālī on 424, 425; and historiography 191–3; Ibāḍī 34, 36, 38, 37, 141, 148; *ikhtilāf al-madhāhib* 146, 152; in India 147, 149, 153, 154; and language 107, 118, 120, 122, 123, 129–30; local 143, 151; medieval stasis 145; morality not distinct from 140; practical works, miscellaneous 150–2; pre-Islamic base 139; principles not analysed in writings 146; procedures 3 (adopted by grammarians) 120, 122, 123, 129–30 (*see also: istiḥsān; istiṣlāḥ; qiyās; raʾy*); public 150, 157; Qurʾān and 46, 139–40, 143, 14, 148; schools xvii, 126, 139 (development) 140–6 (major works) 146–53; (*see also individual schools, viz.*: Ḥanafite; Hanbalite; Malikite; Shafiʿite); secretaries and 155; Shiʿite 19, 141–2, 148 (*see also* Ibāḍī *above*); subsidiary sources 148; of succession 149; textbooks 143, 151–2; and theology 1, 2–3, 19; *see also: fatāwā; furūʿ al-fiqh; sharīʿah; uṣūl al-fiqh*
laws of war (*siyar*) 142, 143–4
Layth b. Kahlān 325
al-Layth b. al-Muẓaffar 110, 111
lead monoxide (litharge) 329
Lebanon 241
Leibniz, Gottfried Wilhelm 437
Leiden glossary 108
Leiden manuscript (alchemy) 331
Lemay, R. 298
Leningrad 475, 476
Leo (Byzantine scholar) 484
letters, diplomatic 163
Lewis, B. 236, 247
lexicography 106–17; abbreviations 114–15; alphabets 108–9; arrangements 108–10; authorities cited 110, 112, 115, 116; contents and method 115–16; dictionaries

described 106, 110–14; effect 116–17; and *Ḥadīth* 107, 112; Islamic vocabulary 115; motivation 116; polyglot dictionaries 107–8, 376–7; roots 109, 110, 117; vocalization 115, 178, 463; word-lists 106–7, 125; *see also*: *ʿarabiyyah*; etymology; al-Khalīl b. Aḥmad; Sībawayhi
libraries xix, 208, 274; Baghdad xix, 293, 480, 482, 484; Dār al-ʿIlm, Cairo 241, 243; Escurial 211, 266; Faṭimid xix, 235; Ismāʿīlī 235, 241, 243, 246; *see also*: archives; Genizah (Cairo)
Libros del Saber de Astronomia 270, 272
Lippmann , E. O. von 333
Lisān al-Dīn b. al-Khaṭīb 175, 185, 503
litanies (*aḥzāb*) 67
litharge (lead monoxide) 329
liturgical literature: Christian 459; Judaeo-Arabic 470
Löfgren, O. 235
logic 76, 96; didactic verse on 501, 503; al-Ghazālī on 425–6, 431; and grammar 125, 127–9, 130, 135, 380, 381; in Ibn Sīnā's synthesis 395, 426; and *kalām* 380; propositional and class 492
Logos 8, 72–4, 453
love: art of; didactic poetry 500; divine 58, 71–2, 443–5
Lughdah al-Iṣfahānī 131
Luʾluʾ, Badr al-Dīn 227
lunar mansions 275, 276, 282, 292, 326, 408
lutf (divine favour) 31
Luṭfī, ʿAbd al-Majīd 509

al-māʾ (glaucoma) 370
maʿārīḍ al-kalām (vagaries of speech) 130
al-Maʿarrī, Abū ʾl-ʿAlāʾ, Aḥmad b. ʿAbdullāh b. Sulaymān 170, 242, 502, 504, 505
al-Maʿarrī, Abū Ghālib 219–20
al-Maʿarrī family 219–20
Macdonald, D. B. 428
macrobiotics 330, 332
Maʿdan al-Aʿmā al-Shīʿī al-Sumayṭī 506
al-Madāʾinī 197
Madelung, W. 236, 247
madrasah (college) 132, 208, 464
maghāzī literature 45, 189, 190
Maghrib: biography 232; historiography 193, 211, 215, 231–2, 455; Ibaḍism 33, 35, 36, 37, 38, 214; Ibn Khurradādhbih's region 309; Jews 463; water-clocks 262
al-Maghribī (vizier) 452
al-Maghribī, Abū ʾl-Ḥasan ʿAlī b. Mūsā b. Saʿīd 231, 239
al-Maghribī, Muḥyī ʾl-Dīn 283
magic 64, 71, 273, 339, 347
magnetism 257, 326
Māhānkard b. Mihrziyār 292
Mahāsiddhānta 251
Maḥbūb b. al-Raḥīl, Abū Sufyān 34, 35
Mahdi, Muhsin 378
Mahdī, Shiʿite 16, 22, 23
al-Mahdī (ʿAbbasid caliph) 196
al-Mahdī, ʿUbaydullāh (Faṭimid caliph) 236, 237, 239, 466
Maḥmūd of Ghaznah (Maḥmūd Yamīn al-Dawlah) 177, 206, 209, 405–6, 416
Maḥmūd b. Zankī, Nūr al-Dīn 226, 227, 228, 267
Māhūya b. Māhānāhīdh 292
Maimonides (Mūsā b. ʿUbaydullāh b. Maymūn): descendants 467–8; *Guide for the Perplexed* 462, 474; medical writings 350, 363, 464–5; Mishnah, commentary on 473; *Mishneh Tōrāh* 471; translations of 472; transliterations into Hebrew letters 462, 464–5, 471
majālis (séances)-literature 239, 242
Majd al-Dīn abū Salamah Murshid 186–7
majmūʿ (nomocanon) 449, 450
al-Majrīṭī, Maslamah b. Aḥmad 338–9, 340
al-Majūsī, ʿAlī b. al-ʿAbbās 348, 354, 356
al-Makīn b. al-Amīn 225
al-Makīn Jūrjīs ibn al-ʿAmīd 458, 459
al-Makkī, Abū Ṭālib 64, 438
Makkīkhā I (Nestorian catholicos) 458
al-Malashāwī, Abū Naṣr Fatḥ b. Nūḥ 38
al-Malaṭī 238
Malāzkird (Manzikert), battle of 241
Mālik b. Anas 42, 143, 144, 145
al-Malik al-Nāṣir Dāwūd 231
al-Malik al-Ẓāhir Ghāzī 226
al-Mālikī 232
Malikite school 11, 141; on *ʿamal* 151; al-Ashʿarī and 8; compendium 147; in Faṭimid Egypt 241; on *furūq* 150; and *ḥiyal* (legal devices) 151; on *ikhtilāf al-madhāhib* 152; Quranic basis 49; on *shurūṭ* 152; on *uṣūl al-fiqh* 141, 148; writings 143, 145
mamarr (transit) 407, 415, 416
Mamlūk era 221, 225, 228, 230, 233, 287
Mamour, P. H. 236
al-Maʾmūn (caliph): makes ʿAlī al-Riḍā heir 21, 485; and Bakhtīshūʿ family 480; and Banū Mūsā 264; Bayt al-Ḥikmah 305, 306, 344, 484; geodetic survey 305, 306–7; patronage 124–5, 276, 301, 304, 305, 306, 484–5; philhellene 166; rationalism 124–5, 495; sciences during reign 249; and translation 304, 305, 306, 344, 484
manāqib see hagiography
Mandaeans 292
mandate, divine (*amr*) 6, 9
Manichaeism 364, 484
Mann, J. 475
al-Manṣūr (caliph): founds Baghdad 293, 478; and Bakhtīshūʿ family 480; and *Sindhind* 302, 479; and translation 302, 479, 481, 482

al-Manṣūr b. abī ʿĀmir 181
Manṣūr b. ʿAmmār 60
al-Manṣūr b. Isḥāq (governor of Rayy) 354, 370
Manṣūr II b. Nūḥ 406
Manṣūr al-Yaman 239, 242
Manzikert, battle of 241
al-manzilah bayn al-manzilatayn (Muʿtazilite doctrine) 6, 131
maps 306, 312, 313, 314, 318, 411
maqāmah (literary genre) 59, 63, 71, 351, 353
maqāmāt (Ṣūfī stations) 439, 506
al-Maqdisī, ʿIzz al-Dīn 70
al-Maqdisī, al-Muṭahhar 206
al-Maqqarī, Aḥmad b. Muḥammad 180
al-Maqrīzī, Taqī ʾl-Dīn Aḥmad b. ʿAlī: *Kitāb al-Ittiʿāẓ* 240, 246; *al-Muqaffaʿ* 240; sources 222, 224, 230, 241, 288, 459
al-Maqsī 287
Marāghah observatory 287
al-Marghinānī, Burhān al-Dīn 147
Mārī b. Sulaymān (ʿAmr b. Mattā al-Ṭīrhānī) 458, 459
maʿrifah (immediate knowledge) 54
Maronite church 450, 451, 457
Marqus b. Qanbar, Abū ʾl-Fakhr 447
Marqus III b. Zurʿah (Coptic patriarch) 458
al-Marrākushī, Abū ʿAlī 286–7
marriage 42, 449
Martín, Ramón 108
Marw oasis 159
Marwān I 481
Marwanids 480, 481
al-Marwazī (Syriac-speaking physician) 492
al-Marwazī, Aḥmad b. ʿAbdullāh Ḥabash al-Ḥāsib *see* Ḥabash al-Ḥāsib
al-Marwazī, Ḥafṣ b. ʿUmar 157
al-Marwazī, Sharaf al-Zamān Ṭāhir 371
Mary the Jewess 332
Maryānos 333, 338
masāʾil (*quaestiones*) xix, 61, 129
Māsarjawayh 343–4, 346, 481
Māsarjis al-Naṣrānī, Abū ʾl-ʿAbbās al-Faḍl b. Marwān b. 455
masḥ ʿalā ʾl-khuffayn ("rubbing the shoes") 26, 42
Māshāʾallāh 293, 294, 297, 299, 478
Mashhad 424–5
Mashriq 33, 34, 309
al-Masīḥī, Abū ʾl-Khayr 350
al-Masīḥī, Abū Naṣr Saʿīd b. abī ʾl-Khayr b. ʿĪsā 348, 350
Massignon, L. 70, 427
Masʿūd b. Maḥmūd 406
al-Masʿūdī, Abū ʾl-Ḥasan ʿAlī: on ancient sources 249, 302; influence in Europe 204, 315, 318; on Ismaʿilism 246; on Ptolemy 305; sources 205, 455
WORKS: *Akhbār al-zamān* 204; *al-Awsaṭ* 204; *Murūj al-dhahab* 204–5, 207, 305, 315, 316
al-Maʿẓūmī 409
materia medica 346, 347, 356, 359, 361–3
mathematics xv, xvii, 248–56, 307; and astrology 407, 415; and astronomy 253–4, 276–83, 411, 418; Banū Mūsā 249; Byzantine 248, 379; decimal place-value system 251, 254; equations 252, 256, 258; Greek influence 248, 251, 282, 479 (*see also individual Greek authors*); Hebrew 251; Indian influence 248, 251, 252, 253, 255, 391; and philosophy 364, 411, 412, 479; theory of mechanics 258; translation 251, 252–3, 489; *see also*: algebra; arithmetic; geometry; trigonometry
mathnawī metre 135
Mattā b. Yūnus (Abū Bishr) 127, 379, 381, 492
al-Maṭwī, Muḥammad 168
mawālī (client, non-Arab Muslim) 194
al-Māwardī 150, 157, 160, 162, 166
Mawdūd b. Maḥmūd 406
Mawhūb b. Manṣūr b. Mufarrij al-Iskandarānī, Abū ʾl-Barakāt 457, 458
al-Mawṣilī, ʿAmmār b. ʿAlī 359–60
al-Mawṣilī, al-Muʿāfā b. ʿImrān 172
al-Mawṣilī, Tāj al-Islām 61
maxims 502
al-Maydānī, Abū ʾl-Faḍl Aḥmad 108
Maymūn al-Qaddāḥ 236
al-Maymūnī, Abū ʾl-Munā Abraham b. Mūsā 467–8, 469
al-Maymūnī, ʿUbaydullāh b. Abraham b. Mūsā 467–8
Mayyāfāriqīn, history of 220
al-Māzinī, Abū ʿUthmān Bakr b. Muḥammad 125
mean, golden 165–6
measles 354, 377
measures, weights and 159, 306
Mecca: histories 206, 212; hospital 491; Ibāḍīs take (129/747) 33; Ibn Rustih on 310; Kaʿbah 13; Malikite school originates in 151; Traditions 43; *see also*: prayer (times); *qiblah*
mechanical technology 250, 260–73; balance 260; controls, automatic 263, 265–6, 270, 273; diffusion of knowledge 272; gears 258, 266–7; hydraulics 258–9, 263, 266; mechanisms with life of own 273; pneumatics 266, 330; pulleys 263, 266, 267; rationale 272–3; universe, representation of 273; *see also*: astrolabes; astronomy (instruments); automata; craftsmen; cranks; time-keeping (clocks); trick vessels; water-raising machines.
mechanics xv, 249, 257, 258–9
medicine xv, xvii, 342–63; anatomy 347, 356; astrology and 347, 363; biographies 172,

174, 179–80, 346, 350; birth control 361; blood, pulmonary circulation of 348, *349*; Byzantine 342; catechisms 345, 348, 489; Christians and 248, 456; clinical approach 290, 343, 345, 377; dictionaries 480 (polyglot) 376–7; didactic verse 498, 501; education in 174, 346–7, 482; encyclopaedias 347–8, 354, *355*, 356–8; ethics 347, 348, 350–4; etiquette 347, 348, 350–1; European medicine influenced by 220, 354, 356, 358, 391; Greek influence 343, 346, 481 (*see also*: Galen; Hippocrates); Hebrew transliterations of Arabic works 471; humoral pathology 347, 356; Indian influence 344, 346; and Islam 342, 350, 361; Jewish contribution 465, 471; Jundishāpūr centre 248, 342, 343, 344, 480; manuals 345, 348; obstetrics 360–1, 494; originality 345–6; paediatrics 360–1; Persian 344; philosophy of 343, 357, 372; popular 348; pre-Islamic 342; procreation 360–1; professionalism 347–54; Prophet and 342, 361; regulation 347, 359; satire against physicians 353–4; *sharḥ* (commentary) 348; specialism 347–8, 352, 375–6; synoptic literature 358–9; textbooks 346, 347, 358; translation 333, 343–5, 354, 362, 480, 486, 487, 489, 492 (*see also under* Galen); *see also individual physicians and*: hospitals; materia medica; ophthalmology; pharmacology

Medina: histories 190, 212; hospital 491; Ibāḍīs take (129/747) 33; Ibn Rustih on 310; laws 141, 151

Melkite church: Arabization 212; Biblical exegesis 447, 447, 447–8; calendar 409; Christology 451; historiography 455, 457, 457–8; theology 450, 452; translation of canon law 449

memoirs *see* autobiography

mendicancy, literature of (*adab al-kudyah*) 506

Menelaus 252, 259, 276, 412

meningitis 358, 377

mercuric oxide 339

mercury 272, 329, 419

Mesopotamia, Upper 212, 261

metallurgy 261, 270, 329, 339

metals, al-Bīrūnī on 419–20

metaphor 71, 73, 290

metaphysics: Greek 392, 429, 433, 436; and mysticism 404; Persian 392; *see also under*: Aristotle; al-Fārābī, Abū Naṣr Muḥammad; al-Ghazālī, Abū Ḥāmid; Ibn Sīnā; al-Kindī, Yaʿqūb b. Isḥāq; Plato

meteorology 300, 407; *see also* weather

metres, poetic 135, 500–1; *see also rajaz*

Meyerhof, M. 344, 346, 359–60

microcosmos 437

miḥnah (inquisition) 485

Mihrān b. Manṣūr 362

Mīkhāʾīl, Bishop of Athrīb and Malīj 450, 451, 452

Mīkhāʾīl, Bishop of Damietta 450

Mīkhāʾīl IV (Coptic patriarch) 458

Mīkhāʾīl b. Badīr 456

mīl (land measurement) 306

milal wa-ʾl-niḥal literature 238

mills 258, 260, 261–2

al-Minqarī, Naṣr b. Muzāḥim 192

Miguel, André 310, 315

miracles: Christianity 454–5; Islam 19, 20, 64, 435, 445, 454–5

miʿrāj of Muḥammad 68

Mirdasid hospital, Aleppo 496

al-Mirghānī, Jaʿfar 68

mirrors 264

"Mirrors for Princes" 165–7, 204, 232

Mishnah 469, 470

Miskawayh, Abū ʿAlī 203–4, 211, 219, 246

missionaries: Christian 137; Ibāḍī 33, 34, 38; *see also daʿwah*

Momigliano, A. 180

monasticism, Christian 372, 450, 459–60

money 193, 208, 419

Mongolian language 108

Mongols 230, 233, 425; Baghdad falls to 231, 319; diplomatic letters to khans 163; Nizārī *daʿwah* and 245; in Syria 230

Monophysite church 481; calendar 409; Christology 451; mathematics and science 248; philosophy 486; Syriac language 212, 248

monotheism *see* unity of God

morality: Christian 459, 460; al-Ghazālī on 438–40; *ḥisbah* manuals 150, 160–1; law not distinct from, in Islam 140; Ṣūfī literature 60–2, 74, 438

Morocco; historiography 213, 214–15

morphology 121, 122, 125, 134, 135

Moses (alchemist's pseudonym) 332

Moses (prophet) 13, 51, 72, 454

Mōsheh b. ʿEzra 470–1

mosques 208, 464; *see also madrasah*

Mosul 206, 227

al-Muʿāfā b. ʿImrān al-Mawṣilī 172

Muʿāwiyah b. abī Sufyān 3, 16, 189, 291

al-Muʾayyad fī ʾl-Dīn al-Shīrāzī 242, 243, 244

al-Mubarrad, Abū ʾl-ʿAbbās Muḥammad b. Yazīd 121, 122, 125–6, 126–7, 128

al-Mufīd Muḥammad b. Muḥammad b. al-Nuʿmān, Shaykh 29–31

muftī 153

muḥaddithūn (Traditionists): biographies 168, 169; in Faṭimid Egypt 241; method of 190, 201, 213

muḥāl (grammatical term) 122, 125

al-Muhallabī, Ḥasan 320

Muḥammad (the Prophet): biography xvii, 506–7 (*see also sīrah*); on Day of Judgement 14; exegesis 40, 43, 44, 48; influence of Jewish and Christian scriptures 484; and Judaeo-Arabs 463; *miʿrāj* 68; and medicine 342, 361; prophethood 10, 13, 51; and rabbis 42; succession to 3, 141; and Ṣufism 72; Traditions on *see sunnah*
Muḥammad (concealed imam, son of al-Ḥasan al-ʿAskarī) 23
Muḥammad b. ʿAbd al-Wahhāb 12
Muḥammad b. ʿAbdullāh b. al-Muqaffaʿ 480–1
Muḥammad b. Aflaḥ 172
Muḥammad b. al-Ḥanafiyyah 16, 17, 196
Muḥammad b. Ibrāhīm 37
Muḥammad b. Ismāʿīl 18, 236, 237–8
Muḥammad b. Karrām 57
Muḥammad b. Mūsā 37
Muḥammad b. Nuʿmān al-Aḥwal (Shayṭān al-Ṭāq) 20, 21
Muḥammad b. Saʿūd 12
Muḥammad b. Shādhān 325
Muḥammad b. ʿUmar b. Shāhinshāh b. ʿUmar (ruler of Ḥamāh) 226
Muḥammad b. Ziyādatullāh 214
Muḥammad b. al-Bāqir (imam) 17, 26, 48
Muḥammad b. al-Jawād 23
Muḥammad b. al-Sammār 69
muhandis (engineer) 252
al-Muḥāsibī, Ḥārith b. Asad: exegesis 59; style 56; *ṭarīqah* works 69, 439; on terminology 70
WORKS: *Ādāb al-nufūs* 66; *Kitāb Fahm maʿānī al-Qurʾān* 59; *Kitāb al-Waṣāyā* 185; *al-Makāsib wa-ʾl-warʿ* 69; *Naṣīḥah li-ʾl-ṭālibīn* 60; *Risālah fī ʾl-Taṣawwuf* 62; *al-Riʿāyah li-ḥuqūq Allāh* 64
muḥdath (caused) 25, 30
muḥtasib (market inspector) 150, 160–1, 359
Muḥyī ʾl-Dīn b. ʿAbd al-Ẓāhir 178
Muḥyī ʾl-Dīn Abū Bakr Muḥammad b. ʿAlī b. al-ʿArabī *see* Ibn al-ʿArabī
al-Muʿizz (Faṭimid caliph) 239, 241
al-Muʿizz b. Bādīs (Zirid) 299
Muʿizz al-Dawlah Aḥmad (Aḥmad b. Buwayh) 294
mūjiz (epitome) xix, 348
muʿjizāt literature 64
Mujmal al-Tawārīkh (anon. Persian history) 224
al-Mukhtār b. abī ʿUbayd al-Thaqafī 16–17, 192
Multan 239
Muʾmin al-Ṭāq (Muḥammad b. Nuʿmān al-Aḥwal) 20, 21
al-Mundaribī, Abū ʾl-Mufaḍḍal 170
Munich Arab. 2570 (manuscript) 458
Munk, S. 474
Munkar (angel) 14
Munqidh family 220–1
al-muqābalah (algebraic term) 256
al-Muqaddasī, Muḥammad b. Aḥmad 240, 261, 305, 312, 314–15, 320
al-Muqammiṣ, Dāwūd b. Marwān al-Raqqī 466
Muqātil b. Sulaymān 46
al-Muqriʾ, Abū Jaʿfar 184
al-Muqtadī (caliph) 361
al-Muqtadir (caliph) 347
al-Muqtanaʿ, Bahāʾ al-Dīn 241
al-Murādī 266
Murjiʾites 3–4
Murshid, Majd al-Dīn abū Salamah 186–7
al-Mursī, Abū ʾl-ʿAbbās 62
al-Murtaḍā, al-Sharīf Abū ʾl-Qāsim ʿAlī b. al-Ḥusayn 31
Murtaḍā al-Zabīdī 106, 115
Mūsā, Banū *see* Banū Mūsā
Mūsā b. Khālid 487
Mūsā b. Maymūn *see* Maimonides
Mūsā b. Shākir 249, 264
Mūsā al-Kāẓim: on attributes of God 24; death and occultation 21–2; imamate 18, 20, 236; on Qurʾān 28, 29
Muṣʿab b. ʿImrān 182
al-Musabbiḥī, ʿIzz al-Mulk Muḥammad b. abī ʾl-Qāsim 211, 241
musajjaʿ see epistolary style
al-Musanī 145–6
mushāhadah (philosophical term) 397
music, 57, 76, 257, 384, 486
musk 257
Muslim b. al-Ḥajjāj 43, 49
Muslim al-Laḥijī 222
mustajīb (candidate for Faṭimid community) 234
al-Mustaʿlī (caliph) 243
al-Mustanṣir, Maʿadd (Faṭimid caliph) 241–3, 244, 352
mustaqīm (grammatical term) 122, 125
al-Mustaẓhir (caliph) 361, 443
al-Muʿtaḍid (caliph) 364, 370, 486, 495, 503
al-Muʿtaḍidī hospital, Baghdad 370
mutʿah (temporary marriage) 42
al-Muṭahhar al-Maqdisī 206
mutakallimūn (theologians) 4, 364, 367–8, 382–3
al-Muʾtaman b. al-ʿAssāl 448, 451, 452, 459–60
al-Mutanabbī, ʿAbd al-Jabbār 503
al-Mutanabbī, Abū ʾl-Ṭayyib Aḥmad b. al-Ḥusayn 498, 502, 504
al-Muṭarrizī 137
al-Muʿtaṣim (caliph) 364, 480
al-Mutawakkil (caliph) 59, 198, 362, 480, 487, 495
Muʿtazilism 4–7, 424; al-Ashʿarī and 8; on attributes of God 5, 27, 30; Baḥya b. Paquda 467; Basran 31; biography 215; and Christianity 454; didactic verse 506; Faṭimids and 242; on free will 6, 27, 30; al-Ghazālī on 430; and grammar 129; and Jews 465; Yaʿqūb b. Isḥāq al-Kindī on 367; on Moses' beatific vision 134; official

standing under al-Maʾmūn 485; on Qurʾān 5, 485; reaction against 424, 495; and Shiʿites 27, 29–30, 31; on sin 6, 131; on unknowability of future 382; al-Zamakhsharī 49, 133, 134
Muṭrān Khalīl Muṭrān 502
muṭṭalaʿ (exegetical term) 52
Muwaffaq al-Dīn b. al-Mutaqqinah, al-Raḥbī 149
muwaḥḥidūn (Wahhābīs) 12
al-Muwaqqit, ʿAlāʾ al-Dīn 471
Muẓaffar al-Dīn al-Baʿlabakkī 471
al-Muẓaffar of Ḥamāh 226
muzdawij verse form 501
mysticism 1; Christian 1; Islamo-Hindu 246; Jewish 468; *see also* Ṣufism
Mzāb 36

"Nabataean" language *see* Aramaic
al-Nābighah al-Dhubyānī 498
al-Nābulusī, ʿAbd al-Ghanī 75
Nagel, T. 237
al-Nahrawālī, Muḥammad b. ʿAlāʾ al-Dīn 326
naḥw see: grammar; syntax
naḥwī (grammarian) 118, 137
naḥwiyyūn (grammarians) 120–1, 123
Nakīr (angel) 14
Nallino, C. A. 276
al-Narshakhī 206
al-Nasafī, Abū Ḥafṣ ʿUmar b. Muḥammad 14
al-Nasafī, Abū ʾl-Ḥasan Muḥammad b. Aḥmad 240
al-Nasawī, Aḥmad 62–3
al-Nasawī, Muḥammad b. Aḥmad b. ʿAlī b. Muḥammad 219
al-Nāshiʾ al-Akbar 238
Nashwān b. Saʿīd 113, 503
Naṣīḥat al-mulūk (*attr.* al-Ghazālī) 166–7
al-Nāṣir li-Dīn Allāh 350
Naṣīr al-Dīn b. al-Ḥusayn al-Ṭūsī 32; on astrology 298; on astronomy 276, 278, 280, 282, 284, 422; on Ḥayy b. Yaqẓān 87; on intuition 397–8; Ismaʿilism 245; theology 32
WORKS: *Īlkhānī zīj* 278; *ʿilm al-taqwīm* 280; *Risālah fī Shakl al-qaṭṭāʿ* 282; *Tadhkirah* 284; *Tajrīd al-iʿtiqād* 32
Nāṣir al-Dīn Maḥmūd 268
Nāṣir-i-Khusraw
al-Nāṣirī, Ibrāhīm 300
al-Naṣīrī, Quṭb al-Dīn Muḥammad al-Marwazī 184
naskh see abrogation
Naṣr, Sayyid Ḥusayn 331, 334
Naṣr b. Muzāḥim al-Minqarī 192
Naṣrallāh, J. 446, 450
naṣṣ (designation) 17
al-Nātalī 392
al-Nāṭifī, Aḥmad 153
nāʿūrah (water-wheel) 262
navigation: celestial 325; compass 257, 326; literature 324–7 (verse) 325, 508
al-Nawawī, Yaḥyā 148
Nawbakht 293, 478; descendants 27, 293, 295, 296, 482
Nawbakht al-Ḥakīm 293, 478
al-Nayrīzī, al-Faḍl b. Ḥātim 283, 298
Naysābūr; Niẓāmiyyah College 425, 427
al-Naysābūrī, Aḥmad b. Ibrāhīm 240
al-Naysābūrī, al-Ḥākim 171
Naẓīf b. Yumn, Abū ʿAlī 451–2
Needham, Sir Joseph 328, 332
Nemesius of Edessa 488
Nemoy, L. 475
neo-Platonism: and alchemy 332; Aristotle and 369; and astrology 297; on creation 401; in education 380; emanation theory 53, 433, 492; Abū Naṣr Muḥammad al-Fārābī and 379, 388; Abū Ḥāmid al-Ghazālī on 433, 496; Ibn Sīnā and 395, 403; Ikhwān al-Ṣafāʾ and 238, 240, 250; Ismaʿilism and 238, 240, 250, 321; Judaeo-Arabic 466–7, 469; Yaʿqūb b. Isḥāq al-Kindī's circle and 369; Muḥyī ʾl-Dīn b. al-ʿArabī and 74; Persian 393; and Ṣufism 68, 496; *Theology of Aristotle* 365, 466, 471, 490; triad 453
neo-Pythagoreanism 486
Nestorian church: Biblical exegesis 447; calendar 409; Christology 451; decline of Syriac language 212; historiography 456, 457, 458; philosophy 486; school 248 (*see also* Jundishāpūr); theology 452; translation 248, 344, 494; *see also*: Elijah of Nisibin; Jundishāpūr
Nestorius 452
Nĕthanʾel b. al-Fayyūmī 468
Neubauer, A. 474
Nicholas (Byzantine monk of Cordova) 495
Nicholas of Damascus 494
Nicholson, R. A. 175
Nicomachus of Gerasa 254, 486
al-Niffarī, Muḥammad 67, 72
Niftawayhi 112
Niger 324
Nisibin; Nestorian school 248
Nissīm b. Yaʿqūb b. Shāhīn 470
Niẓām of Burhānpūr, Shaykh 154
Niẓām al-Mulk (vizier, d. 485/1092) 167, 246, 425
Niẓāmī ʿArūḍī Samarqandī 405
Niẓāmiyyah colleges 425, 427
Nizār b. Maʿadd 244
Nizārī *daʿwah* 242, 243, 244–5, 246, 247
Nizwā party 38
Noah 72
Nöldeke, T. 475
nomocanons (*majmūʿ*) 449, 450
Nonnus, Bishop of Nisibin 448

noria (*nāʿūrah*, water-wheel) 262
North and South Arabs 113
Nubia, history of 241
Nūḥ II b. Manṣūr 390
Nukkarites 34
al-Nuʿmān, Abū Ḥanīfah (al-Qāḍī) 148, 214, 216, 239, 242
numerals 254–5, 391; sexagesimal notation 255, 278
numerology 335, 486
Nūr al-Dīn Maḥmūd b. Zankī 226, 227, 228, 267
al-Nūrī, Abū ʾl-Ḥusayn 60, 69, 71–2
al-Nuṣayrī 300
al-Nushūʾ abū Shākir 459, 460
al-Nuwayrī, Aḥmad 215, 224, 240, 246, 321–2

oases 159
Obermann, J. 428
obituary notices 218, 228
observational method: alchemy 336, 337; al-Bīrūnī 259, 419–20, 422; Abū Naṣr Muḥammad al-Fārābī 383, 384; Ibn al-Haytham 258, 259; Ibn Sīnā 343, 356; medicine 290, 343, 345, 377; Abū Bakr Muḥammad b. Zakariyyāʾ al-Rāzī 290, 337, 363, 372, 377
observatories 287–8, 484
obstetrics 360–1, 494
occult sciences 391; *see also* esoteric works
occultation of imam 17, 20, 21–2, 23, 26, 29, 30–1
occurrence, theory of 433, 435–6
Ockley, Simon 104–5
oculists (*kaḥḥālūn*) 352, 359
omens, celestial 291–2, 364, 407
oneirocritics 174
Onomasticon Arabicum 176–7
ontology/number theory 486
ophthalmology 345, 359–60, 370, 375, 490
optics 257–8
oral tradition 197; *Ḥadīth* 170; historiography 189, 193–4, 195, 220; Ibāḍī 34–5; navigational literature 325; of scholarship, through travel 322; transition to written 41
Oriental (*ishrāqī, mashriqī*) wisdom 88, 90, 91–2, 95, 96, 100–1, 468
Orontes, river 258
orthography 115, 119, 178, 463, 471
Ostanes 332
Ottomans 246
Oxford University 473–4

paediatrics 360–1
Pahlavi literature and translations: astrology 290, 292–3, 294, 295; astronomy 251, 294; historical 166, 212; mathematics 251; *see also Kalīlah wa-Dimnah*
Palestine 223, 446
Palmyra; observatory 484
Panchatantra 165, 183
panegyric 206–7, 209–10, 222–3, 245
paper: availability xix, 207; manufacture 261, 333, 483
Pappus 251, 252, 260
papyri 190, 197
parables 68, 498
parallax 277
parallelism 156
Paris 235, 318
participation, Zoroastrian theory of 398–9
Path, literature of Ṣūfī 68–70
Patricius *see* Abū Yaḥyā b. al-Baṭrīq
patronage 124–5, 206, 293, 324; *see also*: Banū Mūsā; al-Maʾmūn; *and under* translation
Paul, St 448
Paulus, H. 474
Pavia, faculty of 354
al-Pazdawī, ʿAbdullāh b. Muḥammad 149
pedagogy 361; *see also under* grammar
Pellat, Charles 176
pension rights 189
Peripatetic school 397–8
Persepolis 249
Persia: administrative literature 158, 159; astrology 290, 292–3, 293–5, 297, 299; astronomy 251, 274, 276, 294; autobiography 183; biography 170, 232; calendar 409; ethics 165, 166; geographical tradition 308; historiography 166, 194, 197, 198, 206–7, 209–10, 212, 219, 224, 232, 249; land grants 157; medicine 344; metaphysics 392; "Mirrors for Princes" 165, 166–7, 232; Muḥyī ʾl-Dīn b. al-ʿArabī's influence 73; Nizārī *daʿwah* 242, 244–5; occult sciences 391; Persian aspects of Ibn Sīnā's thought 390, 391, 392, 395, 398–9; pharmacy 362; philosophy 87, 393; poetry 73; and secretaries 164; Shuʿūbiyyah and 133; statecraft 155, 165, 166, 249; Ṣufism 71, 75; words borrowed from 116; *see also*: Pahlavi; Zoroastrianism
Persian language: glossaries 108; translations (to Arabic) 194, 249, 407, 481, 509 (from Arabic) 209
Peters, F. E. 485
Petrus de Regio 300
Petry, Carl F. 176
Phaedrus 508
pharmacy 339, 347, 352, 356, 357, 361–3, 489; al-Bīrūnī on 375, 406, 420–1; Greek 362, 487; Indian 362; Persian 362; Abū Bakr Muḥammad b. Zakariyyāʾ al-Rāzī on 375–6; specialization established 375–6; *see also* materia medica
Philo of Byzantium 263, 265
Philo Judaeus 491
philology xv; Christian Arabic 449; Judaeo-

Arabic 465, 468–9, 475; secretaries and 155; *see also*: grammar; language; lexicography; Qur'ān (linguistic studies)
philosopher's stone 330
philosophy (*falsafah*) xvi, 76–105; of alchemy 338; Arabic language adapted to express 249; and astrology 297, 367; and astronomy 76, 291; al-Bīrūnī's disdain for 422; Christian 396, 460, 494; defined 1–2; didactic verse on 501, 503, 504; education 234, 364–5; al-Ghazālī's effect on 445; grammar and 118, 125–6, 127–9, 137; Greek influence xvi, 77, 128, 166 (*see also individual authors*); *ishrāqī* (Oriental) *see separate entry*; Ismā'īlī 240; Judaeo-Arabic 465, 466–8, 469; literary nature 76–8; mathematics and 364, 411, 412, 479; of medicine 343, 357, 372; Mu'tazilites and 4, 5; Persian 87, 393; philosopher and the city 87–98; political 379, 387, 388; popular (*dhā'i'ah*) 86–7; and prophecy 99, 367, 369, 371; range 78; and reason 1, 164, 432–5; and religion 99, 379, 380–2, 384–5, 400–4, 437, 494 (and *kalām*) xv, xvi, 51, 78–9, 424 (religious encyclopaedias on) 459, 460; Ṣabians and 486; style of writing 76–8, 80; Ṣufism and 57, 68, 468, 496; theology harmonized with 51, 78–9, 424; *see also individual philosophers and systems and* logic
phlebotomy 268, 352, 377
phonology 121, 122, 133–4, 135, 463
physics 5, 250, 256–60, 365, 384, 433; Greek 294, 429
Pilgrimage (*ḥajj*) 10, 33, 323, 427, 508
pillars of Islam 10
pilot-books 508
Pingree, D. 276, 417
plagiarism, concept of 321
Plato xvi; and Aristotle 78–87, 365, 369, 378; in educational curriculum 380; Abū Naṣr Muḥammad al-Fārābī on 80–1, 82–6, 379, 387, 388, 493; al-Ghazālī and 428; Ya'qūb b. Isḥāq al-Kindī on 491; literary style 77; on manual work 262; metaphysics 365, 369, 378, 379, 387, 388; myths 68; and participation (Iranian theory) 398; on pious ascetic 83, 84–6; translation 483, 488, 489, 493
  WORKS: *Laws* 493; *Republic* 387, 486, 489; *Timaeus* 482
  see also neo-Platonism
Plato of Tivoli 296
pleurisy, Ibn Sīnā on 391
Plotinus xvi, 77, 365, 366, 398
Plutarch 492
pneumatics 266, 330
Pococke, E. 473
poetics 77, 78
poetry: alchemical 337; astrological 300; biography of poets 172, 173; al-Bīrūnī's autobiographical 406; Abū Naṣr Muḥammad al-Fārābī on 384; geographers cite 309, 320; Hebrew 464, 470; historical content 188, 239; Islamo-Hindu mystical (*ginān*s) 246; lexicographical citation 110, 112, 116; Persian 73; poetics 77, 78; pre-Islamic 45, 113, 116; Ṣufī 58; *see also* didactic verse
poisons 363, 487
polemical literature: on 'Abbasid revolution 196; and Basran-Kufan dispute 126, 133; didactic verse 506; Faṭimid 240; Judaeo-Arabic 185, 466; against *kalām* 493
politics: Ibn Sīnā 390–1; philosophy of 379, 387, 388, 442–3; and religion 189; and theology 3–9
Polyglot Bibles 473
polyglot dictionaries 107–8, 376–7
polytheism (*shirk*) 12
Pontano, Giovanni Gioviano 298
Poonawala, I. K. 235
Pope, letters to the 163
Porphyry 487–8, 491
Portuguese in India 326–6
Posidonius 306
postal service (*barīd*) 158, 164, 201, 308
Poznanski, S. 475
prayer: ablutions before 26, 42; direction of *see qiblah*; Ibāḍī dispute on communal 34; Jewish prayer-book 470; pillar of Islam 10; Quranic exhortations 140; Ṣufism 67–8; times 275–6, 283, 284–5, 306, 412; Wahhābīs on 12
predestination: al-Ghazālī 436, 441–2; Jabrites 4; al-Ma'arrī 504; and *rizq* (life-wages) 14; *see also* freedom
pre-Islamic period 194; didactic verse 498, 502; historiography 193–4, 309; language *see 'arabiyyah*; law 139; medicine 342; poetry 45, 113, 116; time-keeping and calendar 409
printing 318, 462–3, 467, 473–4
Proclus xvi, 365, 366–7, 433, 488, 494, 497
procreation, medical literature on 360–1
Profatius 287
pronunciation *see* phonology
prophecy and prophets 13, 73–4; historiography on 193, 194; Muḥammad's prophethood 10, 13, 51; and philosophy 99, 367, 369, 371; Shī'īs on 19, 25
"prophets, tales of the" (*qiṣaṣ al-anbiyā'*) 194
proverbs 110, 498
provinces, learning in 250, 368
Psalms, Book of 447
psychology 5, 361, 395
psychosomatic medicine 357
Ptolemy, Claudius: and astrology 292, 294, 295, 296, 298, 299, 416, 481; astronomy 274,

Ptolemy, Claudius: (*cont.*)
394; climes 303; cosmos, concept of 479; enduring influence 122, 307; geography 303–5, 306; mathematics 251, 253; modifications to models 284; translation of 276, 288, 303–4, 365, 481, 484, 486, 488
WORKS: *Almagest* (*Megale Syntaxis*, *Majisṭī*) 251, 253, 303, 418; *Apotelesmatika* (*Tetrabiblos*, *Kitāb al-Arbaʿah*) 292, 295, 298, 481, 482; *Geographia* 303–5, 306; *Handy Tables* 279
pulleys 263, 266, 267
pulse, Ibn Sīnā on 357
Pumpeditha; Jewish academy 464
pumps *269*, 270
punishment, judicial 42–3
Pythagoras 179, 254, 338, 346; neo-Pythagoreanism 486

Qabʿah, ʿAmr b. ʿAbdullāh b. Layth 182–3
qabbālāh 468
qabīḥ (grammatical term) 122, 125
al-Qabīṣī, Abū ʾl-Ṣaqr ʿAbd al-ʿAzīz b. ʿUthmān 299
Qābūs b. Wushmagīr 405, 407
qadar see predestination
Qaddaḥid line of imams 236
qaddāḥūn (cataract couchers) 359
al-Qāḍī al-Fāḍil, ʿAbd al-Raḥmān b. ʿAlī 223–4, 228
Qāḍikhān, Fakhr al-Dīn 153–4
Qādiriyyah 68
*qāḍī*s 150, 151, 184
al-Qādisī 218
Qāfiḥ, Y. 475
Qaḥṭān 368
al-Qalhāti, Abū ʿAbdullāh Muḥammad b. Saʿīd 38
al-Qālī 111, 112
al-Qalqashandī, Aḥmad 162–3, 202, 246
al-Qalyūbī, al-Wajīh Yūḥannā 448
qāmūs (dictionary) 114
*qanāt*s (canals) 252, 258
qānūn (Islamic neologism) 115
al-Qarāfī, Aḥmad b. Idrīs 150
Qaraites 462, 466, 468–9, 470, 472, 475
Qarāmiṭah (Carmathians) 202, 237–8, 239, 242
qaṣaṣ technique 71
al-Qāshī, Ibn Bābā 224
Qāsim b. Muḥammad 141
al-Qaṣrānī, Abū Yūsuf Yaʿqūb b. ʿAlī 297
al-Qayrawān 168, 215, 465–6, 466–7, 470
Qays al-Mārūnī 455
Qayṣar, Abū Isḥāq ʿAlam al-Riʾāsah Ibrāhīm b. Kātib 449
Qayṣar b. Musāfir Taʿāsīf 258
al-Qazwīnī, Abū Ḥātim Maḥmūd b. al-Ḥasan b. Muḥammad 152
al-Qazwīnī, Zakariyyāʾ b. Muḥammad 320–1
qiblah 275–6, 283, 285–6, 306, 411–12, 422
al-Qifṭī, ʿAlī b. Yūsuf 230; on ancient world 169, 179; *Ikhbār al-ʿulamāʾ* 174, 347; on Ptolemy 304; on Abū Bakr Muḥammad b. Zakariyyāʾ al-Rāzī 373; selection of subjects 169, 171, 264, 421
al-Qirqisānī, Yaʿqūb b. Isḥāq 466, 470
qiṣaṣ al-anbiyāʾ ("tales of the prophets") 194
qiyās (analogy) 3; Christian use 453; and grammar 120–1, 123; Ibn Sīnā on 356, 396–7, 398, 399; in jurisprudence 121, 141, 143, 144, 145, 148; in Sunnī theology 10
quadrants, astronomical 286–7
al-Quḍāʿī 211, 241
al-qudamāʾ al-khamsah (pre-eternal principles) 372
Qudāmah b. Jaʿfar 132, 157, 158
qudrah (ability to act) 6, 8, 9, 441
al-Qudūrī 147
al-Quhandizī 137
Qumm 23–7, 206, 209
al-Qummī, Abū al-Ḥasan ʿAlī b. Ibrāhīm 24, 48
al-Qummī, Saʿd b. ʿAbdullāh 238
Qurʾān and Quranic exegesis xv, xvi, 40–55, 139–40; *ʿarabiyyah* 107, 124; Christianity and 452–3, 484; Companions assemble 43; creation issue 5, 8, 13, 34, 435, 485 (Shiʿite view) 20, 21, 22, 25, 28–9, 30; dating (*asbāb al-nuzūl*) 44–5; on freedom 6; *ghayb* (mystery) 8; Abū Ḥāmid al-Ghazālī on 431; golden calf story 53; Hebrew transliteration 462; Ibāḍī view 34, 37, 38; Ibn Sīnā reconciles philosophy with 395, 396, 399–400, 400–3; identification (*taʿyīn*) 44–5; imprecision 41, 44–5, 119; inimitabilty 13, 49, 50, 124, 471; interpolation 41–3; *isnād*s and exegesis 47; *isrāʾīliyyāt* 45; Judaeo-Christian context 484; and law 46, 139–40 (as root of law) 139, 140, 143, 144, 148; lexicographical citation 110, 112, 115, 116; linguistic studies 9–10, 45–9, 107, 119, 124; literary style 156; marriage, temporary 42; Muʿtazilites on 5, 485; proof-verses 45–6, 49; rational analysis 49–52; reciters 172; revelation, scheme of 395; script 41, 119; secretaries and 164; Shīʿīs (on creation issue) 20, 21, 22, 25, 28–9, 30 (exegesis) 48, 50, 51; Ṣufism and 52–5, 59, 64; *sunnah* and 43, 47; and Sunnī theology 10; Abū Jaʿfar Muḥammad b. Jarīr al-Ṭabarī 46–7, 48, 124, 146, 191, 199, 200; textual criticism 41–3, 119; translations 11, 462; written exegesis 43–4; Yemeni Jewish literature cites 468; *ẓāhir* 47
CITED: *ii: 42* 42; *255* 64; *iii: 18* 49–50; *19* 50; *93* 42; *105* 40; *173* 45; *iv:14* 40; *24* 42; *59* 40; *80* 40; *v:6* 42; *12* 41; *vi.153* 40; *vii.143*, 134; *157* 41; *ix.3* 41; *xii.2* 45; *xvi.44* 40; *148* 53;

xxxiv.2 43; *xxvi.78–82* 53; *xxxvi* 64; *xxxvii.107* 53; *xlii.11* 452; *xlviii.9* 41; *lix.2* 53–4; lxix.17 22
see also: abrogation
al-Qurashī, Idrīs ʿImād al-Dīn al-Anf 244
Quraysh, tribe of 443
al-Qurṭubī, Abū ʾl-Qāsim Ṣāʿid b. Aḥmad b. Ṣāʿid 302
al-Qurṭubī, ʿArīb b. Saʿd 201, 203, 214, 455
al-Qurṭubī, Muḥammad b. Aḥmad 48–9
al-Qurṭubī al-Andalusī, ʿUmar b. ʿAbd al-Raḥmān 179
al-Qushayrī, Abū ʾl-Qāsim ʿAbd al-Karīm 64, 65, 66, 70, 74, 438
Qusṭā b. Lūqā 455, 456, 491, 492
Qusṭanṭīn, Maḥbūb 457
al-Qusyān, Antioch; church 455
quṭb (pole, head of the hierarchy of *awliyāʾ*) 72–3
Quṭb al-Dīn al-Shīrāzī 284, 422
al-Quwayrī 492

rabbis, Muḥammad and 42
al-Rabīʿ b. Ḥabīb al-Farāhīdī 34, 35, 38
Rābiʿah al-ʿAdawīyyah 58
Rabīʿ al-Raʾy 180–1
al-Radāʿī, Aḥmad b. ʿĪsā 508
Rādhāniyyah merchants 309
Rafiḍites 429
al-Raghūnī 217
al-Raḥbī Muwaffaq al-Dīn b. al-Mutaqqinah 149
Raʾīs al-Ḥasan b. Ṣalāḥ Munshī Birjandī 245
rajʿah (return of imam) 17, 22, 23, 26–7, 29, 32
rajaz metre 325, 447, 498, 500–1
ramad (trachoma) 345, 359, 360
Ramaḍān 10
ramal metre 501
Raṣābī, T. 475
Raʾs al-ʿAyn, monks from 343
raṣd (al-Maʾmūn's geodetic survey) 305, 306–7
Rashīd al-Dīn Ṭabīb, Faḍlullāh 224, 245
Rashīd al-Dīn Sinān 224, 245, 246
rationalism *see*: Muʿtazilism; reason *raʾy* (individual reasoning) 3, 141, 143, 145
Rayḥānah bint al-Ḥasan 413
Rayṭah bint al-Ḥārith 173
Rayy 27, 370
al-Rāzī, Abū ʾl-ʿAbbās Aḥmad b. ʿAbdullāh b. Muḥammad 212
al-Rāzī, Abū Bakr Aḥmad b. Muḥammad b. Bashīr 214, 227
al-Rāzī, Abū Bakr Muḥammad b. Shādhān 71
al-Rāzī, Abū Bakr Muḥammad b. Zakariyyāʾ xviii, 370–7; alchemy 328, 335–7, 338, 340, 341; on authority and dogma 371, 377, 496; autobiography 185–6; bibliography 488; character 370–1; on creation 372; dissemination 377; on Galen 372; life 370, 374; and medical astrology 363; on medicine 344, 345, 354, *355*, 356, 358, 377, 420; observational method 290, 337, 363, 372, 377; on ophthalmology 375; on pharmacy 375–6; philosophy 240, 371–2, 496; polyglot lexicon 376–7; on prophets 371, 493; *al-qudamāʾ al-khamsah* (eternal principles) 372; Quranic exegesis 50–2
WORKS: *al-Adwiyah al-murakkabah* (formulary) 376; *al-Aqrabādhīn al-mukhtaṣar* 375; *Fī anna al-Ṭabīb al-Fāḍil faylasūf* 372; *Fī Makhārīq al-anbiyāʾ* 371; *Fī ʾl-Shukūk ʿalā Jālīnūs* 372, 375; *Fi-ʾstinbāṭ al-asmāʾ* 376–7; *al-Fuṣūl* 375; *al-Ḥāwī fī ʾl-ṭibb (Continens)* 345, 348, 354, 356, 373–4, 374–5, 377; *al-Jadarī wa-ʾl-ḥaṣbah* 377; *al-Jāmiʿ al-kabīr* 374–6; *Kitāb al-ʿIlm al-ilāhī* 372; *Kitāb al-Khawāṣṣ* 377; *Kitāb al-Manṣūrī fī ʾl-ṭibb*, 354, 355, 377;
Kitāb Ṣaydalat al-ṭibb 375; *Kitāb al-Sīrah al-falsafiyyah* 185–6, 370–1, 374–5; *Man lā yaḥḍuruhu al-ṭabīb* 377; *al-Ṭibb al-mulūkī* 377; *al-Ṭibb al-rūḥānī* 371
al-Rāzī, Abū Ḥātim Aḥmad b. Ḥamdān b. Aḥmad 238, 240, 371
al-Rāzī, Abū ʾl-Haytham 170
al-Rāzī, Abū Muḥammad ʿAbd al-Raḥmān b. abī Ḥātim Muḥammad b. Idrīs 173
al-Rāzī, Abū Zakariyyāʾ Yaḥyā b. Muʿādh 66
al-Rāzī, Fakhr al-Dīn abū ʿAbdullāh Muḥammad b. ʿUmar 14–15, 32, 50–2, 460
al-Rāzī, ʿĪsā b. Aḥmad b. Muḥammad b. Bashīr 214
Rāzī, Shāhmardān 282
reason and reasoning: al-Ashʿarī on 8; Christian proof of monotheism 452; classifications of 369, 383; and dogmatism 371; and faith 8, 389, 431–2, 445; Ibāḍīs and 34; Muʿtazilites on 5, 7; and philosophy 1, 431–5; rational exegesis of Qurʾān 49–52; and revelation 367–8. 395; Shīʿīs on 31, 32; and theology 2, 124–5; *see also under*: al-Fārābī, Abū Naṣr Muḥammad; al-Ghazālī, Abū Ḥāmid
refraction, atmospheric 258
regionalism in literature 207, 209
religion 1; histories of sects and schisms 205–6; and politics 189; secular and political interpretation 384–5; *see also individual religions and sects, and* philosophy (and religion)
Renassia, Yūsuf 472
responsa, legal 153, 470
resurrection 14, 22, 401–3; return of the imam from death or occultation (*rajʿah*) 17, 22, 23, 26–7, 29, 32
revelation: astrology as stemming from antediluvian 297; and faith 389; Abū Naṣr Muḥammad al-Fārābī on 385–6; law, revealed *see sharīʿah*; nature of Islamic 40, 395; and philosophy 400–3, 404, 494; and reason 367–8, 395; theology on 2, 13

Revelation, Book of 449
rewards and punishments 100, 403, 440
Rhazes *see* al-Rāzī, Abū Bakr Muḥammad b. Zakariyyāʾ
rhetoric 77, 78, 115, 125, 384, 471
Rhetorius 294
ribā (interest) 140
rice-husking machine 261
Riḍwān b. al-Saʿātī 267, 270
Riḍwān b. al-Walakhshī 187
al-Rifāʿī, Aḥmad 61, 62, 74
rigour, academic 481
risālah see epistles
road-blocks 158
Robert of Ketton 255, 341
Roger II of Sicily 318
Roget, Peter 107
Roman, J. 465, 473
Rome: ancient 169, 194, 290 (law) 153; printing in C16th 318
al-Rudhabārī 60, 66
al-Rūdhrāwarī, Abū Shujāʿ Ẓāhir ʾl-Dīn Muḥammad 204, 246
al-Ruhāwī, Isḥāq b. ʿAlī 351, 456
Rūm, embassy to 311
al-Rummānī 111, 128, 129, 131, 135
Rūs 309, 311, 323
al-Ruṣāfī, Maʿrūf 502
Ruska, J. 333, 336
Rustamids 214
Rustāq party 38
ruʾyah (visibility) *see under* God

Saʿadyah b. Dāwūd al-ʿAdanī 473
Saʿadyah Gaʾon b. Yūsuf al-Fayyūmī: exegesis 468; *Kitāb al-Amānāt* 466; life 466; prayer book 470; translation of Bible 466, 472, 473, 474; uses Arabic script 462
al-Saʿātī, Muḥammad 267
sabab (motivating cause) 46, 48
al-Ṣabbāgh 61
al-Ṣābiʾ, Abū Isḥāq Ibrāhīm b. Hilāl 156, 163, 202–3, 206
al-Ṣābiʾ, Hilāl b. al-Muḥassin 164, 203, 204, 205, 211, 228
Ṣābiʾ family of Ḥarrān (historians) 202–3, 204
Ṣabian sect 170, 202, 248, 364, 484, 486
Sachau, E. 415
Sacy, Silvestre de 241
Saʿd al-Dīn Khiḍr 228
al-Ṣafadī, Khalīl b. Aybak 176, 226, 488
Ṣafī ʾl-Dīn, ʿAbd al-Muʾmin al-Baghdādī 320
safīr (ambassador of concealed imam) 23
Ṣafwān al-Anṣārī 502–3
al-Ṣaghānī 114
ṣaghāʾir (venial sins) 6
al-Ṣaḥābah *see* Companions
Sahara 314, 317
al-Ṣāḥib Ibn ʿAbbād (Ismāʿīl b. ʿAbbād) 110–11, 163
Sahl b. Abbān 325
Sahl b. Bishr al-Isrāʾīlī, Abū ʿUthmān 295
Sahl b. Hārūn 484
Sahl al-Tusṭarī 52–3, 60, 61, 62
al-Sahlī, Abū ʾl-Ḥasan Sahl b. Muḥammad 338
Saḥnūn b. Saʿīd 145, 214
Saʿīd b. Aḥmad b. Saʿīd al-Qurṭubī, Abū ʾl-Qāsim 302
Saʿīd b. Baṭrīq (Melkite patriarch) 451, 457–8
Saʿīd b. Hārūn 484
Ṣāʿid b. al-Ḥasan b. ʿĪsā, Abū ʾl-ʿAlāʾ 181
Saʿīd b. Hibatullāh, Abū ʾl-Ḥasan 359, 361
Saʿīd b. Khurāsānkhurrah 292
Saʿīd b. al-Musayyib 141
Saïdi, O. 211
saints, Ṣūfī 63, 64, 65, 72–3
sajʿ (rhymed prose) 67, 156, 178, 315, 447, 459
al-Sajāwandī, Sirāj al-Dīn abū Ṭāhir Muḥammad 149
al-Sakkāk, Muḥammad b. al-Khalīl 23
Salafiyyah 12
ṣalāh (prayer) 10
Ṣalāḥ al-Dīn Yūsuf al-Ayyūbī: biography 177, 207; histories of 222–3, 226, 227, 228; panegyric 222–3; reconquest of Jerusalem 221, 223
Salāmān and Absāl (anon.) 87
Salamiyyah; imam in hiding at 237
salicin 362–3
Salio of Padua 296
Saljūq period 31; al-Ghazālī's "Mirrors for Princes" for 166–7; historiography 218–19, 226; land tenure 157; Zirid alliance against Faṭimids 241
Salmān of Ḥarrān 484
al-Samʿānī 218
al-Samarqandī, Abū ʾl-Fatḥ Saʿīd b. Khafīf 278
al-Samarqandī, Abū Layth Naṣr b. Muḥammad 153
Samawʾal b. Yaḥyā al-Maghribī 185
al-Samhūdī 212
Ṣanʿāʾ 212, 235, 243
Sanjar b. Malik-Shāh 427
Sanskrit, transition from 249; astrology 290, 293; astronomical works 248, 251, 417; al-Bīrūnī and 406, 416, 417; geography 302; *Panchatantra see Kalīlah wa-Dimnah*; *Siddhāntas* 251, 253 (*Sindhind*) 302–3, 481
al-Sanūsī, Abū ʿAbdullāh Muḥammad b. Yūsuf of Tlemcen 15
al-Saqaṭī 160–1
sāqiyah (water-raising device) 262
al-Sarakhsī, Aḥmad b. al-Ṭayyib 364, 368
al-Sarakhsī, Muḥammad 144
ṣarf see morphology
al-Sarrāj, Abū Naṣr ʿAbdullāh b. ʿAlī 64, 72
al-Sarrāj al-Ṭūsī 439

Sarton, G. 485
Sāsān b. Sāsān b. Bābak b. Sāsān 184
satire 353–4, 503–4, 506
satr (period of concealment) *see under* Faṭimids
Sauvaget, J. 322
Sawād of Iraq 157, 309, 310
Sāwīrus of Antioch 448
Sāwīrus b. al-Muqaffa' (Bishop of al-Ashmūnayn): Bible commentaries 447, 448; *Kitāb al-Siyar* 222, 457, 458; theological treatises 451, 452
ṣawm see fasting
Sayf al-Dawlah 299, 379, 498
Sayili, Aḥmad 288
al-Ṣaymarī, Abū 'l-'Anbas Muḥammad b. Isḥāq 296–7
Sayyid, Ayman Fu'ād 211, 245, 247
al-Sayyid al-Ḥimyarī 506–7
Sbath Manuscripts 452
Schechter, S. 475
Schnurrer, C. F. 474
schools: Christian canon law on 450; Greek, in Asia Minor 248; *see also* education *and under*: law; theology
Science of Generation 335
sciences xvii, 248–51; Byzantine 248, 379; classifications xv, xvi, 131–2, 250, 392–3, 411; development of Arabic 121, 248–51, 263, 482; Euclid's concept of theoretical 479; foreign influence 248–8 (Greek) 166, 248, 249, 263, 282; human 366; Judaeo-Arabic 465; and theology 51; *see also individual sciences*
scripts: Arabic (ambiguity) 115, 178, 463, 471 (calligraphy) 65, 162, (manuals on 162, 163 (Quranic) 41, 119; Hebrew 462, 463, 471; Syriac 119, 462; *see also* transliteration
secretaries (*kuttāb*), sing. *kātib*) 155; art of (*kitābah*) writings in 157–8, 161–2; *durrā'ah* (sleeved coat) 164; education 156, 157, 161–3; *esprit de corps* 164; and historiography 198, 203; manuals for xvii, 162, 163, 198, 308; Persian culture 164; and Shu'ūbiyyah 164
Secretum Secretorum (*Sirr al-asrār*) 483
Sédillot, J.J. 287
Sédillot, L. A. 287, 288–9
sentence (*jumlah*) 122, 125
Sergius of Ra's al-'Ayn 343, 488
sermons, Ṣūfī 59
Servius Sulpicius 122
Seth 13
sex, literature on 361, 507–8
sexagesimal notation 255, 278
sexes, separation of 150
Sezgin, F. 107, 189, 274, 288, 333, 343
al-Sha'bī 141
al-Shabistarī, Sa'd al-Dīn Maḥmūd 73
Shādhān b. Baḥr, Abū Sa'īd 298
al-Shādhilī, Abū 'l-Ḥasan 'Alī 61, 62, 64, 67
Shādhiliyyah 68
Shāfi' b. 'Alī 178
al-Shāfi'ī, Muḥammad b. Idrīs 43, 142, 144–5, 149
Shafi'ite school 141; analytical work 146; al-Ash'arī and 7; biography 173; foundation 145–6; Abū Ḥāmid al-Ghazālī on 425; *ḥiyal* (legal devices) 151–2; on public law 150, 157; on roots of law 149; writings 144–5, 147–8; Yemeni historiography 222
shahādah (creed) 10, 25
al-Shahrastānī, Abū 'l-Fatḥ Muḥammad b. 'Abd al-Karīm b. Aḥmad 238, 244
al-Shahrazūrī 410
shakk (doubt) 34
shakkāziyyah (astrolabe) 286
al-Shammākhī 35
Shams al-Dawlah (amir) 390, 391
al-Sha'rānī, 'Abd al-Wahhāb 61, 74, 75
sharḥ (commentary) 348
Sharḥ al-ma'rifah (anon.) 69
sharī'ah (law) xvii, 1, 2, 143; caliphate and 142; Shi'ite view 19; Ṣufism and 55, 70
al-Sharīf al-Juwwānī 241
al-Sharīf al-Murtaḍā 31
al-Shaṭṭanūfī 61, 62
shawāhid (citations) 116
al-shawkah (might) 443
Shawqī, Aḥmad 502, 508
al-Shaybānī, Abū 'Ābdullāh Muḥammad 142, 143–4, 145, 152
al-Shaybānī, Abū 'Amr Isḥāq b. Mirār 112
al-Shaybānī, Abū Ghālib 223–4
al-Shaybānī, Ibrāhīm b. Muḥammad 161
Shayṭān al-Ṭāq (Muḥammad b. Nu'mān al-Aḥwal) 20, 21
Shayzar, castle of 186, 221
al-Shayzarī, Abū 'l-Ḥasan 'Alī 311
she'elot u-teshuvot (legal responses) 153
Shī'ah xv, 16–32; on abrogation 18, 28, 30; on attributes of God 20, 21, 22, 23, 24–5, 27, 28, 30 (anthropomorphism) 21, 27 (visibility) 28; *badā'* 16–17, 18, 25, 28, 30, 32; biographical dictionaries 215; on creation 20, 21, 22, 25, 28–9, 30; didactic verse 506–7; early theologians 20–1; exegesis 48, 50, 51; factions, writings on 238; on faith 25–6, 29, 30; Faṭimid viziers and 245; formation xv, 3–4; on freedom 20, 21, 25, 27, 29, 30; Hishām b. al-Ḥakam, school of 21–3; historiography 198, 239; history after Buwayhids 31–2; imamate 3, 16–20, 25, 26, 27, 29, 30–1; *istiṭā'ah* 20, 21, 25; law xvii, 19, 141–2, 148; Mahdī 16, 22, 23; materialism 23, 27; and Mu'tazilism 27, 29–30, 31; occultations 17, 20, 21–2, 23, 26, 29, 30–1; on Qur'ān; creation issue 21, 22, 25, 28–9, 30; on

Shīʿah (*cont.*)
prophets 19, 25; *rajʿah* (return of imam) 17, 22, 23, 26–7, 29, 32; on reason 31, 32; on resurrection 22; on *sharīʿah* 19; Shumayṭī sect 506; on sin 3; and Sunnism 196, 485; *taqiyyah* 18, 26, 29, 30, 32, 36; Traditionists 23–7, 28, 29, 31, 32; Twelver sect 48, 148; *see also*: Ismaʿilism; Zaydī sect
Shihāb al-Dīn (Ismāʿīlī governor of Qūhistān) 245
ship-mills 261
shiʿr taʿlīmī see didactic verse
al-Shīrāzī, al-Muʾayyad fī ʾl-Dīn 242, 243, 244
al-Shīrāzī, Quṭb al-Dīn 284, 422
shirk (polytheism) 12
Shujāʿ, Abū Kāmil 256
al-Shumayṭī, Maʿdan al-Aʿmā al-Shīʿī 506
Shumayṭī sect 506
shūrā (consultation) 443
shurūṭ (sing. *sharṭ*) (legal documents) 152
Shuʿūbiyyah 113, 133, 164, 310, 368; and Jews 464, 471
Shuyūkh al-ḥirfah (Shaykhs of the Craft) 74
Sībawayhi, Abū Bishr ʿAmr b. ʿUthmān 119–23; and Basran-Kufan antagonism 126; cites Qurʾān and *Ḥadīth* 136; commentaries on *Kitāb* 129; creates grammar 106, 122–3; evidence on early grammar 119–21; and al-Khalīl b. Aḥmad 121; *Kitāb* 119–23, 122–3, 125, 130; legal training 122; life 122; rare word patterns in 132; successors 111, 124, 125, 127, 128, 131, 134
Sibṭ Ibn al-Jawzī 167, 203, 217, 218, 228, 229, 231
Sicily 167, 215, 226, 309
Siddhāntas 253; *Sindhind* 302–3, 481
siege warfare 333
Siirt, Chronicle of 458
Sijistān 33
al-Sijistānī, Abū Ḥātim Sahl b. Muḥammad 131
al-Sijistānī, Abū Yaʿqūb 240
al-Sijzī, Abū Saʿīd Aḥmad b. Muḥammad 283, 286, 299, 413
Simʿān b. Kalīl b. Maqārah 447, 448
sin 3, 6-7, 34, 37, 131
Sinān, Rashīd al-Dīn 224, 245, 246
Sinān b. Thābit 347
Sind, Pakistan 245, 246
Sindhind 302–3, 481
al-Sindī, ʿAbd al-Ḥamīd 170
sine 253, 278–9, 302
Sionita, Gabriel 473
siphonic action 263, 266
al-Sīrāfī, al-Ḥasan 127
sīrah (biography) 168
sīrah (biography of Prophet) xvii, 45, 63, 140, 168, 89, 193, 507
sīrah (pl. *siyar*, Ibāḍī writings) 35, 36
Sīrat ʿAntar 168
Sirr al-asrār (*Secretum Secretorum*) 483
Sithon, Menasheh of Aleppo 473
Sitruk, Issakhar 472
siyar (laws of war) 142, 143–4
siyāsah xvii, 165
Skoss, S. 475
Slavonic peoples 318
smallpox 354, 377
Smith, Margaret 428
social history 176, 242
society: and philosophy 87–98; and religion 384–5
Socrates: Abū Naṣr Muḥammad al-Fārābī and 379, 388; in "Histories of the Ancients" 85; Yaʿqūb b. Isḥāq al-Kindī on 364; Abū Bakr Muḥammad b. Zakariyyāʾ al-Rāzī on 51, 185–6, 371–2; self-knowledge 388
Soghdians 409
solar apogee 418
soothsayers, pre-Islamic (*kāhins*) 156
Soranus 361
soul 98, 99–100, 365, 386–7, 400
Spain: alchemy 340–1; al-Bakrī on 317; Christian Arabic literature 455; Christian reconquest 225; diffusion of learning to 102; grammarians 468, 469; *ḥisbah*, manuals of 160; historiography 193, 213–14, 215, 231–2, 455; Jews in 461, 465–6, 467, 468, 469, 471; letters to kings of 163; map *313*; mathematics 96; philosophy 95–8, 368; translation schools 362, 461, 468, 469, 472, 495; Umayyad rule 213, 481, 495; water-clocks 262; *see also* Cordova
specific gravity 259, 419–20
speech (*kalām*) 8, 25, 121, 122, 130
stars: fixed 275, 276, 292; navigation by 325
statecraft 155, 165–7, 249
statics 257
steelyard clepsydra 260
Steinschneider, M. 473, 474
Stephanus of Alexandria 346
Stephanus Byzantinus 297
Stephanus son of Basilius (Iṣṭifān b. Bāsil) 362, 487
Stern, S. M. 236, 237, 247
Stockholm manuscript (alchemy) 331
Stoicism 8, 332, 493
stoning, death by 42–3
Storey, C. A. 274
story-telling *see* tales
Strassburg University 475
Strauss, Leo 378
Su Sung water-clock 266
succession, law of (*ʿilm al-farāʾiḍ*) 149
Successors 47, 48, 169, 171
Sūdānī troops of Faṭimid state 241
al-Ṣūfī, ʿAbd al-Raḥmān b. ʿUmar 280, *281*, 282
Ṣufism xvi, 56–75; *Adab al-Sulūk* 66–7; admonitions 60; allegory 56, 68, 70, 71;

anthropology 437–8; apologetic 64, 70–1; asceticism 52, 54, 58, 74; *awrād* 67–8; Baḥya b. Paquda and 467; Basran 59; biography 56, 62–3, 172, 177 (*see also* hagiography); brotherliness 74; celibacy 74; converts 58; correspondence 59, 61–2, 70–1; degeneration of literature 57, 64; didactic works 56, 59; divine converse, literature of 67–8; early literature 58–9; epistles (*risālah*) 61–2, 65; erudition 75; ethics 74; etiquette literature 66–7; foreign language literature 71; *futuwwah* 74; Abū Ḥāmid al-Ghazālī and 11, 62, 101–2, 424, 426, 431, 445, 496; gnosis 57, 69, 71, 72, 468; hagiography *see separate entry*; Ḥanbalism and 12; history after al-Ghazālī 445; humour 66, 71; invocations 67; *ishrāqī* school 468; and Jews 467–8, 469; *kalām* 11; Kufa 59; lexical derivations 70; literary style 56–8, 65; Logos theme 72–4; love, theme of 58, 71–2; and magic 71; *manāqib* works 60–1, 65; miracles 64, 445; morality 60–2, 74, 438; moralizing literature 60–2; and Muḥammad 72; narratives, short 60; novice training 65, 66; parables 68; Path, literature of (*ṭarīqah*) 68–70; Persian 71, 75; and philosophy 57, 68, 468, 496; poetry 58; prayers 67–8; problems and answers 61; *qaṣaṣ* technique 71; and Qurʾān 52–5, 59, 64; reference literature 64–5; saints 63, 64, 65, 72–3; sermons 59; and *sharīʿah* 55, 70; story-telling 71; *ṭarīqah* 68–70; and Umayyads 59; on unity of God 69; veneration, literature of 64; virtue, literature of 74; *see also* hagiography
Ṣufrīs 33
Sufyān al-Thawrī 143
sugar-cane crushing machinery 261
Suhrāb, Ibn Sarābiyūn 305, 307
al-Suhrawardī, Ḍiyāʾ al-Dīn ʿAbd al-Qāhir 66
al-Suhrawardī, Shihāb al-Dīn ʿUmar 65
al-Suhrawardī al-Maqtūl, Shihāb al-Dīn Yaḥyā b. Ḥabash 64, 68, 87, 468
al-Sulamī, Abū ʿAbd al-Raḥmān: apologetic 70; biography 61, 63; denounced 53; etiquette writings 66, 67; exegesis 53, 59; moralizing literature 59, 61; testament 60
WORKS: *Jawāmiʿ ādāb al-ṣūfiyyah* 66; *Maqāmāt al-awliyāʾ* 61; *Sulūk al-ʿārifīn* 67; *Ṭabaqāt al-ṣūfiyyah* 63; *ʿUyūb al-nafs wa-mudāwātuhā* 69
al-Ṣulayḥī, ʿAlī b. Muḥammad 242, 243, 244
Ṣulayḥī dynasty of Yemen 222, 241–2, 242–3
Sulaymān b. Gabirol 467
Sulaymān al-Mahrī (the Merchant) 322, 325, 327
Sulaymān b. Ruḥaym 468–9
Sulaymān b. Yasār 141
al-Ṣūlī, Abū Bakr Muḥammad b. Yaḥyā 161–2, 164, 205, 499
sulphur 329
Sumer; didactic poetry 498
Sūmra dynasty of Sind 245
Sunbād (Ispahbad) 292
sundials 286, 287
sunnah 1, 10; grammar and 130; and Qurʾān 43, 47; as root of law (*uṣūl al-fiqh*) 140, 143, 144, 148–9
Sunnī Islam: and Faṭimids 234, 241, 245; al-Maʾmūn attempts to reunite with Shīʿah 20–1, 485; theology xv, 1–15; *see also individual aspects*
Sura, Academy of 464, 466, 477
Surat, India 246
surgery 352, 359
surveying 252, 263; al-Maʾmūn's, of length of degree 305, 306–7
Suryān 451
Suter, H. 274
al-Suyūṭī, Jalāl al-Dīn 53, 146
Sylvius 354
syntax 118, 121, 122, 134, 135; morphology separated from 125; of Qurʾān 45, 46, 49
Syria: archives 191; astronomy 287; Ayyubid era 225–30, 244; Christians 446, 451; and conquest of West 213; dialect 219, 220; Faṭimid rule 220–1, 234, 244–5, 457; geography 230; historiography 217, 219–21, 223, 225–30, 457; law 142; Mamlūk era 221, 228, 287; Mongol invasion 230; Nizārī *daʿwah* and 244–5; sundials 287; Umayyads and tradition 197–8; *see also individual cities*
Syriac language: Christian literature 212, 447, 462; glossaries 108; historiography 212, 457; philosophy 77, 248; script 119, 462; Ṣūfī literature 71; translations from Greek 119, 248, 294, 480, 483, 488 (astrology) 290 (medicine) 343 (philosophy 77, 248 (retranslated into Greek) 248, 343, 449, 487; transliteration 462; words borrowed from 116

Taʿāsīf, Qayṣar b. Musāfir 258
ṭabaqāt (biographies) 153, 171, 189, 194–5
al-Ṭabarī, Abū Ḥafṣ ʿUmar b. al-Farrukhān 293, 295, 296, 481
al-Ṭabarī, Abū Jaʿfar Muḥammad b. Jarīr: exegesis 44, 46–7, 48, 124, 146, 191, 199, 200, 452; historiography 165, 198, 199–201, 214, 264 (continuations of *Taʾrīkh*) 201, 203, 210, 217, 224, 227, 228, 229, 455–6 (translation into Persian) 209; on Ismaʿilism 246; jurisprudence 146, 152, 199; objectivity 200, 209; as polymath 191, 199; sources 124, 142, 191, 195, 197, 198, 199–200, 202, 209, 464
al-Ṭabarī, ʿAlī b. Rabbān 345–6, 350, 357
Ṭabaristan, history of 203
al-Ṭabarsī, al-Faḍl b. al-Ḥasan 48
al-Tābiʿūn *see* Successors

Tabin, Yemen 507
tadbīr al-mulk (basis of kingship) 165
tafsīr see Qurʾān and Quranic exegesis
Tāhart 33, 36, 214
al-Ṭaḥāwī, Abū Jaʿfar Aḥmad 14, 152
Ṭāhir b. Aḥmad b. Bābashādh, Abū ʾl-Ḥasan 132–3, 182
Ṭāhir b. al-Ḥusayn 295
Ṭāhir Dhū ʾl-Yamīnayn 165, 166
Tāj al-Dīn b. ʿAṭāʾallāh ʿAbbās al-Sakandarī 60, 62
Tāj al-Islām al-Mawṣilī 61
Tajikistan 246
Tāj-nāmah (Pahlavi work) 166
tajribah (experimentation) 356
al-Takrītī, Abū Naṣr Yaḥyā b. Jarīr 451, 456, 459
al-Takrītī, Abū Rāʾiṭah 451, 452, 453, 454
ṭalab al-riʾāsah (pursuit of leadership) 127
Ṭalāʾiʿ b. Ruzzīk 222, 245
tales 71, 168, 273, 470; *see also*: fables; *Kalīlah wa-Dimnah*
Ṭālib al-Ḥaqq *see* al-Kindī, ʿAbdullāh b. Yaḥyā
talion, law of 449
Tamīm b. al-Muʿizz 239
al-Tamīmī, Ismāʿīl 241
al-Tamīmī, Muḥammad b. Umayl 337–8, 340
Tāmir, ʿĀrif 247
Tammām b. ʿĀmir b. ʿAlqamah 503
tamyīz (grammatical term) 125
tangent 253, 278–9, 412, 413
Tanḥūm b. Yūsuf Yerūshalmī 469, 474
taqdīr (interpolation) 42, 46, 125–6
Taqī ʾl-Dīn b. Maʿrūf 270, 287
taqiyyah (precautionary dissimulation) 18, 26, 29, 30, 32, 36
taqlīd (imitation) 11, 34, 51
taqsīm (grammatical term) 128, 133
taqwīm (ephemerides) 279–80
Ṭarafah b. al-ʿAbd 502
tarbiyat al-ḥudūd (training for Faṭimid *dāʿīs*) 234
taʿrīf (biography) 168
taʾrīkh (history) 188–9, 197
Taʾrīkh Baghdād 174, 218
ṭarīqah (Ṣūfī Path) 68–70
ṭarīqah Muḥammadiyyah (Wahhabism) 12
tarjamah (pl. *tarājim*, biography) 168
tarjamah dhātiyyah (modern Ar., autobiography) 183
tashbīh see anthropomorphism
tashkīk (ambiguity) 397
taʿṭīl (denying God all attributes) 8
tawḥīd see unity of God
al-Tawḥīdī, Abū Ḥayyān 204
taʾwīl (esoteric interpretation) 12, 41, 54, 234, 243
ṭawīl metre 501
taxation 142, 156–7, 159–60, 301, 449, 499–500
taʿyīn al-mubham (exegetical term) 44–5, 46
tayman (geographical region) 309
Ṭayyib b. al-Āmir 243
Ṭayyibī *daʿwah* 242, 243–4, 246
technology *see* mechanical technology
temperaments, four 343, 356
testaments (*waṣāyā*), Ṣūfī 60
testimony 140, 152, 449
textbooks 143, 368–9; *see also*: grammar (pedagogy); medicine
al-Thaʿālibī, ʿAbd al-Malik b. Muḥammad 107, 162, 167, 173, 210
Thābit b. Qurrah al-Ḥarrānī: astronomy 279, 280, 282–3, 298; Ṣabian background 485–6, 495; translator 249, 254, 264, 304, 482, 485–6, 494, 495, 497; trigonometry 282–3
Thābit b. Sinān 202
Thaʿlab 126, 130
Thaʿlabah b. Ḥāṭib 172–3
Themistius 482, 488, 497
Theodore abū Qurrah 451, 484
Theodore of Mopsuestia 448
Theodosius 492
theology (*kalām*): apologetics 2; *ʿaqīdāt* (compendia) 14–15; authority 3–4, 304, 371; on Day of Judgement 14; defined 1–2; development of discipline xv, 47; didactic verse 498, 501, 503, 504; dogma 12–14, 14–15, 429; and grammar 128; Judaeo-Arabic 466–8, 484; and laws 1, 2–3, 19; linguistic study of Qurʾān 9–10; and logic 380; methods criticized 12, 382–3, 493; and natural sciences 51; and philosophy xvi, 10–11, 51, 78–9, 380, 393, 424, 428; pillars of Islam 10; and politics 3–9; reason and 2, 124–5; resurrection 14; revelation 2, 13; schools 4, 9, 12 (*see also individual schools*); secretaries and 155; *see also*: creation; freedom; God, attributes of; Qurʾān; resurrection; Traditionists; Traditions; unity of God; *and under individual religions, movements and sects*
Theophilus (teacher of Mattā b. Yūnus) 492
Theophilus (Thawfīl al-Rāhib) 456
Theophilus of Edessa (Thawfīl b. Tūmā) 295, 296, 297, 457, 497n
Theophrastus 494, 497
Thomas Aquinas, St 393
Thousand and One Nights 273
Thrasymachus 85
thunderstorm, Fakhr al-Dīn al-Rāzī on 51
ṭibb al-ʿāmmah (popular medicine) 348
Tibbetts, G. R. 326, 327
al-Tibr al-masbūk fī naṣīḥat al-Mulūk ("Mirror for Princes") 166–7
tidal mills 261
Tigris, river 261
Tijāniyyah 68
timber, lamination of 270
time-keeping: astronomical 284–6; al-Bīrūnī's

survey of known world 408–9; clocks 261, 268, 270, 272 (*see also* water-clocks); steelyard clepsydra 260; sundials 286, 287
Timothy I (Nestorian patriarch) 451
al-Tirmidhī, Muḥammad b. ᶜAlī al-Ḥakīm: apologetic 70; on etiquette 66; hagiography (*Kitāb Khatm al-wilāyah*) 61, 64, 72; moralizing works 60, 61; on path 69; synopsis of Qurʾān 59
Tobias b. Mōsheh 472
Toledo 286, 341
tolerance 371, 428
toothpicks, didactic verse on 501
Torah 13
touchstone 329
toys, mechanical 262
trachoma (*ramad*) 345, 359, 360
Traditionists: early 143; Shiᶜite 23–7, 28, 29, 31, 32; *see also: muḥaddithūn*; *mutakallimūn*
Traditions xv: *āthār* 139, 140, 141; and biography 141, 142, 168; canonical status 127; Christian reference to 452; Companions and 43, 47, 48, 139, 140, 141, 168; and historiography 195; Ibn Ḥanbal on 145; as root of law (*uṣūl al-fiqh*) 139, 140, 148–9; on rulers 192; Ṣūfī criticism 53; *see also*: *Ḥadīth*; *isnād*s; Traditionists
Traini, R. 235
transits (*mamarr*) 407, 415, 416
translation movement xv, 477–97; beginnings 480–4, 495; end of movement 494–7; Ḥunayn b. Isḥāq 487–90 (*see also under* Ḥunayn); after Ḥunayn 491–4; under al-Maʾmūn 484–5; patronage 481, 482, 483, 484–5, 485–6, 487 (Banū Mūsā) 264, 484, 485–6, 487 (Hārūn al-Rashīd) 481, 482 (Khālid b. Yazīd) 301, 333 (al-Maʾmūn) 484–5; pragmatic motivation 483, 485, 496–7; in Spain 363, 461, 468, 469, 472, 495; systematic organization 483; Thābit b. Qurrah 485–6 (*see also under* Thābit); *see also under individual authors, under individual languages, viz*: Armenian; Berber; French; Geᶜez; Greek; Hebrew; Latin; Pahlavi; Persian; Sanskrit; Syriac; *and under*: Bible; Christian Arabic literature; Qurʾān
transliteration: Hebrew 462, 463, 464–5, 471–2; Syriac 462
Transoxiana 157, 159
travellers 186, 322–4; dissemination of scholarship 207; geographers 314, 315, 316; technical information from 261
Treveris, Peter 362
tribes, Arab 33, 189, 190, 443
trick vessels 263, 264–5, 268, 270, 272
trigonometry 253–4; al-Bīrūnī on 283, 288, 412–13, 418; chords 253, 302, 421; and land management 160; sine 253, 278–9, 302; spherical 288, 411, 415 (and astronomy) 253–4, 277, 278–9, 282–3; tangent 253, 278–9, 412, 413; words used instead of symbols 256
Tübingen 474
al-Tujībī 59, 71
al-Ṭulūnī, Abū ᶜAlī Khalaf 360
Ṭulunid period in Egypt 210, 298
Tunis 174–5
Turkish language 71, 108, 165
Turks in Faṭimid Egypt 240, 241, 245
al-Ṭurṭūshī, Ibn abī Randaqah 167
Ṭūs 424–5, 427
al-Ṭūsī, Abū Jaᶜfar Muḥammad b. al-Ḥasan 31, 48
al-Ṭūsī, Naṣīr al-Dīn b. al-Ḥusayn *see under* Naṣīr al-Dīn
al-Ṭūsī, al-Sarrāj 439
al-Tustarī, Sahl 52–3, 60, 61, 62
Twelver Shiᶜites (Ithnā ᶜAshariyyah) 48, 148, 236

ᶜUbaydullāh b. ᶜAbdullāh b. ᶜUtbah 141
ᶜUbaydullāh b. Abraham b. Mūsā b. Maymūn 468
ᶜUbaydullāh b. Jibrāʾīl 456
ᶜUbaydullāh al-Mahdī 236, 237, 239, 466
al-ᶜUkbarī 137
Ullmann, M. 363
Ulugh Beg 277, 278, 279, 283, 482
ᶜUmān 33, 34, 36–7, 38
ᶜUmar I b. al-Khaṭṭāb 17, 172, 192
ᶜUmar II b. ᶜAbd al-ᶜAzīz 59, 192, 210, 216, 301
ᶜUmar al-Khayyām 254, 256, 259
ᶜUmārah b. abī ʾl-Ḥasan al-Ḥakamī 184–5, 222, 245
al-ᶜUmarī, Aḥmad b. Yaḥyā b. Faḍlullāh 321, 322
Umayyad era: caliphate of Cordova 213, 481, 495; genealogy 195; geographical literature 301; Ibaḍism 33; local historical documents 190; Ṣufism 59; Syrian tradition 197–8; translation 481, 495
Umayyah b. abī ʾl-Ṣalt 498
ummah see community
Union of Soviet Socialist Republics 246, 420, 475, 476
unity of God (*tawḥīd*) 2, 13; Almohads and 11; Ashᶜarī view 8; Christian view 452–3; Galen and 489; *ghayriyyah* 453; Judaeo-Arabic view 466; Muᶜtazilites on 5; Shiᶜite view 23; Ṣūfī view 69; Sunnī theology 2, 5, 8, 10, 13, 51, 393
universe, representation of 273
al-Uqlīdisī, Abū ʾl-Ḥasan Aḥmad b. Ibrāhīm 255
al-ᶜUrḍī, Muʾayyad al-Dīn 284, 287, 422
ᶜurf (customary law) 141
ᶜUrwah b. al-Zubayr 141
Usāmah b. Murshid b. Munqidh, Abū ʾl-Muẓaffar 182, 186–7, 221, 231

ᶜ*ushr* (tax) 157
uṣūl al-fiqh ("roots" of law) 139, 140–1, 143, 144, 148–9, 152, 425
usurpation, rights of 144
usury 140
al-Uswānī 241
al-ᶜUtuqī 241
ᶜUṭārid b. Muḥammad al-Ḥāsib 282, 419
ᶜUṭbah, ᶜAbd al-Raḥmān 171–2
al-ᶜUtbī, Abū ᵓl-Naṣr Muḥammad 177, 206, 209
ᶜUthmān (caliph) 17
ᶜUzayr (Ezra) 292

vacuum 384
Vajda, G. 475
Valens 294, 297
valves, conical 266
Vasco da Gama 326
Vattier, P. 230
Vaux, Carra de 284, 428
Vesalius 354
Vitruvius 260, 263
vizierate: ascendancy 155, 205; Egyptian 222, 245; histories and biographies 163, 205, 208, 222, 245; *wizārah* (treaties on art of) 162; *see also* Barmakids
vocalization of scripts 115, 178, 463

waᶜd (promises) 6
Wādī Daᶜwān 34
Wahbiyyah Ibaḍism 34
Wahhabism 12
al-Wāḥidī 53
waᶜīd (admonitions) 6
Wakīᶜ, Abū Muḥammad Bakr b. Ḥayyān 153
Walzer, R. 479
waqf (religious endowment) 149–50
al-Wāqidī 192
al-Waqqāshī 102
war, laws of (*siyar*) 142, 143–4
al-Warathānī, ᶜAbd al-Wāḥid 62
al-Warjalānī, Abū Yaᶜqūb Yūsuf b. Ibrāhīm 38
al-Warjalānī, Abū Zakariyyāᵓ Yaḥyā b. abī Bakr 232, 239
al-Warrāq, Abū Bakr Muḥammad b. ᶜUmar 70
al-Warrāq, Muḥammad b. Yūsuf 215
waṣāyā (testaments) 60, 68
Wāṣil b. ᶜAṭāᵓ 4–5
al-Wāsiṭī, Taqī ᵓl-Dīn 62
water-clocks 262, 264, 266, 267–8, 272; Archimedean 263, 267, 268
water dispensers 270
water-mills 258, 260, 261–2
water-raising machines 262, 270, *271*; pump *269*; wheels 258, 261
Wathīmah 192
al-Wāthiq 305, 480
Watt, W. M. 427
wazīr (Islamic neologism) 115; *see also* vizierate
al-Wazzān, Ḥusayn 66
weather 198–9, 275; *see also* meteorology
weights and measures 159, 306
Wensinck, A. J. 428
West, Muslim: historiography 213–15, 227, 231–21; al-Ṭabarī on 201; theoretical astronomy 284; *see also*: Africa, north; Maghrib; Spain
wheat, extraction-rates of 161
Wheelock, Abraham 175
William of Aragon 298
willow used in medicine 362–3
windmills 262
witchcraft 361
wizārah (art of vizier) 162
word of God 64; Christ as 453; *see also* Logos
word-lists 106–7, 125
world-map 314
Wright, William 125
writer's cramp 374
writing, introduction of 41, 188, 189

Xenophon 178

al-Yāfiᶜī, ᶜAfīf al-Dīn 64
al-Yaḥshūr (falcon) 182
al-Yaḥsūbī, ᶜIyāḍ b. Mūsā 170, 173
Yahuda, A. S. 475
Yaḥyā b. ᶜAbd al-Muᶜṭī 135
Yaḥyā b. abī Manṣūr 276
Yaḥyā b. Ādam 157, 159
Yaḥyā b. ᶜAdī, Abū Zakariyyāᵓ 127–8, 447, 451, 453, 454; school of 493–4
Yaḥyā b. al-Baṭrīq 363, 482–3, 484
Yaḥyā b. Ḥakam al-Ghazāl 503
Yaḥyā b. Ḥamzāh al-ᶜAlawī 238
Yaḥyā b. Hārūn 487
Yaḥyā b. Jarīr al-Takrītī, Abū Naṣr 451, 456, 459
Yaḥyā b. Khālid al-Barmakī 293, 295, 499
Yaḥyā b. Manṣūr 482
Yaḥyā b. Saᶜīd al-Anṭākī 219, 241, 457
Yaḥyā b. Yaḥyā al-Laythī of Cordova 143, 144
Yaḥyā al-Naḥwī (John Philoponus of Alexandria) 365, 433
Yaḥyā al-Nawawī 148
Yaḥyā Yehūdāh b. Balᶜam, Abū Zakariyyāᵓ 469
Yaᶜqūb b. Ṭāriq 253
al-Yaᶜqūbī, Ibn Wāḍiḥ 198–9, 200, 304, 309–10, 311
Yāqūt b. ᶜAbdullāh al-Ḥamawī: biography; (*Irshād al-arīb*) 170, 174, 178, 230, 312, 503; (anecdotes in) 181 (on al-Bīrūnī) 405, 406, 422 (al-Ṣafadī omitted) 226; geographical works 304, 312–15, 320, 508; method 178; sources 184, 459
Yazīd b. Muᶜāwiyah 16
al-Yazīdī, Abū Muḥammad 123, 126
al-Yāzijī, Nāṣīf 502

Yefet b. ʿAlī 469, 474
Yehūdāh ha-Lēvī, Abū ʾl-Ḥasan 467
Yehūdāh b. Mōsheh 300
Yehūdāh b. Quraysh of Tāhart 469, 474
Yemen: astronomy 279–80; Ayyubid era 231, 244; didactic verse on 507, 508; Faṭimids 238, 239, 242–3, 246; historiography 212–13, 222, 231, 239, 245; Ibāḍīs 33, 34, 38; interest in languages 108; Judaeo-Arabic literature 468, 475, 476; Ottoman conquest 246; Shafiʿites 222; Ṣulayḥid state 222, 241–2, 242–3; Ṭayyibī *daʿwah* 243–4, 246; Zaydīs 213, 222
Yuʾannis b. ʿAbdullāh, Abū Ṣāliḥ 449
Yūḥannā b. Ḥaylān 379
Yūḥannā b. Māsawayh 346, 353, 484, 487
Yūḥannā b. al-Ṭabarī 456
Yūnān 368
Yūnus b. ʿAbd al-Raḥmān 22, 23, 24
Yūsuf b. Ibrāhīm al-Baṣīr, Abū Yaʿqūb 466, 470
Yūsuf b. Waqār of Toledo 468

al-Zabīdī, Abū ʾl-Fayḍ Muḥammad Murtaḍā 106, 115
Zacuto, Abraham 472
al-Ẓāfir (Faṭimid caliph) 243, 245
Ẓāfir al-Ḥaddād 245
ẓāhir (exegesis) 47, 52
al-Ẓāhir, al-Malik 226
al-Ẓāhir Baybars 178
Ẓāhirīs 137, 148
al-Zahrāwī, Abū ʾl-Qāsim 363
al-Zajjājī, Abū ʾl-Qāsim 128–9, 130, 131, 132
al-zakāh see alms
al-Zamakhsharī, Abū ʾl-Qāsim Maḥmūd b. ʿUmar 49–50, 52, 108, 113, 133–4
Zangids 227, 245
al-Zaqqāq, ʿAlī 151
Zarādusht 292–3, 297, 299
al-Zarqālī 286
zarqāliyyah (type of astrolabe) 286
al-Zawzanī 108
Zayd b. ʿAlī 17, 141–2, 148
Zaydī sect 17, 213, 240; legal works 141–2, 148; in Yemen 213, 222
Zayn al-ʿĀbidīn b. Nujaym 146
Zeno 296
*zīj*s (astronomical tables) 251, 276–8, 279, 285, 288, 305, 457; computer-aided study 283; *ghurrat al-zījāt* (Sanskrit) 417; *Zīj al-Arkand* 302, 303; *Zīj al-Shāh* (Pahlavi) 251
Zirids 214, 240, 241, 299
al-Ziyādī, Abū Ḥassān 197
ziyārāt literature 64
zodiacal signs 275
Zoroastrianism 5, 170, 294, 398–9, 429
Zosimus of Panopolis 332
al-Zubaydī al-Ishbīlī 110
Zucker, M. 475
Zuhayr b. abī Sulmā 498, 502
al-Zuhrī, Ibn Shihāb Muḥammad 193
ẓuhūr (realization of Ibāḍī state) 33–6
Zurārah b. Aʿyān 20
Zurayʿids of ʿAdan 243
al-Zurqānī 143